AMERICAN GOTHIC

six decades of classic horror cinema

JONATHAN RIGBY

SIGNUM BOOKS

This one is for my father
– who in 1933 saw *The Mummy* at the Ambassador Cinema on Salford's Langworthy Road –
and my mother
– who seven years later saw *The Mummy's Hand* at the Weaste on Eccles New Road.
Their first film together as a married couple was *The Thing from Another World*,
at Manchester's Gaiety Cinema in August 1952.

This edition published in Great Britain
in 2017 by Signum Books, an imprint of
Flashpoint Media Ltd
173 Mill Road
Cambridge
CB1 3AN

American Gothic was originally published
by Reynolds & Hearn Ltd.

A CIP catalogue record for this book is
available from the British Library.

ISBN 978 0 9955191 3 8

Edited by Marcus Hearn
Designed by Peri Godbold

Printed and bound in China by
1010 Printing International Ltd.

Picture Credits

Front endpaper
Life Without Soul (1915): William W Cohill, Lucy Cotton, Percy Darrell Standing
The Show (1926): Betty Boyd ('Neptuna, Queen of the Mermaids')
The Great Gabbo (1929): Erich von Stroheim, Otto
The Last Performance (1929): Conrad Veidt
The Cat Creeps (1930): Lilyan Tashman, Elizabeth Patterson
Thirteen Women (1932): Myrna Loy, Ricardo Cortez
Secrets of the French Police (1932): Gwili André, Gregory Ratoff
Oliver the Eighth (1934): Stan Laurel, Oliver Hardy, Mae Busch
The Florentine Dagger (1935): Donald Woods, Margaret Lindsay
Dante's Inferno (1935): various damned souls
Maid of Salem (1936): Halliwell Hobbes, Claudette Colbert
The Hunchback of Notre Dame (1939): Charles Laughton

Half-title page
The Last Warning (1928): Mme Carrie Daumery

Frontispiece
Frankenstein (1931): Boris Karloff

Contents page
Dr Jekyll and Mr Hyde (1919): John Barrymore
The Man Who Laughs (1927): Conrad Veidt
Mystery of the Wax Museum (1932): Lionel Atwill
The Cat and the Canary (1939): Paulette Goddard
The Leopard Man (1943): James Bell, Jean Brooks
The Thing from Another World (1951): James Arness
Terror in the Midnight Sun (1958): Lars Åhrén

Back endpaper
Ladies in Retirement (1941): Ida Lupino
The Man in Half Moon Street (1943): Helen Walker, Nils Asther
Dead Man's Eyes (1944): Lon Chaney Jr
The Unseen (1944): Gail Russell, Richard Lyon
The Spider Woman Strikes Back (1945): Brenda Joyce, Gale Sondergaard
Strangler of the Swamp (1945): Rosemary LaPlanche, Charles Middleton
The Woman in White (1947): Eleanor Parker
The Neanderthal Man (1952): Robert Shayne
Man in the Attic (1953): Constance Smith, Jack Palance
Cult of the Cobra (1954): Ruth Carlsson
The Wasp Woman (1958): Susan Cabot
Return of the Fly (1959): Ed Wolff

Photo Acknowledgments

Photofest NYC
pages 6, 8, 31, 37, 39, 63, 69, 74, 77, 80, 81, 107, 117, 174, 209, 245, 271, 280, 282, front endpaper picture 2

The Joel Finler Collection
pages 5 (top right), 14, 41, 60, 61, 112, 131, 154, 163, 170, 194, 234, 243, 249, 259, 285, 301, 336

Contents

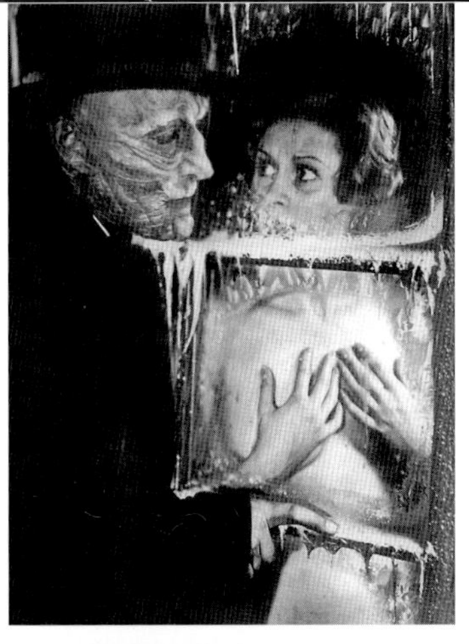

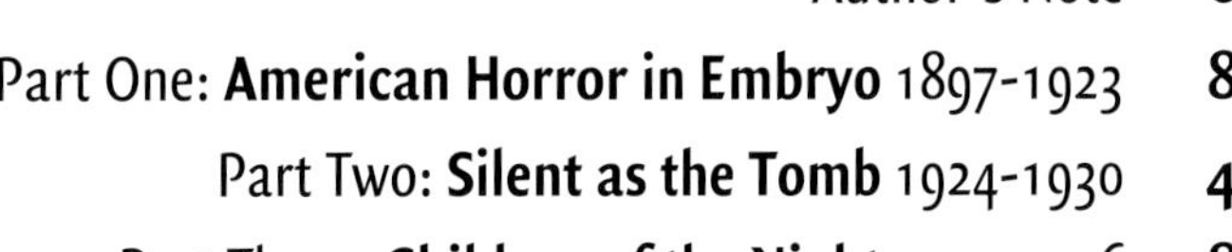

Author's Note

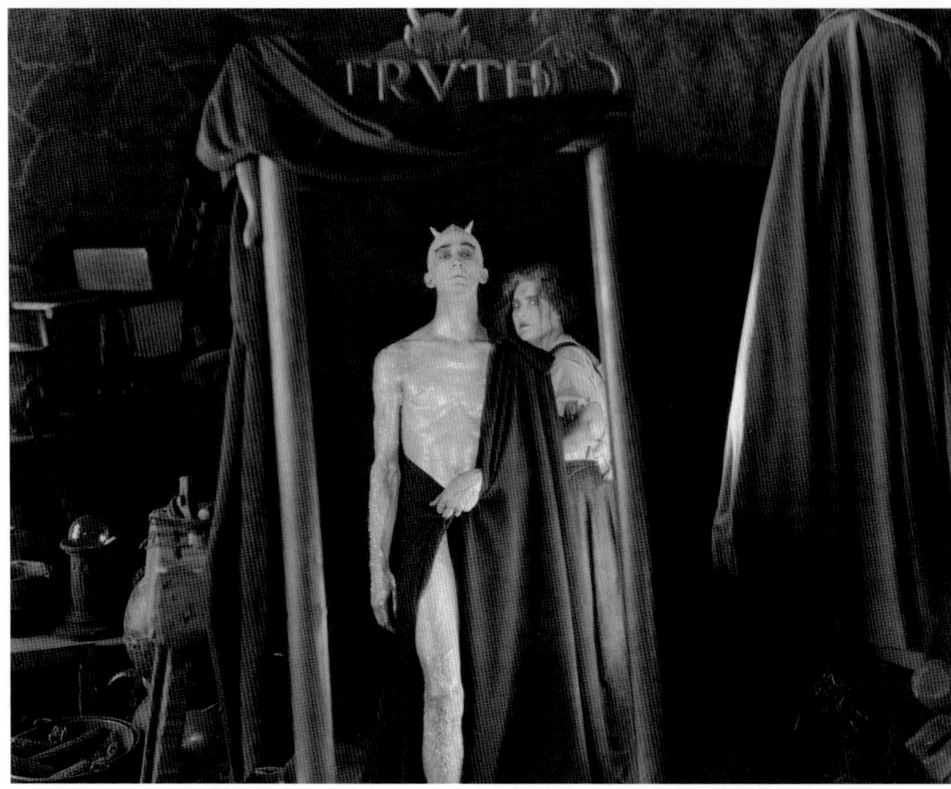

"A perfect cloven-hoofed Satan." Osgood Perkins and Maude Hill in the presumed missing *Puritan Passions* (1923)

This book began, in a roundabout sort of way, with a clandestine glimpse, some time in 1972, of the opening reel of James Whale's *Frankenstein*. Circumstances were restricted in that I could only watch through the gap between the door and the door-frame; inside, viewing in sanctioned comfort, were my father and eldest brother. Even at that early age I was aware that my position was strangely similar to that of Colin Clive and Dwight Frye (secretly watching a midnight burial through the bars of a cemetery monument) in the film itself.

A mere 28 years later, my first book came along. It was called *English Gothic* and in 2007 it gave rise to a follow-up – *American Gothic*. Another nine years on, a third book in the sequence, *Euro Gothic*, was published. So now, in 2017, I'm delighted to have been given the opportunity to revise and expand *American Gothic* so that all three volumes can be made available in uniform editions.

Horror itself, of course, is far from uniform; given the shape-shifting often portrayed in them, it seems appropriate that horror films constitute perhaps the most amorphous and wide-ranging of all genres. This was particularly true in the early years when their various elements coalesced only gradually into what Walter Kendrick, in *The Thrill of Fear*, contemptuously dubbed 'genrefication'. The business of selecting films that qualify for inclusion in *American Gothic* was therefore an unscientific one, relying mostly on subjective impressions of what constitutes horror.

Because the American tradition is so rooted in the mystery-comedy mechanics of Broadway's thriller hits of the 1920s, I've tried to be inclusive where 'old dark house' pictures are concerned, even though some are hardly horror films in the accepted sense. There are so many of them, however, that various borderline items – notably *The Ghost in the Garret* (1920), *In the Next Room* (1930) and *The Ghost and the Guest* (1943) – have had to be excluded, along with a ton of short films in similar vein, among them such alluring titles as *The House of a Thousand Trembles* (1922),

Creeps (1926) and *They Shall Not Pass Out* (1929). And, just as old dark houses bled into the emergent horror genre, so horror iconography seeped into the 1940s vogue for film noir and the 1950s boom in science fiction. In these cases I have been less indulgent, focusing only on films that seem to me to have indisputable horror content.

As well as subjective impressions, there were also some specific criteria designed to keep the book within manageable bounds. Short films and serials, for example, have been treated selectively; 'chapter-plays', in fact, are only considered in the silent period, when their cliff-hanging iconography introduced several motifs that would crop up in the horror features of a later generation. Amateur films have been omitted, the same applying to animation (with one exception; it crops up in 1953) and children's films. The last of these criteria entailed the exclusion of Roy Rowland's 1952 oddity *The 5,000 Fingers of Dr T*, a nightmarish Dr Seuss musical fantasy that bombed at the time but has since become a cult.

These criteria also apply, of course, to the 111 major titles selected as representative of American horror from 1914 to 1959. I decided to add an extra proviso for these films, however – the exclusion of such 'lost world' fantasies as *King Kong* and *Creature from the Black Lagoon*. The key titles, incidentally, are mainly concentrated in Parts Two to Five, a 20-year period that strikes me as American horror's most fertile prior to the upheavals of the 1960s. Worth noting, too, is the fact that many of the films discussed in Parts One and Two are described as 'lost'. Again, this is an unscientific term in that a lost film can always, happily, turn up again; to cite just two examples, *The Magician* and *Mystery of the Wax Museum* were considered lost until relatively recently. Either way, an interesting question arose as to whether to include lost films among the book's major titles. Interesting because, obviously, I couldn't offer a personal response to them. I decided to do so only in the case of two especially significant Lon Chaney titles, *A Blind Bargain* and *London After Midnight*.

In revising the book I've made relatively few alterations to the first five sections, but Part Six has been augmented and, indeed, Part Seven is entirely new. In the first edition I took the story up to 1956, when the initiative in international horror production passed to the UK; this seemed appropriate given that *The Black Sleep*, the major title with which I closed the book, had been double-billed in the US with *The Quatermass Xperiment*, the film that kicks off the main narrative of *English Gothic*. A decade on, however, I've decided to add another three years in order to wind things up at the cusp of the 1960s. Any film is fair game, in fact, if it went into production prior to 30 November 1959 – which is when Alfred Hitchcock began shooting the genre game-changer that was *Psycho*.

Now for a few nuts and bolts. Quotations within the text are numbered in order that their source can be found in the relevant appendix; given the ready availability of both papers' collected film columns (complete with indexes), quotations from *Variety* and the *New York Times* are the only exceptions to this. The years attached to films are, wherever possible, those of production, not necessarily release, meaning you'll find plenty of dates that differ from the standard ones given in other sources. And in the credits accompanying each of the major films, unbilled actors are gathered together at the end of each cast list under the heading 'uncredited', while technical personnel who went similarly unacknowledged are indicated individually by means of an asterisk.

Nobody researching vintage American horror can fail to be indebted to the works that have gone before, particularly those by astute genre historians like Greg Mank, Tom Weaver and Michael F Blake. More direct assistance, particularly in acquiring copies of hard-to-find films, was rendered by David Miller and the late Mark A Miller (no relation), with various stubborn stragglers supplied by Tom Johnson, Kim Newman and Josephine Botting. The hunt for photographs was just as wide-ranging, chief conspirator, again, being David Miller. Particularly remarkable contributions were made by Jan 'Sister Grimm' Garfield and Neil Pettigrew, with other items being supplied by Richard Dacre, Tony Hillman, Ted Okuda, Bryan Senn and Melynie Withington. My thanks, too, to Kate Brown, Andrew Cartmel, James Clatterbaugh, Sara Dee, Tony Foy, David Hanks, Rachael Hewer, David J Hogan, Steve Knight, Martin Pavey, Philip Spedding, Paul Taylor, and the staff of the BFI's invaluable reference library.

As for this new edition, thanks are due to my publisher, Marcus Hearn, for enabling the whole thing; to Kevin Lyons, who proved a research associate without peer (just as he did on *Euro Gothic*), and to the splendid Peri Godbold, who has been designing these books quite brilliantly for 17 years now. And a final thank you to my wife Claire, who has been as tolerant of teenage werewolves and sentient severed heads as any husband could wish.

Jonathan Rigby
London
July 2017

Part One

Miser, moneybox and "ghoul vision" – Ralph Lewis being taught a familiar lesson in *The Conquering Power* (1921)

American Horror in Embryo 1897-1923

Think of the classic horror films produced in the USA in the first half of the 20th century and two indelible images spring immediately to mind – Bela Lugosi in the impeccable aristocratic regalia of Count Dracula and Boris Karloff in the shrunken, proletarian suit of Frankenstein's Monster. Both images were derived from European sources – a Bram Stoker novel published in 1897 and a Mary Shelley one from some eight decades earlier – and the actors embodying them were from Lugos in Hungary and Forest Hill in south-east London respectively.

Karloff and Lugosi were merely the most prominent of the numerous Europeans, both before and behind the camera, who put their stamp on American horror pictures. There was nothing unusual about this; after all, Hollywood itself had been built up by émigrés from Hungary (Adolph Zukor, William Fox), Germany (Carl Laemmle) and Poland (Louis B Mayer, Sam Goldwyn, all four Warner brothers). But the preponderance of Old World artistes involved in the production of America's collective nightmares was appropriate given the fact that the New World had always been at something of a historical disadvantage where Gothic subjects were concerned.

The trouble lay in the very word 'new'; Gothic was concerned with antiquity, with ancient terrors rising from a barbarous mediaeval past to give life to the familiar dramatis personae of horrid fiction: persecuted heroines, satanic villains, madmen, fatal women, vampires, doppelgängers. But when the English writer Ann Radcliffe published her seminal Gothic novels of the 1790s, Americans who had just emerged from their struggle for independence could trace back their history little more than 170 years.

GOTHIC MODELS

In the Gothic strain popularised by Mrs Radcliffe, the focus of anxiety was almost invariably a Gothic castle or abbey (there were numerous variations), a forbidding edifice designed, in Radcliffe's words, to induce "a sensation of sublimity rising into terror – a suspension of mingled astonishment and awe." Reeling from just these impressions, the hero of Radcliffe's *The Romance of the Forest* "surveyed the vastness of the place, and as he contemplated its ruins, fancy bore him back to past ages." The atavistic horror of "past ages," with the castle at its centre, gave the original Gothic novels their potency. Across

the Atlantic, however, "past ages" were an unknown quantity to a people for whom 1620 was Year One.

The legacy of Puritanism, however, held its own taint of atavism. In the summer of 1692, the insecurities of an emerging nation, hedged about as it was by the uncharted wilderness and what Cotton Mather called *The Wonders of the Invisible World*, became manifest in a witch-hunting mania that swept through Massachusetts, in particular the Essex County coastal settlement of Salem.

A massively influential Congregationalist minister and friend of the Salem magistrates, Mather widely disseminated his belief that "the Devil has made a dreadful Knot of *Witches* in the Country, and by the help of *Witches* has dreadfully increased that Knot," ascribing to the practitioners the intention "of Rooting out the Christian Religion from this Country, and setting up instead of it, perhaps a more gross *Diabolism*, than ever the World saw before." In the fearful atmosphere propagated by Mather, petty personal jealousies were stoked into hysteria by the malicious fabrications of a few teenage girls, making Salem's Gallows Hill the site of a grotesque miscarriage of justice that claimed at least 25 lives.

A propensity towards paranoia and conspiracy theories, spreading like a cancer from officialdom to the mass of ordinary Americans and resulting in the unreasoning persecution of supposed subversives, was to resurface several times in the succeeding centuries. A hundred years after Cotton Mather's voluminous writings, such concerns gave the first American attempts at Gothic fiction an acute and forward-looking psychological slant that set them apart from their exotic Old World models. Charles Brockden Brown, widely taken to be America's first professional man of letters, established his reputation in the dying days of the 18th century with grimly macabre novels like *Wieland; or, The Transformation*, moving the Euro-centric motifs of Mrs Radcliffe and her imitators to specifically American locales and using them to illuminate specifically American social concerns. *Wieland*, for example, is a cautionary tale of the 'God told me to' variety – a religious maniac is persuaded to massacre his wife and children by voices he takes to be divine.

In the wake of Brockden Brown came Washington Irving, whose 1819 anthology *The Sketch Book of Geoffrey Crayon, Gent* included such whimsical fantasies as *Rip Van Winkle* and *The Legend of Sleepy Hollow*. Mid-century, Nathaniel Hawthorne had a very personal stake in New England's ancestral shame, one of his forebears having been a presiding magistrate at the Salem witch trials; he exorcised this Puritan shadow in such allegorical novels as *The Scarlet Letter* and *The House of the Seven Gables* and mordant short stories like *Young Goodman Brown*. And by the end of the 19th century the Civil War veteran Ambrose Bierce added his unique brand of bitter cynicism to the ghostly tales comprising his 1893 anthology *Can Such Things Be?*

Despite these writers' efforts to locate Gothic fictions in recognisably American surroundings, early filmmakers would largely ignore them in favour of European sources, with their evocation of apparently more authentic, because more ancient, terrors. Irving's skittish tales proved popular, however, and Hawthorne's *The Scarlet Letter* was transferred to film no fewer than six times prior to the famous M-G-M version of 1926. Bierce and Brockden Brown would be ignored entirely, though Bierce's *An Occurrence at Owl Creek Bridge* finally yielded an eye-catching silent short, *The Bridge*, directed by Hungarian émigré Charles Vidor in 1929.

But there was one American writer – a contemporary of Hawthorne's – who overcame the prejudice towards European models, inspiring numerous films of varying degrees of fidelity. In the years following his death in 1849, the works of Edgar Allan Poe incurred plenty of lordly put-downs from fellow writers. "An enthusiasm for Poe," opined Henry James, "is the mark of a decidedly primitive stage of reflection," while Paul Elmer More offered the stereotypical view of horror fans in any age when he declared that "Poe is the poet of unripe boys and unsound men." Despite such judgments, Poe gathered plenty of posthumous adherents, Baudelaire and Debussy among them, and his influence was to prove pervasive.

His horror stories built on the psychological concerns of Brockden Brown, several of them reading like case histories from 20th century psychiatry; one, *The Fall of the House of Usher*, successfully transfers the Gothic castle of Mrs Radcliffe to an American locale, its decrepitude and final collapse applying as much to the family (or 'house') within it as the building itself. And, in presenting his first anthology, *Tales of the Grotesque and Arabesque*, in 1839, Poe firmly refuted the idea that his stories were just another product of the vogue for German-style Gothic. "If in many of my productions terror has been the thesis," he wrote, "I maintain that terror is not of Germany, but of the soul – that I deduced this terror only from its legitimate sources, and have urged it only to its legitimate results."

But, for all his popularity with filmmakers a century hence, Poe's dictum that "terror is not of Germany" was a notion Hollywood would take some convincing of.

Legacy of Puritanism: Lillian Gish, branded 'A' for 'adulteress', in *The Scarlet Letter* (1926)

FIRST STIRRINGS

When William McKinley, the 25th President of the United States, was assassinated in September 1901, his successor, Theodore Roosevelt, offered a "square deal" to the American people, instituting progressive policies aimed in particular at reforming the monopolistic practices and widespread corruption of big business. And yet the term of Roosevelt's presidency, which ended in 1909 – and that of his trust-busting successor, William Howard Taft, which extended to 1913 – saw the first tentative steps of a new industry whose monopolistic practices would thrive unchecked until 1948.

At the turn of the 20th century, the American public was happy to ascribe the remarkable new invention of moving pictures to Thomas Alva Edison. This, after all, was the man who had previously given them such staples as the light bulb and the phonograph. The truth, however, was rather more complex. Edison himself had little interest in the process, leaving the technicalities of perfecting a slot-machine prototype, the Kinetoscope, to his English associate W K L Dickson. And, having been persuaded against his better judgment to move on to a projection system, Edison took the credit for the Vitascope from its happy-to-oblige inventor, Thomas Armat.

The latter process was given a public demonstration at Koster and Bial's Music Hall in New York on 23 April 1896. Edison saw no future in moving pictures other than as a short-lived novelty, just as the Lumière brothers – who had demonstrated their own Cinématographe in Paris the previous December – advised the inquisitive stage magician Georges Méliès not to waste his time on it. The combined lack of vision of Edison and the Lumières prompted Gilbert Seldes to observe, rather brutally, that "The moving picture had to be taken away from the inventors by aggressive and ignorant men without taste or tradition, but with a highly developed sense of business, before it could be transformed from a mechanical toy into the medium of the first popular art."[1]

The time of the fledgling movie moguls, however, was not yet. The early years of the burgeoning

industry were given over, instead, to mavericks and magicians. Méliès, for example, was a true visionary. Undaunted by the Lumières' dismissive attitude, he bought a projector from the English pioneer Robert W Paul and, rejecting the documentary capabilities of the new invention, opted to use its magical properties in the creation of fantasy subjects he called féeries.

While Méliès perfected his studio at Montreuil, the American industry began to coalesce around New York and New Jersey. But, where Britain's pioneers had their very own answer to Méliès in George Albert Smith, the Thomas Edison Company was relatively slow to exploit the new medium in a similar style. In December 1898, however, 75 feet of film were devoted to a subject called *The Cavalier's Dream*, showing an old witch turning into a young beauty together with an appearance from Mephistopheles himself.

The same character would reappear in a March 1900 release called *The Mystic Swing*, which, given that it was distributed by both Edison and the Selig company of Chicago, was in all likelihood a Méliès import. The same month, ghosts were added to the Edison repertoire in *Uncle Josh in a Spooky Hotel* and *Uncle Josh's Nightmare*, additions to a popular homegrown series featuring Charles Manley. The former was typical of the slapstick approach taken to such themes: at the midnight visitation of a ghost, both Josh and his landlord receive spectral slaps in the face, each thinking the other has done it, with a predictable altercation to follow.

Without a Méliès to push the medium forward, the American industry lagged well behind the French equivalent at this early stage. In November of 1900, however, Edison's horizons would be broadened considerably by the arrival of Edwin S Porter, who was put in charge of Edison's brand-new rooftop studio on New York's East 21st Street. By his own admission Porter was an inveterate 'tinkerer' and, having made an in-depth study of Méliès' techniques, he would shortly revolutionise the nascent industry.

Of Edison's competitors, the Philadelphia studios of Siegmund Lubin came up with a comedy called *The Haunted House* as early as August 1899, around 159 feet of hick hotelier Silas Hayseed being tormented in his bedroom by first a ghost and then Satan himself. Edison's chief rival, however, was New York's American Mutoscope and Biograph Company, set up in 1895 under the supervision of Edison's former collaborator, W K L Dickson. Biograph depicted "His Satanic Majesty himself" in an April 1900 release called *The Prince of Darkness*, though his depredations are fairly innocuous, amounting to no more than bedevilling a drunkard as he tries to get undressed for bed.

Located between 13th and 14th Streets at 841 Broadway, in May of the same year the Biograph studio would create (and blow to pieces) a monstrous insect in *The Troublesome Fly*. In December, *Davy Jones' Locker* offered ample evidence of the fact that the rehashing of old material was a well-established practice even at this early date. The film depicted a skeleton frolicking on the deck of a capsized ship, but its effects were cannibalised from two earlier Biograph titles, *Wreck of the Schooner 'Richmond'* and *The Dancing Skeleton*, both from as far back as 1897. Another film recycling the *'Richmond'* documentary footage – and also issued in December 1900 – was *Neptune's Daughters*, which, with the 1899 subject *The Ballet of the Ghosts* superimposed, conjured spectral ballerinas from the surf. Biograph also created skeletons en masse to show the fate of the complacent members of *The Thirteen Club*, released in November 1905. All these items featured on camera G W 'Billy' Bitzer, who was to loom large in the rapid development of motion pictures in the following decade.

By this time, Edwin S Porter had shaken the burgeoning industry into an awareness of its untapped potential with the December 1903 release of *The Great Train Robbery*, its exciting tableaux organised into a coherent 740-foot narrative, complete with stunning highlights like gun-toting George Barnes firing directly at the audience. The film proved so profitable that it sparked off a boom in so-called nickelodeons, which were for the most part empty storefronts converted into makeshift screening rooms. These proved a magnet for sensation-hungry working men and by 1907 were attracting over two million patrons every day. But exhibitors were keen to maximise their profits by attracting a different kind of audience – specifically women and the middle class in general.

This drive towards the gentrification of the humble nickelodeon led to a reliance on subjects drawn from literature and the stage, the majority filmed with the kind of fixed-camera, front-and-centre inflexibility *The Great Train Robbery* had repudiated. Even Porter back-pedalled in the wake of his own innovations; with his pronounced veneration for the stage, he would eventually join Adolph Zukor in setting up the Famous Players Film Company, progenitor of Paramount. In the meantime, amid the slew of nickelodeon product was Essanay's December 1908 version of Dickens' *A Christmas Carol* and a Biograph adaptation of Robert Louis Stevenson's *The Suicide Club* the following May.

Competition was fierce and turnover correspondingly rapid. Ferenc Molnár's satirical play *The Devil* premiered on Broadway on 18 August 1908, making a Stateside star of the patrician English actor George Arliss. Cashing in with commendable speed, Porter's potted Edison version came out on 10 September, with D W Griffith's for Biograph lagging behind somewhat, only emerging on 2 October. Not to be outdone, Vitagraph and Selig produced bizarre variants imagining the hair-raising effects of merely attending the Arliss production, in *He Went to See the Devil Play* and *The Devil, the Servant and the Man* respectively.

Edison pressed on with adaptations of Nathaniel Hawthorne (*Lord Feathertop*, *The House of the Seven Gables*), Rider Haggard (a November 1908 digest of *She*) and Stevenson (*The Imp of the Bottle*), as well as concocting another version of *A Christmas Carol* (featuring the soon to be ubiquitous character actor Marc McDermott) in December 1910. The company was also responsible for a Hawthorne-style Puritan witch-burning in the April 1909 release *In the Days of Witchcraft*, as well as a standard-issue haunted house item from September of the same year called *'Tis Now the Very Witching Time of Night*.

The need to upgrade the moving pictures' prestige was an urgent one, given that anything perceived as appealing to the working classes inevitably attracted the killjoy attentions of moralists and reformers. Indeed, by November 1907 the Chicago city council had endowed the Chief of Police with the power to grant or withhold picture permits. Over in New York, meanwhile, an official move to abolish the nickelodeons altogether resulted in the institution, in January 1909, of the National Board of Censorship of Motion Pictures. Its name amended in 1915 to the National Board of Review, this was an attempt by exhibitors to police their product from within rather than yield it up to the outside interference of reformers.

Though the word 'censorship' had made its baleful entrance into the industry's lexicon, the torrent of nickelodeon product showed no sign of abating, and fantastic subjects continued to appear in the repertoire of the five- and ten-cent theatres. Amid the riot of enticing titles – from Vitagraph's *The Ghost Holiday* to Selig's *The Witch's Cavern*, from Edison's *The Ghost's Warning* to Urban's *The Witches' Spell* – Poe-type themes surfaced via Biograph (premature burial in *The Golden Supper*, 1910) and Vitagraph (the walling-up of a murder victim in the same year's *The Mystery of Temple Court*). Shakespeare was adapted more directly, with Vitagraph's April 1908 version of *Macbeth* sporting the euphonious subtitle *Shakespeare's Sublime Tragedy*.

Wilkie Collins was a popular source too, with Selig and Urbanora offering versions of *The Moonstone* in 1909 and 1911 respectively, the story seeming to spark off a vogue for 'yellow peril'-flavoured yarns about the malefic influence of exotic jewellery appropriated by presumptuous westerners. The catalogue of curse-encrusted gems ranged from Lubin's *The Bloodstone* in 1908 through such toothsome, albeit interchangeable, titles as *The Curse of the Hindoo Pearl*, *The Green Eye of the Yellow God*, *The Death Stone of India*, *Diamond of Disaster*, *The Mystery of the Fatal Pearl* and *The Jewel of Death*.

The motif would retain its potency well into the 1930s, and several other themes later to find expression in the talkies were previewed before the First World War. The shivery potential of wax museums was initiated in *The Professor and His Waxworks* (1907), the wilful behaviour of substitute body parts in *The Thieving Hand* (1909) and the fusion of animals with humans in *The Key of Life* (1910), an Edison production in which a kitten was transformed by Hindu magic into a feral cat woman.

EARLY ARCHETYPES

With the nickelodeon proprietors' increasing hunger for high-class (and pre-sold) subject matter, it's unsurprising that the most recognisable horror subject in the first decade of the 20th century should owe its inception to a stage play. Back in 1886, the popular matinée idol Richard Mansfield had immediately seen the star potential in Robert Louis Stevenson's just-published novella *Strange Case of Dr Jekyll and Mr Hyde*, engaging Thomas Russell Sullivan to dramatise it and first staging the play in Boston in May 1887. He continued playing Jekyll and Hyde for 20 years, popularising the story to such a degree that a rival adaptation, by Luella Forepaugh and George F Fish, appeared in 1897.

It was this version that Colonel William Selig of the Chicago-based Selig Polyscope Company happened to catch a performance of early in 1908. He immediately engaged the troupe to go before his cameras during the day, spending a week shooting a *Dr Jekyll and Mr Hyde* that ran to 1035 feet and even included the raising and lowering of the curtain. As Selig's publicists put it, the result showed "the transformation of the moral and physical character of Dr Jekyll from the admirable gentleman and scholar to the ferocious brute of a maniac known as Mr Hyde," and it was ready for release to the nickelodeons on 7 March. Here began the tradition of fitting Dr Jekyll with a neglected fiancée, also that of recasting Hyde's elderly victim as her interfering

father (in this case a vicar). Some sources identify the film's uncredited star as prolific actor-director Hobart Bosworth, others as the famous actor-manager Thomas E Shea. Frank Oakes Rose, meanwhile, is proposed as the star of a rival Kalem production directed the same year by Sidney Olcott.

Two years after Selig's Jekyll and Hyde, Friday 18 March 1910 saw the release of the first film version of Mary Shelley's *Frankenstein*, billed as "a liberal adaptation" and with the prestigious name Edison attached to it. Shot in the third week of January at Edison's studio in the Bronx, it was directed by James Searle Dawley, a former playwright and protégé of Edwin S Porter.

His techniques looking increasingly staid by comparison to the kind of films D W Griffith was turning out at the rival Biograph Studio, Porter had been removed as Edison's production head as recently as November 1909. To judge from *Frankenstein*, however, Dawley was by no means qualified to help the Edison Company compete in an increasingly cut-throat business. The kind of in-your-face experimentation Porter had brought to *The Great Train Robbery* back in 1903 is nowhere to be seen; on the contrary, *Frankenstein* consists in the main of stagey tableaux shot in unvarying long-shot. But Dawley's scenario nevertheless takes a surprisingly imaginative approach to what the Edison publicists called "the mystic and psychological problems that are to be found in this weird tale."

At a mere 975 feet (around 16 minutes), the film is typical of literary adaptations of the period, boiling down the bare bones of the original into a handful of not always coherent vignettes. Barely has Frankenstein (Augustus Phillips) been established as an impetuous 18th century medical student than he's discovered in his laboratory endeavouring to "create into life the most perfect human being that the world has yet known." A skeleton sits upright in a chair, offering a memento-mori mockery of his pretensions, and behind iron-clad double-doors stands a massive cauldron into which Frankenstein sprinkles various chemicals, coming across as equal parts mediaeval alchemist and gourmet chef.

The ensuing creation sequence, which Frankenstein watches through an observation window set into the iron doors, makes very effective use of reversed footage, with lumps of offal gradually attaching themselves to an exposed rib-cage, absurdly attenuated arms waving all the while and a head gradually becoming discernible amid enveloping flames. When out and about, however, Charles Ogle's Monster is rather less impressive. Like Caliban as

Robert Louis Stevenson's "Gothic gnome" first emerged from actor-manager Richard Mansfield in 1887

played by Beerbohm Tree, he's a mass of shaggy hair and taloned hands, with only his extremities (unnaturally high forehead, comically exaggerated feet) providing any foretaste of the Karloff Monster that would follow 21 years later.

In the film's concluding passages (staged in Frankenstein's drawing room rather than Shelley's Arctic), Dawley makes inventive use of a prominently displayed full-length mirror, in which the Monster and Frankenstein's unnamed sweetheart (Mary Fuller) are made to seem like opposing aspects of Frankenstein's soul. Remarkably, the Monster is finally reduced to nothing more than a reflection in the glass, "the evil in Frankenstein's mind" being safely consigned to oblivion as the lovers embrace.

In showing the Monster being vanquished by the power of love, the film comes over like an odd premonition of Murnau's *Nosferatu*, and in depicting him as a projection of Frankenstein's mind it provides a naïve but effective twist on Shelley's doppel-gänger theme.

If Ogle's reflection suggests that the Monster has a soul after all (albeit no more than a neglected fragment of its creator's), the next *Frankenstein* adaptation refuted the notion even in its title. According to its publicity, the Ocean Film Corporation's *Life Without Soul* was "a dramatic masterpiece, pulsating with heart interest, interwoven with a love tale of sacrificial devotion." Directed by Colonel Joseph W Smiley, it was shot on location in Georgia and Florida, together with studio work in New York, in October 1915 and tradeshown on 21 November.

By February of the following year, the fledgling Ocean set-up was out of business, having been taken over by former distributor Harry Raver, who attempted to revive interest in *Life Without Soul* by splicing into it documentary footage relating to reproductive cycles in fish. Running to five reels, and with its extensive location footage augmented by specially staged landslides and such, *Life Without Soul*, now lost, was clearly a much more spectacular production than its Edison forebear. That the latter was already forgotten is made clear by *Variety*'s verdict that "the novelty of the idea for filming will be sure to create a healthy demand for the [Ocean] picture."

Modernising the story, Jesse J Goldburg's scenario called for scientist Victor Frawley (William A Cohill) to fall asleep while reading the Shelley novel, dreaming that he creates a soulless creature (Percy Darrell Standing) that kills Frawley's little sister (Pauline Curley), best friend (Jack Hopkins) and fiancée (Lucy Cotton) when denied a mate. An Englishman, Standing received a warm welcome from critic Edward Weitzel: "He is awe-inspiring, but never grotesque, and indicates the gradual unfolding of the creature's senses and understanding with convincing skill. At times, he actually awakens sympathy for the monster's condition, cut off as he is from all human companionship."[2]

Cover star of the 15 March 1910 issue of the *Edison Kinetogram*: Charles Ogle's Caliban-like monster in *Frankenstein*

Between the Edison and Ocean attempts at *Frankenstein* came an intriguing variant called *Naidra, the Dream Woman*, released on 4 December 1914 and telling the story of an elderly scientist who brings into being a beautiful but emotionless female. All his attempts to stir her feelings come to naught – these include showing her a pair of young lovers, a mother cooing to her baby and a couple weeping over the grave of their dead child – until a young organist wins her love merely by paying a call. Unfortunately, a narrative cop-out common to *Life Without Soul* and many other films of the period is indicated even in the title – as Naidra and the younger man are about to kiss, the scientist starts up from what was only a troubling dream. The film's publicity referred explicitly to the myth of Pygmalion and Galatea, though it also seems reminiscent of Hans Heinz Ewers' 1911 novel *Alraune*.

Naidra was a product of one of the classiest independent production companies of the day, Thanhouser, which made its films in an abandoned ice-rink at New Rochelle, New York. Earlier in 1914, the company was responsible for *The Miser's Reversion*, issued on 24 March and widely taken to be the first film to use a series of dissolves to change an actor's facial features. The actor in question was 36-year-old Sidney Bracey, playing a septuagenarian so obsessed with regaining his youth that he trades his own daughter for a swig at a Maharajah's elixir. He overdoes it, however, and reverts to an ape, poetic justice given his parallel obsession with Darwinism. A similar 'gag' would be employed 20 years later in the Laurel and Hardy short *Dirty Work*, by which time apes had become an almost omnipresent threat in 'old dark house' thrillers, with Bracey himself playing supporting roles in two such, *The Monster Walks* and *The Intruder*.

The dissolves used in *The Miser's Reversion* could have come in handy back in 1911, when Thanhouser put together a third version of *Dr Jekyll and Mr Hyde*, this one starring future director James Cruze and studio favourites Florence LaBadie and Marie Eline (the so-called Thanhouser Kid). Released on 16 January 1912, the film was directed by Lucius Henderson and played as a short-and-sharp parable about the personality-changing dangers of drug addiction. Jekyll is a young-ish man with conspicuously white hair who, in this version, "becomes the accepted suitor of the minister's daughter." He subsequently bludgeons the old man to death when involuntarily taken over by Hyde, though the murder is discreetly veiled by a cutaway to the fiancée running for a policeman.

Lasting a mere 11 minutes, what survives of Henderson's picture cuts smartly to the chase, packing in a number of transformations alongside Hyde's vaguely delineated trampling of a little girl and eventual death by self-administered poison. The film would acquire a measure of intrigue some 50 years later when Thanhouser regular Harry Benham (who had been the Maharajah in *The Miser's Reversion*) claimed to have played not only the ill-fated minister but also Hyde. "In those days pictures were turned out like a butcher grinds out sausage," he added, "but this one was slower because of the delays in changing the characters, so it lasted over a week ... much to [Edwin] Thanhouser's chagrin!"[3] At a distance of nearly a century, Benham's claims are impossible to substantiate; to judge from the surviving footage, Cruze did indeed play the black-haired, gremlin-like Hyde after all.

James Cruze – or possibly Harry Benham – as a provincial doctor's baser self in *Dr Jekyll and Mr Hyde* (1911)

Thanhouser's high-class product occasionally admitted other grisly subjects, notably a 1911 attempt at Rider Haggard's *She* with Marguerite Snow as Ayesha and James Cruze as her reincarnated lover, and a 1915 version of *The Picture of Dorian Gray*. Also in 1915, an original subject titled *A Call from the Dead* (aka *From the River's Depths*) involved a revived corpse avenging its own murder.

The Thanhouser *Jekyll and Hyde*, meanwhile, had been followed by another from Charles Urban, whose two-reel 1913 version featured Murdock MacQuarrie in the title roles and utilised a Kinemacolor process invented by G A Smith of England's pioneering 'Brighton school'. Despite the Brighton connection, and the assertion by several commentators that the film is British, it was actually made by Urban's US operation. And, thanks to Smith's prohibitively complex system of double-speed projectors and red-green filters, the film was barely seen – or even reviewed. Eighteen years on, MacQuarrie would play a small role in the famous Paramount talkie based on the same story.

Another 1913 rendition of *Dr Jekyll and Mr Hyde* was much more widely visible than Urban's. Directed by Herbert Brenon and starring the extremely popular 33-year-old character star King Baggot, the film was a product of Carl Laemmle's IMP (Independent Motion Pictures) Company, which had recently been incorporated with several others into the Universal Film Manufacturing Company, an outfit which in time would play a decisive role in the development of American horror.

This first attempt in the field features a fresh detail that would be perfected in most later versions of the Jekyll and Hyde story, namely Jekyll's philanthropic interest in his charity patients. Balancing this, it shows Hyde beating a defenceless boy on crutches and making an impish nuisance of himself in low-grade pubs. Compared to the Thanhouser version, the film benefits from an increased running time and the relative leisure with which Brenon can unravel the story. The scenario also shows a certain wit, as when Hyde presents Jekyll's domestic staff with a note from their master saying, "Treat him [Hyde] as myself." And there's an early view of what was to become a Universal staple, with an angry mob pursuing Hyde to his lodgings, only to be confounded when Jekyll emerges to greet them instead.

Baggot's Hyde is as bow-backed, buck-toothed and shag-haired as previous incarnations, often to risible effect, though contemporary opinion was more indulgent. "The leading man of the

IMP company outdoes himself," commented George Blaisdell in *Moving Picture World* on 1 March. "In the periods when Mr Baggot portrays Mr Hyde the horror of it holds you." Predictably, parodies were quick to follow, notably Warners' 1914 production *Dr Jekyll and Mr Hyde Done to a Frazzle* and, the following year, Lubin's *Horrible Hyde* and Vitagraph's *Miss Jekyll and Madame Hyde*.

Running on parallel lines where fantastic subjects were concerned, Charles Urban and Edwin Thanhouser not only produced separate Jekyll and Hyde pictures; back in 1911 they both produced films called *The Mummy*. Urban's showed the resurrection of a mummy in the standard 'it was all a dream' mode, while Thanhouser's depicted the revivification of an Egyptian princess by electricity. Long before the Tutankhamen expedition of 1922, which would initiate a King Tut craze worldwide and in turn inspire Universal's *The Mummy* in 1932, the theme of Ancient Egyptians being magically revived was already a popular one, with titles coming in from Britain (*The Vengeance of Egypt*, *The Wraith of the Tomb*) and France (*La Momie du Roi*, *The Romance of the Mummy*). In the US, Edison set the pattern with a 1909 fragment called *The Egyptian Mystery*, in which a pendant salvaged from a tomb confers on the wearer the ability to make things disappear.

The theme of reincarnated princesses and love stretching across the centuries – seemingly cannibalised from Rider Haggard's *She* and Bram Stoker's *The Jewel of Seven Stars* – was particularly prevalent, cropping up in such films as J Farrell MacDonald's *When Soul Meets Soul* (Essanay 1912), Fred W Huntley's *Through the Centuries* (Selig 1914), George D Baker's *The Dust of Egypt* (Vitagraph 1915), A E Christie's *His Egyptian Affinity* (Nestor 1915) and Charles Bartlett's *A Modern Sphinx* (American Film Company 1916). Men disguising themselves as mummies, generally for comic effect, was almost as popular a theme, featuring in two Kalem productions, *The Egyptian Mummy* (1913) and *The Missing Mummy* (1915), as well as Nestor's *When the Mummy Cried for Help* (also 1915).

A revived mummy acting as a matchmaker for modern lovers was a more outré notion but director Lee Beggs handled it nevertheless, in another film titled *The Egyptian Mummy* but this time made for Vitagraph in 1914. A number of current or future stars appeared in these early Egyptological romances: Francis X Bushman in *When Soul Meets Soul*, Antonio Moreno in *The Dust of Egypt* and 15-year-old Constance Talmadge, the so-called Vitagraph Tomboy, in the second *Egyptian Mummy*.

In 1915, Talmadge and her sister Norma would go out to California and be contracted by the great D W Griffith, under whose aegis Constance would achieve immortality the following year in Griffith's massive epic *Intolerance*. As already noted, Griffith too had started his film career in New York, turning out nearly 500 Biograph one-reelers between 1908 and 1913, ranging freely across a whole range of yet-to-coalesce genres. One of the first of these films, *The Princess in the Vase*, predated even Edison's *The Egyptian Mystery* in dusting off Ancient Egyptian artefacts, in this case the ashes of a cremated princess. From these the woman herself is wondrously reconstituted in the agitated dream of an Egyptologist played by Griffith himself.

ABOUT TO GIVE BIRTH

Among Griffith's other Biograph subjects was a prototype biopic called *Edgar Allen Poe*, the mis-spelling of Poe's middle name counting as an egregious error for a man with as pronounced a literary bent as Griffith. The Poe centennial celebrations having taken place on 19 January 1909, Griffith shot his film at Biograph's Broadway studio on the 21st and 23rd, putting it before the public as "one of the most artistic films ever produced" on 8 February. The result showed Poe (Herbert Yost) composing *The Raven* (complete with the relevant bird looking on from atop a bust), submitting it to an initially underwhelmed publisher, then returning in triumph to his wife Virginia (played by Griffith's own wife, Linda Arvidson), who has predictably expired in the interim. "My God, she is dead!" he gasps, flinging himself despairingly across her body.

Later the same year, Griffith and his cameraman, Billy Bitzer, made another Poe subject, though *The Sealed Room* – released in September – failed to acknowledge its origin in *The Cask of Amontillado*. With Renaissance lovers Henry B Walthall and Marion Leonard walled up by the latter's avenging husband (Arthur Johnson), the source was nevertheless pretty plain, though Balzac's *La Grande Bretèche* may have been in the back of Griffith's mind too.

A film that anticipated the Poe centennial had been issued on 27 November 1908. Shot in Brooklyn's Prospect Avenue, the Crescent Film Manufacturing Company's *Sherlock Holmes and the Great Murder Mystery* was the third Holmes picture ever released in the USA, showing Holmes rushing to the rescue of a young man accused of murdering his fiancée; she has actually been killed by a gorilla escaped from a ship's hold. The idea is intriguing in that it takes Poe's *The Murders in the Rue Morgue* and substitutes Holmes

for Poe's C Auguste Dupin – who had been Conan Doyle's model for Holmes in the first place.

Other Poe projects included Edison's *Lunatics in Power*, a May 1909 release that burlesqued Poe's *The System of Dr Tarr and Prof Fether*, paying homage to the original in that the escaped lunatics climactically tar and feather their victim. The first of several films called *The Raven* followed in April 1912, produced in Fort Lee, New Jersey by the US branch of the French company Eclair. In this, the anonymous director showcased location footage of the Fordham cottage in which Poe spent the last three years of his life, as well as trotting through tableaux culled variously from *The Gold Bug*, *The Black Cat*, *The Murders in the Rue Morgue*, *The Pit and the Pendulum*, *A Descent into the Maelstrom*, *The Premature Burial* and, inevitably, *The Raven* – all presented as visions that impel Poe (Guy Oliver) to take up his pen and write.

The Pit and the Pendulum itself went on to form the basis of a three-reeler of the same name released by the Solax Film Company in July 1913. Directed by Solax co-founder Alice Guy Blaché, and starring Solax regular Darwin Karr, this was advertised in barnstorming style as "A Blood-curdling Classic! The screen story vibrates with all the virility and vitality of Poe's incomparable pen! The scenes mirror Poe's compellingly gruesome but not repellent verbal rhapsody!" George Lessey's *The Bells*, an Edison production released the same month, concerned an arranged marriage in which the unhappy bride is saved when the church burns down, taking her unappetising bridegroom with it. Unsurprisingly, the film was dismissed by contemporary critics as a catchpenny production trading on Poe's name and having nothing to do with his original poem. In this, it would turn out to be something of a trailblazer.

An early Poe contrivance (complete with mis-spelled name): Eclair's 1912 two-reeler *The Raven*

D W Griffith was moved to turn to Poe again in the spring of 1914, by which time he had made the momentous journey west; indeed, the industry itself had undergone some revolutionary changes. Filmmakers had first shown an interest in Hollywood and its environs early in 1907, when Colonel Selig of Chicago ordered west coast location work for his version of *The Count of Monte Cristo*, and by 1913 most of the major companies had taken root in California.

As well as being attracted by the state's sunshine and scenery, many independents were lured there as a means of eluding the gun-toting agents of the Motion Picture Patents Company. Formed in 1908 to protect Edison's doubtful claims to ownership of the mechanisms involved in film production, the combine comprised, among others, Biograph, Vitagraph, Selig, Kalem, Essanay and Lubin. The resultant monopoly was bitterly resisted, in particular by IMP's Carl Laemmle, the future founder of Universal. Eventually destroying the Edison combine via the Sherman Anti-Trust Law, Laemmle had already made a seismic contribution to the burgeoning industry by the simple expedient of revealing the name of his most popular star: Florence Lawrence. He did this in March 1910, sending her, a month later, to St Louis to make a personal appearance alongside King Baggot. There she was greeted by an unruly mob of passionate admirers and the notion of the film star was officially born.

It was during this tempestuous period that Griffith established himself at the Mutual facility, located at the intersection of Hollywood and Sunset Boulevards. His new Poe film – *The Murderer's Conscience* – was the last of four Griffith features issued between April and July 1914, the others being *The Battle of the Sexes*, *The Escape* and *Home Sweet Home*. Though not formally released until 24 August, the film, retitled *The Avenging Conscience or "Thou Shalt Not Kill"*, was first seen in Pasadena on 16 July. By then, Griffith was fully occupied with his epoch-making feature *The Birth of a Nation*, which had begun filming on the fourth of that month.

A young Poe enthusiast is blocked by his mean-spirited, and one-eyed, uncle from marrying his sweetheart. He promptly murders the older man, sealing up his corpse behind the fireplace. Assailed by his conscience, together with a blackmailer and an imperturbable detective, the

THE AVENGING CONSCIENCE or "Thou Shalt Not Kill"

Majestic Motion Picture Co 1914
seven to eight reels; silent
produced March/April

Cinematographer: G W [Billy] Bitzer*; Assistant Camera: Karl Brown*; Editors: James Smith*, Rose Richtel*; Musical Accompaniment: S L Rothapfel*; Scenario: D W Griffith [from the Edgar Allan Poe story *The Tell-Tale Heart* and poem *Annabel Lee*]; Director-Producer: D W Griffith

Henry [B] Walthall (the Nephew); Blanche Sweet (the Sweetheart); Ralph Lewis (the Stranger); George Siegmann (the Italian); uncredited: Spottiswoode Aitken (the Uncle); Josephine Crowell (the Mother); Robert Harron (the Grocery Boy); Walter Long (second detective); Mae Marsh (the Maid); Wallace Reid (doctor); with George A [André de] Beranger, Donald Crisp

Artistically, Mr Griffiths [sic] has put on a beautiful picture in *Conscience*. It lives up to his reputation, from scenes and situations to photography ... To picture people *The Avenging Conscience* will prove a study, it is so well done. To the public it will be an everlasting lesson that ... you may fool everybody but you can't fool yourself, for yourself is Conscience. *Variety*

We were doing a picture called *The Avenging Conscience* ... [which was] all about the murderous moods of a man long overdue for the loony bin. This called for symbolism, and I somehow became promoted to the symbolism department, mostly, I imagine, because shooting natural symbolism takes a lot of time and mine wasn't worth very much, so they could spend it freely. *Karl Brown [Adventures with D W Griffith, 1973]*

A Motion Picture Classic montage of Henry B Walthall's Poe-inspired murderer in *The Avenging Conscience* (1914)

young man finally hangs himself, the girl meanwhile flinging herself off a cliff. He then wakes to realise it was all a dream, and is united with his sweetheart after all.

The Avenging Conscience begins with a very Poe-like tableau – to the right, a sheet is drawn over a bedridden young woman, with sundry actors scattered across the frame in appropriate attitudes of bereavement and, at screen left, a baby's crib hovered over by a haggard man wearing an eyepatch. This turns out to be the doting uncle who, in Griffith's scheme, is roughly equivalent to the cantankerous old murder victim in Poe's *The Tell-Tale Heart*. The eyepatch presumably conceals the "vulture eye" specified by Poe, and to compensate for its non-appearance Spottiswoode Aitken adopts a suitably vulture-like stance as the shabby-genteel uncle, particularly after a title card announces that his nephew is heading "INTO MANHOOD Working with one idea centered on a great career."

This idée fixe seems to consist of reading plenty of Edgar Allan Poe; the opening paragraphs of *The Tell-Tale Heart* are reproduced, along with a plate depicting Poe himself and a snatch of the poem *Annabel Lee*. That the nephew (Henry B Walthall) is already an unhealthy specimen is indicated by a letter he receives from his sweetheart, which she signs "She whom you have chosen to name Annabel" – not a very cheering pet name, given the necrophile subtext of Poe's poem. At a garden party, Griffith then presents "THE CONTRAST." These charming scenes of Bobby Harron and Mae Marsh as a grocer's boy and ladies' maid were presumably intended to show how a healthy young couple behaves (unencumbered by Poe mania and an intransigent uncle), but they're so tenuously connected to the main narrative as to seem irrelevant.

In the aftermath of this sunlit interlude, Griffith tries to curry some sympathy for the uncle. Aitken is seen forlornly touching his elbow to indicate that, unlike the young people, he has no one to link arms with; he also attempts to interact with a baby and, on returning home, mimes stroking the hair of the absent Walthall. The latter, at Aitken's insistence, has reluctantly broken off his engagement, after which he sits disconsolately on a park bench and Griffith inserts the ominous intertitle, "THE BIRTH OF THE EVIL THOUGHT Nature one long system of murder – the spider, the fly and the ants."

The idea that life is nothing more than a vampiric food-chain seems indebted more to the Renfield character in Stoker's *Dracula* than anything in Poe, and Griffith illustrates it with vivid images of a spider closing on its prey while a nearby horde of ants seethes tumultuously over a dead wasp. Walthall grins approvingly at the carnage and, disturbingly, starts talking to himself.

At this point, Griffith discreetly sets up the 'it was all a dream' ending, a plot resolution that can never have seemed satisfactory but was to become positively infuriating as filmmakers continued to fall back on it in future decades. (As noted above, the first significant reprises of the device came in *Naidra, the Dream Woman* and *Life Without Soul*.) Walthall goes home, inspects a heavily symbolic wilted flower drooping in its vase, briefly recollects the devouring

spider, then nods off in his chair. The moment is given no special emphasis, so that the viewer is taken in completely by the ensuing action. Walthall throttles the old man in an argument over money, while a swarthy Italian labourer looks on through a gap in the blinds, dragging on his cigarette and grinning contentedly to himself at the grotesque spectacle. Aware that the "The Plan of a Fevered Brain" is already going seriously awry, Walthall pays off the Italian and bricks up Aitken behind the fireplace.

The delusions with which Walthall is subsequently afflicted consist of the phantom uncle groping his way out of concealment during a visit from the sweetheart, later coming through Walthall's bedroom window and looming over his pillow. Praying for deliverance, Walthall has a vision of Jesus on the cross together with the illuminated legend "THOU SHALT NOT KILL" – clearly one of Moses' original tablets, this last is cleverly articulated to look like a tombstone. Walthall's interview with a persistent detective features the expected reminders of "the beating of the dead man's heart" (a clock pendulum, the drumming of the detective's pencil, the impatient tapping of his foot), whereupon Griffith, presumably realising that such sound-based conceits were insufficient to get the crisis across in a silent film, introduces another vision. This one is of capering, fire-breathing imps and a skeleton that embraces Walthall as he sits tethered in a chair.

The film features several of the sophisticated devices for which Griffith and Billy Bitzer were to become famous (back-projection and split-screen among them), and is unaffectedly acted by Griffith's ace stock company. The 36-year-old Walthall, however, seems oddly matched with Griffith's extremely popular teenage protégée Blanche Sweet, who wasn't yet 18 – unless this was another Poe reference on Griffith's part, Poe having married a 13-year-old when he was 26. Walthall nevertheless garnered high praise, *Motion Picture Classic* hailing his performance as "a marvel of character-drawing and of the dragging forth of the innermost emotions. In this Walthall was almost uncanny, and every movement of the man ... was caught by the audiences with painful reality."[4]

In 1915, Griffith would return to the theme of a murderer bedevilled by a manifestation of his conscience (in this case, a "blood-boltered" ghost), acting in a supervisory capacity on an eight-reel *Macbeth* directed by John Emerson. "D W Griffith had great ambitions for the movies, and he was always trying to better them," explained Emerson's wife Anita Loos, remembering also that "it was a long step, because Shakespeare without Shakespearean dialogue was a little bit hazardous. I know that in the credits there was a line which said, 'By William Shakespeare. Titles by Anita Loos.'"[5] Adding immeasurably to the film's prestige, British stage luminaries Herbert Beerbohm Tree and Constance Collier were engaged to play the Macbeths.

Writer-producer Sol A Rosenberg and writer-director Robert Goodman produced a Poe film of their own in the form of a Paragon Photo Plays version of *The Murders in the Rue Morgue*, released, like *The Avenging Conscience*, in the momentous month of August 1914. What information survives about this production suggests that it was a forerunner of the 1951 film *The Man with a Cloak*, in that "the author" – ie, Poe himself – is domiciled in Paris and helps solve a murder there.

The following year Charles J Brabin directed *The Raven* for Essanay, cannily carrying over Henry B Walthall from *The Avenging Conscience* and dubbing him "The image of Poe, a man of the same mould and temperament."[6] In the film itself, however, Walthall's face is carefully superimposed over a portrait of the real Poe and looks nothing like him. An opening title card describes the film as "A romance of Edgar Allan Poe by George C Hazelton. Founded upon Mr Hazelton's widely known novel and play." The crude biopic that follows dramatises the titular poem as if its events actually happened to Poe himself. The raven's ominous croaks of "Nevermore" are rendered in a font made up of human bones, and the film's other felicities include a door-knocker that knocks by itself and the superimposition of a skull over a glass of wine.

Released on 8 November 1915, *The Raven* was urged upon exhibitors as "the most ethereally artistic and soul-stirring drama of the year" and featured Warda Howard in multiple roles as the women in Poe's life. Destined to marry arch vamp Theda Bara, director Charles Brabin was a Liverpudlian who had begun his career with Edison; much later, he would direct *The Mask of Fu Manchu* for M-G-M.

In the wake of his leading role as Benjamin Cameron in *The Birth of a Nation*, Walthall was one of the most famous actors in the world when he made *The Raven*. Opening in New York in March 1915, Griffith's Civil War epic also made stars of various other members of his stock company (Mae Marsh, Lillian Gish, Bobby Harron), in addition to determining the career paths of his army of assistant directors, among them Raoul Walsh, Victor Fleming, W S Van Dyke, Donald Crisp, Erich von Stroheim and Jack Conway.

As well as proving massively influential in its technical and artistic innovations (so much so that it would appear almost run-of-the-mill within a few years), *The Birth of a Nation* also proved the massive influence the new medium could exert in society at large – albeit, in this instance, a baleful one. Its openly racist scenes extolling the Ku Klux Klan as "the savior of white civilization" led, in November 1915, to the resurrection of a terrorist organisation that had lain dormant since 1869. And yet the heated controversy surrounding the film ensured that nobody could afford to ignore it – not even the middle classes and the intelligentsia.

Here, at last, was the breakthrough. A well-heeled audience that wouldn't have dreamt of entering a humble nickelodeon to watch a naïve two-reeler was now prepared to sit through a film that lasted a staggering three hours, and to do so, moreover, in a legitimate theatre charging legitimate theatre prices. So began the drive to convert the natural home of the moving picture from an empty storefront to the aptly named 'picture palace'. To live up to this new-found prestige, filmmakers followed Griffith's pioneering example in bringing a startling new sophistication to the medium. And the studios, in their turn, began to coalesce into multi-million-dollar concerns that, by the 1920s, would qualify the picture business as America's fourth largest industry.

SHADES OF WAR

While Griffith and Bitzer were perfecting the very grammar of film-making, other practitioners were perpetuating the special effects spirit of Méliès, with the movie camera's ability to achieve apparently wondrous transformations resulting in several films concerned with lycanthropy.

Vitagraph's *The Reincarnation of Karma*, for instance, was directed by Van Dyke Brooke in 1912 and showed an Indian priestess (Rosemary Theby) transformed into a snake. The following year, the Bison company – distributed by the fledgling Universal – produced the first werewolf picture, a now-lost two-reeler called simply *The Werewolf* and released in December 1913. Directed by the prolific Canadian producer-director Henry McRae, Ruth Ann Baldwin's story concerned a Navajo sorceress (Lule Warrenton) who sends out her daughter Watuma (Phyllis Gordon) to attack the white man's settlements in lupine form, with a no-nonsense dissolve to transform Gordon into a real white wolf. Essanay's July 1915 release *The Inner Brute* trod similar ground, retaining Warda Howard from the same company's *The Raven* in a peculiar story of a man struggling with bestial tendencies, having been born to a woman frightened by a tiger while pregnant.

Inevitably, transformation effects were used for comic purposes too, notably in Fred J Balshofer's 1917 five-reeler *The Haunted Pajamas*. Vessel of an Oriental curse, the titular silk pyjamas transform one man into a Chinese warrior and another into glamorous Carmel Myers. Another silent temptress, Seena Owen, had starred in Majestic's much more serious *The Fox Woman* (1915). Taken from a novel by John Luther Long of *Madame Butterfly* fame, Lloyd Ingraham's film featured Owen as an American schemer in contemporary Japan who conforms to legendary descriptions of the soul-stealing 'Fox Woman'.

Prototype mad scientists were also available. In 1915, Tom Moore starred in and also directed a Kalem two-reeler called *The Secret Room*, which told an off-colour story of a doctor attempting to implant the soul of a healthy young man into the body of his retarded son. Even nastier, Harry Pollard's 1917 release *The Devil's Assistant* had lustful Dr Lorenz (Monroe Salisbury) turning the unfortunate Marta (Margarita Fisher) into a drug addict and being destroyed by a well-timed lightning bolt when he tries to rape her in a mountain cabin. And two years later, Fischer Features' *A Scream in the Night* (co-directed by Leander de Cordova and Burton L King) involved a crazed Darwinian scientist, Professor Silvio (John Webb Dillon), cultivating a feral jungle girl called, provocatively, Darwa (Ruth Budd).

Maurice Costello and Ethel Grandin were the draws in Erbograph's 16-part mad-science serial *The Crimson Stain Mystery* (1916)

The most conspicuous of these early mad scientists was Dr Burton Montrose, as played by Thomas J McGrane in a 16-chapter Erbograph serial called *The Crimson Stain Mystery*, which began its cliffhanging run on 21 August 1916. Like so many after him, Montrose's efforts to elevate the human race have precisely the opposite effect; the mutant products

of his experiments club together as a secret terrorist organisation and their depredations are chronicled in such alluringly titled instalments as 'The Brand of Satan', 'The Demon's Spell', 'The Phantom Image' and 'The Infernal Fiend'. The final episode, 'The Unmasking', sees their shadowy leader exposed by dogged detective Harold Stanley (Maurice Costello) as Dr Montrose himself.

The Crimson Stain Mystery was directed by T Hayes Hunter, who had already shown an abundance of commercial acumen in co-writing a Kalem production called *The Vampire* with its director Robert G Vignola. Shot in New Jersey in September 1913, this cautionary tale of a young man ensnared by a calculating 'vamp' had a killer selling point in the notorious 'Vampire Dance' performed by Bert French and the serpentine Alice Eis, which had already scandalised polite society and even got the couple arrested. Here, however, they were paid $2000 by the Kalem executives to immortalise it on film.

Hunter showed similar astuteness in casting two of the biggest names of the period, Maurice Costello and Ethel Grandin, in *The Crimson Stain Mystery*. For Carl Laemmle, Grandin had succeeded both Florence Lawrence and Mary Pickford as the IMP Girl, starring in an IMP adaptation of *Jane Eyre* and also in George Loane Tucker's 'white slavery' sex shocker, *Traffic in Souls*. For his part, Costello was a director as well as a matinée idol; in 1912, for example, he had collaborated with Van Dyke Brooke on a Vitagraph production called *Conscience*. Also known by the more come-hither title *Chamber of Horrors*, this showed an estranged young couple providentially reunited in an after-hours wax museum, the wife (Rose Tapley) because she's homeless and the husband (Costello) because he's fulfilling a wager. The result: he falls dead from shock, she goes insane. The 'stuck in a wax museum overnight' plot would prove a popular one, particularly for the comedic purposes of films like Jack White's *Spooks* (1922).

At this formative stage of the cinema's development, the fertile field of serial cliffhangers offered several embryonic pointers to the horror motifs brought to fruition in later decades. The year 1916, for example, yielded not only *The Crimson Stain Mystery* but Pathé's *The Mysteries of Myra*, which was appetisingly advertised as 'Fifteen Chapters of Science versus the Supernatural'. Here, Jean Sothern's Myra was cast very much in the mould of Pearl White in *The Perils of Pauline* and *The Exploits of Elaine* – indeed, scenarist Charles W Goddard was responsible for all three – and in the final chapter, 'The Thought Monster', she encountered a Frankenstein-type monstrosity created by the so-called Grand Master of the Black Order.

Alice Eis and Bert French performing their scandalous routine in Cliffside, New Jersey for the Kalem hit *The Vampire* (1913)

Three years later, master escapologist Harry Houdini would have a similar run-in with a prototype Frankenstein's Monster in Burton L King's 15-chapter serial *The Master Mystery*. Filmed in Yonkers by B A Rolfe Productions, this was Houdini's film debut and a massive hit in the spring of 1919. Floyd Buckley played the Automaton, a cartoonish-looking robot (closer to the Tin Man of *The Wizard of Oz* than the robot Maria of *Metropolis*) containing the brain of a dead man. Co-author Arthur B Reeve had been behind *The Exploits of Elaine* with Charles W Goddard, so Houdini's tight squeezes here are conceived on predictably fiendish lines: acid vats, electric chairs, descending elevators, even mechanical garrottes.

Houdini's film celebrity did not go unnoticed by other stage prestidigitators; in the UK, magician David Devant appeared in *The Great London Mystery* and, in the US, hypnotist J Robert Pauline made his one-and-only film appearance in the 1920 serial *The Mystery Mind*. Written by Arthur B Reeve again, this had Pauline's hypnotic hero protecting a young heiress not only from the titular menace but also The Phantom Face and The Evil Eye. In certain respects, *The Mystery Mind* may already have seemed old hat in 1920; with its emphasis on hypnotism and prominent use of an ape-man, it was reminiscent of Otis Turner's Universal serial of 1915, *The Black Box*.

The macabre and outré plot points that surfaced regularly in the chapter plays – such as the disembodied hand included among the audience-grabbing ingredients of another Universal serial, Stuart Paton's *The Voice on the Wire* (1917) – would occasionally crop up in more prestigious productions, and at the most unexpected moments. The Jesse L Lasky Feature

A ghost of the German Romantics revived: Conrad Veidt in *Das Cabinet des Dr Caligari* (1919)

The progress of these formidable competitors, however, was inevitably hamstrung by the war in Europe. As an effective counterbalance to the American industry, they would never fully recover from it.

At the outbreak of war in August 1914, Germany, too, was gaining a reputation that promised to equal those of France, Sweden and Italy. Four years later, however, the story seemed, at first, a very different one. Crushed and humiliated, Germany would nevertheless produce a long strong of dazzlingly imaginative films which had a huge impact on filmmakers the world over. In the aftermath of a war that had wiped out a whole generation, many of the subjects were profoundly morbid in tone, putting Germany at the head of the horror film tradition just as it had formerly been in at the birth of the horrid novel. As Lotte Eisner memorably put it, "the ghosts which had haunted the German Romantics revived, like the shades of Hades after draughts of blood."[7]

When, late in 1919, the 26-year-old Conrad Veidt was engaged by Erich Pommer's Decla-Film Gesellschaft to appear in a picture called *Das Cabinet des Dr Caligari*, he was already well versed in the crepuscular nightmares characteristic of German film studios. Earlier that year, he had appeared in two 'portmanteau' chillers, Richard Oswald's *Unheimliche Geschichten* and F W Murnau's *Satanas*; in the latter, Veidt was the Devil himself, wearily traversing three historical epochs in the style of Maturin's Gothic classic *Melmoth the Wanderer*. Now, the writer of *Satanas*, Robert Wiene, assumed the director's chair for *Caligari*, casting Veidt as Cesare, a somnambulist sent out to kill by an insane carnival mountebank called Dr Caligari (Werner Krauss). The analogy to the millions of young men who had recently been sent out to kill, and be killed, by lunatic governments was a transparent one and, on its premiere at Berlin's Marmorhaus on 26 February 1920, the film was a sensation.

Nightmare scenarios, often attended by the kind of Expressionist production design so bizarrely applied to *Caligari*, soon became commonplace. Veidt himself would play Ivan the Terrible in another portmanteau, Paul Leni's *Das Wachsfigurenkabinett*, together with a tormented concert pianist in Wiene's *Orlacs Hände* and a man shadowed by his own doppelgänger in Henrik Galeen's *Der Student von Prag*. Elsewhere,

Play presentation *Unconquered* was directed by Frank Reicher some 15 years ahead of his memorable performance as Captain Englehorn in *King Kong*. Here, Beatrice DeMille's straightforward tale of domestic cruelty was bizarrely augmented with voodoo details in which Tully Marshall (in blackface) proposes to sacrifice a small boy to propitiate his voodoo queen (Jane Wolfe).

Unconquered was released on 31 May 1917, by which time President Woodrow Wilson had finally precipitated the USA into a war that had been raging in Europe for nearly three years. By the end of the year close to ten million Americans had joined up, with the number exceeding 24 million by the end of hostilities in November 1918. Out among the West Coast orange groves, Hollywood would be by no means immune to the seismic impact of the Great War. Film production dropped noticeably in 1917, and many of the titles that were produced were unedifying features of the hiss-the-Hun variety. (If nothing else, these jingoistic knock-offs at least gave Erich von Stroheim his start as a succession of sadistic Prussian officers.) But, in the long run, the war would guarantee America's final ascendancy over the motion picture industry.

Before August 1914, US dominance was far from assured. In a medium still unencumbered by language barriers, France, Sweden and especially Italy were major players; Griffith himself was inspired to make *Intolerance* in an attempt to outdo the staggering visual innovations of Giovanni Pastrone's 1914 epic *Cabiria*.

F W Murnau would concoct an unauthorised *Dracula* adaptation in *Nosferatu* and a breathtaking version of Goethe's *Faust*, while Galeen went on to direct Paul Wegener and Brigitte Helm in a tale of an artificially created femme fatale called *Alraune*. By that time (1927), Wegener had starred as a clay robot in several versions of *Der Golem* and Helm had played a shimmering metal one in Fritz Lang's *Metropolis*, both of which would exercise a decisive influence over Hollywood renditions of *Frankenstein*.

Indeed, artificial life was already a well-worn theme in Germany, Otto Rippert having scored a huge hit in 1916 with his six-part serial *Homunculus*. Where France offered the black-masked Fantômas, Britain the avenging Ultus, and America the winsome Pearl White, Germany's serial masterwork showcased a superman (Olaf Fønss) forged in a laboratory and climactically extinguished by a thunderbolt.

When *Caligari* premiered in New York on 3 April 1921, the reviewer for *Picture-Play* magazine, in addition to calling the film "as pleasant as a trip through a lunacy ward," made an unusually astute prediction in the magazine's June issue: "Although you may never see *Doctor Caligari*, you ought to know about it because you will feel its influence in other pictures that are to come. It contains the germ of a great production idea, and while American directors have not had the courage to blaze new trails away from convention, they probably will not be slow to follow a good road once it has been pointed out to them." This proved all too true. As well as cannily importing such talents as Paul Leni and F W Murnau, US studios would also employ indigenous directors who were more than willing to obey the film's enticing tag-line, "Du musst Caligari werden" – "You must become Caligari."

Long before the film exercised its alien influence to the full, American critics had sought to get the measure of it by invoking a native author. The *New York Times*' estimate of *Caligari* as "a fantastic story of murder and madness such as Edgar Allan Poe might have written" was echoed in *Motion Picture News* ("like a page from Poe"), *Variety* ("a mystery story told in the Poe manner") and *Picture-Play* ("a story that might have been conceived by Edgar Allan Poe"). The comparison was a reasonable one, given that Poe had offered his own take on the enduring German theme of the doppelgänger as long ago as 1839, when he drew on his schooling in, of all places, Stoke Newington for a tale called *William Wilson*.

But even as *Caligari* was being produced at the Lixie-Atelier in Weissensee, across the Atlantic three different US film companies were turning to a British manifestation of the same theme.

THE PERSONIFICATION OF A CRAWLING POWER

In 1920, former Keystone Kop Hank Mann took the lead in a two-reel Arrow burlesque of Stevenson's *Dr Jekyll and Mr Hyde*, a topical target in that no fewer than three straight-faced versions had emerged in April of that year. One, F W Murnau's *Der Januskopf*, was an unauthorised treatment starring Conrad Veidt; it doesn't seem to have got beyond Germany and is now lost altogether. The other two were available to US filmgoers for direct comparison, and writer-director J Charles Haydon's five-reel version for the Pioneer Film Corporation was bound to come out the loser. Indeed, Haydon himself appears to have declined an on-screen credit.

Seasoned screen villain Sheldon Lewis was the star of one of three 1920 releases entitled *Dr Jekyll and Mr Hyde*

With a contemporary New York setting the better to skimp on the budget, Haydon's *Dr Jekyll and Mr Hyde* reshuffles Stevenson's characters so that Jekyll is engaged to Bernice Lanyon (Gladys Field), daughter of a doctor friend. When the atheistic Jekyll is thrown over in favour of "Bernice's chum since childhood," Danvers Carew (Leslie Austin), Jekyll's vengeful alter ego beats Carew to death with a cane, an atrocity which, along with Hyde's other depredations – handbag-snatching, unmotivated arson, flinging test tubes at a cat – causes the intertitles to brand him "An Apostle of Hell."

Though Bernice gets about in an automobile and urges Jekyll to join her in golfing sessions at the local Country Club, Haydon's location-heavy gloss of modernity does not extend to his lumpen direction. The transformations are easily achieved (in the first, a convenient cut-away to a hat-brushing butler does the trick), though an elementary double-exposure is employed for Hyde's vision of Carew's finger-pointing ghost. This forlorn reminiscence of Griffith's *Avenging Conscience* is supplemented at the end by another; from a shot of Hyde awaiting death in the electric chair, Haydon jumps to Jekyll starting awake in his seat, gratefully telling Bernice that "I believe in God – I have a soul – and – and I still have you!" Yet again, it was all a dream.

DR. JEKYLL AND MR. HYDE

Famous Players-Lasky Corporation 1919
6335 feet; silent
production began November

Cinematographer: Roy Overbaugh; Art Directors: Robert M Haas [architecture], Charles O Seessel [decorations], Clark Robinson*; Assistant Director: Shaw Lovett*; Screenplay: Clara Beranger, from the novel by Robert Louis Stevenson [and play by Thomas Russell Sullivan*]; Presented by: Adolph Zukor; Director: John S Robertson

John Barrymore (Dr Jekyll/Mr Hyde); Martha Mansfield (Millicent Carew); Brandon Hurst (Sir George Carew); Charles Lane (Dr Richard Lanyon); J Malcolm Dunn (John Utterson); Cecil Clovelly (Edward Enfield); Nita Naldi (Gina); uncredited: George Stevens (Poole); Louis Wolheim (music hall proprietor)

I left the picture cold, not to say clammy, but eager to sing the praises of J Barrymore and his sincere and quite amazing performance in this famous dual role, by which he reaches the peak of his screen achievements. Eager also to declare it to be the finest bit of directing John Stewart Robertson has ever done, and a job that places him with the first half dozen intelligent directors in the field. *Photoplay*

I grant you John Robertson did wonders with it and our cameraman was a perfect angel from Heaven, but I really don't know enough about pictures to give an expert opinion on it. I've always thought that my acting in it was not too bad, but beyond that I am not prepared to go.
John Barrymore [quoted in The Picturegoer, March 1924]

Bottled spider: John Barrymore's Hyde consorts with music-hall manager Louis Wolheim in *Dr Jekyll and Mr Hyde* (1919)

Haydon's Jekyll and Hyde was Sheldon Lewis, a seasoned serial villain of the clutching-hand variety who in 1914 had actually played 'The Clutching Hand' in *The Exploits of Elaine*. His snaggle-toothed Hyde, kitted out in slouch hat and black mac like an Edwardian child molester, is given one imaginative moment; as he kisses a skull, we half expect him to murmur "Alas, poor Yorick! I knew him, Horatio." But in all other respects Lewis' Hyde is an absurdity, gurning energetically even as he goes to the electric chair.

The film was produced by Louis Meyer, not to be confused (as he has been for eight decades) with the mighty Louis B Mayer of the yet-to-be-formed M-G-M. This lower-level Meyer was the entrepreneur behind 'vamp' actress Virginia Pearson, who also happened to be Mrs Sheldon Lewis. Meyer's version of *Dr Jekyll and Mr Hyde* was copyrighted on 16 April 1920, less than three weeks after the New York opening of a film with exactly the same title. A brief inspection of the rival production's credits – a Famous Players-Lasky picture distributed by Paramount-Artcraft, with John Barrymore heading the cast – makes it clear that the Pioneer version grew out of an already well-established tradition, that of fly-by-night filmmakers slinging together a cheapskate rip-off of a prestige production in record time.

The lion's share of the Famous Players production had been shot, like *Caligari*, in the closing weeks of 1919. In it, scenarist Clara Beranger came up with some variations on Stevenson's plot that were to have a profound effect on almost all subsequent adaptations. More importantly to contemporary audiences, the film showcased a bravura star turn from a gifted matinée idol with a pronounced appetite for the grotesque.

When taken to a low-life music hall by his venal prospective father-in-law Sir George Carew, the virtuous Dr Henry Jekyll is so disturbed by the unworthy feelings stirred in him by dancer-cum-prostitute Gina that he determines on a new experiment. Drinking a specially concocted potion, he becomes the degenerate Edward Hyde, enslaving Gina, threatening Jekyll's fiancée Millicent, murdering Carew and finally killing himself.

On Saturday 6 March 1920, Barrymore opened to huge acclaim at Broadway's Plymouth Theatre in the title role of *Richard III*. Despite the plaudits, the play was taken off prematurely and its star admitted to a White Plains sanitarium; the strain of filming additional scenes for *Dr Jekyll and Mr Hyde* at Adolph Zukor's 56th Street studio in Manhattan while rehearsing Richard at the Plymouth had finally taken its toll.

During his convalescence, Barrymore dramatised his own duality by means of a watercolour self-portrait, depicting the so-called 'Great Profile' fused with a hideous, octopoid spider. Loitering in the Bronx Zoo, Barrymore had become fascinated by a reddish-grey tarantula, calling it "the personification of a crawling power ... just like Richard the Third."[8] *Dr Jekyll and Mr Hyde* was released some three weeks after Barrymore's Plymouth premiere, and the spider imagery crept in there too, with Hyde depicted as a hobbling arachnid low-life in a pointy hat, which, when doffed, reveals a cranium of precisely the same shape. The parallels to Barrymore's Richard (whom Shakespeare describes as "a bottled spider") were no doubt inescapable to contemporary audiences. And if the star's nervous breakdown was brought on in part by visions of wall-to-wall tarantulas, they can't have been any worse than the truly hideous nightmare sequence contained in the film itself.

In it, Jekyll reposes uneasily in a four-poster bed, his aquiline left profile turned fetchingly to camera. Suddenly, a huge, and very hirsute, spider emerges to the right of the bed, scuttles rapidly over the ottoman at its foot and thence onto the counterpane. Jekyll reaches out a hand to fend it off, but it crawls on top of him in an obscene embrace – it's around this time that we notice it has Hyde's face – and then, via an elementary double-exposure, is absorbed into him. He wakes, of course, as a leering and triumphant Hyde. The scene derives its power not only from the ghastly metaphor of a man's hidden desires arising from sexual congress with a tarantula, but also from the artless crudity with which it's put over. A second viewing confirms that, yes, the monster is just Barrymore in his Hyde make-up with the spider-body literally attached to his back. Two of its eight legs are his own, and he's even got his trousers on. But this gaslit grotesquerie from a vanished era remains among the most repugnant images ever committed to celluloid.

"The Screen's Greatest Actor in a Tremendous Story of Man at His Best and Worst," screamed the ads, and Barrymore didn't disappoint. Though narcissistic, his Jekyll is nothing less than a paragon of virtue; as his fiancée's wily father puts it, "no man could be as good as he looks." When taken by Carew to the Victorian equivalent of a pole-dancing establishment, Jekyll seems to conceive his high-minded scheme in traumatised response to getting his first erection.

Barrymore's Hyde, meanwhile, is a genuine monstrosity. His first appearance is a triumph of gestural acting (Barrymore resorting to make-up only after an uninterrupted take in which his face and body-language effect the transformation unaided), and his climactic murder of Carew remains an awesome outburst of animal ferocity. Everything about him – the distorted countenance gradually worsening as the film progresses, the hideously elongated fingers, the strangely phallic head, the gratuitous biting of Carew's neck – is strikingly similar to the cadaverous bloodsucker played by Max Schreck in F W Murnau's *Nosferatu* some 18 months later.

The film made a huge impact in its day. "It will easily become the most talked-of picture of the time," observed Burns Mantle in *Photoplay*'s June issue. "A door and two windows were broken by the crowds that tried to see it on its first showing in New York. It may tour the country to the tune of similar crashes." Today, however, the picture looks more antiquated than many of its surviving contemporaries, due in large part to John S Robertson's pedestrian direction and a nondescript supporting cast; of several expendable male characters, the 29-year-old Cecil Clovelly looks ridiculous in an Am Dram old-age make-up as Enfield.

British import Brandon Hurst is an exception, however, giving Carew a watchful man-of-the-world hauteur ideally attuned to Beranger's wholesale lifting of the character from Wilde's Lord Henry Wotton in *The Picture of Dorian Gray*. There's nothing subtle about the script's cheerful piracy here; one of Sir George's intertitles actually reads, "The only way to get rid of a temptation is to yield to it."

Indeed, after Barrymore's central performance, Beranger's script remains much the most interesting feature of the film. It touches on Jekyll as drug fiend (Barrymore irresistibly suggests a state of wild-eyed 'cold turkey' as he waits for his manservant to bring home the relevant chemicals), and even hints that the steadily deteriorating Hyde is a victim of some peculiarly virulent STD, a condition passed on to the increasingly hollow-eyed Gina. And, as Hyde skulks through low-life settings worthy of Thomas Burke's 1916 anthology *Limehouse Nights*, we're left to ponder on whether Beranger's real purpose was to show the patrician Jekyll's 'evil' nature as merely his working-class side struggling to get out.

Deeply dubious though the analogy might be, it throws up some of the film's most striking images: underprivileged patients in Jekyll's "human repair shop" looking like a sequence of weathered daguerrotypes; Hyde's hook-nosed landlady underlit by the pallid effulgence of a gas lamp; a man with, seemingly, no nose reposing among the down-and-outs in an opium den. Most significantly, the Beranger scenario firmly established the Madonna-Whore convention of providing Jekyll with two contrasted women to choose between. The winsome fiancée, Millicent, handily reflects the outwardly respectable side of his nature, with his other self mirrored by the earthy and exotic prostitute Gina – or, as the music hall barker euphemistically calls her, "the fimous h'Italian dancer."

If, in its East End scenes, the film's echoes of Burke's *Limehouse Nights* anthology were deliberate, art director Robert M Haas was probably influenced more by a recent film based on Burke's book than by the book itself. Shot in just 18 days and released in May 1919, D W Griffith's *Broken Blossoms* was based on Burke's story *The Chink and the Child*. Here, Griffith enlisted the soft-focus help of master lighting cameraman Hendrik Sartov (in addition to his usual confederate, Billy Bitzer) in bringing limpid beauty to a heavily atmospheric parable of racism and domestic violence. In it, fragile East End teenager Lucy Burrows (Lillian Gish) is regularly brutalised by her prizefighter father (Donald Crisp), briefly rescued by "Chink storekeeper" Chen (Richard Barthelmess), and finally killed when her father finds out about the relationship.

Lillian Gish as brutalised Limehouse waif Lucy Burrows in *Broken Blossoms or The Yellow Man and the Girl* (1919)

With Gish whirring round and round inside a closet as Crisp batters his way through, the film's climactic scene builds to a truly terrifying crescendo. "It had to be spontaneous, the hysterical terror of a child," Gish later explained. "Well, when I came to play the scene in front of the camera, I did it as I'd planned – spinning and screaming terribly (I was a good screamer; Mr Griffith used to encourage me to scream at the top of my voice). When we finished, Mr Griffith was very pale. There was a man from *Variety* at the studio, and Mr Griffith called him in and made me go through the scene again for him. It was so horrific that the man from *Variety* brought up his breakfast."[9]

In a post-war Hollywood firmament dominated by such luminous stars as Gish, Mary Pickford and the Talmadge sisters, *Dr Jekyll and Mr Hyde*'s two female leads, Martha Mansfield and Nita Naldi, were to suffer very different fates. Tragically, Mansfield burned to death in November 1923 as a result of a flicked cigarette butt on the set of *The Warrens of Virginia*. Earlier that year, she had starred opposite Barrymore's rival Hyde, Sheldon Lewis, in John G Adolfi's *The Little Red Schoolhouse*, in which a murderer (Lewis) is magically exposed when his face is etched onto a schoolhouse window by a bolt of lightning.

Though based on a play by Hal Reid, the film's deus ex machina twist was extremely similar to that of Augusta Wilson's 1887 novel *At the Mercy of Tiberius*, which had been filmed twice already: first by Thanhouser's Eugene W Moore as *God's Witness* in 1915, then by Fred LeRoy Granville as *The Price of Silence* in 1920. In Wilson's story, though, the entire murder tableau is sketched out on the windowpane, not just the guilty face. The 1920 version was a co-production between Sunrise Pictures and the British impresario G B Samuelson, who issued the film in the UK several months ahead of its US release, also restoring Wilson's original title.

Subsequent to *Dr Jekyll and Mr Hyde*, Nita Naldi would become known as 'Queen of the Vampires' and be perfectly matched opposite Rudolph Valentino in both *Blood and Sand* and *The Cobra*. She also appeared

in a star vehicle for a more unlikely film star, Harry Houdini, in Burton L King's *The Man from Beyond* (1921). Co-written by Houdini and made by his own production company, this traded on his personal interest in reincarnation and life after death, casting him as a man hewn from a block of ice in the Arctic and revived 100 years after his death. The snowbound opening is effective, with the cryogenically suspended Houdini presented as a "figure stark and stiff within its icy tomb – its features frozen in a snarl of hate." But the remainder is a disappointingly routine melodrama, culminating in a spot of free advertising for *The New Revelation*, a 1918 book by Houdini's chum Sir Arthur Conan Doyle.

By the time Naldi assumed the title, the cult of the so-called 'vamp' was thought to be on its last legs. The confusion between the out-and-out undead vampire and the briefly fashionable vamp (a sexually predatory female busting any number of Edwardian taboos) had thrown up plenty of tantalising but non-supernatural titles, notably the above-mentioned Kalem hit of 1913, *The Vampire*, and its 1914 sequel *The Vampire's Trail*. But the cult had originated, like *Dracula*, as far back as 1897, with the exhibition of Philip Burne-Jones' scandalous canvas 'The Vampire', in which the actress Mrs Patrick Campbell hovers hungrily over a prostrated young man. The painting inspired the artist's cousin, Rudyard Kipling, to write a poem of the same name, itself the cue for a smash-hit Broadway play of 1909, *A Fool There Was*.

William Fox's film version was released in January 1915, making a star of Theodosia Goodman, comely daughter of a Cincinnati tailor. The studios' publicity machine having acquired untold sophistication since the 1910 revelation of Florence Lawrence, Goodman was transformed by Fox into Theda Bara – daughter of the Nile, born in the shadow of the Sphinx, her name an anagram of 'Arab Death', etc etc. "This deadly Arab girl," noted Terry Ramsaye in 1926, "was a crystal-gazing seeress of profoundly occult powers, wicked as fresh red paint and poisonous as dried spiders. The stronger the copy grew, the more it was printed. Little girls read it and swallowed their gum with excitement."[10] For some four years, Bara enjoyed a pulling power exceeded only by Charlie Chaplin and Mary Pickford, her position as the screen's first sex symbol immortalised in the famous *A Fool There Was* intertitle, "Kiss me, my fool!"

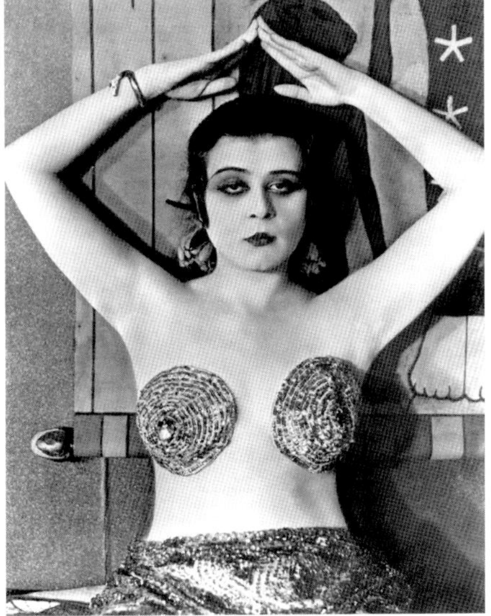

Theda Bara: Cincinnati's "deadly Arab girl" in characteristically smouldering pose (1917)

By 1925, Bara was well aware of her pervasive influence. "I disagree with the statement that the vamp is dead; she is too sturdy and resilient and wily to be killed off," she maintained. "What are [Nita] Naldi and [Barbara] LaMarr if not vampire types? Their appeal is mostly physical. Thus, the technique has changed somewhat. But the motif is the same."[11] Bara's example was also followed by Valeska Suratt, Alma Rubens and Louise Glaum, among others, while her 'look' – eyes positively smouldering with mascara and, as Ramsaye put it, "her full lips a livid scarlet in a large white face, so that it looked as if all the blood in her head had concentrated in her mouth" – predated the 'Goth' style by some seven decades. More immediately, it would be transposed onto male Latin lovers of the Valentino variety prior to mutating, with a pleasing circularity, into the slickly venomous form of Bela Lugosi's genuine vampire, Count Dracula.

Pray Don't Tell Them How It Ends

Theatregoers thrilling to John Barrymore's "foul lump of deformity" in *Richard III* – and perhaps condescending also to catch his screen performance as Mr Hyde – were in for another shuddery treat within six months. A long-running play called *The Bat* not only modernised the 'Gothic castle' motif for a generation gearing up for the Jazz Age, it also provided the catalyst for that mode taking root in picture palaces too. Clutching hands, sliding panels, masked murderers, hidden treasures, screams in the night – all these hoary old tricks gained a new and vaguely tongue-in-cheek currency via *The Bat*.

The play took a circuitous route to the stage. It originated as *The Circular Staircase*, a novel by Pittsburgh's Queen of Crime, Mary Roberts Rinehart, serialised in *All-Story Magazine* from November 1907 and issued in book form the following year. "The

Circular Staircase was intended to be a semi-satire on the pompous and self-important crime story," Rinehart explained in her autobiography, though critics, to her surprise, claimed that "I had made the first advance in the technique of the crime story since Edgar Allan Poe!"[12] Telling of an elderly New York society lady who takes a summer's lease on the ironically named Sunnyside, Rinehart's story also involves a dying banker, a bogus gardener, a stash of bank securities in an attic room, and an embittered housekeeper who confesses to killing the banker's son at the foot of the titular staircase.

In 1915, Edward J Le Saint directed a five-reel version of *The Circular Staircase* for Selig Polyscope, with Eugénie Besserer in the lead. Not content with this, Rinehart turned to her dramatist friend Avery Hopwood, concocting with him a much-altered stage version named after an entirely new character, The Bat, a black-masked master criminal owing something to the Fantômas figure popularised in France by Louis Feuillade.

Crane Wilbur: Pearl White's leading man, author of *The Monster*, and (much later) screenwriter of *House of Wax*

This character would give the property the kind of spooky glamour a murderous old housekeeper couldn't provide, while his disguise as Detective Anderson qualifies the play as the first in a line of 'the policeman did it' stories that eventually included Agatha Christie's *The Mousetrap*. And, in applying up-to-the-minute ratiocination to a long discredited genre, Rinehart revealed herself as a late-blooming descendant of Mrs Radcliffe twice over: the Gothic castle was reconfigured as a labyrinthine 'old dark house', while its apparently supernatural trappings were revealed – again as per Mrs Radcliffe – as the machinations of scheming human beings.

The Bat accordingly opened at the Morosco Theatre on 23 August 1920, running for a whopping 867 performances and netting in all some $9 million. "The authors botched their work by allowing a farcically frightened maidservant to rip open the suspense whenever possible," noted theatre historian J C Trewin, pinpointing a tendency that would bedevil so many subsequent films in similar vein. "Even with this bawling, with the steeping of the stage in a sickly green, and with a failure to make any of the action mildly credible," he added, "*The Bat* managed to flap to a success with a public that liked to be told a story, and did not much mind how improbable it was ... Many more terrors would follow, as fast as dramatists could invent them and directors direct."[13]

Indeed they would. John Willard's *The Cat and the Canary* arrived at the National (now Nederlander) Theatre on 7 February 1922 and ran for the best part of a year, during which time Crane Wilbur's *The Monster* opened on 9 August at the 39th Street Theatre and notched up 101 performances. Then on 24 October *The Last Warning*, adapted by Thomas F Fallon from a Wadsworth Camp novel, began a run of 238 performances at the Klaw Theatre.

Occasionally these plays threw up a showy leading role for a suitably mesmerising actor; in *The Monster*, for instance, Wilton Lackaye came to the mad Dr Ziska direct from the umpteenth revival of his famous Svengali. But mainly they were concerned with moving various puppet figures around the crepuscular recesses of country houses (in *Bat* and *Cat*), an abandoned lunatic asylum (in *The Monster*) and an old 'dark' theatre (in *The Last Warning*). And all of them traded on the familiar 1920s jingle, "If you like this play, please tell your friends / But pray don't tell them how it ends." On top of this, the genre's obvious indebtedness to the kind of 'clutching hand' movie serials of the previous decade was confirmed by the participation of Crane Wilbur. Author of *The Monster*, he had previously starred opposite Pearl White in *The Perils of Pauline*.

There were several exotic variants on the formula, with the inky blackness of night exchanged for sweat-stained bouts of murder and miscegenation in the tropics. Audience-grabbing potboilers like Leon Gordon's *White Cargo* (1923) and *Aloma of the South Seas* by John B Hymer and LeRoy Clemens (1925) would eventually throw up a wildly sleazy and sadistic mutant called *Kongo*, produced at the Biltmore Theatre in 1926. Chester DeVonde and Kilbourn Gordon's play gave Walter Huston a barnstorming showcase as a berserk 'White God' in darkest Africa, also inspiring two film versions. This kind of native sadism was presumably more congenial than the blood-drenched Gallic excesses of Le Théâtre du Grand Guignol.

Though a British equivalent had run in London for three years, Georges Renavent's American Grand Guignol, which opened at the Grove Street Theatre in Greenwich Village in December 1927, met with an indifferent reception.

Inevitably, many of Broadway's mystery plays crossed the Atlantic to London's West End. In 1922, *The Bat* and *The Cat and the Canary* were produced at the St James's and Shaftesbury Theatres respectively, the former featuring Eva Moore as Miss Van Gorder, Arthur Wontner as Detective Anderson and Claude Rains as Billy the butler. *The Monster*, meanwhile, made a belated appearance at the Strand in 1928. Another such, *The Gorilla*, actually did better in the West End than on Broadway. Written by Ralph Spence, a Ziegfeld Follies regular who could command $10,000 per picture as a Hollywood titles-writer, this one opened at London's New Oxford Theatre in June 1925 and totted up 134 performances. The advertising showed an acute awareness of a tradition already so ingrained that Spence could afford to parody it: "Now – outbats *The Bat* – outcats *The Cat and the Canary* – outwarns *The Last Warning*. You'll laugh – roar – howl and scream."

The Jazz Age appetite for howling and screaming was obviously so vast that homegrown British variants weren't slow to follow, and some of them were to prove just as durable. Arnold Ridley's *The Ghost Train* inspired several film versions, together with a Broadway transfer starring Eric Blore and Claudette Colbert. Edgar Wallace's *The Terror* went on to sire the second all-talking picture made in Hollywood, while *The Silent House*, in which John G Brandon and George Pickett located their 'old dark house' on Barnes Common, remained on home ground, being filmed at Walton-on-Thames in 1929. Like Spence, Ben Travers would send up the whole trend in his 1927 Aldwych farce *Thark*, featuring a butler named Death and a 'haunted bedroom' routine that was to be much imitated.

By that time, however, the British strain had thrown up a play that was to have a decisive effect on the future of Hollywood horror. Provincial actor-manager Hamilton Deane opened his cost-conscious adaptation of Bram Stoker's *Dracula* at Derby's Grand Theatre in August 1924. By St Valentine's Day of 1927 it had reached London's Little Theatre, provoking unmixed critical condescension and a Broadway transfer some eight months later. Though exploiting the trend, the crucial difference between *Dracula* and its fellows was its unblushing admission that the Count really *was* a blood-drinking revenant, rather than exposing him in the final tableau as the kind of earthbound villain featured in *The Bat*. When Universal translated that crucial difference to film in 1930, the effect would be revolutionary.

In the meantime, the 1920s' vogue for Broadway mystery-thrillers had three notable precedents, all of which had been translated to film well before *The Bat* took up residence at the Morosco. Bayard Veiller's *The Thirteenth Chair* had opened in November 1916, running for 328 performances and inspiring a 1919 six-reeler from the Acme Pictures Corporation. Here, a blackmailer sitting in the thirteenth chair at a seance is murdered, his killer only being revealed by means of an elaborate trick played out at a further seance. Written and directed by the famous Gaumont comedian Léonce Perret, this gave the plum part of medium Mme LaGrange to Marie Shotwell. Veiller's English wife, Margaret Wycherly, had made a big hit in the part on stage, but had to wait until the 1929 remake to repeat her performance.

Going back still further, Earl Derr Biggers' 1913 novel *Seven Keys to Baldpate* was adapted for the stage by George M Cohan and opened in New York in September of the same year, clocking up 320 performances. Its story – of a pulp novelist trying to write a 24-hour novel at a supposedly untenanted inn, only to be bedevilled by a series of mysterious interlopers – was first filmed in Australia in 1916. The following year, Cohan himself starred opposite Anna Q Nilsson in an Artcraft production directed by Hugh Ford, after which the property was revived with astonishing regularity.

A 1920 send-up, *Seven Bald Pates*, was concocted by future horror specialists William Beaudine and W Scott Darling, after which there was a Famous Players-Lasky version in 1925 and a 1929 talkie from the fledgling RKO, who proceeded to wheel the story out again in 1935 and 1947. The last version to date, *House of the Long Shadows*, was made in Britain as late as 1982, complete with Cohan's postmodern double-twist – (a) all the mysterious characters are revealed as actors, and (b) the action turns out to be that of the novel the writer was engaged in all along.

An even earlier precedent for the clutching-hand comedy-thriller had been set with the March 1909 opening of *The Ghost Breaker*, "a Melodramatic Farce in Four Acts" by Paul Dickey and Charles W Goddard. Dickey would go on to play a memorably villainous Guy of Gisbourne opposite Douglas Fairbanks in *Robin Hood*, while Goddard would be the originator of the classic Pearl White serials *The Perils of Pauline* and *The Exploits of Elaine*. Their play, meanwhile, would have a very long life.

Having been revived on Broadway in the spring of 1913, by Christmas the following year it had been transferred to film as a glamorous product of the Jesse L Lasky Feature Play Company. The star of both Broadway manifestations of the play, English actor H B Warner, was retained as Warren Jarvis, whose efforts to recover a valuable locket for Aragon princess Maria Theresa (Rita Stanwood) range from New York and Kentucky to a supposedly haunted castillo in Spain. Co-directed by Lasky's director-general Cecil B DeMille and former Edison associate Oscar C Apfel, this was the only film version to adhere at all closely to the original play.

Lasky revived the property in 1922, the result directed by Alfred E Green and reaching cinemas in September. This time, the play was extensively made over as a vehicle for all-American heart-throb Wallace Reid; the scenarist responsible, Walter DeLeon, would render the story even less recognisable 18 years later as a Bob Hope comedy special. As before, Warren Jarvis (Reid) agrees to help exorcise the family seat of the lovely Maria Theresa (Lila Lee), though this time the uniquely saturnine character star Arthur Edmund Carewe enlivens proceedings as the conniving Duke d'Alva, who has trumped up a fleet of so-called ghosts to get his hands on hidden treasure. *Variety*'s judgment of 15 September noted that "The sets are elaborate and the photography [by William Marshall] good, but it looks as though Reid had made up his mind that he was going to do as little work as possible in this picture, and possibly conspired with the script writer and director to help him out."

Wallace Reid stows away in the heroine's trunk in *The Ghost Breaker* (1922)

MANSLAUGHTER, MURDER AND MONKEY GLANDS

Prior to his starring role as Warren Jarvis in *The Ghost Breaker*, Wallace Reid had 'form' where Gothic subjects were concerned. In 1917 he had appeared in DeMille's *The Devil-Stone* (a feature-length treatment of the old 'curse-encrusted gems' scenario) and, four years before that, he'd played the title role in a version of *The Picture of Dorian Gray* produced by the New York Motion Picture Corporation. If, by 1922, Reid's performance as Warren Jarvis appeared somewhat listless, it was hardly surprising. Not only did he make a remarkable total of nine features that year, he was also in the toils of morphine addiction, dying, aged 30, on 18 January 1923. He had been hooked on the drug by studio executives eager to get him through the 1919 filming of James Cruze's *The Valley of the Giants* after he sustained injuries in a train crash.

Reid's death was an acute embarrassment to the film business not because of its own culpability but because of the way it added to the stench of corruption that was beginning to form around Hollywood. The suicide in September 1920 of boyish Griffith star Bobby Harron had been succeeded, cataclysmically, by the September 1921 arraignment of Roscoe 'Fatty' Arbuckle for manslaughter, then the unsolved murder on 1 February 1922 of the well-known director William Desmond Taylor.

As it turned out, the stew of apparent corruption in Hollywood was just a pale shadow of the far more serious evils sanctioned by the easy-going but vapid President Warren Harding, whose coinage of the grotesque word 'normalcy' had strongly appealed to Americans worn out by nearly a decade of Woodrow Wilson's high-flown idealism. The Harding administration had its own share of mystery suicides and even sex scandals (as revealed by Harding's mistress after his death), with million-dollar 'graft' sensations to boot. But, despite these 'real world' scandals, it was clear that the Hollywood studios were going to have to clean up their act.

Within six weeks of the Taylor murder, and against a rising tide of anti-Hollywood feeling, panicked studio heads acted to avert the threat of federal censorship by incorporating the Motion Picture Producers and Distributors Association (MPPDA). To head this self-regulating body, they appointed Will H Hays, who as postmaster-general had engineered the success of President Harding. As Kevin Brownlow puts it, Hays "had no knowledge of motion pictures. Yet he was to have more influence on their development – or retardation – than any single figure since Thomas Edison."[14] This was no consolation to Roscoe Arbuckle, who, though exonerated, had seen his career destroyed, his reputation skewered in particular by the all-powerful newspaper magnate William Randolph Hearst.

Some months before the scandal broke, Arbuckle had made his contribution to the ubiquitous 'comedian in a phoney haunted house' field, starring opposite Lila Lee in James Cruze's *The Dollar-a-Year Man*, a Famous Players feature issued in April 1921. The same year, Buster Keaton made his own contribution to the trend via the opening section of *The Balloonatics* and the entirety of *The Haunted House*, the latter featuring a plot device – "the bank cashier and his band of counterfeiters" tricked out as ghosts – derived from *The Ghost Breaker*. Probably the first such film in the post-war period was the Harold Lloyd short *Haunted Spooks* (1920), which preceded similar haunted house hi-jinks in Lloyd's *I Do* (1922) and the feature-length *Dr Jack* (1924), in which his climactic masquerade as an escaped lunatic was a direct take-off of *The Cat and the Canary*. Another Lloyd feature, *Hot Water* (1924), saw him mistaking his accidentally chloroformed mother-in-law (Josephine Crowell) for a ghost, just as a little black boy providentially dunked in flour ('Sunshine Sammy' Morrison) had been misinterpreted in *Haunted Spooks*.

Despite these parodies, haunted houses were still being handled with a straight face by other filmmakers. Among them was the British-born Vitagraph veteran J Stuart Blackton, whose *The House of the Tolling Bell* featured a supposedly dead old man residing in the cupola of a spooky old house in order to observe his heirs' behaviour under stress. May McAvoy was the love interest and, simplifying the casting process, Blackton cast his studio manager, William R Dunn, as the chief villain. Released in September 1920, Blackton's film was followed in October by Ernest C Warde's *The House of Whispers*, in which J Warren Kerrigan and Fritzi Brunette were tenants of an apartment block honeycombed with secret passages and beset by ghostly sounds – as so often, the work of crooks.

Working a minor variation on the usual routine, Albert Ray's August 1921 release *A Midnight Bell* set its ghostly thrills in a deserted church, showcasing 'real' ghosts alongside the predictable underground passage leading to the local bank. Finally, Lloyd Ingraham's *At the Sign of the Jack o' Lantern* centred on a young couple obliged by the terms of a will to entertain obnoxious guests and petrifying ghosts in their New England home.

Ingraham's film came out in January 1922. The same month saw the unveiling of the picture Roscoe Arbuckle had been working on when the tragic events of 5 September 1921 came to light. A James Cruze fantasy-comedy called *Ek*, it had since experienced a title change to *One Glorious Day* and a leading-man change to Will Rogers. As a mild-mannered psychology professor intrigued by spiritualism, Rogers succeeds in liberating his soul from his body, only for an anarchic, bug-eyed spirit called Ek (short for ectoplasm) to take up residence before he can get back in.

A much more visceral experiment had been undertaken in Marshall Neilan's serial-style feature *Go and Get It*, a "Sensational, Mile-a-minute Melodrama of Newspaper Life" made in April 1920 and released by First National three months later. Here, an intrepid reporter (Pat O'Malley) traces a rash of brutal revenge killings to an ape that has had its brain swapped

Noah Beery contemplates his caged creation (Bull Montana) in *Go and Get It* (1920)

with that of a gangster (Walter Long), the surgeon responsible, Dr Ord (Noah Beery), being the first to go.

The ape-man, Ferry – a much more alarming character than the female hybrid featured the previous year in *A Scream in the Night* – was played by Louis 'Bull' Montana, an Italian wrestler brought to Hollywood under the patronage of Douglas Fairbanks. (He would later play a similar role in *The Lost World*, written, like *Go and Get It*, by Marion Fairfax.) Neilan cajoled several real-life journalists, among them the famous sports writer Ring Lardner, into endorsing the film, and in its mood of hot-off-the-presses verisimilitude *Go and Get It* anticipated the hard-boiled style of the company that would later subsume First National, Warner Bros. In its parallel mood of outrageous non-verisimilitude, the film anticipated Paramount's *The Monster and the Girl* by two decades.

Only a year or two elapsed, however, before the skittish Darwinian details of *Go and Get It* were refashioned into an out-and-out grim-faced shocker from the Goldwyn company. Faced with Wallace Worsley's *A Blind Bargain*, *Variety*'s 'Skig' was unimpressed, dismissing it as "Another addition to the 'horror' situation so prevalent in fiction, theatre and on the screen for the past year." Despite Skig's seen-it-all nonchalance, the film was considered – by Goldwyn executives, at any rate – as something of a hot potato, thanks to a plot that fused the contemporary gland-grafting theories of Dr Serge Voronoff with fiction's master vivisectionist Dr Moreau, and in the process aggravated the still inflammatory sore of Darwinism.

In need of cash, Robert Sandell agrees to be an experimental guinea pig for the apparently philanthropic Dr Lamb. Given eight days in which to live it up at Lamb's expense, Sandell realises too late that Lamb's hunchbacked assistant was formerly an ape; only when Sandell has been strapped to the operating table does the vengeful hunchback uncage one of Lamb's other subjects, a colossal beast-man which savages Lamb to death.

The film was actually based, not on H G Wells' 1896 novel *The Island of Dr Moreau*, but on *The Octave of Claudius* by Barry Pain, which was published a year later. J G Hawks' scenario deviated from the original in several ways, retaining Pain's so-called 'octave' (the eight-day period of grace before Sandell submits to Lamb's 'blind bargain') but making the young hero not only an aspiring author but a veteran of World War I. Hawks also gave Dr Lamb a more spectacular demise; in the novel he's murdered by his long-suffering wife.

In the process, Hawks provided Lamb with much of the trademark rhetoric later to issue from any number of movie mad scientists. Referring to the monstrosity that will ultimately destroy him, Lamb boasts that "He was the first sacrifice that science demanded in a marvellous biologic [sic] experiment. I took him one hour from death, a wasted maniac, and gave him the life and virility of a powerful animal. This time I will reverse the process of transfusion. The blood in your veins shall flow in the ape's!" Hawks also made the film's indebtedness to contemporary news reports very obvious indeed, notably in an intertitle purporting to be one of Dr Lamb's vainglorious diary entries: "French scientists claim that by grafting the glands of an anthropoid ape to the human body they have renewed the youth of old men. I shall outdo their achievements – I shall not permit men to grow old. I shall preserve youth indefinitely."[15]

Goldwyn's publicity agents also emphasised this point. The customary spotlight was thrown on the film's leads – pre-eminently the gifted character star Lon Chaney, but also beleaguered hero Raymond McKee and Buster Keaton's regular co-star Jacqueline Logan. In addition, the film's pressbook proposed several hyperbolic tag-lines, including the generic "A mad physician tears the veil of secrecy from life's profoundest secrets" and the more pertinent "Will the gland of the Ape bring humanity eternal Youth?"

Yet it was this very theme that caused the Goldwyn company numerous post-production headaches. Though made in October 1921, the film was only sneak-previewed in the last week of November 1922. The hiatus may in part have been due to corporate upheavals; deeming him responsible for such suspiciously arty manoeuvres as the importation of *Caligari*, Goldwyn stockholders had ejected the company's president, Sam Goldwyn, that very year. But the response to the film's sneak preview betrayed every sign of panic, particularly in light of the recent formation of the MPPDA. In a matter of days, *A Blind Bargain* was drastically cut down to remove its more controversial elements, with a hand-coloured ball sequence added to bulk up the (still slim) running time. After this brutal surgery, the film opened at the Capitol in New York City on 3 December.

Sadly, *A Blind Bargain* now appears to be irretrievably lost; surviving stills show Chaney looking slickly Mephistophelean as Dr Lamb and convincingly simian as his hunchbacked assistant. For Chaney, however, this dual role constituted little more than a business-as-usual display of versatility. Indeed, such was the public perception of Chaney's protean brilliance that a quip attributed to Marshall Neilan – "Don't step on it [a spider or some such] – it might be Lon Chaney" – became a popular 1920s catchphrase.

The post-war fascination with Serge Voronoff's monkey-gland theories was also reflected in a glamorous literary adaptation produced by William Randolph Hearst's Cosmopolitan Pictures, an outfit mainly concerned with pushing Hearst's mistress Marion Davies. To this end, a wildly popular Marie Corelli novel called *The Young Diana* became a Davies showcase, with a dowdy spinster, still smarting from her two-decades-old jilting, having those 20 years eradicated by a conniving scientist researching the elixir of youth. Unfortunately, the film, directed by Albert Capellani and Robert G Vignola, winds up by invoking the already mildewed 'it was all a dream' clause. Seen, then as now, more as Hearst's pampered protégée than the accomplished comedienne she was, Davies nevertheless earned high praise from *Motion Picture Classic*'s Laurence Reid, who also observed that "money has been scattered with a lavish hand to accomplish the last word in elaborate mounting" and that "Pedro de Cordoba's playing of the scientist [Dr Dimitrius] is a study in poise and finesse."[16]

Released in August 1922, *The Young Diana* seems to have sparked off a vogue for rejuvenation fantasies, leaning heavily on the modish Voronoff angle while pointing forward to the quick-fix wonders of plastic surgery. By December 1923, Frank Lloyd's *Black Oxen* was offering Corinne Griffith as an Austrian Countess made over by surgical means. While this one was based on a Gertrude Franklin Atherton novel, Roy William Neill's *Vanity's Price*, made by the appropriately named Gothic Pictures and released in September 1924, was an original scenario in which Anna Q Nilsson took advantage of her restored youth to give her caddish ex-husband (Stuart Holmes) a good horse-whipping. Ironically, the film's writer was Paul Bern, one of the Goldwyn employees who had been charged with the post-production emasculation of *A Blind Bargain*.

Cornering the market in this limited area, Anna Q Nilsson moved from playing a celebrated actress in *Vanity's Price* to a British aristocrat in *One Way Street*, a First National release from April 1925. John Francis Dillon's film took a Beale Davis novel of the same title and arbitrarily grafted on the rejuvenation angle merely to exploit the trend, even showing Nilsson's Lady Sylvia withering into decrepitude when placed under stress.

At the opposite extreme to glamorous stars like Marion Davies, Corinne Griffith and Anna Q Nilsson, the kind of ape-men featured in

A BLIND BARGAIN

Goldwyn Pictures 1921
4473 feet; silent
included colour sequence
produced October/November

Cinematographer: Norbert Brodin; Art Director: Cedric Gibbons; Editor: Paul Bern; Assistant Director: James Dugan; Scenario: J G Hawks, from the novel *The Octave of Claudius* by Barry Pain; Director: Wallace Worsley

Lon Chaney (Dr Lamb/The Hunchback); Raymond McKee (Robert Sandell); Virginia True Boardman (Mrs Sandell); Fontaine LaRue (Mrs Lamb); Jacqueline Logan (Angela Marshall); Aggie Herring (Bessie); Virginia Madison (Angela's mother)

Exactly what it is the doctor wants to do and why his resourceful wife never thinks of putting him in an asylum are questions avoided by the rambling story, for, if considered, there wouldn't be any story and the chance to show Mr Chaney in contrasted roles would be last [sic] – until some one turned up with a real plot and conceivable action. *New York Times*

When I directed *The Penalty* ... I said: "This is the best thing I have done!" When I read the story, *The Octave of Claudius* ... I said: "If I can put on the screen all that is in this story, it will triumph over *The Penalty*." When I saw *A Blind Bargain* on the screen, I was thrilled as though it were entirely new to me. "It *has* triumphed over *The Penalty*! It is the biggest picture I have ever made!" *Wallace Worsley [quoted in original pressbook]*

Semi-simian: Lon Chaney appeals to Jacqueline Logan in *A Blind Bargain* (1921)

Goldwyn's *A Blind Bargain* – indeed, apes in general – were to enjoy a remarkable omnipresence in the 1920s, remaining conspicuous well into the 1940s. Henry Lehrman's *On Time*, for example, was released by Truart in March 1924 and included an obvious nod to the Goldwyn film. Submitted to a series of trials that result in both marriage and a movie contract, a young man tangles, at one point, with a mad doctor bent on removing his brain and replacing it with that of a gorilla. The young hero was played by Richard Talmadge (actually stunt man Sylvester Metzetti assuming a surname that would associate him with Hollywood princesses Constance and Norma) and the film was written by Ralph (*The Gorilla*) Spence and Garrett Fort, who would later be involved in Universal's *Dracula* and *Frankenstein*.

STABBED IN THE VESTIBULE

Amid all this activity, *The Bat* and its near relation, *The Cat and the Canary*, were proving so profitable on tour that film rights were initially withheld. One person especially frustrated by the non-availability of *The Bat* was none other than D W Griffith, who in the summer of 1922 went ahead and made a *Bat* of his own.

At the end of the war Griffith bestrode the industry like a colossus, forming United Artists in tandem with Charlie Chaplin, Mary Pickford and Douglas Fairbanks, then, on completion of the masterful *Broken Blossoms*, electing to move back to New York. Despite the huge success of *Way Down East* in 1920, his Mamaroneck studios soon began to suffer financially; Griffith's interest in making an ersatz *Bat* was therefore evidence of his increasingly rudderless efforts to appeal to popular taste – in short, to have another hit. Unsurprisingly, the result would be widely seen as a retrograde step, returning the master to his earliest days at Biograph, notably to his nail-biting 1909 cliffhanger *The Lonely Villa*. Indeed, the new film's working title was the very similar *The Haunted Grange*.

Attributing the scenario to his alter-ego "Irene Sinclair, young Kentucky authoress," Griffith was canny enough to engage the services of Henry Hull, leading man of Broadway's *The Cat and the Canary*. He also sent out Hendrik Sartov to brave the elements when the Mamaroneck facility was buffeted by a hurricane that swept across Long Island Sound on 11 June 1922, incorporating the tempestuous footage into the film's climax. The financing for the picture only came through four days later, courtesy of the Central Union Trust Company, to whom Griffith already owed half a million dollars. Presumably as a sardonic in-joke, this is precisely the sum stashed away in the film's old dark Louisville house.

Though under pressure from her grasping mother to marry the devious J Wilson Rockmaine, Agnes Harrington loves the true-blue John Fairfax instead. When the latter's ancestral home is reopened for the purposes of a house party, a murderous, black-cloaked figure arrives in quest of an illicit stash of money. In the teeth of a violent storm, Rockmaine is unmasked as the killer and Agnes learns that she is actually an orphan – and an heiress to boot.

One Exciting Night, as it became known, remains significant in that it codified many of the *Bat*-derived motifs later to proliferate in hordes of 'old dark house' pictures. Indeed, by 1940 a British reviewer could preface his critique of Paramount's *The Ghost Breakers* with the sage observation that "When, years ago, D W Griffith made *One Exciting Night*, he started a cycle of films which has never ceased."[17]

"A Comedy Drama of Mystery Under the Personal Direction of D W Griffith" trumpet the opening titles, but there are signs from the outset that Griffith was fatally unsure of what kind of film he was making. His intertitles downplay the enterprise as "our little effort" while simultaneously puffing it up as an "absolute departure from all the OLD METHODS of story telling." The truth of the matter is that, in discarding the old methods – and, more importantly, in striving to put Mary Roberts Rinehart's lawyers off the scent – Griffith came up with a scenario so garbled it almost defies synopsis.

The film begins with an African safari prologue to establish the unhappy circumstances of the heroine's birth, and this gives the director of *The Birth of a Nation* the opportunity, within the first five minutes, to show a pith-helmeted white woman shuddering in revulsion at a black servant. The same servant turns up later as a saturnine butler in the pay of a Scotland Yard investigator, while a romance is taking place below stairs between black handyman Romeo Washington and a so-called "colored maid." The relationship is identical to that of Mantan Moreland and Marguerite Whitten in the much later *King of the Zombies*, but it's depressing to note that, in the Griffith film, all three of the supposedly black actors are actually, as *Variety*'s 'Libbey' tartly noted, "white, working under [burnt] cork." On top of this, Romeo's briefly glimpsed family are shown as so lazy they're barely sentient, while Romeo himself sports a stolen war decoration – a terrible insult to all the African-Americans who had served (in segregated units) in the Great War.

Presumably to lend weight to so 'frivolous' a subject, Griffith garnishes the film with faux-portentous references to "The mystery of greed" and "GREED – the killer!" A certain fusty Victorianism

"There's something out there that ain't human..."
C H Crocker-King and Porter Strong (in blackface)
in *One Exciting Night* (1922)

attaches to Griffith's prose elsewhere; he won't, for example, say "A mysterious figure" when he can say "A figure mysterious" or "There is no greater torment than jealousy" when he can say "Than jealousy – no greater torment!" The literary tone sits uneasily with Griffith's imagery, which makes a reasonable stab at engendering the requisite chills – periodic long shots in which the house is hovered over by a giant silhouetted hand, the black-cloaked interloper passing through a lumber room hung with ghostly white sheets, the flickering eyes of the killer seen through slatted window blinds, and a surprisingly savage scene in which a young man in Harold Lloyd specs is repeatedly stabbed in the vestibule.

Griffith's muse at the time, Carol Dempster, makes a fetching heroine and also a highly proactive one, being quite prepared to fling herself bodily at the villain and wrestle him to the floor. And the climactic storm is a staggering tour de force, vividly reasserting Griffith's bravura techniques as hero and heroine pursue the killer into the great outdoors, where Dempster becomes trapped under an accumulation of broken branches, a tree totters precariously above her, and Henry Hull (mascara streaming in the maelstrom) struggles against his handcuffs to release her.

"There's something out there that ain't human," quakes Romeo at one point, referring to a skull-faced 'thing' that has competed for attention with the killer himself. In a surprisingly topical touch, it's finally revealed as nothing more than "the bootleggers' trick to frighten people away" – a canny reflection of the fact that the passage of the 18th Amendment, ushering in the era of Prohibition, not only marked a victory for the Temperance Union but also a bonanza for organised crime. As for the 'crooks disguised as bogies' subplot (which was by no means original even in 1922, as noted above), its prominent use in a D W Griffith picture would prove a bonanza for future filmmakers, being reiterated countless times on both sides of the Atlantic; first up was a slapstick parody, *One Spooky Night*, concocted by former Keystone supremo Mack Sennett.

Running a whopping 110 minutes, Griffith's film premiered in Boston on 10 October prior to general release on Christmas Eve. For all its faults, it did the trick for Griffith commercially, leading him ten years later to consider mounting a talkie remake, with Sartov's storm footage recycled for the occasion. It didn't happen.

ONE EXCITING NIGHT

D W Griffith Inc 1922
11,500 feet; silent
produced June/July

Cinematographers: Hendrik Sartov, Irving B Ruby*; Art Director: Charles M Kirk*; Special Effects: Edward Scholl*; Musical Director: Albert Pesce*; Story: Irene Sinclair [D W Griffith]; Director-Producer: D W Griffith

Carol Dempster (Agnes Harrington); Henry Hull (John Fairfax); Porter Strong (Romeo Washington); Morgan Wallace (J Wilson Rockmaine); C H Crocker-King (the Neighbor); Margaret Dale (Mrs Harrington); Frank Sheridan (the Detective); Frank Wunderlee (Samuel Jones); Irma Harrison (colored maid); Percy Carr (the Butler); Charles E Mack (a guest); uncredited: Grace Griswold (Auntie Fairfax); Herbert Sutch (Clary Johnson)

Mr Griffith's thriller resembles a couple of mystery melodramas that have attained popularity upon Broadway. He believes in emphasizing the spooky note to the limit ... The picture may be called a success from the standpoint that it serves in furnishing an evening of excitement. But we expect bigger things from the man who gave us *Broken Blossoms*, *Way Down East*, *Intolerance* and *The Birth of a Nation*. *Motion Picture Classic*

Perhaps this picture appears like a hasty work. It is the exact opposite. There is no more difficult thing than to put mystery and suspense on the screen.
D W Griffith [reprinted in Schickel, *D W Griffith: An American Life*, 1984]

With both *The Cat and the Canary* and *One Exciting Night* under his belt, Henry Hull's mystery-thriller cachet was further exploited in *The Last Moment*, a J Parker Read production released through Goldwyn in June 1923. Here he's a bookish young man, ironically named Hercules Napoleon Cameron, who is shanghaied by brutish sea captain 'The Finn' (Louis Wolheim) and finds himself headed for the South Seas alongside beautiful Alice Winthrop (Doris Kenyon). At the height of a storm, a caged ape-man, 'The Thing' (Jerry Peterson), breaks free and wipes out the crew, only for Cameron to experience an uncharacteristic burst of heroism and drown the beast. After this hair-raising encounter, Hull would steer clear of spooky subjects to the extent that, by 1935, his starring role in Universal's *WereWolf of London* seemed like left-field casting.

Lustful captain and shanghaied damsel in the seafaring melodrama *The Last Moment* (1923)

The copyright bottle-neck created by Mary Roberts Rinehart would finally be freed in 1925, when the rights to *The Bat*, denied to D W Griffith, were won by director-producer Roland West. Two years before, West had adapted a hit play of his own in the form of *The Unknown Purple*, which was released in October 1923. Here, Griffith graduate Henry B Walthall played inventor Peter Marchmont, who, having been framed by his former wife Jewel (Alice Lake) and her partner James (Stuart Holmes), returns from prison to exact his revenge. With the aid of a purple beam that confers invisibility on him, he sets the conniving couple at loggerheads prior to calmly marrying Jewel's sister Ruth (Helen Ferguson). A contemporary notice in the *New York Sun* dubbed the result "a first cousin to the trashy old *Fantomus* [sic] series," dismissed West's scenario as "worth ten cents any day in the canned goods market of melodrama," and likened the titular beam (tinted a fetching purple) to "a ham vaudeville spotlight searching for an actor."[18]

Roland West was familiar with vaudeville spotlights, having already made a mint as a vaudeville performer. By the same token, he could afford to ignore reviews such as this. Something of a dilettante, he had no financial imperative to be a film director and turned out his highly idiosyncratic pictures by arrangement with his friend Joseph M Schenck of United Artists. *The Unknown Purple* had originated back in 1912 as an unused movie scenario; turned into a play by West and Carlyle Moore, it opened on Broadway in September 1918 and proved a smash hit. After making the film version, West was planning to direct a picture starring Schenck's wife, Norma Talmadge, at the Ufa studios in Neubabelsberg. Nothing came of the idea, but it makes the darkly Germanic chiaroscuro of his later films seem all the more intriguing.

The Unknown Purple may have cut no ice with the *New York Sun*, but in the mid-1930s there were a couple of indications that Hollywood hadn't forgotten it. As well as being echoed in the very title of Universal's *The Invisible Ray*, it was explicitly recalled in the opening reel of M-G-M's *The Devil-Doll*, in which Walthall (in his last film) played another inventor escaping from prison, though in this case leaving the revenge plot to his fellow escapee. And it turns out to be a much nastier revenge than Walthall's in *The Unknown Purple*, which amounted to little more than the inventor being a kind of invisible Banquo and frightening his ex-wife's dinner guests.

GEMS OF LITERATURE

In addition to adaptations of plays (or rip-offs of same), filmmakers had a rich source of literature to draw upon, and not just the pulp bestsellers exemplified by *The Young Diana* and its ilk. November 1922, for example, saw the release of Edward Venturini's *The Headless Horseman or The Legend of Sleepy Hollow*, in which Ichabod Crane was played by the internationally famous Ziegfeld Follies star and homespun humorist Will Rogers.

Washington Irving's original story had been filmed in fragmentary form twice before, both times as just *The Legend of Sleepy Hollow* – by Kalem in 1908 and Eclair in 1912. Here, however, it was extended to seven reels, enjoyed the facilities of Melrose Avenue's Tec-Art Studios and was adapted with unusual fidelity. An early shot of "the famous chief of [Sleepy Hollow's] legion of ghosts" – extending a skeleton hand to summon its steed – is succeeded in the final minutes by a suitably hell-for-leather chase as Crane

is pursued by the phantom, though this time, of course, it turns out to be a mean-spirited prankster in disguise. In between is a great deal of folksy 18th century character comedy distinguished only by some glimmering location photography.

Washington Irving had previously been adapted via multiple versions of *Rip Van Winkle*, though the Selig director Hardee Kirkland made a more interesting selection from Irving's works in adapting *The Devil and Tom Walker* in 1913, casting William Stowell and Harry Lonsdale in the titular roles. Irving's barbaric, soot-blackened Devil doing business with a mean-spirited hick in a New England swamp was far removed from the suave central figure of *Puritan Passions*, a 1923 production derived from the sardonic parables of Irving's successor, Nathaniel Hawthorne. The picture was a product of the Film Guild, a New York-based organisation patterned by director Frank Tuttle after the Theatre Guild.

As remembered by Mary Astor, who was only 16 when she appeared in the film, "They were not hardened manufacturers of movies; they were young, well educated, enthusiastic, and withal a bit snobbish and full of high-sounding theories about the moving pictures as an art form."[19] Astor would make the move to Hollywood in April 1923, appearing opposite John Barrymore in *Beau Brummell*. *Puritan Passions* was one of the last films she made prior to the move and, having opened on 2 September, was belatedly endorsed in the *New York Times* in mid-October. "A picture which has enlisted careful study and unlimited pains," enthused the anonymous reviewer, who also called it "an unique effort, a bold photoplay" and "a singular film, weird, but nevertheless gripping."

Osgood Perkins' demonic Dr Nicholas manufactures a Golem-like scarecrow in *Puritan Passions* (1923)

Unfortunately, like *A Blind Bargain*, *Puritan Passions* appears to be one of the legions of lost films, which is doubly regrettable given its obvious attempt to forge a specifically American species of 'folk' horror tale – a folk tale filmed, moreover, on location in Salem. The source was Percy Mackaye's 1908 stage play *The Scarecrow; or The Glass of Truth*, derived in its turn from Hawthorne's *Feathertop*. Hawthorne's creepy notion of man-made simulacra coming to unexpected life, in this case a scarecrow, had bled through into such diverse films as a 1908 Biograph item called *The Snowman* and Edison's *Lord Feathertop* from the same year. Here, the sub-Frankenstein theme was fused with a generous helping of Goethe's *Faust*, with the so-called Dr Nicholas perfecting a Mirror of Truth to show people what they really are. "When Dr Nicholas glances at his reflection," noted the *New York Times*, "he sees a perfect cloven-hoofed Satan."

Concocted by Tuttle and James Ashmore Creelman (future writer of *King Kong*), the scenario concerns the efforts of Goody Rickby to have her belated revenge on Gillead Wingate, the pompous Town Beadle whose hypocritical unwillingness to acknowledge their bastard child resulted in its death. To help her, Dr Nicholas endows a scarecrow with life, and, fashioning it as the handsome Lord Ravensbane, has it strike up a romance with Wingate's ward, Rachel – further twisting the knife by informing Wingate that the boy is his presumed-dead illegitimate son. Dr Nicholas is thwarted, however, when the scarecrow falls in love with Rachel for real.

In addition to Astor's Rachel, the cast featured Glenn Hunter as the scarecrow and Osgood Perkins as the insidiously plausible Dr Nicholas. Perkins – whose son Anthony would achieve immortality nearly 40 years later as the tragic anti-hero of Alfred Hitchcock's *Psycho* – by all accounts stole the show. "His smile," reported the *New York Times* reviewer, "is something of which to beware, the conjuring in his crafty face is forbidding, and his wheedling causes one to shrink at its success."

Perkins' hoary New World demon had been preceded by several other films dealing with satanic pacts, notably the 1915 productions *The Devil's Toy* and *The Black Crook*. James Young's *The Devil* – a January 1921 release based on Molnár's 1908 play of the same name – was more significant in that it allowed George Arliss to repeat his stage triumph in a vehicle that had inspired numerous rip-offs in the nickelodeon era. Here, the devious Dr Muller heartily approves of a fashionable new canvas called 'The Martyr – Truth Crucified by Evil', seeking to prove the thesis by sundering a pair of young lovers. Coaxing the girl to his apartment, he is confounded by the magical appearance of a shimmering crucifix and spontaneously combusts.

Other literary properties were similarly plumbed on a regular basis. Honoré de Balzac's 1831 novel *La Peau de chagrin* (The Wild Ass's Skin), in which the titular hide confers wishes on the owner at a heavy price to his soul, was filmed by Ernest C Warde in 1920 as *The Dream Cheater*, a British version appearing the same year under the title *Desire*. Three years later, George D Baker concocted yet another for the Goldwyn company, the property this time called *Slave of Desire* and juxtaposing vamp Carmel Myers with good girl Bessie Love. The Goldwyn title change was glossed by *Variety*'s 'Bell' as "a concession, of course, to the supposed liking of the rank and file picture fans for flashy titles," though he feared for the film's chances, given that such audiences "are so used to trash and junk it is difficult to interest them in anything that even slightly borders on the highbrow."

Balzac was also the source of Metro's *The Conquering Power*, a modernised version of the 1833 novel *Eugénie Grandet*. This July 1921 release reunited the winning team of director-producer Rex Ingram, screenwriter June Mathis and stars Alice Terry and Rudolph Valentino, whose *The Four Horsemen of the Apocalypse* had come out in March and turned a staggering profit of $4 million. Previously filmed by Eclair in 1910, Balzac's bitter story of star-crossed lovers was here fitted with an absurd happy ending and was a relative failure in commercial terms. But it greatly enhanced Ingram's reputation as one of the supreme stylists of the silent screen. According to the *New York Evening Post* for 23 July 1921: "Mr Ingram's groups fall, dissolve and fall again into pictures so well composed that one regrets the necessity for continuous movement ... and we make bold to recommend it to those, if any, who are sceptical of the screen as an instrument of beauty."

A Dubliner by birth, Ingram added to his talent for pictorial beauty a pronounced taste for the grotesque. *Four Horsemen* had included in its epic tale of the Great War a macabre tableau of its title characters riding out, and in *The Conquering Power* Ingram collaborated with the brilliant cinematographer John F Seitz on what the film's pressbook dubbed "spirit photography." A veteran of Griffith's *The Birth of a Nation*, Ralph Lewis loses his mind in grand style as the miserly Père Grandet, trapped in his own strongroom and finally being killed by a sentient chest of gold – but not before it has disgorged taloned "ghoul visions" to torment him.

Ingram had previously essayed the Poe-type theme of premature burial in both *Black Orchids* (1916) and *The Reward of the Faithless* (1917). Based on a story of Ingram's own, *Black Orchids* starred Cleo Madison and would later be remade by Ingram as *Trifling Women*, in which Barbara LaMarr inherited the role of a wayward young vamp horrified into rectitude by a cautionary tale recounted by her father. As *Variety* explained it, "Zareda, a product of the Orient with supernatural powers, meeting with great success in her assumed role of sorceress, succumbs to her vanity, and at the apex of her triumph pays with her life to learn for her sins." Not that *Variety*'s 'Sime' swallowed this corpse-strewn saga of a necromantic temptress for one minute. "Its chief feature," he sneered, "is a trained chimpanzee [actually played by a well-known Hollywood orang-outan called Joe Martin]. The animal had an eerie appearance ... but did nothing sensational."

The *New York Times* reviewer was just as contemptuous, particularly of Ingram's finger-wagging framing story: "To attach a moral to this pure shocker is to make the moral look foolish. The effort was made, apparently, for the sake of the censors and the twelve-year-old minds among fans, but it is inconceivable that even such as these will be impressed." With notices like that, Ingram's nine-reel Gothic romance was a commercial disaster on its release in October 1922, despite featuring a very plausible Valentino substitute in Ramon Novarro. Ingram's trademark 'pictorialism' – embodied not only in the gorgeous lighting effects and trailblazing 'matte' shots of Seitz but also in Leo Kuter's meticulous art direction – also counted for little to contemporary audiences.

Hollywood's star orang-outan Joe Martin, cast as simian familiar to a female necromancer in *Trifling Women* (1922)

As was the case in Ingram's lurid spectaculars, in the early 1920s Edgar Allan Poe tended only to get in by the back door, filmmakers lifting his themes rather than his stories. A typical example was issued by Universal in the first month of the decade. In Douglas Gerrard's *The Phantom Melody*, Monroe Salisbury played an Italian nobleman who, on returning from the front, is immured alive in his family vault by a money-grubbing cousin. And, on its blink-and-you'll-miss-it appearance in June 1922, William J Scully's *Annabel Lee* purported to be derived from Poe's poem of the same name. But this so-called "Joe Mitchell Chapple 'heart-throb' feature" was described in *Variety* as having been "modernized and fictionized to a degree that must have caused Poe's ghost to walk."

The range of other literary sources was wide, taking in contemporary authors of substance (Jack London), contemporary authors due to be more or less forgotten (Gelett Burgess, Joseph Hergesheimer) and even grand opera (Richard Wagner). An improbable subject for the silent screen, the latter was featured in Lloyd B Carleton's *The Flying Dutchman* (1923), which used the old *Avenging Conscience* trick of a man falling asleep while reading – in this case, Wagner's *Der fliegende Holländer* – and imagining himself as the cursed captain of a spectral ship.

Gelett Burgess' 1907 novel *The White Cat* was the source for Universal's *The Untameable*, directed by Herbert Blaché in 1923. Here, Gladys Walton alternated between two different personalities – demure Joy and vampish Edna – under the hypnotic control of a doctor (John Sainpolis) who is out to get her money. (The film was also known as *The Two Souled Woman*; confusingly, an earlier adaptation, directed by Elmer Clifton five years before and starring Priscilla Dean, was called *The Two-Soul Woman*.) Also in 1923, Joseph Hergesheimer's *Wild Oranges* became a Goldwyn production of the same name, directed by the young King Vidor and featuring a number of long-lived motifs – a ruined house on an island off Georgia, a maniac threatening the handful of inhabitants, an unleashed dog that finally tears the maniac's throat out.

A few years earlier, Metro had engaged Edward Sloman to direct *The Star Rover* (1920), based on Jack London's 1915 novel about a doctor, accused of murder, who regresses to past lives while undergoing a sustained bout of police brutality. Sloman's film was one of several unusually outré prison pictures of the period, among them Universal's *The Trembling Hour*, which was directed in 1919 by one of D W Griffith's closest associates, George Siegmann. With location scenes filmed at San Quentin, this yoked an up-to-the-minute premise (ex-con returns from World War I with severe shell-shock) to a hoary conclusion (a murder unjustly pinned on him is solved by the victim's twin masquerading as a ghost).

Another such was Finis Fox's *The Bishop of the Ozarks*, a February 1923 release in which an escaped convict masquerades as a kindly minister in the Ozark mountains, becomes chaplain of the local gaol, and is alarmed when his pretty ward comes under the hypnotic influence of a malevolent doctor. The same year, Universal went back behind bars for William Parke's *Legally Dead*, which featured an anti-capital punishment campaigner being hanged for a crime he didn't commit and being resurrected with a shot of adrenaline. Universal had previously revived the dead in Clem Easton's 1915 picture *The Eleventh Dimension*, which itself followed the World Film Corp's 1914 smash *Lola*. In this adaptation of Owen Davis' play of the same name, director James Young cast his wife, Clara Kimball Young, in the role of a woman who returns as a soulless, amoral vamp.

MURDEROUS, HIDEOUS, REPULSIVE

By the beginning of 1923, Lon Chaney and Wallace Worsley – star and director of *A Blind Bargain* – had moved on to the biggest picture of their respective careers. *The Hunchback of Notre Dame* was a Universal 'Super Jewel', so designated to distinguish it from Universal's general run of programmer product. Its staggering production cost of well over $1.25 million distinguished it from most other pictures of the period, too; indeed, it was reasonably described in Universal's own publicity as "The Greatest Screen Attraction of the Age."

Victor Hugo's 1831 novel *Notre Dame de Paris* had already been filmed half a dozen times, though only once in the US. J Gordon Edwards' 1916 version – as its title, *The Darling of Paris*, suggests – subordinated Glen White's Quasimodo to Fox's prize vamp, Theda Bara, oddly cast as Esmeralda. The Universal *Hunchback* was focused decisively on Quasimodo himself ("an inhuman freak, a monstrous joke of Nature," according to the film's intertitles), and the role was a logical development for Chaney, who, though a cast-iron superstar of the silent era, nevertheless seemed like a bizarre anomaly in an industry devoted to God-like glamour and audience wish-fulfilment. Chaney felt a deep-seated kinship, instead, with society's dispossessed, employing his mastery of stage make-up to create a gallery of grotesques, twisted sometimes in mind, sometimes in body, and frequently both.

His attractiveness to picturegoers in the supposedly carefree Jazz Age was therefore a complex one, leading film historian Denis Gifford to speculate on the nature of "his world appeal at a time when genuine grotesques, the victims of war, begged at every street corner."[20] It's an alluring theory, developed at length by David Skal in his 1993 book *The Monster Show* – that, whether they were conscious of it or not, Chaney's devoted admirers saw in his hideous disguises a nightmare reflection of the disfigured war veterans all around them.

Born in Colorado Springs to deaf-mute parents in 1883, Chaney entered the film business in 1913, making a major impact six years later in George Loane Tucker's *The Miracle Man*. His performance as a supposedly crippled con-man called Frog was a tour de force and set the pattern for his career. The following year he was playing grotesques of literature like Fagin and Blind Pew, as well as a legless gangster in Wallace Worsley's gruesome crime melodrama *The Penalty*, released by the Goldwyn company in August 1920. The latter caused a censorship outcry with its story of the disabled Blizzard plotting against the doctor who accidentally amputated his legs in childhood – proposing to do the same to the doctor's prospective son-in-law, then to fuse the boy's severed limbs to his own stumps.

A further indication of Chaney's future was provided by his performance as mad sculptor Henri Santodos in the 1920 feature *The Glory of Love*. Based on a novel of the same name by 'Pan' (aka Leslie Beresford), the film fell victim in post-production to front-office queasiness about its content, Paramount eventually unloading it onto the Hodkinson Corporation, which released the picture in January 1923 as *While Paris Sleeps*. The film's director, Maurice Tourneur, had come to America at the behest of the Eclair company and, like Rex Ingram, was convinced of cinema's potential as high art. As a sometime student of Rodin, he was presumably amused by Pan's hokey story of a Latin Quarter sculptor intent on turning his model's boyfriend into one of his exhibits. The boy was played by John Gilbert, a former assistant of Tourneur's who would go on to superstar status in such films as *The Big Parade* and *Flesh and the Devil*.

To get Chaney for the title role in *The Hunchback of Notre Dame*, Universal were forced to bury the hatchet over a salary dispute that had driven the star away from the studio some years earlier. When the film began shooting on 16 December 1922, Universal had been in existence for ten years, having evolved from Carl Laemmle's earlier IMP company and taken root in a 230-acre section of the San Fernando Valley grandiloquently dubbed Universal City. Nineteen of these acres were requisitioned for *Hunchback*'s sprawling recreation of 15th century Paris, while the film's proverbial cast of thousands necessitated the first use of a PA system on a film set. ("This picture," as *Time* magazine put it, "is a legitimate example of

Lon Chaney's Quasimodo is swept up in "the uprising of the bums" in *The Hunchback of Notre Dame* (1923)

movie elephantiasis ... done on the Gargantuan scale of which only cinema directors can conceive."[21]) Completed on 3 June 1923, the result opened at Carnegie Hall on 30 August and was a smash hit, vindicating the faith vested in it by Laemmle and his brilliant young production executive, Irving Thalberg.

Chaney, in particular, was a sensation; indeed, his Quasimodo – wholly grotesque yet authentically pitiful – indulges in wild bursts of atavistic behaviour that retain their power nearly 100 years later. Though the film is a brutal historical melodrama rather than the straight-ahead horror of *A Blind Bargain*, the ghoulish impact of Chaney's performance was so great that the normally hard-nosed industry bible, *Variety*, lost all its characteristic acumen when assessing its commercial prospects. "Produced as it is," commented 'Sime', "*The Hunchback of Notre Dame* may become a detriment to the box office it plays for." He also pointed out that the film "is a two-hour nightmare. It's murderous, hideous and repulsive ... No children can stand its morbid scenes, and there are likely but few parents seeing it first who will permit their young to see it afterward."

Though Chaney remains its centrepiece, the film's enduring power owes a great deal to the fact that it is by no means a one-man show. As well as its epic scenes of the Feast of Fools and the climactic insurrection of the Paris underclass (or, as 'Sime' called it, "the uprising of the bums"), *Hunchback* boasts a truly deluxe supporting cast. Patsy Ruth Miller and Norman Kerry are delightful as the imperilled Esmeralda and her equivocal Captain of the Guard love interest, while three of the silent screen's most compelling character actors are visible elsewhere – Brandon Hurst as the cloak-twitching villain Jehan, Ernest Torrence as the imposing King of the Beggars, and Tully Marshall as a hatchet-faced Louis XI. Unhappily, Marshall's contribution is severely truncated in surviving prints of the film, a general release version shaved down by some 2000 feet from the cut seen during the film's original New York playdates.

In the wake of *Hunchback*, Universal executives would succeed only once in luring Chaney away from the newly formed M-G-M, but he had taught them an important lesson nevertheless. Picturegoers may have been besotted by the athletic derring-do of Douglas Fairbanks, the winsome heroics of Mary Pickford, the Latin smoulder of Rudolph Valentino and the exotic allure of Pola Negri. But they also had a queasy fascination for human monsters of the Lon Chaney variety, characters inspiring in them, as per the original Aristotelean recipe, both pity and terror.

Part Two

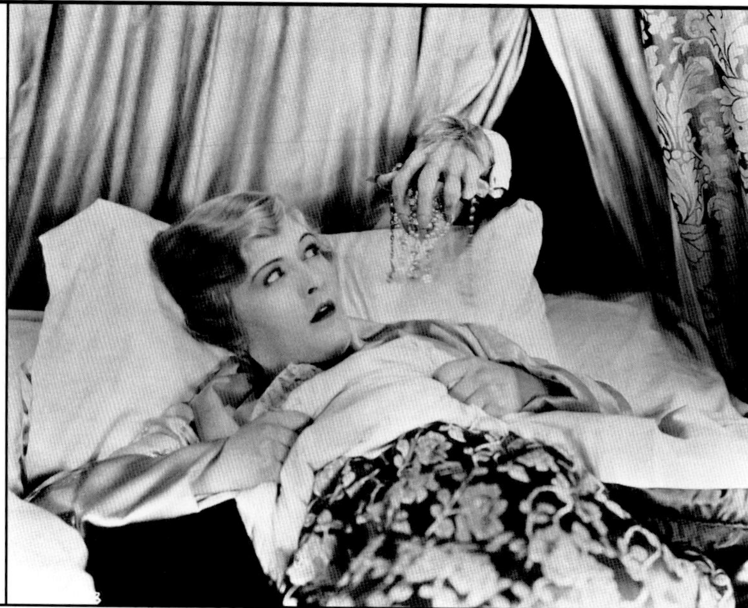

Laura La Plante encounters the classic clutching hand in *The Cat and the Canary* (1927)

Silent as the Tomb 1924-1930

After a shaky start, American prosperity in the 1920s snowballed at an unprecedented rate. Calvin Coolidge's assertion that "This is a business country; it wants a business government" set the tone for an economic boom shared out between pretty much every industry bar agriculture. Emblematic of the boom was the decade's massive expansion of automobile sales; emblematic, too, in its way, was the mint to be made from bootlegging and gangsterism. The arrival of Prohibition in January 1920 was an ironically Puritanical measure, given that the upcoming decade would, in all other departments, sweep away Edwardian restraints with wild abandon. But it ensured that the trade in illicit alcohol would reach fantastically profitable heights, as well as entailing the violent deaths of many of the racketeers involved.

Much the most glamorous emblem of the new prosperity was provided by Hollywood. Just as President Coolidge conferred mystical significance on the nation's get-rich-quick philosophy when observing that "The man who builds a factory builds a temple," so Hollywood fashioned a new religion in which some 700 dreams a year were turned out in its factories and shipped worldwide to those increasingly ornate temples of wish-fulfilment called picture palaces. The dreamers worshipping at them numbered in their millions, and the inscrutable idols enshrined in the charmed circle of the silent screen became like gods. In 1927, Samuel L 'Roxy' Rothapfel was keenly aware of this when describing his newly opened Roxy Theatre – with its 6214 seats, commanding proximity to New York's Times Square and Gothic architectural extravagances – as "the Cathedral of the Motion Picture."

For all the ultra-modern gloss of Jazz Age decadence in which Hollywood's products were steeped, many of them enshrined a double standard of the 'having your cake and eating it' variety. In Fox's 1924 version of *Dante's Inferno*, scenarist Edmund Goulding offered a sardonic critique of post-war prosperity by sending a millionaire slum landlord to Hell and back. And he did it by returning to the already mildewed 'it was all a dream' motif. Just as penny-pinching as he had been in *The Conquering Power*, Ralph Lewis undergoes a Scrooge-like change of heart as a result of a diabolical vision carefully modelled on Gustave Doré's original illustrations.

The vision is also a highly eroticised one, director Henry Otto presumably having realised that, if Cecil

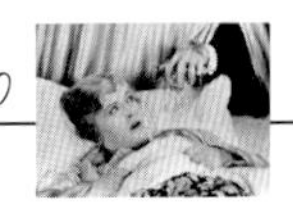

B DeMille could smuggle salacious material into his films under cover of adapting the Bible, then he could do the same via a supposedly moralistic view of Purgatory. "There is more nudity among the writhing figures than has hit the screen in an age,"[1] observed *Photoplay* approvingly. Nudity (or artfully deployed bodystockings) aside, Otto's film was little different from humble offerings of the previous decade. Edmund Lawrence's *The Warning*, for example – also known as *The Eternal Penalty* – was a December 1915 release in which Henry Kolker played an alcoholic condemned to Hades who, on waking, realises that it was all a 'mend your ways'-type dream.

WEIRD TALES, GRIM COMEDY

If *Dante's Inferno* looked askance at the nation's accumulating wealth in its high-minded finger-wagging, then its luridly over-ripe realisation of Hell was in line with the 'let it all hang out' mentality attendant on that wealth. With money flowing in, America entered into a hedonistic splurge of consumerism unparalleled in its history. The same note of excess was struck in the zealous adulation lavished on sports heroes like 'Babe' Ruth, Jack Dempsey and the future Tarzan, Johnny Weismuller – and, of course, on the god-like movie stars projected many times larger than life in the nation's cinemas.

Writhing figures in the lower depths: an alluring lobby card for *Dante's Inferno* (1924)

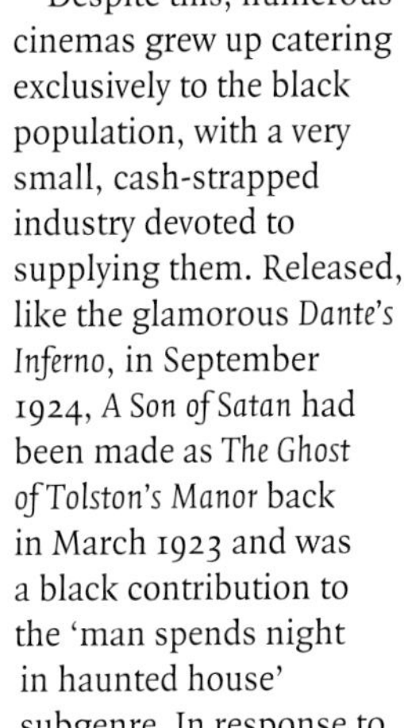

It cropped up even in the ghoulish fascination for murderers like Nathan Leopold and Richard Loeb, teenage 'thrill-killers' who in 1924 became stars of a more dubious kind thanks to the post-war explosion in tabloid newspapers and 'confession' magazines. The same explosion engendered the heyday of 'pulp' magazines, luridly jacketed descendants of the mid-Victorian penny dreadfuls. The most famous of these was *Weird Tales*, edited initially by Edwin Baird but acquiring its characteristic stamp under the stewardship of Farnsworth Wright. Established in March 1923, the magazine became notorious the following year with the publication of C M Eddy Jr's *The Loved Dead*, a studiedly offensive, and wildly overwritten, confessional from a homicidal necrophiliac. Needless to say, the extremes of horror featured in the pulps would find no direct echo in Hollywood.

Eddy's story was one of many that was whipped into shape by *Weird Tales'* high-minded eminence grise, H P Lovecraft. Lovecraft's own stories bore chilly titles like *The Colour Out of Space*, *The Whisperer in Darkness* and *The Shadow Over Innsmouth*, fashioned an entire cosmological backdrop related to loathsome 'others' patiently awaiting an opportunity to re-colonise the earth, and inspired a posthumous cult of impressive proportions. Yet no official screen adaptation would be attempted until 1963.

For all the enthusiasm with which many Americans danced the Black Bottom or brewed up bathtub gin (or, for that matter, revelled in the queasy horrors of *Weird Tales*), there were plenty of others who were not beneficiaries of the nationwide binge. Farmers and production workers were entirely excluded from the boom, while The National Association for the Advancement of Colored People faced an uphill struggle just getting their constituents the vote.

Despite this, numerous cinemas grew up catering exclusively to the black population, with a very small, cash-strapped industry devoted to supplying them. Released, like the glamorous *Dante's Inferno*, in September 1924, *A Son of Satan* had been made as *The Ghost of Tolston's Manor* back in March 1923 and was a black contribution to the 'man spends night in haunted house' subgenre. In response to the demeaning use of blackface comedians in films like Griffith's *One Exciting Night*, the Micheaux Film Company appears to have larded *A Son of Satan* with a host of inflammatory ingredients, the New York censor board complaining vociferously about its scenes of uninhibited drinking and crap games, plus the stoning of a cat and the strangulation of a woman. The film starred Andrew S Bishop and was written, produced and directed by the great African-American film pioneer Oscar Micheaux.

At the opposite end of the scale, 1924 also saw the amalgamation of Goldwyn, Metro and Louis B Mayer Productions into Metro-Goldwyn-Mayer; William Randolph Hearst's Cosmopolitan Pictures was also part of the deal, a useful circumstance given the might of Hearst's press empire. The combine's first production started shooting on 17 June, was based

Tragic clown Lon Chaney corners venal aristocrats Marc McDermott and Tully Marshall in *HE Who Gets Slapped* (1924)

on a play by Leonid Andreyev and cost $172,000. The project had been initiated by the 25-year-old Irving Thalberg, who, having been behind Universal's *The Hunchback of Notre Dame*, was now ensconced at M-G-M and had brought Lon Chaney with him. The director was the brilliant Swedish import Victor Sjöstrom (Anglicised to Seastrom for American audiences) and the film was *HE Who Gets Slapped*.

Opening on 9 November, the result did fantastic business, making a profit of nearly $350,000 and conferring immense prestige on the new venture at first try. Given the increasingly formulaic nature of Hollywood product, this outcome was by no means guaranteed, for *HE Who Gets Slapped* is a bitterly ironic parable concerning, as the first intertitle puts it, "the grim comedy of life." In it, Chaney is a self-absorbed scientist whose "startling theories about the Origin of Mankind" are appropriated, along with his wife, by an aristocratic benefactor. In "a supreme gesture of contempt," he reinvents himself as HE, a Parisian clown whose act involves being repeatedly slapped in the face by a platoon of other clowns. When the appalling Baron moves in on the beautiful bareback rider whom HE has fallen in unrequited love with, HE arranges for the Baron and the girl's duplicitous father to be torn apart by a lion, then wanders into the teeming arena to bleed to death in the girl's arms.

The role of a tragic, clown-faced martyr further enriched the Chaney mystique; reciprocally, Chaney enriched the role with his unmistakable brand of burning intensity. But, even beyond Chaney, the film is full of the unspoken eloquence unique to the silent screen, brilliantly juxtaposing the youthful beauty of John Gilbert and Thalberg's future wife, Norma Shearer, with the raddled old aristocrats scheming to part them, Marc McDermott and Tully Marshall. It also has Ford Sterling in the role of HE's clown mentor, Tricaud. Having achieved immortality as Chief Teheezel of the Keystone Kops, Sterling no doubt had his own opinion of his supposedly comic circus duties here, which involve tearing the symbolic heart out of HE, burying it, then giving him full funeral honours with a cortege of clowns.

As a European art film transplanted to Hollywood, Sjöstrom's picture is hamstrung by a series of po-faced intertitles that climax with "What is – death?

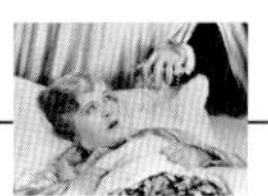

What is – life? What is – love?" And yet it exudes a potent lyricism that transcends such half-baked philosophising. And, by a strange quirk, its plot device of a naïve man having his work pirated by an unscrupulous sponsor would be appropriated by future remakes of the epoch-making film Chaney was about to make for Carl Laemmle.

IN AND OUT OF MAKE-UP

In October 1924, Chaney returned to Universal for what would turn out to be the last time. When, some 12 months earlier, he had acquired the rights to Gaston Leroux's 1911 novel, *Le Fantôme de l'opéra*, Universal had envisaged making it for just $100,000. On its eventual release in September 1925, the film's tortuous production had swollen the final budget to over $630,000.

The director assigned to the project, Rupert Julian, had earned kudos at Universal when he took over *The Merry-Go-Round* from the wayward Erich von Stroheim; that film's stars, Mary Philbin and Norman Kerry, subsequently turned up alongside Chaney in *The Phantom of the Opera*. Julian's militaristic inflexibility on the *Phantom* set pleased nobody, least of all Chaney, who, according to some reports, resorted to directing parts of the film himself. What's certain is that, after an LA preview in January 1925, Universal engaged Edward Sedgwick to concoct a more slam-bang finale and add some romantic scenes featuring Ward Crane. A San Francisco try-out in April resulted in the film being further fiddled with, this time with the addition of comic Chester Conklin. When *Phantom* finally opened in New York in September, Crane and Conklin were nowhere to be seen, the film having undergone yet more surgery at the hands of director Lois Weber. It proved a phenomenal smash regardless, earning Universal a profit of nearly $540,000.

Erik, the so-called 'opera ghost', resides five cellars deep in the catacombs of the Paris Opera. From his habitual seat in Box Five, he spies pretty understudy, Christine Daaé, and determines to elevate her to the level of prima donna. She recoils at sight of his horribly disfigured face, however, and plots to elope with her aristocratic fiancé Raoul. In response, Erik abducts her before being beaten to death by the mob and flung into the Seine.

That Universal spared no expense on *The Phantom of the Opera* is obvious from the opulence of its settings – the reproduction of the interior of the Paris Opera would remain in use for decades – and from the 'cast of thousands' nature of its masque and mob scenes. Christine's journey into the Phantom's subterranean quarters smacks of a mythological descent into the Underworld, complete with Erik sculling his private gondola across "a black lake" in an echo of Charon crossing the River Styx. The art direction gives a distinctive touch to each of the five levels through which they pass, including a particularly startling honeycomb of vaulted passageways which Erik traverses with the aid, rather surprisingly, of a horse.

The Bal Masque sequence is another showstopper, briefly abandoning the film's subtle tints and tones for a blast of two-colour Technicolor. With a nod to Edgar Allan Poe, Erik parades among the revellers in Red Death disguise. "Beneath your dancing feet," he intones, "are the tombs of tortured men – thus does the Red Death rebuke your merriment!" The only trouble with this section is the limited palette of early Technicolor. The preponderance of scarlet cummerbunds, tutus and peacock feathers adorning the other guests diminishes the impact of Erik's own crimson garb, which in Poe's original was the only splash of red in the entire composition.

The reference to "the tombs of tortured men" reminds the viewer of the grim legacy of the opera house, its surface glitz concealing catacombs formerly used as a prison during the Paris Commune. Erik himself, we learn, dates from the Franco-Prussian conflict. Our complete 'backstory' on the character is given to us, rather crudely, via a card index brandished at the camera by saturnine Secret Service man Ledoux. Under the bald heading "ERIK," it reads: "Born during the Boulevard Massacre. Self educated musician and master of Black Art. Exiled to Devil's Island for criminal insane. ESCAPED NOW AT LARGE." This brief summary begs more questions than it answers, failing, in particular, to explain Erik's disfigurement. Subsequent versions would put it down to acid-scarring, but Chaney's masterful make-up suggests something unpleasantly congenital.

And what a frightful visage it is, a shrunken death's-head applied to a living man. Its shock revelation was the horror high-point of the silent era and still packs a punch. It's artfully staged in order to make a double impact; with Christine positioned behind Erik as she removes his mask, our shock is immediately succeeded by hers when he furiously turns in his seat to face her. The horror is intensified as Christine recoils and Erik advances on her in a brilliant subjective shot. His finger thrust accusingly at the camera, the terrible rictus looms over her in blurred close-up as she begins to lose consciousness. Erik won't let her, however. In the scene's final

Lon Chaney's Erik rebukes the revellers in the guise of Poe's Red Death in *The Phantom of the Opera* (1924)

THE PHANTOM OF THE OPERA

Universal 1924
8464 feet; silent
includes Technicolor sequences
production began 29 October

Cinematographers: Charles Van Enger*, Virgil Miller*, Milton Bridenbecker*; Colour Supervision: Edward Estabrook*; Art Directors: E E Sheeley*, Sidney Ullman*; Consulting Artist: Ben Carré*; Editor: Gilmore Walker*; Technical Director: A H Hall*; Ballet Master: Ernest Belcher*; Screenplay: Elliott Clawson* ('from the celebrated novel by Gaston Leroux'); Titles: Walter Anthony*; Presented by: Carl Laemmle; Director of post-production material: Edward Sedgwick*; Director: Rupert Julian

Lon Chaney (The Phantom [Erik]); Mary Philbin (Christine Daaé); Norman Kerry (Vicomte Raoul de Chagny); Arthur Edmund Carewe (Ledoux); Gibson Gowland (Simon Buquet); John Sainpolis (Comte Philip de Chagny); Snitz Edwards (Florine Papillon); Mary Fabian (Carlotta); Virginia Pearson (Carlotta's mother); uncredited: Olive Ann Alcorn (La Sorelli); Alexander Bevani (Mephistopheles); Edward Cecil (Faust); Bruce Covington (Monsieur Moncharmin [manager]); George Davis (man at Christine's dressing room door); Cesare Gravina (manager); Carla Laemmle (prima ballerina); Grace Marvin (Martha); John Miljan (Valentin); Bernard Siegel (Joseph Buquet); William Tryoler (orchestra director); Anton Vaverka (prompter); George B Williams (Monsieur Richard [manager]); Edith Yorke (Mama Valerius)

nb: Carlotta was played in the 1925 release by Virginia Pearson, who subsequently played the character's mother in the 1929 part-sound reissue

I wasn't fooled or scared one bit by Lon Chaney as the reputed, ghastly Phantom ... When Mr Chaney pulled off his mask with an air of going "Boo!" I felt like saying, "Don't you 'boo' at me, Lon Chaney, and take that false face off right away. A great big boy like you scaring the children!" ... If you are frightened by pumpkin heads and black cats, you will like *The Phantom of the Opera*. Picture-Play

It was a terrific strain, because Chaney and Julian wouldn't talk to each other. I had to be the messenger boy. Rupert would say, "Tell Lon to do this," and I'd go over and tell Lon, "He wants you to do this," and Lon would say, "Tell him to go to Hell." I'd go back and I'd say, "He says to go to Hell." So Lon did whatever he wanted. Charles Van Enger [quoted in American Cinematographer, October 1989]

masterstroke, he pulls her up and actually laughs as we read the pitiful intertitle: "Feast your eyes – glut your soul, on my accursed ugliness!" Only then, perversely, does he hide his face.

In *Life* magazine, playwright Robert E Sherwood, having enthusiastically dubbed the film "spook melodrama at its wildest and weirdest", pointed out that "The acting, though undistinguished, is appropriate to the general tub-thumper quality of the story. In other words, it is of the variety that is usually known as 'ham'."[2] Mary Philbin's mannered performance as Christine certainly lives up to this judgment, but so, surprisingly, does Chaney's. Saddled with an obscurely motivated psychopath who is featureless in every sense, he relies on uncharacteristically operatic gestures to bring the character alive, with some especially outrageous posturing reserved for his crimson-cloaked eavesdropping on the young lovers. He creates a sublime effect when cornered by the crowd at the end, pretending to be carrying a concealed grenade prior to a cackling revelation that his hand is empty after all. But, like Bela Lugosi and Dracula, we're left with the impression that Chaney's most famous performance is by no means his best.

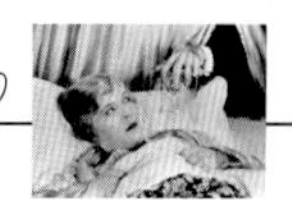

The acting honours are stolen, in fact, by Arthur Edmund Carewe's dark-eyed and watchful Ledoux (his early appearances milked for maximum 'could he be the Phantom?' effect), and the film is memorable for several other understated pleasures. The intertitle proclaiming "Behold! She is singing to bring down the chandelier!" is framed against a striking, purple-tinted silhouette of the Phantom. An ill-fated stagehand whispers of the opera ghost while clutching a prop severed head which, rather charmingly, opens its eyes during his recitation. And a memorably desolate shot of Raoul opening Christine's masque invitation is bathed in a subdued amber light and framed by marble pillars.

In the final reel, Raoul and Ledoux descend into the catacombs and are subjected to a series of improbable tortures that make Rupert Julian seem like a poor man's Louis Feuillade. The film falls apart completely at this point, only rallying with a red-tinted scene of the mob lighting their torches and the final mad pursuit at the climax. Here, incidentally, Erik sprints insanely past the Notre Dame cathedral frontage which had played so large a part in Chaney's previous Universal shocker.

The showbusiness bible, *Variety*, issued a dire warning against the trend towards pictures like *Phantom*: "It is impossible to believe there are a majority of picturegoers who prefer this revolting sort of a tale on the screen. It is better for any exhibitor to pass up this film or 100 like it than to have one patron pass up his theatre through it." The reviewer conceded ruefully, however, that "Universal is evidently out to establish itself as the champ ghost story-telling firm among film producers. There can be no question of its supremacy after seeing this one."

Well before the equivocal reactions to *Phantom* came in, Lon Chaney had rounded out 1924 by appearing in an independent production for Roland West. While waiting for the rights to *The Bat* to become available, West had chosen to adapt another Broadway mystery-thriller, Crane Wilbur's *The Monster*. In converting it to the screen, West took up residence in the former Clune Studio on Melrose Avenue, then run by the Tec-Art company, and promised a "first-class mystery melodrama with heaps of laughter."[3]

In Danburg Indiana, trainee detective Johnny Goodlittle and his romantic rival, Amos Rugg, find themselves in the local sanitarium, apparently untenanted since Doc Edwards left for Europe. In fact, the good doctor is imprisoned in the bowels of the building with two other unfortunates. Above ground, the asylum has been taken over by former inmate Dr Ziska, who proposes to learn the secret of life by experimenting on Johnny's sweetheart, Betty Watson...

The Monster opens at full tilt, with a storm raging at dead of night, a black-eyed fiend perched high in a tree and a colossal mirror lowered into the path of an oncoming automobile. Confused by the sight of another car apparently heading straight for him, the driver swerves and crashes, whereupon a second conspirator emerges from the ground, his white breath pluming on the night air. "A human monster watched with cat-like eyes for a victim," an intertitle has informed us, leaving us unprepared for the surprise emergence of another. With one perched aloft and the other apparently erupting from the very earth, the scene carries an authentically nightmarish edge.

After this, the film lapses briefly into sunlit character comedy, a mode West was clearly uncomfortable with. Johnny Goodlittle's efforts to convince his fellow Danburghers that he's a competent detective are reminiscent of Buster Keaton's in *Sherlock, Jr* but considerably less engaging. Instead, West reserves his invention for Dr Ziska's spooky sanitarium. Abounding as it does in concealed chutes, collapsible beds, divans that sprout arms and mute black-face giants levitating from ottomans, it isn't hard to work out that the lunatics have taken over this asylum.

Though the comic tone harks back to Poe's *The System of Dr Tarr and Prof Fether*, there remains something highly disturbing about Ziska and his three deranged confederates. Even the apparently harmless Daffy Dan is first encountered by Johnny, at the height of another storm, emerging from some bushes and adjusting not only his rain-slicked mac but also his trousers, leaving us uncertain as to whether Dan merely has a weak bladder or is an out-and-out flasher.

As for the others, Caliban is a monolithic, ever-scowling Nubian played by the conspicuously non-Nubian Walter James (who was retained from the Broadway original). And the black-eyed Rigo, though wizened in appearance, is frighteningly athletic, particularly when he corners Johnny atop a storm-lashed telegraph pole and gleefully slashes the cables on which our hero is precariously balanced. As a result, Johnny is propelled through an open window, hurtles down several banisters, is ejected through the front door and crashes into Rigo again on his way out. A truly dazzling set-piece, this too smacks of Buster Keaton, though the man who famously broke his neck while making *Sherlock, Jr*

Hallam Cooley and Johnny Arthur assailed by lunatics Walter James, Knute Erickson, Lon Chaney and Frank Austin in *The Monster* (1924)

THE MONSTER

Tec-Art / Roland West Productions 1924
6425 feet; silent
produced November/December

Cinematographer: Hal Mohr; Editor: A Carle Palm; Production Manager: W L Heywood; Screenplay: Willard Mack, Albert Kenyon (from the play by Crane Wilbur); Adaptation: Roland West; Titles: C Gardner Sullivan; Director-Producer: Roland West

Lon Chaney (Dr Ziska); Gertrude Olmstead (Betty Watson); Hallam Cooley (Watson's head clerk [Amos Rugg]); Johnny Arthur (the under clerk [Johnny Goodlittle]); Charles A Sellon (the constable); Walter James (Caliban); Knute Erickson (Daffy Dan); George Austin (Rigo); Edward McWade (Luke Watson); Ethel Wales (Mrs Watson); uncredited: Herbert Prior (Doc Edwards)

As always, Lon Chaney does excellent work in an unusual character role. He appears as the sinister surgeon in charge [of the asylum] and scores heavily, although his role is secondary to that of Johnny Arthur as the boob detective. *Moving Picture World*

Lon Chaney taught me to make up. In my first pictures I must have looked quite like Lon Chaney ... Mother would sit and watch him ... She got so good at it that when I would try to do it myself, she would say, "Honey, you are smudging. Now Lon would never put it on like that."
Gertrude Olmstead [quoted in Slide, Silent Players, 2002]

would have spurned the very visible wires and pulleys used in achieving it.

"I've found a hidden passage," Betty remarks at one point, adding, "it goes straight down into the dark!" Taking their cue from this, some commentators have sniffed a Freudian motive in the accoutrements with which West kits out the asylum – subterranean chutes from which victims plop out onto soft sofas comprising Exhibit A. But Ziska himself carries a sufficient whiff of sexual perversion to make such assumptions a side-issue. For Lon Chaney, fresh from *HE who Gets Slapped* and *The Phantom of the Opera*, the Ziska role must have seemed like a pretty negligible diversion. But he brings to it, nevertheless, all the uncanny force of personality which made him such a uniquely powerful screen presence. And the uncanny force seems all the more potent for being unadorned by make-up.

We learn from the deposed Dr Edwards that Ziska "was once a famous surgeon." Like Rigo, he is first encountered at a great height, not up a tree but frowning down at Johnny, Amos and Betty from an upper landing. With his silk dressing gown and long cigarette-holder, Ziska resembles a sort of fanged Noël Coward, grinning an insane welcome through clouds of cigarette smoke. His eyes burn balefully even when he makes a courtly offer to provide Betty with separate accommodation; in a nicely creepy touch, it turns out to be a spartan cell with nothing in it but a hospital bed. Chaney allows himself only one rhetorical gesture – to accompany the classic intertitle, "The fools sent me a man when it is a woman I want!" – prior to expounding his diabolical plan in an underground laboratory. In intertitles that would be repeated as spoken dialogue ad infinitum

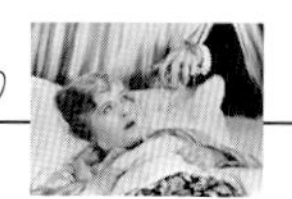

in the years to come, he tells Amos that "You are about to witness the most remarkable operation ever attempted by man."

Ziska's apparatus includes an electric chair, for some reason, as well as the doped-up Betty stretched out on a hospital gurney. (As Ziska peels off the sheet covering her, West briefly teases the audience with the possibility that she's nude, just as, a little earlier, the hands encircling her on the collapsible couch seemed poised to attach themselves to her breasts.) "With the aid of that death chair," Ziska informs Amos, "I shall transfer your soul into her body!" Inevitably, Ziska is himself manhandled into the chair and the unwitting Caliban flicks the switch. West gives us a glimpse of smoke billowing from Ziska's silhouetted form prior to a close-up of his rubber-gloved hands twitching and then going limp. It's a memorably nasty end to an otherwise good-natured film.

Though they appear incongruous to modern viewers, the comic elements of *The Monster* were par for the course to contemporary audiences. Typically frivolous was Alfred Santell's independent feature *Fools in the Dark*, which arrived in cinemas in August 1924, borrowed Patsy Ruth Miller from *The Hunchback of Notre Dame*, lumbered her with a mad scientist father, and called on the Marines, no less, to help her out in the final reel. And spooky happenings in slapstick two-reelers were ten-a-penny. Among others, Johnny Arthur (hapless hero of *The Monster*) turned up in *Scared Silly*, portly comic Bert Roach in *That's the Spirit* and the unwashed urchins of Our Gang in both *Shivering Spooks* and *Spook Spoofing*. Our Gang's producer, Hal Roach, was also responsible for such titles as *Scared Stiff* and *The Haunted Honeymoon*, while future Roach star Stan Laurel appeared in *Dr Pyckle and Mr Pryde*, a 1925 two-reeler for producer Joe Rock.

SHAPES IN THE DARK

Last thing in 1925, on 16 December, the humble Lee-Bradford Corporation released *Wolfblood*, a Ryan Brothers production subtitled *A tale of the forest* and starring Broncho Billy Anderson's sometime leading lady, Marguerite Clayton. When lumber-camp foreman Dick Bannister sustains a severed artery, his love rival Dr Horton is forced to transfuse lupine blood into him. The operation is abetted by a black-hearted lumberjack who, himself a "half-breed", tells all his fellows that Dick is now "half wolf". Dick himself begins to believe it, remembering "the weird tales of the Loup Garou of the Far North – The Wolf in human form!" and concluding that "I am a beast! I'm one of the pack!" Running in the forest with phantom wolves, he attempts suicide by throwing himself off the aptly named Wolf's Head Rock, but is saved by the selfless love of his doe-eyed sweetheart.

More a lumber-country love triangle than a horror picture, *Wolfblood* was directed by Bruce Mitchell and George Chesebro; the latter also played the hallucinating Dick. Twenty years later, its cinematographer, R Leslie Selander, would direct a much more literal lycanthrope in the shape of *The Catman of Paris*, while another 1940s picture, *The Mad Monster*, would pick up *Wolfblood*'s blood transfusion angle and produce a fully fledged wolf man.

The bizarre plot developments of *Wolfblood* were in line with the sinister details that sometimes crept into Westerns of the period. Cowboy superstars William S Hart and Tom Mix eschewed such indulgences, but lesser lights Hoot Gibson and Tom Tyler turned up in *Spook Ranch* (1925) and *Terror* (1928) respectively, while Ken Maynard was the draw in both *The Haunted Ranch* (1926) and *Phantom City* (1928). In 1940 – having been stricken with arthritis – Tyler would make a suitably stiff-limbed Kharis in *The Mummy's Hand*.

Outdoors adventures of the Ken Maynard variety were a world away from well-heeled theatrical adaptations like *The Return of Peter Grimm*, a 1926 Fox release based on a 15-year-old stage hit by David Belasco. This was the template for a subgenre that was to become very popular during the Second World War, that of whimsical and well-intentioned ghosts who return to 'sort things out' on terra firma. Alec B Francis was the ghost in Victor Schertzinger's film, a role taken over by Lionel Barrymore in a 1935 RKO remake. Another spooky strain popularised on stage, the haunted house melodrama, was already finding itself cross-fertilised into mainstream pictures for the sake of atmospheric set-dressing. In the DeMille presentation *Bachelor Brides*, for example, director William K Howard had fun with the faux-Scots eeriness of the so-called Duncraggen Towers, while another 1926 release, Edward Sedgwick's M-G-M farce *Tin Hats*, came complete with a spectral suit of armour and titles penned by Ralph (*The Gorilla*) Spence.

The rights to Broadway's original spooky-house melodrama, Mary Roberts Rinehart's *The Bat*, finally became available in 1925, and Roland West snapped them up with alacrity. The latest production in West's now ten-year-old partnership with Joseph Schenck, the result became a sustained homage to Louis Feuillade's super-criminal serials of the previous decade. Shot in December and released in New York on 14 March 1926, it prompted yet another permutation in the property's already convoluted history – this time a novelisation, attributed to Rinehart but actually written by Stephen Vincent Benet.

Master criminal The Bat is poised to rob the Oakdale Bank when he sees another crook absconding with the $200,000 in question. He pursues his rival to the country estate of the bank's supposedly deceased president, which the wealthy Cornelia Van Gorder has leased for the duration. The so-called Detective Moletti is finally exposed as The Bat when he stumbles into a bear-trap laid by Miss Van Gorder's scatter-brained maid.

THE BAT

Feature Productions 1925
8219 feet; silent
produced December

Cinematographer: Arthur Edeson; Art Director: William Cameron Menzies; Editor: Hal C Kern; Technical Effects: Ned Herbert Mann; Production Managers: Frank Hall Crane, Hal C Kern, Thornton Freeland; Screenplay: Roland West (based on the play by Mary Roberts Rinehart and Avery Hopwood); Continuity [ie, Scenario]: Julian Josephson; Titles: George Marion Jr; Production Executive: Joseph M Schenck; Director-Producer: Roland West

[in order of appearance] André de Beranger *(Gideon Bell)*; Charles Herzinger *(man in black mask [Courtleigh Fleming])*; Emily Fitzroy *(Miss Cornelia Van Gorder)*; Louise Fazenda *(Lizzie Allen)*; Arthur Housman *(Richard Fleming)*; Robert McKim *(Dr Wells)*; Jack Pickford *(Brooks Bailey)*; Jewel Carmen *(Miss Dale Ogden)*; Sojin Kamiyama *(Billy [butler])*; Tullio Carminati *(Moletti)*; Eddie Gribbon *(Detective Anderson)*; Lee Shumway *(The Unknown)*

Secret panels; creeping fingers; shapes in the dark – they're all in *The Bat*, and you can enjoy them and still get a good sound night's sleep afterwards ... Mary Roberts Rinehart certainly started something when she wrote the story; and Roland West, who directed the picture, left no crime uncommitted to give you a good time. *Screenland*

When Sojin was first considered for the part of the Japanese butler in *The Bat*, it was decided by director Roland West that his appearance lacked a certain sinister quality necessary to the role – his teeth were too perfect, his smile too bland ... The following day Sojin ... came into the room where West sat dictating ... and smiled fiendishly, horribly, at the surprised director. For there, protruding from the corners of his mouth, were two short tusks ... "I have plenty teef," he said. *'How Sojin Does It'* [from *Picture-Play*, June 1927]

Heroine Jewel Carmen, dowager Emily Fitzroy, maid Louise Fazenda and private dick Eddie Gribbon, potential victims of *The Bat* (1925)

Released through United Artists, *The Bat* was advertised as "a comedy-mystery-drama ... [with] the stirring tempo of a thousand terrors, gasps and LAUGHS!" West's emphasis on comedy no doubt helped make the film palatable to audiences unused to seeing bat-faced murderers looming into colossal close-up; as the *New York Times* put it the day after the premiere, "People in the theatre yesterday were distinctly affected by the spine-chilling episodes, and they were relieved by the comedy interludes."

To bolster the film's comic credentials, West engaged two performers indelibly associated with Mack Sennett's Keystone comedies of the previous decade, both of them on hand to deflate the audience's apprehension by parodying it. As the ham-handed "Bloodhound Anderson – Super-Sleuth of Oakdale County," Eddie Gribbon acts so frightened he can't hold his revolvers steady, while Louise Fazenda's hysterical maid wears absurd pyjamas and sets up a full-throated caterwauling at the slightest provocation. Both are likely to test the patience of modern viewers, though Gribbon does some delightful pistol-swerving business in the concluding attic scenes and Fazenda is by no means as irksome as Maude Eburne in West's talkie remake. Fazenda's Lizzie is, however, conspicuously younger than the 40 her employer tartly describes her as – an unfortunate gaffe in that it destroys the joke of Lizzie claiming coyly to be 22.

All in all, the film's mixture of laughter and chills is more adroitly achieved than West's previous venture into the same territory in *The Monster*. The balance is maintained by an unusually strong cast, among them Robert McKim, whose prissy waxed moustache tips us off in advance that the shifty Dr Wells isn't to be trusted, and the fresh-faced Jack Pickford (brother of Mary) as the fugitive bank clerk Brooks Bailey. Best of all, English character actress Emily Fitzroy is delightfully dry and sardonic as the imperturbable Miss Van Gorder, embodying exactly the description provided in the accompanying novel: "patrician to her finger-tips, independent to the roots of her hair ... [with] a humorous and quenchless curiosity in regard to every side of life."

West cast his wife, Jewel Carmen, as Miss Van Gorder's niece Dale, and her show of sustained fright during her climactic encounter with The Bat is a remarkable one. Previously seen only

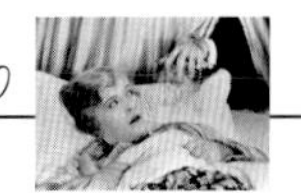

as an athletic shadow sporting a fuzzy headpiece and elongated ears, The Bat is here shown full-face and advancing implacably into the camera lens. Though the snout and ears have so far recalled Bottom in *A Midsummer Night's Dream*, we're now treated to something much nastier: a bristling set of tusk-like fangs and a really alarming view of Tullio Carminati's unhinged, kohl-rimmed stare. It may as well be Leatherface of *The Texas Chain Saw Massacre* with the ears of Bugs Bunny attached, making it clear that the influence of *The Bat* extended not only to comic-book characters like Batman and Diabolik, but also to the weirdly masked killing machines of Italian giallo films and US slasher flicks.

The Batman connection is inescapable, notably when a circular light containing a silhouetted bat plays across the walls of the Fleming mansion. ("A lot of excitement over a moth-miller on a headlight," chuckles Dr Wells as he gets out of his motor-car.) And it is in its visual properties that *The Bat* makes its strongest impact, with West's restless experimentation abetted by three gifted collaborators – cinematographer Arthur Edeson, designer William Cameron Menzies and effects wizard Ned Mann.

The film's opening passages are distinguished by three of Mann's groundbreaking miniatures, first a New York skyline, then the provincial Oakdale Bank, finally the castellated splendour of the Fleming mansion itself, all of them lit by the full moon and attended by a fluttering bat. The mansion's interiors are conceived on an epic scale, with 18-foot doors and a maze of zig-zagging staircases, a palatial monument to 1920s grandiloquence. (Rather than an old dark house, this is most decidedly a new dark house; indeed, the youthful bank clerk confesses to having been privy to the architectural discussions.) And Edeson's chiaroscuro lighting takes full advantage of the German Expressionist style filtering into US features at the time – the apprehensive heroine, candle in hand, framed against a threatening expanse of black doorway space; a blinding flashlight beam hurled down the main stairway as The Bat shoots the banker's dissolute nephew; the doctor's shadowed arm attenuated on the banisters in a shot reminiscent of *Nosferatu*.

West also indulges some of his more bizarre sideline witticisms. Preceded, inevitably, by a lowering shadow, Sojin's hollow-cheeked Japanese butler sports outsized teeth echoed later by The Bat himself, while the ridiculous Lizzie, for all her exaggerated terror of The Bat, wears a two-pronged white headpiece similar to the master criminal's monstrous ears. There are also off-the-wall stylistic flourishes like the insertion of a diagonal intertitle ("Give me that blueprint!") in the above-mentioned flashlight beam. West also gets to replicate some of the rooftop tomfoolery previously indulged in *The Monster*. This time, Brooks, Anderson, Lizzie, even Miss Van Gorder herself, ascend to the roof for a farcical interlude involving plenty of ropes and pulleys.

The delay in getting *The Bat* onto film had already entailed the peculiar circumstance of a rip-off – Griffith's *One Exciting Night* – reaching the screen nearly four years in advance of the genuine article. And now, less than a fortnight after West's film made its New York bow, came another. One of only two films from the independent outfit Otto K Schreier Productions, *Midnight Faces* ticks every available box – a late uncle's will, a lurking Oriental menace, a midnight marauder skulking around in slouch hat and uplifted cape, a resident black cat, a frightened black servant, a sinister butler and housekeeper, and, of course, plenty of secret passageways.

But the film's writer-director, Bennett Cohn (who had recently written the script for *Wolfblood*), works some interesting variations on the standard clichés. The uncle turns out not to be dead, the Chinaman is a good guy, the black cat lasts only a few seconds before lapping up some poisoned wine. And the black valet – euphoniously named Trohelius Washington Snapp – is played by a black man, which is certainly a progression from Griffith's 'burnt cork' procedure. The actor in question is Martin Turner, whose selection of intertitle wisecracks (eg, "Boss, mah nerves departed hours ago") makes him a clear precursor of such latterday comedians as Willie Best and Mantan Moreland.

Clean-limbed leading man Francis X Bushman Jr finally bests the chief villain in a ferociously prolonged fight that ascends to the roof and down again, though the unmasking of the maniac as a character previously advertised as paraplegic comes as no surprise whatever. The film is interesting for eschewing studio sets and being filmed on location; unfortunately, Claymore Point, apparently located "at the edge of a dismal swamp on a Florida Bayou" and carrying about it "a graveyard smell," is rather a nice-looking place and Cohn struggles to infuse it with much atmosphere. But, as rip-offs go, *Midnight Faces* is unusually engaging and intelligent, and it's a shame that, after it, Cohn and his witty titles-writer Bennett Sheldon went straight back to their usual diet of low-budget Westerns.

While Roland West was preoccupied with an up-to-the-minute Broadway smash (and Bennett Cohn was concocting an elaborate carbon-copy), another independent filmmaker, London-born I E Chadwick, reached back over 50 years to a theatrical property made famous by Henry Irving. Based by melodramatist Leopold Lewis on an Erckmann-Chatrian original called *Le Juif polonais*, *The Bells* had begun its triumphal progress in November 1871. The play was made over by Chadwick as a vehicle for John Barrymore's elder brother Lionel, though the film's opening intertitles made no secret of Barrymore's momentous predecessor in the leading role, reminding the viewer that "The most notable performance of the play was that of the late Sir Henry Irving." The direction was entrusted to James Young, who was no stranger to literary adaptations, having directed the 1923 film of *Trilby* and acted in Maurice Tourneur's 1915 version.

> *Alsace, Christmas 1868. Mathias is an innkeeper, mill-owner and all-round pillar of the community with aspirations to becoming Burgomaster. Unfortunately, he owes over 6000 francs to another local dignitary, Jerome Frantz. After a travelling Warsaw Jew has visited the inn and shown off his gold-crammed money belt, Mathias waylays him in the snow and kills him. But both his appointment as Burgomaster and his daughter's wedding day are poisoned for him by "His tormentor – CONSCIENCE."*

Though *The Bells* shares its title with an Edgar Allan Poe poem, its actual Poe flavour is more in the vein of *The Tell-Tale Heart*, with the guilty Barrymore succumbing to aural torments previously suffered by Henry B Walthall in *The Avenging Conscience*. As before, it was a brave move to make a silent movie predicated so completely on sound; with the shaking of sleigh-bells returning to haunt Mathias at unpredictable intervals, it was presumably left to individual theatres to provide their own rendition of what Mathias dismisses in the play as "the blood rushing to my head" and "this jangling in my ears."

The murder scene itself is not very arrestingly handled; from Mathias' impetuously uplifted axe, Young cuts to syrupy spots of blood puddling in the snow, then to the expiring Koweski shaking the fateful loop of sleigh-bells at his murderer, and finally to the Jew's horse bolting in alarm. But the gradual escalation of Mathias' numerous 'guilt trips' is treated more confidently, starting immediately post-murder as he skulks through a flour mill and runs slap-bang into a dangling noose. And the amount of dramatic irony on offer is also effective. When news of the murder gets out, Mathias visibly quails on hearing that "the body cannot be found, only a glove – and a cap cleft with a sharp axe." Whereupon his unsuspecting father-in-law explains to the bystanders that "Mathias has a tender heart – he cannot stand hearing of such violence."

The optical tricks employed as Mathias sinks deeper into despair are smoothly done, starting with a phantom manifestation of the shuddering bells and a disembodied hand pointing accusingly through them. When Mathias counts out his ill-gotten gains and finds blood forming miraculously on his hands, his frantic efforts to wipe it away are irresistibly reminiscent of Macbeth's mournful line, "Will all great Neptune's ocean / Wash this blood clean from my hand?" *Macbeth* is also recalled when Mathias disrupts his own daughter's wedding reception; indeed, Macbeth's "never shake / Thy gory locks at me" would have been quite appropriate here as an intertitle, given our glimpses of Koweski's ghost with blood seeping from its scalp and down its face.

For most of the film, Barrymore relies on the watery pallor of his eyes to suggest a well-meaning but weak-willed man, only indulging in gestural extravagance (and on quite a grand scale) in a pleasingly absurd scene in which Mathias defiantly sits down with Koweski's ghost in order to play cards with it. For horror fans, however, *The Bells* occupies a small corner of motion picture history thanks to its uncannily prescient casting of the 38-year-old Boris Karloff as a sideshow mesmerist. In a role much expanded from the Leopold Lewis play, Karloff presides at the local carnival, levitating a local maiden and boasting portentously of making "criminals confess their crimes and good men tell of their good deeds."

The carnival has other disturbing features – notably a flock of revellers skipping about in stovepipe hats and grotesquely enlarged potato-face masks – but Karloff's shark-like grin and Dr Caligari get-up are enough to disconcert Mathias in themselves. And when Koweski's brother turns up with a reward of 30,000 francs (the same amount Mathias has set aside as his daughter's dowry), the fact that he brings the grinning mesmerist with him makes Mathias lose his cool completely.

In what must have been a deliberate evocation of the old Griffith picture, an intertitle then announces "The dream of – accusing conscience!" In a strikingly composed shot, the fantasy courtroom here is bisected by a huge shaft of light from a central window, picking out Karloff's hungry mesmerist and a mob of black-garbed accusers lurking in the shadows. What with this lot and the hatchet-faced Gustav von Seyffertitz occupying the judicial bench, the cards are clearly stacked against Mathias by this stage, and he duly expires of a heart attack back in his room as the ghost utters its characteristic mantra of "Peace be with you." It's an anticlimactic

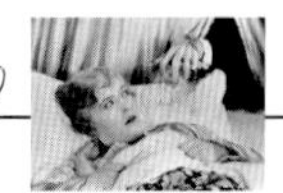

Bedevilled by guilt: Lionel Barrymore encounters a noose in a flour mill in *The Bells* (1926)

end to a modestly conceived (and presumably modestly budgeted) picture, but one with enough charm to make even its amber-tinted romantic interludes of damsels and gendarmes larking about in haywains seem strangely beguiling.

A *Bells*-type scenario had previously surfaced in the form of Jacques Jaccard's *Unseen Hands*, an Encore Pictures production released in May 1924. In this, Wallace Beery is cash-strapped opportunist Jean Scholast, who sabotages a life-or-death operation being undergone by his elderly benefactor and proceeds to marry the widow (Fontaine LaRue). Escaping with her fortune to Arizona, he is tracked down many years later by her son (Jack Rollins) and plunges to his death on mistaking the boy for the shade of his victim. A British trade reviewer noted that "The atmosphere of the French scenes is created in numberless characteristic touches, obviously carried out under the knowing eye of a Frenchman." And, in praising Beery's performance, the reviewer made the *Bells* comparison explicit: "In the scenes showing the murderer's dread of his own conscience there are moments worthy of an Irving or a [Feodor] Chaliapine."[4]

For his part, Lionel Barrymore graduated to serial killing at M-G-M's behest in Chester Franklin's *The Thirteenth Hour* (1927), in which two-faced criminologist Professor Leroy is brought low by a detective's faithful dog. "He would come through the window with a well-trained snarl," Barrymore recalled, "then jump on me affectionately and ask for a romp. In the end, they had to mistreat and deceive that dog in order to have him make-believe that I was a bad man. They underfed him for two days, then put a sirloin steak in my wig. He almost tore me to pieces."[5] With murders committed at the stroke of 1.00 am and the Professor's creepy house bristling with mechanical traps for the unwary, the result moved *Variety*'s 'Sid' to suggest that "Barrymore probably snickers to himself over these roles." In between prestige engagements like co-starring with Gloria Swanson in Raoul Walsh's *Sadie Thompson*, no doubt he did.

After *The Bells*, Edgar Allan Poe was confined for the remainder of the silent era to two brief appearances in the burgeoning avant-garde, both of them in 1928. *The Tell-Tale Heart* – its title adjusted to *The Telltale Heart* – emerged as a dazzling 24-minute short courtesy of filmmaker Charles F Klein. "Maurice Barber presents it, but it might have been presented by the author himself, if he were still in the flesh, for it has the stark realism of Poe's pen, his cold precision, his unrelenting exactitude," enthused Welford Beaton, influential editor of *The Film Spectator*. "It is screen literature, as cruelly beautiful as the author wrote it. It uncovers another screen genius in the person of Charles F Klein ... [who] is a man whom pictures need."[6] Sadly, the 30-year-old Klein relapsed into obscurity after this

THE BELLS

Chadwick Pictures 1926
6300 feet; silent
produced April

Cinematographer: William O'Connell; Lighting Effects: Percy Harris*; Technical Director: Earl Sibley; Screenplay: James Young (from the play *Le Juif polonais* by Emile Erckmann and Alexandre Chatrian); Presented by: I E Chadwick; Director: James Young

Lionel Barrymore (Mathias); Caroline Frances Cooke (Catharine); Gustav von Seyffertitz (Jerome Frantz); Lorimer Johnston (Hans); Edward Phillips (Christian); Lola Todd (Annette); Laura Lavarnie (fortune teller); Boris Karloff (mesmerist); E Allyn Warren (Baruch Koweski/ Jethro Koweski); uncredited: John George (mesmerist's assistant); Otto Lederer (pedlar)

Workmanlike and effective production in which Lionel Barrymore gives a strong performance ... The figure of the Jew himself is rather lacking in romance ... In all essentials, however, the mounting is most effective, and this may be regarded as a very adequate representation of a story which has long proved its popular appeal. *The Bioscope* [UK]

Lionel [Barrymore] was a stimulating man – a marvellous, a great man. Because my make-up for this part was a conventional Svengali-like job, Lionel sat down and on an envelope sketched an idea for [James] Young and the make-up person. What he sketched was Caligari.
Boris Karloff [quoted in *Films in Review*, August-September 1964]

Melville Webber as the unnamed guest who witnesses *The Fall of the House of Usher* (1928)

extraordinary effort, in which he took charge not only of the direction but also the titles, trick photography and some heavily *Caligari*-styled sets, only delegating the camerawork to Leon Shamroy.

"A picturization of Edgar Allan Poe's immortal classic of the same name" announces the opening title, after which an unusually lengthy written extract from Poe's original gives place to a black cat skulking over crazily angled rooftops. The protagonist, brilliantly played by the chiselled Otto Matiesen, is identified only as "The Insane" and is obviously modelled physically on Poe himself. The murder sequence, complete with "KILL KILL KILL" burning itself into the image and a subtly superimposed hammer to indicate the victim's steadily decreasing heartbeat, is a true tour de force, and is followed up at the end by another as Matiesen crumbles under the collective glare of the investigating policemen.

In the meantime, Klein works a few inventive variations on Poe. "I will give you a beautiful grave, my friend," Matiesen murmurs as his eyes move to the floorboards, one of which, in a delightfully telling moment, wobbles slightly when he later arranges chairs for the officers. And a strange, triangular mirror is produced by one of the policemen in order to facilitate a distorted close-up of Matiesen, after which the officer, somewhat prematurely, pronounces: "His eyes ... there is no guilt."

Made in Rochester, New York, *The Fall of the House of Usher* is by no means as straightforward as Klein's film. The pioneering work of experimental filmmakers Melville Webber and James Sibley Watson, it too was heavily influenced by *Caligari*. Announcing itself as "a fantasy on the theme by Edgar Allan Poe," the film rejects narrative almost completely in a dizzying 15-minute accumulation of surrealist imagery. As the monied publisher of influential arts journal *The Dial*, Watson had introduced T S Eliot to American readers, and for help with the *Usher* script, he reportedly co-opted modernist poets Ezra Pound and e e cummings.

Starting with a kaleidoscopic view of Poe's opening pages, Webber and Watson move on to multiple coffins floating in black space and a stark dinner table scene in which the Lady Madeline (played by Watson's wife Hildegarde) recoils in horror from an unspecified delicacy under the domed lid of a silver dish. The Ushers' unnamed visitor subsequently turns up, white-faced save for a prominent stripe down his nose; this is Melville Webber himself. Black-gloved hands fondle the coffined, catatonic Madeline prior to her being nailed in, after which Usher (Herbert Stern) takes to wandering the house and obsessively miming the fateful hammer blows.

Madeline presents a very ghoulish spectacle indeed on her emergence from the tomb, and the whole thing winds up with childrens' building blocks splashing into water to represent the climactic collapse of the house. In perfecting a cinematic equivalent to the poetic principles behind *The Dial*, Webber and Watson came up with an ingenious solution to the old *Bells* problem of how to represent the subterranean sounds that bedevil Usher. Up they pop in animated characters, one letter at a time: "B-E-A-T, C-R-A-C-K, S-C-R-E-A-M..."

A third avant-garde short from this period was concocted by Robert Florey and Slavko Vorkapich, French and Serbian émigrés respectively. In 1927 they expended a mere $200 on the now-lost *Johann the Coffin Maker*, in which Agostino Borgato invited several living dead into his workshop and finally climbed into a custom-built casket with a personification of Death itself. While Vorkapich became a master of montage, Florey would continue to direct, later playing a hotly debated role in the genesis of Universal's *Frankenstein*.

THE BIOGRAPH EFFECT

In the mid-1920s, the young actresses made famous by D W Griffith in the previous decade were growing into maturity in different ways. Dorothy Gish and Mae Marsh were in England, making *Nell Gwynn* and *The Rat* respectively. Blanche Sweet was starring in early versions of *Anna Christie* and *Tess of the d'Urbervilles*. Pre-eminent among this group, Mary Pickford was turning out major hits for her own film corporation and Lillian Gish was riding high at the newly formed M-G-M in King Vidor's *La Bohème*.

Gish's next project brought her together with Victor Sjöstrom, director of *HE Who Gets Slapped*, on a prestigious adaptation of a novel deemed unfilmable by the watchful Will H Hays. *The Scarlet Letter* nevertheless went into production on 25 January 1926, with Gish bringing her own special brand of luminosity to a role for which she was theoretically unsuited. The strapping Hester Prynne of Nathaniel Hawthorne's original – condemned by her Puritan community to wear an embroidered 'A' for 'Adulteress' – was converted into a delicate flower, almost dwarfed by the very large infant (Joyce Coad) selected to play her lovechild Pearl. The Swedish star Lars Hanson was brought over to play the girl's father, the Revd Arthur Dimmesdale, sharing a gorgeously idyllic brookside tryst with Hester and finally expiring on the pillory when confessing his guilty secret to the community at large.

The beauty of Sjöstrom's images, much enhanced by the photography of Griffith's former cameraman Hendrik Sartov, stamped *The Scarlet Letter* as an art film but didn't prevent it from turning a handsome profit of nearly $300,000. Acknowledging the parity of Sjöstrom's repressed Swedish style with the Puritan subject matter, *Picture-Play*'s Norbert Lusk noted that "Victor Seastrom's direction is that of a master, and the Scandinavian's sympathy with the traditions of our rock-bound New England is strongly manifested in every scene."[7]

In a classic instance of the kind of rationalisation that characterised the 1920s' attitude to Gothic motifs, the hideous 'A' branded into Dimmesdale's chest – in Hawthorne, a stigmatic manifestation of his guilt – is explained away by a graphic scene in which Dimmesdale brands himself in an extreme of masochistic remorse. Balancing this, Gish's former Griffith co-star, Henry B Walthall, is deeply frightening as Hester's long-lost husband, particularly in a baleful close-up when he reappears unexpectedly on her doorstep. The novel had previously been adapted several times, notably a 1913 version with Griffith's wife, Linda Arvidson, in the lead; a feeble talkie version from 1934 saw Walthall reprising his role opposite Colleen Moore in her final film.

After a couple of intervening pictures, Lillian Gish was reunited with Sjöstrom for *The Wind*, which started shooting on 29 April 1927. Gish had hit upon the film's source novel herself; given that it was written by Dorothy Scarborough – author in 1917 of one of the earliest critical histories of Gothic literature, *The Supernatural in Modern English Fiction* – it's appropriate that the film version should forge a truly elemental terror from the arid landscape of the West. To achieve this, cast and crew endured the 120° heat of the Mojave desert, nearly 150 miles from Hollywood, as well as a constant bombardment of sand driven at them by the propellers of nine aeroplanes. For Gish, the ordeal was a blistering counterbalance to Griffith's *Way Down East*, which in March 1920 had exposed her to the full force of a Connecticut blizzard.

"This is a wonderful, but almost terrible part for me," she explained to English journalist Margaret Chute on location. "I am a gently reared Southern girl who goes to live in Texas, in strange, miserable surroundings; and the villain of the drama is not a living man, but The Wind – that ceaseless wind, which blows in Texas till it drives human beings crazy ... It drives me to such a state of frenzy that in the end I murder a man; and then I try to bury his body in the sand. I do bury it; but the Wind blows the sand away..."[8] The climactic scene is a triumph of silent film acting to equal Gish's hysteria in *Broken Blossoms*. Increasingly deranged, she watches through the cabin window as the wind remorselessly exposes her attacker's submerged corpse, its death-mask features gradually becoming

Lillian Gish as "a gently reared Southern girl" driven insane by *The Wind* (1927)

visible through the whirling sand. When the door of the cabin is forced open, however, it is not the dead man's hand that pulls her from her hiding place but that of her husband (Lars Hanson again).

Though a late masterpiece of the silent era, *The Wind* was perhaps just a little *too* late; by the time of its much-delayed release on 23 November 1928, talking pictures were all the rage and the unrelenting grimness of *The Wind* made it a commercial failure. It remains uniquely powerful, however, for its almost Shakespearean use of the unbridled elements as an index to a disintegrating mind, and for its hallucinatory image of a white stallion bucking and plunging in the eye of the storm. Is it a phantom manifestation of the North Wind, as per Indian myth? Or a symbol of the ungovernable drives the demure Letty tries to block out? Or, for the incorrigible rationalists in the audience, merely a stray horse from the herd her husband is out rounding up?

Lillian Gish wasn't the only former Biograph girl who translated old-style melodrama into a new and more mature form of American Gothic. From her debut in 1909, Mary Pickford had risen to the level of 'America's Sweetheart', forming United Artists in 1919 with Chaplin, Griffith and her future husband Douglas Fairbanks, in the meantime keeping the company supplied with hit films produced by her own Pickford Corporation. She played the last of her celebrated juvenile roles in *Sparrows*, which was completed just prior to her 34th birthday in April 1926 and was a much grimmer proposition than such trademark Pickford properties as *Pollyanna* and *Little Annie Rooney*.

Deep in Southern swamp country, Mr and Mrs Grimes maintain an illicit baby farm. When the only child of millionaire Dennis Wayne is kidnapped, the baby is lodged at the Grimes place and placed in the care of the oldest of the Grimes' charges, 'Mama' Molly. Becoming nervous about the encroaching police investigation, Grimes determines to dispose of the Wayne baby in the swamp, whereupon Molly leads the children in a life-or-death escape attempt.

From *Little Annie Rooney*, the canny Pickford retained several top talents, including director William Beaudine, cinematographers Charles Rosher and Hal Mohr, and designer Harry Oliver. The 14-year-old Walter 'Spec' O'Donnell was also kept on, here playing Mrs Grimes' moronic teenage son, Ambrose. The story, meanwhile, was concocted by Winifred Dunn, and so steeped is it in Dickensian gloom, recalling *Oliver Twist* in particular, that it comes as a major surprise to the contemporary viewer when such modern conveniences as automobiles and motor-boats put in an appearance. And yet this was the film's trump card. For all its elaborately upholstered touches of Gothic horror, it was firmly grounded in a social evil – baby farming – that had been exposed by the Juvenile Protective Association of Chicago as recently as 1917.

According to Pickford's own estimate, she departed so decisively from her usual heartwarming tactics in *Sparrows* that her vast public was somewhat put off; though there was a reasonably healthy ration of Pickford's winning comedy and melting sentiment on offer, there was also the ghastly figure of Gustav von Seyffertitz's Mr Grimes to contend with. The opening intertitle says it all: "The Devil's share in the world's creation was a certain southern swampland – a masterpiece of horror. And the Lord appreciating a good job, let it stand." After a long look at a brilliant William Johnson miniature of Grimes' benighted homestead, hedged about by quicksands and overhanging trees, we're next treated to a splendidly laconic follow-up: "Then the Devil went himself one better – and had Mr Grimes live in the swamp."

Hovering malefically around a gnarled tree, Grimes comes complete with a paralysed hand, hump back and leg-dragging limp. And in von Seyffertitz's hawk-like countenance and skeletal frame, it's hard to resist the conclusion that Max Schreck's Nosferatu has flown west and fetched up in a Louisiana bayou. Sneering at a letter from the unfortunate mother of his youngest charge, Grimes crushes the enclosed doll prior to tossing it in the nearest bog. A uniquely powerful piece of silent shorthand, this sequence is subsequently revealed to be no mere metaphor. For, as the dull-witted Mrs Grimes warns him, "Some day you'll shove one too many in the swamp" – and it's clear she's not just referring to dolls.

Constructed on the backlot of Pickford's studio on Santa Monica Boulevard, the fetid setting through which Grimes moves is a miracle of production design. Of the film's three cinematographers, two – Rosher and Karl Struss – were soon to collaborate with F W Murnau on the miraculous lighting effects of *Sunrise*, and they achieve a similar limpid beauty here, especially in a dream sequence in which the sleeping Molly is unaware that the baby in her arms has expired. By means of a gorgeous optical effect, the colossal door of Grimes' barn becomes a picture frame for an idyllic vision of Jesus tending a flock of lambs. It's as if we're looking through an Edwardian proscenium arch, the tableau made all the more powerful when, miraculously, Jesus steps into the barn to gather the dead Amy into his arms and take her to the proverbial better place.

The scene no doubt made *Sparrows* a three-hanky affair for 1920s filmgoers, but it retains a naïve power

Mary Pickford leads her orphan brood into the terrors of the swamp in *Sparrows* (1926)

in light of the implicit question contained in the film's opening intertitles: if God is so benevolent, how is it that he condones the manifold evils in the world, Grimes in particular? Molly's indomitable faith is more than a match for such spiky paradoxes, however. She merely assures the children that Jesus "was born in a barn – just like this," and is herself almost Christ-like as she leads her urchin flock into the terrors of the swamp.

And here is the nerve-jangling set-piece for which the film is best remembered, with the children inching across a gradually collapsing tree branch as slithering alligators swarm hungrily below. Pickford went along with studio publicity that suggested the children were in direct proximity to the alligators, castigating director Beaudine for his cavalier attitude to the children's safety – somewhat unfairly, given Hal Mohr's subsequent revelation that the whole thing was done via double-exposure and that "There wasn't an alligator within ten miles of Miss Pickford. Do people think we were crazy?"[9]

The abduction of the well-heeled (and conspicuously well-fed) Wayne baby brings the plot to a head, as well as seeming uncannily prescient of the 1932 Lindbergh kidnapping case. Grimes, befitting his name, is swallowed up in the all-pervading mud, but Beaudine's handling of Grimes' comeuppance is disappointingly reticent, cutting the scene off while he's still only up to his waist. In any case, Grimes' death acts merely as a cue for an almost zany coda in which Molly finds herself in charge of a runaway motor-launch prior to settling in, 'sparrows' included, at the palatial Wayne mansion. Though cowboy star Roy Stewart is thoroughly charming in the unlikely role of Dennis Wayne, these skittish closing scenes are belaboured for some 15 minutes, as if Pickford was at pains to convince her fans she hadn't made a grim and grisly Gothic thriller after all.

SPARROWS

Pickford Corporation 1926
7763 feet; silent
copyright date 30 April
UK title: Human Sparrows

Cinematographers: Charles Rosher, Hal Mohr, Karl Struss; Art Director: Harry Oliver; Editor: Harold McLernon; Properties: Irving Sindler*; Electrical Effects: William [S] Johnson; Collaborators [ie, assistant directors]: Tom McNamara, Carl Harbaugh, Earle Browne; Screenplay: C Gardner Sullivan (based on a story by Winifred Dunn); Titles: George Marion Jr;

Producer: Mary Pickford*; Director: William Beaudine

Mary Pickford (Molly); Roy Stewart (Dennis Wayne); Mary Louise Miller (Doris Wayne [the baby]); Gustave von Seyffertitz (Mr Grimes); Charlotte Mineau (Mrs Grimes); 'Spec' O'Donnell (Ambrose); Lloyd Whitlock (Bailey); Monty O'Grady (Splutters); Billy Butts, Jack Lavine, Billy Jones, Muriel McCormac, Florence Rogan, Mary Frances McLean, Sylvia Bernard, Seeseell Ann Johnson, Camille Johnson (the children); uncredited: A L Schaeffer (Bailey's confederate); Mark Hamilton (hog buyer)

The choice of *Sparrows* was a singular one for Mary Pickford to make, but no one can deny that she has done the picture surpassingly well. The subject is gloomy, and some of the horrors recall Dickens, yet the darkness is shot through with many laughs. Indeed, so heavily does the hand of melodrama smite *Sparrows* that the picture passes beyond the bounds of credibility.
Picture-Play

My picture *Sparrows* wasn't too successful, comparatively speaking ... In the swamp scene, I had to carry some children along a narrow board – five or six inches wide – across an alligator-infested pool ... [and] it was so terrifying for many people seeing babies in such danger that *Sparrows* didn't do as well as it might have done.
Mary Pickford [quoted in Brownlow, The Parade's Gone By, 1968]

FAUSTIAN PACTS AND MAIDEN'S BLOOD

By the time his former protégées were making films like *The Scarlet Letter* and *Sparrows*, D W Griffith was widely perceived to have had his day. On the collapse of his Mamaroneck venture, he was forced to sign away his independence to Adolph Zukor of Paramount, who handed him an unrealised Cecil B DeMille project about, appropriately enough, a Faustian pact. This was *The Sorrows of Satan*, based on a purplish novel by Marie Corelli that had already been filmed in England in 1916.

The November 1925 issue of *Photoplay* announced the alliance with the full bombast of Paramount's publicity department: "Some critics feel they can pick out the place where Shakespeare's art reached its richest period. So it is with that master director David Wark Griffith ... In freedom from all worry and with the resources of the world's foremost film organisation at his disposal, D W Griffith is now in the golden age of his art." Rarely has PR puff sounded more hollow and sanctimonious, for the filming of *The Sorrows of Satan* was a Byzantine affair in which the projected budget of $650,000 ballooned, through internal Paramount politics rather than Griffith extravagance, to nearly a million. Having gone into production on 1 March 1926, the result was released in October and proved a bona-fide disaster.

Smooth devil Adolphe Menjou tempts Ricardo Cortez with Lya de Putti in *The Sorrows of Satan* (1926)

The Sorrows of Satan concerns a luckless novelist, Geoffrey Tempest, who cries out in despair that "I'd sell my soul for money – if there were a Devil to buy it!" Right on cue, lightning flashes outside his garret and the dapper, silk-hatted Prince Lucio Riminez announces that "The money I hold in trust for you ... will make you one of the richest men in the world." Tempest is persuaded by the Prince to reject his sweetheart, fellow writer Mavis Clare, and marry the exotic Princess Olga instead. Love wins through in a saccharine conclusion, but not before the Prince has come out with the tantalising intertitle, "Perhaps it is time to show you who I really am!"

Unfortunately, this only happens in the last five minutes, though the image of Tempest recoiling from an enveloping bat-winged shadow would become familiar to a whole new generation when used as the cover photo for the 1979 Bauhaus single *Bela Lugosi's Dead*. Though nicely acted by Adolphe Menjou (Riminez), Ricardo Cortez (Tempest) and Carol Dempster (Mavis), the remainder of the film is a society melodrama of the simultaneously exotic and stodgy sort so prevalent in the 1920s. It does, however, contain an outrageously suggestive shot of Lya de Putti's Olga making eyes at the Prince while wrapping her bee-stung lips round a cigarette.

By 1926, the 33-year-old Rex Ingram – creator of the macabre tableaux featured in *The Conquering Power* and *Trifling Women* – had become exasperated by the new breed of 'supervisors' breathing down the necks of Hollywood directors, the kind of bean-counting functionaries who, it has been suggested, deliberately sabotaged *The Sorrows of Satan* to discredit Griffith once and for all. Anxious to avoid a similar fate, Ingram decamped to the south of France, where he renovated (and eventually purchased) the old Victorine Studio in Nice. Though Ingram made his pictures for M-G-M, he pointedly referred to them merely as 'Metro-Goldwyn' productions, thanks to his profound loathing of the 'supervisor' supreme, Louis B Mayer.

First in line was *Mare Nostrum*, in which Ingram cast his wife, Alice Terry, as a German spy mystically converted into the goddess Amphitrite and reunited with her drowned lover (Antonio Moreno) in the depths of the ocean. Next was a bizarre adaptation of W Somerset Maugham's 1908 novel *The Magician*, in which Maugham had offered an acid caricature of the self-styled Satanic guru Aleister Crowley, whom he'd met in Paris and cordially loathed. Among Ingram's assistants on the film was the young Michael Powell, who would become one of Britain's most distinctive directors, and the result opened in New York on 24 October 1926.

Consulting ancient manuscripts, the insane Dr Oliver Haddo has ascertained the secret of creating artificial life. The chief ingredient is the heart's blood of a maiden, and his efforts to ingratiate himself with the innocent sculptress Margaret Dauncey include taking her on a trance-induced tour of Hades. Fortunately for Margaret, Haddo's eventual experiment in his remote, castellated laboratory is thwarted by the intervention of her fiancé, Dr Arthur Burdon.

Variety's 'Fred' accused *The Magician* of "having too much of a Continental angle to appeal generally." Eight decades later, that Continental angle makes the

film a fascinating artefact. For not only does it serve as a vintage travelogue, complete with glimpses of the Café de Paris in Monte Carlo, the Dôme and the Parc Monçeau in Paris, and the mountain village of Sospel; it also offers a selective snapshot of the arts in 1920s France. Ballet is represented by Hubert Stowitts, the American dancer who had partnered Pavlova and starred in the 1924 Folies-Bergère, sculpture by Paul Dardé (who furnished Ingram with Margaret's colossal figure of a contemplative demon) and theatre by Firmin Gémier of the Comédie Française, whom Ingram retained as directorial consultant, also giving him the important role of Margaret's elderly guardian, Dr Porhoët.

Cinema, however, was represented by a German import. The hooded eyes and massive Tartar countenance of Paul Wegener were ideally suited to Maugham's Crowley substitute, who's described in the novel as "a big stout fellow, showily dressed in a check suit." Haddo is first seen as one of the white-coated onlookers at the operation Arthur performs to save Margaret's life. (In a gripping sequence, the head of the demon sculpture has toppled over and crushed her underneath it.) Hands splayed against the glass, Haddo pooh-poohs the minor business of saving a life, explaining that creating one from scratch is much more challenging.

His initial transgressions are relatively minor – visiting the Library of the Arsenal and tearing out a vellumed page from an ancient grimoire, then presenting Margaret with a flower in the park despite a sign saying "Défense de toucher aux fleurs." By the end, however, Arthur's intervention in his great experiment causes Haddo to go completely berserk – flinging knives, chairs, chemicals – even biting Arthur's hand as their titanic struggle propels him into a suitably Hellish furnace.

That torn-out page, of course, is a recipe for "The Creation of Human Beings by Alchemistry," the (unspecified) ingredients of which should "be kept at a Temperature of 115 Degrees Fahrenheit" and supplemented with "the Heart Blood of a Maiden ... of fair Skin, golden Hair, [and] Eyes that are blue or grey." This is a reasonable description of Ingram's wife Alice Terry, whose winsome Margaret therefore enters into a Trilby-Svengali relationship with Haddo. She takes care, however, to reassure the stricken Arthur that "I have *never been Haddo's wife* ... We are married in name only!" Haddo has his own way of cementing their relationship – he gives her a hallucinogenic tour of Hell, complete with a Witches' Sabbat, Stowitts as a lascivious faun who abandons a scantily clad brunette in order to turn his attentions to

THE MAGICIAN

Metro-Goldwyn 1926
6960 feet; silent
production ended June

Screenplay: Rex Ingram (based on a story by W Somerset Maugham); Director-Producer: Rex Ingram

Cinematographer: John F Seitz; Art Director: Henri Menessier; Editor: Grant Whytock; Sculptures: Paul Dardé*; Production Manager: Harry Lachman; Assistant Directors: Firmin Gémier*, Michael Powell*, Harry Lachman*; Executive [Director]: George Noffka;

Alice Terry (Margaret Dauncey); Paul Wegener (Oliver Haddo); Firmin Gémier (Doctor Porhoët); Iván Petrovich (Arthur Burdon); Gladys Hamer (Susie Boyd); Henry Wilson (Haddo's servant); [Hubert] Stowitts (dancing faun); uncredited: Michael Powell (man with balloon); Claude Fielding, Gerald Fielding (fauns)

Its extreme beauty makes it impossible to dismiss this picture as a piece of crude sensationalism. Simple in construction with little originality, the Svengali-Frankenstein story so grips by sustained horror that its imperfections are ignored. For this the personality of Paul Wegener is mainly responsible. *The Bioscope* [UK]

I feel sure that Rex would have played Conrad Veidt in the part if he had not recently seen *The Golem* ... But Wegener was chosen, and so we were saddled with a pompous German whose one idea was to pose like a statue and whose one expression to indicate magical powers was to open his huge eyes even wider, until he looked about as frightening as a bullfrog.
Michael Powell [A Life in Movies, 1986]

Paul Wegener consults his formula for "The Creation of Human Beings by Alchemistry" in *The Magician* (1926)

the white-robed Margaret, and Haddo himself in black draperies, his hair teased into Mephistophelean horns.

This striking sequence clearly had an effect on Ingram's assistant Harry Lachman, who nine years later would use similar imagery in his remake of *Dante's Inferno*. *The Magician*'s chief influence, however, would be on the Frankenstein pictures later directed for Universal by James Whale. The homunculus Haddo is working on is never seen; indeed, the climactic experiment seems designed merely to extract from Margaret the vital ingredient only she can provide. But the "ancient sorcerer's tower ... beyond the town of Sospel" in which Haddo

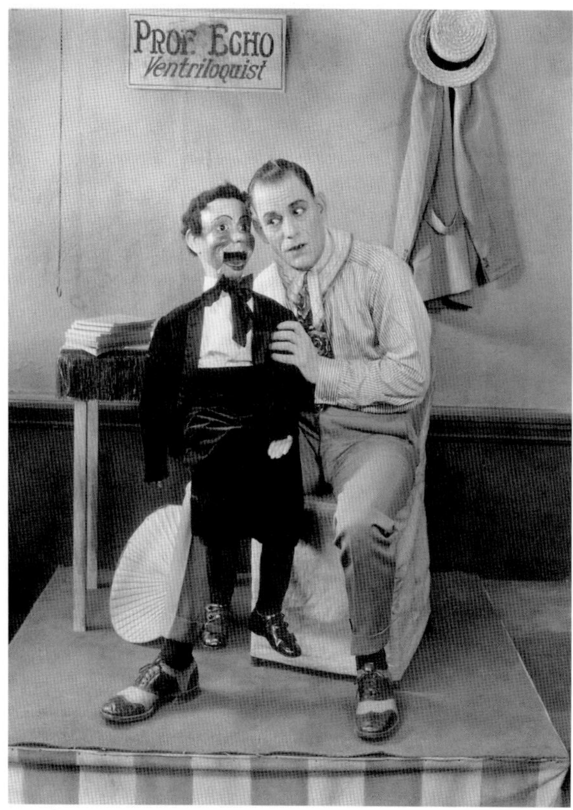

Lon Chaney's Echo performs his 'vent' routine in *The Unholy Three* (1925)

conducts his researches is strikingly similar to the one subsequently seen in *Bride of Frankenstein*, and its climactic detonation is identical.

Inside, Haddo pours smouldering liquids into glass beakers, prepares his wicked-looking surgical knives and lords it over a gnome-like assistant, who goes to answer the door at the foot of a twisting staircase. All these would recur in *Frankenstein*. There are agreeable pre-echoes of Universal's *Dracula*, too, with a frightened local observing that "Neither man nor beast will venture near the Sorcerer's tower at night," while, at the end, Arthur and Margaret descend the tower stairs in much the same way that Jonathan and Mina ascend theirs.

As well as pointing forward to *Frankenstein*, the film's final reel – with Margaret lashed to an operating table, Haddo hovering over her, Arthur and Dr Porhoët rushing to the rescue – has its roots in what the *Variety* review called "the old days when the serials were the feature attractions of the average picture bills." Ingram was certainly well aware of the hokiness of his material here, playing it on a grand scale and even allowing for a bit of farce when the midget assistant, thrown clear of the apocalyptic blast, loses his trousers in the process.

Indeed, Ingram's sense of humour in *The Magician* is almost as strong as his pictorial bent. In particular, Haddo's self-amused response when he overhears Arthur saying that "He looks as if he had stepped out of a melodrama" is a delight. And, after so signally failing to create life in Ingram's film, Wegener (who had himself played an artificial man in three versions of *Der Golem*) would redeem himself the following year in Henrik Galeen's *Alraune*, where his experiments in artificial insemination give rise to the vampiric Brigitte Helm.

LET'S GET GRUESOME

Though Roland West was clearly very much at home in old dark houses, and Rex Ingram, too, had a pronounced appetite for the baroque and the bizarre, it was another director who was extolled in *Motion Picture Classic* as "a stylist among stylists. Almost a specialist. The murky, the grotesque, the gruesome, the mystifying, is his stock in trade. Give this man a Lon Chaney characterization, a mystery concoction of his own weaving, and he can tell a story as masterly as one of Poe's."[10]

Born in Louisville in 1880, Tod Browning had begun his film career at Biograph in 1913, later moving to Hollywood with his mentor, and fellow Kentuckian, D W Griffith. Before all this he had been a performer in an itinerant 'rivershow', the most outré of his several specialities being a 'Hypnotic Living Corpse' routine in which Poe's favoured theme of premature burial was played out for the sensation-hungry hordes of rural America. Browning's career as a Hollywood director nearly ended as soon as it began, when his fondness for alcohol resulted in a 1915 car crash that severely injured Browning and fellow Griffith associate George Siegmann and killed the promising comedian Elmer Booth outright. Recovering, Browning became a force at Universal via several films starring Priscilla Dean, in two of which – *The Wicked Darling* and *Outside the Law* – he made the acquaintance of Lon Chaney. The chance to direct Chaney in *The Hunchback of Notre Dame* was lost, however, when Browning's alcoholism worsened in the early 1920s.

Emerging from several blacklisted years, Browning made an astonishing comeback with *The Unholy Three*, which started its 25-day schedule at M-G-M just before Christmas 1924. The film was based on a 1917 novel by Clarence Aaron 'Tod' Robbins, whose work Browning would turn to again in the 1930s, and it starred Lon Chaney, fresh from his moonlighting jobs on *The Phantom of the Opera* and *The Monster* and

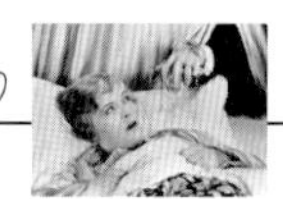

now signed up with M-G-M's Irving Thalberg on a permanent basis.

With *The Unholy Three*, Browning finally began to exploit the shabby carnival milieu in which he had grown up, and with Chaney's shape-shifting genius attached, the film was hailed as "one of the finest pictures ever made" in *Photoplay*'s 'Shadow Stage' section for July 1925. ("However," added the reviewer, "we don't recommend it for the children.") It subsequently rated third on Mordaunt Hall's *New York Times* list of the Ten Best films of the year, ahead of such evergreens as *Ben-Hur* and *The Gold Rush*. And it appeared on similar lists compiled by fan magazines, trade publications and mainstream journals alike.

The story that had so startling a cross-over appeal was a thoroughly bizarre one, particularly for being set down in front of glamour-fixated audiences in the Roaring Twenties. As adapted by Waldemar Young, Robbins' story involved a sideshow ventriloquist, Echo (Chaney), in league with strongman Hercules (Victor McLaglen) and midget Tweedledee (Harry Earles). Dragged up as a little old lady, Echo runs a store selling supposedly 'talking' birds, and, with Tweedledee disguised as a baby, he successfully 'cases' the homes of well-heeled bird-buyers. Despite the high level of weirdness, Young recalled in 1936 that "As far as I know it is the only one [of my films] for which but one script was written, which was shot from the first draft of the screenplay. I wrote it, and have written Heaven knows how many more, but *Unholy Three* was the only one shot without revision of even one line."[11]

Among the plaudits, *Picture-Play*'s Sally Benson observed that "To me it is a fine picture, about the best I have ever seen," also noting that "I have never seen suspense so deliberate and so terrifying. It has the gripping quality of Poe's story *The Pit and the Pendulum*."[12] Perhaps Benson was actually thinking of *The Murders in the Rue Morgue*, for the film's climax can still leave a contemporary viewer open-mouthed in amazement. When The Unholy Three are set at loggerheads – inevitably, by a beautiful carny girl (Mae Busch) – the duplicitous midget unleashes Echo's pet gorilla on the unsuspecting strongman. The latter is killed by the ape, but not before himself killing the midget. Browning's scenes of a crazed chimpanzee, gnashing its fangs and flailing madly around miniaturised sets, remain among the most jaw-dropping in silent cinema.

Browning's next picture started in April 1925 and was released on 27 September, a mere six weeks after *The Unholy Three* began its blockbusting run. *The Mystic* was based on a story of Browning's own, worked up into a scenario by the faithful Waldemar Young. In it, Conway Tearle gains access to Gladys Hulette's fortune by means of the phoney conjuration of her father's spirit, finally returning the money in remorse and following the prettiest of his gypsy spiritualists (Aileen Pringle) back to Hungary.

Despite Pringle's startling Erté-designed costumes, the result was lost in the excitement surrounding *The Unholy Three*, as well as being compared unfavourably to it in reviews that didn't shrink from pointing out the films' plot similarities. "Tod Browning, famous director of crook stories, cannot come within sight of *The Unholy Three* with this," noted the 'Shadow Stage' reviewer in the November issue of *Photoplay*. "If you like spooky thrills – go – but not the children." In an era devoted to the debunking of so many old certainties, Browning's film was one of several that took the Victorian obsession with spiritualism and depicted it as a mere bag of tricks; only the year before, for example, Universal had offered picturegoers a murderous medium in Chester M Franklin's *Behind the Curtain*. The trend, of course, was in perfect accord

Police inspector DeWitt Jennings collars Hungarian fakers Robert Ober, Mitchell Lewis and Aileen Pringle (modelling a fetching Erté creation) in *The Mystic* (1925)

Director Tod Browning relaxes with Lon Chaney on the M-G-M set of *The Road to Mandalay* (1926)

with the rationalisations endemic to Broadway's contemporaneous mystery-thrillers.

After directing Lon Chaney as a Limehouse gangster in *The Blackbird* and a one-eyed smuggler in *The Road to Mandalay*, Browning concocted one of the most beguiling of all his films, *The Show*, which was shot in October and November of 1926 as *Cock o' the Walk*. John Gilbert was here cast against type as feckless carny Cock Robin, "ballyhoo man at the Palace of Illusions." The setting, as per *The Mystic*, is Hungary, with Robin playing John the Baptist in a sideshow sketch with his very own Salome (Renée Adorée), whose spirituality eventually converts him in an affecting subplot involving her blind father (Edward Connelly). The rest of the picture is more in Browning's usual vein, with Lionel Barrymore as a gimlet-eyed psychopath called The Greek, who plots to behead Robin for real and, in a remarkable low-angle shot, almost succeeds. He is finally trapped in Salome's attic with a large poisonous reptile – presumably Browning's take on the 'trapped with a lion' conclusion of *HE Who Gets Slapped*.

Gilbert and Adorée had recently played an American soldier and a French farm girl in King Vidor's *The Big Parade*, which made well over $3 million for M-G-M. On its release on 22 January 1927, *The Show* was far too outré to make anything like that sum, but it remains fascinating for its foreshadowing of Browning's *Freaks* and for its emphasis on the dismemberment fantasies so characteristic of him.

Robin's entourage includes a glamorous trio of bogus curiosities comprising "Arachnida the Human Spider" (the disembodied head of Edna Tichenor suspended in a giant spider's web), plus Zalla Zarana as "Zela the Half Lady" and Betty Boyd as "Neptuna, the Queen of the Mermaids." ("You're hired as freaks ... not vampires!" the jealous Salome cries out at one point.) There's also a phantom female hand that collects the ticket stubs of eager punters. More startling than any of these is a brutal decapitation scene for Gilbert – done in the context of his stage act, of course, but still highly effective, especially when his head keeps on talking from its position on Salome's platter. In 1932, this routine would be lifted in toto for M-G-M's jungle shocker *Kongo* – an apt tribute given that the film was a remake of another Browning picture, *West of Zanzibar*.

A character called Cock getting his head chopped off inevitably attracted the attention of critics influenced by the voguish 1920s interest in psychoanalysis. Whether viewed from a Freudian perspective or not, Browning's signature style was by this time becoming increasingly recognisable, inspiring journalist Joan Dickey to pre-empt François Truffaut and other auteur theorists by some three decades in a 1928 Browning profile. "In the long run," she wrote, "it is more than likely that the directors will be recognized as the real authors of the screen. They, rather than the script writers, are the stylists."[10]

In reviewing Browning's next film, *The Unknown*, *Variety*'s 'Sid' facetiously suggested that "Every time Browning thinks of Chaney he probably looks around for a typewriter and says 'Let's get gruesome.'" In the midst of the 1920s' New Morality, with young Americans emancipating themselves in every direction while enthusiastically absorbing second-hand accounts of Havelock Ellis and Sigmund Freud, Browning's kinky scenarios of unrequited love and physical dismemberment must have seemed like dire warnings from a more grim-faced and atavistic age. If so, with *The Unknown* Browning outdid himself. According to a contemporary notice in the *New York Sun*, "the picture might have been written by Nero, directed by Lucretia Borgia, constructed by the shade of Edgar Allan Poe and lighted by a well-known vivisectionist."[13]

A wanted criminal masquerading as an armless knife-thrower, Alonzo is secretly in love with the circus owner's daughter, who has a pathological aversion to

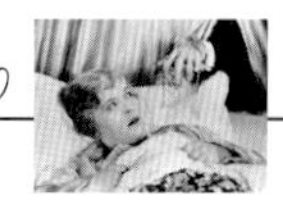

men's hands. When Nanon's father discovers that Alonzo has arms after all, Alonzo is forced to strangle him. Nanon witnesses the murder but knows only that the killer has a double-thumb on one hand. To win her love and also rid himself of his incriminating arms, Alonzo blackmails a surgeon into amputating them...

The Unknown went into production as *Alonzo the Armless* in February 1927 and cost $217,000. It remains the most extreme of all the Browning-Chaney collaborations, though Browning himself, through his title-writer Joseph Farnham, chose to slip this uniquely twisted narrative to unsuspecting moviegoers as if it were merely a harmless anecdote told by some waggish barfly. As the opening intertitle puts it: "This is a story they tell in old Madrid ... it's a story they say is true."

What follows is tightly coiled into a remarkably short and sharp 55 minutes, Browning not wasting so much as a second as his wild tale of amour fou unwinds to its terrible end. As the proud and swarthy Alonzo, Chaney's naked emotional vulnerability is even more impressive than his disappointed scientist in *HE Who Gets Slapped*. As he watches Nanon being chatted up by the good-hearted circus strongman Malabar, his face shades, in a miracle of understated pantomime, from gimlet-eyed resentment to soft fellow-feeling in an instant. And, when Nanon gives him a sisterly kiss, the deluded Alonzo's response – seen only by us and his diminutive assistant Cojo – is beautifully done, telling us all we need to know about the way in which unrequited love can be perverted into a kind of masochism.

As for the kind of masochism seen by several critics as the motivating force behind Chaney's performances, it's shown in action here as Cojo diligently sets about stripping his master of his stripey sweat-shirt, revealing first an imprisoning corset and then, after the laborious unlacing procedure, the genuinely surprising fact that Alonzo has arms after all. Browning is so completely master of his material that he can afford to make this revelation a mere 15 minutes in, where others might have sprung it as a big 'third act' surprise several reels later.

And it's immediately followed by three further audience body-blows – telling us, first, that Alonzo has a double-thumb on one hand; second, that he's wanted by the police; and finally, that underneath that benevolent exterior he might just be a bit bonkers. Exulting in his immunity from police investigation and outlining his plans for Nanon's troublesome father, Chaney's face breaks into maniacal laughter that immediately cranks the film up to a different, more alarming level.

Following the brutal murder sequence, Browning makes room for some grim humour when a sour-faced policeman instructs Cojo to have his fingerprints taken and a twinkling Alonzo waggles his toes to indicate that he has the perfect alibi. And, with Nanon slowly falling under Malabar's spell after all, the romantic scenes are genuinely affecting, much enhanced by a delightfully open-faced performance from Chaney's *Phantom* co-star Norman Kerry; also by Browning's strange device of shooting these sequences through a screen of what looks like burlap wallpaper.

THE UNKNOWN

M-G-M 1927
5521 feet; silent
production began 7 February

Cinematographer: Merritt Gerstad; Art Directors: Cedric Gibbons, Richard Day; Editors: Harry Reynolds, Errol Taggart; Wardrobe: Lucia Coulter; Screenplay: Waldemar Young, from a story by Tod Browning; Titles: Joseph Farnham; Producer: Irving Thalberg; Director: Tod Browning

Lon Chaney (Alonzo); Norman Kerry (Malabar); Joan Crawford (Nanon); Nick de Ruiz (Zanzi, Nanon's father); John George (Cojo); Frank Lanning (Costra); uncredited: Dismuki (armless double for Chaney); Louise Emmons (gypsy woman); Julian Rivero (theatre patron); John Sainpolis (surgeon)

I don't think Tod Browning ever will give us a great picture as he is too firmly addicted to all the moss-grown methods of constructing one ... In a measure he has a fine pictorial eye and succeeds in intriguing our visual sense without making any appeal to our brains. It is too bad that the fine actor of *Mr. Wu* [Chaney] is wasted in such a grotesque offering as *The Unknown*. *The Film Spectator*

Lon Chaney was my introduction to acting. The concentration, the complete absorption, he gave to his characterization filled me with such awe I could scarcely speak to him ... He never slipped out of character. Watching him gave me the desire to be a real actress.
Joan Crawford [quoted in *Films in Review*, December 1956]

Joan Crawford confides in the supposedly armless Lon Chaney in *The Unknown* (1927)

The fulcrum of the plot, however, remains Alonzo's fateful decision to have his arms removed for real, whereupon Browning cuts to a waiting surgeon dwarfed by the arid whiteness of his operating theatre. After a giant close-up of the surgeon's fob-watch as it ticks towards midnight, we next see Alonzo and Cojo skulking down a shadowy corridor to keep their blackmailing appointment. John Sainpolis, having been dragged to a watery grave by Chaney in *The Phantom of the Opera*, contributes a very nice cameo here as the rather prissy, but presumably venal, surgeon.

From this point, Browning piles on the dramatic irony with a trowel. Alonzo's convalescence is intercut with Malabar and Nanon's burgeoning romance (including her absurdly rapid conversion to liking men's hands after all), and the stage is set for a sublimely painful scene in which the returning Alonzo learns of their impending marriage. Malabar's new stage act involves being attached to two straining horses – by his arms, naturally – and Alonzo's jealous attempt at nobbling the machinery features a prominently displayed poster for *Othello*. He finally pushes Nanon from under the hooves of one of the flailing horses and is trampled to death for his pains. By a curious coincidence, Hammer's 1961 remake of *The Phantom of the Opera* would wind up with a very similar self-sacrificing gesture.

For critics convinced of Browning's supposed castration complex, the kinky dismemberments featured in *The Unknown* are like gold dust; certainly, that very peculiar double-thumb would have delighted Freud himself. On top of all this, *The Unknown* is memorable for a performance of heart-touching luminosity by the young Joan Crawford, whom we first see parading in the ring as Alonzo literally shoots the clothes off her, revealing the Amazonian Nanon in a kind of Romany bikini. On the brink of attaining stardom as the ultimate jazz-baby in Harry Beaumont's *Our Dancing Daughters*, Norma Shearer's sometime stand-in makes Nanon a genuinely bewitching figure.

After *The Unknown*, Browning and Chaney next collaborated on *London After Midnight*, which at the time of writing remains much the most famous 'lost' horror picture of the silent era. Scripted once again by Waldemar Young from a story by Browning himself, it went into production on 25 July 1927 as *The Hypnotist*, a title it would retain in the UK. In it, Browning and Chaney offered their own variation on the 'old dark house' routine, fitting it with a rationalist wrap-up in the well-established tradition of Mary Roberts Rinehart.

Scotland Yard's Inspector Burke seeks to establish that the five-year-old suicide of Sir Roger Balfour was actually murder by means of an elaborate vampire charade. Already discomfited by the seeming presence of vampires on the derelict Balfour property, Sir James Hamlin is hypnotised into re-enacting his crime, which was triggered when Sir Roger refused him the hand of his daughter Lucille.

LONDON AFTER MIDNIGHT

M-G-M 1927
5692 feet; silent
production began 25 July
UK title: The Hypnotist

Cinematographer: Merritt Gerstad; Art Directors: Cedric Gibbons, Arnold Gillespie; Editor: Harry Reynolds; Wardrobe: Lucia Coulter; Screenplay: Waldemar Young, from a story by Tod Browning; Titles: Joseph Farnham; Producer: Irving Thalberg; Director: Tod Browning

Lon Chaney (Burke); Marceline Day (Lucille Balfour); Henry B Walthall (Sir James Hamlin); Conrad Nagel (Arthur Hibbs); Polly Moran (Miss Smithson); Percy Williams (butler); Edna Tichenor (Bat Girl), Claude King (The Stranger); Jules Cowles (Gallagher); with Andy MacLennon

To me the funniest thing in it is Lon Chaney's acting ... as the hump-backed runt with all the teeth. I can't understand why he was in the picture. The make-up no doubt pleased Lon, but that is not sufficient reason. However, the whole thing is too utterly silly to warrant detailed criticism. There is about one reel of story embellished by six reels of utter rot. The Film Spectator

I'm particularly lucky in carrying out my ideas by having an artist like Lon to take on guises and disguises of the most grotesque nature. The more grotesque, the better Lon likes them. You have probably read how much he suffers in some of his make-ups. That isn't publicity. He will do anything ... for the sake of his pictures. *Tod Browning* [quoted in Motion Picture Classic, March 1928]

Lon Chaney as "the runt with all the teeth" in *London After Midnight* (1927)

Having been shot on the briefest schedule and smallest budget ($152,000) of any of Chaney's M-G-M assignments, *London After Midnight* earned the studio a whopping profit of over $540,000. (This despite the potential confusion caused by another Metro picture on release in late 1927, the Norma Shearer vehicle *After Midnight*.) It was the occasion of one of Chaney's most grotesque and painful make-ups (including the use of wire loops in his eye sockets, screwed tight just before each take to create the requisite fried-egg effect), and also the occasion for Browning to expound his well-known manifesto regarding the 'debunking' of the supernatural.

"It may sound incongruous," he told Joan Dickey during production, "but mystery must be made plausible. In our latest release, *The Hypnotist*, we use a lot of ghosts and grave spirits and bats. Now, nobody believes in ghosts and grave spirits except children and maybe some dark-complexioned Southerners. But people *would* believe in your ghost if they found out later he was a detective solving a murder crime. The plausibility of that doesn't lessen the thrills and chills in the least. On the contrary, it increases them, because the audience is not asked to believe the horrible *impossible*, but the horrible *possible*."[10]

Browning's worries about audience laughter seem disingenuous, coming from a man whose most celebrated mystery had put a sour-faced gangster into grandmother drag and a cigar-chewing midget into a baby's bib. And as for his 'horrible possible' formula, he was to eat his words in spectacular style when engaged to direct *Dracula* in 1930, having presumably decided by then that mainstream audiences were just as susceptible to the supernatural as infants and "dark-complexioned Southerners."

In the meantime, Browning's strategy succeeded in making *London After Midnight* an out-and-out cheat. Just as *The Bat* had featured a fake detective who turned out to be the 'monster', so Browning's story has a fake vampire who turns out to be the detective. But even though the vampires are exposed as fakes, they remain the first such creatures seen in any American film, and the movie was no doubt startling to contemporary audiences on that score alone. As Young's script evocatively put it, "Inside the deserted house two strange creatures are descending the staircase. One of them, a man, is as strange a creature as the eyes ever beheld. He wears a black beaver hat and a black coat and his face is the pallor of death. The other figure, a woman, is clothed all in black and the sleeves to her dress are long, like wings, giving her the appearance of a bat. Her face, too, is of a deathly pallor."[14]

With imagery like that, the film's New York run presumably acted as an intriguing complement to the Broadway production of *Dracula*, which was heading towards its third month when the film opened on 17 December. Indeed, *London After Midnight* is likely to have been Browning's attempt at a rights-dodging *Dracula* cash-in in the same way that Griffith had previously ripped off *The Bat* as *One Exciting Night*.

Unfortunately, the only visual evidence that remains of *London After Midnight* is a scattering of production stills, though they're certainly pretty mouth-watering in themselves. The cobwebbed majesty of Cedric Gibbons and Arnold Gillespie's sets (depicting a Balfour mansion that has taken a mere five years to fall into Gothic decrepitude), together with the shark-toothed countenance of Chaney's bug-eyed vampire and the wraith-like beauty of Edna Tichenor's 'Bat Girl', have helped to make *London After Midnight* a kind of Holy Grail for film archivists around the world. But, with the lion's share of Browning's footage given over to a rather stodgy detective story and Polly Moran's hyperventilating 'comedy relief' parlourmaid, it's probable that the film would be a profound disappointment if disinterred.

THE UFA EFFECT

Like *The Bat*, John Willard's *The Cat and the Canary* had to wait some time before being filmed. Having premiered on Broadway in February 1922, it only went into production as a so-called Universal 'Jewel' some five years later. By this time, Hollywood moguls were busily coaxing German filmmakers across the Atlantic, and, with his own Teutonic origins, Universal's Carl Laemmle was among the most zealous. His prize catch was the cherubic Paul Leni, a gifted scenic designer whose graduation to film director had thrown up the remarkable, Ufa-distributed 'portmanteau' picture *Das Wachsfiguren-kabinett* (Waxworks).

That Leni was the ideal choice to transfer Willard's Broadway smash to film was proved in spectacular style by the finished product. In the estimate of the *New York Times*' Mordaunt Hall, Leni's *Cat* "is the first time that a mystery melodrama has been lifted into the realms of art."

Twenty years after his death, the surviving relatives of eccentric millionaire Cyrus West gather at his mansion overlooking the Hudson to hear the reading of his will. Annabelle West is named as the heir, but only if her sanity can be proved beyond a doubt. Moments later, a homicidal lunatic is reported to be on the loose – but all is revealed as a plot by the unhinged second heir to drive Annabelle insane.

THE CAT AND THE CANARY

Universal (Jewel) 1927
7713 ft; silent
copyright date 31 March

Cinematographer: Gilbert Warrenton; Art Director: Charles D Hall; Supervising Editor: Lloyd D Nosler; Editor: Martin G Cohn; Music: James C Bradford*; Screenplay: Alfred A Cohn; Adapted by Robert F Hill and Alfred A Cohn from the stage play by John Willard; Titles: Walter Anthony; Story Supervisor: Edward J Montagne; English-speaking liaison: Robert F Hill*; Presented by: Carl Laemmle; Director: Paul Leni

Laura La Plante (Annabelle West); Creighton Hale (Paul Jones); Forrest Stanley (Charles Wilder); Tully Marshall (Roger Crosby); Gertrude Astor (Cecily Young); Flora Finch (Aunt Susan); Arthur Edmund Carewe (Harry Blythe); Martha Mattox (Mammy Pleasant); George Siegmann (the guard); Lucien Littlefield (Ira Lazar [the doctor]); uncredited: Joe Murphy (milkman); Billy Engle (taxi driver)

A night of scares and thrills is promised to all who see this picture. It is of particular interest to the discriminating as the first American picture to be made by that great German producer and technician, Paul Levi [sic]. He has got a great deal more out of the theme than was possible on the stage. The eerie effects achieved are wonderful. The Picturegoer [UK]

What was special about the silent films was the pantomime. You had to get over the story without words. The scripts actually had dialog in those days. We didn't learn the lines but we got over the idea ... I got up as high as $3500 a week at Universal. The idea that anybody would pay me that much was paralysing.
Laura La Plante [quoted in Young, Let Me Entertain You: Conversations with Show People, 1988]

To a director trained in the psychologically probing school of German Expressionism, Willard's hoary narrative must have seemed trite at best. Undaunted, Leni determined to make *The Cat and the Canary* as visually striking a calling-card as he could muster. There are good-natured references to his German confreres – a shadowed hand falling across the sleeping heroine is straight out of *Nosferatu*, and a whole character is made-up to resemble Dr Caligari. (As the psychiatrist who makes a late arrival to assess Annabelle's state of mind, Lucien Littlefield's bald dome, ratty comb-over and spidery hands are reminiscent, too, of Barrymore's Mr Hyde.) There are also any number of beguiling little camera tricks – the hypochondriac millionaire dwarfed by the multiple spires of his castle as they morph into the medicine bottles to which he's enslaved; a yawning skull superimposed over the cowardly hero as another character explains the dire portent of West's portrait falling from the wall; the complex mechanism of a grandfather clock striking 12 as the relatives gather at midnight.

Leni jazzes things up further with drolly off-the-wall intertitles in which exclamations like "GHOST!" and "Gosh what a spooky house!" take on a juddery existence of their own. He also makes masterful use of Charles D Hall's towering interiors, notably when the camera 'becomes' the deceased owner's restless shade as it patrols the castle's dusty corridors, vast curtains billowing fearfully at his approach.

In addition to Hall's sets, Gilbert Warrenton's camerawork is the decisive factor that separates Leni's *Cat* from that other progenitor of the 'old dark house' subgenre, Roland West's *The Bat*. There, West's feats of queasy chiaroscuro were accomplished by a camera that never moved; here, Warrenton's camera conjures up a remarkable fluidity. Hall's sets, too, stand in stark contrast to the sleek, ultra-modern grandeur favoured by West. Hall opts for a crumbling, cobweb-strewn antiquity that would be carried over, pretty much intact, to Universal's first volley of all-talking Gothic horrors.

A couple of details, however, seem to have been playfully lifted from *The Bat*. There, the shadow of a moth was grotesquely enlarged by the headlights of a motor-car; here,

Doe-eyed heroine Laura La Plante and sour-faced housekeeper Martha Mattox in *The Cat and the Canary* (1927)

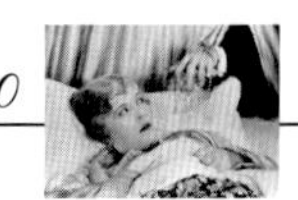

a wavering flashlight beam scans the house in search of the safe, which is later revealed to contain a fluttering moth. This is an especially creepy detail, revealing as it does that the safe and its contents have not lain undisturbed for the requisite 20 years. Indeed, in the playfully paranoid atmosphere cooked up by Leni, even the pores of Lawyer Crosby's nose, seen in massive close-up as he prepares to start reading the will, take on potentially dread significance. The mood of foreboding is further underlined by the will-reading itself, which, in its circular arrangement of high-backed ecclesiastical chairs, suggests a seance rather than a legal formality.

Leni also excels in the big fright set-pieces – the taloned hand that reaches from the woodwork to snatch Crosby into the next world; the same hand plucking the priceless diamond necklace from Annabelle's throat (previously tinted a pale midnight blue, the screen switches to a livid red as she surges up from her sleep, an agitated intertitle screaming "HELP!"); above all, the shock discovery of Crosby's corpse, propped upright behind yet another secret panel.

Of the actors, Creighton Hale's worm-turns comic-relief hero seemed laboured even in 1927, but the ubiquitous Tully Marshall is a standout as the desiccated attorney, as is Martha Mattox as his dark-eyed opposite number, the ironically named Mammy Pleasant. Asked how she's got along for two decades as sole occupant of her late master's cobwebbed abode, she mutters only, "I don't need the living ones."

The climax brings with it an entirely unpredicted sting in the tail just as redolent of German Expressionism as Leni's visual sense. Though the red herrings are plentiful (the saturnine Arthur Edmund Carewe, in the role originated on stage by John Willard himself, is the best of them), the culprit turns out to be the mild-mannered Forrest Stanley. The bulbous eye, the tusk-like fangs, even the Cat's whiskers are mere props, all of them a great deal less frightening than the bleary-eyed gaze of genuine insanity brought by Stanley to a character previously represented as true-blue and just a little bland. It's a truly disquieting end to a picture that laid out the Universal style in virtually all its particulars, requiring only the arrival of Dracula and Frankenstein to give birth to the horror film proper.

In the meantime, one of Leni's most distinguished associates from back home was also in Hollywood. Conrad Veidt had come over in September 1926 at the personal invitation of John Barrymore to appear in Alan Crosland's *The Beloved Rogue*, a florid rendition of the Friml operetta *The Vagabond King*. This featured Barrymore as François Villon and Veidt as Louis XI, the actor's efforts to conceal his towering 6'3" stature resulting in a crouched grotesque that had the fan magazines reaching for the predictable Lon Chaney comparisons. Signed up thereafter by Universal, Veidt only got together with Leni in September 1927. Budgeted at a cool $1.5 million, *The Man Who Laughs* saw Leni promoted from 'Jewel' status to directing a mammoth Universal 'Super Jewel'.

1690. On the execution of his father Lord Clancharlie, ten-year-old Gwynplaine is taken by gypsies and given a permanent fixed grin by their resident surgeon. He grows into manhood as a wildly popular feature of provincial sideshows, and at Southwark Fair he's spotted by the capricious Duchess Josiana. Though Josiana's lascivious interest in him results in his restoration to the House of Lords, Gwynplaine prefers to flee to the continent with his blind sweetheart, Dea.

Victor Hugo's 1869 novel *L'Homme qui rit* had been earmarked as a Lon Chaney vehicle back in April 1924, only a matter of weeks after Universal had put their version of Hugo's *The Hunchback of Notre Dame* into general release. With its grim emphasis on facial disfigurement and the freakshow exploitation of same, the Chaney-free end product was no doubt watched with considerable interest by Chaney's collaborator Tod Browning.

Indeed, Leni's bustling scenes of low-life ogling at Southwark Fair – though garnished with an up-to-the-minute mobile camera in homage to E A Dupont's *Varieté* – devolved in a straight line from Wiene's *Das Cabinet des Dr Caligari* and his own *Waxworks* to James Young's *The Bells* and on to Browning's *The Show* and *The Unknown*. Here is Conrad Veidt on display once again, not as Wiene's shadowy somnambulist but as "The incomparable Gwynplaine with his variety of drolleries." Being silent, the film is understandably sketchy about what those drolleries might consist of, but the unwashed crowds that turn out to fête him seem unconcerned by whatever nominal jokes he has up his sleeve. Instead, they're ready to roll in the aisles merely at sight of his hideous rictus grin – an early triumph, incidentally, for Universal's new make-up man, Jack P Pierce.

The upper crust, of course, are no better. Several of their number – notably Duchess Josiana's nitwit fiancé, Lord Dirry-Moir – look like congenitally in-bred lunatics, and they too fall about at sight of Gwynplaine. Dressed in ducal finery and in the presence of Queen Anne herself, Gwynplaine finally rises up in revolt and utters the immortal intertitle, "A Queen made me a Lord – But first, *God made me*

Conrad Veidt and Mary Philbin in exultant mood in Universal's 'Super Jewel' adaptation of *The Man Who Laughs* (1927)

THE MAN WHO LAUGHS

Universal (Super Jewel) 1927
10,223 *feet; silent with Movietone music and effects*
production began 1 *September*

Cinematographer: Gilbert Warrenton; Technical and Art Directors: Charles D Hall, Joseph Wright, Thomas O'Neil; Editors: Maurice Pivar, Edward [L] Cahn; Make-up: Jack P Pierce*; Costumes: Dave Cox, Vera West; Technical Research: Prof R H Newlands; Production Staff [ie, assistant directors]: John M Voshell, Jay Marchant, Louis Friedlander [later Lew Landers]; Adaptation and Continuity [ie, Screenplay]: J Grubb Alexander, May McLean*, Marion Ward*, Charles E Whitaker* (based on the novel *L'Homme qui rit* by Victor Hugo); Titles: Walter Anthony; Story Supervision: Dr Bela Sekely; Production Supervision: Paul Kohner; Producer: Carl Laemmle; Director: Paul Leni

Mary Philbin (Dea); Conrad Veidt (Gwynplaine/Lord Clancharlie); Julius Molnar Jr (Gwynplaine as a child); Olga Baclanova (Duchess Josiana); Brandon Hurst (Barkilphedro); Cesare Gravina (Ursus); Stuart Holmes (Lord Dirry-Moir); Sam DeGrasse (King James); George Siegmann (Dr Hardquanonne); Josephine Crowell (Queen Anne); Charles Puffy (innkeeper); 'Zimbo' (Homo the wolf); uncredited: Carmen Costello (Dea's mother); Nick de Ruiz (Wapentake); John George (coachman); Torben Meyer (spy); Joe Murphy (Hardquanonne's messenger); Edgar Norton (Lord High Chancellor); Jack Goodrich, Frank Puglia (clowns)

nb: the billing order for Philbin and Veidt was reversed outside the USA

The Man Who Laughs **has a quality all its own. It is bitter, mordant, macabre – a delight to the discriminating, because such pictures are few and far between ... [and] it seems impossible that any one should fail to be engrossed by its strange story, nor fascinated by its atmosphere of evil beauty.** *Picture-Play*

Paul Leni ... was the director of my picture, *The Man Who Laughs*, and we were all very happy about it. It was the Victor Hugo story of the man whose lips were cut away so that he has to go through life forever smiling ... It took some months to make. Sometimes I felt 'The Man Who Laughs' never wanted to smile again. *Conrad Veidt ['The Conrad Veidt Story', Sunday Dispatch 4 November 1934]*

a man!" It's a short distance from this to the heartfelt cry of John Merrick in *The Elephant Man* (1980) that "I am not an animal! I am a human being! I am a man!" Merrick, too, graduates from freakshow humiliation to the highest of high society, only to learn that man's inhumanity to man knows no class barriers. In both films, the confined coterie of the travelling show is identified as a safe haven, a tight-knit community founded on fellow-feeling and compassion.

Soon after *The Man Who Laughs*, Tod Browning would make this the governing theme of *Freaks*, in which he cast Moscow Art Theatre graduate Olga Baclanova as the exemplar of able-bodied heartlessness. As the smouldering Duchess Josiana in Leni's film, she presents an alternative response to disfigurement which, in its way, is more repulsive than anything Browning imagined. Observing Gwynplaine's platform performance from an upper balcony, Josiana's bosom heaves in barely sublimated orgasm. And when the muffled Gwynplaine is delivered to her palatial boudoir, she moves in for a kiss and widens her eyes at sight of his tombstone teeth in as frank a display of sexual arousal as any actor has achieved. To the jaded palate of a pampered aristocrat like Josiana, extreme disfigurement is the final forbidden thrill.

Lon Chaney's co-star from *The Phantom of the Opera*, Mary Philbin, is on hand as Josiana's polar opposite Dea, whose love is spiritual rather than fleshly and whose frizzy blonde wig is irresistibly suggestive of a halo. Veidt, meanwhile, fashions a uniquely disturbing fusion of horror and humour. Peeking out bashfully from the sideshow curtains, the white-faced Gwynplaine could easily pass for one of the more grotesque slapstick clowns of the silent era – Larry Semon, for example. And to point up the paradox, Brandon Hurst gives Gwynplaine's chief antagonist,

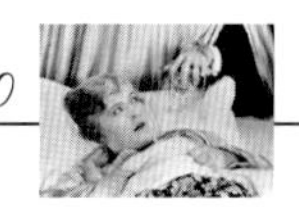

the newly elevated court toady Barkilphedro, a real whiff of pantomime sulphur, a whiff made all the more potent by the fact that Barkilphedro used to be a jester himself.

With his *Cat and the Canary* collaborators Gilbert Warrenton and Charles D Hall, Leni ensured that the film remains a visual feast, setting a high standard with its opening scenes devoted to Gwynplaine's travails as a little boy. These pack a considerable emotional punch, with the boy turfed off the Comprachicos' departing ship (and what a remarkable group of plug-uglies these gypsies are), wandering the snowbound and gibbet-studded Cornish coast and finally stumbling upon a dead woman cradling a still-living baby. Ominously, a couple of ravens drop into the scene only moments after Gwynplaine has picked up the child – who turns out, of course, to be the blind Dea.

The film's happy ending was widely seen as a grievous betrayal of Hugo's novel for the sake of the US audience, and a full reel of Gwynplaine sprinting to the docks with Barkilphedro's minions in hot pursuit is certainly pretty wearing. Even here, however, the film's angry mob of torch-wielding Londoners – directly descended from *Phantom*'s torch-wielding Parisians – was to be repeated in any number of Universal's more straight-ahead horrors. The sequence also gives us a gratifying shot of Barkilphedro having his throat torn out by Gwynplaine's trusty wolfhound.

Despite this audience-pleasing finale, the film did better as an export than in the US itself; as *Photoplay*'s 'Shadow Stage' critic put it in May 1928, "This picture may get by in Europe under the name of Art, but in this country it will have little interest." At least one American audience member was paying close attention, however. The young Bob Kane would derive The Joker from Veidt's Gwynplaine just as surely as he derived Batman from *The Bat*.

WALL-TO-WALL APES

In November 1927, while *The Man Who Laughs* was still in production, US cinemagoers were treated to a lurid Fox production which appears not to have survived. Richard Rosson's *The Wizard* was a very loose remake of a French film of 1913, Victorin Jasset's *Balaoo*, which had been urged upon American exhibitors with the memorable injunction that "This tragedy of the footprints on the ceiling will jam any theatre."

The new version featured Hollywood's Grade-A continental menace, Gustav von Seyffertitz, as Professor Paul Coriolos, who plots an appalling revenge on the family responsible for his son's execution; the instrument of that revenge is "a fiend-faced ape" of his own devising (played by Greek wrestler George Kotsonaros). The vacuity of the by-the-numbers storyline was brought into sharp focus by *Variety*'s 'Sid': "It's all very annoying until the cub reporter (Mr [Edmund] Lowe) gets on the trail. He's got to get a big story or lose his job ... Coriolos, a dirty dog at best, uses the whip once too often and dies at the hands of the 'thing' he has conceived. Anne [Leila Hyams] shoots the beast, Stanley phones his beat on the town's blood-curdling mystery and obtains himself a bride. Write and play down to your audience. They did."

The *Balaoo* template would prove a remarkably durable one – in England, it would inform a cheapskate quota quickie of 1932 called *Castle Sinister*, and in the USA it would be directly remade in 1942 as *Dr Renault's Secret*. But here it seems to have had the currently voguish ingredients of a knockabout mystery-thriller grafted onto it to detrimental effect. The *New York Times*, for example, called *The Wizard* "quite a good entertainment weakened by the levity forced upon it. This subject really has enough of a story to deserve more serious treatment" – noting also that "Gustav von Seyffertitz, who impersonates the mad surgeon, does some capital acting."

Norman Trevor and Leila Hyams at the mercy of Gustav von Seyffertitz and his "fiend-faced ape" (George Kotsonaros) in *The Wizard* (1927)

As well as borrowing from Broadway's horror-comedy trend, the film formed part of a brief fad for 'selective' tinting, with the action presented in standard black-and-white save for a few showstopping details. Deploring what he called Fox's "tinting complex," 'Sid' drew attention to a birthday cake with luminescent candles, the flash of Leila Hyams' revolver as she guns down the rampaging ape-man, even the robe worn by the thing as a disguise – "it's unquestionably yellow," 'Sid' sneered. Given these contemporary responses, William K Everson may have been right when he suggested in 1974 that *The Wizard* "is perhaps most sorely missed as a major gap in our knowledge of [Frank] Good's camerawork in the silent period."[15]

That *The Wizard* was derived from an old newspaper serial by Gaston Leroux, whose *The Phantom of the Opera* had recently proved such a hit for Universal, was presumably the main reason Fox made it. Another reason, perhaps, was the sensational splash Darwinian theories had lately been making in the nation's newspapers. The Anti-Evolution League had been set up in 1924 with a view to outlawing the teaching of Darwinism in schools, and the following summer a Dayton schoolteacher called John Thomas Scopes was arraigned for contravening Tennessee's Butler Act. The show trial that followed drew world attention to the momentous clash between local Fundamentalist William Jennings Bryan and the brilliant advocate Clarence Darrow. His "fool religion," as Darrow called it, having been utterly discredited, Bryan collapsed and died only a few days after the trial ended.

As if subconsciously compelled to further inflame the sores left behind by the Scopes trial, Hollywood's extraordinary preponderance of apes and ape-men in this period – a preponderance also reflected in the pulp magazines – was by no means confined to picturegoers' continuing love affair with Tarzan, nor would it let up for another decade or two. The stars of *The Wizard* were no strangers to the trend; in 1926, Gustav von Seyffertitz had encountered a homicidal ape in Archie Mayo's melodrama *Unknown Treasures*, while George Kotsonaros had played a similar character in Howard Bretherton's *While London Sleeps*. The latter saw canine superstar Rin-Tin-Tin earning his $6000-a-month pay cheque by foiling the schemes of Limehouse master criminal 'London Letter' (Otto Matiesen) and his attendant beast-man, the 'Monk'.

When dogs like Rin-Tin-Tin (or Silverstreak, or Fido, or Lightning, to name just a few of Rinty's competitors) displayed anthropomorphic qualities, they were venerated by picture patrons just as much as Colleen Moore or Clara Bow. When apes did the same thing, the spectre they presented of man's ancestral past made them figures of horror. (Albeit frequently as mere horror 'props' in films not chiefly concerned with horror.) And the horror was apparently most pronounced across the Atlantic. Kotsonaros suffered the ignominy of being eliminated entirely from the UK release of *While London Sleeps*, an early warning from the British Board of Film Censors of the intolerant attitude that would have serious repercussions some ten years later.

Back in the USA, *Photoplay* could afford to make sport of the Scopes trial, noting "the similarity between the actions of Hollywood stars and orang-outans" and imagining a debate on the subject presided over by an orang-outan dignitary called Judge Jiggs, who claimed to have "seen a picture in which a man named Bull Montana [was] made up to look like a monkey, but he had yet to see the monkey who would make up to look like a man."[16] This kind of satire did nothing, of course, to stem the simian stampede issuing from the studios. Montana himself, for example, supplemented his ape impersonations in *Go and Get It* and *The Lost World* with another, in Alvin J Neitz's 15-chapter serial *Vanishing Millions* (1925). In addition, Sam Baker essayed the title role in Warners' frenetic farce *The Missing Link* (1927), the old Triangle studio played host to an apparently act-based story called *The Ape* in 1928, and Pathé's ten-part serial *The Fire Detective* (1929) stirred in the obligatory 'throwback' in Chapter Seven.

Presented to the critics only a week before *The Wizard* was yet another ape-fixated subject, First National's *The Gorilla*. This, too, appears to be a 'lost' film. A farcical adaptation of the 1925 Broadway show written by Ralph Spence, *The Gorilla* demonstrated, as had *The Missing Link*, that the ape threat could be played for laughs as well as chills. Directed by Alfred Santell, the film cast ex-Keystone comic Charlie Murray and perennial hard-nosed investigator Fred Kelsey as Garrity and Mulligan, a pair of bungling detectives on the trail of whoever murdered elderly miser Cyrus Townsend (Claude Gillingwater). There's a murderous gorilla at large, too, eventually revealed to be the miser's friend Stevens (Walter Pidgeon) in gorilla disguise. Predictably, the culprit is exposed, not by Garrity and Mulligan, but by their chief suspect, Townsend's secretary (Gaston Glass), who turns out to have been a detective all along.

Presumably with Murray in mind, the *New York Times* declared that "*The Gorilla* is very much as if Mack Sennett in a restrained mood had turned to Edgar Allan Poe's *The Murders in the Rue Morgue*," while *Photoplay*'s 'Shadow Stage' for January 1928

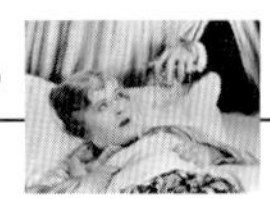

noted that "The episodes in which the gorilla chases Murray through the house, over the roof and down the chimney, as well as the battle in the cellar of the old mansion, will rock any audience." *Variety*, meanwhile, praised the "expert treatment of lighting values and perspective" in the work of Arthur Edeson, future cinematographer of *Frankenstein*. With pretty heroine Alice Day robed in filmy white for her climactic Beauty and the Beast confrontation, surviving stills suggest that Pidgeon's bow-legged ape get-up was entirely in keeping with a film aimed at laughs rather than chills.

Another ape disguise featured in Fox's *The Monkey Talks*, only this time it was a more cuddlesome chimp rather than the traditionally fearsome gorilla. First unveiled in February 1927, the film was directed by Raoul Walsh and adapted by L G Rigby from the René Fauchois play *Le Singe qui parle*, which had opened at Broadway's Sam H Harris Theatre in December 1925. Retained from the stage version was the diminutive French actor Jacques Lerner, playing circus performer François Faho, who perfects an ingenious chimpanzee impersonation for the purposes of a con-trick but finds himself sold as a pet to the beautiful Olivette (Olive Borden). Inevitably, the hirsute 'Jocko' falls in love with her, and the apparently innocuous action therefore bristles with unrequited kinkiness of the Tod Browning variety.

The film's circus backdrop and forbidden love theme also recall Sjöstrom's *HE Who Gets Slapped*, and the likeness is confirmed when Jocko arranges for the villains to walk, literally, into the lion's den. Confusingly, when Olivette is threatened with a fate worse than death by a real ape, the latter is played by yet another man in a monkey suit, with the climactic battle between Jocko and the supposedly genuine article being played out in silhouette. Lerner's make-up, incidentally, was designed by Jack P Pierce shortly before his defection to Universal and *The Man Who Laughs*.

After his troubled time as nominal director of *The Phantom of the Opera*, Rupert Julian was bound to encounter one of Hollywood's omnipresent apes at some time or other, and it finally happened in a film harking back to Poe's *The Murders in the Rue Morgue*. Despite top-lining the glamorous Jacqueline Logan – who, as leopard trainer Paula, is deputed by the police to solve a series of murders in a travelling carnival – the acting honours in *The Leopard Lady* were reportedly stolen by Alan Hale's robust Caesar, whose trained gorilla turns out to have perpetrated the killings at his behest. The gorilla was played by a 25-year-old Filipino make-up artist called Charles Gemora, his first such performance in a simian career that would stretch to 1953. "Film features like this don't make it tough for the opposition," sneered *Variety*. "Here's a mystery thriller that's a perfect fit for the third-grade houses."

Alice Day swoons into the accommodating arms of *The Gorilla* (1927)

Welford Beaton, however, was more indulgent, drawing attention to the cinematography of John J Mescall (who in the 1930s would graduate to films like *The Black Cat* and *Bride of Frankenstein*) and reflecting on Hollywood's resistance to Grand Guignol subjects in general: "Blood-and-thunder stuff is provided for us so seldom that when we do get a dose of it, provided it be well done, it is a most welcome change of diet. I don't think we have changed a great deal since the time melodramas flourished and murder was regarded as high class entertainment. [Rupert] Julian proves himself a splendid murderer."[17]

The next Tod Browning-Lon Chaney collaboration featured only a cameo role for a chimpanzee. "Fate had made him a crippled monster," drooled the ads for *West of Zanzibar*, "so he took his revenge on Life!" Made in July 1928 and released on Christmas Eve, the film was derived from the shocking Charles DeVonde-Kilbourn Gordon play *Kongo*. This time, it was Welford Beaton's 18-year-old son Donald who

Straight from the so-called Cesspools of Hollywood: Lon Chaney torments Mary Nolan in *West of Zanzibar* (1928)

poured cold water on the result from the influential pulpit of *The Film Spectator*. "It is getting so that Lon Chaney's name warns theatregoers of a bad picture, and with Tod Browning an atrocity is assured," he began, noting also that "Chaney's once considerable acting ability has been atrophied by the parts he has had to play until he has about three expressions left."[18]

Admittedly, Chaney's expressions in *West of Zanzibar* don't go much beyond those of a cigar-chomping Cheshire Cat, but they're perfectly attuned to Browning's impishly comic take on the DeVonde-Gordon play. Chaney is the disabled Phroso, a sometime music-hall conjuror who has established himself as an all-powerful 'white Voodoo' in darkest Africa. Railing against Crane, his late wife's lover (Lionel Barrymore), Phroso pronounces vengefully that "He made me this thing that crawls ... *now I'm ready to bite!*" The biting involves bringing up Crane's daughter Maizie (Mary Nolan) in the most squalid circumstances imaginable, though the laugh's on Phroso when Crane reveals that the girl is Phroso's daughter after all.

The freakish black comedy of *West of Zanzibar* ranges from Crane's wild hilarity on realising his enemy's mistake to Phroso's crazy, wheelchair-bound St Vitus Dance while trying to pull a final fast one on the credulous natives. Some contemporary critics saw the joke. "This is mad, weird, grotesque, and completely nutty melodrama," opined the January 1929 issue of *Motion Picture*, adding, "You will get lots of laughs out of it." Others didn't, notably *Harrison's Reports*, which on 5 January headed its review 'An Outpouring of the Cesspools of Hollywood', calling the stage original "this horrible syphilitic play" and the film itself "this piece of filth." In fact, Browning refers to Maizie's enforced prostitution and a local doctor's drug addiction in such elliptical terms they could easily be missed, paving the way for a much more uncompromising talkie remake, *Kongo*, in 1932.

As well as adding a number of sadistic details (and restoring the ferocious Walter Huston to his old stage role), the new version would appropriate some of the ritual masks, together with a bug-eyed voodoo idol, used in *West of Zanzibar*. Voodoo had figured already in Frank Reicher's 1917 film *Unconquered* (discussed in Part One) and John B O'Brien's *Those Who Dare* (1924), which chronicled a voodoo-inspired mutiny on board a cursed ship called The Swallow. In addition, Ben Wilson's 15-part serial *The Power God* (1925) featured revived corpses and Ernest Stern's *The Witching Eyes* (1929) a lustful voodoo witch doctor.

The old standby of exotic jewellery exercising a malefic influence over its owners was meanwhile being kept going almost single-handedly by scenarist Arthur Hoerl. His adaptation of Harold MacGrath's play *The Drums of Jeopardy*, directed by Edward Dillon in 1923, was followed five years later by Scott Pembroke's *The Black Pearl*, in which Lila Lee was surrounded by the whole paraphernalia of cursed gems, death threats pinned by daggers and an edge-of-the-seat will-reading. After that, the sinister emeralds of *The Drums of Jeopardy* were trotted out again for George B Seitz's talkie remake of 1931.

For their part, Browning and Chaney remained in exotic climes for their next film, *Where East is East*. Produced in January and February 1929, this was another instance of Chaney resisting the move into talkies, instead scowling his way through a ludicrous, but highly engaging, melodrama that plays like a 'Greatest Hits' gazetteer of Browning and Chaney's most cherished preoccupations. With the exception of the director's beloved sideshow milieu, they're all here. The sweat-stained Oriental setting and parent-child plot convolutions are familiar from both *The Road to Mandalay* and *West of Zanzibar*, while the 'death by liberated gorilla' climax is straight out of *The Unholy Three*.

In what would later be classed as an erotic thriller, Estelle Taylor smoulders magnificently as a mixed-race vamp using her "heathen tricks" to seduce the straitlaced fiancé of her own daughter (Lupe Velez). Chaney is the scarfaced, tiger-trapping father who, in desperation, eradicates Taylor's overwhelmingly threatening sexuality by loosing his pet gorilla on her – intriguingly, a female of the species called Rangho.

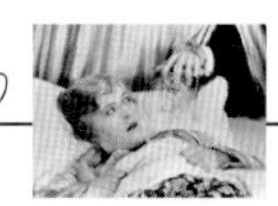

"From the instant a close-up and caption calls attention to a captive gorilla," noted 'Land' in *Variety*, "the smart pupils will easily and correctly surmise that it is the plot function of this gorilla to remove the evil woman at the critical moment." The *New York Herald Tribune*, meanwhile, wondered facetiously whether, in addition to the unusually subdued role of 'Tiger' Haynes, Chaney also played the ape. (In fact, it was the inescapable Charles Gemora.) At one point in the film, the spineless fiancé (Lloyd Hughes) observes that "This is all like a poem of Kipling's" – a sly acknowledgment, not only of where Browning came by the title for his earlier film *The Road to Mandalay*, but also of Kipling's role in propagating the predatory 'vamp' character, of which Taylor's performance remains perhaps the definitive example.

Another, more harmonious father-daughter relationship: Lupe Velez teases scar-faced Lon Chaney in *Where East is East* (1929)

THE TERROR TALKS

"The star system dominating the picture industry since its inception is about to be tagged for the junk heap," announced *Variety* on 28 November 1928. "Total eclipse of many old-time favorites seems inevitable." This alarming (and, as it turned out, rather premature) statement confirmed the worst fears of many denizens of the movie colony, who had by then been apprehensive about the coming of talking pictures for over 12 months. Warner Bros had first used their Vitaphone process to add a synchronised score and sound effects to the John Barrymore vehicle *Don Juan*, which opened in New York on 6 August 1926. Then came the epoch-making premiere of *The Jazz Singer* on 6 October 1927, its selected musical and talking interludes incorporating Al Jolson's prescient phrase, "You ain't heard nothin' yet." And finally, Warners' first all-talking picture, *The Lights of New York*, was unveiled on 6 July 1928.

"Even if you haven't heard so much as a single chirrup from a Vitaphone, or a Movietone [M-G-M's competing system]," suggested *Picture-Play*'s Edwin Schallert, "you must naturally take some token of this amazing new *racket* ... That the whole talking-picture situation will assume the proportions of a veritable revolution is undoubted. Moviedom will be turned into topsy-turvydom by the new development."[19] So it proved, with stars by the dozen lining up for their all-important voice tests in a state of virtual terror. In the meantime, Broadway actors (and directors) were flocking to Hollywood to take advantage of a situation exemplified by Jesse Lasky's insistence that Paramount productions should be advertised with the ludicrous slogan, 'With Casts That Can Talk.'

In the meantime, *Variety* offered its own prediction of the gauche clunkiness of early talkies, which would for several years seem a poor substitute for the technical perfection attained by silent pictures, in the glum assertion that "We're in for a new deal, and the game is dated right back to the rules of 1915." Despite such sage warnings, the death knell was finally rung on the silent era when Warners' second Al Jolson vehicle, *The Singing Fool*, racked up close to $6 million; it had cost a mere $388,000. Unlike *The Lights of New York*, however, *The Singing Fool* was only a 'part-talkie'. For their second fully fledged talking feature, Warner Bros hit upon an Edgar Wallace adaptation called *The Terror* and released it on 6 September 1928.

If sound films offered the questionable virtue of screeds of drawing-room dialogue – plus the much more exciting use of, say, machine-gun fire in crime pictures – then it was obvious that the screen's thriller-chillers would benefit no end from crashes of thunder, creaking doors, moaning winds, screams in the night, the whole works. This *The Terror* duly got, together with the wheezing of a toad familiar called Squeegee and the eerie organ extemporisations of The Terror himself. On top of all this, the film's pressbook offered a classic example of Hollywood's inability to define this nascent strain of scary entertainment, be it silent or sound. Among the tag-lines recommended to prospective exhibitors were such ugly mixed metaphors as "Funniest Fright Film!" and "Creepiest Crook Film Ever!"

The massively popular Edgar Wallace was establishing the British Lion studio in Beaconsfield

The world's second all-talking picture: John Miljan teases May McAvoy in *The Terror* (1928)

while Hollywood conferred such unexpected import on *The Terror*. His original play had given *The Bat* a Home Counties makeover, locating its monk-like hooded maniac and stash of sought-after loot in a country house lately converted into an inn. On film, director Roy Del Ruth apparently flouted the wax museum immobility of the talking picture by offering a giddy overhead shot of a seance and having Barney McGill's camera hurtle on rollers into a shrieking face. But, tellingly, these and other showstopping moments were filmed silent. Elsewhere, the film was all-talking in the most literal sense, with no titles of any sort, never mind intertitles, to spoil the novelty. As the film's bumbling detective, Edward Everett Horton, remembered it, "*The Terror* had no titles at all and even the opening credits and the words 'The End' were intoned, and Conrad Nagel's voice informed the audience of the time and place of each scene."[20]

The rest of the cast included the ubiquitous Louise Fazenda as a medium and Frank Austin as a creepy butler, a role he would repeat two years later in *The Laurel-Hardy Murder Case*. (He had already appeared as the lunatic Rigo in *The Monster*, styling himself George Austin on that occasion.) Jolson's co-star from *The Jazz Singer*, May McAvoy, was cast as the heroine and suffered from Mordaunt Hall's careless reference in the *New York Times* to her voice as "shy and shrinking, a lisping peep." This was the seed of a May McAvoy myth almost as persistent as the mistaken notion that John Gilbert failed in the talkies thanks to an effeminate voice. The vengeful enmity of Louis B Mayer was the more likely explanation in Gilbert's case, the faulty apparatus of the time the probable cause in McAvoy's.

Whatever the quality of the film's recording (and the recordings are all that remain, the picture itself being lost), the British trade paper *Bioscope* acknowledged that "Acting was generally on a fairly high level, and much was done to compensate for poor story values and appallingly bad production," adding that "The house was impossibly theatrical; it bore no resemblance to a place of human habitation. Feasibility was all thrown out of the window to make room for cobwebs and other eerie appurtenances."[21]

And the film's providential importance as the world's second talkie ensured it pride of place in the same issue's editorial. "It would be easy to dismiss *The Terror* by saying that it was a terror," wrote John Cabourn, "but ... the question which every sensible person had in his mind when he visited the Piccadilly Theatre last week was not whether *The Terror* was a good talkie but whether talkies were going to be good at all ... *The Terror* as a film may not be brilliant, but, as a talking film, it is in the highest degree suggestive. To criticise it on the ground of indistinct sibilants or puerile scenic inconsistencies is to miss the entire omen."[22]

At Universal, meanwhile, Paul Leni may well have found the challenge of talkies less galling than the fact that the script for his *Man Who Laughs* follow-up was a virtual carbon copy of his first American film, *The Cat and the Canary*. *The Last Warning* was based on a Broadway hit of the 1922-3 season that at least had the self-reflexive wit to be set in an old 'dark' theatre rather than an old dark house. Universal had bought the rights for $15,000 back in June 1927, but had moved slowly on the property thanks to vacillation over whether to make it as a talkie or not. As M-G-M had done with *West of Zanzibar*, *The Man Who Laughs* had been fitted by Universal with a sound effects track courtesy of the Vitaphone competitor, Movietone. Now that some form of talk was deemed indispensable, *The Last Warning* finally went into release in January 1929 as a silent with token talkie sequences – a curious compromise that kept audiences in a peculiar state of unease, wondering when the talking would actually start.

On Broadway, actor-manager John Woodford is killed during a performance of The Snare *and his murder never solved. Several years later, producer Arthur McHugh decides to revive the play and reopen the long-dark Woodford Theatre. He assembles much the same personnel and tries to quiet their fears that Woodford's ghost haunts the theatre. This is difficult given the presence of a masked maniac in the flies.*

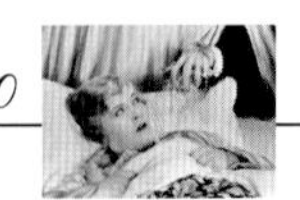

Backstage phantom: Margaret Livingston, Laura La Plante, Montagu Love, John Boles, Mack Swain, Bert Roach and 'Slim' Summerville in *The Last Warning* (1928)

Making what would turn out to be his last film, Leni seems to have determined on demonstrating just what was being lost in the changeover to talkies, transforming the hoary theatrics of *The Last Warning* into a sensational showcase of the silent screen's capabilities. He did this initially via a trick recycled from *The Cat and the Canary*, though here much magnified – a dazzlingly inventive use of the already outmoded intertitle.

The first spins into view like a roulette wheel, proclaiming "Broadway, Electric Highway of Happiness – Street of Night Clubs, Theatres, Laughter," prior to strobing like a neon light and giving way to a breathtaking montage of scenes from the Great White Way. High-stepping chorus girls are superimposed over the neon glare of Madison Square Garden and the Greenwich Village Follies – even the fruity sensation Josephine Baker is briefly glimpsed in the melange – and then a police car plunges onto the scene and comes to a halt outside the Woodford

THE LAST WARNING

Universal (Jewel) 1928
6171 feet; silent version: 5999 feet
silent with Movietone effects track and talking sequences
produced August

Cinematographer: Hal Mohr*; Art Director: Charles D Hall*; Editor: Robert Carlisle*; Music: Joseph Chernivasky*; Screenplay: Alfred A Cohn, Robert F Hill, J G Hawks [adaptation], Alfred A Cohn [continuity], Tom Reed* [titles], from the play by Thomas F Fallon and novel by Wadsworth Camp; Editor in Chief [ie, Story Supervisor]: Edward J Montagne; English-speaking liaison: Robert F Hill*; Associate Producer: Carl Laemmle Jr; 'A Carl Laemmle Special'; Director-Producer: Paul Leni

Laura La Plante *(Doris Terry)*; Montagu Love *(Arthur McHugh)*; Roy D'Arcy *(Harvey Carleton)*; Margaret Livingston *(Evelynda Hendon)*; John Boles *(Richard Quayle)*; Bert Roach *(Mike Brody)*; Mack Swain *(Robert Bunce)*; Burr McIntosh *(Josiah Bunce)*; Mme Carrie Daumery *(Barbara Morgan)*; 'Slim' Summerville *(Tommy Wall)*; 'Buddy' Phelps *('Buddy')*; Torben Meyer *(Gene)*; D'Arcy Corrigan *(John Woodford)*; Tom O'Brien *(first detective)*; Fred Kelsey *(second detective)*; *uncredited:* Charles K French *(doctor)*; Francisco Marán *(Jeffries)*; Ella McKenzie *(Ann)*; Harry Northrup *(coroner)*; Pat Harmon, Charles McMurphy *(policemen)*

This could have been a gorgeous mystery story, but it's an obvious cross between *The Phantom of the Opera* and *The Terror*, with none of their consistency or power. It has a distinguished cast, with massive sets and effective, futuristic photography, but there's no story.
Photoplay

That was a very fun picture to make. Leni was a wonderful little guy [who] could speak very little English, and he had manners of directing that were truly of the silent era ... It was supposed to be a haunted theatre, and he had these wild chases through the thing. It was like a three-ring circus.
Hal Mohr [quoted in Film Comment, September 1974]

Theatre. In another of Leni's nods to his German confreres, this time to the monstrous factory of Fritz Lang's *Metropolis*, we notice that the theatre frontage bears a discreet resemblance to a human face.

The action within is grippingly done, with tension screwed to a high pitch as Fred Kelsey barges his way through all the shiftless theatre types in his usual role of a hard-nosed Irish police inspector. (Though billed as 'second detective', he's very much in charge.) We're also given ample evidence of Universal's determination to get their money's worth from the old *Phantom of the Opera* stage, which was already proving just as recyclable as the cathedral façade built for *The Hunchback of Notre Dame*.

A flashback to Woodford's on-stage demise reveals *The Snare* as a tacky-looking 'Gay Hussars' kind of piece, after which Hal Mohr's camera ducks dexterously under the lowering curtain in order to catch John Boles uttering the generic intertitle, "Quick! Is there a doctor in the house?" Let loose in the former Paris Opera, Mohr goes absolutely wild, the camera's vertiginous movements rivalling even the trapeze shots in E A Dupont's *Varieté*.

On the re-opening of the theatre, Leni inserts a few self-amused nods to *The Cat and the Canary*. A caretaker opens a drawer to reveal the dust-laden scripts of *The Snare* and, when a spider scuttles crankily across them, we're irresistibly reminded of Lawyer Crosby disinterring Cyrus West's 20-year-old documents and finding a moth fluttering inside the safe. Most obviously, Lawyer Crosby's death-plunge is re-staged when McHugh breaks into Woodford's old dressing room ("It's like rifling a tomb – but I have to do it!") and the new leading man staggers out of a secret panel prior to pitching forward across the divan. Other effects are new, such as a headline montage in which the assembled newspapers rise up like skyscrapers against a view of the theatre façade, a gauzy subjective shot in which Carrie Daumery sees her companions through a face-full of cobwebs, and a dazzling entrance for Margaret Livingston, who steps nonchalantly through another cobweb and heads flirtatiously for the theatre owner while Mohr homes in on her shapely legs.

Livingston, whose character turns out to be an undercover policewoman, had recently played the vampish 'Woman from the City' in Murnau's *Sunrise*. Similarly, Montagu Love, cast in the plum part of the watchful McHugh, had been Lillian Gish's abuser in *The Wind*. More to the point as far as Universal were concerned, top-billed Laura La Plante had starred in Leni's *The Cat and the Canary*. ("No reason for Miss La Plante being in the picture other than her name," sniped *Variety*. "She does little or nothing except look frightened and scream every so often, the May McAvoy scheme of *The Terror*.") In addition, Leni was given a couple of ex-Sennett clowns to punch up the comedy – the mountainous Mack Swain and the pencil-thin 'Slim' Summerville.

Despite the high calibre of his actors, Leni was clearly uninterested in them, and even less so in the story. For the viewer, this results in 'style over content' fatigue about two-thirds of the way in, but Leni recovers with a barnstorming finale in which the cheese-faced maniac causes havoc in the flies and Mohr's camera swings giddily in pursuit. Astonishingly, the stage flats all fly up on cue to expose the killer, who is located, and unmasked, in the belly of a clock. The sequence anticipates the backstage set-pieces featured in John Brahm's *The Lodger* and Alfred Hitchcock's *Torn Curtain*, but it's never really been bettered.

Both *The Terror* and *The Last Warning* had been preceded in March 1928 by Paramount's *Something Always Happens*, in which Film Guild veteran Frank Tuttle put Esther Ralston into a mock haunted house, complete with Noble Johnson as 'The Thing'; this, however, was a silent. The all-talking gauntlet of *The Terror* was finally taken up by Lewis Seiler, who surrounded Helen Twelvetrees with peculiar hotel guests in Fox's February 1929 release *The Ghost Talks*. More entertaining than either of these was James Parrott's silent short *Habeas Corpus*, which was filmed over several nights in July 1928 and located the ace comic team of Stan Laurel and Oliver Hardy – engaged by a mad professor as a latterday Burke and Hare – in a Culver City cemetery. The film was an elaboration of the graveyard sequence in the previous year's *Do Detectives Think?*, in which Stan and Ollie encountered Noah Beery's formidable 'Tipton Slasher'.

THREE FOR FIRST NATIONAL

As the mania for talking pictures took hold, First National could counter Universal's German acquisition, Paul Leni, with their very own Danish import, Benjamin Christensen. A sometime opera singer and theatre director, in 1919 Christensen had started researching *Häxan* (aka *Witchcraft Through the Ages*), which, with a budget of a million Swedish crowns, would cost the Svensk Filmindustri conglomerate over ten times the budget of a normal feature. The result, a kind of early drama-documentary about mediaeval diabolism, was finally unveiled in 1922 and was banned in many territories; as well as casting himself as Satan, Christensen had heaped on sufficient nudity and graphic horror to make the film seem a good 50 years ahead of its time.

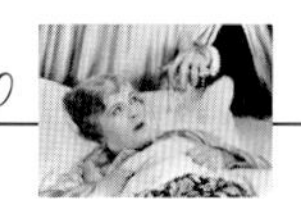

Despite, or maybe because of, the controversy, Christensen found his way to Hollywood and made two films for M-G-M, featuring an omniscient Satan in the otherwise straightforward Norma Shearer vehicle *The Devil's Circus* and directing Lon Chaney in a melodrama of revolutionary Russia called *Mockery*. He moved on to an embattled combination of Jules Verne and Technicolor, *Mysterious Island*, before leaving M-G-M in protest at producer interference. His replacement, Maurice Tourneur, would leave Hollywood for good for the same reason; the film was completed by its screenwriter, Lucien Hubbard.

First National stepped into the breach and, despite Christensen's uniquely grisly back-catalogue, assigned him three projects that fell firmly into the skittish, but still popular, horror-comedy mould. All three were made more or less back-to-back and opted for the 'part-talkie' route taken by *The Last Warning* rather than the all-talking approach of *The Terror*. In doing so, they were able to make use of Vitaphone itself, First National having recently been absorbed by Warner Bros.

Star comedian Chester Conklin encounters singing somnambulist Eve Southern in *The Haunted House* (1928)

The first of the Christensen trio was based on one of the few Broadway mystery-thrillers that had as yet gone unfilmed. The Owen Davis play *The Haunted House* (subtitled 'An American Comedy in Three Acts') dated back to September 1924; to adapt it, First National engaged two figures who would be common to all Christensen's horror-comedies – titles writer William Irish (nom de plume for Cornell Woolrich) and scenarist Richard Bee, who in fact was Christensen himself, working, for this first film, in collaboration with the Hungarian writer Lájos Biró. Also common to all three films were cinematographer Sol Polito, editor Frank Ware, leading lady Thelma Todd and saturnine character actor William V Mong.

Though *The Haunted House* is now lost, its derivative ingredients are clear enough from contemporary reports. The group of heirs foregathered to learn the dying wishes of an eccentric millionaire are familiar from *The Cat and the Canary* (literally in the case of Flora Finch, who was cast as a desiccated old woman in both films). The secret stash of bonds hidden somewhere in the supposedly haunted house is a direct lift from *The Bat*, and the bizarre characters therein, including a mad doctor (Montagu Love) and a female somnambulist (Eve Southern), could have stepped straight out of *The Monster*. The millionaire eventually pops up to explain that all the terrifying apparitions are merely actors from Central Casting, part of a scheme to put his heirs under the microscope and see what they're really like. Even the twist is compounded equally of *London After Midnight* and *Seven Keys to Baldpate* (ghoul actors), together with the much older *House of the Tolling Bell* (heirs under scrutiny).

Christensen and cinematographer Sol Polito reportedly eschewed Leni-like distorted angles and showstopping lighting effects, instead creating a mood of unease by positioning the camera virtually at floor level and shooting up at the actors. In *Variety*, 'Bige' lamented that the Davis play, a calculated send-up of the whole *Cat and the Canary* mode, had been played straight by Christensen, "with no attempt to get a tongue-in-the-cheek laugh."

That Christensen drained the film of comedy seems unlikely given the presence of former Sennett star Chester Conklin (who received rave notices for his performance), but 'Bige' reserved his biggest gripe for the then-familiar teething troubles characteristic of the new technology: "*The Haunted House* should get some shrieks and laughs, though it isn't as good as another recent boogy-man thriller, *The Terror*. The latter had an added kick in its dialog. Nothing vocal to *Haunted House* outside of two songs by the sleep-walking girl, both post-production insertions. Synchronisation of the song stuff was badly handled, with the player [Eve Southern] and the sound always out of kilter and neither starting nor finishing together."

The Haunted House was put before the public in the first week of November 1928, by which time Christensen was embroiled in his second consecutive shocker. This was based by Christensen and Woolrich, not on a play, but on a just-published novel by Abraham Merritt, a 44-year-old journalist who was a mainstay of the Hearst publication *American Weekly*. Just as a later

Thelma Todd is released from her designer coffin by whiskery William V Mong in *Seven Footprints to Satan* (1928)

SEVEN FOOTPRINTS TO SATAN

First National 1928
5405 feet; silent version 5237 feet
silent with Vitaphone effects, music and talking sequence
produced November/December

Cinematographer: Sol Polito; Editor: Frank Ware; Make-up: Perc Westmore*; Screenplay: Richard Bee [Benjamin Christensen], based on the novel by Abraham Merritt; Titles: William Irish [Cornell Woolrich]; Presented by: Richard A Rowland; Producer: Wid Gunning; Director: Benjamin Christensen

Thelma Todd (Eve); Creighton Hale (Jim); Sheldon Lewis (the Spider); William V Mong (the Professor); Sojin [Kamiyama] (Sojin); Laska Winters (Satan's mistress); Ivan Christy (Jim's valet); DeWitt Jennings (Uncle Joe); Nora Cecil (old witch); Kalla Pasha (Professor Von Viede); Harry Tenbrook (Eve's chauffeur); Cissy Fitzgerald (old lady); Alonzo [later Angelo] Rossitto (the dwarf); Thelma McNeill (tall girl); uncredited: Charles Gemora (ape); Loretta Young (victim); Louis Mercier, Julian Rivero (Satanists)

You won't get very excited over this so-called mystery story ... There are gorillas and dwarfs and weird characters who strut through the picture ineffectually. Thelma Todd manages to look both beautiful and frightened while Creighton Hale makes his knees stutter. It's a hodge podge. *Photoplay*

It is no longer possible for a clever director to mould his material as he could before the talkies came. The captions that once helped the screen actress along are gone. She has to put her own captions across, and on her ability to do so depends her success ... Beauty alone cannot achieve victories.
Thelma Todd ['How I Was Groomed for Stardom', *Film Weekly* 30 June 1933]

Merritt novel, *Burn Witch Burn!*, would be unrecognisably adapted as *The Devil-Doll*, Christensen's film bears very little relation to the original; indeed, Merritt reportedly broke down and wept on seeing it. Presumably First National just wanted to get their hands on Merritt's uniquely appetising title – *Seven Footprints to Satan*.

Preparing an expedition to darkest Africa, young millionaire Jim Kirkham is shanghaied instead into a strange New York house where, along with his fiancée Eve, he encounters a host of extremely strange people. At the mercy of a secret society presided over by the so-called Satan, Jim finally realises that the whole evening has been orchestrated by Eve and his uncle Joe as a means of dissuading him from his African adventure.

The touch of a master filmmaker is evident from the film's very first shot, in which Christensen establishes a mood of intrigue via an extreme close-up of Jim's hand inserting bullets into a revolver. "He's bought enough cartridges to supply a whole army," says Jim's shifty manservant to the cigar-chewing Uncle Joe, who is subsequently gifted with some very droll dialogue – pooh-poohing Jim's determination to uncover "the oldest civilisation in the world," for instance, with the bombastic pronouncement, "But you've never even explored your own back garden!"

The arrival of the beauteous Eve reveals the expert comedienne Thelma Todd, stunningly costumed in cloche hat and fur trimmings; she urges Jim to attend a soirée at her father's house and thus sets the convoluted plot in motion. After the apparent theft

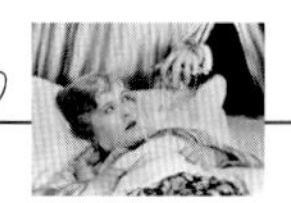

of "the famous Romanoff emerald" and the gunning down of some of the guests, Christensen stages a dazzling stampede of tuxedoed grandees, with Jim and Eve being deputed to fetch the police. They end up instead in a mysterious house containing the most outrageous assortment of weirdos featured in any film before or since – "types as grotesque as in the dreams inspired by imperfect digestion," as a British trade reviewer aptly put it.[23]

First up is a wizened, imp-like and palpably insane doorman, swiftly followed by an exotic beauty in a startlingly brief black mini-dress, a bearded dwarf concealed behind a sliding panel, and a freakishly eyebrowed concierge who makes Mammy Pleasant in *The Cat and the Canary* seem benign by comparison. The intention was clearly to outstrip the crazy crew featured in Roland West's *The Monster*, who numbered a paltry four. Here, the outré collection embraces the inevitable marauding gorilla, a hysterical girl who claims that "Satan has decreed I should receive a hundred lashes," a werewolf-whiskered Professor, and finally the frightful Spider, a shag-haired, tombstone-toothed monstrosity in a dress, getting about on crutches and played with relish by the old serial villain, Sheldon Lewis.

Christensen is in complete control of his material, allowing Jim's charming responses to the rising tide of weirdness ("Excuse me, I'd like to pop home for a moment") to co-exist with some genuinely alarming set-pieces. At one point, a screaming girl, struggling to keep her pursuers behind a closed door, is seen only as a pair of ankles; she finally flees, whereupon the door opens and the camera discloses two pairs of patent leather shoes taking off in pursuit, followed by the hirsute feet of the gorilla and then the baleful draperies, club foot and crutches of the Spider. The girl is then seen manacled to a pillar, the camera dropping down once more to show her ankles being secured by the ape's hairy paws.

Christensen also inserts three horizontal 'wipes' as Jim and Eve explore the various levels of the house, eventually reaching a grand hall in which the black-cowled Satan moves among the well-heeled guests like the fateful 'mummer' in Poe's *The Masque of the Red Death*. With so many levels and so many freakish characters, the film would be a natural in the 21st century for conversion into a PlayStation game, and in the final reel it turns into a 'sudden death' quiz show presided over by the extravagantly plumed Sojin, late of *The Bat*. In a triumph of production design, Jim is required to ascend a shimmering staircase with steps helpfully illuminated from '1' to '7', Sojin maintaining a similarly illuminated scoreboard and Jim showing unwonted courage in trying to save Eve from harm.

In bending Merritt's original novel to the prevalent 'spooky house' mode, *Seven Footprints to Satan* is, of course, an out-and-out travesty. Merritt's Satan, for example, is a corpulent, seven-foot abomination with sapphire-blue eyes and a weirdly musical utterance, "the exact opposite of the long, lank, dark Mephisto of opera, play and story." Here, he's merely Uncle Joe in a silken gaberdine and hood. But, taken on its own terms, Christensen's film is a lavishly appointed masterpiece of the horror-comedy mode, with particularly engaging performances from Creighton Hale and Thelma Todd.

As Jim, Hale's scaredy-cat schtick doesn't go much beyond forming his mouth into a scandalised 'o' and goggling through his Coke bottle spectacles, but he's much more fun here than he was in Leni's *The Cat and the Canary*. Todd is unaffected and natural, showing a sparky comic intelligence that would be tragically snuffed out seven years later. Though she was Christensen's leading lady in all three of his horror-comedies, she was in real life the girlfriend of another horror specialist, Roland West, who in 1935 would be implicated in her unsolved murder.

Christensen's third comedy-thriller was originally intended to be an adaptation of the recent Broadway play *Sh, the Octopus*, which in the end had to wait until 1937 to be filmed. Instead, *The House of Horror* followed *Seven Footprints to Satan* into release with indecent haste, appearing on 28 April 1929. This one was apparently a 'Richard Bee' original, garnished with 'William Irish' dialogue and titles by Tom Miranda, but its plot mechanics were all too familiar from the previous films.

By this time, Louise Fazenda and Chester Conklin (the latter retained from *The Haunted House*) were themselves so familiar that their characters were called Louise and Chester. An Ohio spinster and her bachelor brother, they come to see their reclusive Uncle Abner (Emile Chautard) at his New York home, where the so-called 'Mystery Man' (William V Mong) is just one of several sinister characters they encounter. Thelma Todd, meanwhile – playing Thelma, naturally – is on the track of a missing gem just as she was in *Seven Footprints to Satan*. And, like both its predecessors, *The House of Horror* finally debunks its spooky proceedings as an elaborate set-up, with Todd revealed as a newspaper reporter on the trail of a good story.

After three films in exactly similar vein, the notices for *The House of Horror* indicated all too clearly that the law of diminishing returns had come into play. "This is some better than *Haunted House* and *Seven*

'Mystery Man' William V Mong unnerves Ohio spinster Louise Fazenda in *The House of Horror* (1929)

Footprints to Satan because of the work of Chester Conklin and Louise Fazenda," commented *Photoplay* in the 'Shadow Stage' section of its May issue. "As far as story is concerned it is as cheap and claptrap as the former efforts ... Pass it up." *Variety*'s 'Waly' went further, dismissing the film as "one of the weakest and most boring afterbirths of pseudo mystery-comedy ... [utilising] every trick in the moth-eaten bag." He also expressed contempt for a Conklin-in-drag sequence and facetiously headed his review "1% Dialog" – apparently, the film's talkie section was over within the first few minutes. On that dismal note, Christensen went back to Denmark, only resuming his native film career after a hiatus of a decade.

SMOKE AND MIRRORS

The theatre setting exploited by Paul Leni in *The Last Warning* was a popular one at Universal. George Melford's *The Charlatan*, another part-talkie, followed Leni's film into release in April 1929. This one reversed the pattern of *HE Who Gets Slapped* in that a circus clown responds to his wife's betrayal by assuming a new identity, that of Hindu mystic Count Merlin, subsequently solving her murder. The double role had originally been intended for Conrad Veidt but eventually went to the English actor Holmes Herbert. Veidt appeared instead as another mesmeric theatrical in *The Last Performance*, yet another Universal Jewel with a theatrical setting – the latter furnished, again, by the old *Phantom* stage.

The fusty sentiment of backstage romance, coupled with the perverse and unrequited longings of the more outré characters within it, was a strange, and strangely popular, combination in the twilight of the 1920s. Lon Chaney had set the pattern with his maudlin-macabre love for Norma Shearer in *HE Who Gets Slapped*, following it up in 1928 with his quasi-incestuous attraction towards the teenage Loretta Young in Herbert Brenon's *Laugh, Clown, Laugh*. Conrad Veidt had already gone down this route via the creepy vaudevillian romance of *The Man Who Laughs*. Reunited with Mary Philbin, he was compelled to do so again in *The Last Performance*, albeit in an infinitely slicker role and with the earlier film's epic trimmings conspicuously absent.

Filmed at the beginning of 1929 under the working titles *Erik the Great* and *The Play Goes On*, the film was delayed in release until November, by which time Veidt had returned to Germany. Universal's publicity for it must have seemed yawn-inducingly familiar even in 1929. "Crackling drama that fascinates and thrills!" screamed the ads. "The romance of a master magician in his hopeless love for his beautiful assistant. Exotic! Exciting!" An 'original' written by James Ashmore Creelman, the plot involved Veidt's saturnine Erik Goff sublimating his love for Julie (Philbin) by eliminating his duplicitous assistant Buffo (Leslie Fenton) in a rigged sword-cabinet illusion, then confessing all and killing himself at the trumped-up trial of Julie's sweetheart, Mark (Fred Mackaye).

The surviving print, much truncated, is completely silent, though the part-talkie version was only seen at a handful of sneak previews anyway. As *Variety* put it, the film "opens in Europe and ends in America, but all of it in every way looks like Europe and its picture product." Chiefly a vehicle for Hal Mohr's continuing bid to outdo Karl Freund's acrobatic camera in *Varieté*, the film was reportedly taken on by director Paul Fejos purely to work with the already legendary Veidt. A former research biologist, Fejos had recently made an ingenious montage of a dying man's kaleidoscopic impressions called *The Last Moment*. *The Last Performance*, however, is notable

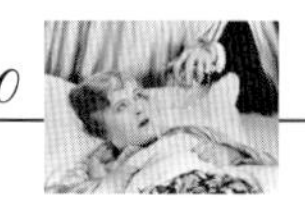

only for Mohr's camera pyrotechnics and Veidt's trademark demonic intensity.

Yet another example of this peculiar subgenre came from a cash-strapped independent called Sono Art World Wide, which cast Erich von Stroheim as a mentally unstable vaudeville ventriloquist in James Cruze's musical extravaganza *The Great Gabbo*. Based on a Ben Hecht story called *The Rival Dummy*, the film was the first feature Cruze made on his acquisition in March 1929 of the old Chadwick Studios, where *The Bells* had been made three years earlier. The result demonstrates all too clearly the degree to which filmmakers were hamstrung by the new technology. Cinematographer Ira Morgan does what he can to keep the camera moving, but for the most part he's locked unwaveringly onto actors who appear ill at ease and self-conscious. Von Stroheim seems merely bored, addressing several of his lines to the rafters and even garbling some of them with every appearance of indifference.

Describing his dummy Otto as "my other half," Gabbo sublimates his emotions through it and in the process drives away his devoted assistant Mary (played by Cruze's then-wife, Betty Compson). "Little Otto there is the only human thing about you," she sniffs, later marrying her new stage partner and performing a heavily symbolic number with him called 'The Web of Love'. (With the stage enmeshed in a colossal spider's web, poor Don Douglas looks ridiculous here in a tie-dyed spider costume.) Realising his love for Mary at the same time as he learns of her unavailability, Gabbo goes to pieces and disrupts another number, 'I'm Laughing', in a forlorn echo of Chaney's mordant hilarity in *HE Who Gets Slapped*.

As well as benefiting from the Deco-Expressionism of Robert E Lee's set designs (and, on its original release, the application of a so-called 'Multicolor' process to its production numbers), *The Great Gabbo* contains a couple of moments that linger in the memory. In one, Otto loses his left eye when punched by his rapidly fragmenting master. In the other, there's a nice doppelgänger frisson when Otto tells Mary "You're the sweetest girl I know" and the tight-lipped Gabbo is revealed in the make-up mirror behind them.

In addition to accommodating Erich von Stroheim, Sono Art World Wide provided sanctuary for another capricious director brought low by the coming of sound. Marshall Neilan's *Black Waters* was officially a British production but was shot by producer Herbert Wilcox at the United Artists facility because of the as yet unperfected sound technology in UK studios. Based on a stage play, *Fog*, by John (*The Cat and the Canary*) Willard, it has insane sea captain 'Tiger' Larrabee (James Kirkwood), backed up by his saturnine aide Jeelo (Noble Johnson), informing his ever-dwindling passengers that he's "giving a party in Hell" to which they're all invited. It opened in the US in April 1929 and in the UK (in a somewhat longer version) a month later.

Having provided the source material for *The Great Gabbo*, Ben Hecht was also the originator, via his story *The Green Ghost*, of M-G-M's *The Unholy Night*, which was made available in both sound and silent versions and was directed by Lionel Barrymore. In this, a group of stuffed-shirt Gallipoli veterans are picked off one by one in "the greatest fog London has ever known," the malefactors finally being revealed (in the style of *The Thirteenth Chair*) via a seance. Sojin is the toothy medium, Li Hung, whose manifestation of the ectoplasmic officers turns out to have been a classic case of smoke and mirrors.

The film begins promisingly, with a beckoning skeleton in tattered robes floating behind the credits plus a coshing, a shooting, a possible rape and an attempted garrotting, all in the first fog-shrouded reel. The survivor of the latter outrage turns out to be Roland Young, perfectly cast as a feckless aristocrat and delighting in a long string of witty lines. (Some are just plain peculiar, however, as when he says of a ghostly ancestor, "Sir Roger, the old wretch, died of some nasty disease like spinach, which turned him quite green.") A still unknown Boris Karloff, with whom Barrymore had acted in *The Bells*, is also in the cast (albeit unbilled), giving a weirdly overdrawn sketch of an Indian solicitor.

Barrymore manages some startling effects, as when Sojin's apparently disembodied head is seen

Exotic beauty Dorothy Sebastian with shell-shocked old soldier John Miljan in *The Unholy Night* (1929)

Bela Lugosi grills Margaret Wycherly and Leila Hyams in *The Thirteenth Chair* (1929), watched by fellow suspects Helene Millard, Mary Forbes, Moon Carroll, Bertram Johns and Holmes Herbert

oscillating in the darkness of an early seance, and later a remarkable tracking shot that glides through multiple bedrooms to reveal the corpses within. But he's defeated by the script's overload of laboured talk and by a communal rendition of 'Auld Lang Syne' that is run through no fewer than four times. "It's an all-talker and a 100% lemon," grumbled 'Waly' in *Variety*, adding: "Worse than the worst would-be thrill meller staged on Broadway and impressing as a pointless soufflé burlesquing them all." And in the January 1930 issue of *Picture-Play*, Norbert Lusk noted that "some persons have snickered in the wrong places" and deplored the film's expository wrap-up on the principle that "when explanation becomes a duty it is a bore to listen to it, because action ceases and talk holds the screen."

With producers still unsure of how to get around the language problem thrown up by the talkie explosion, M-G-M also offered a French version of the film, *Le Spectre vert*. Directed by the distinguished Belgian filmmaker Jacques Feyder, this featured Georges Renavent, organiser of New York's Grand Guignol experiment, in the doctor role played in the US version by Ernest Torrence.

The Ben Hecht double of *The Great Gabbo* and *The Unholy Night* saw release just two days apart, on 12 and 14 September 1929 respectively. Indeed, the Ziegfeld-style 'Multicolor' production numbers of the former provided a rather stilted record of the gaiety and exuberance of the Roaring Twenties a matter of weeks before they were silenced by the cataclysmic events of Tuesday 29 October. The Wall Street Crash entailed a loss of $30 billion on the New York Stock Exchange, permanently bursting the ever-inflating bubble of the wild and feckless Jazz Age. And, with speculation by individuals having undergone a remarkable increase as recently as 1928, it wasn't just fat-cat money men who had their dreams destroyed.

NEW VERSIONS FOR OLD

As the talkie revolution gained ground, producers betrayed a signal lack of imagination in remaking numerous properties that had recently been popular as silents. Among the first of these was Tod Browning's new version of *The Thirteenth Chair*, which earned M-G-M a profit of close to $150,000 and was based on the 1916 play by Bayard Veiller.

Veiller's tale of murder among the governing classes in Calcutta, and of the seances contrived by the mysterious Mme Rosalie LaGrange to expose the killer, offered a much-publicised showcase for the new technology in its scene of a second murder taking place in the gloom of one of Mme LaGrange's performances. The ensuing Babel of panic issuing

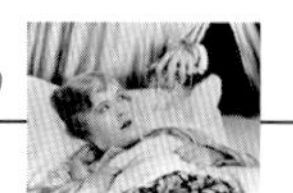

from a darkened screen was judged such a winner the whole palaver was repeated at film's end; unfortunately, the scene was effectively satirised in a picture released the same month. Harold Lloyd's first talkie, *Welcome Danger*, included just such an interlude, with the screen going black and only the sound remaining – Lloyd's sardonic comment on the visual primitivism imposed by the mania for talking pictures.

As it turned out, Browning's final day on *The Thirteenth Chair* – 16 July 1929 – would mark his last appearance at Metro's Culver City studios for over two years. The final film under his M-G-M contract, it must have seemed to Browning an unusually anodyne project, entirely free of the outrageous plot contrivances characteristic of his earlier films; the application of sound was presumably judged challenge enough, without having to deal simultaneously with armless knife-throwers or transvestite jewel thieves.

For the purposes of posterity, the film is distinguished only by an eye-catching turn from Bela Lugosi as Inspector Delzante. Fresh from his career-defining Broadway run in *Dracula*, Lugosi was seventh-billed but dominates the extremely creaky proceedings with an over-the-top but agreeably portentous performance – an odd transformation for a character conceived by Veiller as Inspector Donohue and intended as comic relief. It also preserves stage star Margaret Wycherly's slightly dodgy Irish accent as Mme LaGrange, together with the kind of laboured, stop-start editing that made the early talkies such a poor substitute for the lately deposed silents.

The phoney spiritualism routine, which Browning had set in stone as long ago as *The Mystic*, showed no drop in popularity as silence gave way to sound. Late-blooming silents included Phil Rosen's *The Faker*, in which Warner Oland played the title part in one of the first films from the fledgling Columbia Pictures, and Albert Ray's *A Thief in the Dark*, "a Chilling Fun-Drama of 'Spooks' and Crooks" with Michael Vavitch in the equivalent role. Paramount's *The Hole in the Wall* opted for the part-talkie route, casting the young Claudette Colbert as a vengeful ex-con who disguises herself as Mme Mystera; it was also one of the films by which director Robert Florey moved from the avant-garde into the mainstream.

While *The Thirteenth Chair* resurrected a property last filmed in 1919, there were other remakes on offer that recycled much more recent material, meaning that picturegoers got to go through the whole 'Broadway mystery-thrillers on film' routine yet again, only this time with a modified version of the Broadway dialogue. The true glutton for punishment could catch talkie retreads of *The Bat*, *The Cat and the Canary* and *The Gorilla* all in the same month – November 1930. Unfortunately, only the remodelled *Bat* survives.

First National's new version of *The Gorilla* appeared first, confusing matters by matching the toothsome Lila Lee with a young Walter Pidgeon; here playing the undercover detective, in the silent version he had been the ape-suited villain. "Mysterious! Hilarious! Stupendous! *The Gorilla* will Give You the Thrill of Your LAFFtime!" screamed the ads. The director was Bryan Foy, a former Sennett gag-man who had kick-started the whole talkie revolution with *The Lights of New York*. "As it comes to the screen," commented the *New York Times'* Mordaunt Hall, "Ralph Spence's play, *The Gorilla*, is more humorous than hair-raising ... Quite a number of the turns [in the plot] were anticipated by some of the spectators, but this did not alter the fact that they enjoyed them when they came."

First National's parent company, Warner Bros, had gone the ubiquitous 'ape' route before. Now lost, Lloyd Bacon's *Stark Mad* offered an 'old dark jungle' scenario in which an Amazonian search party discovered an enlarged simian chained to the floor in a Mayan temple. Available in both silent and talkie versions, the film opened in February 1929, its pre-echoes of the colossal *King Kong* obviously being lost on contemporary audiences. "Elevated eyebrow gentry will sneer at this sort of entertainment," was *Variety*'s pithy judgment.

Next up in November 1930 was Rupert Julian's *The Cat Creeps*, Universal's talkie remake of *The Cat and the Canary*. Just in case anyone was unclear what they were in for, the legend "while the canary sleeps!" was inserted beneath the title in the film's publicity material. The film had gone into production in the first week of July with Rupert Julian as director; the actors assembled for what *Variety* dubbed "a revival of a popular play type vogue that has gone cold" included Helen Twelvetrees (beleaguered heroine), Raymond Hackett (bumbling hero) and Neil Hamilton (smoothly insane killer), plus Montagu Love as the creepy warder and the incomparable Lilyan Tashman in the role previously played by Gertrude Astor.

Later to make a remarkable impact in Paramount's *Murder by the Clock*, Tashman was one of the paradoxical success stories of the talkie upheaval, her career being boosted by the new process rather than abruptly terminated. As Walter Ramsey put it at the time, "Lilyan Tashman's throaty contralto gives her a lightness and a humanness that her silent roles never revealed. In fact, Lilyan introduced, in *Bulldog Drummond*, the vamp with a sense of humor."[24] As showcased in *The Cat Creeps*, however, Tashman's throaty contralto is unavailable for inspection, the film being lost.

The same applies to the Hispanic voices featured in Universal's Spanish language version, filmed at night on the same sets under the true-to-Willard title *El gato y el canario*. Lupita Tovar and Antonio Moreno were the stars, and the result opened in Mexico City a week or so after the New York premiere of its English-speaking parent, by which time the film had been retitled *La voluntad del muerto* (literally, 'The Dead Man's Will'). Carl Laemmle was so impressed by the Leni-like atmospherics perfected by director George Melford and Universal's head of foreign production, Paul Kohner, that he ordered the flavourless English version reshot in the same manner. The famously self-willed Rupert Julian apparently acceded to this humiliation with uncharacteristic good grace.

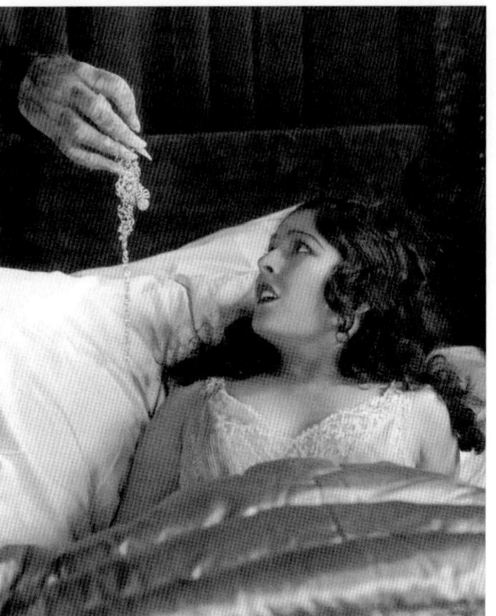

Lupita Tovar in Universal's Spanish-speaking version of *The Cat Creeps*, *La voluntad del muerto* (1930) [see also pages 42 and 182]

Like the executives at First National and Universal, the maverick director-producer Roland West was convinced by the coming of sound that there was more mileage to be had from an old property. His remake of *The Bat* began shooting – at night, as was his wont – at the United Artists studio in July 1930, with the action captured not only on conventional 35mm cameras but also (at West's own expense) in an innovative widescreen format called Magnifilm. West was not alone among filmmakers in his enthusiasm for the format, but there was a serious obstacle in that very few cinema owners were inclined to welcome a further technological crisis so soon after being traumatised by the conversion to sound. Indeed, only a month after the November opening of what became known as *The Bat Whispers*, the MPPDA more or less outlawed further widescreen experiments.

During her summer retreat at the country residence of vacationing banker Courtleigh Fleming, New York dowager Miss Cornelia Van Gorder is attended by her pretty niece Dale, hyperventilating maid Lizzie Allen, an unjustly 'wanted' bank clerk masquerading as her gardener – and, during a protracted night of mystery and terror, none other than shadowy criminal mastermind The Bat. At stake is a cool $500,000 looted from Fleming's bank...

Though it follows the plot of West's original film pretty faithfully, in all other respects *The Bat Whispers* represents a complete re-imagining of the property. The charmed circle of silent film gave license to West's most abstract flights of fancy, but, five years later, the received notion of the talkies' enhanced 'realism' encouraged him to ground the absurd events in more prosaic soil.

Right from the start, the ill-fated Mr Bell, whose murder gets the plot going, is a long way from the weirdly sinister figure he was in 1926. In the same way, Sojin's discreetly fanged Japanese butler has become a slack-jawed Caucasian caretaker, played by Spencer Charters on a wearisome note of hyperactive comic relief. These character re-alignments are in tune with the massive sets devised by Paul Roe Crawley. Though a protégé of William Cameron Menzies, Crawley replaces Menzies' Deco abstractions in the earlier film with a Fleming mansion Miss Van Gorder could conceivably live in.

The Bat himself is stripped of the exaggerated bat-faced mask he wore in 1926, reverting to the black-hooded look of the original Broadway play. He's fitted instead – in the opening chase sequences, at any rate – with a foot-dragging limp, a nonsensical detail given that, elsewhere, he's agility and athleticism personified. (The foot-dragging business seems especially ridiculous given that he's meant to be in pursuit of someone who's got hold of the half-million he'd marked as his own.) Now that he's played by West's permanently scowling protégé Chester Morris rather than Dalmatian import Tullio Carminati, his alias has changed back from Detective Moletti to the original Detective Anderson of the play, but any 'whodunit' possibilities are thoroughly scotched by West's spookily underlit emphasis on Morris' beetling brows, leaving no doubt as to who The Bat really is.

For all his championing of Chester Morris (who had been Oscar-nominated for his role in West's previous film, *Alibi*), the actors were by no means West's priority. Instead, he turned *The Bat Whispers* into a triumph of style over substance, firmly rejecting, in

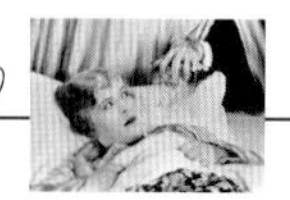

particular, the talkies' imprisonment of the moving camera. This was ironic, given that in *The Bat*, when there were no such constraints, West's camera never moved. Now, perversely, he went wild, encouraging technical wizard Charles Cline to come up with, among other innovations, an early version of the zoom. Making inspired use of miniatures, West has the camera swoop down the façade of a clocktower, flash headlong across a cityscape, hurtle towards Oakdale in the guise of a rattling locomotive and, most impressively, pursue Detective Anderson as he vaults over a balustrade and sprints towards the Fleming garage. For 1930, these scenes are staggering in their virtuosity.

Nor is West's trademark Expressionist shadowplay confined to the frequently repeated image of The Bat's bristling silhouette framed against a panelled window. It also adds portentous weight to less loaded moments, as when Detective Anderson eavesdrops on Una Merkel's Dale as she makes a shadowy telephone call. West can also throw the audience for a loop with occasional unexpected angles, as in a bizarre set-up in which the camera hovers omnisciently, judgmentally, above Anderson's presentation of his bogus badge to the hick detective engaged by Miss Van Gorder.

Elsewhere, unfortunately, West's indifferent handling of the dialogue keeps the camera rigorously front and centre in the manner of a photographed proscenium arch. This has two consequences – (1) the plot somehow becomes even less comprehensible than it was in the silent version, and (2) the actors vacillate unpredictably between bland wishy-washyness and grotesque overplaying. Maude Eburne's supposedly comic antics as Lizzie are trying in the extreme, and of the other actors Grayce Hampton is pretty much alone in striking exactly the right self-amused note as the stately Miss Van Gorder.

On top of this, West fumbles some of the moments that came off best in the silent, notably the execution of Richard Fleming on the stairs and Dale's climactic entrapment by The Bat. Another memorable moment from the original film – the projected bat silhouette that would give rise to Bob Kane's iconic 'Bat Signal' – is dropped altogether in favour of an elaborate bit of business with a collapsing portrait, a routine that seems to have been lifted wholesale from Leni's *The Cat and the Canary*. As a stylistic exercise, however, *The Bat Whispers* was beyond state-of-the-art for its day, so it's hardly surprising that after only

THE BAT WHISPERS

Feature Productions-Art Cinema Associates 1930
85 minutes; shot in standard and 'Magnifilm' formats
production began mid-July

Cinematographer: Ray June; Wide Film photography: Robert H Planck; Special Photography: Edward Colman, Harry Zech; Art Director: Paul Roe Crawley; Editor: James Smith; Editor (Magnifilm version): Hal C Kern; Sound: J T Reed, O E Lagerstrom; Electrical Effects: William McClellan; Special Technician: Charles Cline; Make-up: S E Jennings; Musical Director: Dr Hugo Riesenfeld; Screenplay: Roland West (from the stage play *The Bat* by Mary Roberts Rinehart and Avery Hopwood); Dialogue Director: Charles H Smith; Presented by: Joseph M Schenck; Director-Producer: Roland West

[in order of appearance] Chance Ward (police lieutenant); Richard Tucker (Mr Bell); Wilson Benge (the butler); DeWitt Jennings (police captain); Sydney D'Albrook (police sergeant); S E Jennings (man in black mask); Grayce Hampton (Cornelia Van Gorder); Maude Eburne (Lizzie Allen); Spencer Charters (the caretaker); Una Merkel (Dale Van Gorder); William Bakewell (Brook); Gustav von Seyffertitz (Dr Venrees); Chester Morris (Detective Anderson); Hugh Huntley (Richard Fleming); Charles Dow Clark (Detective Jones); Ben Bard (The Unknown)

This is your one-time friend, *The Bat*, disguised in a modern dress called Magnifilm. There are ... all the usual ingredients of a thriller directed by Roland West, with emphasis on effective and artistic camera angles ... Most people will enjoy it, even if they have seen it before in one form or another. *Motion Picture*

That was directed by Roland West, and he worked at night only. He didn't want any producers coming around telling him how to do anything ... He worked all night long, and we had a big meal at midnight – that was our dinner. It was seven weeks, and I think I lost about 15 pounds on the picture. *Una Merkel [quoted in Film Fan Monthly, January 1971]*

Chester Morris eavesdrops on Una Merkel's emergency phone call in the talkie version of an old property, *The Bat Whispers* (1930)

one more film – *Corsair*, also starring Chester Morris – the sated West lost interest in the capabilities of film and retired.

Unlike West, The Bat did not retire, though he would take a lot longer to re-emerge than his feline and anthropoid confreres. *The Cat and the Canary* and *The Gorilla* – also, in a minor key, *The Last Warning* – would be made over again in 1939. In the same year, Mary Pickford purchased the rights to *The Bat* and proposed to star Humphrey Bogart and Lillian Gish in it. Nothing came of the idea, however, and another 20 years would elapse before Allied Artists put together a tacky remake aimed at 1950s bobbysoxers. With an intriguing circularity, this one was written and directed by the septuagenarian Crane Wilbur, author of *The Monster*.

THE REST IS NOT SILENCE

In the meantime, the new crop of reheated Broadway adaptations was accompanied by a couple of stage transfers that were being put on camera for the first time. Edmund Lawrence's *The House of Secrets* (1929) came from the Poverty Row outfit Chesterfield, faithfully following Sydney Horler's play in sending its hero to an inherited pile in the UK, complete with dungeons, a lurking Oriental and a hunt for a piratical hoard. The following year, George B Seitz's *Midnight Mystery* – based on Howard Irving Young's play *Hawk Island* – was one of the first productions from the fledgling RKO, locating Betty Compson and Hugh Trevor in a storm-laden castle on an island off the coast of Maine.

Trapped in an old dark house: Oliver Hardy and Stan Laurel in the three-reel parody *The Laurel-Hardy Murder Case* (1930)

New or old, all these 'old house' potboilers were subjected to an all-talking parody that was shot, with impeccable timing, in May 1930. Running rather superfluously to three reels rather than the team's customary two, James Parrott's *The Laurel-Hardy Murder Case* puts Stan and Ollie at the centre of a will-reading, and resultant murder investigation, in a spooky old house, with Fred Kelsey barking his way through his perennial police inspector role. The ensuing confusion, which features not only a black cat but also a bat tangled in a bed sheet, is untypically laborious. There's an extended 'haunted bedroom' routine in *Thark* mode, and the boys end up dodging a Sweeney Todd-style revolving chair and tussling instead with a very nasty, knife-wielding granny who turns out to be a man in drag. If this was Laurel and Hardy's nod to *The Unholy Three*, it would have its own influence three decades later in the form of *Psycho*.

The Unholy Three was a topical reference given that it, too, had just received the inevitable 1930 makeover. Filmed at M-G-M between 26 March and 24 April, the new version was directed by Jack Conway and reproduced the original in most of its essentials, even down to a carnival barker's near-the-knuckle introduction for an undulating belly dancer: "This is the dance that broke the Sultan's thermometer." Venturing into talkies for the first time, Lon Chaney was back as Echo the ventriloquist, wittily making use of a range of different voices to set against his 'Man of a Thousand Faces' reputation. Whether he would have preferred Tod Browning back in the director's chair is not known, though it seems unlikely given his laissez-faire attitude to their partnership. "I've had good directors," he once said. "Tod Browning and I have worked so much together he's called the Chaney director. I like his work. I think Victor Seastrom and Benjamin Christonson [sic] are great directors. Their values are finer. But I really don't worry over who they hand me."[25]

Like Chaney, the German-born midget Harry Earles (real name: Kurt Schneider) was retained from the 1925 version. A truly demonic baby-faced presence in the silent, here, unfortunately, he proves every bit as incomprehensible as the baby he impersonates. Ivan Linow, meanwhile, took over from Victor McLaglen as the strongman and Lila Lee from Mae Busch as the beautiful Rosie O'Grady. The story's comedic possibilities – which had made several studios reject Tod

Browning's pitch back in 1924 – are amplified by the addition of sound into virtual farce, particularly when Browning's nightmarish 'chimpanzee on miniaturised sets' climax is turned into a run-of-the-mill case of Charles Gemora rampaging in a gorilla suit. Yet as an outrageously deranged black farce the story holds up pretty well.

Lon Chaney struggles to maintain control over Ivan Linow, Lila Lee and Harry Earles in the all-talking remake of *The Unholy Three* (1930)

The film opened in New York on 3 July. "If Metro had gone at the thing with the sole intention of destroying one of its most valuable assets," complained Welford Beaton, "it could not have acted with greater wisdom. *The Unholy Three* is a fearful thing and the country is not warming up to it. It presents Chaney without the glamour that he had in silent pictures, and reveals him as a very ordinary actor of less than star calibre."[26] This is unfair, given that (a) the film grossed nearly a million worldwide and (b) Chaney gives a powerful performance that suggests his destiny could just as easily have been in the soon-to-be-fashionable gangster pictures as the soon-to-be-fashionable horror pictures. Not only can he rap out a line frequently misattributed to James Cagney ("You dirty rat") with aplomb, but in his Grandma O'Grady disguise he displays a sly satirical wit, notably when reassuring a sanctimonious parrot-fancier that "This bird used to belong to Aimee Semple McPherson."

So popular was Lila Lee in the new medium that she followed *The Unholy Three* with a nervous breakdown brought on by the pressure of her talkie commitments, retiring for a time to an Arizona sanitarium. But the question of whether Chaney would prove just as popular in talking pictures soon became an academic one; indeed, his final line in the film ("I'll send you a postal card") was almost the last anyone would hear from him. Succumbing to throat cancer, he died, aged 47, on 26 August. According to some accounts, in its final stages the disease rendered him mute – a grim indication that the tortured eloquence of his silent films was his true metier after all.

On the news of Chaney's death, a two-minute silence was observed in all Hollywood studios and the M-G-M flag was flown at half-mast, accurately reflecting the nation's shock at the passing of its most offbeat film star. His one-of-a-kind status had recently been confirmed by the failure of two Chaney-type projects in which Universal proposed to feature someone else; a mooted sequel to *The Phantom of the Opera* and a remake of *The Hunchback of Notre Dame*, both set to star Conrad Veidt, hadn't got beyond the planning stages. On top of this, the original *Phantom* had been reissued in January 1930, tricked out with a score, sound effects and talking sequences – and proved a hit all over again, despite Chaney being conspicuously absent from the added dialogue.

The Bat himself, Chester Morris, was meanwhile being mooted for the title role in an all-new Universal project. The role had earlier been earmarked for Veidt, who would have been ideal for the part but had elected to return to Germany to perfect his English. On top of this, Paul Leni, the supreme visual stylist tipped to direct the Veidt version, had died on 2 September 1929 from blood poisoning brought on by an infected tooth; he was 44. Now, in the wake of another premature death – that of Lon Chaney – the project would suddenly come together with unwonted speed. And with Chaney's old associate, Tod Browning, attached as director.

That property was *Dracula*.

Part Three

Bela Lugosi and Boris Karloff rake over ancient enmities in *The Black Cat* (1934)

Children of the Night 1930-1936

In the wake of the Stock Market crash in October 1929, what would become known as the Great Depression began in earnest. Over 1300 banks went to the wall in 1930 alone, a figure that would nudge 2300 in 1931. The year after that, unemployment figures were estimated at anything between 12 and 16 million, though President Herbert Hoover gave no credence to such estimates and consistently resisted calls for federal intervention.

The film industry initially seemed impervious to the decline, with the new vogue for talkies, and the escapism they offered, entailing US ticket sales in 1930 of some 90 million per week. For a three-year stretch starting in 1932, however, this figure would plummet by one-third.

It was also at this time that further steps were taken to pacify the increasingly vociferous complaints of moral reformers. Back in 1927, Will Hays of the MPPDA had set up the Studio Relations Committee (SRC) under the directorship of Colonel Jason S Joy, with the purpose of implementing a list of 'Don'ts and Be Carefuls' devised by studio executives Sol Wurtzel (Fox), Irving Thalberg (M-G-M) and E H Allen (Paramount). Among the Don'ts were "pointed profanity," "licentious or suggestive nudity" and "any inference of sex perversion." Among the Be Carefuls: "brutality and possible gruesomeness," "surgical operations" and "excessive or lustful kissing."

By 1930, the campaigning of powerful Catholics like Martin Quigley and Joseph I Breen resulted in the formalisation of these loosely expressed principles into the so-called Production Code. For a period of four years, producers would pay little more than lip service to the Code, resulting in a halcyon period devoted to mature and hard-hitting pictures nowadays referred to as 'pre-Code' – ie, pre-dating the July 1934 establishment of the Production Code Administration. Despite the fact that the Code's provisions would initially prove unenforcable, in 1930 Will Hays was delighted with the document, announcing it to the world on April Fool's Day.

GRIM TALES OF A FAR-OFF COUNTRY

In November 1930, Lewis Milestone's *All Quiet on the Western Front* won for Universal a coveted Academy Award for Best Picture. The film had been pushed through in the teeth of widespread studio opposition

by the diminutive Carl Laemmle Jr, whose general managership of Universal City dated back to April 1929, when it had been bestowed on him by his equally diminutive father as a 21st birthday present. Now, seemingly careless of the fact that the studio was haemorrhaging millions as the first anniversary of the crash came around, Laemmle Sr was so intoxicated by the prestige value of Milestone's film that he gave his blessing to some of Junior's wilder whims, even those he personally found distasteful. Among these was the resurrection of *Dracula*, a production idea that had lain dormant since the departure of Conrad Veidt and the death of Paul Leni.

For its Broadway transfer in October 1927, Hamilton Deane's stage adaptation of *Dracula* had itself been adapted by journalist and playwright John L Balderston. In August 1930, therefore, Universal acquired rights in both the Bram Stoker novel and the Deane-Balderston play derived from it. Among the writers charged with the project was the novelist Louis Bromfield, whose epic script was quietly sidelined when censorship and budgetary considerations dictated an approach cleaving more closely to the play.

Casting was similarly fraught; in Veidt's absence, the list of actors under consideration for the title role included Paul Muni, Ian Keith, John Wray and William Courtenay. (The latter had scored in a misterioso role in Broadway's *The Spider*, which was later filmed without him.) At the last minute, the part went to Dracula's Broadway originator Bela Lugosi, who turned 48 during filming and, iniquitously, was paid only a quarter of the fee lavished on the film's ineffectual hero, David Manners. Lugosi had been born close to the site of Stoker's novel and was therefore ideally placed to recount, as Dracula puts it, "some rather grim tales of my far-off country."

Filming was concluded by 15 November, with retakes undertaken in December and January. The finished product opened at the Roxy in New York City on Thursday 12 February 1931, and it proved to be a radically new kind of screen entertainment. As we have seen, mystery fans were by then habituated to discovering that a film's apparently supernatural goings-on had all been mocked up by human agencies; had all, in a manner of speaking, been done with mirrors. To these audiences, the scene in *Dracula* in which Van Helsing stumbles on the fact that the Count has no reflection must have struck with the force of a thunderbolt. For here, at last, was a film in which a mirror was used, not to fake a supernatural manifestation, but to confirm it in all its awful reality.

Renfield, a British estate agent, journeys to Transylvania to complete a sale to Hungarian nobleman Count Dracula. The Count turns out to be a vampire, enslaving Renfield, sailing to England, moving into a ruined pile adjoining a mental home and precipitating the death of young Lucy Weston. Before he can do the same to Lucy's friend Mina Harker, he is tracked down by Dutch specialist Professor Van Helsing and transfixed with a stake.

Something of the film's freakish novelty was reflected in Donald Beaton's review in the *Film Spectator*. As well as puzzling over the fact that "*Dracula* ... is one of the hardest pictures to criticise that I have come across in a long time," he also observed that "Bela Lugosi, as Dracula, was quite adequate. Having never met a vampire, I don't know exactly how one should act, but I presume that Lugosi is all right."[1] To audiences whose very lifeblood seemed to be draining away in the wake of the Stock Market crash, the super-smooth, tuxedoed aristocrat embodied by Lugosi was a lot more than all right; at one stroke, he established in the popular imagination exactly how a vampire should act.

Of course, this image owed nothing to the atavistic predator embodied in Stoker's book. Instead, it was an accident of dramatic expediency, originating in Hamilton Deane's cost-conscious decision to 'domesticate' Stoker's vampire into the kind of character who would be admitted into his victims' drawing rooms. This literal lounge lizard was further emasculated by the film's addition of ludicrous lines like "To die, to be really dead: that must be glorious" – an effort, presumably, to give Dracula a conscience; maybe even curry some sympathy for him. But Lugosi was too canny to go down that road, happily remaining a monolithic exemplar of absolute evil while relishing the Gothic poetry of Stoker lines like "Listen to them: children of the night. What music they make." In many ways he seems like a blood-lusting ghost of the recently deceased Jazz Age, a Valentino gone rancid, with a touch of sexual ambiguity provided by bee-stung lips that wouldn't have disgraced Clara Bow.

But, for all the iconic force of Lugosi's performance, one frequently has the impression of an actor who has been left to his own devices, badly needing a firm directorial hand to stop him from drawing out a simple line like "We will be leaving tomorrow evening" to ridiculous lengths. And the other actors seem equally rudderless. Edward Van Sloan (a veteran, like Lugosi and Herbert Bunston, of the Broadway production) has just the right air of Old World implacability for Van Helsing, but long exposure to Lugosi on the boards

Bela Lugosi sweeps Helen Chandler into the lower depths of Carfax Abbey in *Dracula* (1930)

DRACULA

Universal 1930
75 minutes; silent version: 78 minutes
production began 29 September

Cinematographer: Karl Freund; Art Director: Charles D Hall; Set Design: Herman Rosse*, John Hoffman*; Supervising Editor: Maurice Pivar; Editor: Milton Carruth; Recording Supervision: C Roy Hunter; Photographic Effects: Frank J Booth*; Set Decorations: R A Gausman*; Make-up: Jack P Pierce*; Wardrobe: Ed Ware*, Vera West*; Screenplay: Garrett Fort, Dudley Murphy*, Tod Browning* ('by Bram Stoker from the play adapted by Hamilton Deane and John L Balderston'); Associate Producer: E M Asher; Presented by: Carl Laemmle; Producer: Carl Laemmle Jr; Director: Tod Browning

Bela Lugosi (Count Dracula); Helen Chandler (Mina); David Manners (John Harker); Dwight Frye (Renfield); Edward Van Sloan (Van Helsing); Herbert Bunston (Doctor Seward); Frances Dade (Lucy); Joan Standing (Briggs [nurse]); Charles Gerrard (Martin); uncredited: Anna Bakacs (innkeeper's daughter); Nick Bela (coach passenger); Daisy Belmore (Englishwoman on coach); Tod Browning (voice of harbour master); Moon Carroll (maid); John George (small scientist); Carla Laemmle (young woman on coach); Wyndham Standing (surgeon); Josephine Velez (nurse); Michael Visaroff (innkeeper); Jeraldine Dvorak, Cornelia Thaw, Dorothy Tree (vampire women)

nb: Joan Standing's role is erroneously credited on screen as 'maid'

When I first read Bram Stoker's novel *Dracula*, I felt suitably creepy and eerie; when I saw what Hollywood had done to it and vampires in general, I felt much more inclined to laugh than to be thrilled. It is wholly artificial, in spite of Tod Browning's efforts with the camera to create a ghostly and ghastly atmosphere. Picturegoer Weekly [UK]

***Dracula* is a story which has always had a powerful effect on the emotions of an audience, and I think that the picture will be no less effective than the stage play. In fact, the motion picture should even prove more remarkable in this direction, since many things which could only be talked about on the stage are shown on the screen in all their uncanny detail.**
Bela Lugosi [1931 radio address, reprinted in *Famous Monsters of Filmland*, April 1963]

seems to have made him unconsciously pick up the same laboured speech rhythms. As Dracula's first victim, Dwight Frye's extremely fey Renfield adds to the peculiar sexual tension of the film's opening section; he later perfects a famously disturbing 'mad' laugh but suffers badly from the script's total ignorance of Renfield's role in the novel. Here, he just breaks out of his cell with boring regularity and does nothing of the slightest consequence.

Unfortunately, the firm directorial hand these actors needed is nowhere in evidence; indeed, Tod Browning seems to have approached the film with almost total indifference, perhaps because it represented so complete a refutation of his old theory of the 'horrible possible'. Even with the celebrated German cinematographer Karl Freund as his lieutenant, Browning ignores any number of opportunities to make the material visually interesting, turning at least two-thirds of the film into a deadening proscenium-arch plod.

In this, he was abetted by a script that shows an almost pathological unwillingness to open the play

out. At one point, David Manners' Harker strides across to the French windows in his plus-fours and says "What's that, running across the lawn? Looks like a huge dog." And yet the audience is given no glimpse of Dracula in werewolf form. At another juncture, we have to take the insane Renfield's word for it regarding the horde of rats offered to him by the Count, and later the key scene of Dracula forcing Mina to drink his own blood is similarly skimped. "He opened a vein in his arm and made me drink," Mina sobs – and, intriguingly, Helen Chandler involuntarily raises a hand to her bosom at this point, as if aware that Stoker had specified Dracula's chest as the source. The sexual connotations of this were obviously too strong for Universal to risk incorporating, even in reported speech.

Where the play does get opened out is in the film's first two reels, which offer a richly atmospheric digest of Stoker's first four chapters. The pleasures here are many, from the opening shot of a coach rattling rustily through the Carpathian mountains (actually California's Vasquez Rocks, augmented by a marvellous Frank Booth glass painting) to the carefully chosen mid-European faces that peer fearfully at Renfield during his respite at the inn. The tour of Dracula's crypt, as well as disclosing to view a possum and an improbably large beetle, features Greta Garbo's stand-in, Jeraldine Dvorak, looming blankly from her casket prior to all three brides congregating in the shadow of a massive spider's web.

When Renfield arrives at the castle, the brides reappear as three bats framed by the ruined arch of a high window, and Dracula's majestic appearance on the staircase is heralded, for no discernible reason, by the shuffling interpolation of armadillos. Again augmented by glass paintings, Charles D Hall's sets – both for Castle Dracula and, later, Carfax Abbey – are truly monumental, lending a suitably shattered magnificence to the site of an ancient, unknowable evil.

Everywhere else, however, the film exudes a slipshod air of making do, of get it in the can and move on, of tragically squandered opportunities. None of this mattered, however, to sensation-hungry audiences of 1931, who turned out in sufficient numbers to make the film Universal's most lucrative release of the year; by 1936, it had reportedly made a profit of over $1 million.

The shortcomings of Browning's film are made all the more conspicuous by a Spanish-speaking version that was shot after-hours by director George Melford. Its producer, Paul Kohner, had recently made over Universal's *The Cat Creeps* as *La voluntad del muerto*; he had also been behind the drive to make *Dracula* a Conrad Veidt-Paul Leni project. Newly ensconced as Universal's head of foreign production, he now had the opportunity to show what that film might have

DRÁCULA

Universal 1930
102 minutes
production began 10 October

[credits as English-language version, except] Cinematographer: George Robinson; Editor: Arturo Tavares; Assistant Directors: Charles Gould*, Jay Marchant*; Dialogue Director: Enrique Tovar Avalos*; Screenplay [Versión Española]: B [Baltazar] Fernández Cué; Associate Producer: Paul Kohner; Director: George Melford

Carlos Villar [Villarías] (Conde Drácula); Lupita Tovar (Eva); Barry Norton (Juan Harker); Pablo Álvarez Rubio (Renfield); Eduardo Arozamena (Van Helsing); José Soriana Viosca (Doctor Seward); Carmen Guerrero (Lucía); Amelia Senisterra (Marta); Manuel Arbó (Martín); uncredited: John George (small scientist)

If the English version of *Dracula*, directed by Tod Browning, is as good as the Spanish version, why the Big U haven't a thing in the world to worry about ... To use [Bela Lugosi's] own words the Spanish picture was "beautiful, great, splendid." *Hollywood Filmograph*

Lupita [Tovar, his future wife] told me she couldn't make enough money at Universal and she was going back to Mexico. I lay awake all night trying to figure a way to change her mind. I went to Uncle Carl and told him that I could make Spanish versions of his pictures for about $35,000 each by using the same sets after the regular company had quit for the night. He agreed to give it a try... Paul Kohner [quoted in *American Cinematographer*, May 1988]

Carlos Villarías enfolds Carmen Guerrero in the Spanish-speaking *Drácula* (1930)

been like. His Dracula, Carlos Villarías, is admittedly no Conrad Veidt, nor even a match for Bela Lugosi. But in all other respects the Kohner-Melford *Drácula* wipes the floor with Browning's *Dracula*.

It commenced production 12 days after the English-speaking version and wrapped a week ahead of it. Released in Mexico City on 4 April 1931, it replicated Browning's film only in its advertising, replacing "The story of the strangest passion the world has ever known" with "La historia de una extraña pasión que el mundo jamás ha conocido." As Conde Drácula, Villarías substitutes a mad glint for Lugosi's unfathomable leer, and his attempts at looking hypnotic aren't always convincing. But he's more prone than Lugosi to outbursts of feral ferocity, and makes up for a faintly comical recoil from Renfield's crucifix with a marvellous yell of indignation when faced later with Van Helsing's.

Villarías reportedly wore the same hairpiece as Lugosi but, curiously, his evening ensemble was deprived of Lugosi's stylish heraldic medallion. There are other intriguing anomalies. Melford leaves out the glass-painted exteriors of Castle Dracula but includes a stunning Carfax exterior that was left out by Browning. The Eliza Doolittle type whom Dracula takes as his first London victim is dropped altogether, while the English women sharing Renfield's coach journey are more strongly identified as bluestockings – which, to judge from the footage here, may have been a 1930s euphemism for lesbians. And, in an explicit nod to *Nosferatu*, Renfield cuts his thumb while slicing some bread; in the English version, he merely snags himself on a paper-clip.

Though Villarías can't match Lugosi's virtually pornographic smirk while watching Renfield suck his bleeding thumb, the eroticism is considerably stepped up elsewhere. In Browning's film it operates on a purely subliminal level; here, the vampire brides literally let their hair down and both Carmen Guerrero's Lucía and Lupita Tovar's Eva (Mina) sport extremely diaphanous negligées.

Most importantly, Melford and cinematographer George Robinson invest the action with all the visual inventiveness repudiated by Browning. The rising of the Count from his coffin is achieved by an eerie pall of smoke, exactly as described by Stoker, and the scenes aboard ship are augmented by shots of Dracula emerging from the hold and Renfield screaming insanely in the haloed orb of a porthole. (The "buque abandonado," called the Demeter by Stoker and the Vesta in the Browning film, is here rechristened the Elsie.) The Count's nocturnal movements between Carfax and Seward's sanitarium are picked out by hellish stripes of light piercing through fog, as is Eva's dreamlike wander across the lawn to meet his embrace. And the film's crane shots, taking in the full sweep of Charles Hall's staircases both in the castle and at Carfax, are noticeably more ambitious than anything in the Lugosi version.

The film can't, of course, overcome the fundamental obstacle of its talky script, and, to make matters worse, we get a fuller rendition of it here. As a result, *Drácula* runs a full half-hour longer than *Dracula* (which was brutally chopped pre-release in an attempt to improve its catatonic pace). At least one major plot point left unresolved in the English version – the destruction of the resurrected Lucy – is nicely tidied up by Melford: over a highly atmospheric shot of cemetery gates, a scream rings out, a bird takes flight from a gnarled tree branch, and Eduardo Arozamena's Van Helsing explains to Harker that "It was a good deed to drive a stake through the heart of that poor girl." But, aside from yielding juicy titbits of this sort, the unexpurgated script finally defeats Melford. Even so, the film's stellar pictorial qualities make it a potent, even poignant, record of what might have been.

VIRTUOSO AND VAMPIRE

While Universal readied *Dracula* for release, John Barrymore was over at Warner Bros playing a similarly mesmeric Hungarian in a film also derived from an 1890s original. George du Maurier's novel *Trilby* had been published three years ahead of Stoker's, and in a very short time its central character, Svengali, had been immortalised on the British stage by Herbert Beerbohm Tree and, in the USA, by Wilton Lackaye. Several film versions had already been made, American ones cropping up in 1915 (with Lackaye) and 1923 (with Arthur Edmund Carewe). The part was ideal for Barrymore, whose obsessive need to subvert his matinée idol image with demoniac characterisations had first struck picturegoers in *Dr Jekyll and Mr Hyde*.

Barrymore had tried something similar in 1925, when he starred as a memorably insane Captain Ahab in a very loose adaptation of Melville's *Moby Dick*, rechristened *The Sea Beast* and directed by Millard Webb. The sadomasochistic highlights included the fiery cauterisation of Ahab's stump following the white whale's removal of his leg, a scene played out again, with added bone-freezing screams, when Barrymore appeared in a 1930 talkie that reverted to Melville's original title. Straight after it, he was ready, in the second week of January 1931, to bring the combined intensity of his Hyde and Ahab to Warners' *Svengali*. The finished film would compete

with Universal's vampire smash even in its publicity, replacing *Dracula*'s "The strangest passion the world has ever known" with come-hither tag-lines like "Weirdest romance ever pictured" and "Strangest lovers the world ever knew."

In fin-de-siècle Paris, the gifted pianist Svengali exercises a hypnotic hold over his beautiful young protégée Trilby. To get her away from her artist sweetheart Billee, Svengali has Trilby fake her own death and tour Europe with him as conductor and operatic diva. Though she doesn't return Svengali's love, Trilby nevertheless follows suit when he collapses and dies during an engagement in Cairo.

"In one masterful performance, John Barrymore redeems a host of uninspired portrayals," noted a fan-magazine reviewer at the time. "His Svengali is brilliantly conceived and played for everything that is in the macabre, bestial characterization."[2] Though introduced to us while cruelly manipulating devoted admirer Mme Honori, who later drowns herself in the Seine, Barrymore's Svengali is played, for the first few reels at any rate, as an affable scoundrel. His toilette involves crudely expectorating into a spittoon and he has sufficient self-knowledge to tell his assistant Gecko that "Our English friends ... have not enjoyed the fragrance of our society for a week." Dunked into a bathtub by two of them, he reposes uneasily among the soap suds like a comical version of an El Greco martyr.

Screenwriter J Grubb Alexander, formerly responsible for Universal's *The Man Who Laughs*, also ensures that Svengali has a way with words, as when he counters Billee's rhapsodic sketch of old England – "green fields and hedgerows, and hollyhocks and primroses" – with a withering litany of "Fog and pneumonia and shopkeepers and flat feet, and boiled beef and cabbage." The star tops off this facetious badinage with a wheezing laugh that sounds more like Lionel than John Barrymore.

But the playful mood is abruptly terminated when Svengali takes advantage of Trilby's persistent headaches to put her under his hypnotic influence. In a tight close-up, his eyes take on a milky-white opaqueness that reportedly chilled contemporary audiences to the marrow; it still packs a punch today. And the scene ends with two statements that anticipate the tragic bond that will develop between Svengali and his muse. "Your headache is here in my heart," croons Svengali. "I will keep it as a souvenir." Billee, meanwhile, warns Trilby that hypnotists have a tendency to "make you kill yourself when they're done with you."

The highpoint of the film is a remarkably fluid nocturnal tour of the Paris rooftops. Starting on a long shot of Svengali's study, the camera skirts round his piano, past a stuffed bird of prey and his street clothes hanging blackly on the wall, then settles on Svengali himself, hunched statue-like in the eerie immobility of a profound trance. From a huge close-up of his luminous and pupil-free eyes, the camera pulls smoothly back through his garret window and floats across a wholly convincing miniature of tiled roofs, angled chimney stacks and

SVENGALI

Warner Bros 1931
79 minutes
production began 12 January

Cinematographer: Barney McGill; Art Director: Anton Grot; Editor: William Holmes; Technical Effects: Fred Jackman, Hans F Koenekamp*; Mr Barrymore's make-up: Johnny Wallis*; Wardrobe: Earl Luick; Music: David Mendoza; Screenplay: J Grubb Alexander (based on the novel [*Trilby*] by George Louis du Maurier); Director: Archie Mayo

John Barrymore (Svengali); Marian Marsh (Trilby O'Farrell); Donald Crisp (the Laird); Bramwell Fletcher (Billee); Carmel Myers (Mme Honori); Luis Alberni (Gecko); Lumsden Hare (Taffy); Paul Porcasi (Signor Bonelli); uncredited: Ferike Boros (Marta); Adrienne d'Ambricourt (Mme Vinard); Yola d'Avril (maid); Henry Otto (audience member with opera glasses)

The Barrymore penchant for doing things the Barrymore way has its advantages, but it has its drawbacks, too. If I am expected to sit up and watch Svengali's eyes turn Lon Chaneywise to water for minutes on end, I object. I object also to the way Barrymore has robbed the piece of its delicious humor. *Hollywood Spectator*

Many times I would leave my dressing room, where I was supposed to be resting, and come to watch Mr Barrymore play his scenes ... Always he was so helpful, and so inspiring to me; and when you're with the greatest, you have to try to come up to his level.
Marian Marsh [quoted in Mank, *Women in Horror Films 1930s*, 1999]

Marian Marsh comes under the hypnotic sway of John Barrymore in *Svengali* (1931)

attic windows. (In its combination of Expressionist lighting and almost cartoon-like architectural abstractions, this shot is, as it were, where Dr Caligari meets Dr Seuss.) A violent gust of wind finally blows Trilby's bedroom windows open, the camera tracking smoothly to her sleeping face nestled on a pillow.

When she later responds to Svengali's call, Trilby finds him sprawled in an armchair, toying with a black cat and framed by the corvine silhouette of the stuffed bird seen earlier – two Poe references in one, and a startlingly effective tableau to boot. The whole sequence has a weird, spell-stopped Gothic atmosphere far outstripping the hypnotic hi-jinks of *Dracula*. And whichever Warners technician was responsible for training the spooky key-lights on Barrymore's eyes had a much steadier hand than his counterpart at Universal.

Though Barrymore's bravura performance is obviously the film's raison d'être, the 17-year-old Marian Marsh makes a delightfully vibrant Trilby. She's not all blonde winsomeness either; when Svengali hypnotises her into showing the passion she does not feel, her display of unwonted carnality is at least as effective as Barrymore's sad and self-disgusted recoil from her embrace. Barrymore has by this stage shaded into an affecting mood of desolation, and in the closing reel achieves a powerful effect when the eyes that have previously smouldered, narrowed, popped and glowed finally fill with tears. Barrymore also gets to quote Hamlet's line "There are more things in Heaven and Earth than are dreamed of in your philosophy" not once but twice. Rephrased any number of ways, this line would crop up repeatedly in subsequent horrors as a catch-all excuse for their increasingly fantastic plot-lines.

As well as a charming nude scene for Marsh's anonymous body-double, *Svengali* contains numerous effective moments, as when director Archie Mayo pulls off a witty bit of misdirection at the news of Trilby's supposed suicide. Cutting directly to what looks like a tombstone (complete with misterioso woodwinds on the soundtrack), he then has the camera circle round for a closer look, revealing it as a milestone pointing to Paris and Brussels. And Mayo's technical team is top-notch, in particular cinematographer Barney McGill and designer Anton Grot, whose vaulted sets have an eerie spaciousness that would be carried over to full-on Warner horrors like *Doctor X*.

Released in May, *Svengali* garnered Oscar nominations for Grot and McGill (though not, surprisingly, for Barrymore himself) and was sufficiently successful to prompt the hasty manufacture of a loose follow-up, the result making it into US cinemas by November. In *The Mad Genius*, Barrymore is a club-footed Russian dancing master, Tsarakov, who masterminds the meteoric success of a young (male) ballet dancer; only a few months before making a massive impact on the nascent horror genre, Boris Karloff passes through briefly as the boy's abusive father. Though entrusted to director Michael Curtiz rather than Archie Mayo, the film otherwise was scrupulously faithful to its original, with Marian Marsh, Carmel Myers and Luis Alberni in the cast and Barney McGill, J Grubb Alexander and Anton Grot among the credits. It did not, however, repeat *Svengali*'s success.

An old protégé of Grot's, William Cameron Menzies, had by this time made the jump from art director to film director. Working for the Fox Film Corporation at Movietone City, in 1931 he turned out two quasi-horrors – *The Spider* and *Almost Married*. The first of these, like *Svengali*, was a late-flowering manifestation of the 1920s vogue for charismatic theatrical hucksters, as seen in pictures like *The Mystic* and *The Charlatan*. Made in June and co-directed by Kenneth MacKenna, it stars Edmund Lowe as Chatrand the Great, who attempts to solve an on-stage murder with an on-stage seance and mind-reading session. As so often in films of this period, it's seriously disfigured by a bad case of comic relief. "El Brendel does some very senseless stuff, and manages to break the continuity of every important scene," complained Dalton Trumbo. "I am wondering if *The Spider* might not have been one of the year's best mysteries if those in charge had not insisted upon spoiling it."[3]

The hoary theatrics of *The Spider* were succeeded by the much more forward-looking *Almost Married*, which Menzies started shooting on 26 October and polished off in three weeks. Based on Andrew Soutar's novel *The Devil's Triangle*, it features Alexander Kirkland as a Bolshevik pianist and compulsive strangler who escapes from a lunatic asylum when his wife (Violet Heming) is smuggled out of Russia by her new husband (Ralph Bellamy). The film survives only in truncated form, but its portrait of a psychopath was deemed unusually penetrating in its time, in part because of Kirkland's remarkable performance and in part because screenwriter Wallace Smith had formerly worked in an asylum. As the pressbook crudely stated it: "Smith's intimate knowledge and complete understanding of mental deficients and raving maniacs ... enabled him to preserve the weird and eerie tempo of the film and at the same time to give it its necessary spark of realism."

Yet again, romance was invoked as a means of advertising the picture ("The Weirdest, Strangest Love Story of the Year"), but an effort to differentiate

it from *Dracula* was evident in the pressbook's contention that "It is thoroughly human and believable in both characters and story and is entirely devoid of any trick plot manipulations." An LA preview on 11 December was abortive, however, and extra material seems to have been shot in March 1932 by Marcel Varnel, the film's running time paradoxically dwindling by some 15 minutes in the process. The result was issued to an indifferent public in July.

The same month, Menzies and Varnel co-directed Fox's *Chandu the Magician*. Having played a similar character in *The Spider*, Edmund Lowe was a natural for the role of the heroic Western yogi, who had become popular on radio and was here plunged into an absurd serial-style adventure distinguished only by the ravishing cinematography of James Wong Howe. *Variety* aptly dismissed the result as "hoke growing out of the development of the horror cycle," while the power-crazed villain was memorably apostrophised in the *New York Times*: "Roxor, a baleful character whose behaviour may be described with the simple information that Bela Lugosi plays the part, is a madman who wants to possess himself of a death ray and destroy the world." Chandu would resurface in a 1934 serial called *Return of Chandu*, which, by a strange quirk, starred Lugosi, not as the villain, but as Chandu himself.

Bela Lugosi, Irene Ware and Edmund Lowe in the hokey Fox fantasy *Chandu the Magician* (1932)

Back in 1931, Warners' *Svengali* had been produced before the impact of *Dracula* made itself felt. By May, however, Paramount had embarked on a mystery-horror subject whose creepy appurtenances were carefully tailored to take advantage of *Dracula*'s notoriety – and the result proved a splendid vehicle for Edmund Lowe's 31-year-old wife, Lilyan Tashman. The advertising for *Murder by the Clock* promised not only "The blood-chilling mystery of a man who is MURDERED TWICE!" but also "Hours of heart-gripping horror" and "Horrors that out-thrill anything ever seen!" Paramount's publicists also ran photos of Tashman's burning-eyed femme fatale under the tantalising heading, "VAMPIRE?"

Having induced her husband Herbert to murder his wealthy Aunt Julia, the malicious Laura Endicott then persuades her besotted boyfriend Tom Hollander to kill Herbert. Next, she cajoles the aunt's idiot son, Phillip, into dispatching Hollander. And when Herbert is restored to life, Laura disguises herself as the apparently resurrected aunt in order to kill him again, this time by fright. She meets her match, however, in the watchful Lieutenant Valcour.

Paramount's less-than-strictly-honest suggestion that Tashman's Laura Endicott is a vampire was made possible, of course, by the continuing confusion between vamps and vampires. Though she may not be the latter, Tashman's performance in *Murder by the Clock* qualifies her as a vamp par excellence.

Unlike Estelle Taylor's smouldering exotic in Tod Browning's *Where East is East*, Tashman is a glacial platinum-blonde socialite in (decidedly pre-Code) figure-hugging lamé. "She's a malicious, designing creature," harrumphs Aunt Julia. "Ought to be hung for a witch." Indeed, Laura drops homicidal suggestions right and left, spinning a web that encompasses Julia, Herbert, Hollander and Phillip in turn. Having emerged from the police station where she has been energetically 'vamping' her imprisoned halfwit cousin, she immediately tries the same thing on the imperturbable Lieutenant Valcour, who tells her that "You have a look in your eyes that is characteristic of two types: inspired geniuses – and killers." This is one of the few occasions when Tashman allows Laura's self-possession to slip; indeed, she looks positively crestfallen. Valcour is wrong, however; the gleam in Tashman's eye is that of an expert comic actress who's treading a fine line

Cop on the case William 'Stage' Boyd, femme fatale Lilyan Tashman and capering lunatic Irving Pichel pose for *Murder by the Clock* (1931)

MURDER BY THE CLOCK

Paramount 1931
76 minutes
produced May/June

Cinematographer: Karl Struss; Art Director: Hans Dreier*; Camera Operators: George Clemens*, Cliff Blackstone*; Assistant Camera: Fleet Southcott*, Al Smalley*; Adapted by [ie, Screenplay]: Henry Myers (from the story [of the same name] by Rufus King and the play [*Dangerously Yours*] by Charles Beahan); Director: Edward Sloman

William Boyd (*Lieutenant Valcour*); Lilyan Tashman (*Laura Endicott*); Irving Pichel (*Phillip Endicott*); Regis Toomey (*Officer Cassidy*); Sally O'Neil (*maid [Jane]*); Blanche Friderici (*Mrs Julia Endicott*); Walter McGrail (*Herbert Endicott*); Lester Vail (*Thomas Hollander*); Martha Mattox (*Miss Roberts*); Frank Sheridan (*Chief of Police*); Frederick Sullivan (*medical examiner*); *uncredited:* Charles D Brown (*O'Brien*); Harry Burgess (*coroner*); Lenita Lane (*Miss Morrow [nurse]*); Guy Oliver (*Emil [cemetery caretaker]*); Willard Robertson (*police captain*); John Rogers (*Jerry Smith [Hollander's valet]*); Matty Roubert (*newsboy*); Dick Rush (*desk sergeant*)

The spectacle of Lil [Tashman] vamping the giant idiot to further her murderous schemes is as shocking as anything on the screen. Irving Pichel is fascinating and terrifying as the idiot who wants to kill, and William Boyd is good as the one man Lil can't vamp. This is really a pretty good blood-curdling piece. *Motion Picture*

Those who have read Rufus King's spine-tingling mystery novel *Murder by the Clock* and thus learned the identity of the culprit in the last gripping paragraphs will find, when they see the film version of this story, that a new murderer has taken the place of the original one supplied by the author ... In fact, the character who committed the dire deed in the novel does not appear in the picture at all. *from original pressbook*

between taking the material seriously and sending it up rotten.

Tashman's delivery is somewhat slow and somnolent, presumably as a means of relishing the dialogue's camp extravagance rather than because of discomfort with the talkie medium; her performance in George Cukor's *Girls About Town*, released only a few months after *Murder by the Clock*, is as slick and rapid-fire as one could wish. She may also have been taking a cue from Edward Sloman's static direction, which takes the film's funereal setting (the Endicott house is positioned across the street from a cemetery) rather too literally. Sloman manages an occasional striking composition, as when the view from Laura's window discloses a street lamp, spidery tree branches, and a newsboy crossing the park while shouting "Maniac escapes!" But he relies for the most part on the ace art direction of Hans Dreier, who creates an arid, wintery graveyard and an impressively vaulted family crypt to go with it.

Rufus King's original novel was the first of 11 featuring Lieutenant Valcour; the film, however, remains Valcour's only appearance on screen. William 'Stage' Boyd – not to be confused with the William Boyd who later became famous as 'Hopalong' Cassidy – is a suitably rock-like presence as Valcour, quick with dour epigrams like "It's a poor murderer that has to be present when the crime is committed" and "We're up against a murderer whose mind works like a clock." Irving Pichel, an aspirant director who had made a big impact in Josef von Sternberg's *An American Tragedy*, is an all-stops-out

hoot as the morbid halfwit, enthusing over knives and strangulation at the dinner table, drooling over Laura's come-hither suggestions in his prison cell, and finally pursuing her round his late mother's crypt with nothing less than rape on his mind.

With its secret panels, contested last will and testament, and silhouetted killer, the film is obviously indebted to *The Cat and the Canary*, and to bolster the impression it has some decidedly incestuous casting. Blanche Friderici and Martha Mattox, here playing the ill-fated Aunt Julia and her sour-faced housekeeper, had both played *Cat*'s Mammy Pleasant (in the Broadway original and the Paul Leni film version respectively). Tashman, too, was fresh from the talkie remake of Leni's film, *The Cat Creeps*. The notion of reviving a dead man in order that he might identify his murderer was derived from F Brooke Warren's time-honoured stage melodrama *The Face at the Window*; the use of adrenaline to do it (injected "right into his heart muscles") was an echo of Universal's 1923 film *Legally Dead*. The film would have an influence of its own, however: the process by which Laura manages to kill the dead man a second time – donning a plaster death-mask of Julia and perambulating outside the window with a trademark tap-tap of the old lady's cane – would soon be picked up in RKO's *The Phantom of Crestwood*.

Murder by the Clock reportedly scared contemporary audiences in a big way, and in the UK it would be withdrawn from exhibition after public protest (an early warning of Britain's institutionalised antipathy towards horror subjects). There are still some chills to be had from Aunt Julia's designer vault; mindful of the fact that her husband Morton was buried alive, she has installed an en-suite foghorn to alert people if the same fate should befall her, and Laura makes calculated use of the eerie wailing at a critical moment. The film also delights in its portrait of a patrician New York family destroying itself through greed and self-interest, and thankfully allots minimum screen time to the romance of a supposedly comical Irish cop and an equally unamusing Irish maid.

The following year, 'Stage' Boyd investigated a similarly gruesome mystery in Mayfair Pictures' *Midnight Warning*. Directed by Spencer Gordon Bennett, this starts with an earbone being found in the fireplace of a hotel room and leads to the discovery that a body was burnt there to prevent an outbreak of bubonic plague. The plot device of a man's sister returning to the establishment to find her brother's booking – indeed, his very existence – steadfastly denied by the staff was a form of urban legend dating back to the 1890s. In 1947 the original period of the story was restored in Anthony Thorne's novel *So Long at the Fair*, which would be made into a memorable British film two years later.

TOO DREADFULLY BRUTAL

In the spring of 1931, Hollywood observers were unsure whether the box-office bonanza enjoyed by *Dracula* was merely a flash-in-the-pan or whether it presaged a genuine trend. To Universal's Junior Laemmle, however, it was obvious that a follow-up of some kind was in order, particularly as Universal remained in dire financial straits.

French filmmaker Robert Florey was accordingly put to work on *Frankenstein*, Laemmle having bought the rights to a stage adaptation of Mary Shelley's book by Peggy Webling and John L Balderston. (Prior to Balderston's usual process of 'streamlining', the Webling original had played at London's Little Theatre in February 1930; another Hamilton Deane production, it had not repeated the success of *Dracula*.) Having prepared a screen treatment with *Dracula* veteran Garrett Fort, Florey went ahead and made a two-reel *Frankenstein* test featuring, among others, Edward Van Sloan, Dwight Frye and, as the Monster, Bela Lugosi. This was an unusually pro-active move given the fact that Florey hadn't been formally assigned to the project as director.

Then on 26 June, only nine days after the completion of Florey's test, another director on the Universal lot wound up production on a film adaptation of the Robert E Sherwood play *Waterloo Bridge*. Impressed with the result, Junior Laemmle offered James Whale his pick of the properties on Universal's schedules. Unfortunately for Florey and Lugosi, Laemmle's offer entailed their summary removal from *Frankenstein*.

An Englishman, James Whale was born in Dudley in 1889 and, after a spell as a POW in Germany, became a prominent designer, director and sometime actor in the post-war West End. In the latter capacity, he had two prophetic engagements in 1928. In *A Man with Red Hair*, a Benn Levy adaptation of Hugh Walpole's shockingly sadistic novel, he played Charles Laughton's grotesque son; in the Grand Guignol play *After Death*, he was a guillotined head brought back to life by electricity. (Both productions were staged, like *Dracula* and *Frankenstein*, at the Little Theatre.) Just as important to Whale's later film career was the gentrified persona he had cultivated in response to his humble origin, coupled with a sophisticated sense of humour that was by turns bitter and whimsical.

Success on a major scale came in January 1929, when Whale's smash-hit production of R C Sherriff's *Journey's*

Frankenstein director James Whale, transplanted from Shaftesbury Avenue to Universal City

End took him first to Broadway to direct a US version and then to Hollywood, where his film adaptation was under way at the Tiffany Studio by Christmas. Some 18 months later, Whale gathered together an august team for *Frankenstein*, several of them – cinematographer Arthur Edeson, designer Charles D Hall and leading lady Mae Clarke – carried over from *Waterloo Bridge*. He also screened the German Expressionist classics *Das Cabinet des Dr Caligari* and *Der Golem*, which, like Rex Ingram's *The Magician*, would exercise a profound influence on the finished product. In addition, he insisted on engaging Colin Clive, star of *Journey's End* on both stage and screen, as Frankenstein.

Another English actor was cast as Frankenstein's creation. In the closing weeks of August 1931, the 43-year-old Boris Karloff was accordingly holed up with make-up expert Jack P Pierce in the so-called 'bug-a-boudoir' that had once housed Lon Chaney. Whale, meanwhile, set about shooting the film's opening sequences. Finally, ten days into Whale's schedule, a monster emerged from Dressing Room Five whose image would sink deep into the pop-culture fabric of the 20th century and beyond.

Henry Frankenstein's research into chemical galvanism and electro-biology bears fruit in the form of a grotesque artificial man, who soon murders both Frankenstein's vindictive assistant Fritz and scholarly mentor Dr Waldman. Having accidentally drowned a peasant girl, the Monster is pursued by the enraged local populace and finally faces his creator in a burning windmill.

In its first ten minutes, *Frankenstein* constituted as severe a test of the nerves as 1931 audiences had ever encountered – this even before the arrival of the Monster. Where *Dracula*'s credit titles played out against a stationary Art Deco bat, *Frankenstein*'s feature clutching hands and revolving disembodied eyeballs, after which Edeson's camera picks out in dispassionate detail all the ghoulish paraphernalia of a hillside burial, finally coming to rest on a forbidding statue of Death itself.

Soon enough, Whale introduces the first of several characteristically irreverent touches: the mourners having departed, the tubby gravedigger spits on his hands in 'business as usual' style and sends clods of earth thudding down onto the exposed coffin. Then, of course, Frankenstein and the twisted Fritz emerge from their concealment, feverishly reversing all the gravedigger's work and, in Frankenstein's case, sending a shovelful of graveyard dirt straight into the face of the watching Death figure.

Whale doesn't let up: the next two scenes are located at a wayside gibbet and in an anatomy class. In the latter, Dr Waldman (played by Van Sloan as a more avuncular version of his earlier Van Helsing) refers to "the dead man before us, whose life was one of brutality, of violence and murder." Setting up the film's most significant distortion of Shelley's original, Waldman draws attention to the cadaver's pickled brain, noting the differences between 'dysfunctio cerebri' and a plain old healthy 'cerebrum' in an adjoining jar. (In his eagerness to hammer the message home, Whale allows the jars' labels to change from daintily typewritten to crudely handwritten from shot to shot.) Inevitably, the marauding Fritz absconds with the dysfunctional brain, and the narrative becomes a grimly tragic tale of predestination just in time for reel two.

Only now does the film try to make sense of these charnel-house manoeuvrings, with Elizabeth (Frankenstein's fiancée) and the stolid Victor Moritz fretting over Henry's weird behaviour in a baronial morning room left over from *The Cat and the Canary*. Though Whale for the most part keeps the film on an admirably tight leash, he slackens off in any scenes not devoted to Frankenstein's great experiment and its gruesome outcome, showing a particular lack of interest in the script's obligatory romantic interludes. In an early example of his variable gift for outré casting, Whale tries to enliven these passages with the blustering comedy of Frederick Kerr's ancient Baron Frankenstein. Unfortunately, Kerr is a figure straight out of P G Wodehouse – one of Bertie Wooster's more dyspeptic uncles, perhaps – and is seriously out of place in the gloomy Tyrolean ambience of *Frankenstein*.

Only later would Whale perfect the seamless fusion of humour and horror so characteristic of him; for now, Kerr is just another out-of-kilter element in a world that isn't fully realised. The hi-falutin' old-school-tie heroics of Colin Clive, for example, sit uneasily beside the Californian twang of the seven-year-old girl whom the Monster accidentally drowns. In the same way, the dazzling solidity of Charles D Hall's lofty watchtower laboratory – and its crackling fusillade of electronic gadgets cobbled together by the Santa Monica inventor Kenneth Strickfaden – are at strange variance with mountaintop exteriors played out against a noticeably slack cyclorama.

With his yen for theatrical effects and waspish fondness for in-jokes, perhaps the rumpled night sky over Goldstadt was Whale's way of pointing up the artificiality, not only of Frankenstein's self-made man, but the whole enterprise. In the same way, he seems to have been blissfully unconcerned about the patently fake dummy that represents Frankenstein's apparent death plunge from the burning windmill. Again, Whale was to become more confident about his in-jokes in later films. For the time being, the only readily identifiable pot-shot here comes in the closing scenes, when the insanely creative Frankenstein attires himself in the jodhpurs and riding boots favoured by the more self-important Hollywood film directors.

None of this is to deny *Frankenstein* its enduring power, much of which derives from the rough-hewn authority endemic to a first attempt. In particular, Whale's gift for theatricality is given a splendid showcase in the creation sequence, which veers from an unmistakable pastiche of the Porter scene in *Macbeth* (Fritz's ungracious welcome to Waldman and company at the watchtower door) to Frankenstein himself arranging his hi-tech props in order to give them the show of a lifetime. "Quite a good scene, isn't it?" he grins. "One man crazy; three very sane spectators."

After the scene's lightning-flashing electrical crescendo and the creator's orgasmic cry of "It's alive," Frankenstein is seen in more reflective mode, puffing on a post-coital cigarette and asking Waldman if he has never wanted to find out "what causes the trees to bud and what changes the darkness into light." Though beautifully played by Clive, this speech is just a prelude to the arrival of the Monster, turning his remarkable face to the camera in what was to become a Whale trademark – three rapidly tightening close-ups that seek to fathom the creature's impenetrable, basilisk stare.

Needless to say, Karloff's Monster is a million miles from the braindead psychopathic brute envisioned in Robert Florey's original treatment. Indeed, Karloff's pantomime is on the highest level throughout – whether expressing puzzled yearning for the sunlight in which Frankenstein briefly bathes him, inarticulate fury at the torments inflicted on him by the jealous Fritz, or childlike excitement during his brief lakeside idyll with the doomed Maria. Most affecting of all, perhaps, is his shrieking hysteria and panic when trapped in the blazing mill. Here, Whale contrives an exciting wrap-up to a third act handled otherwise in slightly desultory fashion; he has carefully replicated Fuseli's *The Night Mare* in his staging of the Monster's encounter with Elizabeth, but is clearly uninterested in the soon-to-be-generic business of vengeful, torch-wielding villagers.

Frankenstein cost Universal some $290,000 and proved a phenomenal success, taking well over a million in its first six months and sparking heated controversy around the world. Heavily trimmed by several state censor boards and also in Britain, it would be banned outright in such territories as Sweden, Italy and Australia. Of its unprecedented catalogue of charnel-house horrors, the Monster's unwitting murder of Maria was perhaps the most contentious. On 14 November, the pre-release estimate of the recently incorporated trade paper *Motion Picture Herald* was unequivocal on this point: "I won't forgive Junior Laemmle or James Whale for permitting the monster to drown a little girl before my very eyes. That job should come out before the picture is released. It is too dreadfully brutal, no matter what the story calls for."[4] It stayed in but only in a truncated form that made the Monster's intentions seem far more sinister; it was finally restored in the 1980s.

Of critical evaluations, the response in *Motion Picture*'s 'Picture Parade' section for February 1932 was typical:

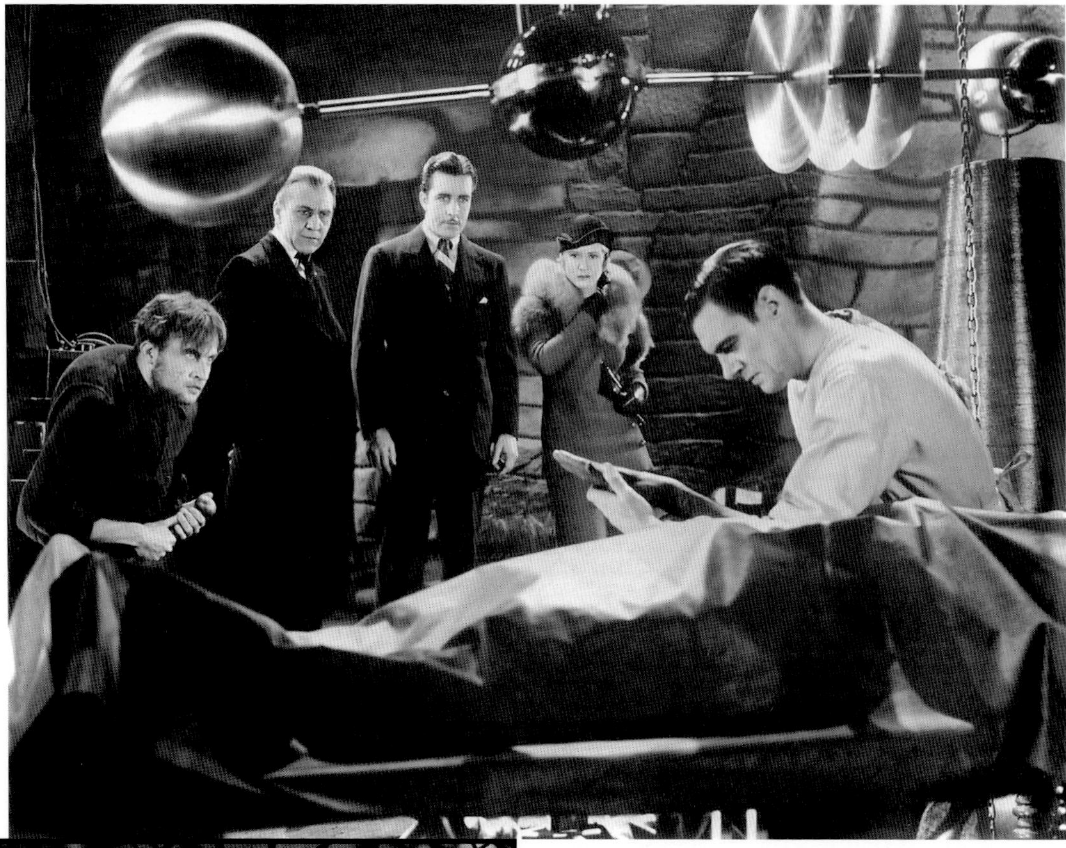

Sane spectators Edward Van Sloan, John Boles and Mae Clarke witness the handiwork of Dwight Frye (left) and Colin Clive in *Frankenstein* (1931)

FRANKENSTEIN

Universal 1931
71 minutes
production began 24 August

Cinematographer: Arthur Edeson; Art Director: Charles D Hall; Set Design: Herman Rosse*; Editors: Maurice Pivar, Clarence Kolster; Recording Supervision: C Roy Hunter, William Hedgcock*; Special Electrical Effects: Kenneth Strickfaden*, Frank Graves*, Raymond Lindsay*; Make-up: Jack P Pierce*; Music: David Broekman*, Bernhard Kaun*; Technical Adviser: Dr Cecil Reynolds*; Screenplay: Garrett Fort, Francis Edwards Faragoh, John Russell*, Robert Florey* ('Based upon the composition by John L Balderston From the novel by Mrs Percy B Shelley Adapted from the play by Peggy Webling'); Scenario Editor: Richard Schayer; Associated [sic] Producer: E M Asher; Producer: Carl Laemmle Jr; Director: James Whale

Colin Clive (Henry Frankenstein); Mae Clarke (Elizabeth); John Boles (Victor Moritz); Boris Karloff (The Monster); Edward Van Sloan (Doctor Waldman); Frederick Kerr (Baron Frankenstein); Dwight Frye (Fritz); Lionel Belmore (the Burgomaster [Herr Vogel]); Marilyn Harris (little Maria); uncredited: Francis Ford (Hans [wounded villager]); Michael Mark (Ludwig [Maria's father]); Joseph North (butler); Cecilia Parker (maid); Maidel Turner (housekeeper); William Yetter (gendarme); Mary Sherman, Arletta Duncan, Pauline Moore (bridesmaids); Ted Billings, Ines Palange, Paul Panzer, Harry Tenbrook (villagers)

One of the finest picture jobs I ever saw on the screen ... As a horrifier it is a tremendous success, but I doubt very much if it will be equally successful as a financial venture ... If your tastes run to the morbid you will enjoy *Frankenstein*. If, however, you have a healthy outlook on life you had better stay away from it. *Hollywood Spectator*

Boris Karloff was not at all pleased with the part of the monster, originally. When he saw the rushes of the picture, he mumbled unhappily to me that the film would ruin his career. But I told him, "Not so, Boris,not so! You're *made*!"
Edward Van Sloan [quoted in Famous Monsters of Filmland, December 1964]

"Children should not be allowed to see this picture. Nervous people should keep away from it. For the strong-stomached, however, it is a new sensation." The anonymous reviewer accurately noted that Karloff "is superb. His make-up is awe-inspiring and he arouses morbid sympathy as well as loathing," concluding with, "A remarkable picture, but one of its kind is enough."

In Britain, meanwhile, *Picturegoer* published a "helpful open letter" addressed to Karloff himself. "So much has been said about this 'repellent and morbid' film that my curiosity is naturally whetted," wrote Burness Martin, "and I rather want to see all the details for myself, but, on the other hand, I doubt whether I could stomach the crimes you commit in the picture. How does it feel to be a monster? I hope they will not condemn you to similar parts, Boris. They say once a thief always a thief, but never let it be once a monster always a monster."[5] Of course, *Motion Picture*'s hope that Hollywood would produce no further horror pictures, and *Picturegoer*'s that Karloff would portray no more monsters, were to fall on deaf ears.

In fact, Karloff went direct from *Frankenstein* to a Columbia gangster melodrama called *In the Secret Service*, directed by John Francis Dillon over a 19-day period in November 1931. By the time it was released the following February, Karloff's sudden monster celebrity had incurred a title change to the more ominous *Behind the Mask* and a publicity campaign that screamed "Who is the murdering monster?" By a curious coincidence, it wasn't Karloff (uneasily cast as an English-accented hoodlum) but his *Frankenstein* co-star Edward Van Sloan, relishing a wonderfully juicy role as a surgeon-cum-drugs baron who performs unnecessary appendectomies and uses the resultant coffins to stash narcotics in. Similarly, in January 1932 Karloff was working on Norman Z McLeod's remake of the old Lon Chaney hit *The Miracle Man*, not in Chaney's old part – that went to John Wray – but as a Chinatown publican.

Primeval Instincts and Rotten Blood

Despite developments over at Universal, spooky-house mysteries were still being ground out by the lesser studios on a regular basis. Written and directed by Alan James, *The Phantom* appeared, like *Frankenstein*, in December 1931, lifting its master criminal and hyperventilating maid from *The Bat* and neighbouring asylum, plus resident mad scientist, from *The Monster*. The result is outstandingly amateurish, with an opening prison break composited from ancient stock footage and several actors who have visibly failed to master their lines. In a nepotistic touch, James (here using the alias Alvin J Neitz) cast his sister, Violet Knights, as the irritating maid, though the only real point of interest is provided by William Jackie as a lanky, German-accented inmate called Oscar. Despite being lumbered with corny lines like "Ever hear that story about Yack and Yill?", Jackie's performance is bizarre in the extreme, a genuine one-off.

Similar films came from Poverty Row companies like Tiffany (Frank Strayer's *Murder at Midnight*, 1931) and Monogram (Phil Whitman's *A Strange Adventure*, 1932). Not to be outdone, Columbia also went the 'will reading in an old mansion' route in Edward Sedgwick's *A Dangerous Affair* (1931). A much more interesting scenario, and a prescient one, featured in George Crone's *Get That Girl* (1932), in which a mad scientist (Fred Malatesta) turned his victims into shop-window dummies. His death, too – savaged by his own guard dogs – was to prove a popular one.

A more intriguing entry was David Howard's *Mystery Ranch*, a Fox horse-opera made in April 1932 from a script by Alfred A Cohn, co-writer of both *The Cat and the Canary* and *The Last Warning*. In it, George O'Brien is an Arizona ranger charged with apprehending a psychopathic rancher, played with chilling containment by Charles Middleton. Later to achieve immortality as Ming the Merciless in Universal's *Flash Gordon* serials, Middleton is attended by a monolithic Apache manservant played by the distinguished black actor Noble Johnson, himself due to take a prominent part in Hollywood's horror cycle.

Middleton's outstanding performance and Joseph August's crepuscular photography make *Mystery Ranch* the cream of a surprisingly large crop of quasi-Gothic Westerns, which ranged across the maniacal killers killers of *Tombstone Canyon* (1932), *The Rawhide Terror* (1935) and *Desert Phantom* (1936) to the mad scientist of *Big Calibre* (1934) and the 'dark house' embellishments of *Haunted Gold* (1932) and *Big Boy Rides Again* (1935). Of these, *Tombstone Canyon* was directed by *The Phantom*'s Alan James and featured, in addition to idiosyncratic cowboy star Ken Maynard, yet another marauding 'Phantom'.

On a much more exalted level, Paramount had more than just *Murder by the Clock* with which to counter the surprise success of *Dracula*. As well as planning films of Hugh Walpole's *A Man with Red Hair* and H G Wells' *The Island of Dr Moreau* (only the second of which would come to fruition), production head B P Schulberg took Warners' *Svengali* as his cue to lure John Barrymore back to Paramount for a reprise of his now 11-year-old *Dr Jekyll and Mr Hyde*. When Barrymore signed with M-G-M instead, Schulberg hit upon Irving Pichel, whose performance in *Murder by the Clock* seemed to qualify him as an ideal Jekyll and Hyde. Director Rouben Mamoulian, however, insisted on Fredric March – who, ironically, had made an impact the previous year as a thinly veiled Barrymore lampoon in Paramount's *The Royal Family*.

Unrivalled as a visual stylist, Mamoulian had two other gifted collaborators in this new take on the R L Stevenson story – Ufa-trained designer Hans Dreier and cinematographer Karl Struss, who four years earlier had shot Murnau's *Sunrise*. Produced at the same time as *Frankenstein*, the final product would be unveiled on New Year's Eve and garner three Oscar nominations (Best Actor, Cinematography and Screenplay). It was advertised, in typically misleading style, as "The weirdest, yet most romantic theme ever played by Fredric March!"

Convinced that "man is not truly one but truly two" – and frustrated by delays imposed by his future father-in-law on his impending marriage to Muriel Carew – Dr Henry Jekyll perfects an elixir that makes him revert to a primeval self whom he dubs Mr Hyde. In this form, he

Miriam Hopkins and director Rouben Mamoulian take tea with the fully made-up Fredric March while shooting *Dr Jekyll and Mr Hyde* (1931)

DR. JEKYLL AND MR. HYDE

Paramount 1931
98 minutes
production ended late October

Cinematographer: Karl Struss; Art Director: Hans Dreier*; Editor: William Shea*; Sound: M M Paggi*; Technical Effects: Gordon Jennings*; Process Photography: Farciot Edouart*; Effects Photography: Frank Bjerring*; Wardrobe: [Travis] Banton*; Make-up: Wally Westmore*; Musical Director: Nathaniel W Finston*; Screenplay: Samuel Hoffenstein, Percy Heath (based on the novel by Robert Louis Stevenson); Presented by: Adolph Zukor; Director-Producer: Rouben Mamoulian

Fredric March (*Dr Henry Jekyll/Mr Hyde*); Miriam Hopkins (*Ivy Pierson*); Rose Hobart (*Muriel Carew*); Holmes Herbert (*Dr Lanyon*); Halliwell Hobbes (*Brigadier-General Carew*); Edgar Norton (*Poole*); Tempe Pigott (*Mrs Hawkins*); *uncredited:* Robert Adair (*Charlie [man with Ivy at music hall]*); Rita Carlisle (*Mrs Lucas*); Pat Harmon (*man at music hall*); Arnold Lucy (*Utterson*); Colonel MacDonnell (*Hobson [Carew's butler]*); John Rogers (*music hall waiter*); Douglas Walton (*student*); Eric Wilton (*Briggs [Lanyon's butler]*); Frank Baker, D'Arcy Corrigan, Murdock MacQuarrie, Eric Mayne (*doctors at lecture*)

I'll say this for the Paramount horror-purveyor: It is amazingly well done in all its essential elements and gives further evidence of the growing importance of Rouben Mamoulian as a director ... The pathological and psychological aspects of Poe's story [sic] are handled with rare intelligence ... Dramatically Mamoulian seems to have no limits. *Hollywood Spectator*

I conceived Mr Hyde as more than just Dr Jekyll's inhibited evil nature. I saw the beast as a separate entity – one who could, and almost did, little by little, overpower and annihilate Dr Jekyll ... To me, those repeated appearances of the beast within him were more than just a mental strain on Jekyll – they crushed him physically as well. Fredric March [quoted in *Screen Book* 1932]

enslaves and finally strangles Soho prostitute Ivy Pierson, later bludgeoning Brigadier-General Carew to death before being shot down by the police in Jekyll's laboratory.

The credit titles of Mamoulian's *Dr Jekyll and Mr Hyde* are accompanied by Bach's Toccata and Fugue in D Minor, a piece which, having been played by Boris Karloff in *The Black Cat* and Bela Lugosi in *The Raven*, would become a horror film staple. Credits over, Mamoulian immediately makes it clear that this *Jekyll and Hyde* is to be the polar opposite of its silent forebear. Where John S Robertson's direction was essentially functional and featureless, Mamoulian loads his film with studiedly poetic effects that are always eye-catching but frequently self-conscious.

As Welford Beaton observed at the time, "Mamoulian opens *Jekyll* with a camera trick which is interesting in a way, but which means nothing."[6] A pioneering exercise in the use of subjective camera, this lengthy sequence only permits us a glimpse of the handsome Jekyll when he scrutinises himself in a mirror. A question mark regarding Jekyll's true identity is immediately implanted in the viewer's mind – and, in a clever touch, Hyde, too, is subsequently introduced in a mirror. But, as Jekyll makes his protracted way to the lecture theatre, the inordinate amount of footage involved finally renders the subjective camera conceit, as Beaton indicated, meaningless. A 1935 reissue, running 81 minutes rather than the original's gruelling 98, sensibly cut this section down to its bare bones; other deletions, however, were more damaging.

As Beaton's testimony suggests, several of Mamoulian's devices seemed heavy-handed even at the time, with an about equal tally of hits and misses. A rain-streaked window, for instance, provides a strikingly poetic metaphor for Jekyll's mood during Muriel's extended absence. Moments later, however, a bubbling cauldron boils over in a laughably blunt parallel to Jekyll's ungovernable passions. Licked by hellish flames, this persistent pot is even accorded pride of place in the film's final frame.

Mamoulian's trademark fondness for statuary is given an airing when Hyde's off-screen strangling of Ivy is coolly observed by an alabaster statue of a winged angel caressing a naked woman; the juxtaposition is bitterly effective given Ivy's earlier description of Jekyll as "an angel." Ivy herself has been described by Hyde as "my bright little bird," and there's a grim wit in Hyde's flight from the strangulation scene, which takes him past a pub called The Bird in Hand. Similar effects, however,

are merely precious, as when Mamoulian's camera glides away from the florid love-talk of Jekyll and Muriel, passing another piece of statuary and settling on a pair of nodding water-lilies.

Shot on a seven-week schedule and with a massive budget of some $500,000, the film offers a lavish recreation of Victorian London, made subtly Expressionist by Hans Dreier but wholly convincing within its own slightly fanciful terms. The opening transformation scene is an imaginative tour de force, starting with a clever alternation of red make-up and red filters to show Jekyll's changing features, later progressing to an unnerving montage sequence as the camera spirals drunkenly around the laboratory. Cinematographer Karl Struss had previously used the red filter technique, except in reverse, for the curing of the lepers in *Ben-Hur*; unfortunately, Jekyll's last few transformations are rendered in the kind of crude lap-dissolves that would become familiar in pictures like *The Wolf Man*.

There are also extremely strong supporting performances from Miriam Hopkins as the ill-fated Ivy and Holmes Herbert as Jekyll's straight-laced friend Dr Lanyon. Tellingly, the former's lodgings are graced by a cheap reproduction of Velázquez's mirror-gazing 'Rokeby Venus', while the latter's desk is surmounted by a large portrait of Queen Victoria.

The script is an unusually sophisticated one, recasting Stevenson's story as a critique of Victorian hypocrisy and, by extension, a parable about the dangers of sexual repression. "Can a man dying of thirst forget water?" Jekyll asks frankly when discussing his separation from Muriel. "If I understand you correctly," replies Lanyon, "you sound almost indecent." Appropriately, equal weight is given to the scenes in which Jekyll and then Hyde encounter the hoydenish Ivy, both scenes bristling with pre-Code explicitness. Playful eroticism predominates in Jekyll's first meeting with Ivy; after lingering on a luscious close-up of her exposed thigh amid a sea of billowing petticoats, Mamoulian then allows the half-faded image of Ivy's naked leg to percolate in Jekyll's mind for fully half a minute. Later, Hyde's sadistic domination of Ivy is brilliantly played by both Hopkins and March. The perverted hunger for sexual fulfilment through emotional torture is perfectly encapsulated in Hyde's phrase "I hurt you because I love you," and their final scene together paints a truly horrifying picture of male-female relations.

The scene is so brutally frank it may well have failed to get past the censors had it been presented in a more 'realistic' context – if Wallace Beery, say, were brutalising Jean Harlow in a 1930s flophouse. The setting here, however, is Victorian London and the aggressor a troglodytic monster. Struss argued strongly against the heavy make-up applied to Hyde, but was overruled because of Mamoulian's determination to present the character as "a replica of our ancestor, the Neanderthal man that we once were, to show the struggle of modern man with his primeval instincts."[7] Maybe Struss was on to something, for the film ends up enshrining a peculiar contradiction: a formidably intellectual director, while throwing at the screen every highbrow trick in the book, simultaneously presents us with the kind of hirsute missing link played in silent days by Bull Montana.

Of course, Fredric March was a much more considerable actor than Montana; indeed, on 18 November 1932 he would pick up an Academy Award for his work here. But, for all the atavistic braggadocio of his Hyde, March's Jekyll is hard to warm to. Hamstrung from the start by the over-careful enunciation of an actor trying to sound English, he ends by tearing a passion to very comprehensive tatters in his tearful leave-taking with Muriel, pitching his performance directly at the Upper Circle rather than the searching intimacy of a picture house.

If March's Neanderthal throwback stirred vague memories of the Scopes trial in cinemagoers' minds, Universal's next horror picture no doubt brought those memories screaming to the front. As a consolation prize for his removal from *Frankenstein*, Robert Florey was assigned to adapt Poe's *Murders in the Rue Morgue*. Fashioning a suitable role for Bela Lugosi, Florey harked back to tests he had made in the mid-1920s for an aborted avant-garde picture called *The Mad Doctor*, in which Michael Visaroff (the gurning innkeeper of Browning's *Dracula*) had played the title role. Florey accordingly created the insane Dr Mirakle, a sideshow mountebank whose Darwinian bent is expressed in the frankest terms possible in the finished film. The Parisian audiences who shout "Heresy!" at him are interchangeable with the members of the Anti-Evolution League who, for a brief moment in 1925, had made a Tennessee schoolteacher the most famous man in America.

Paris, 1845. The sideshow act of Dr Mirakle has as its centrepiece his captive gorilla Erik. After hours, the doctor's determination to establish "man's kinship with the ape" causes him to inject Erik's blood into a prostitute, with fatal consequences. Having instructed Erik to abduct young Camille l'Espanaye (in the process killing her mother), Mirakle is turned on by the ape, which is itself gunned down by Camille's medical student fiancé, Pierre Dupin.

Charles Gemora threatens Bert Roach, watched by Sidney Fox, Leon Waycoff, Bela Lugosi and Edna Marion, in this gag shot from *Murders in the Rue Morgue* (1931)

MURDERS IN THE RUE MORGUE

Universal 1931
62 minutes
production began 19 October

Cinematographer: Karl Freund; Art Director: Charles D Hall; Set Design: Herman Rosse*; Editors: Maurice Pivar, Milton Carruth; Sound: C Roy Hunter; Special Effects: John P Fulton; Process Shots: Frank D Williams*; Make-up: Jack P Pierce*; Musical Director: Heinz Roemheld*; Technical Adviser: Harold Salemsen*; Screenplay: Tom Reed, Dale van Every ('based on the immortal Edgar Allan Poe classic'); Adaptation: Robert Florey; Added Dialogue: John Huston; Associate Producer: E M Asher; Producer: Carl Laemmle Jr; Director: Robert Florey

Sidney Fox (*Mlle Camille l'Espanaye*); Bela Lugosi (*Doctor Mirakle*); Leon Waycoff [*later Leon Ames*] (*Pierre Dupin*); Bert Roach (*Paul*); Betsy Ross Clarke (*Mme l'Espanaye*); Brandon Hurst (*Prefect of Police*); D'Arcy Corrigan (*morgue keeper*); Noble Johnson (*Janos, the Black One*); Arlene Francis (*woman of the streets*); *uncredited:* Ted Billings (*carnival goer*); Herman Bing (*Franz Odenheimer, German tenant*); Agostino Borgato (*Alberto Montani, Italian tenant*); Elspeth Dudgeon (*waterfront crone*); Charles Gemora (*Erik [the ape]*); Charles Hamilton Greene (*sideshow barker*); Harry Holman (*landlord*); Edna Marion (*Mignette*); Torben Meyer (*Danish tenant*); Charles T Millsfield (*bearded sideshow patron*); Monte Montague (*workman*); Dorothy Vernon (*tenant*), Michael Visaroff (*second sideshow barker*); Christian J Frank, John T Murray (*gendarmes*); Charlotte Henry, Polly Ann Young (*girls*)

I have enough to worry about without getting excited over an ape's infatuation for the delightful little Sidney Fox, as I am asked to do when I view *Rue Morgue* ... It interested me chiefly by confirming my opinion that Florey is a director of marked ability. That is all I got out of it. I was indifferent to everything else in it. *Hollywood Spectator*

I wrote the *Rue Morgue* adaptation in a week ... I used the same device I employed in my *Frankenstein* adaptation. Bela Lugosi became Dr Mirakle – a mad scientist desirous of creating a human being – not with body parts stolen from a graveyard and a brain from a lab, but by the mating of an ape with a woman. *Robert Florey [quoted in Bojarski, The Films of Bela Lugosi, 1980]*

Just as James Whale had bagged *Frankenstein* over the head of Florey, so Florey bagged *Rue Morgue* over the head of the originally mooted George Melford. And, having completed the film on 13 November, Florey was able to reactivate it in December, with close to $25,000 added to the original budget thanks to the meteoric success of *Frankenstein*. By 8 January the following year, however, the SRC's Jason Joy was writing to Carl Laemmle Jr with a prophetic response to the film's strongest scene. "Because the victim is a woman in this instance, which has not heretofore been the case in the other so-called 'horror' pictures recently produced," Joy wrote, "[local] censor boards are very likely to think that this scene is overdone in gruesomeness."[8]

Indeed they did, more often than not lopping it out altogether, together with Mirakle's more inflammatory Darwinian pronouncements. In it, Mirakle pinions a semi-clad prostitute to cruciform beams in his makeshift laboratory (actually the old watchtower cellar from *Frankenstein*) and transfuses Erik's blood into her. "If you only last one more minute, then we shall see," Lugosi tells her in a sublimely unhinged apotheosis. "We shall know if you are to be the bride of science!" Disgusted by the failure of his experiment, his subsequent railings are among the most memorable in the Universal catalogue: "Your blood is rotten – black as your sins. You cheated me; your beauty was a lie!" By this time she's dead, however, and, having kneeled in strangely religious supplication at her dangling feet, Mirakle turns to his troglodyte helper (Noble Johnson) and utters a line repeated by mad scientists a thousand times down the decades: "Janos: get rid of it. Get it away!"

Prior to front-office tampering, this eye-poppingly sadistic set-piece was to have come at the very outset of the picture; even awkwardly displaced by a reel or two, it remains the film's high point. Elsewhere, Lugosi is saddled with a Beethoven perm and a highly unbecoming uninterrupted eyebrow, but lends his agreeably peculiar cadences to lines like "Erik is only human, mademoiselle – he has an eye for beauty." That

one – penned, perhaps, by future director John Huston, one of many writers involved in the film – was an especially cheeky 'up yours' to the Anti-Evolutionists.

The acting elsewhere in the film is unusually sub-standard. Sidney Fox won the Camille role in preference to Bette Davis and ended up billed above Lugosi, but remains a simpering and unengaging heroine. Worse, Bert Roach (a veteran of Leni's *The Last Warning* and King Vidor's shattering 1928 drama *The Crowd*) plays the hero's cherubic friend Paul in a limp-wristed style redolent of the 'sissy' characters then popular in Hollywood. D'Arcy Corrigan, however, is a delight as "that old ghoul down at the morgue," accepting the arrival of Mirakle's body with just as much detachment as he previously accepted Mirakle's victims.

Florey clearly wasn't concerned with his actors; instead, he did his best to construct a Hollywood response to the Expressionist masterpiece *Das Cabinet des Dr Caligari*. The result is good to look at but marked by a fatal confusion of intent. With cinematographer Karl Freund as co-conspirator, Florey transplanted Germanic angles and painted shadows onto designs otherwise influenced by Florey's French favourite, Daumier – and the cross-fertilisation is no more successful than Mirakle's. Tellingly, Florey and Freund knew each other's languages and reportedly confused cast and crew by alternating between French and German. On the plus side, this linguistic confusion fed in to the film's second-best scene (derived, like virtually nothing else in the picture, from Poe's original), in which Herman Bing, Agostino Borgato and Torben Meyer create a genuinely funny explosion of polyglot cross-purposes.

Pre-Code sadism: ape specialist Charles Gemora encounters burlesque dancer Sally Rand in *The Sign of the Cross* (1932)

Though Florey obviously had to commodify *Caligari*'s art-house template to the demands of mainstream US audiences, the parallels between the two films finally become ridiculous when one considers Florey's answer to the ethereal menace of Conrad Veidt's Cesare. What Florey gives us instead is the ubiquitous Charles Gemora in one of his trademark ape suits. And confusion reigns even here, for Erik's close-ups are given over – not to Gemora, nor even to a genuine gorilla – but to an elderly chimpanzee, footage of which was captured at the Selig Zoo. On top of all this, the inane Paul mistakes Erik for a baboon. Whatever he is, it's clear that the one thing Erik isn't is what Poe originally prescribed – an orang-outan. The effect is laughable, and the ape's climactic abduction of Camille across the crazily articulated rooftops of Florey's Paris isn't much better.

The continued popularity of apes was a hangover from the silent period and made the early 1930s something of a boom time for Charles Gemora. The natural successor to Bull Montana, Gemora's speciality owed its inception to his work with make-up guru Perc Westmore on the 1927 version of *The Gorilla*. As noted in Part Two, Gemora subsequently made his debut in his self-devised gorilla suit in Rupert Julian's *The Leopard Lady*. As a startling indication of the flexibility of his gorilla act (and the continuing confusion between comedy and horror), Gemora moved straight from throttling Bela Lugosi at Universal to cavorting in a tutu for Laurel and Hardy in *The Chimp*. Also on the Roach lot, he would put the wind up Roach's female Laurel and Hardy equivalents, Thelma Todd and ZaSu Pitts, in another 1932 release, *Seal Skins*.

Further up the Hollywood ladder, Gemora was used at Paramount the same year to deepen the artfully contrived depravity of Cecil B DeMille's *The Sign of the Cross*, which also featured Joyzelle Joyner's frankly lesbian 'Dance of the Naked Moon', Charles Laughton's thoroughly gay Emperor Nero, Claudette Colbert's naked breasts in a creamy glaze of asses' milk, and gladiatorial contests unrivalled in their gruesomeness. Most notoriously, Gemora had appeared in *Ingagi*, a bogus travelogue that combined genuine nature footage dating back to 1914 with crudely mocked-up 'verité' sequences shot at the end of 1929. Exploiting exactly the kind of bestiality *Murders in the Rue Morgue* could only hint at, on its release in March 1931 it raked in a cool $2 million (more like $4 million, according to some sources) prior to being withdrawn from circulation.

Describing *Ingagi* as "the supreme cinematic joke of the decade," *Motion Picture*'s Charles Grayson reported that "The bright young men of Congo Pictures [entrepreneur Nathan M Spitzer, director William Campbell and writer Adam Hull

Shirk] ... were shrewd enough psychologists to foresee that pickings were to be had from a picture based on the theme of illicit traffic between animals and human beings ... Despite an enormous barrage of suspicion, and even guffaws and jeers from the more skeptical, it scored tremendously. Let him deny it now who will, I doubt that there is a solitary member of all the many audiences of that film who did not feel his pulses accelerate when the gorilla came fumbling through the foliage toward the woman who, according to the custom of her tribe, awaited him."[9] The film was finally exposed as a hoax when one of Gemora's subordinate simians filed suit for unpaid wages; Gemora later claimed to have filmed the gorilla sequence himself at a cost of $5000 (hiring the bare-breasted native maiden from Central Casting), selling it on to Spitzer for $7000.

Ingagi was merely the most disreputable manifestation of a persistent 'jungle' vogue that would throw up such classy pictures as Paramount's *White Woman* and RKO's *Bird of Paradise*. For M-G-M, the nearly $950,000 profit they made on W S Van Dyke's *Trader Horn* prompted them to make *Tarzan, the Ape Man*, which began shooting under Van Dyke's direction at Hallowe'en 1931. A massive hit on its release the following April, it concluded with a hair-raising sacrifice by pygmies to their eight-foot gorilla deity, Johnny Weissmuller's Tarzan coming to the rescue with an elephant stampede, then blinding the monster and finally cutting its throat. The lustrous sequel, *Tarzan and His Mate*, would be released two years later and featured a similarly gruesome throat-stabbing for a mechanical crocodile.

The influence of *Ingagi* extended much further than bargain-basement jungle exploiters like *Love Life of a Gorilla*, *Forbidden Adventures in Angkor*, *The Beast of Borneo* and the entirely unrelated *Son of Ingagi*. For the 'gorilla sacrifice' sequences of both *Ingagi* and *Tarzan, the Ape Man* would be clearly reflected in the biggest jungle adventure of them all, *King Kong*.

MORE THAN USUALLY MACABRE

"Buy a bottle of nerve tonic, throw away your cigarettes, and start your serious training for the screen 'thriller' season," advised the news column of Britain's *Picturegoer Weekly* early in 1932. "The fan has to be hard-boiled in these days of competitive film 'frightfulness'. I wonder how you will like *Freaks*, the latest contribution to the Hollywood 'horrors'. This has been devised specially so that a collection of side-show monstrosities – men and women without arms and legs, dwarfs, and 'living torsos' – may add their hideous deformities to the sinister atmosphere of an apparently more than usually macabre movie drama."[10]

The question as to how UK picturegoers would respond to M-G-M's *Freaks* turned out to be an academic one, for it would be banned outright by the BBFC and remain banned until 1963. It faced a rough ride in the USA too, its running time pared down by some 25 minutes before achieving a New York run in July 1932. Within a month, it was pulled from distribution and, much later, offloaded onto exploitation distributor Dwain Esper for a mere $50,000, finding a new life in provincial grindhouses under such titles as *Nature's Mistakes* and *The Monster Show*.

In Mme Tetrallini's circus, beautiful trapeze artist Cleopatra marries doting midget Hans only to start systematically poisoning him in order to get hold of the money he has recently inherited. Hans soon becomes wise to her plan, however, and the assembled community of circus 'freaks' decide to teach her a lesson, performing appalling surgery on Cleopatra and her strong man confederate, Hercules, at the height of a violent thunderstorm.

In the closing months of 1931, *Freaks* had shared M-G-M's stages with such films as 'Woody' Van Dyke's above-mentioned *Tarzan, the Ape Man* and George Fitzmaurice's luscious Garbo vehicle *Mata Hari*. The latter would earn a profit of over $1 million; the *Freaks* fiasco, by contrast, incurred a loss of $164,000. But, having eagerly re-engaged Tod Browning after the smash success of *Dracula*, the quixotic Irving Thalberg had sanctioned the film on the admirable principle that he would shoulder the responsibility if it turned out badly. For his part, Browning presumably considered *Freaks* the logical solution to the calamitous loss of his old associate Lon Chaney. Deprived of Chaney's gallery of grotesques conjured from a make-up box, the obvious answer was to hire the genuine article.

The film saw Browning in his element, directing a tale of the sideshows in which he'd grown up, basing his scenario on a 1923 story by Tod Robbins of *The Unholy Three* fame, and climaxing the grisly business with an orgy of castration – and not merely the symbolic variety this time. The stories surrounding the film are well known: writer F Scott Fitzgerald throwing up when faced with Browning's cast in the studio canteen, Metro production supervisor Harry Rapf trying to get the production shut down, audience members at the film's LA preview running out in horror. Simply put, Depression audiences who had quaked at the

decorous villainies of Lugosi's Dracula weren't ready for such a thoroughgoing exercise of Browning's trademark obsessions. As Leonard Wolf aptly puts it, "*Freaks* has attained a kind of immortality as an example of what happens when a great director makes a monumental error of judgment. He leaves behind a film that squirms with the vitality of incoherence."[11]

The film's squirm-inducing incoherence stems from a fatal double-standard at its core, a double-standard that has been debated back and forth for decades. Why did Browning spend an entire film pointing up the winning humanity of his disabled cast members only to undo all his good work in a Grand Guignol climax of unparalleled ghastliness? Why did he turn a plea for understanding into the most garish kind of exploitation, returning motion pictures to the sideshows from which they sprang?

In truth, there are plenty of signs from the outset that Browning's interest in his cast was essentially voyeuristic and prurient, pandering to the very same leanings in his audience by showing off, in the words of the film's carnival barker, a host of "living, breathing monstrosities." Living and breathing, perhaps – but not, as Browning is at pains to point out, fully functional. The entire film turns on questions of repressed and frustrated sexuality, questions posed, more often than not, in the nudge-nudge tones of a garrulous, loud-suited barfly. As well as making fun of the trans-sexual Josephine-Joseph ("Don't get her sore, or he'll bust you in the nose"), the film directs plenty of pre-Code sniggers at the Siamese twins and the complicated aspirations of their 'healthy' fiancés. Indeed, the plot strand that motors the whole film is equally salacious – that a midget could have any realistic hopes of satisfying "the most beautiful big woman [he's] ever seen."

Referred to at one point as "that big horse," Cleopatra is a memorable distillate of sexual evil as played by Olga Baclanova, who replaced the originally mooted Myrna Loy. (In the same way, Venus and Hercules went to Leila Hyams and Henry Victor rather than the hoped-for Jean Harlow and Victor McLaglen.) And the big-boned, vaguely mannish allure of Cleopatra serves notice that Browning's web of sexual ambiguity will extend even to the 'normal' characters. We have the clownish Rosco togged up as a blonde-wigged "Roman lady"; the affable Phroso kidding Venus with the line, "You shoulda caught me before my operation"; even Hercules absent-mindedly perfuming himself with an atomiser confiscated from Venus.

This blurring of the 'normal' and the 'abnormal' reaches critical mass in, as a silent picture intertitle

FREAKS

M-G-M 1931
61 minutes
production began 9 November
banned in the UK

Cinematographer: Merritt B Gerstad*; Art Directors: Cedric Gibbons*, Merrill Pyer*; Editor: Basil Wrangell*; Sound: Gavin Burns*; Screenplay: Willis Goldbeck*, Leon Gordon*; Dialogue: Edgar Allan Woolf*, Al Boasberg* ('suggested by Tod Robbins' story Spurs'); Executive Producers: Irving Thalberg*, Harry Sharrock*; Director-Producer: Tod Browning

Wallace Ford (Phroso); Leila Hyams (Venus); Olga Baclanova (Cleopatra); Rosco Ates (Roscoe); Henry Victor (Hercules); Harry Earles (Hans); Daisy Earles (Frieda); Rose Dione (Madame Tetrallini); Daisy Hilton, Violet Hilton (Siamese twins); Schlitze (herself); Josephine Joseph (half woman-half man), Johnny Eck (half boy); Frances O'Connor (armless girl [fair]); Peter Robinson (human skeleton); Olga Roderick (bearded lady); Koo Koo (herself); [Prince] Randion (The Living Torso); Martha Morris (armless girl [dark]); Zip and Pip [Jennie Lynn, Elvira Snow] (pinheads); Elizabeth Green (bird girl); Angelo Rossitto (Angeleno); Edward Brophy, Matt McHugh (Rollo Brothers); uncredited: Ernie Adams (sideshow patron); Louise Beavers (maid); Sidney Bracey (butler); Albert Conti (Dubois [landowner]); Murray Kinnell (sideshow barker); Michael Visaroff (Jean [groundsman])

Here is a horror picture which out-horrors anything heretofore conceived to make you gasp. *Freaks* is by far the most daringly executed plot we have ever seen on the screen. Only people with exceptionally strong constitutions can sit through it. *Frankenstein* is a bed-time story by comparison. *Motion Picture*

Tod Browning. I loved him. He say, "... Now I show you with whom you are going to play. But don't faint." I say, "Why should I faint?" So he takes me and shows me all the freaks there ... He shows me little by little and I could not look. I wanted to cry when I saw them. They have such nice faces, but it is so terrible. *Olga Baclanova* [quoted in Kobal, *People Will Talk*, 1985]

"Can a full grown woman truly love a midget?" Olga Baclanova doses Harry Earles with poison in *Freaks* (1931)

dubs it, 'The Wedding Feast'. The tableau here is surely one of the most painful ever filmed – the joyful passing of a 'Loving Cup' from mouth to mouth, the bizarre chant of "Gooble-gobble, we accept her, one of us," and Cleopatra's final rebellion at the attempted blurring, surging back from the table with a convulsive cry of "Dirty – slimy – FREAKS!" And, in a truly awful moment, we realise that she has flung the contents of the Loving Cup over the diminutive Angeleno, supplementing the gesture with the terrible words, "You FILTH! Make me one of you, will you?"

In the climax, of course, the 'freaks' do exactly that, advancing inexorably on their victims through the mud and slush of a nocturnal cloudburst, in the process becoming exactly what Cleopatra described them as: dirty and slimy. Unforgettable in its impact, Browning's handling of the scene remains a masterpiece of horror. So much so that, after it, the shock revelation of Cleopatra's fate can only seem like an Absurdist punchline. Squawking like Emil Jannings in *The Blue Angel*, she is not only horribly disfigured but also kitted out in a feathery chicken-suit, making it clear that her bottom half has somehow gone missing. In an excised shot, Browning indicated that Hercules, too – looking pudgy and singing in an unnaturally high voice – had been relieved of his genitalia.

The brutally symbolic justice of the sideshow is here in perfect accord with the remorseless logic of the film's sexual preoccupations. Ironically, in making a film aimed so unwaveringly at the groin, Browning succeeded only in emasculating himself. For, after it, he would be widely dismissed as a spent force in the film industry, never again recapturing the power and privilege he had formerly enjoyed.

The shocking debacle that was *Freaks* helped to consolidate industry suspicions that, for all the financial success of *Frankenstein* and prestige value of *Dr Jekyll and Mr Hyde*, the horror craze was a passing one and was already on the wane. To some extent, these suspicions were motivated by wishful thinking, given the censorship headaches involved in making horror pictures and the swelling opposition to them voiced by women's groups and religious organisations.

Though published by the hard-line Catholic Martin Quigley (one of the key architects of the 1930 Production Code), the *Motion Picture Herald* of 23 July 1932 was relatively unfazed by M-G-M's disastrous horror show, merely observing that "If *Freaks* has caused a furore in certain censor circles the fault lies with the manner in which it was campaigned to the public. I found it to be an interesting and entertaining picture, and I did not have nightmares, nor did I attempt to murder any of my relatives."[12] The reference to "the manner in which it was campaigned" reflected a growing conviction that, if horror films had to be on the agenda, the ballyhoo surrounding them should show good taste and not brandish the red rag of 'horror' too brazenly. That half the trouble caused by horror pictures was vested in their lurid advertising was to be a long-lived argument; as late as the mid-1980s, the UK censor banned a number of so-called 'video nasties' as much for their over-the-top packaging as their frequently innocuous content.

UNUSUAL TIMES, UNUSUAL PICTURES

Whatever coy euphemisms were carefully introduced into a film's advertising, the vociferous complaints of moral reformers continued unabated, occasionally being echoed by ordinary filmgoers. One such was 'TMW' of New York City, who, in the course of *Motion Picture*'s $20 letter for May 1932, opined that "we must be on the high road to becoming a race of morons. Witness the success of the recent horror pictures ... I am no pessimist, but it is my opinion that we are fast approaching the time when nothing but that which is of a sadistic tendency will satisfy our warped emotions. In plain words, we are harking back to the dark ages, and the producers are serving us along those lines."[13]

TMW's reference to the dark ages was an instructive one, given that the worsening grip of the Depression had led several film critics to speculate on the peculiar appeal of horror pictures at a time of national crisis. After all, the two great exemplars of Hollywood's horror craze were figures of peculiar, if unspoken, potency to Depression-hit audiences: at one extreme of the monsters' social scale, there was the smoothly predatory aristocrat Count Dracula; at the other, the grotesquely disadvantaged proletarian represented by Frankenstein's Monster.

And in the summer of 1932, an independently produced horror picture came along that introduced a still more diabolical figure – necromantic zombie master 'Murder' Legendre, whose solution to the labour crisis was splendid in its simplicity. With its Haitian sugar mill staffed entirely by dead people, *White Zombie* was urged on exhibitors with the knowing tag-line "Unusual Times Demand Unusual Pictures."

In Haiti, plantation owner Beaumont becomes obsessed by the beautiful Madeline Short, who is soon to marry another man. With the help of voodoo master 'Murder' Legendre, Beaumont contrives her apparent death at the altar, only to himself fall victim to Legendre's paralysing drugs at the latter's clifftop castle. Legendre is finally toppled over

the precipice by the half-zombified Beaumont, leaving the recovered Madeline in the arms of husband Neil.

Made in under a fortnight for $62,500 (a phenomenal sum by Poverty Row standards), *White Zombie* achieved the distinction of being distributed by United Artists, and its impressive box-office takings helped to quell the trade papers' idea that the horror craze was over.

The Halperin brothers (director Victor and producer Edward) had got together a remarkable array of talent – cinematographer Arthur Martinelli, 'glass shot' experts Conrad Tritschler and Howard Anderson, British novelist Herbert Farjeon as dialogue director, and Dracula himself, Bela Lugosi, in the one-dimensional but iconic role of 'Murder' Legendre. In addition, night shooting at Universal City yielded numerous sets from such films as *Dracula*, *Frankenstein* and *The Hunchback of Notre Dame* (even the ecclesiastical chairs from *The Cat and the Canary* make an appearance), together with the participation of Universal's make-up ace Jack Pierce. Sporting stellar production values, a host of inventive camera effects and a uniquely ominous atmosphere, the result was touted, in true *Dracula-Svengali* mode, as "The Weirdest Love Story in 2000 Years."

Fitted by Pierce with an exaggerated widow's peak and eyebrows almost as extravagant as those in *Murders in the Rue Morgue*, Lugosi is on top form here in a role expertly tailored to his bizarre brand of screen magnetism. Carving a wax image of Madeline prior to melting it in the flame of a gas lamp, he casts a conspiratorial upward glance at his beady-eyed vulture familiar, later appearing superimposed in Madeline's wine glass as she stammers out the words "I see Death." Towards the end, having trapped the unwary Beaumont merely because he "refused to shake hands once," Legendre accompanies his victim's slow petrification with the self-amused observation that "It is unfortunate you are no longer able to speak. I should be interested to hear you describe your symptoms." And, to add to his Mephistophelean aura, Martinelli favours Lugosi with some of the most hypnotic close-ups of his career.

Simply put, Lugosi's Legendre is the very image of a fairytale Demon King. Madeline, too – subsumed in "lethargic coma or lifeless sleep" – is Sleeping Beauty in the flimsy disguise of a 1920s flapper. Nor do the mythic overtones of Garnett Weston's script stop there; as well as replaying the charnel house details of *Romeo and Juliet*, Weston works a sinister first-reel twist on *Cinderella* when Legendre appropriates Madeline's scarf in place of a discarded slipper.

For all its nominal setting in 1932, the film has an atmosphere of fusty timelessness (if that isn't a contradiction in terms) that is much enhanced by Victor Halperin's ossified taste in actors. As well as insisting that only 15 per cent of a talkie should be composed of dialogue, he retained the services of three actors strongly identified with silent pictures.

WHITE ZOMBIE

Amusement Securities / a Halperin production
1932
69 minutes
produced March

Cinematographer: Arthur Martinelli; Art Director: Ralph Berger; Editor: Harold MacLernon; Sound: L E Clark; Special Effects: Harold Anderson; Art Effects: Conrad Tritschler; Make-up: Jack P Pierce, Carl Axcelle; Music: Guy Bevier Williams, Xavier Cugat*; Musical Director: Abe Meyer*; Production Assistant: Sidney Marcus; Technical Director: Herbert Glazer; Assistant Director: William Cody; Dialogue Director: Herbert Farjeon; Screenplay: Garnett Weston; Producer: Edward Halperin; Director: Victor Halperin

Bela Lugosi (Murder Legendre); Madge Bellamy (Madeline); Joseph Cawthorn (Dr Bruner); Robert Frazer (Beaumont); John Harron (Neil); Brandon Hurst (Silver); George Burr MacAnnan (Von Gelder [zombie]); Frederick Peters (Chauvin [zombie]); Annette Stone (first maid); John Printz (Latour [zombie]), Dan Crimmins (Pierre [witchdoctor]); Claude Morgan (Minister of the Interior [zombie]); John Fergusson (Marquis [zombie]); Velma Gresham (second maid); uncredited: Clarence Muse (coach driver)

Necromancers waved their sinister hands from the screen of the Rivoli yesterday [29 July 1932] ... And half way through the picture ... an actor wistfully remarked: "The whole thing has me confused; I just can't understand it." That was, as briefly as can be expressed, the legend for posterity of *White Zombie*. *New York Times*

We never went off the Universal lot. Even the night exteriors on the backwoods roads were shot there. All the night shots were night for night. My uncle always made sure it was possible to recognise the source of the light in those scenes. In so many shows today they just ignore the light source.
Enzo Martinelli (second assistant cameraman) [quoted in *American Cinematographer*, February 1988]

Brandon Hurst waits on Bela Lugosi, Madge Bellamy and Robert Frazer in *White Zombie* (1932)

As the equivocal Beaumont, Robert Frazer is an almost camp figure, complete with permed hair and jodhpurs. Madge Bellamy's Madeline has the chalk-white face and bee-stung lips of a corpse even before her interment. And Neil is played by John Harron (brother of the more famous Bobby) with the loose-limbed amiability of a fully paid-up Drones Club member.

The film abounds in genuinely creepy set-pieces: Legendre and Beaumont advancing through cruciform grave-markers to a nocturnal chorus of frogs, dogs and cicadas; Madeline undergoing a funeral in reverse, her zombie entourage processing over a hill overhung by Spanish moss; Neil venturing gingerly into her now empty tomb, the camera lingering for a seeming eternity before his traumatised scream rings out from within. Showing Beaumont the zombie workers in his sugar mill, Legendre points out sardonically that "They work faithfully. They are not worried about long hours." Nor are they distracted when one of their number topples soundlessly into the cane-shredder, a horrid little aside slipped in by Halperin with cunningly underplayed insouciance. On top of this, Halperin finds room for a brief spot of pre-Code erotica. With the virginal Madeline dressed only in her lingerie and wedding veil, the scene caters for a very particular taste.

Artwork for *Drums o' Voodoo* (1933) under its 1940 reissue title *She Devil*

If Legendre is the Demon King, he must necessarily be counterbalanced by a suitably omniscient Van Helsing figure, and one of the wonders of the film is that the benevolent Dr Bruner, brilliantly played by Joseph Cawthorn, provides a very light dusting of 'comic relief' without losing any of his required authority. Admittedly, he's lumbered with a tedious running gag regarding a refill for his Meerschaum pipe (regrettably, the film even winds up on a repetition of it). But his 'opposite side of the same coin' credentials are firmly established when he notes that "Because I'm a preacher, they [the locals] think I'm a magician." He then explains the whole business of zombiedom to Neil in a remarkable uninterrupted take that lasts a whopping five minutes. We're treated next to some stunning glass shots of Bruner and Neil on the beach, dwarfed by the towering hulk of Legendre's clifftop fortress, and Legendre finally gets his just deserts in a stirring finale staged in the castle itself.

The business of zombiedom had been explained to the public at large by William Seabrook's anthropological study *The Magic Island*, published in 1929. In introducing the concept to cinemagoers, the Halperin brothers triggered the production of two ultra-low budget voodoo pictures that somehow managed to ignore zombies altogether. In March 1933, director Arthur Hoerl (scenarist, ten years previously, of *The Drums of Jeopardy*) took J Augustus Smith's one-act play *Louisiana* and turned it into a 70-minute picture shot at New York's Atlas Soundfilm Studios. Also known in production as *Voodoo*, the result was released to the nation's limited pool of 'black' cinemas as *Drums o' Voodoo* over 12 months later.

In it, Laura Bowman is a voodoo priestess, Aunt Hagar, who settles the hash of a duplicitous seducer by striking him blind; Gus Smith himself plays the community's ex-con minister. The film survives only in mutilated condition, but enough remains to make its attribution to International Stageplay Pictures seem unusually apt. Like Selig's *Dr Jekyll and Mr Hyde* from 1908, it's essentially a filmed record of a current stage production, with even exteriors rendered as painted flats. As 'Bige' put it in *Variety*, "picture appears to have been produced in one room, not too large."

A couple of months later, Gus Smith turned up in a supporting role in *Chloe – Love is Calling You*, which began shooting at Florida's Sun Haven Studios in the last week of May 1933. This is a very different proposition, with an abundance of sunlit location photography, an apparently unfaked alligator fight for the mixed-race hero, and a sustained score from Erno Rapee, the man who contributed a saccharine love song to Universal's *The Man Who Laughs*. Indeed, the picture owed its inception to another saccharine love song, George Henninger's famous 1927 ballad 'Chloe'.

Though by turns static and episodic, *Chloe* is slickly made and has an engaging star in Olive Borden, a former Mack Sennett bathing beauty who here plays

the titular Chloe, bedevilled by the knowledge that, though not looking it, she is of black parentage. "You's black as your blood, you is," insists her voodoo-practising 'mother' Mandy (Georgette Harvey). But in an apparently joyful resolution that leaves her free to marry her whiter-than-white lover, it's discovered that Chloe is actually Betty Anne, long-lost daughter of the white-suited Colonel against whom Mandy has been plotting. The Colonel himself dismisses voodoo as "just a mixture of savagery, gin, mumbo-jumbo and drum beating." But the film's climactic ritual is a bit more impressive than that, with a blazing fire in a forest clearing, Mandy resplendent in top hat and tails, and Chloe stretched out as a helpless human sacrifice.

Much of *Chloe*'s relative proficiency can be attributed to its slumming director Marshall Neilan, who, according to the film's UK pressbook, "devoted several months to a personal investigation of voodoo practices" and in the film "duplicated in minute detail several voodoo ceremonials that he witnessed." Whatever the truth of this – and despite the film's unequivocally racist message – *Chloe* works up quite a head of steam in its last-reel contrast between an all-white garden party and the untrammelled wildness in the woods.

Also starting production in the last week of May 1933 was a 'black' subject with considerably loftier aspirations. Shot independently in New York, Dudley Murphy's *The Emperor Jones* was based on Eugene O'Neill's 1920 play of the same name and distributed by United Artists. Considerably simplifying O'Neill's original, the film was nevertheless a controversial one in its day, with a Pullman porter (Paul Robeson) becoming an island dictator, being rebelled against by his fellow blacks, suffering *Macbeth*-style ghostly visions, being bedevilled by a witch doctor and finally succumbing to a silver bullet. By the time of the film's release in September, attentive picturegoers may have noted its similarity to a couple of bona-fide horror pictures, *Kongo* and *Island of Lost Souls*. In those, however, the role of jungle and/or island overlord was less provocative, being entrusted to white men.

Synthetic Flesh and the British at Home

Under youthful production head Darryl F Zanuck, Warner Bros had acquired a reputation for gritty and fast-moving pictures bearing the urgent stamp of tomorrow's tabloid headlines. Via Mervyn LeRoy's *Little Caesar* and William Wellman's *The Public Enemy*, Zanuck had launched a gangster cycle viewed by the MPPDA with just as much alarm as the horror mode inaugurated by Universal. Warners had made a few isolated chillers of their own in the dying days of the silent era – the all-talking *The Terror*, two versions of *The Gorilla*, Benjamin Christensen's three haunted house pictures – but such fripperies now seemed a world away from the urban realism of the Warners house style.

But the proven profitability of macabre subjects was something no Hollywood studio could afford to ignore, and, in casting about for a new shocker subject, Warners hit upon a 1928 play, *Terror*, written by Howard W Comstock and Allen C Miller. Reaching Broadway on 9 February 1931, it had been retitled *Doctor X* to avoid confusion with the Edgar Wallace property filmed by Warners three years previously. The studio's film version got under way in March 1932 under the direction of Hungarian émigré Michael Curtiz. To force this bizarre tale of a cannibalistic serial killer into the prevailing Warners mould, it had become a newspaper story. Who better, then, to play the wisecracking reporter than Lee Tracy, who had played Hildy Johnson in the original Broadway production of *The Front Page*.

The so-called Moon Killer has struck six times in as many months, partially eating his victims and using a scalpel unique to Dr Xavier's Academy of Surgical Research. Retreating to his Long Island mansion, Xavier assembles his staff in order to identify the guilty man. The culprit is revealed as Dr Wells, previously not suspected thanks to his missing arm but in fact the inventor of a synthetic flesh designed to "make a crippled world whole again."

As Hollywood's first out-and-out shocker to sport an aggressively contemporary setting (excepting the half-arsed modernisation applied to *Dracula* and *Frankenstein*), *Doctor X* is well served by its typically hard-nosed veneer of Warners realism. Via Tracy's feckless newshound, comments are passed on both Prohibition (in the basement of Xavier's palatial home, he stumbles across a still and murmurs, "I wonder where they bottle it?") and the Depression itself ("I've got to get something on this story," he pleads, "or I'll have to join the army of the unemployed"). Though saddled with some dismally inane gags, Tracy was no doubt a personable identification figure to 1930s audiences; his final 'worm turns' tussle with the Moon Killer reportedly elicited screams of panic wherever the picture played.

The film also saw the horror debuts of Lionel Atwill and Fay Wray, the former a sleek 47-year-old Englishman (hailing from Croydon) who had earned a high reputation on Broadway, the latter an

The deeply dubious staff members of Dr Xavier's Academy of Surgical Research: Harry Beresford, John Wray, Arthur Edmund Carewe and Preston Foster in *Doctor X* (1932)

DOCTOR X

Warner Bros-First National 1932
77 minutes; shot in b/w and Technicolor versions
production began 19 March

Cinematographers: Richard Towers (b/w), Ray Rennahan (colour); Art Director: Anton Grot; Editor: George Amy; Sound Recording: Robert B Lee*; Photographic Effects: Fred Jackman*; Make-up: Perc Westmore*, Ray Romero*; Mask Effects: Max Factor Co; Music: Bernhard Kaun*; Vitaphone Orchestra conducted by Leo F Forbstein; Technical Adviser: Dr C E Warrener*; Screenplay: Earl Baldwin, Robert Tasker (from the play by Howard W Comstock and Allen C Miller); Screen Treatment: George Rosener*; Production Supervisor: Hal B Wallis*; In Charge of Production: Darryl F Zanuck*; Director: Michael Curtiz

Lionel Atwill (Dr Xavier); Fay Wray (Joanne Xavier); Lee Tracy (Lee Taylor); Preston Foster (Dr Wells); John Wray (Dr Haines); Harry Beresford (Dr Duke); Arthur Edmund Carewe (Dr Rowitz); Leila Bennett (Mamie [maid]); Robert Warwick (Police Commissioner Stevens); George Rosener (Otto [butler]); Willard Robertson (O'Halloran [detective]); Thomas Jackson (editor); Harry Holman (Mike [cop on the beat]); Mae Busch (madame at speak-easy); Tom Dugan (Deputy Sheriff); uncredited: Josephine Gillerman (murdered woman); Selmer Jackson (night editor)

Manufactured thrills in a typical 'horror' film. The chief attraction is some excellent comedy relief by Lee Tracy ... The film's big moments are obviously intended to be those showing the doctor's amazing experiments. But ... there is a bigger thrill for filmgoers who respond to horror stuff laid on with a trowel in the actual revelation of the murderer – a ghastly scene of its type. *Film Weekly* [UK]

The primary purpose of set designing is to establish the mood of the story. In *Doctor X*, that mood is mystery, of course, but we have tried to build menace into the sets. Those criss-crossed attic beams, for example, give a cramped sensation even before you know that beneath them a man is in danger. Anton Grot [quoted in original pressbook]

auburn-haired 24-year-old from Alberta who had come to prominence opposite Erich von Stroheim in *The Wedding March*. As Xavier's plucky daughter Joan, Wray gives as good as she gets in several Benedick-and-Beatrice exchanges with the persistent Tracy; she also shares a brief seashore idyll with him in a delightful scene shot at Laguna Beach. As Dr Xavier, Atwill is essentially the reddest of red herrings but brings a strangely kinky undertow to apparently innocuous lines like "Locked in the human brain is a little world all its own," an approach that was to become his trademark.

Xavier's staff are a highly entertaining bunch, too. Played by former opera singer Preston Foster, Dr Wells keeps a living human heart in his laboratory and coolly detaches a rubber glove from his empty left-hand sleeve. The scar-faced Dr Rowitz (Arthur Edmund Carewe) has lost an eye and stares out from behind a smoked-glass monocle, meanwhile speaking of his researches into "lunacy – from the word luna, meaning the moon." Dr Duke (Harry Beresford) is a whingeing, wheelchair-bound neurotic with a club-foot. And Dr Haines (John Wray) is first shown in Mephistophelean silhouette and has a copy of a saucy magazine, 'French Art', concealed among his research papers. Even Xavier's butler Otto is creepily lit for maximum beetle-browed effect, though his cod-sinister antics seem to have been included merely to provide the audience with another red herring and actor-writer George Rosener with a consolation prize for having his original *Doctor X* screenplay rejected.

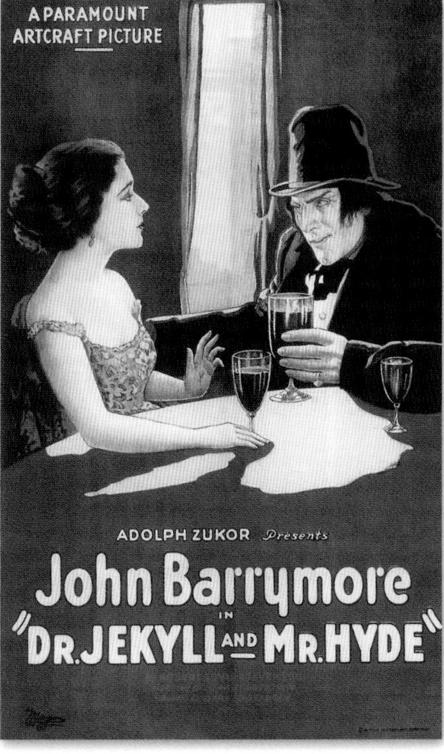

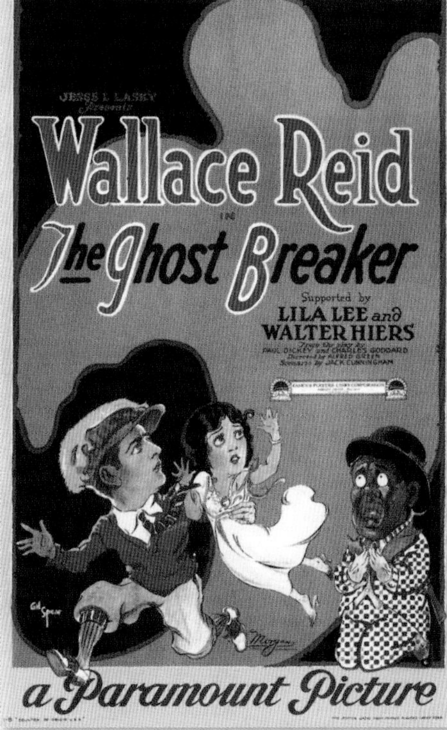

ABOVE LEFT: Poe's murderer with attendant memento mori in *The Avenging Conscience* (1914)

ABOVE RIGHT: Magnetic advertising for the first of 16 instalments of *The Crimson Stain Mystery* (1916)

FAR LEFT: Nita Naldi and John Barrymore advertising the 1920 smash *Dr Jekyll and Mr Hyde*

LEFT: Early horror-comedy, direct from the stage – *The Ghost Breaker* (1922)

TOP LEFT: Johnny Arthur meets Walter James, one of several nightmarish characters featured in *The Monster* (1924)

TOP RIGHT: Sumptuous Spanish artwork for *The Magician*, filmed on the French Riviera in 1926

ABOVE: British flyer for M-G-M's Hawthorne adaptation, *The Scarlet Letter* (1926)

RIGHT: Emily Fitzroy, Jewel Carmen, Jack Pickford, Louise Fazenda and Eddie Gribbon, all in search of *The Bat* (1925)

Three from 1927 – Gertrude Astor and Flora Finch in *The Cat and the Canary*, Lon Chaney and Joan Crawford in *The Unknown*, and Conrad Veidt and Olga Baclanova in *The Man Who Laughs*

RIGHT: Thelma Todd assailed by Montagu Love in *The Haunted House* (1928)

BELOW LEFT: Reissue lobby card for *Dracula* (1930), featuring Edward Van Sloan and Bela Lugosi

BELOW RIGHT: British programme cover advertising *Frankenstein* (1931) during the film's first London run

BOTTOM LEFT: Queen Victoria joins Holmes Herbert and Fredric March in *Dr Jekyll and Mr Hyde* (1931)

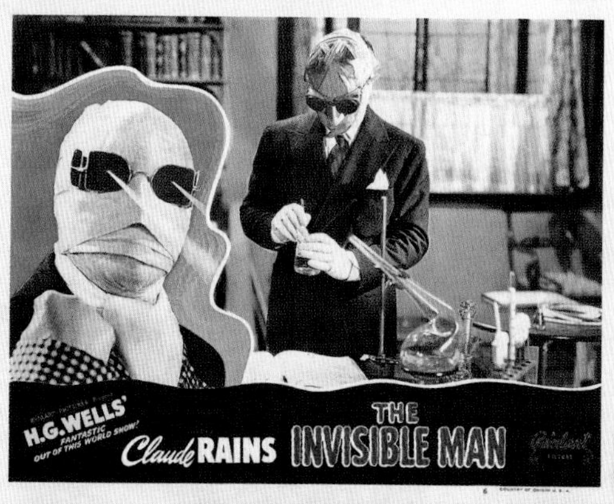

Top left: Boris Karloff traumatises Bramwell Fletcher in *The Mummy* (1932)

Above left: Claude Rains as the titular maniac in a reissue lobby card for *The Invisible Man* (1933)

Above right: Paramount's sadist extravaganza *Murders in the Zoo* (1933)

Left: Kathleen Burke, Richard Arlen and assorted beast-men in *Island of Lost Souls* (1932)

LEFT: Columbia's West Indies melodrama *Black Moon* (1934)

ABOVE: Peter Lorre and Frances Drake in the classic amputation melodrama *Mad Love* (1935)

BELOW: Universal's magisterial super-sequel, *Bride of Frankenstein* (1935)

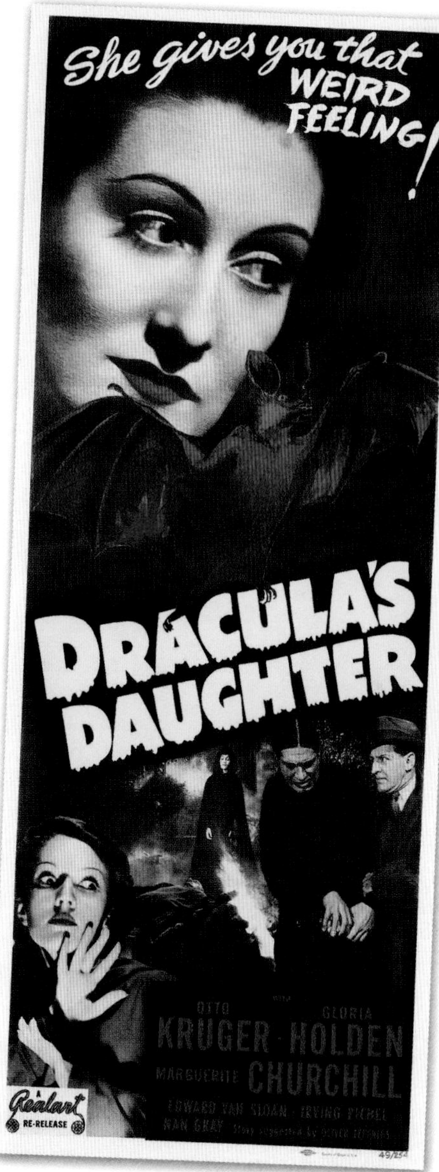

ABOVE AND RIGHT: Striking reissue artwork for *The Walking Dead* (1935), with Karloff, and *Dracula's Daughter* (1936), in which Gloria Holden provided the 'weird feeling'

BELOW LEFT: *Son of Frankenstein* (1938) kickstarted a major genre renaissance

BELOW RIGHT: Warners' expertise in crime stories was mixed with mad science for *The Return of Doctor X* (1939)

TOP LEFT: Nina Mae McKinney, 'the black Garbo', in *The Devil's Daughter* (1939)

ABOVE: Basil Rathbone's regal profile was ideal for Sherlock Holmes in Fox's *The Hound of the Baskervilles* (1939)

LEFT: Spanish advertising for Universal's would-be historical epic *Tower of London* (1939)

BELOW: British herald for *Before I Hang* (1940)

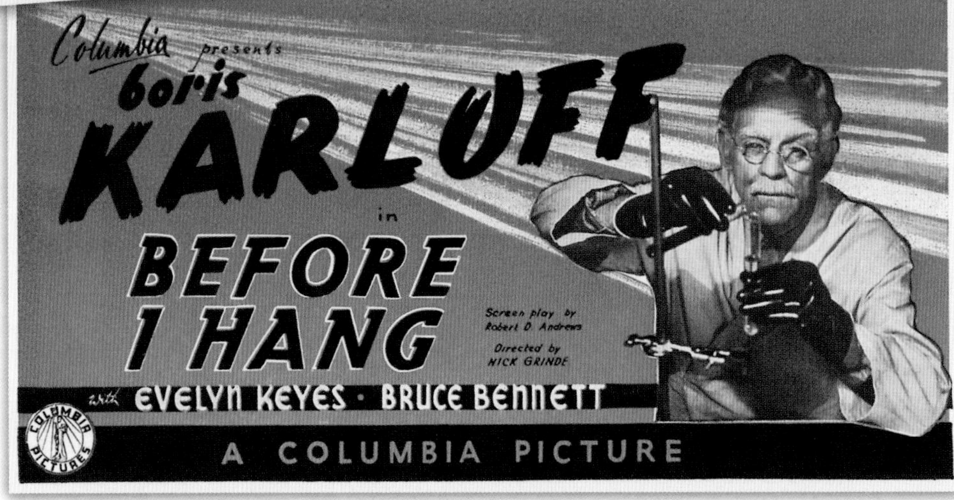

Later to prove himself one of cinema's supreme stylists in such films as *Casablanca* and *Mildred Pierce*, Curtiz comes up with a host of arresting tableaux, from the opening atmospherics of a fog-wreathed wharf to a stunning shot of the full moon as Tracy's editor leans inquiringly out of his upper window. He also makes the most of Anton Grot's brilliant set designs, which include Xavier's unfeasibly large library and an Art Deco riot of shimmering glass tubes in his climactic experiment.

A fanatical disciplinarian, Curtiz put his cast and crew through working days that lasted anything up to 20 hours, their discomfort increased by the ferocious heat of the assembled Technicolor cameras. Though the two-strip Technicolor process was already old-hat as far as audiences were concerned, Warners felt obliged to get their money's worth from a contract signed way back in 1929, and as a result *Doctor X* was made available in both colour and black-and-white versions. With Warners' own Richard Towers in charge of the monochrome cut, Technicolor specialist Ray Rennahan was brought in for the colour version, favouring considerably more bizarre camera angles and making the most of the bilious green-and-pink palette available to him.

Xavier's elaborate re-enactment of the killings is an appropriately bizarre transcription of a famous episode in *Hamlet*, and the Moon Killer's unscheduled appearance in it does not disappoint. With Joan in direst peril as Xavier and his associates strain madly against their experimental restraints, the scene is a dazzlingly edited tour de force. "What difference did it make if a few people had to die?" gloats the transmogrified Dr Wells. "Their flesh taught me how to manufacture arms, legs, faces that are human!"

The preceding scene of Wells' transmogrification in action is shot through pulsing electrical waves as he ladles on the revolting slop he calls "synthetic flesh." Fashioning himself a conical head like Barrymore's Hyde and then applying a wig similar to Chaney's Phantom, Wells looks down at himself in a tray of rippling chemicals like some mediaeval alchemist turned preening Narcissus. The scene achieves an apex of horror bordering, in some indefinable way, on the obscene. It certainly makes a nonsense of Warners' lily-livered advice to exhibitors to "avoid any suggestion of horror or shock" in their publicity.

One of several pre-Code features of *Doctor X* is Tracy's early visit to a waterfront cathouse, with the inimitable Mae Busch cast as the joint's peroxide madam. A silent star in the 1920s, Busch had co-starred with Lon Chaney in *The Unholy Three*. But in the talkies she became, like Anita Garvin and Thelma Todd, a familiar face in Laurel and Hardy's two-reel comedy shorts.

After *The Laurel-Hardy Murder Case* in 1930, the team made three further horror-comedies and gave Busch pride of place in the best of them. The first, *Dirty Work*, was filmed in August 1933 and cast Lucien Littlefield (the sinister doctor of *The Cat and the Canary*) as a mad scientist who regresses Ollie to a derby-wearing chimpanzee. *The Live Ghost* followed in November 1934, with the scary Walter Long as the captain of a supposedly haunted ship. Between these two came a minor masterpiece called *Oliver the Eighth*, directed by Lloyd French in January 1934 and featuring Busch as a psychopathic widow who, at the climax, is seen pulling on surgical gloves and floating obsessively down a corridor, sharpening twin kitchen knives in rhythmic strokes. The scene in which she puts a blade to the unconscious Ollie's upturned throat – with Stan trapped helpless in a closet – is, in its own way, one of the nastiest moments in 1930s cinema.

Also on the Roach lot, the Thelma Todd-ZaSu Pitts series had been supplanted by one featuring Todd and Patsy Kelly. These two faced James Parrott's *The Tin Man* in 1935, in which the bald and crabby character actor Clarence Wilson sets a robot onto them. Other comedians faced much the same spooky threats that had characterised the silent era; the fallen star Harry Langdon, for example, appeared in *Shivers* (1934) for Columbia and *Goodness, a Ghost* (1940) for RKO.

The template for all these pictures was, of course, the durable subgenre of the 'old dark house' mystery-thriller, which back in April 1932 had received its definitive treatment courtesy of Universal and James Whale. J B Priestley's 1927 novel *Benighted* had been issued in America as *The Old Dark House*, and under this generic title Whale fashioned what is arguably his masterpiece.

> *Three travellers are forced by a landslide to stay the night at the isolated Welsh home of the Femm family; later the number of benighted visitors is increased by two. As explained by the family's 102-year-old paterfamilias, all the Femms are crazy to one degree or another. Indeed, one of them is a pyromaniac and is kept locked in the attic. Until, that is, the brutish butler becomes drunk and lets him out...*

In its genteel yet devastating lampoon of the British at home, *The Old Dark House* is a film just as personal to Whale as was the circus milieu of *Freaks* to Tod Browning. Whale was here marking out a tricky territory that was to become uniquely his own, maintaining a delicate balance between humour and

Melvyn Douglas and Charles Laughton grapple with Boris Karloff in *The Old Dark House* (1932); Raymond Massey, Lillian Bond, Gloria Stuart and Eva Moore look on

THE OLD DARK HOUSE

Universal 1932
72 minutes
production began 18 April

Cinematographer: Arthur Edeson*; Art Director: Charles D Hall*; Editors: Maurice Pivar*, Clarence Kolster*; Sound: C Roy Hunter*, William Hedgcock*; Special Effects: John P Fulton*; Set Decoration: R A Gausman*; Make-up: Jack P Pierce*; Music: Bernhard Kaun*; Screenplay: Benn W Levy; Additional Dialogue: R C Sherriff* (from the novel [*Benighted*] by J B Priestly [sic]); Associate Producer: E M Asher*; Presented by: Carl Laemmle; Producer: Carl Laemmle Jr; Director: James Whale

Boris Karloff (Morgan); Melvyn Douglas (Penderel); Charles Laughton (Sir William Porterhouse); Lillian Bond (Gladys); Ernest Thesiger (Horace Femm); Eva Moore (Rebecca Femm); Raymond Massey (Philip Waverton); Gloria Stuart (Margaret Waverton); John [Elspeth] Dudgeon (Sir Roderick Femm); Brember Wills (Saul Femm)

The vexed question of the horror film again rears its ugly head (and rears is the word) with the arrival this weekend of the latest James Whale-Boris Karloff excursion into the realms of the unnatural. To give them their due, Messrs Whale and Karloff have progressed since the day when they dabbled in the crude though diverting sensations of *Frankenstein*. There is a new and welcome restraint about their work. *Film Weekly* [UK]

***The Old Dark House* was very interesting for a Southern California girl like myself. My first impression of James [Whale] was that he was very austere, very cold, very 'English'; very removed from the scene ... The English contingent had tea at 11 and four, and neither Melvyn [Douglas] nor I were ever asked!** Gloria Stuart [quoted in Mank, *Hollywood Cauldron*, 1994]

horror through an artful dose of Old World irony. Though luxuriating in sunny California, he was perfectly placed to recreate a typically inclement night in the old country. "West End Stars in Hollywood's British Film" announced Britain's *Film Weekly* on 20 May, *Kinematograph Weekly* following this up on 3 August with "Universal Goes British." Unsurprisingly, the result did a great deal better in the UK than in America. Priestley himself, meanwhile, took British producers to task for not picking up the novel themselves.

In truth, Priestley was much better served by the deluxe treatment Junior Laemmle accorded his story; nothing comparable could have been produced by, say, Julius Hagen, whose outfit at Twickenham Studios had a reputation at the time for blood-and-thunder subjects. Priestley was also done a favour (though he most certainly wouldn't have agreed) by Whale and his playwright associates Benn Levy and R C Sherriff, who skimped on much of the novel's populist philosophising and focused instead on the grim comedy to be had from the clash of five 'normal' Britishers with the five grotesque Femms.

In the person of Roger Penderel – "war generation, slightly soiled" – the film retains just enough of the jaded post-war malaise that Priestley's novel sought to anatomise. Played with a nicely self-amused twinkle by Melvyn Douglas, he's first discovered in typically nonchalant pose in the back of the

Wavertons' car, rain lashing down as his friends engage in a beautifully observed marital spat in the front. And when, in a memorably forbidding shot, the exterior of the Femm house is picked out in the Wavertons' headlights, we see that designer Charles D Hall has rightly eschewed the baroque extravagances of *Dracula* and *The Cat and the Canary*. Instead the house is a lumpen, featureless block of a uniquely British variety, with shallow steps leading to a front door behind which lurks the film's top-billed star.

Though the picture was put together as a vehicle for Boris Karloff, Whale smoothly undercuts the mute and half-mad butler, Morgan, on his very first appearance. Opening the door to disclose only a sliver of his distorted face, he mumbles incoherently and closes the door again, prompting a sublimely droll response from Penderel: "Even Welsh ought not to sound like that." Later, Karloff indulges in some characteristically eloquent mime while serving at the dinner table, lingering with the vaguest sense of sexual threat over Gloria Stuart's luminous Margaret Waverton. And when Morgan finally gets her alone, he proves a terrifying antagonist, Whale cutting in for his trademark three-step view (moving from a close-up of Morgan's face to a tight focus on first his eyes and then his mouth) and giving us a good look at Jack Pierce's brilliantly understated make-up design.

The real focus, however, is on Whale's West End imports Ernest Thesiger and Eva Moore. As the emaciated Horace, Thesiger is given a grand entrance down the central staircase, his remarkable nostrils advancing into close-up as flames from the fireplace dapple the walls in a hellish glow. Whether slyly confessing to being on the run from the police or commending his sister's flower arrangements moments before tossing them on the fire, Thesiger is a desiccated delight, precisely encapsulating a particular kind of lapsed late-Victorian, sniping acidulously at society's restrictions but too craven to do anything about them.

While Horace looks like a malnourished provincial bank manager, his sister Rebecca has the fleshy, leathery look of a gypsy fortune-teller. This is a wonderful irony, given the sexual repression that simmers so dangerously beneath her lip-smacking outbursts of religious mania. Inveighing against "laughter and sin," Rebecca takes a prurient interest in Margaret's "long straight legs" and plants a liver-spotted hand on the younger woman's décolletage with the cheery observation that her flesh will rot just as surely as her bias-cut satin gown. This gruesome interview is succeeded by a Whale tour de force in which Margaret recollects Rebecca's leering face in a multiplicity of distorting mirrors, with close-ups of Morgan's watchful features cut in for good measure. After that, Whale sends Margaret flashing in panic down a corridor as lace curtains billow tempestuously at the windows – the director's explicit nod to Leni's *The Cat and the Canary*, a film he greatly admired.

The late entrance of a boorish self-made Yorkshireman and his happy-go-lucky chorus girl companion provides the cue for more wonderfully idiomatic dialogue; "I've never seen such a night in all my born natural," booms Charles Laughton, here making his Hollywood debut. But by this stage Whale is making ready for a dramatic gear-change, exchanging the whimsical eeriness of the film's first half for a straight-faced crescendo of madness and mayhem.

To this end, the entrance of the homicidal Saul has been well prepared. First, Horace has stumbled in pronouncing that "Morgan is the – the butler" (he meant to say 'keeper'). Second, Philip Waverton has gone upstairs for a lamp and, in a splendidly creepy sequence, discovered abandoned food outside a padlocked door. Finally, Margaret and Philip encounter the bedridden Sir Roderick in his plushly appointed chambers and are told that "Saul is the worst." (In one of Whale's more bizarre inside jokes, the old man is played by a piping old woman in wispy beard and striped pyjamas.) When Saul at last appears, he is at first just a disembodied hand attached to a banister, later disclosing to view the frightened features of a diminutive sexagenarian in carpet slippers.

A double-bluff is in operation, of course. Brilliantly played by Brember Wills, Saul tells the perspiring Penderel that "flames are really knives" and displays demoniac agility in trying to kill Penderel and torch the house. In the aftermath, Karloff creates a sublime effect as he sobs over Saul's broken body, and Whale has the doting Gladys, cradling the apparently dead Penderel, come out with a self-reflexive cry of "He's alive!" And so *The Old Dark House* ends, a film with a peculiarly sophisticated tone like no other before or since. As such, it was too much of an 'acquired taste' for contemporary audiences, and will disappoint seekers after mere monster mayhem even today.

A year later, the crepuscular gloom of Charles Hall's *Old Dark House* sets would be plushly refurbished for a charming quasi-horror called *Secret of the Blue Room*, a remake of the 1932 film *Das Geheimnis des blauen Zimmers*. Gloria Stuart was retained too, alongside the suave Hungarian import Paul Lukas and *Doctor X* himself, Lionel Atwill (making his first of 19 appearances for Universal). Kurt Neumann's film is set on "just the sort of night to tell good, goose-fleshy stories" – and on this cue Atwill's Baron von Helldorf recalls three unsolved deaths that occurred two decades before in the apparently haunted Blue Room of his isolated Bavarian schloss. After this, inevitably, history starts to repeat itself, with the modern intrigue containing plot points lifted from Conan Doyle's *The Hound of the Baskervilles* and *The Empty House*.

A consistently entertaining appendage to *The Old Dark House*, *Secret of the Blue Room* cost the studio a mere $69,000. Subsequent Universal managements obviously thought the property was ideally suited to cheap thrills, cranking out two bargain-basement remakes played largely for comedy – John Rawlins' *The Missing Guest* (1938) and Leslie Goodwins' *Murder in the Blue Room* (1944).

As well as making his mark at Warner Bros and Universal, Lionel Atwill was also snapped up by various Poverty Row outfits. In April 1933, for example, he made a Monogram potboiler called *The Sphinx* for director Phil Rosen. Cast as nefarious twin brothers, he no doubt delighted Depression-hit filmgoers in his choice of financier fat cats as victims. As the cop on the case puts it, "If we're gonna suspect everybody in this country that's sore on stockbrokers, we're gonna be getting out indictments for half the population of the United States."

Intriguingly, *The Sphinx* and *Secret of the Blue Room* were on release at the same time as Rouben Mamoulian's *The Song of Songs*, in which Atwill starred opposite Marlene Dietrich in one of Paramount's most lustrous offerings of the year. This was a knack that Bela Lugosi might well have envied. For, however grisly his proliferating horror vehicles, Atwill retained a strong presence in more mainstream productions, re-teaming with Dietrich in Josef von Sternberg's *The Devil is a Woman* and with director Michael Curtiz for Warners' *Captain Blood*.

SHOCKERS FROM SELZNICK

Eva Moore, the grotesque Rebecca Femm of *The Old Dark House*, had a more intimate kind of British colony around her than even James Whale could muster. Also in Hollywood that spring were her daughter Jill Esmond and son-in-law Laurence Olivier, both of them working for the quixotic David O Selznick, the recently appointed vice-president in charge of production at Hollywood's newest studio, RKO.

Esmond's RKO career yielded a peculiar little number called *Thirteen Women*, a so-called 'woman's picture' which had a female serial killer as its central figure. In fact, Vivienne Osborne in Paramount's *Supernatural* would be left to take the crown as the cinema's first 'hands-on' example of the breed. In *Thirteen Women*, Myrna Loy's Ursula Georgi goes the more subtle, and frankly improbable, route of 'willing' her victims to kill themselves via her association with C Henry Gordon's pencil-moustached Swami Yogadachi, whom she also disposes of. Based on an episodic bestseller by Tiffany Thayer, the film clocks in at just under an hour and, despite the title, only manages to tick off about half a dozen of the former sorority girls on Ursula's hit list. Among them is Irene Dunne's Laura, who eventually manages to put an end to the 'Horoscope Murders' in a train-bound climax that offers Ursula a chance to state her case. "Do you know what it means to be a half-breed, a half-caste in a world ruled by whites?" she spits. "You and the others wouldn't let me cross the colour line."

Typecast at the time in Oriental femme fatale roles, Myrna Loy accepted the Ursula Georgi part only after Zita Johann (soon to star in *The Mummy*) had been fired. Even so, Loy is strikingly shot in hypnotic close-ups comparable to Lugosi's in *White Zombie*, and she's a good deal more interesting than any of her victims. But for all its charms – including a high level of location work, even a car chase – George Archainbaud's film remains compromised by a familiar double-standard. Though apportioning a token share of sympathy to the mixed-race villainess, the film trades chiefly on depicting her as an unknowable, slant-eyed 'other', referred to by the cop on the case (Ricardo Cortez) as a "half-breed type" and by his subordinate as "that Hindu dame."

Another Tiffany Thayer adaptation of 1932 was the Fox Film Corporation's lurid Clara Bow vehicle *Call Her Savage*, and this was similarly questionable in that it attributed its heroine's ungovernable temper to her being partly Native American, a peculiar state of affairs given that Thayer's own wife had precisely the same lineage. On a lower level, the Tiffany company (no relation) released H Bruce Humberstone's *Strangers of the Evening* in May of the same year. Based on Thayer's novel *The Illustrious Corpse*, this featured no racial slurs but plenty of missing corpses in a convoluted 'old dark morgue' scenario.

Ricardo Cortez also played the lead in a cracking little murder-mystery called *The Phantom of Crestwood*, directed by J Walter Ruben and released just ahead of *Thirteen Women*. Rarely has RKO's 'A Radio Picture' masthead seemed more appropriate, for the picture was the culmination of a hook-up with NBC's Red Network, which broadcast its own radio version of the story in six episodes, starting on Friday 26 August. "Hear It on the Air! See It on the Screen! $6000 reward for solving this mystery! YOU can be the

detective in this astounding crime thriller!" screamed the ads, with the canny proviso that "all but the final chapter will be given on the air." To find out whodunit, you had to see the film.

Karen Morley and Anita Louise (on floor) under threat from a luminous death mask in *The Phantom of Crestwood* (1932)

With apparently amoral heroines proliferating in Hollywood pictures, British actress Karen Morley got the opportunity in *The Phantom of Crestwood* to provide her own version of a role model that was scandalising censor boards up and down the country. "You didn't know that you'd all been gambolling on the same green, did you?" she sneers at the four shifty-eyed men whom she has gathered at the storm-laden Casa de los Andes. She aims to 'retire' and, collectively, demands $425,000 of them to keep her mouth shut, explaining that "I'm quitting early, gentlemen, before I'm on the rummage counter." Among her former lovers are a prospective senator and a wealthy financier, the latter played by the normally incorruptible H B Warner. How satisfying it must have been for Depression audiences to see these venal hypocrites laid low, especially when Cortez – as a friendly gangster forced into playing detective on the discovery of Morley's corpse – spits out, "What a bunch of mangy pillars of society!"

Some genuinely spooky moments are provided by the perambulations of a luminous death-mask (an effect borrowed from *Murder by the Clock*), worn by the grieving father (Ivan Simpson) of a young man destroyed by Morley some weeks before. The killer, however, turns out to be Warner's patrician sister (Pauline Frederick). "The woman is insane with family pride," Cortez explains, allowing her a dignified exit as she slips serenely off a cliff. Henry Gerrard's artfully suffused photography gives the clifftop scenes a memorably melancholic quality, and only a series of flashbacks mid-film slows the pace of an unusually engaging programmer.

That RKO were serious about their horror-mystery pictures was indicated by the studio's acquisition of the legendary British crime writer Edgar Wallace, who had come to Hollywood at Selznick's invitation in November 1931. Wallace was the most successful novelist in the world and his books were already being transferred to the screen on a regular basis; one such adaptation, Columbia's *The Menace*, had been directed by Roy William Neill as recently as September, combining plastic surgery, a disfigured hero, a Hallowe'en party and numerous creepy curios with an embarrassed Bette Davis.

At RKO, Wallace was assigned a story idea by jungle picture specialist Merian C Cooper, and a preliminary screenplay called *The Beast* laid out the bare bones of a powerfully allegorical tale – a giant ape, revered as a god on an uncharted island, is brought in chains to civilisation and reasserts his dominance through the nobly suicidal gesture of scaling the recently completed Empire State Building. Nobody at this early stage can have guessed that the resultant film, *King Kong*, would rapidly acquire the status of a pop-cultural myth, least of all Edgar Wallace himself, who died suddenly on 10 February 1932.

Cooper pressed on without him, drawing his filmmaking partner Ernest B Schoedsack into the project alongside the brilliant stop-motion animator Willis O'Brien, whose work on an abandoned project called *Creation* was adapted to provide the ape with a suitable range of prehistoric adversaries. O'Brien had previously created the dinosaurs for First National's 1924 Conan Doyle adaptation *The Lost World*, as well as toying with the notion of an animated monster in a projected First National *Frankenstein* in 1928. With *King Kong*, however, he achieved a personal apotheosis, fashioning a beast whose brute ferocity co-exists with an engaging variety of human emotions, elevating him from noble savage to fully fledged tragic hero.

"We have had plays and pictures about monsters before, but never one in which the desired effect depended so completely on the increased dimensions of the monster," claimed William Troy in *The Nation*. He also drew attention to the nature of Kong's tragic flaw with the skittish observation that "if the love that Kong felt for the heroine was sacred, it suggests a weakness that hardly fits in with his other actions; and if it was, after all, merely profane, it proposes problems to the imagination that are not the less real for being crude."[14] Anatomically improbable though it is, Kong's fascination for Fay Wray makes him a profoundly vulnerable figure even as he trashes New York City, offering a cathartic orgy of civic destruction for Depression-era picturegoers to delight in.

Alongside its magnificent Max Steiner score and intriguingly self-reflexive storyline (involving a gung-ho jungle filmmaker not a million miles removed from Merian C Cooper himself), *King Kong* also has its share of horror – Kong brutally snapping open the jaws of a Tyrannosaurus, chewing and/or stomping on fleeing Skull Island natives, plucking a screaming New Yorker from her bed and, realising that she isn't Fay Wray, flinging her nonchalantly to the sidewalk. But the emotion it primarily evokes is one of awe at arguably the most immaculately conceived adventure-fantasy Hollywood has produced.

The film opened in New York City on 2 March 1933 at both the RKO Roxy and the Radio City Music Hall. Unveiled in Hollywood on the 24th, it made $2 million within 12 months – just as well, given that the previous year had entailed a bruising loss for RKO of $10 million. Its smash-hit status caused a whimsical sequel, *The Son of Kong*, to be hurried into production in April 1933, in which Kong's captor (pursued, hardly surprisingly, by outraged litigants) returns to Skull Island and encounters a chummy 12-foot specimen called Little Kong.

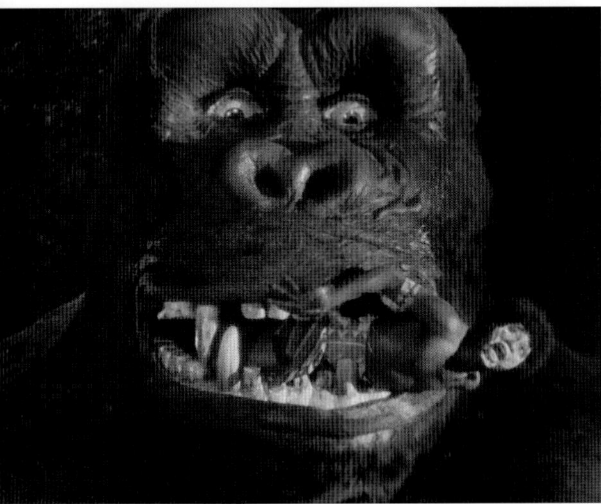

Graphic monster mayhem in the classic 1933 release *King Kong*

While Willis O'Brien was perfecting *Kong*'s stop-motion marvels, the film's live-action sequences got under way in earnest in June 1932, utilising the jungle sets (together with performers Robert Armstrong and Fay Wray) from an unusually gripping thriller Cooper and Schoedsack had dashed off the previous month. For *The Most Dangerous Game*, actor Irving Pichel – the murderous brute of *Murder by the Clock* – was brought in as dialogue director. The action sequences, meanwhile, were fashioned by Schoedsack and editor Archie Marshek into a shattering tour de force matched only by *Kong* itself. Based on an award-winning Richard Connell short story from 1924, *The Most Dangerous Game* would be subject to any number of remakes, acknowledged or otherwise. But the original – produced in three weeks for $217,000 and earning RKO a modest profit of $75,000 – remains unsurpassed.

Bob Rainsford's yacht has gone down and, having been washed ashore on an isolated tropical island, he stumbles into a Gothic fortress inhabited by a Crimean Count expelled from Russia during the revolution. They discover a shared enthusiasm for hunting, but Rainsford soon realises that Zaroff – attended now only by a few baleful-looking Cossacks – has grown bored of conventional methods and has "invented a new sensation."

Early in the film's development, Bruce Cabot, square-jawed hero of *King Kong*, had petitioned for the role of Zaroff and even commissioned special photos of himself in character. With amazing impudence, RKO's PR department would use one of these pictures in early ads for the film – ads that simultaneously name-checked the actor who actually got the part. This was West End star Leslie Banks, who was appearing on Broadway in P G Wodehouse's *Springtime for Henry* when the call from Selznick came through. Though he later turned up in any number of classic British films – from *The Man Who Knew Too Much* to *Went the Day Well?* – *The Most Dangerous Game* would remain Banks' only American picture and Zaroff his most memorable role.

Zaroff's introduction is obviously modelled, to a virtually parodic degree, on Bela Lugosi's in *Dracula*. (Schoedsack and Cooper gave the game away in

Clean-limbed leads Joel McCrea and Fay Wray threatened by West End import Leslie Banks in *The Most Dangerous Game* (1932)

this regard by elevating Connell's General Zaroff to the status of Count.) As the waterlogged Rainsford stumbles upon Zaroff's Gothic pile, the door opens apparently of its own accord and Zaroff is revealed on the massive staircase in Dracula-like evening dress. He then sashays down the steps into close-up with a self-deprecating utterance of "Welcome to my poor fortress" – and as he does so it's hard to resist the conclusion that this Count is 'gay' in a sense of the word that was only just beginning to gain currency at the time.

Aided by some very nifty dialogue by James Ashmore Creelman, Banks quickly makes clear, however, that Zaroff's orientation is a great deal more complicated and infinitely more sinister. Zaroff's motto is "Kill – then love," and while elaborating on his theory that "Only after the kill does man know the true ecstasy of love," he has a masturbatory tendency to finger the livid head-wound he received from a Cape buffalo – and this after a fetishistic fondling of a tiger skull's fangs. "We barbarians know that it is after the chase, and then only, that man revels," he explains. "What is woman – even such a woman as this – until the blood is quickened by the kill?" And his dishonourable intentions towards the beauteous Eve Trowbridge (washed up like Bob, but from a different shipwreck) are made all the more appalling when we realise that his preferred aphrodisiac prey are human beings.

THE MOST DANGEROUS GAME

RKO Radio 1932
63 minutes
production began 16 May
UK title: The Hounds of Zaroff

Cinematographer: Henry Gerrard; Art Director: Carroll Clark; Editor: Archie S Marshek; Sound: Clem Portman; Location camera: Nick Musuraca*; Make-up: Wally Westmore*; Music: Max Steiner; Screenplay: James Ashmore Creelman (from the O Henry Prize Winning Collection story by Richard Connell); Executive Producer: David O Selznick; Associate Producer: Merian C Cooper; Directors: Ernest B Schoedsack, Irving Pichel

Joel McCrea (Bob); Fay Wray (Eve); Robert Armstrong (Martin); Leslie Banks (Zaroff); Noble Johnson (Ivan); Steve Clemento (Tartar [Achmed]); William B Davidson (Captain); Dutch Hendrian (Genghis); uncredited: Clem Beauchamp (steward); James Flavin (First Mate); Charles Hall (helmsman); Hale Hamilton (Bill Woodman); Landers Stevens (Doc); Martin Turner (cook); Arnold Grey, Phil Tead (passengers)

For sustained thrills, for suspense that steadily mounts to the very last scene, this picture of the ghastly sport of a madman on a lost and lonely island will be very hard indeed to top ... A new screen personality, Leslie Banks, will trouble the dreams of sensitive folk with his remarkable characterization of the sinister huntsman. Don't miss sixty of the most exciting minutes of your life. *Motion Picture*

Leslie Banks, who played Count Zaroff in *The Most Dangerous Game*, was an astonishingly interesting actor, a very distinguished British actor. He looked like he'd had a stroke. He had something wrong with one eye and it gave him a really scary expression. It didn't hurt that picture at all!
Fay Wray [quoted in Scarlet Street, March-April 1998]

The realisation is confirmed when Eve and Bob venture into Zaroff's mysteriously locked Trophy Room. Here we have the time-honoured 'forbidden room' scenario, stretching back at least as far as Bluebeard's blood-soaked closet and so effectively realised that RKO cut out numerous juicy details before release. What survives is still strong stuff. By the light of Bob's candle we see on the wall a withered human head, and moments later Eve stumbles across a large jar containing another, its hair waving in preserving fluid like an anemone. For 1930s audiences, this must have been a real shocker, confirming all their worst fears about Russian aristocrats. Not for British punters, however; chief censor Edward Shortt did a little 'decapitation' of his own in this scene.

The film's script constitutes a simplistic, but nevertheless effective, rite of passage for the blandly self-assured Rainsford, nicely played by Joel McCrea. Beginning with the glib statement that "The world is divided into two kinds of people: the hunters and the hunted," he ends stuck up a tree with Eve, harried by Zaroff's baying hounds and ruefully admitting that "Those animals I cornered; now I know how they felt." *The Most Dangerous Game* has its share of flaws; Banks overdoes his retroflexed 'r' sounds in a fairly half-hearted attempt at a Russian accent, and, as played by Robert Armstrong, Eve's sozzled brother richly deserves his fate. (He has only one vaguely amusing moment, when he wonders if Rainsford subscribes to the bizarre 1920s craze for flagpole-sitting.) But the mood of ghastly foreboding established in the film's first section – and the breathless excitement of Zaroff's protracted game of "outdoor chess" in the second – make it one of the most powerful entries in Hollywood's initial wave of horror thrillers.

The chase sequences, captured in grimly beautiful images by cinematographer Henry Gerrard, are also immeasurably enhanced by the pulsing music composed by RKO's longtime MD, Max Steiner. Based around an ominous three-note motif (figuring in Zaroff's piano improvisations as well as in the film's action highlights), Steiner's sustained score, like his subsequent one for *King Kong*, was highly unusual in a film industry as yet reluctant to apply much more than perfunctory 'library' cues at a picture's beginning and end.

As *The Most Dangerous Game* went into release, RKO were close to completing a film that recycled a high proportion of its sets. *Secrets of the French Police*, which wrapped on 14 September, was directed by comedy specialist Edward Sutherland and written by diverse hands, among them left-wing novelist Samuel Ornitz, humorist Robert Benchley and *Murder by the Clock* author Rufus King. The latter, perhaps, was responsible for the film's bizarre third act, in which a vaguely outré police procedural takes a startling turn into the 'mad lab' school of horror picture.

The film was ostensibly a vehicle for Gwili André, a strikingly beautiful starlet whom Selznick saw as RKO's answer to Greta Garbo. Here, she plays Parisian flower-seller Eugénie Dorain, who is kidnapped by a mad Russian aristocrat and passed off, via hypnosis, as the presumed-dead Princess Anastasia. Her abductor, ripely played by the future director Gregory Ratoff, is the reptilian General Moloff. "Source of wealth unknown, mother Manchu princess, father Russian nobleman, trace of insanity on father's side," explains plucky Surêté detective St Cyr (Frank Morgan). His castle is, of course, Zaroff's; even his retinue's Cossack tunics were reportedly borrowed from *The Most Dangerous Game*. (His pet mastiff looks familiar too.) Moloff's basement, however, is given over, not to human heads, but to petrified cats.

The film's grisly details include Eugénie's father having his windpipe severed, a waterlogged corpse with its face bashed in, and a Rolls-Royce caused to crash by a specially rigged cinema screen projecting the image of an oncoming car. (A witty technological update of a routine featured in Roland West's *The Monster*.) Now we're treated to a twist suggesting that RKO were well aware of First National's plans to make *Mystery of the Wax Museum*. Coating his dead mistress (Kendall Lee) in plaster, Moloff adds her to an impressive collection of similar sculptures. And, moments before the police crash in, he's shown draining off Eugénie's blood and claiming that she'll be "the most beautiful statue I have ever made." Having been handcuffed, he flings himself at his own machinery and is electrocuted; a close-up of his hands bursting into flame, like Lee's briefly glimpsed nude scene, would certainly have been deleted had the film been made two years later.

While *Secrets of the French Police* was in production, an embattled RKO adaptation of the W W Jacobs perennial *The Monkey's Paw* was also being made; under consideration by Universal, the property had been cheekily snapped up by Selznick instead. Starting the film on 12 August, director Wesley Ruggles left behind him only half an hour's worth of material, despite shooting the script precisely as written. Ernest B Schoedsack was accordingly brought in to direct a lengthy North West Frontier prologue devised by Merian C Cooper, explaining how garrulous old soldier C Aubrey Smith acquired the fateful paw in the first place. After all that, the film's release on 13 January the following year saw it rubbished by critics and granted virtually no bookings. Pretty much unseen then, it's even less viewable today, qualifying as a lost film.

This is a shame, for, as well as its reportedly authentic British feel, the film featured a stop-motion paw created by key *King Kong* technicians Marcel Delgado and Orville Goldner; on Ivan Simpson's

utterance of his first wish, it miraculously clenched its fist as a preternatural wind buffeted Simpson's Chelsea home. Less enticingly, Simpson's tragic sequence of wishes, which comes close to reuniting him with his zombie son (Bramwell Fletcher), was explained away by screenwriter Graham John as a dream. And, given Selznick's eleventh-hour efforts to boost the film to feature length, the estimate of *Motion Picture* magazine was an ironic one. "Take out several reels of this mystery picture and you would have an excellent and substantial thriller short," it began. "There is one superb scene where a knocking on the door will bring gasps and screams from an audience, but on the whole the story is padded, and the denouement ... will have the effect of making the onlooker feel 'sold'."[15]

SADIST-EXOTICA AT M-G-M

RKO's *The Most Dangerous Game* – together with its upcoming twin, *King Kong* – provided ample proof that the sweat-stained ambience of jungle pictures was still a popular one. With the profits from *Tarzan, the Ape Man* rolling in, M-G-M needed no reminding of the fact, and in the summer of 1932 Irving Thalberg gave the go-ahead for two further jungle melodramas, one in 'tropical sex shocker' vein and the other closer to the sadistic ambience of *The Most Dangerous Game*.

Victor Fleming's *Red Dust* accordingly went into production on 22 July, inaugurating the uniquely raw sexual chemistry between Clark Gable and Jean Harlow. Less than a fortnight later, the film was joined at Culver City by a torrid remake of the studio's old Tod Browning thriller, *West of Zanzibar*. This time it reverted to the title of its stage original, *Kongo*, cost M-G-M a trifling $157,000 and earned a decent profit of $82,000. It offered picture patrons the chance to see the extraordinary Walter Huston in the role he had played at the Biltmore Theatre in the spring of 1926, the same role that had gone to Lon Chaney in the earlier picture. William Cowen's film also offered patrons the chance to revel in (or recoil from, according to taste) some of the most transgressive thrills of the pre-Code era.

In the Belgian Congo, 'Dead Legs' Flint is a former stage magician venerated by the natives as a white God. Flint blames his disability on his former business partner Gregg, whose grown daughter he has kidnapped and placed in the degenerate surroundings of a whorehouse. Learning, to his horror, that Ann is his own child rather than Gregg's, Flint's plan to smuggle her to safety is overheard by the natives, who vengefully fling him on a sacrificial pyre.

Apparently unfazed by the scandal created by *Freaks*, Metro's publicity department pulled out every salacious stop in ballyhooing *Kongo*. As well as promising that the film contained "greater thrills than *Trader Horn* [and] finer romance than *Tarzan*," the ad mats enticed prospective viewers with such delights as "A 'White Devil' in a Wheel-Chair," "A passion-flower of the jungle, slave of love to a madman," "The Black Avalanche of Savage Killers" and "Lovers facing the ritual of flaming sacrifice to Devil Worshippers."

Though suggesting a 'cast of thousands' extravaganza rather than the claustrophobic chamber-piece *Kongo* actually is, these tag-lines are otherwise quite close to the mark. To adapt the Chester DeVonde and Kilbourn Gordon play, Thalberg had engaged the author of a similarly sweat-stained stage success, *White Cargo*. This was Brighton-born Leon Gordon, who had previously co-written *Freaks* for Thalberg. He was familiar, therefore, not only with jungle melodramatics but also with legless avengers slithering through mud, which Walter Huston does quite a lot of in *Kongo*.

The feral intensity of Huston's performance remains shocking even today. Reminding himself of Gregg's betrayal by keeping a sign – 'HE SNEERED' – on permanent display, Flint hoists himself up to his secluded living quarters to share with one of his cronies his insane scheme of revenge. "He made me

"He sneered..." Smooth C Henry Gordon gives berserk Walter Huston some unwelcome news in *Kongo* (1932)

be," deadpans the enervated Dr Kingsland. The latter, in the parlance of the day, has 'gone native' via his addiction to a form of local 'weed' (Flint dunks him in a leech-infested swamp as a cure), and gets from Conrad Nagel a decidedly 'out there' performance that's occasionally reminiscent of Dwight Frye's Renfield. Similarly, Virginia Bruce gives a wildly baroque, yet touching, performance as the persecuted Ann, succumbing both to swamp fever and a counter-productive enslavement to brandy. On top of this, there's an extraordinary, unrehearsed moment in which Flint's chimp familiar (played by the same animal that had been such a hit in *Tarzan, the Ape Man*) literally punches her in the face.

If Kingsland is addicted to dope, Ann to alcohol and Flint to dreams of vengeance, the fourth point of this combustible quadrangle, Tula, is a gleeful martyr to sex addiction. Described in the pressbook as "a copper-skinned Portuguese minx," Tula is played by the delectable Lupe Velez in barely-there costumes that leave little to the imagination. Like all the characters (particularly the sculptural, loincloth-clad natives), she's slathered in a fetishistic sheen of mock-perspiration that makes one wonder how much Metro spent on baby oil for this film. Tula is also subject to one of Flint's most sadistic sports, when he's only just diverted from twisting her tongue with a bit of cheese-wire.

Despite running for a then unusually long 86 minutes, the film suffers from a yawning narrative gap after Ann is first encountered in the convent. Her initial meeting with Flint – and subsequent 'graduation' to what she euphemistically calls "a 'house' in Zanzibar" – is left out entirely, an omission which the *New York Times*' Mordaunt Hall put down to the fact that "The censors have evidently scowled at parts of this production."

The film also has its share of racist jibes, one of the milder ones being Flint's observation apropos missionaries that it "takes them a lifetime to Christianise a native and I can undo it all in two minutes with one lump of white sugar." It also has

KONGO

M-G-M 1932
86 minutes
production began 2 August

Cinematographer: Harold Rosson; Art Director: Cedric Gibbons; Editor: Conrad A Nervig; Sound: Douglas Shearer, Fred Morgan*; Assistant Director: Earl Taggart*; Screenplay: Leon Gordon (based upon the play by Chester DeVonde and Kilbourn Gordon); Producer: Irving Thalberg*; Director: William Cowen

Walter Huston (Flint); Lupe Velez (Tula); Conrad Nagel (Kingsland); Virginia Bruce (Ann); C Henry Gordon (Gregg); Mitchell Lewis (Hogan); Forrester Harvey (Cookie); Curtis Nero (Fuzzy); uncredited: Everett Brown (native); Charles Irwin (Carl); Sarah Padden (nun), Queenie (Kong [chimp])

As lurid a tale of hatred and revenge as ever Lon Chaney played in, but without his genius to make it come to life ... For those who like their jungle stories filled with horror, here is strong meat, but children should stay home and study their geography. *Photoplay*

I get letters ... from certain groups of people who say that they would never want to know or even to meet up with anyone so brutal as the man in *Kongo* ... Others write me that they know I would make the perfect husband and father and friend, because of *Abraham Lincoln* and *American Madness* ... They ask, "What kind of man *are* you, anyway? Black or white? Beast or human? Saint or devil?" *Walter Huston [quoted in Picturegoer Weekly, 14 January 1933]*

half a man," he raves, pointing out also that Gregg's convent-bred daughter will soon be "degraded, polluted – her name smouldering from the Cameroons to Zanzibar!" Huston's frenzy of hatred here is genuinely hair-raising – and further enhanced by a brilliant make-up job that sends an elongated scar running into the corner of his mouth, which at the opposite corner sprouts a weirdly symmetrical cigar.

The cigar would recur nine years later when Huston played a different kind of devil in RKO's *All That Money Can Buy*, a film that also repeats, perhaps at Huston's prompting, one of *Kongo*'s pithier dialogue exchanges. "Well, I'll be..." gasps Flint at one point. "You *will*

a slight-of-hand decapitation for Tula that's copied from Tod Browning's *The Show*, and an almost hallucinatory set-piece in which a native girl is offered up for voodoo sacrifice and the traumatised Ann stands shrieking among the weirdly masked celebrants. She then tears back inside, is manhandled by Flint's drunken cronies, briefly falls out of her blouse in escaping, interrupts Kingsland as he carouses with a bunch of native girls, and is jumped on by the chimp again before finally passing out. Virginia Bruce therefore takes the crown as the most put-upon heroine of 1930s horror.

Going into production just four days after *Kongo* was an M-G-M exotic of a different, but no less sadistic, kind. Sax Rohmer's Oriental menace, Dr Fu Manchu, had first appeared in print in 1913, and by 1932 he had been played in Sir Oswald Stoll's Cricklewood studio by Harry Agar Lyons and in Paramount's Hollywood one by Warner Oland. The latter had starred in Rowland V Lee's *The Mysterious Dr Fu Manchu* and *The Return of Dr Fu Manchu* in 1929 and 1930 respectively, later appearing briefly in Lloyd Corrigan's *Daughter of the Dragon* (1931), where centre stage was given over to the bewitching Anna May Wong as Fu's daughter. Irving Thalberg was no doubt acutely conscious of the fact that the cherubic, soft-spoken Oland wouldn't frighten anyone. For his Fu Manchu, no less a screen threat than Boris Karloff would do.

When the sword and mask of Genghis Khan are located by a British expedition, the evil Dr Fu Manchu and his sadistic daughter Fah Lo See devise a range of fiendish tortures to get the relics for themselves. Identified as "Genghis Khan come to life again," Fu Manchu urges his assembled Asian warlords to "kill the white man and take his women" – only for Scotland Yard's Nayland Smith to turn Fu's own death-ray on the assembled hordes.

Produced through William Randolph Hearst's Cosmopolitan subsidiary, *The Mask of Fu Manchu* had the distinction of numbering among its writers John Willard, author of *The Cat and the Canary*. The script, however, was an unfocused hodge-podge, remaining so despite extensive revisions being cobbled together on an almost daily basis. On top of this, production was halted briefly at the end of August, when Charles Vidor was replaced by Charles Brabin, director, back in 1915, of Essanay's *The Raven*.

The film bears traces of its troubled genesis throughout, with the plot, such as it is, developed in desultory style and viewer interest maintained only by the wraparound luxuriance of M-G-M's presentation. The barbaric statuary created by Cedric Gibbons' art department is in the same vein as the shimmering Shiva to whom Garbo had offered a sinuous dance in *Mata Hari* just 12 months previously. The tomb of Genghis Khan, in particular, is a triumph of elegant desolation, complete with goose-pimpling details like a tarantula emerging from an empty eye-socket when the archaeologists dislodge the coveted mask.

The Oriental gowns created by in-house designer Adrian are just as eye-catching, and M-G-M also had the good sense to engage freelance gadget-man Kenneth Strickfaden, whose crackling death ray is a spectacular contrivance. Brabin, however, could have handled some of the more hands-on electrical highlights with greater tact, in order to make it less obvious that Karloff was doubled in them by Strickfaden himself.

Hiring Strickfaden was an obvious nod to Universal's *Frankenstein*, and neither did Karloff's gorgeously caparisoned Fu Manchu escape the built-up boots familiar from his most famous role. Karloff's first appearance – hideously reflected in a distorting mirror as he quaffs a smoking potion à la *Dr Jekyll and Mr Hyde* – remains the strongest image in the film. Playing Fu as a grinning bisexual gargoyle, Karloff nevertheless brings a veneer of sweet reason to the script's several sadistic set-pieces, as when he submits Sir Lionel Barton to "the torture of the bell" and explains that "The percussion and the repercussion of sound against your ear-drums will soften and destroy them until the sound is magnified a thousand times."

Being familiar with Freud, Myrna Loy was staggered by the undisguised sexual sadism of her role as Fah Lo See. Having been touted as a vamp by Warner Bros as long ago as 1926, by 1932 she was sick to death of the label, and it shows. Despite her cries of "Faster, faster, faster!" as the handsome hero is whipped, she barely registers as Fah Lo See – certainly by comparison to her mesmeric turn in RKO's *Thirteen Women*. The other supporting actors, bar Lawrence Grant's plucky Sir Lionel, are virtually negligible in their impact. As Nayland Smith, M-G-M stalwart Lewis Stone gives a phoned-in performance of the worst kind, and Karen Morley – so good in *The Phantom of Crestwood* and as Paul Muni's moll in *Scarface* – is seriously overpitched as the jodhpured heroine. To be fair, she was probably severely put-out by the expulsion of Vidor, whom she married in November.

In a *Boy's Own* adventure of this vintage a bit of unaffected racism is to be expected, but *The Mask*

Oriental schemers Myrna Loy and Boris Karloff with true-blue hero Charles Starrett in *The Mask of Fu Manchu* (1932)

THE MASK OF FU MANCHU

M-G-M 1932
['a Cosmopolitan production']
72 minutes
production began 6 August (suspended); resumed 3 September

Cinematographer: Tony Gaudio; Art Director: Cedric Gibbons; Editor: Ben Lewis; Sound: Douglas Shearer; Special Effects: Warren Newcombe*; Electrical Properties: Kenneth Strickfaden*; Make-up: Cecil Holland*; Gowns: Adrian; Music: William Axt*; Animal Supervisor: Jack Allman*; Screenplay: Irene Kuhn, Edgar Allan Woolf, John Willard (from the story by Sax Rohmer); Director: Charles Brabin

Boris Karloff (Dr Fu Manchu); Lewis Stone (Nayland Smith); Karen Morley (Sheila); Charles Starrett (Terrence Granville); Myrna Loy (Fah Lo See); Jean Hersholt (Von Berg); Lawrence Grant (Sir Lionel Barton); David Torrence (McLeod); uncredited: Ray Benard (Corrigan); Willie Fung (steward); Steve Clemente (knife thrower); Ferdinand Gottschalk (Dr Nicholson); Allen Jung (coolie); Tetsu Komai (swordsman); James B Leong (guest); Chris-Pin Martin (potentate); Lal Chand Mehra (Indian prince); Edward Peil Sr (spy); C Montague Shaw (Dr Fairgyle); E Allyn Warren (Goy Lo Sung); Victor Wong (attendant in opium den)

The latest of the bugaboo symposiums arrived at the Capitol yesterday [3 December 1932] ... It is Fu's whimsical notion ... to set about conquering the world and stamping out the hated palefaces ... It is Scotland Yard's intention to frustrate Fu if it takes all Winter – and at the Capitol the new film does manage to convey the unhappy impression that it is taking at least that long. *New York Times*

That script was really the last straw ... yet when Roddy McDowall tricked me into seeing it recently, it astonished me how good Karloff and I were. Everyone else just tossed it off as something that didn't matter, while Boris and I brought some feeling and humor to those comic-book characters.
Myrna Loy [Myrna Loy: Being and Becoming, 1987]

of Fu Manchu is something else again. As well as Sheila branding Fu a "hideous yellow monster," Nayland Smith paints an apocalyptic portrait of the world overrun by the Chinese: "Should Fu Manchu put that mask across his wicked eyes, and take that scimitar into his bony, cruel hands, all Asia rises." In one of several choice slurs, he finally handles the longed-for scimitar and sneers: "They *believe* in a bauble like this? Will we ever understand these Eastern races?" Worst of all, the film's epilogue presents gap-toothed Willie Fung (fresh from fetishistically admiring Jean Harlow's lingerie in *Red Dust*) as a Chinaman who knows his Hollywood place – ie, as a shipboard flunky striking the dinner gong for the whites.

In the early 1990s, attempts were made to cut the more contentious moments, 60 years too late, in the name of 'political correctness'. But, racism aside, what really sinks the film is the tedious jumble of serial-style hi-jinks with which it concludes. Crudely undercranked fisticuffs vie with totally suspense-free torture sequences to make these scenes a very boring slog indeed. As designer of the Oscar statuette, Cedric Gibbons works in a neat in-joke for Fu's diabolical operating theatre, in which oiled-up Nubian slaves are artfully arranged into a semi-circle of living Oscars. But, beyond that, these scenes are distinguished only by the startlingly high level of homo-eroticism applied to the nappy-clad hero, stretched out at Fu's mercy in a posture normally reserved for the heroine.

When Charles Brabin bumped Charles Vidor from *The Mask of Fu Manchu*, he had himself just been bumped from M-G-M's *Rasputin and the Empress*, which instead devolved upon Richard Boleslavski. Cannily conceived by Thalberg as a historic teaming of John, Lionel and Ethel Barrymore, the result was a headache from start to finish. Starting on 22 July, the film took a mammoth 17 weeks to shoot, had many of its lecherous details cut in advance of its 23 December premiere, and was finally sued in a British court by Prince Youssoupoff, who had collaborated in the assassination of the real-life Rasputin a mere 16 years before. M-G-M reportedly settled out of court to the tune of $250,000.

The Rasputin role had originally been proposed for Karloff or Lugosi before the 'three Barrymores for the

price of one' angle came up; instead, it gave Lionel Barrymore a barnstorming showcase, particularly in a climactic scene which, though trimmed, remains startlingly gruesome. The bludgeoning battle between Rasputin and John's so-called Prince Chegodiev concludes with Rasputin rising from the floor, streaming with blood and grimly insisting that "The great day of wrath is coming." Thoroughly unnerved, Chegodiev finally submerges him in the Neva, shrieking "Anti-Christ! Drown in the lake of Hell!" The preternatural persistence of Rasputin, coupled with the goggle-eyed hysteria of his assassin, gives the scene a genuinely nightmarish quality.

Lionel Barrymore hypnotises Tad Alexander's haemophilia away in *Rasputin and the Empress* (1932)

LOVE AND CRIME AND DEATH

By the closing months of 1932, the fortunes of Bela Lugosi and Boris Karloff were radically different. Lugosi's star was already tarnished by his willingness to headline Poverty Row productions like Edwin L Marin's *The Death Kiss* (a vacuous 'murder on a movie set' mystery that nevertheless provides a fascinating look at the workings of its parent studio, Tiffany). This, together with a careless attitude to business dealings, resulted in his filing for bankruptcy in October. Karloff, by contrast, would soon be in a position to hold Universal to ransom over a promised pay rise, later becoming a co-founder of the Screen Actors' Guild and the recipient of juicy roles in non-horror pictures like *The Lost Patrol* and *The House of Rothschild*.

And Karloff's ascendancy was enthusiastically bolstered by the nation's fan magazines, which accorded him the 'new Chaney' title that had briefly been mooted for Lugosi. "Boris Karloff – is it coincidence? – is now repeating on the Universal lot Chaney's spectacular career," claimed *Photoplay*'s Kathryn Dougherty. "Yet he is not another Chaney. His methods and effects are distinctly individualistic ... It is easy to conceive of Karloff ten years from now, when the names of other outstanding actors of the day shall have practically been forgotten, still holding an undisputed eminence. Chaney's and Karloff's names should go down, linked together, in motion picture history."[16]

While Lugosi signed up to play a virtually unrecognisable werewolf in Paramount's *Island of Lost Souls*, his rival was being enthroned as 'Karloff the Uncanny' and starring in two major pictures simultaneously. When *The Mask of Fu Manchu* finished at M-G-M on 21 October, only a week or so remained before time was called on another Karloff vehicle, this time back at his home studio. This one had originated as a fanciful treatment, *Cagliostro*, written by Nina Wilcox Putnam and Richard Schayer. Handed on to John L Balderston, who in 1922 had covered the opening of Tutankhamen's tomb for the *New York World*, it became a radically different Egyptological romance called *Im-Ho-Tep*. Then, halfway through production, it acquired a more uncompromising title – *The Mummy*.

> *Egypt, 1921. Archaeologist Ralph Norton foolishly intones the life-giving words of the Scroll of Thoth over the inert mummy of Imhotep. Eleven years on, the rejuvenated Imhotep presents himself to the Whemple expedition under the pseudonym Ardath Bey, recognising in Frank Whemple's sweetheart Helen Grosvenor a reincarnation of his 3700-year-old love, Princess Anck-es-en-Amon. His plans to make Helen like himself are finally foiled by the intervention of Isis, whose statue reduces him to dust.*

Though enthused by the meteoric success of *Frankenstein*, Carl Laemmle was also disconcerted by the bitter controversy stirred up by it. As a result, on 1 September the UK trade paper *To-Day's Cinema* had announced *The Old Dark House* with the headline, "The First of Eerie Hair Raisers – NO MORE HORROR – Hollywood's New Entertainment Vogue – The 'Eerie' Picture." Closely following *The Old Dark House* into release, *The Mummy* was presumably conceived as another 'eerie' item rather than an all-out shocker.

Boris Karloff offers Zita Johann a dream of "love and crime and death" in *The Mummy* (1932)

THE MUMMY

Universal 1932
72 minutes
production ended 30 October

Cinematographer: Charles Stumar; Art Director: Willy Pogany*; Editor: Milton Carruth; Special Effects: John P Fulton; Make-up: Jack P Pierce*; Music: James Dietrich*; Screenplay: John L Balderston, from the story by Nina Wilcox Putnam, Richard Schayer; Associate Producer: Stanley Bergerman*; Presented by Carl Laemmle; Producer: Carl Laemmle Jr; Director: Karl Freund

Boris Karloff (Imhotep); Zita Johann (Helen Grosvenor); David Manners (Frank Whemple); Arthur Byron (Sir Joseph Whemple); Edward Van Sloan (Doctor Muller); Bramwell Fletcher (Ralph Norton); Noble Johnson (the Nubian); Kathryn Byron (Frau Muller); Leonard Mudie (Professor Pearson); James Crane (the Pharaoh); uncredited: Eddie Kane (Dr LeBarron); Tony Marlow (Inspector); Pat Somerset (Helen's dance partner); Leland Hodgson, C Montague Shaw (gents in Cairo nightclub)

nb: Henry Victor is credited on screen as 'The Saxon Warrior' but was deleted from the final print

Fresh from his amiable massacres in *The Mask of Fu Manchu*, Boris Karloff – now billed austerely as Karloff the Uncanny – is spreading desolation at the Mayfair. That there is a place for a national bogey man in the scheme of things was fulsomely demonstrated by the crowds that clicked past the box office yesterday [6 January 1933] ... But most of *The Mummy* is costume melodrama for the children. New York Times

The director, Karl Freund, really was a terrible sadist ... He said, "In one scene you have to be nude from the waist up." ... He wanted me to have a fit, you see ... But, instead, I said, "It's all right with me if you can get it by the censors!" *Zita Johann* [quoted in *Filmfax*, February-March 1998]

Whether *The Mummy* moves at a funereal plod or with appropriately dreamlike languor is a matter of taste. The masterful quality of its opening reel, however, is incontestable. After a close-up of an elderly archaeologist reassembling the fragments of a heavily hieroglyphed mosaic, his young assistant's first line is also the film's first line: "Trying to teach me a lesson in patience, Sir Joseph?" Patience of a peculiarly long-lasting variety will turn out to be the distinguishing characteristic of Imhotep; in the meantime, we know already that this hot-headed young Englishman will be undone by his own impetuosity. As the camera sidles tantalisingly around the invaluable casket found alongside Imhotep, we know that Norton will be unable to resist opening it. We know, too, that his mumbled reading of the parchment within will have a devastating effect.

The lingering close-up that follows – of Imhotep propped upright in his sarcophagus as Norton breathes the fateful words off-camera – is at once Freund's impish homage to the awakening of Cesare in *Das Cabinet des Dr Caligari* and arguably the most disquieting moment in Hollywood's horror cycle thus far. In place of Conrad Veidt's wide-eyed stare of unspeakable terror, Karloff substitutes just the tiniest glimmer of returning consciousness under the heavy eyelids. Then the camera coolly observes his desiccated hands as they slip silently from their funerary bindings.

The mummy's hands remain a focus of horror throughout – reaching slowly for the scroll as Norton looks on in mounting hysteria; leaving behind a dusty, five-pointed print for Sir Joseph to find on his return; much later staining Helen's forearm with graveyard earth. For now, the scene closes on Norton's classic line, "He went for a little walk. You should have seen his face..." Earning a little bit of cinema immortality, Bramwell Fletcher's insane laughter here strikes a profoundly disturbing chord, outdoing even Dwight Frye's in *Dracula*.

Dracula, in fact, remains the film's reference point throughout, Balderston merely rehashing its

It plays, in fact, more like a macabre tone-poem, rendered in images of limpid beauty by director Karl Freund and distinguished by the sombre sonority of Karloff's performance. Unfortunately, it remains a poem that doesn't quite scan. In the hands of a former cinematographer whose grasp of pacing was no match for his genius with imagery, its fundamentally faulty metre doesn't so much ebb and flow as lurch from point to point.

characters and situations in the Egyptian context he was so familiar with; by coincidence, one of his suggested titles for the film – *Undead* – was also Bram Stoker's working title back in 1897. We even have David Manners and Edward Van Sloan playing pretty much the same roles as in the earlier film.

Van Sloan is exceptional as the occult expert Dr Muller, and it's a pleasure to hear him give lipsmacking force to a naked threat Van Helsing would never have permitted himself: "If I could get my hands on you," he says, mere inches from Ardath Bey's face, "I'd break your dried flesh to pieces." And, where Van Helsing presented Dracula with an image of his true self (a soulless blank) in a mirror, we're here given an identical set-up in which Muller gives Bey an image of his true self (a shrivelled mummy) in a ten-year-old snapshot. Finally, confirming Van Helsing's kinship with Sherlock Holmes, Muller wears his bow-tie in the prescribed Holmesian fashion and loses no time in gathering tell-tale ashes into an envelope.

Karloff's stately presence as Ardath Bey suggests the agonising passage of 3700 years with admirable economy, and to bolster his 'Karloff the Uncanny' repute, effects expert John Fulton provides several chilling close-ups in which Bey's parchment face pulses with a neon-lit glare of unfathomable malevolence. As a mood piece, the film is also made memorable by the oneiric fluidity of Charles Stumar's camera and a sacrificial climax played with all the spell-stopped solemnity of an underwater ballet. In addition, the Mojave Desert proves a convincing stand-in for the Valley of the Kings, Zita Johann's gamine Helen Grosvenor is an appropriately exotic heroine, and Jack Pierce's make-up (for both Imhotep and the more presentable Ardath Bey) is on a par with his iconic work on Frankenstein's Monster.

Balderston's scenario for *The Mummy* would give rise in future years to some strange cross-fertilisations. In the course of rejigging his own *Dracula* script, he appears to have lifted several details from another Bram Stoker story, *The Jewel of Seven Stars*. The reincarnation theme of Stoker's 1903 novel dovetailed neatly not only with Balderston's own 1926 play *Berkeley Square* but also with another script he was working on for Universal in 1932. This was an adaptation of Rider Haggard's 1886 adventure yarn *She*, in which, contrary to *The Mummy*, the ageless lover is female and the reincarnated love object a man. Bizarrely, the reincarnation angle of *The Mummy* – introduced by Balderston in an effort to differentiate it from *Dracula* – would later become a feature of the more simple-minded retellings of *Dracula* itself, starting with *Blacula* in 1972.

Universal's rights in *She* were eventually sold on to RKO, who finally got around to filming it in March 1935. Here, Imhotep's promise to Helen that he will "awaken memories of love and crime and death" is echoed by Ayesha's assurance to Leo Vincey that "Dreams are only memories in the endless flow of time." The film is chiefly a showcase for the stunning design work of Van Nest Polglase, the stirring music of Max Steiner, and the first (and last) film appearance of stage star Helen Gahagan. To satisfy the horror constituency, it also boasts a scary sequence in which Nigel Bruce's Holly comes close to having a white-hot helmet attached to his head by a horde of troglodyte cannibals. He's saved by the intervention of that time-honoured hatchet-faced menace Gustav von Seyffertitz, here playing High Priest Billali.

As the much-anticipated Ayesha, Gahagan comes across like an Oxford-educated Boadicea, her non-existent chemistry with Randolph Scott contriving to sink the film irretrievably. Her first appearance, however – a wraith-like silhouette speaking mournfully from behind a wall of billowing smoke, finally uttering a piercing scream on recognising Scott as her long-dead lover – is a truly bewitching moment. Though directed by Irving Pichel and Lansing C Holden, the film bears the unmistakable stamp of its producer Merian C Cooper, and not merely through the reappearance of the massive gateway from *King*

Helen Gahagan contemplates "the endless flow of time" in the RKO epic *She* (1935)

Kong. The film was somewhat scaled down from Cooper's original specifications (among the casualties: Technicolor and *Kong* animator Willis O'Brien), but it's still pretty colossal. In particular, the outrageous ceremonials and elaborate dance routines at the end seem like a high-camp retread of Griffith's *Intolerance*.

THE MENTAL LON CHANEY

Just as spooky-house mystery-thrillers were by no means dead on screen, they still showed occasional signs of life on Broadway. One such, *The Black Tower* by Ralph Murphy and Helen Baxter, reached Los Angeles and San Francisco in April 1932; retitled *Murdered Alive*, the West Coast production had the added bonus of Bela Lugosi as mad sculptor Dr Orloff. The play briefly caused legal complications for Warner Bros-First National, who were anxious to capitalise on the success of *Doctor X* and had bought an unpublished story called *The Wax Works* by Charles S Belden. Getting together many of the key components of the earlier film – Lionel Atwill, Fay Wray, Michael Curtiz, Anton Grot, Technicolor – the studio put *Wax Museum* into production at the end of September.

> *London, 1921. Gifted sculptor Ivan Igor is apparently consumed in a fire started by his insurance-hungry business partner. Twelve years later, in New York, Igor opens a lavish new attraction called the London Wax Museum, but sassy young newshound Florence Dempsey suspects that he has a uniquely labour-saving approach to creating his exhibits. What she doesn't suspect is left to her friend Charlotte to find out – that Igor is himself coated in wax to conceal his atrocious disfigurement.*

Unlike *Doctor X*, the new film was shot, at Technicolor's insistence, only in colour. And, on its release in February 1933, it had acquired the fuller title *Mystery of the Wax Museum*. Though the last-minute addition of the word 'mystery' was an obvious indication that Warners were still unwilling to go for all-out Grand Guignol, the film's prologue remains one of the great set-pieces of Hollywood horror. Here, the exterior sets previously used for *Doctor X*'s New York waterfront became a damp London side street – and, incidentally, caused the British censor to demand the removal of the title card 'London 1921', lest it prove prejudicial to London's only real waxworks, Mme Tussaud's.

In an ironic foreshadowing of what is to come, our first view of Ivan Igor is a close-up of him massaging a waxen female torso, puffing meanwhile on an extremely foolhardy cigarette. His cash-strapped business partner, the ironically named Worth, dismisses "all this artistic nonsense," points out that the Chamber of Horrors at Walston Lane is a true moneyspinner, and flourishes a Fire Insurance certificate in Igor's face. A clumsy struggle ensues, during which Igor is sent sprawling against a shelf of waxen body parts – a severed head goes flying – while his "children," as he calls them, begin to suppurate and smoulder all around him.

The clash between the refined, velvet-jacketed sculptor and the beefy, venal financier positions Igor as the classic misunderstood artist, thus encouraging a measure of sympathy for him on his removal to New York. His children – immobile on their plinths and podia, their skins glistening like glacé fruit even as they slither away in the ferocious heat – watch the pathetic struggle between art and commerce with perfect inscrutability, offering a grotesque parody of bodily corruption and, more specifically, a horrible image of what happens to Igor off-camera.

Dissolving to 1933, Ray Rennahan's Technicolor camera allows a roseate pink to predominate rather than the gangrenous greens of *Doctor X*. Curtiz immediately plunges the viewer into the hectic gaiety of a New York New Year's Eve, complete with cascading confetti, silly hats, hooting horns – and a sheeted corpse being bundled into a waiting ambulance. In the morgue, *Doctor X*'s 'corpse rising up on its slab' routine is dutifully repeated ("embalming fluid: it makes 'em jump," explains a mortician), soon after which a slouch-hatted grotesque arrives in search of the recently deceased Joan Gale. Lifting a sheet, the monster reveals the silhouetted profile of Joan while simultaneously concealing his own hideous features. The soundtrack, meanwhile, resonates to the thing's extremely laboured breathing, making the story's necrophile implications as blatant as possible.

Igor's New York establishment, of course, turns out to be as much a temple of necrophilia as a temple of beauty; as his junkie associate Professor d'Arcy puts it, "the whole place is a morgue." Igor himself is a perfect image of the castrated artist, lamenting that "Never since these hands were burnt have I created anything; I've only been able to direct the work of others." (In this he provides an echo of *Doctor X*'s armless villain and anticipates the emasculated pianist of *Mad Love* and the black-gloved surgeon of Hammer's Frankenstein pictures.) Despite these intriguing themes, the film's characteristic Warner Bros emphasis on newspaper realism finally drowns out its Gothic flourishes, making it a less satisfactory fusion of the two styles than *Doctor X*. At least the investigative Florence – gifted with absurd lines like "I gotta make news if I have to bite a dog" and

High-minded sculptor Lionel Atwill smoking an extremely ominous cigarette in *Mystery of the Wax Museum* (1932)

winningly played by Glenda Farrell – is a more engaging character than was Lee Tracy's reporter in the earlier film.

The film's catalogue of pre-Code straight-from-the-streets verisimilitude includes explicit references to drug addiction, live-in lovers, pornographic magazines and bootlegging; the latter, in fact, is the newest enterprise of Igor's old business partner. There's also a charming little cheesecake sequence between Florence and her room-mate Charlotte. Reference is made to rival horror pictures (upbraiding one of his assistant artists, Igor says, "You must have studied with a sideshow of freaks") and to other Warner products (Worth ends up as a mummified 'stiff' like James Cagney in *The Public Enemy*). Unfortunately, this stew of ingredients makes the middle section of the film awkwardly choppy and episodic. Throughout it all, however, Rennahan models the human figures just as lovingly as the wax ones, creating an almost 3-D effect at times – an effect that would become literal in the film's remake 20 years later.

Finally, to balance the splendid opening, there's the famous climax in which Charlotte is inducted into Igor's shimmering subterranean laboratory, its central, circular vat resembling an alchemical cauldron brought up to date. Beating against Igor's face, Charlotte sees it crack open like an egg to reveal what Florence has previously likened to "an African war mask." The scene's shock value was reportedly extreme back in 1933, though nowadays it's slightly compromised by the unconvincing punch-up that ensues when the police break in. Atwill, however, memorably articulates Igor's shame and self-disgust, eventually toppling, with a grim inevitability, into his own white-hot wax.

Starting as far back as the 1907 fragment *The Professor and His Waxworks*, and taking in Paul Leni's memorable *Das Wachsfigurenkabinett* in 1923, wax museums were to become something of a horror staple. Having anticipated *Mystery of the Wax Museum* via the play *Murdered Alive*, Bela Lugosi would also provide a small footnote to it in December 1932, when he played waxworks proprietor Professor Strang in the Mascot serial *The Whispering Shadow*. And, as noted above, *Wax Museum* had also been anticipated by RKO's *Secrets of the French Police*; indeed, a plot strand involving houseflies poisoned by formaldehyde had

MYSTERY OF THE WAX MUSEUM

Warner Bros-Vitaphone 1932
80 minutes; Technicolor
production began 26 September

Cinematographer: Ray Rennahan; Art Director: Anton Grot; Editor: George Amy; Sound: Everett A Brown*; Process Photography: Rex Wimpy*; Wax Figures: L E Oates*, assisted by H Clay Campbell*; Make-up: Perc Westmore*, Ray Romero*; Gowns: Orry-Kelly; Music: Cliff Hess*; Vitaphone Orchestra conducted by Leo F Forbstein; Color Consultant: Natalie Kalmus*; Screenplay: Don Mullaly, Carl Erickson (from the story by Charles S Belden); Production Supervisor: Henry Blanke*; In Charge of Production: Darryl F Zanuck*; Director: Michael Curtiz

Lionel Atwill (Ivan Igor); Fay Wray (Charlotte Duncan); Glenda Farrell (Florence Dempsey); Frank McHugh (Jim); Allen Vincent (Ralph Burton); Gavin Gordon (George Winton); Edwin Maxwell (Joe Worth); Holmes Herbert (Dr Rasmussen); Claude King (Mr Golatily); Arthur Edmund Carewe (Professor D'Arcy); Thomas Jackson (detective); DeWitt Jennings (police captain); Matthew Betz (Otto/Hugo); Monica Bannister (Joan Gale); uncredited: Bull Anderson (janitor); James Burke (newspaperman); Frank Darien (autopsy surgeon); James Donlin (morgue attendant); Robert E Homans (desk sergeant); Perry Ivins (copy editor); Edward Keane (doctor); Robert Emmett O'Connor (Joe Kelly [cop]); Pat O'Malley (plainclothes man); Lon Poff (thin man); William B Davidson, Guy Usher (detectives)

This picture, done in color, tops the horrors of the year. It is so well-conceived, mounted and acted that its horrors become plausible ... It would be unfair to take away any of your thrills by touching on the story, which is enacted only too well for your peace of mind. See it by all means – but don't take the kids. Motion Picture

He [Michael Curtiz] was very exacting. I liked him, we got along fine, but he worked people to death. We all collapsed one night on *Wax Museum*. He worked us for 23 hours! We all had hysterics and collapsed. They had to let us have the next day off to stay in bed.
Glenda Farrell [quoted in Photon # 20, 1971]

been deleted from *Wax Museum*'s script when it was realised RKO had already filched it.

Two years later, Warners themselves would echo *Wax Museum* in Robert Florey's *The Florentine Dagger*. Loosely based on a Ben Hecht novel, this cast Donald Woods as a young man driven almost to suicide by the baneful influence of his ancestors; as he tells C Aubrey Smith's crusty psychiatrist, "The ghosts of the Borgias still walk in me." On Smith's advice, he writes a Borgia play that becomes a big hit, falling in love with the leading lady (Margaret Lindsay) but succumbing to despair again when her impresario stepfather (Henry O'Neill) is found stabbed to death with a Borgia dagger. Starting on 20 December 1934, Florey had only 18 days and $135,000 to make the film. Bolstering it with his trademark Expressionist lighting and skewed camera angles, he ensures that the action is consistently eye-catching despite a sluggish rhythm imposed by on-the-set rewriting of Tom Reed's slung-together screenplay.

In retrospect, the most interesting thing about the film is its third act revelation of the killer and of the thoroughly despicable nature of the victim. Years before, O'Neill had attempted to kill his wife (Florence Fair) by setting her dress on fire; now, her ruined face is concealed by a mask and she kills O'Neill when he tries to force himself on his own stepdaughter. In the character of Floria, Florey's film not only points back to *Mystery of the Wax Museum* but also provides an unmistakable model for Georges Franju's grisly 1959 masterpiece, *Les Yeux sans visage*.

Florey had dealt with facial disfigurement in the Poverty Row drama *Face Value* as long ago as 1927. Harping on similar themes, by December 1935 he was shooting *The Preview Murder Mystery* for Paramount, in which Frances Drake is involved in a series of film studio murders that turn out to be the work of a presumed-dead star whose face was badly burned during a fire scene.

Despite the hideous make-up he sported in *Mystery of the Wax Museum*, Lionel Atwill was by now acquiring a reputation, in the words of *Motion Picture*'s Faith Service, as 'The Mental Lon Chaney'. Straight after *Wax Museum*, he moved on to a Poverty Row item called *The Vampire Bat*, which bore the humble imprimatur of the Majestic Picture Corporation but was given a little lustre by the use of standing sets at Universal City, a shortcut previously taken by the Halperins on *White Zombie*. Still convinced that the horror craze was soon to fade out, *Variety*'s 'Rush' described this one as a "Shiver picture, well enough done but coming along too late in the cycle to figure in the money."

A series of murders in the Tyrolean community of Kleinschloss is popularly attributed to a vampire. After bat-fancying village idiot Herman is pursued to his death by a lynch mob, the level-headed Karl Bretschneider unmasks Dr Otto von Niemann instead. Claiming that "from the lives of those who have gone before I have created life," von Niemann proposes to sacrifice both Karl and his fiancée Ruth to a bloodthirsty, sponge-like creature resident in his laboratory.

'Rush' would soon have to eat his words. Keenly anticipating its UK release, the British trade paper *Kinematograph Weekly* reported that "*The Vampire Bat* has been playing to big business in practically every town since its recent release in America ... On the occasion of the world premiere [on 20 January 1933] at the Winter Garden Theatre, New York, *The Vampire Bat* was held over for a second week. The Orpheum Theatre, Boston, took $16,500 in one week for this Majestic film, and when one considers that the house record for this theatre only stands at $20,000, this is a tribute to the drawing power of *The Vampire Bat*."[17] Though not on the money-spinning level of *White Zombie*, the film's success was a clear indication that the horror boom was far from over, nor was it confined to the product of the major studios.

The robust box-office returns for *The Vampire Bat* remain hard to explain, however. Though the script is by Edward T Lowe (who ten years earlier had co-written *The Hunchback of Notre Dame* for Universal), the film's agglomeration of borrowed motifs isn't done with the kind of self-reflexive wit that would later characterise M-G-M's *Mad Love*. Instead, *The Vampire Bat* is unadulterated computer product. It takes an 'everything but the kitchen sink' approach: there's a sculpted bat behind the opening credits as in *Dracula*; a lynch-mob pursuit, complete with baying hounds, à la *Frankenstein*; a rooftop prowler as per *Murders in the Rue Morgue*; a palpitating thing in a tank akin to Dr Wells' preserved heart in *Doctor X*. And so it goes on.

And, given that certain actors were becoming just as emblematic of the burgeoning genre as plot devices, the film is also a triumph of casting by numbers. From *Doctor X*, we have Lionel Atwill and Fay Wray; from *The Old Dark House*, Melvyn Douglas; plus Maude Eburne from *The Bat Whispers* and Robert Frazer from *White Zombie*. Lionel Belmore and Dwight Frye play pretty much the same roles (splenetic burgomaster and gibbering idiot) they previously essayed in *Frankenstein* and *Dracula*; even Rita Carlisle gets to repeat her bedridden old lady routine from *Dr Jekyll and Mr Hyde*. The film's aroma of used goods is further emphasised by its use of the village set

from *Frankenstein* and the impressive interiors of *The Old Dark House*. Briefly bucking the backward-looking trend, Atwill's von Niemann gets to foreshadow *Bride of Frankenstein*'s Dr Pretorius when he describes coffee as "My one weakness."

What the film has to offer on its own account is a spooky opening, with bats taking flight at the nocturnal scream of the latest victim, and a few compensatory visual felicities as the plot progresses. The killer's approach to the bedridden Martha is memorably achieved with an unpredictable series of subjective camera moves, first sweeping down the ominous bulk of a clocktower before swallowing the victim in the folds of the killer's cloak. And the demise of Dwight Frye's Herman in the so-called Devil's Well (actually LA's Beachwood Canyon) benefits from plenty of torch-lit chiaroscuro.

There's also a delightful last-reel confrontation in which a gimlet-eyed Atwill explains himself in bravura style to the quailing Fay Wray. Though the US pronunciation of 'laboratory' must have stuck in his throat, Atwill is impressively demented as he extols his creation of "living, growing tissue – life that moves, pulsates, and demands food for its continued growth. Ha! You shudder in horror. So did I, the first time. But what are a few lives when weighed in the balance against the achievement of biological science?" The 'thing' itself, unfortunately, is the size of a bathroom sponge and about as impressive. Equally lame is a climactic laboratory tussle in which von Niemann and his murderous confederate, Emil, succeed in shooting each other to death off screen.

The picture's chief asset, however, is Melvyn Douglas, who was no doubt surprised to find himself back on the *Old Dark House* sets so soon and in such lowly circumstances; indeed, his disenchantment with Hollywood soon had him heading back east to the Broadway stage. An expert boulevardier trapped in a straight-faced penny dreadful, Douglas' cocked-eyebrow condescension when dealing with the credulous burghers of Kleinschloss – "Good night, gentlemen; don't let the vampires get you!" – no doubt mirrored his own tongue-in-cheek attitude to the project. Set against Douglas, unfortunately, is Maude Eburne, a kind of poor man's Marie Dressler whose 'comic' interludes disfigure *The Vampire Bat* just as surely as they did *The Bat Whispers*. The film's closing shot – in which, having inadvertently overdosed on Epsom Salts, she charges up the *Old Dark House* stairs in search of the nearest lavatory – is the most unedifying yet seen in a Hollywood horror film.

As well as the murder-mysteries *Tangled Destinies* (1932) and *Fifteen Wives* (1934), director Frank Strayer made three other horror pictures, all of them of such severely limited visual excitement that *The Vampire Bat* stands out like a freak accident. (Or, more likely, a tribute to cinematographer Ira Morgan, with whom Strayer did not collaborate on the remaining films.) Some 12 months prior to making *The Vampire Bat* for Majestic, Strayer had knocked out the promisingly titled *The Monster Walks* for another Poverty Row outfit, Action. Released in February 1932, the result is a stodgy and static retread of the kind of 'ape in an old dark house' quasi-horrors of the silent period, with a blatant quote from *The Cat and the Canary* when

THE VAMPIRE BAT

Majestic 1932
62 minutes
production ended 19 November

Cinematographer: Ira H Morgan; Art Director: Daniel [Charles D] Hall; Editor: Otis Garrett; Sound: Dick Tyler; Musical Director: Abe Meyer*; Screenplay: Edward T Lowe; Executive Producer: Larry Darmour*; Producer: Phil Goldstone; Director: Frank Strayer

Lionel Atwill (Otto von Niemann); Fay Wray (Ruth Berlin); Melvyn Douglas (Karl Bretschneider); Maude Eburne (Gussie Schnappman); George E Stone (Kringen); Dwight Frye (Herman Gleib); Robert Frazer (Emil Borst); Rita Carlisle (Martha Mueller); Lionel Belmore (Gustave Schoen [burgomaster]); William V Mong (Sauer); Stella Adams (Georgianna); Harrison Greene (Weingarten); uncredited: Fern Emmett (Gertrude [Martha's nurse]); William Humphrey (Dr Haupt); Carl Stockdale (Schmidt); Paul Weigel (Holdstadt)

Thrill melodrama admirably produced and directed with unusually strong cast. Packs powerful punch. Developments of a clever plot are skilfully handled and the direction is expert ... One of the best independent features seen this season. *Film Daily*

In *The Vampire Bat* I exposed a faked monster – and let a breathlessly waiting world know that Epsom Salt has a scientific name ... After consultation with Helen [Gahagan, his wife] in northern California, ... [I] went to studio head Sam Goldwyn to ask for my contract's termination.
Melvyn Douglas [See You at the Movies: the Autobiography, 1986]

Lionel Atwill expounds his atrocious scientific theories to Fay Wray in *The Vampire Bat* (1932)

Vera Reynolds' heroine is menaced by a hirsute hand emerging from a sliding panel. Strayer also roped in *Canary*'s saturnine housekeeper, Martha Mattox, to play more or less the same part.

The set-up is a numbingly familiar one: a Darwinian research scientist has died and, as the relatives gather for the reading of the will, a large, and apparently homicidal, chimpanzee flings itself around in a basement cage. Robert Ellis' script has the hero's black retainer – played by Willie Best but credited as Sleep 'n' Eat – point out that "I had a gran'pappy that looked something like him, but he wasn't this active." Almost as demeaning is the role of the housekeeper's half-wit son, played by Russian-born Mischa Auer prior to his becoming a comic character star in A-pictures like *You Can't Take It With You*. In addition to *The Monster Walks*, Auer spent a lot of his time in 1932-3 toiling in the spooky-house doldrums, playing saturnine mystics in both *Sinister Hands* and *Sucker Money*, being upstaged by a Kenneth Strickfaden death ray in *Murder at Dawn*, and starring opposite Henry B Walthall in a jungle variant called *The Flaming Signal*.

For his part, Frank Strayer moved on to Invincible, for whom he shot *The Ghost Walks* in November 1934 from a script by Charles Belden of *Wax Museum* fame. In this – yet another flagrant rip-off of *The Cat and the Canary* – that play's asylum warder turns out to be the escaped lunatic in disguise, finally tethering several of the dramatis personae in an underground room and proposing to perform plastic surgery on them. A dyspeptic Broadway producer and his effeminate assistant have been tricked by an enterprising playwright (John Miljan) into spending the night at his storm-tossed mansion, where a group of undercover actors are on hand to perform the writer's new play with the visitors unknowingly mixed up in the action.

Johnny Arthur, sometime boob hero of Roland West's *The Monster*, is not very funny as the prissy secretary, but Richard Carle is a delight as his short-fused boss. Belden's script is littered with archly self-reflexive gags that can only elicit a groaning endorsement from the viewer. "Not enough action for me," observes Arthur of the unfolding drama. (Faced with an eye-swivelling portrait, he also comes out with the already generic cry, "It's alive!") Carle, meanwhile, grumbles accurately that "This isn't a horror play, it's a bedroom farce."

By July 1935, Strayer was at work on another Invincible potboiler, this time a retread, not of *The Cat and the Canary*, but of his own *The Vampire Bat*. *Condemned to Live* has a moderately intriguing prologue set "in the darkest depths of Africa." Against an encroaching tattoo of jungle drums, a woman is about to give birth when she is attacked by a very large, and surprisingly convincing, bat. (The 'death in childbirth while in Africa' angle is an odd reminder of the prologue to Griffith's *One Exciting Night*.)

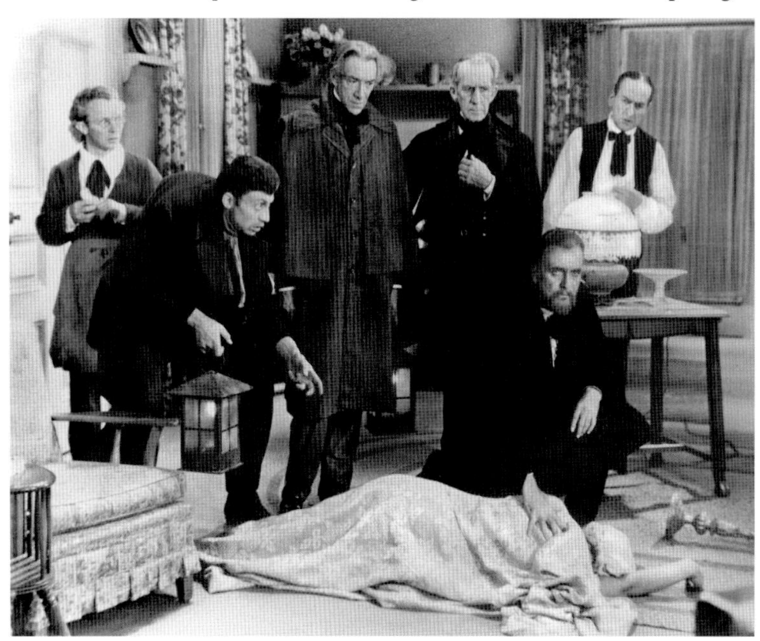

Another exsanguinated victim is discovered by Mischa Auer (with hunchback), Pedro de Cordoba, Carl Stockdale, Edward Cecil and Ralph Morgan (kneeling) in *Condemned to Live* (1935)

The remainder of the film is set some 40 years later in "a peaceful village in another land," where the saintly Professor Kristan has a sanctimonious platitude for every occasion and profound feelings of self-doubt when a rash of killings paralyses the community, killings popularly attributed to a vampire bat. "It's incredibly odd that I was unconscious during every one of these crimes," he agonises. "And these headaches: what are they?"

The answer, of course, is that Kristan is subject to homicidal fugues brought on by his prenatal misfortune, fugues which involve Ralph Morgan developing a bad squint and a severe attack of asthma. Karen de Wolfe's stilted screenplay and Strayer's stagey direction wring zero excitement from the film's peculiar cross-fertilisation of vampirism with *Dr Jekyll and Mr*

Chief beast-man Hans Steinke, master vivisectionist Charles Laughton and 'Panther Woman' Kathleen Burke in *Island of Lost Souls* (1932)

Hyde, and it's further hobbled by an excruciating mixture of classy but clueless character actors (Morgan, Pedro de Cordoba, Mischa Auer) with utter stiffs like romantic leads Russell Gleason and Maxine Doyle. Like *The Vampire Bat*, the film is lent a bit of spurious glamour by standing sets at Universal. Also like *The Vampire Bat*, it features people flinging themselves to their deaths when pursued by lynch mobs into a cave – in this case, Professor Kristan and his devoted hunchback assistant, Zan.

PARAMOUNT MENAGERIE

Despite major hits like DeMille's *The Sign of the Cross*, Paramount went into receivership in the first week of February 1933, filing for bankruptcy some six weeks later. Fortunately, Lowell Sherman's Mae West showcase, *She Done Him Wrong*, had been released in January and would eventually make in excess of $2 million. Also on release that month was *Island of Lost Souls*, in which DeMille's epicene Nero, Charles Laughton, was cast as H G Wells' remorseless animal experimenter Dr Moreau. The film would be rejected by no fewer than 14 local censor boards and banned altogether in the UK, a fate that had previously befallen M-G-M's *Freaks*. In *Variety*, 'Waly' had sounded the warning bell with the ominous observation that "Literally the [film's] proper title is *Island of Lost Freaks*. It is decidedly a freak picture..."

> *Stranded at sea, Edward Parker finds himself on a remote South Seas island belonging to the exiled vivisectionist Dr Moreau. Discovering that the deformed natives were all animals prior to Moreau's intervention, he is disgusted by the doctor's scheme to mate him with the part-feline Lota. When Parker's fiancée Ruth arrives and her ship's captain is killed at Moreau's command, the beast-men rise in revolt and drag the doctor to an atrocious death in his own 'House of Pain'.*

'Waly' had a point. Replacing the genuine circus curios of *Freaks* with vivisected beast-men turned out by Wally Westmore's make-up department, *Island of Lost Souls* shows every sign of having been designed as a riposte to Tod Browning's picture, a curious aspiration given the earlier film's notoriety as a studio-shaming disaster area.

As a combustible cocktail of sex and horror, *Island of Lost Souls* is arguably even stronger than

ISLAND OF LOST SOULS

Paramount 1932
72 minutes
production began 26 September
banned in the UK

Cinematographer: Karl Struss; Art Director: Hans Dreier*; Sound: Loren Ryder*, M M Paggi*; Special Effects: Gordon Jennings*; Camera Operators: George Clemens*, Otto Pierce*; Assistant Camera: Fleet Southcott*, Paul Cable*; Make-up: Wally Westmore*; Music: Arthur Johnston*, Sigmund Krumgold*; Screenplay: Waldemar Young, Philip Wylie ('from a novel [*The Island of Dr Moreau*] by H G Wells'); Director: Erle C Kenton

Charles Laughton (Dr Moreau); Richard Arlen (Edward Parker); Leila Hyams (Ruth Thomas); Bela Lugosi (Sayer of the Law); Kathleen Burke (the Panther Woman [Lota]); Arthur Hohl (Montgomery); Stanley Fields (Captain Davies); Paul Hurst (Donahue); Hans Steinke (Ouran); Tetsu Komai (M'ling); George Irving (the Consul); uncredited: Harry Ezekian (Gola); Rosemary Grimes (Samoan girl); Robert Kortman (Hogan); with Evangelus Berbas, Joe Bonomo, Buster Brodie, Jack Burdette, Buster Crabbe, Robert P Kerr, John George, Alan Ladd, Robert Milasch, Constantine Romanoff, Jack Walters, Duke Yorke

There comes a time when fantasy becomes too fantastic. If this picture ... doesn't come under this criticism, it is close to the border line between astonishment and absurdity ... The make-up man ran amuck with the droves of hideous, half-human creatures who snarl and gibber at the mention of the House of Pain where they were created. Their revenge on their creator is quite too horrible. *Motion Picture*

I had a subjective camera shot there again, as in *Dr Jekyll and Mr Hyde*, when the evil doctor is murdered by the creatures on the island, and he looks up and sees the vivisectional instruments over him like a kind of forest of steel. I admired [Erle] Kenton; he had a greater command of the English language than anyone I ever worked with.
Karl Struss [quoted in Higham, Hollywood Cameramen: Sources of Light, 1970]

Freaks, supplanting the sniggering prurience of the 'impossible' liaison between a blonde bombshell and a midget with the wildly distasteful promise of some bestial 'action' between an all-American boy and a bikini-clad exotic who was formerly a panther. On top of this, the horrendous final reel – in which the vengeful creatures swarm over the screaming Moreau in his own hi-tech operating theatre – is an obvious spin on *Freaks*' similar climactic uprising. It's interesting, too, that Paramount cast *Freaks* veteran Leila Hyams as Parker's fiancée and engaged Waldemar Young as co-adapter of Wells' book; though he hadn't written *Freaks*, he was nevertheless a longstanding collaborator of none other than Tod Browning.

Nobody was better pleased with the British censor's decision than H G Wells himself, who considered the film a vulgarisation of his 1896 novel *The Island of Doctor Moreau*. In addition to the familiar theme of irresponsible science, Wells had intended the book as a parable of social conditioning and the evils of imperialism – and, despite his qualms, the film doesn't entirely abandon these themes. The social conditioning is marvellously played out by Bela Lugosi as the fur-faced Sayer of the Law, reverently intoning "Not to spill blood. That is the law. Are we not men?" as the creatures parrot his mantra in a dreadful, dirge-like undertone. And Charles Laughton's Moreau – wielding a bull-whip, nattily attired in a crisply laundered white suit, and noting sardonically that "The natives are restless tonight" – is a truly frightening blend of Frankenstein and an overfed colonial overseer.

The film also retains Wells' echoes of *The Tempest*, casting Moreau as a kind of techno-Prospero with a whole tribe of misshapen Calibans at his command. The exploitational masterstroke, of course, was to add a feral Miranda to the mix in the luscious form of Lota the Panther Woman, "throbbing," as Paramount's publicity department put it, "to the hot flush of love!" To cast the part, the studio launched a nationwide 'Panther Woman' contest, with a 19-year-old Chicago model called Kathleen Burke eventually chosen out of some 60,000 eager applicants. Though dismissed in *Variety* as "little more than a *White Cargo* bit," Burke repaid Paramount with a memorably wistful performance, perplexed by what Moreau calls "a woman's emotional impulses" and only revealing her feral nature when her nails dig into Parker's back during their poolside clinch.

For those in search of symbolism, Lota's gesture is no different to the orgasmic response of normal, non-panther-derived women, making Parker's horror at discovering her taloned hands a powerful symbol for male fears of 'inappropriately' demonstrative women. Moreau's horror at Lota's relapse is memorable, too, consisting of a blisteringly effective scene in which he notes "the stubborn beast flesh creeping back" and Lota squirms in mortal terror as he insists that "This time I'll burn out all the animal in her!"

Moreau has previously displayed a kind of academic lasciviousness when throwing Lota in Parker's path, saying, of all the comically generic lines he could think of, "Well, I'll leave you two young people together." With the breakdown of his scheme, he turns his attention to Parker's newly arrived fiancée Ruth, a traditionally non-demonstrative ingenue who is duly threatened with beast-rape when the hirsute Ouran breaks through the bars of her room. Though no stranger to overstatement, Laughton carefully underplays Moreau and is all the more chilling for it. At only 32 he was theoretically too young to play a scientist who boasts of having been hounded out of Britain 20 years ago; perhaps to counteract this, his smoothly pancaked face, chiselled goatee and drawn-on eyebrows suggest a man who has himself been subjected to plastic surgery.

Balancing him is Bela Lugosi, an actor never knowingly underplayed, whose over-ripe vocal technique lends a massive freight of tortured emotion to his final repudiation of Moreau. "You made us in the House of Pain," he wails. "You made us – *things*! Not men! Not beasts! Part men, part beasts. *Things*!" Whereupon a succession of his outraged companions surge into massive close-up, one of them displaying a devilish cloven hoof where his right leg should be. Even today, the uprising of the beasts is nightmarish in its sustained intensity, and includes a grimly satisfying shot of taloned hands smashing Moreau's instrument cases as they reach for the scalpels within.

That *Island of Lost Souls* stills packs such a primal charge is a tribute to Erle C Kenton's coolly unsensational direction (as a former portrait photographer and vaudeville animal exhibitor, he was perhaps the ideal man for the job) and, particularly, to the limpid cinematography of Karl Struss. As well as capturing the clammy fogs of Catalina Island, where the exterior shots were taken, Struss also repeats (not once, but twice) his *Dr Jekyll and Mr Hyde* trick of having characters cast small shadows on a brick wall, shadows that become unfeasibly huge as their owners take to their heels and run.

The film's co-writer, Philip Wylie, moved on to another Paramount shocker, this time co-written with Seton I Miller rather than Waldemar Young. To direct *Murders in the Zoo*, Paramount engaged British-born Edward Sutherland, who had recently made *Secrets*

of the French Police for RKO but was better known for his work with master comedian W C Fields. Here, however, he was dealing with Lionel Atwill at his most gloatingly sadistic and, as the film's pressbook put it, "16 truck-loads of wild animals and venomous reptiles from the Selig Zoo." Released at the end of March 1933, the result ended up being banned in, among other places, Sweden, Australia and Germany, which in January had come under the control of Adolf Hitler's National Socialists.

Millionaire animal trapper Eric Gorman uses a fund-raising dinner at the Municipal Zoo as a means of dispatching his wife's lover, Roger Hewitt. When Evelyn discovers the dried mamba head with which her husband committed the crime, Gorman silences her by tumbling her into the alligator pond. When he tries to poison the zoo's resident toxicologist, however, he ends up tightly constricted in the coils of a colossal python.

Murders in the Zoo remains a delightful picture, not much more than a programmer as far as Paramount were concerned but realised with all the professional lustre the studio had at its command. Apart from a prologue set in French Indo-China (and somewhat reminiscent of the old Lon Chaney vehicle *Where East is East*), the setting – presumably New York – is definitely of the 1933 here-and-now. The sleekly functional sets of Hans Dreier yield to the Gothic mode only in the heavy formality and abundant curios of Gorman's forbidding home, and even then only to the smallest degree.

The realities of the Depression aren't flinched from, either. The zoo's curator complains of having had his budget cut four times, the idealistic doctor lays off several staff members with the words "I know you boys have families; I hate to let you go but there's nothing else I can do," and Gorman himself tells a future victim that "You're one of the few fortunates who still have a little [money] left."

The horror of the film's exotic prologue is played for all its worth, so much so that it would have been impossible under the terms of the Production Code, enforced only a year later. A man is seen being held down in a jungle clearing by native bearers as Gorman does a bit of brutal crochet work. "A Mongolian prince taught me this, Taylor," he says with the sadistic relish of a connoisseur. "An ingenious device for the right occasion." The victim later lurches into screen-hogging close-up to reveal ghastly sutures criss-crossed over his mouth – a fitting punishment, according to Gorman's atavistic code, for attempting to kiss Gorman's wife.

The next man to cross Gorman is removed via the elaborate expedient of an invitation-only banquet in the zoo's Carnivora House, the murder weapon being a severed snake's head with envenomed fangs. Sutherland plays up the latent absurdity of bejewelled New York dowagers sitting down to dine among an assortment of caged big cats, only to execute a dramatic lateral camera movement, sweeping away from the inane speech being given by the zoo's press agent to the tuxedoed victim

MURDERS IN THE ZOO

Paramount 1933
66 minutes
production began late December 1932

Cinematographer: Ernest Haller; Art Director: Hans Dreier*; Sound: Loren Ryder*; Music: Rudolph G Kopp*, John M Leipold*; Musical Director: Nat W Finston*; Animal Trainer: Chubby Guilfoyle*; Screenplay: Philip Wylie, Seton I Miller; Additional Dialogue: Milton H Gropper*; Associate Producer: E Lloyd Sheldon*; Director: Edward Sutherland

Charlie Ruggles (Peter Yates); Lionel Atwill (Eric Gorman); Gail Patrick (Jerry Evans); Randolph Scott (Dr Woodford); John Lodge (Roger Hewitt); Kathleen Burke (Evelyn Gorman); Harry Beresford (Professor Evans); uncredited: Duke Green (stevedore); Ethan Laidlaw (Reardon); Edward McWade (Dan [zookeeper]); Bert Moorhouse (desk clerk); John Rogers (steward); Edwin Stanley, Walter Walker (doctors); Jane Darwell, Samuel S Hinds, Cyril Ring (zoo patrons); Stanley Blystone, Eddie Boland, Sydney D'Albrook, Lee Phelps, Syd Saylor (reporters)

Generally, the effect is apt to be more ludicrous than thrilling and even Lionel Atwill's polished acting as the murderer is insufficient to make the part at all convincing ... but the support is sound as far as it is given opportunities, and includes Kathleen Burke, the much publicised 'Panther Woman' of *Island of Lost Souls*, which we have not been permitted to see here yet.
Picturegoer Weekly [UK]

All women love the men who are capable of mental cruelty. All women love the men they fear ... Which brings me back to horror – and the probably helpless love of it in every heart, male or female ... There is something about horror that is horribly compelling. Is it because we see our possible selves in these dark mirrors? Lionel Atwill [quoted in *Motion Picture*, July 1933]

Cheshire Cat Lionel Atwill and former Panther Woman Kathleen Burke in *Murders in the Zoo* (1933)

surging up in his chair and falling contortedly to the floor. Later, Gorman reveals himself as a close relative of Count Zaroff – clearly turned on in the aftermath of the kill, he importunes Evelyn even as she accuses him of murder. "You don't think I sat there all evening with an eight-foot mamba in my pocket, do you?" he scoffs. "Why, it would be an injustice to my tailor."

Whether written by Wylie or Miller, the outrageously Freudian nature of this wisecrack can't have been lost on Atwill, whose own outré inclinations would be disastrously exposed in a so-called 'orgy' trial in 1941. For now, in a Hollywood landscape studded with degenerate hunchbacks and mesmeric Hungarians, he adopted an unusually sophisticated approach to screen villainy, explaining to interviewer Faith Service that "the abnormal people are not always the people who behave abnormally, or even erratically. The abnormal person, as noted by Krafft-Ebbing, is very likely to be your quiet, well-behaved partner at the family bridge table."[18] Applying this philosophy to Eric Gorman, he created a memorably suave sociopath. A cold-hearted predator more in love with animals than humans, Gorman extols "their primitive emotions" and lives by a similar, and disarmingly simple, code – "They love, they hate, they kill."

Atwill does not receive top billing, however. Still liverish about fully committing themselves to the horror boom – and no doubt mindful of the unrelieved slew of sadistic horrors that was *Island of Lost Souls* – Paramount extended that accolade to Charlie Ruggles instead. Brother of director Wesley Ruggles, his inept PR man is a former alcoholic seemingly terrified of any animal larger than a hamster. Though Ruggles' comic-relief schtick has dated badly (and he's saddled with some unusually vulgar pre-Code quips to boot), he remains a reasonably engaging presence and doesn't disrupt the film's sadistic highlights.

Elsewhere, Gail Patrick and Randolph Scott give a slickly professional sheen to underdeveloped roles and the former Panther Woman, Kathleen Burke, is outstanding as the luckless Evelyn, eloquently expressing a loathing of Gorman that the audience wholeheartedly shares. The climax, too, is a corker, with the cornered Gorman unleashing the big cats (amazing footage here of a savage brawl between leopards and lions) prior to stumbling into the embrace of a 20-foot boa constrictor. Atwill was reportedly so taken with this creature that he not only performed his own stunts with it but also took it home to add to his private menagerie, a story that may well be apocryphal but which nevertheless has a sufficiently Gormanesque ring to be alluring.

STRANGE POWERS

The presidential election of November 1932 resulted, unsurprisingly, in a landslide victory for Franklin Delano Roosevelt, whose promises of "a New Deal for the American people" were backed up by a campaign song insisting that 'Happy Days are Here Again'. With the thoroughly demoralised Herbert Hoover consigned to history, Roosevelt proved a dynamic force, setting up a network of 'alphabet agencies' to combat the effects of the Depression. Among numerous measures designed to maximise government revenue and create new jobs, he even repealed Prohibition on 20 March 1933, less than three weeks after his inauguration.

Chief among the alphabet agencies was the National Recovery Administration, which by July would be the subject of some gentle satire in James Whale's latest horror-fantasy, *The Invisible Man*. In an orgy of anti-social violence, the disembodied voice of the title character cheerfully parrots the NRA slogan "We do our part" even as he lobs a stone through the window of a local grocer's. This was an odd piece of satire, however, in that the film was set in England rather than the USA.

As noted above, the month of Roosevelt's inauguration saw the bankrupt Paramount at its lowest ebb. As far as film fans were concerned, however, nothing seemed amiss. In addition to *Island of Lost Souls* and *Murders in the Zoo*, the studio's production slate for the 1932-3 season included a very different chiller, exchanging jungle histrionics for the impeccable good manners of a high-society novelette. Impressed, like everyone else in Hollywood, by the financial returns of the humble *White Zombie*, Paramount executives had offered Victor and Edward Halperin the chance to do something similar with the high-gloss resources of a major studio. The result, *Supernatural*, went on release a mere three weeks after *Murders in the Zoo*.

Attempting to prevent the soul of executed Greenwich Village murderess Ruth Rogen from entering another person, well-meaning psychologist Dr Houston achieves precisely the opposite, the infected person being young millionairess Roma Courtney. Grieving for her deceased twin brother, Roma has recently consulted phoney spiritualist Paul Bavian, who happens to be the man who betrayed Rogen to the police. Now Roma entices Bavian to her yacht with the purpose of strangling him...

In Paul Bavian, the Halperins had a conniving protagonist in the well-worn tradition of 1920s pictures like *The Mystic* and *The Faker*. As played by Allan Dinehart, he comes across like the sleazier twin brother of Melvyn Douglas in *The Old Dark House*. A hearse-chasing opportunist par excellence, Bavian's down-at-heel apartment has a black cat standing sentry and an array of machinery within that includes a phoney disembodied hand and an illegally acquired death-mask of young John Courtney. And, in a ploy reminiscent of the mediaeval flashback in Paramount's 1919 version of *Dr Jekyll and Mr Hyde*, he sports a signet ring containing some nameless poison, and this becomes central to the film's most memorable scene. Exasperated by his interfering landlady, he cheerfully shakes her hand and watches calmly as she recoils from the scratch she receives, the pair of them laughing hysterically as she subsides onto the sofa and keeps asking "It's only a joke, isn't it?" The performances here, from both Dinehart and Beryl Mercer, are first-rate.

The scene comes early in the picture, but there's plenty to enjoy elsewhere. Overwhelmed by the wraparound luxuriance of the Paramount machine, Victor Halperin predictably failed to recreate the eerie ambience of *White Zombie*. But there's still an agreeable frisson to be had from the subtle supernatural touches he introduces into the clean lines of Hans Dreier's chic settings. When Ruth's soul is accidentally liberated, rain is pouring down outside Dr Houston's plush apartment-cum-laboratory. Ruth's dead eyes flash open through "galvanic action" and the intrusion of the supernatural is gently indicated by the billowing of drapes and the riffled pages of a magazine. Later, Bavian contrives to show bogus 'spirit writing' emerging in the folds of a handkerchief, with the added irony of his phoney seance being the scene of the genuinely supernatural transmigration of souls between Ruth and Roma.

Later to achieve immortality through such evergreen comedies as *Twentieth Century* and *Nothing Sacred*, Carole Lombard achieves the transition with much arching of her already dramatic eyebrows, as well as a super-subtle gradation of make-up and stop-frame photography. Processes of this sort drove the already combustible Lombard to distraction; though dialogue director Sidney Salkow remembered Halperin as "a sweet mild-mannered gentleman," he also recalled Lombard's contemptuous cry of "This guy [Halperin] ought to be running a deli" and the more generalised "Who do you have to screw to get off this picture?"[19] Shaken also by the Long Beach earthquake on Friday

SUPERNATURAL

Paramount 1933
65 minutes
production began 16 February

Cinematographer: Arthur Martinelli; Art Director: Hans Dreier*; Sound: Loren Ryder*; Second Camera: Jockey Feindel*, Roy Eslick*; Assistant Camera: Eddie Adams*, Al Smalley*; Gowns: [Travis] Banton*; Music: Karl Hajos*, Howard Jackson*, Milan Roder*; Dialogue Director: Sidney Salkow; Screenplay: Harvey Thew, Brian Marlow; Story and Adaptation: Garnett Weston; Producer: Edward Halperin; Director: Victor Halperin

Carole Lombard (Roma Courtney); Allan Dinehart (Paul Bavian); Vivienne Osborne (Ruth Rogen); Randolph Scott (Grant Wilson); H B Warner (Dr Houston); Beryl Mercer (landlady); William Farnum (Hammond); Willard Robertson (warden); George Burr MacAnnan (Max); Lyman Williams (John Courtney)

The transmigration of personality gives the picture a new and absorbing theme and its possibilities are turned into arresting drama, the backgrounds of which have an irresistible, eerie fascination ... Here is something off the beaten track, which, at the same time, meets all the demands expected of a popular thriller. *Kinematograph Weekly* [UK]

At 5.10 pm, March 10, 1933, the set suddenly started to rumble ... To all of us it was the Long Beach earthquake (it took 52 lives). To Carole it was 'Lombard's Revenge'. I watched her ... stride to Victor Halperin huddled outside the still-swaying stage and point a finger at him. "Victor – *that* was only a warning!" *Sidney Salkow* [in Peary (ed), *Close Ups: The Movie Star Book*, 1978]

Executed murderess Vivienne Osborne possesses beautiful millionairess Carole Lombard in *Supernatural* (1933)

10 March, the demoralised Halperin was reportedly no match for Lombard's barbs.

Despite her belief that she was 'slumming' it in such a preposterous project, Lombard looks sensational in various slinky numbers designed by Travis Banton and also brings an agreeably vindictive edge to her climactic assault on the amorous Bavian. "Now do you recognise me?" she spits. "I *am* Ruth Rogen. I'm going to kill you before I leave this body you like so much."

In a strikingly effective credits sequence, Halperin sought to bolster the validity of Garnett Weston's story by interleaving bolts of lightning with portentous quotes from Confucius, Mohammed and Saint Matthew. He also claimed to have done substantial research with his brother Edward, including a Pasadena interview with the Julian Sisters that entailed the conjuration of deceased showbiz luminaries like Thomas H Ince, Jack Pickford and David Belasco. But the confusion of intent behind the picture is plain from Paramount's pressbook contention that "*Supernatural* is a sympathetic treatment of spiritualism, and at the same time an exposé of the methods used by crooked mediums in duping the public." On top of which, the 'transmigration of souls' angle – which would find an echo in later British shockers like *Frankenstein Created Woman* and *The Asphyx* – is not only garbled to start with but also listlessly put over by scientist H B Warner.

The film gets away from Halperin in its final third; the business aboard Roma's yacht is sloppily done until Roma gets down to the matter at hand, ie, strangulation. But it's still watchable for Arthur Martinelli's dexterously mobile camera and for probably the first fully fledged female serial killer in cinema history. Ruth Rogen, we're told, "killed each of her three lovers after a riotous orgy in her sensuous Greenwich Village apartment." She's played by Vivienne Osborne, who had come to prominence in the Broadway and West End productions of the steamy miscegenation drama *Aloma of the South Seas* and here gives nasty conviction to lines like "If I could use my hands for just a few minutes..."

Carole Lombard was mooted for another Paramount shocker in 1933, *Dead Reckoning*. Eventually made by director Paul Sloane as *Terror Aboard*, Shirley Grey substituted for Lombard in a gruesome story co-written, like *Supernatural*, by Harvey Thew. Having concluded *Supernatural* with a long sequence set aboard a yacht, Thew played out the entire action of *Terror Aboard* on a similar vessel. As Paramount's PR put it, "Death stalks the deck of a pleasure ship" – with a crazed ship owner disposing of everyone present, "each in a different but ghastly fashion." Undaunted, heroine Shirley Grey travelled to England two years later to appear opposite Bela Lugosi in a similar picture, an early Hammer production called *The Mystery of the Mary Celeste*. Monogram, meanwhile, put William Nigh to work on a 1934 variant of *Terror Aboard* called *Mystery Liner*, adapted from an Edgar Wallace original.

Supernatural's phoney medium, Allan Dinehart, moved on in April 1934 to make Max Marcin's *The Love Captive*, a forgotten Universal melodrama in which Dinehart left the huckster role to Nils Asther, who plays a duplicitous hypnotist exposed by Dinehart's crusading lawyer. Also in 1934, hypnotism was the crux of Paramount's *The Witching Hour*, based on an Augustus Thomas play previously filmed by Paramount in 1921. The director then was the ill-fated William Desmond Taylor; now, the property (for the most part a rather windy courtroom drama) was handed to Henry Hathaway. Concerning a young man who commits a murder when accidentally placed under hypnosis by his father-in-law, it also features a spectral cameo for the defence counsel's deceased sweetheart (Gertrude Michael). The producer was playwright Bayard Veiller, the screenwriter his son Anthony, and the unwitting hypnotist was played by *Terror Aboard* veteran John Halliday.

The most hypnotic eyes in Hollywood, however, belonged to Bela Lugosi. Back in March 1933, while Carole Lombard was doing battle with his old associate Victor Halperin at Paramount, Lugosi was starring in a convoluted melodrama for producer Bryan Foy called *He Lived to Kill*. Lugosi's simultaneous commitment to Paramount's W C Fields vehicle *International House* reportedly necessitated that the Foy film be shot at night. Perhaps as a result, by the time of its release in June, it had acquired the nondescript title *Night of Terror*.

> *Professor Rinehart is found murdered in his laboratory just as his nephew Arthur is preparing to demonstrate a suspended animation formula. Several people are suspected of the crime, including the old man's assembled heirs and two Hindu servants. But when further murders ensue, Arthur is free from suspicion, having been buried alive in the sight of several fellow scientists. Until, that is, his underground casket is discovered to be empty...*

Directed by Benjamin Stoloff, *Night of Terror* was distributed by Columbia, a studio that had so far held aloof from the horror bandwagon set in motion by Universal. Further indications of the studio's half-heartedness were provided by the finished product,

Mystic manservant Bela Lugosi (centre) with Mary Frey, Tully Marshall, Sally Blane and Wallace Ford in *Night of Terror* (1933)

which is yet another pedestrian retread of *The Cat and the Canary*, shot in 13 days flat and not much more ambitious than a Poverty Row equivalent like *The Monster Walks*. And, depressingly, all it can contrive for its top-billed menace is a red-herring role as saturnine Hindu manservant Degar, whose dialogue consists almost entirely of "I want to warn you of danger" and clichéd variants thereof.

One moderately effective scene in *Night of Terror* involves Degar's mediumistic wife, Sika, presiding at a seance designed to identify the killer. "It's the face of a madman," she breathes. "It's very plain. Oh, it's – " Inevitably, she is impaled through the back of her chair before she can continue, confirming the suspicion that the film's writers have taken a brief detour from *The Cat and the Canary* into *The Thirteenth Chair*. Thinking back to the juicy part he had taken in Tod Browning's talkie remake of that property, Lugosi no doubt had cause to reflect on the absurdity of Columbia's description of Degar as an "exacting leading role" and on the bitter truth of another pressbook statement: "Hollywood has scribbled a little card of classification that has limited the screen roles of Bela Lugosi since his international success in the title role of *Dracula*." Perhaps as a consequence of these reflections, Lugosi overplays Degar's gnomic pronouncements to the point of caricature.

His first appearance, however, is a hoot. Alerted by a noise, Tully Marshall's Professor Rinehart goes to his laboratory door and, instead of opening it, unhinges one of its panels – and there, perfectly framed, is Lugosi's face, eyes smouldering satanically under a chic-looking turban. The use of the name Rinehart was presumably a sly nod to the author of *The Bat*, while the casting of Tully Marshall was a gesture to its near-relation, *The Cat and the Canary*. Indeed, Marshall's showstopping death plunge in that film is replicated here when Detective Bailey opens the front door to admit the plummeting corpse of Rinehart's gardener. By 1933, however, this may have been another reference to James Cagney's 'delivered to the door' demise in *The Public Enemy*.

NIGHT OF TERROR

Foy Productions 1933
64 minutes
production began 1 March

Cinematographer: Joseph A Valentine; Technical [ie, Art] Director: W L Vogel; Editor: Arthur Hilton; Sound: Lambert Day*; Assistant Camera: Walter Rankin*; Assistant Director: Leslie Nielson*; Screenplay: Beatrice Van, William Jacobs; Story: Willard Mack; Producer: Bryan Foy*; Director: Ben Stoloff

Bela Lugosi (Degar); Wallace Ford (Tom Hartley); Sally Blane (Mary Rinehart); Tully Marshall (Richard Rinehart); Bryant Washburn (John Rinehart); Gertrude Michael (Sara Rinehart); George Meeker (Arthur Hornsby); Mary Frey (Sika); Matt McHugh (Detective Bailey); Edwin Maxwell (maniac); uncredited: Frank Austin (doctor); Pat Harmon (Dooley); Eric Mayne (Professor André); Dave O'Brien (young man in car); Oscar Smith (Martin)

If you have a penchant for thrillers you will like this one, which employs all the old devices to get a thrill, and includes amongst its humorous interludes the dumb detective and the petrified nigger. There is just a touch of love interest to complete the mixture, which is conventional but well photographed. *Picturegoer Weekly* [UK]

Due to the fact that Bela Lugosi ... was busy during the day working on a picture at another studio, it was found necessary to film scenes for Columbia's new murder-mystery drama ... during the eerie hours between two and six o'clock in the morning ... Little Sally Blane screamed with real fright the first time that Lugosi unexpectedly ... bared his whitened and sepulchral face to her startled eyes. *from original pressbook*

The gardener is a victim, not of the duplicitous schemer within the house, but of an obscurely motivated 'maniac' outside it. In *The Cat and the Canary*, of course, these two characters turned out to be one and the same; the business of separating them only makes the maniac seem like an irrelevance. He does give the opening a certain zing, however. Emerging from foliage by the light of the full moon, he spies on a young couple spooning in a parked car prior to stabbing them to death. And at the end, despite having been killed, he rises up from the floor of the Rinehart cellar to address the audience directly. "If you dare tell anyone how this picture ends," he gurns, "I'll climb into your bedroom window tonight and tear you limb from limb," etc. Unfortunately, the bulky Edwin Maxwell – last seen in *Mystery of the Wax Museum* and here sporting the standard get-up of slouch hat, fangs and shaggy fright-wig – can only remind British viewers of the comic actor Ronnie Barker in one of his more outré disguises.

According to the film's pressbook, "Columbia was anxious to film a murder-mystery with a little different twist," providing just that with the bookish Arthur's ghoulish experiment in being buried alive. Willard Mack, a theatrical producer-cum-playwright who had previously adapted *The Monster* for Roland West, claimed to have had this plot point in the back of his mind for five years. In practice, however, it seems like a modish attempt to update *The Cat and the Canary* to the *Frankenstein* era via a dash of Edgar Allan Poe.

The film does have its moments, notably a striking credits sequence shot through the distorting lens of a crystal ball, a scene in which Degar gives a policeman a euphemistically named "Oriental cigarette," and a dangling skeleton silhouetted on the window blind as the maniac breaks into the Rinehart house. It also has the familiar percentage of self-satisfied 'comedy relief' wiseacres, though, in the form of Wallace Ford and Matt McHugh (both veterans of Tod Browning's *Freaks*), they're slightly more engaging than usual. Less so is the insulting use of a stammering black chauffeur, perpetually frightened and lumbered with lines like "If I was to meet that there maniac I would become famous – I would be the first man to fly without wings."

That Columbia could sponsor a simple-minded mystery-thriller like *Night of Terror* was proof that Whale's wickedly parodic *Old Dark House* had fallen on deaf ears. Indeed, plenty of lower-level filmmakers continued to plough the well-worn furrow with undiminished gusto.

On release in August 1932, for instance, was Albert Ray's *The Thirteenth Guest*, which enlivened its regulation 'last will and testament' plot with flavoursome dialogue by *Scarface* author Armitage Trail and engaging young leads Ginger Rogers and Lyle Talbot. H Bruce Humberstone's *The Crooked Circle* followed in September, anticipating not only *Night of Terror*'s suspended animation theme but also its sinister attendant Hindus; the script was by Ralph (*The Gorilla*) Spence. By October, Max Hoffman and Albert Ray (producer and director of *The Thirteenth Guest*) were at work on *The Intruder*, transferring the action to an uncharted island and throwing a gorilla into the mix, together with Mischa Auer as a sort of feral Robinson Crusoe, custodian of a caveful of skeletons. And in 1933, Hoffman and Ray got Lyle Talbot and Ginger Rogers together again for *A Shriek in the Night*, the result belying its title in that it contains no creepy embellishments whatever, aside from a nasty scene in which a janitor tries to feed Rogers into his basement furnace.

Back in 'old house' vein, fans of the form were likely to OD on its spooky accoutrements in 1933. They could take a choice, for example, between Columbia's *Before Midnight*, a 'family curse' detective drama directed by Lambert Hillyer, or *Before Dawn*, an RKO 'find the loot' item made unusual by the inclusion of a pretty psychic (Dorothy Wilson) whose powers are genuine. The latter also benefits from the impressive triumvirate of director Irving Pichel, screenwriter Garrett Fort and recently deceased original author Edgar Wallace. Lower down the scale were two pictures featuring Vivienne Osborne, the vengeful murderess of *Supernatural* – *The Phantom Broadcast*, a Monogram cheapie directed by Phil Rosen, and Ray Enright's *Tomorrow at Seven*, in which Osborne starred opposite Chester Morris; like *The Crooked Circle*, this one was written by Ralph Spence.

Alternatively, fans could catch Richard Thorpe's splendidly titled *Strange People*, a Chesterfield quickie (filmed, like *The Vampire Bat*, on the *Old Dark House* set) in which an elaborate murder charade is set up to persuade a bunch of jurors to reconsider their guilty verdict; inevitably, a real murder ensues. The following year, Thorpe's assistant, Melville Shyer, cropped up as full-fledged director of a Progressive Pictures variant called *The Murder in the Museum*, in which *White Zombie*'s John Harron investigates the killing of a local politician in a sideshow straight out of the Tod Browning recipe book. The Sphere Museum contains a disembodied female head as per *The Show*, belly dancers similar to those in *The Unholy Three*, and an armless sketch artist reminiscent of *The Unknown*. There's also a flashing-eyed mummy in the lumber room and a touching performance from top-billed Henry B Walthall (himself a Browning veteran), playing a "Bibliophile [hiding] under the charlatan's robe" of a carnival prestidigitator.

By April 1935 thrill-hungry picturegoers were presented with a more than usually accomplished rip-off of *The Cat and the Canary*, a Mascot potboiler called *One Frightened Night*. Bullishly advertised as "The Swellest 'Who-Done-It' Ever Filmed," Christy Cabanne's film features some charming variations on the usual routine – the elderly millionaire (played with relish by Charley Grapewin) is still very much alive, and two blondes show up claiming to be the same

heir; one of them is duly killed. The cast also includes such 'old house' veterans as Fred Kelsey and Lucien Littlefield, with *Night of Terror*'s Wallace Ford offering light relief as a fast-talking vaudevillian.

UNIVERSAL IN FLUX

By the beginning of 1933, Universal was in sufficiently dire straits to necessitate a studio shutdown, complete with laying-off of staff and suspension of contracts. The hiatus was lifted on 1 April, by which time Boris Karloff was in London making *The Ghoul* for Gaumont-British. On his return, he precipitated a further crisis when discovering that the Laemmles proposed not to honour an agreed salary increase. On 1 June, Karloff walked out, sending the Laemmles scrambling to set up an even more lucrative contract for him, which they did in July.

In the meantime, Universal's latest fantasy had been left without a leading man. James Whale hit instead upon the British stage actor Claude Rains, whose smokily sophisticated tones would be ideal for a character who is dominant yet barely discernible. H G Wells' *The Invisible Man* was one of the first properties picked up by the studio in the wake of *Dracula*, since when it had gone through a wide variety of outlandishly unfaithful screenplays (including attempts by future directors Preston Sturges and John Huston) before James Whale's playwright friend, R C Sherriff, hit upon the ingenious expedient of going back to the book.

Dr Jack Griffin has been experimenting with Monocane, a drug that renders him (a) invisible and (b) insane. Enlisting former associate Kemp in his plan to initiate a reign of terror, Griffin responds to Kemp's betrayal by causing a train wreck, later murdering Kemp himself. When his tracks are revealed by a snowfall, he is gunned down by the police and, dying, tells his sweetheart Flora that "I meddled in things that man must leave alone."

Universal had also picked up a recent Philip Wylie novel called *The Murderer Invisible*, which may have fed into Sherriff's script via the conversion of Griffin into a murderous megalomaniac. Though delighted with the finished film, Wells' only complaint related to this possibly Wylie-derived detail; hardly surprising, given Wells' disgust at Wylie's recent adaptation of *The Island of Dr Moreau*. Observing that "instead of an invisible man we now have an invisible lunatic," Wells called it "a liberty he could not condone." Whale's unruffled response was that "in the minds of rational people only a lunatic would want to make himself invisible anyway."[12]

THE INVISIBLE MAN

Universal 1933
71 minutes
production began 30 June

Cinematography: Arthur Edeson, John J Mescall*; Art Director: Charles D Hall; Editor: Ted Kent; Sound: William Hedgcock; Special Effects Photography: John P Fulton; Make-up: Jack P Pierce*; Music: Heinz Roemheld*; Screenplay: R C Sherriff (based on the novel by H G Wells); Producer: Carl Laemmle Jr; Director: James Whale

Claude Rains (Dr Jack Griffin); Gloria Stuart (Flora Cranley); William Harrigan (Dr Kemp); Henry Travers (Dr Cranley); Una O'Connor (Jenny Hall); Forrester Harvey (Herbert Hall); Holmes Herbert (Chief of Police); E E Clive (Police Constable Jaffers); Dudley Digges (Chief of Detectives); Harry Stubbs (Police Inspector Bird); Donald Stuart (Inspector Lane); Merle Tottenham (Milly); uncredited: Walter Brennan (cyclist); Robert Brower (elderly farmer); Dwight Frye (reporter); Mary Gordon (screaming woman); Violet Kemble Cooper (woman); John Merivale (newsboy); Monte Montague (bobby); John Peter Richmond [later John Carradine] (tall man in telephone booth); Jameson Thomas (doctor); Ted Billings, D'Arcy Corrigan (villagers)

My recollection is that when, too many years ago, I read *The Invisible Man*, I revelled in its farcical situations ... But in the film version it has become a tragedy. It is, however, none the worse for that, and without such treatment we should miss a railway accident of the highest merit and a pretty good motor accident too. Punch [UK]

When she had got it all typed out my secretary [at Universal] said it was too long ... "But you don't have to worry," she said. "The story department has had a lot of experience in cutting scripts down. If you leave it to them they'll soon get ten pages out of it." But I didn't want that to happen at any price ... The only thing was to start afresh and write the screenplay over again.
R C Sherriff [*No Leading Lady*, 1968]

"There must be a way back. God knows, there's a way back..."
Claude Rains as *The Invisible Man* (1933)

Despite Wells' reservations, Griffin's Monocane-induced monomania was to exercise a powerful influence on future films. The lunatic schemes of scientific over-reachers in silent serials had, by necessity, been only vaguely articulated; here, though, was a mad scientist whose plans for world domination came in the immaculate prose of R C Sherriff. "Suddenly I realised the power I held, the power to rule, to make the world grovel at my feet," Griffin exults. "Power to walk into the gold vaults of the nations, into the secrets of kings, into the Holy of Holies. Power to make multitudes run squealing in terror at the touch of my invisible finger!"

The Nietzschean note struck here wasn't lost on contemporary observers, who were all too aware of Adolf Hitler's recent appointment as German chancellor. Echoing a classic line spoken by the film's befuddled provincial bobby – "How can I 'andcuff a bloomin' shirt?" – E V Lucas of the British magazine *Punch* headed his review 'The Whiteshirt Movement'. Though Lucas didn't elaborate, he was obviously referring to the Fascist 'blackshirt' faction headed by Oswald Mosley, whose clenched fist and declamatory hectoring precisely paralleled Hitler and, for that matter, Griffin. Appropriately, Griffin proves to be the most thoroughgoing mass murderer of any featured in horror pictures of the period; he kills 100 people at a stroke via a train derailment, picks off another 20 when search parties are sent out, cold-bloodedly sends Dr Kemp to his death and brains a sceptical police inspector out of sheer devilment.

In Whale's typically impish style, this profoundly frightening character is inserted into a thoroughly cosy British milieu. *The Old Dark House* had offered a deliciously well-observed microcosm of British life; *The Invisible Man* expands on this sardonic view of Whale's fellow countrymen, starting with a crowded provincial pub and ending on a massive police dragnet. Like the earlier film, the result could easily be mistaken for a product of Elstree or Twickenham after a significant cash infusion; even William Harrigan's rather transatlantic Kemp could be the kind of minor US name routinely imported by British producers.

The film's first act, detailing the havoc Griffin wreaks in the rural village of Iping, is the closest to Wells' book, with two of Whale's favourite West End performers – E E Clive and Una O'Connor – well to the fore. Whale's outré taste in actors was variable, however. Clive is a delight as Constable Jaffers and was to be even funnier in *Bride of Frankenstein*; O'Connor is a caterwauling bore as the Lion's Head landlady and was to be even worse in *Bride*.

Fortunately, the opening scenes are sufficiently gripping that such anomalies can be overlooked. There is a marvellous sense of desolation in the very first shot – a snow-covered country lane, with the darkly foreboding figure of Griffin winding his way towards a forlornly angled road sign. And the intrigue at the Lion's Head reaches a fantastic crescendo as Griffin performs a triumphant striptease in front of Jaffers and a motley crew of gobsmacked villagers. (Among them, such familiar Universal faces as Ted Billings and D'Arcy Corrigan.) In his flight, Griffin not only overturns a grandfather clock (as previously happened in *The Old Dark House*), he also flings bicycles, overturns perambulators, smashes windows and, later, splashes ink in a policeman's face.

Liberated from the constraints of his physical self, it's as if Griffin also liberates what Poe called the imp of the perverse – in this he resembles Fredric March's initially skittish Mr Hyde – and Whale plays the resultant mayhem for all the sinister farce it's capable of. Even when we know that Griffin is a dangerous psychopath, Whale still has him performing schoolboy pranks like swiping the helmet from one policeman and 'debagging' another.

There's nothing funny, however, about the cat-and-mouse game he plays with the unpleasant but unfortunate Dr Kemp, during which Rains puts a really chilling spin on lines like, "There's no need to be afraid, Kemp. We're partners; bosom friends." Kemp's brutal demise is a real shocker, adding interest to a perfunctory closing act in which Whale's enthusiasm seems to have waned somewhat. Through it all, though, the special photographic effects of John P Fulton remain astonishing to behold, and were especially staggering to contemporary audiences still reeling from *King Kong*.

In the wake of his remarkable performance in *The Invisible Man*, Claude Rains was unceremoniously dropped by Universal, leaving him free in May 1934 to appear in *Crime Without Passion*, an independent production from the legendary team of Ben Hecht and Charles MacArthur. Shot at Paramount's former East Coast facility in Long Island, this features Rains as a high-handed defence advocate who disintegrates rapidly after killing a man in a nightclub. Intriguingly, the film is augmented at beginning and end by stunning surrealistic montages devised by Slavko Vorkapich and Leo Lippe. The Furies of Greek legend – "three sisters of Evil who lie in wait for those who live dangerously and without Gods" – are seen rising up from a puddle of blood to careen laughingly through the canyons of New York City. Fraye Gilbert, Dorothy Bradshaw and Betty Sundmark would have

been ideal casting for the vampire brides in *Dracula*; on top of this, they caused red faces at the MPPDA, which noted that "the costumes of the 'Furies' are so light as to constitute indecent exposure prohibited by the Code."[12]

The second in Hecht and MacArthur's ill-fated production programme, *The Scoundrel*, appeared in April 1935 and starred the British actor-playwright Noël Coward as a callous publisher who dies in a plane crash and returns as a ghost. Another Hecht-MacArthur project, *The Monster*, was planned for Coward but finally appeared in 1940 as a Paramount production called *The Mad Doctor*, with Basil Rathbone in the Coward role. Strangely, its origin as a Hecht-MacArthur script went entirely unmentioned.

After *Crime Without Passion*, Claude Rains was finally recalled by Universal to star in Edward Ludwig's *The Man Who Reclaimed His Head*, a thoughtful treatise on war profiteering shamelessly advertised as a horror picture. Despite the incidental detail of Rains decapitating Lionel Atwill and carrying his head around in a valise, it's nothing of the sort. When it was released on Christmas Eve of 1934, Rains was at work on Stuart Walker's *The Mystery of Edwin Drood*, in which his opium-addled choirmaster murders David Manners' title character on, appropriately, Christmas Eve. A diverting, lavishly appointed and occasionally eerie attempt at completing Charles Dickens' unfinished novel, the film proved a disappointment at the box-office. Maybe Dickens fans were put off by the misleading full moon, complete with attendant bats, that Universal appended to the posters.

Presumably in response to the increasingly strident lobbying of religious and women's groups for the Production Code to be strengthened, Universal had become noticeably reticent about horror subjects. Unwilling to make out-and-out shockers, the studio nevertheless decorated otherwise innocuous films with horror trimmings (if only in their advertising) in an attempt to retain its horror constituency while not inflaming censors; a particularly limp example was Richard Thorpe's *Secret of the Chateau*, a Sûreté whodunit issued in December 1934.

In this new mood of caution, Junior Laemmle would be utterly confounded by the wayward cowboy star Ken Maynard, whose *Smoking Guns* added a malaria-ridden swamp, man-eating alligators, a supposedly haunted house, a creepy Texas graveyard, a troop of outlaws disguised as ghosts and a Hallowe'en night climax to an otherwise conventional revenge plot. Previewed in April 1934 under its production title, *Doomed to Die*, this was directed by Alan James and proved to be the last of Maynard's lucrative, Universal-sponsored series.

Master of montage Slavko Vorkapich and "sister of evil" Fraye Gilbert, working together on the nightmarish prologue to *Crime Without Passion* (1934)

In 1934, Universal's reticence was echoed elsewhere in Hollywood, though a Svengali-type hypnotist appeared in Warners' *The Man with Two Faces* (directed, like *Svengali*, by Archie Mayo) and elements of horror crept into two films based on the works of crime writer Philip MacDonald. Metro's *The Mystery of Mr X* was directed by Edgar Selwyn and features Robert Montgomery as a Raffles-like gentleman thief implicated in the slayings of nine London policemen. The whistling killer is finally revealed as Leonard Mudie (the cultured Professor Pearson of Universal's *The Mummy*), and the story proved sufficiently durable for M-G-M's British arm to mount a 1952 remake called *The Hour of 13*.

The other MacDonald adaptation, Ralph Murphy's *Menace*, has Gertrude Michael as the prime target of an escaped lunatic out to avenge the deaths of his brother and two sisters. The original tragedy, set in East Africa, is a lightning-flashing tour de force, but the remainder devolves into a standard-issue 'who will die next?' melodrama. Like the contemporaneous *The Witching Hour*, *Menace* was made for Paramount by producer Bayard Veiller and scripted by his son Anthony.

Another asylum escapee appeared in Howard Bretherton's *Return of the Terror*, which started shooting on Valentine's Day 1934 and was issued in July. This Warner Bros-First National production wasn't a further experiment in the racy Grand Guignol of *Doctor X* and *Mystery of the Wax Museum*, but rather a modernised retread of the studio's second all-talkie, *The Terror*. In it, a doctor (John Halliday) escapes from the asylum in which he's been incarcerated, becoming a bodeful presence at the rest home he was formerly superintendent of. The killer, however, turns out to be a young doctor (Lyle Talbot) who appropriated the older man's X-ray device. The storm-wracked scene of Halliday's escape is excitingly done, and the cast – Mary Astor, Irving Pichel, J Carroll Naish, even the tiresome Maude Eburne – is deluxe. But the film's whodunit credentials are flimsy in the extreme, leaning heavily on misdirection; "unless you can pry some advance information out of the ushers, the identity of the man in the black raincoat will come as pretty much of a shock," grumbled André Sennwald in the *New York Times*.

In its reiteration of all the moth-eaten spooky house clichés, *Return of the Terror* was in line with the continuing proliferation of similar films from Poverty Row producers, among them a tedious Monogram quickie shot in January 1934 called *The House of Mystery*. Directed by the once-distinguished William Nigh, this one has all the expected ingredients: Hindu domestic staff, a cretinous detective, a murderer disguised as an ape, a Western desecrator living in fear of retribution from an Eastern cult, a medium strangled in the dark of an impromptu seance. The source was a play by Adam Hull Shirk (one of the co-conspirators in the notorious *Ingagi*), and when the property was remade by Monogram and Nigh as a 1940 Karloff vehicle called *The Ape*, all the ingredients save the titular gorilla were chucked out.

While *Return of the Terror* was in production at First National, Universal overcame its reticence sufficiently to get behind a long-gestating project rejoicing in the triple threat of Boris Karloff, Bela Lugosi and Edgar Allan Poe. *The Black Cat* was entrusted to the 34-year-old Austrian director Edgar G Ulmer, whose film career stretched back to Wegener's *Der Golem*, on which he had served as a set decorator. The film was shot for a mere $96,000 in just 19 days, three of them given over to retakes designed to change Lugosi's character from a depraved avenger to a more noble one.

A degree of narrative incoherence was the inevitable result, the film being dismissed in *Variety* as "sub-normal". That word might nowadays be glossed as 'art-house', for *The Black Cat* is as unclassifiable a one-off as Browning's *Freaks* or Whale's *The Old Dark House* – and saturated in a more pervasive aura of death and decay than either of them.

Honeymooning in Eastern Europe, Peter and Joan Alison become enmeshed in the bitter enmity between Dr Vitus Werdegast and war criminal-cum-Satanist Hjalmar Poelzig. Earmarking Joan for sacrifice, Poelzig is foiled by Werdegast, who has not only discovered his wife's corpse suspended in a basement sarcophagus but also that his daughter Karen – Poelzig's wife – has now been killed in her turn. Werdegast flays Poelzig alive prior to detonating the subterranean explosives on which Poelzig's fortress is built.

The enduring fascination of *The Black Cat* derives as much from its labyrinthine impenetrability as its innovative cinematography and art direction. It develops at a calm, unhurried, even stately pace, blooming finally into an untrammelled orgy of madness and torture but suffused throughout with the cold hues of the grave. And over it all hangs the baleful spectre of the First World War.

Early on, a garrulous taxi driver picks up the unwitting Mr and Mrs Alison at Gömbös station and offers a gruesome sketch of the house that is to be the site of the main action: "The ravine down there was piled 12-deep with dead and wounded men. The little river below was swollen red, a raging torrent of blood. That high hill, yonder, where Engineer Poelzig now lives, was the site of Fort Marmaros. He built his home on its very foundations. Marmaros – the greatest graveyard in the world!" The house itself, though whipped up by Ulmer and Charles D Hall at a cost of only $3700, is a shimmering marvel of Art Deco futurism (even featuring digital clocks). Yet the taxi driver has made it very clear that it is built to the most time-honoured of Gothic blueprints. Its dreadful subterranean secrets aren't limited to the fact that it's built astride the corpses of 10,000 men. In addition, it is literally undermined by a cache of dynamite and its cellars are decorated with the bodies of Poelzig's former sacrificial victims, necrophile glamour girls suspended upright in glass sarcophagi.

The traditional castle of Gothic literature, with its several levels and murky lower depths, is frequently characterised as an image of the subconscious mind. If so, Fort Marmaros provides a bewildering index to Ulmer's, a man described as Kafkaesque by his own wife (Shirley Kassel, who served as continuity assistant here). The dense texture of the film jostles crafty in-jokes with what appear to be darker insights. Poelzig's surname, for example, was borrowed from *Der Golem*'s art director Hans Poelzig (intriguingly, art directors in German cinema at the time were known as architects), while his twin interests of Satanism and architecture make him an unholy fusion of

Bela Lugosi and director Edgar G Ulmer on the set of *The Black Cat* (1934)

Aleister Crowley and Le Corbusier. The theme of tainted heredity characteristic of Henrik Ibsen's doom-laden dramas is in there too, a derivation signalled by the use of the Ibsenite name Hjalmar and even the casting of Egon Brecher, an actor famous for playing the title role in Ibsen's aptly named *The Master Builder*.

As for the film's gallery of aberrant psychology, Werdegast's ailurophobia (as Poelzig helpfully glosses it, "an intense and all-consuming horror of cats") is just the beginning; Ulmer seems to tip the entire contents of *Psychopathia Sexualis* into the mix, from incest and necrophilia to plain old-fashioned sadism. The whole thing is slathered in musical cues cunningly adapted by Heinz Roemheld from Liszt (mainly), Brahms, Schumann, Tchaikovsky, Beethoven, Schubert, Chopin and Bach. Classical music was another of Ulmer's obsessions, and the result is that rare thing, a 1930s horror picture burdened, not by too little music, but by far too much.

The film is constructed as a contest between three men for the soul of the virginal Joan Alison, the contestants describing themselves as "one of Austria's greatest architects," "one of Hungary's greatest psychiatrists" and "one of America's greatest writers of unimportant books." The latter is played by David Manners, who gives a nice spin to some witty lines (apropos of Poelzig, for instance: "If I wanted to build a nice, cosy, unpretentious insane asylum, he'd be the man for it") but is inevitably outmanoeuvred by his co-stars. And this, of course, is as it should be, for Peter Alison, though a likable enough New World man, can only appear slick and vacuous by comparison to the deep repository of hatred and ancient evil represented by Werdegast and Poelzig.

These Old World antagonists are ideally presented by Karloff and Lugosi at the height of their powers. The former portrays Poelzig as a chalk-faced demon in black silk, rising like *Nosferatu* from the bed he shares with Werdegast's daughter, presiding with awful solemnity over the climactic Black Mass, and gloating understatedly over classic lines like "Even the phone is dead."

Though subordinate to Karloff in matters of billing and remuneration, Lugosi actually has the better part. Poelzig has fabulous lines to speak and plenty

THE BLACK CAT

Universal 1934
68 minutes
production began 28 February
UK title: The House of Doom

Cinematographer: John J Mescall; Art Director: Charles D Hall; Editor: Ray Curtiss; Sound: Gilbert Kurland; Special Photographic Effects: John P Fulton*; Camera Effects: David S Horsley*; Make-up: Jack P Pierce*; Wardrobe: Edgar G Ulmer*, Vera West*, Ed Ware*; Musical Director: Heinz Roemheld; Screenplay: Peter Ruric (from a story by Peter Ruric and Edgar G Ulmer, 'suggested by the immortal Edgar Allan Poe classic'); Production Supervisor: E M Asher*; Producer: Carl Laemmle Jr*; Director: Edgar G Ulmer

Karloff (Hjalmar Poelzig); Bela Lugosi (Dr Vitus Werdegast); David Manners (Peter Alison); Jacqueline Wells [later Julie Bishop] (Joan Alison); Egon Brecher (the Majordomo); Harry Cording (Thamal); Lucille Lund (Karen); Henry Armetta (the Sergeant); Albert Conti (the Lieutenant); uncredited: Luis Alberni (steward); André Cheron (conductor); George Davis (bus driver); Anna Duncan (Poelzig's maid); Tony Marlow (patrolman); Alphonse Martell (porter); John Peter Richmond [later John Carradine] (organist); Paul Weigel (stationmaster); Michael Mark, Paul Panzer (Satanists who abduct Joan); Frazer Acosta, Virginia Ainsworth, King Baggot, Duskal Blane, Symona Boniface, John George, Lois January, Peggy Terry, Harry Walker (other Satanists)

Because of the presence in one film of Boris Karloff, that jovial madman, and Bela Lugosi, that suave fiend, this picture probably has box office attraction. But otherwise, and on the counts of story, novelty, thrills and distinction, the picture is sub-normal. *Variety*

In preparing the script, which I also had a hand in, we had come up with some very interesting, very supernatural undertones that had to be cut ... Censorship in the thirties was even worse than now, and people couldn't take things like the character of Karen resembling the physical characteristics of a cat. *Edgar G Ulmer [quoted in Modern Monsters, August 1966]*

of sinister poses to strike, but the vengeful, half-mad yet strangely heroic Werdegast acquires a genuinely tragic dimension that Lugosi plays to the hilt, in the process walking off with the film. He brings with him a doom-laden freight of self-knowledge from the minute he enters the Alisons' train compartment and jolts their rinky-dink dance record out of synch. At the opposite end of the film, he applies himself to punishing Poelzig with such unhinged gusto that the line "That's what I'm going to do to you now, Hjalmar: flay the skin from your body, slowly, bit by bit" contains all-new Lugosi pronunciations for both 'flay' and 'slowly'. It's a majestic performance and arguably Lugosi's finest hour.

The flaying scene, done for the most part in shadow-play, was astonishingly sadistic in its time. It also carries a genuine aroma of Poe, like a more hands-on version of Montresor's revenge on Fortunato in *The Cask of Amontillado*. The periodic appearances of a black cat are merely token gestures; the real Poe atmosphere is provided by Poelzig's ghoulish gallery of former mistresses and Ulmer's spellbinding, subjective-camera tour of the cellars. "Did we not both die here in Marmaros 15 years ago?" Poelzig asks Werdegast in funereal voice-over. "Are we any the less victims of the war than those whose bodies were torn asunder? Are we not both the living dead?"

When issued on 7 May, *The Black Cat* became Universal's top-grossing film of the year, earning a profit of $140,000. Its morbid atmosphere of perversion was so ingrained that the custodians of the Production Code seemingly missed many of Ulmer's offensive details, even allowing it to be reissued four years later without cuts.

This was especially remarkable given that the Catholic Legion of Decency had been set up a mere nine days prior to the film's original release. Giving focus to the firestorm of Catholic opposition to Hollywood salaciousness, and in particular to the studios' cavalier attitude to the Production Code, the Legion's formation was followed in short order by the abandonment of the Studio Relations Committee, which on 11 July 1934 was supplanted by the Production Code Administration. Under the supervision of Joseph Breen, the PCA insisted on approving scripts prior to production and on suppressing films altogether if they were not granted a PCA 'seal'. Breen and his cohorts were now empowered to prune films of any details offending against a dozen major categories. These were Sex, Vulgarity, Obscenity, Profanity, Crimes Against the Law, Costume, Dances, Religion, Locations, National Feelings, Titles and the more generalised Repellent Subjects.

POVERTY ROW AND BELOW

To Joseph Breen, 'Repellent Subjects' might very well have been a euphemism for horror films, and the first to attract his ire was a humble Liberty Pictures production called *The Crime of Doctor Crespi*. This was the brainchild of Hungarian émigré John H Auer and was shot in eight days in September 1934 at New York's old Biograph studio. "My confidential information," Breen informed Will Hays the following January, "is to the effect that the picture is probably the most revolting and nauseating picture which has ever been photographed."[20] Two months later, having viewed it, he demanded cuts in no fewer than 13 of its scenes. Distributed by Republic, it finally came out in October 1935, the posters bestowing on its star, Erich von Stroheim, a sobriquet first attached to him in the First World War – 'The Man You Love to Hate.'

When his former assistant, Stephen Ross, is badly injured in a car crash, Dr André Crespi bows to the pleas of Ross' wife Estelle to perform a life-saving operation, despite his bitterness over Ross having taken Estelle from him five years before. Though the procedure is a success, Crespi signs a death certificate for Ross prior to administering a catalepsy-inducing drug. Growing suspicious, two of Crespi's fellow doctors dig Ross up and, cornered, Crespi calmly shoots himself.

Given its bogus attribution to Edgar Allan Poe, *The Crime of Doctor Crespi* was presumably inspired by Universal's success with *The Black Cat*. And, despite its lengthy wait to reach the paying public, it may well have been caught by somebody at Universal in sneak-preview form, for its basic premise – unlucky-in-love surgeon takes fiendish advantage of an automobile smash – is remarkably similar to *The Raven*, which Universal would make in 1935.

The credits, however, do not inspire confidence, contriving, as they do, to mis-spell Poe's middle name twice. This turns out to be a temporary aberration, however, for *The Crime of Doctor Crespi* is a lean and economical shocker with some genuinely startling set-pieces. The tentative romance between Crespi's subordinate Dr Arnold and staff nurse Miss Rexford would qualify as padding in most other pictures but is engagingly played here, while the comic relief (involving an Italian man whose wife has just produced quintuplets) is tactfully confined to the opening and closing minutes.

Most importantly, the film is distinguished by a mesmerising star performance. Von Stroheim's attitude to the film was one of civilised contempt, but it never shows. His acting in talkies had come on in leaps and bounds since *The Great Gabbo* in 1929; among other things, he had been aptly cast as maniac film director Erich von Furst in George Archainbaud's 1932 film *The Lost Squadron*. His Dr Crespi is similarly capricious and combustible, at once supremely relaxed and frighteningly wound up, shifting from reasoned debate to volcanic tirades in the blink of an eye.

Von Stroheim gives Crespi a number of interesting tics that never come over as merely tricksy. After the successful operation on Ross, Crespi settles down at his desk, taps his nose nonchalantly, lights his cigarette, checks the time (5.50), then produces a death certificate and calmly records '6.15' in the 'time of death' panel. And Von Stroheim is at the top of his form when he visits the morgue and lifts the sheet over his rival's inert body, crooning juicy lines like "I hoped and prayed for the chance to pay you back some day, with compound interest" as cinematographer Larry Williams shoots up at his gloating face from a low angle.

The operation on Ross is tensely done, with some particularly nasty sound effects, and is prefaced by a charming bit of gallows humour. "Good gosh, I wish the old man [Crespi] would give me a chance at the trephining," says a junior surgeon as he scrubs up. "You know, a good trephining job would establish me." There are a few pleasing ironies thrown in too, including the fact that Mrs Ross, whose husband has been in a car accident, is a petroleum heiress.

The premature burial of Crespi's rival involves a really riveting bit of location shooting, with the camera travelling down into the grave, soil cascading onto the lens, a tolling bell and cheesy organ music on the soundtrack, and a furious exchange of extreme close-ups for Crespi, Mrs Ross and the presiding minister. Ross is then dug up under cover of night by Crespi's two subordinates (with graverobbing on the agenda, we now realise why Dwight Frye was cast in the otherwise straight role of Dr Thomas) and, as they attempt an autopsy, Ross emerges from his catatonic state at the stroke of midnight.

THE CRIME OF DOCTOR CRESPI

J H A Pictures / Liberty 1934
63 minutes
production began 19 September

Cinematographer: Larry Williams; Art Director: Wm Saulter; Editor: Leonard Wheeler; Sound: Clarence Wall; Make-up: Fred Ryle*; Musical Director: Milton Schwarzwald*; Story: John H Auer ('suggested by Edgar Allen [sic] Poe's *The Premature Burial*'); Adaptation [ie, Screenplay]: Lewis Graham, Edwin Olmstead; Associate Producer: Herb Hayman; Director-Producer: John H Auer

Erich von Stroheim (Dr Crespi); Harriet Russell (Mrs Ross); Dwight Frye (Dr Thomas); Paul Guilfoyle (Dr Arnold); John Bohn (the dead man [Ross]); Geraldine Kay (Miss Rexford); Jeanne Kelly [later Jean Brooks] (Miss Gordon); Patsy Berlin (Jeanne [daughter]); Joe Verdi (Di Angelo); Dean Raymond (minister)

The Crime of Dr Crespi ... is an old story brought up to date ... The production is crude in spots and not all of the acting is on a par with Von Stroheim's playing of the principal role, but the film develops a real atmosphere of horror that is dramatically effective. *New York Sunday News*

If God is good, I will be able to play comedy roles in which I was featured for many seasons on Broadway and in which no producer of motion pictures will give me a chance! And may it take place before I go 'batty' – playing idiots, half-wits and lunatics for the talking screen!
Dwight Frye [quoted in original pressbook]

The pay-off is delightfully ghoulish in a 'He's behind you' sort of way. As Crespi's night nurse, Miss Gordon, prattles on the phone about how good-looking the dead man was, he's actually right behind her, shambling down a shadowed corridor and finally reaching her just as she sighs, "You never do get near the good ones." When Ross confronts Crespi himself, the doctor is tipsy and takes him for a ghost, soon afterwards committing suicide and slumping serenely across his desk. In a final imaginative touch, the dark shape on the screen behind him looks initially like blood, but turns out to be the silhouette of Crespi's very own memento mori – a pygmy skeleton that stands, like some Art Deco knick-knack, on his drinks cabinet. Like the burial sequence, this little detail suggests Auer had seen Carl Dreyer's French film *Vampyr*.

The role of Miss Gordon, who screams the place down when the supposed corpse taps her on the shoulder, was taken by a pretty 18-year-old called Jeanne Kelly, who was at the time a protégée of Von

Stroheim's. Among her other early pictures was a voodoo obscurity called *Obeah*, made by Arcturus Pictures, written and directed by F Herrick Herrick and released in February 1935. Having changed her name to Jean Brooks, she would make an indelible impression in the horror films produced by Val Lewton in the 1940s.

Distant echoes of Poe could be heard in two other 1934 productions. Proceeding from diametrically opposed extremes of the filmmaking spectrum, one is a glossy Paramount item adapted from a well-heeled Broadway play, the other a film so close to the bottom of the exploitation barrel it occupies the shadowy area where legitimate filmmaking shades over into illicit 'stag' movies.

Based on a shocking Broadway hit by Elizabeth McFadden, Paramount's *Double Door* was reviewed in the *New York Times* under the alluring banner 'Horror in an Old Mansion'. Similarly, its star Mary Morris (making her one and only film appearance) was ballyhooed by Paramount's publicists as "the most deadly menace the screen has ever known" and "the Female Frankenstein of Fifth Avenue." As the monomaniacal head of the Van Brett clan, Morris is rather like Pauline Frederick in *The Phantom of Crestwood* – "insane with family pride" – and for much the same reasons. She wants to prevent the 'unsuitable' Ann (Evelyn Venable) from marrying her nephew Rip (Kent Taylor), and to that end imprisons her in a secret chamber. The young Ann Revere – retained, like Morris, from the stage version – plays her downtrodden younger sister, who has endured a character-forming spell of her own in the secret room.

The Hungarian Charles Vidor – previously ousted from the director's chair on *The Mask of Fu Manchu* – puts his Ufa training to good use in examining the shadowed recesses of the Van Brett brownstone but fails to control his actors, who come across as either over-the-top (Morris) or merely wimpish (everyone else). Only in the film's final reel do Paramount's pressbook machinations make any sense; Ann having been liberated from her living death, everything is left clear for the predictable irony of the mad spinster becoming irretrievably trapped in the vault herself. The horror of Poe's *The Premature Burial* is nicely touched upon here, but elsewhere the picture is sluggishly paced and compromised by a central performance too obviously derived from the stage.

The fourth Poe-inflected film of 1934, *Maniac*, predictably did better business when reissued as *Sex Maniac*. As the hucksterish entrepreneur who would eventually take the despised *Freaks* off Metro's hands, director Dwain Esper was perfectly placed to pretty much invent the cross-fertilisation of horror and sexploitation, and as such the humble *Maniac* was way ahead of its time. Written by Esper's wife Hildegarde Stadie, the film concerns a vaudeville impressionist, Maxwell, whose enslavement to mad scientist Dr Meirschutz ends in him gunning the doctor down and assuming his identity. He also walls up the body in his rat-infested basement, not noticing that the doctor's black cat, Satan, has got in with it. The cat, by this time, is missing an eye, Maxwell having gouged it out and eaten it while observing that "It's not unlike an oyster. Or a grape. But the gleam has gone."

Untroubled by the newly enforced Production Code thanks to his policy of exhibiting his pictures in sideshows and burlesque houses, Esper also throws in some topless women, a heart suspended in a jar (the cat eats it), an open-eyed corpse and a cat 'farmer' who cheerfully admits to harvesting his charges' pelts. There's also a conniving wife, Mrs Buckley, who claims that her husband "thinks he's the orang-outan murderer in Poe's *Murder of the Rue Morgue*" [sic] – which he certainly does after being accidentally dosed by Maxwell with "super-adrenaline". Maxwell's estranged wife finally has a vicious 'cat' fight with Mrs Buckley in the cellar and, when the police break it up, they also find Meirschutz and the eyeless, but still living, cat behind the wall. Maxwell ends up behind bars, by now thoroughly possessed by his role, still babbling about "the gleam" and proclaiming his bogus Meirschutz as "my supreme impersonation."

Incoherent, inept, not far from demented but genuinely transgressive for its time, *Maniac* is all of a piece with other Esper exploiters like *Sex Madness* and *How to Undress in Front of Your Husband*. It comes complete with supposedly educational title cards

explaining such terms as dementia praecox and paranoiac, but perhaps the most intriguing thing about it is the presence as Esper's assistant director of J Stuart Blackton Jr, son of the distinguished British film pioneer J Stuart Blackton. Indeed, Junior's sister Marion turns up briefly as a garrulous neighbour and offers her own version of a standard horror film cliché: "To my notion, those that monkeys with what they got no business to gets queer sooner or later."

Cut from much the same marginal cloth as *Maniac* was a Bud Pollard production called *The Horror*, which, according to film historians George E Turner and Michael H Price, was so obscure it was reviewed only in Japan. Made in Long Island in five days in September 1932, it featured Lon Chaney lookalike Leslie King as a US businessman who smuggles an Indian idol into America. Its vengeful guardians cause havoc one storm-laden night, unleashing a python and a gorilla on King and his wife (Nyrida Mantez). In the course of fighting the ape, King changes, for some reason, into a hideous monster and then wakes up from what was only a bad dream. Incredibly, the enterprising Pollard recut and retitled the film 11 years later as a moralistic warning against delirium tremens, marketing the result to religious groups. "Pollard's ineptitude as a director," observe Turner and Price, "is central to any understanding of *The Horror* ... Its sanctimonious condensation, *John the Drunkard*, is uniquely wretched."[21]

HIS MONSTER'S VOICE

In August 1934, James Whale's Dr Frankenstein, Colin Clive, could be seen in a Monogram adaptation of *Jane Eyre*, playing the saturnine Mr Rochester opposite M-G-M's Virginia Bruce. Directed by Christy Cabanne, this is an oversimplified 64-minute digest of Charlotte Brontë's Gothic classic, though by Monogram's penurious standards something of a deluxe super-production. Only the following week, however, Monogram put out another one, a Reginald Barker version of Wilkie Collins' *The Moonstone* with a very good-value cast headed by David Manners, Jameson Thomas and Gustav von Seyffertitz.

For Colin Clive fans, the Monogram *Jane Eyre* was just a prelude to Clive's long-awaited return to his most famous role – though he would be upstaged in it, not merely by Boris Karloff, but also by the former Horace Femm, Ernest Thesiger. Having back-pedalled on out-and-out horror for some two years, Universal plunged boldly into 1935 with a majestically conceived sequel to their biggest horror hit. *The Return of Frankenstein*, as it was originally called, at first held zero appeal for James Whale, who was reluctant to go over old ground. He finally accepted a script by Broadway playwright William Hurlbut and, given complete autonomy by Junior Laemmle, determined to make the picture as baroque and idiosyncratic a sequel as he could. The long-awaited *Bride of Frankenstein* accordingly went into production on 2 January.

> *Frankenstein's Monster is not dead, having fallen through the flames of the burning windmill into the millpond beneath. Frankenstein isn't dead either, but his recuperation is marred by his old tutor Dr Pretorius, who proposes a new experiment on the Biblical principle that "male and female created He them." To "add a little force to the argument," Pretorius has the Monster kidnap Frankenstein's fiancée Elizabeth, whereupon Frankenstein agrees to collaborate in fashioning a mate for the Monster...*

Bride of Frankenstein opens in grand style with a bit of directorial rug-pulling that proves characteristic of the whole film. The camera tracks towards a forbidding castle miniature lit by bolts of lightning, finally gliding, not into a dank and crepuscular crypt, but a vast and airy salon inhabited by three richly attired Regency exquisites; to underscore the surprise, the misterioso theme of the opening credits shifts seamlessly into a charming minuet.

By introducing us to Byron, Shelley and Mary Wollstonecraft, Whale was concerned, in part, to appease the guardians of the Production Code by having Mary explicitly state the novel's moral. (Unfortunately, the only thing the PCA thought explicit in this prologue was Elsa Lanchester's ample décolletage; their other objections to the film were numerous, focusing on its blasphemous utterances and high body-count.) Whale also offered a facetious compliment to his target audience, equating horror fans with Byron and Shelley, no less, when Mary tells the poets that "Such an audience needs something stronger than a pretty little love story."

So begins what purports to be Mary's own sequel, and to realise it Universal spared no expense, gracing the film with world-class settings from Charles D Hall, gorgeous chiaroscuro from cinematographer John J Mescall and a magisterial Franz Waxman score. All three reach a remarkable crescendo in Whale's epic creation sequence, which is fashioned by editor Ted Kent into a tour de force "as awesome," enthused *Variety*, "as a page from Genesis." In a typically arch Whale in-joke, the end-product is Elsa Lanchester again, who modelled her feral hisses on the swans in Regent's Park and whose electrified hair and make-up were the iconic outcome of Whale's collaboration with Jack Pierce.

Boris Karloff descends into the catacombs and stumbles across a potential consort in *Bride of Frankenstein* (1935)

BRIDE OF FRANKENSTEIN

Universal 1935
75 minutes
production began 2 January

Cinematographer: John J Mescall; Art Director: Charles D Hall; Editors: Ted Kent, Maurice Pivar*; Sound: Gilbert Kurland*; Special Electrical Properties: Kenneth Strickfaden*; Photographic Effects: John P Fulton, David Horsley*; Make-up: Jack P Pierce*; Music: Franz Waxman; Orchestra Conductor: Bakaleinikoff; Screenplay: William Hurlbut, Edmund Pearson*; Adaptation: William Hurlbut, John L Balderston ('suggested by the original story written in 1816 by Mary Wollstonecraft Shelley'); Producer: Carl Laemmle Jr; Director: James Whale

Karloff (The Monster); Colin Clive (Henry Frankenstein); Valerie Hobson (Elizabeth); Ernest Thesiger (Doctor Pretorius); Elsa Lanchester (Mary Wollstonecraft Shelley/The Monster's Mate); Gavin Gordon (Lord Byron); Douglas Walton (Percy Bysshe Shelley); Una O'Connor (Minnie); E E Clive (Burgomaster); Lucien Prival (butler [Albert]); O P Heggie (hermit); Dwight Frye (Karl); Reginald Barlow (Hans); Mary Gordon (Hans' wife); Ann Darling (shepherdess); Ted Billings (Ludwig); uncredited: Norman Ainsley (little Archbishop); Maurice Black (gypsy); Arthur S Byron (little King); Kansas DeForrest (little ballerina); Elspeth Dudgeon (old gypsy woman); Neil Fitzgerald (Rudy [Irish graverobber]); Brenda Fowler (mother); Helen Gibson (woman); Marilyn Harris (schoolgirl); Josephine McKim (little mermaid); Charlie Murphy (gendarme); Helen Parrish (communion girl); Sarah Schwartz (Marta); Peter Shaw (little Devil); Lucio Villegas (priest); Joan Woodbury (little Queen); John Carradine, Nat Clifford (huntsmen in hermit sequence); Robert Adair, Jack Curtis (huntsmen in shepherdess sequence); Walter Brennan, D'Arcy Corrigan, Rollo Lloyd, Murdock MacQuarrie, Joseph North (villagers)

There is nothing in *The Bride of Frankenstein* at the Tivoli to scare a child ... This is a pompous, badly acted film, full of absurd anachronisms and inconsistencies. It owes its one moment of excitement less to its director than to the strange electric beauty of Miss Elsa Lanchester. *The Spectator* [UK]

To this day, nine out of ten photographs I get in the mail for autographing are of the Bride ... It's sometimes pleasant to have very young kids in markets or in the street recognise you as the Bride of Frankenstein. Because, changed as I have, obviously, I apparently haven't turned into a type that looks like everybody else.
Elsa Lanchester [Elsa Lanchester Herself, 1983]

Her entrance forms the logical, and genuinely tragic, conclusion to the Monster's travails. In a deluxe restatement of highlights from the first film, these include a misunderstanding with a half-drowned shepherdess, a pursuit (and mock-crucifixion) by mutinous villagers, and an incursion into the bedroom of Frankenstein's fiancée. Now, rejected by the artificial female on whom he'd set so much store, the Monster's awful realisation that "She hate me – like others" is sublimely moving. Answering Pretorius' cry of "Get away from that lever! You'll blow us all to atoms!" with the simple truism that "We belong dead," he initiates a suitably apocalyptic explosion.

As in *The Black Cat*, Karloff was billed here, in the manner of the otherwise very different Garbo, as just that: Karloff. He protested in vain, however, against the introduction of what the publicity department called "His Monster's Voice." Though Pretorius later takes credit for it, the Monster is taught to speak by a blind hermit, and the brief experience of human companionship provided by the hermit (beautifully played by O P Heggie) gives Karloff the opportunity, despite his reservations, for some of his most miraculous moments, expertly balancing comedy, pathos and undiminished awe.

Whale himself doesn't manage this balancing act quite so smoothly. In fact, the huntsmen who destroy the Monster's idyll are emblematic of Whale's two-pronged method in turning *Bride of Frankenstein* into an outrageously lurid, but seriously unbalanced, black comedy. One of them is the young John Carradine, whose spasm of goggle-eyed histrionics is emphatically of the 'theatre theatrical'. The other is the British comic Nat Clifford (aka Frank Terry), whose cheery Cockney schtick, familiar to modern viewers from Laurel and Hardy's *Midnight Patrol*, is deliberately contrasted with Carradine's aristocratic over-emphasis.

The same dichotomy is present in Whale's handling of the actors throughout, and it leads to some grotesque lapses in the director's usual good taste. On the Carradine model, Gavin Gordon's Byron is a ridiculous agglomeration of retroflexed r's; speaking of his "r-r-relish in savouring each separate horror," he claims, all too accurately, to "r-r-roll them over on my tongue." It's obvious, too, that Valerie Hobson's embarrassingly overplayed outburst about "a figure like Death" was performed to Whale's exact specifications; her sensitive performances in later films make this very clear. On the Nat Clifford model, Una O'Connor's sustained low-comedy caterwauling is more unbearable even than her performance in *The Invisible Man*. She was a particular favourite of Whale's, but when the Monster encounters Minnie early on, one bitterly regrets the fact that he doesn't kill her while he has the chance.

Whale's absolute favourite, of course, was Ernest Thesiger, and here he showed much better judgment. Thesiger's Dr Pretorius, aptly described by Minnie as "a very queer-looking old gentleman," is a Satanic tempter of the most engaging kind. In a nod to Horace Femm's tipple of choice, Pretorius toasts "a new world of gods and monsters" with gin drunk out of a laboratory beaker; having described the drink as "my only weakness," he later says exactly the same about the cigars he offers the Monster. Both of them outcasts in their different ways, Pretorius and the Monster forge their unholy alliance in a cobwebbed charnel house, the scene carrying a strong whiff of necrophilia given that the bones laid out in front of them are destined to form the Monster's mate. Thesiger's interplay with Karloff here contributes to one of the most memorable vignettes in the picture.

Sadly, Thesiger is also central to a vignette that's memorable for the wrong reasons. At Whale's insistence, a scene was written into Hurlbut's script in which Pretorius shows Frankenstein his own creations – whipped up, as Pretorius gruesomely puts it, "from seed" (presumably his own). Six stunted homunculi in glass jars whom Pretorius has characterised and costumed as king, queen, devil etc, these creatures' 'comic' antics and cartoonish squeaking constitute Whale's most egregious miscalculation of all.

After the delicate balance of humour and horror showcased in *The Old Dark House* and *The Invisible Man*, Whale was perfecting in *Bride of Frankenstein* the then-unknown quantity called 'camp', and for the most part the results are a delight. But, faced with Pretorius' miniature creations, one becomes aware of a director who is out of control. Ambivalent about directing the film in the first place, he condescended to do so only on his own terms – and those terms occasionally included a frank display of contempt for his material. None of this, however, harmed the picture's barnstorming box-office performance, which saw Universal earning a profit of just under $1 million.

Only 17 at the time, Valerie Hobson had been inducted into the ranks of Universal's featured players via a film aimed at planting the Frankenstein theme in a drama-documentary context. *Life Returns* came about when German filmmaker Dr Eugene Frenke got hold of some footage from the University of Southern California and cajoled Universal into putting up the money to help him build a film around it. On 22 May 1934, Dr Robert E Cornish had apparently restored life to a dead dog; by October, Frenke was filming a painfully cheap and schmaltzy tale of a doctor's small son having his deceased pet, Scooter, similarly resurrected. Onslow Stevens is the feckless doctor, Hobson his ill-fated wife, with top billing reserved for the briefly glimpsed Cornish. Like the scientific breakthrough it memorialised, Cornish's film debut led nowhere.

Universal sensibly buried *Life Returns*, and the doctor's only further contact with the film business involved loaning Warner Bros his motorised operating table for the Karloff vehicle *The Walking Dead*. His achievement obviously made an impression on filmmakers, however, with veiled reference being made to it even in such low-rent surroundings as Dwain Esper's *Maniac*.

BOGUS VAMPIRES, RELUCTANT WEREWOLVES

In January 1935, the hissing female monster of *Bride of Frankenstein* was paralleled over at M-G-M by another. This was Carroll Borland, a 20-year-old Berkeley drama student and Bela Lugosi protégée who had won a Metro talent competition akin to Paramount's 'Panther Woman' contest. The prize was the role of Luna, a bewitching graveyard Lolita featured in Tod Browning's *Vampires of Prague*. Going into production ten days after *Bride* – but due to be released ten days

MARK OF THE VAMPIRE

M-G-M 1935
61 minutes
production began 12 January

Cinematographer: James Wong Howe; Art Director: Cedric Gibbons; Associate Art Directors: Harry Oliver, Edwin B Willis; Editor: Ben Lewis; Sound: Douglas Shearer; Photographic Effects: Warren Newcombe*; Make-up: Jack Dawn*, William Tuttle*; Gowns: Adrian; Screenplay: Guy Endore, Bernard Schubert; Additional Dialogue: H S Kraft*, Samuel Ornitz*, John L Balderston*; Story: Tod Browning*; Producer: E J Mannix*; Director: Tod Browning

Lionel Barrymore (Professor [Zelen]); Elizabeth Allan (Irena); Bela Lugosi (Count Mora); Lionel Atwill (Inspector Neumann); Jean Hersholt (Baron Otto); Henry Wadsworth (Fedor); Donald Meek (Dr Doskil); Jessie Ralph (midwife [crone in graveyard]); Ivan Simpson (Jan [butler]); Franklyn Ardell (chauffeur); Leila Bennett (Maria); June Gittelson (Annie); Carol [Carroll] Borland (Luna); Holmes Herbert (Sir Karrell [Franz]); Michael Visaroff (innkeeper); uncredited: Guy Belis (Englishman [Ronnie]); James Bradbury Jr (third vampire); Egon Brecher (coroner); John George (gypsy); Rosemary Glosz (inkeeper's wife); Mme Lesovosky (crone at inn); Claire Vedara (Englishwoman)

Horror being a precious commodity in the cinema and a potent lure to the box-office, it is not altogether surprising this week to discover that two Broadway houses – the Mayfair and the Rialto – have avidly laid claims to the same picture. Its name is *Mark of the Vampire* ... Like most good ghost stories, it's a lot of fun, even though you don't believe a word of it.
New York Times

He [Tod Browning] was a great big negative. "Carroll, I want you to walk in front of Lugosi. You're gonna be holding a candle, so look out for your hair." "What am I supposed to do?" "Walk over and down the steps and walk out." That was it. He simply expected Lugosi and me to go be vampires.
Carroll Borland [quoted in *Scarlet Street*, Fall 1993]

Bela Lugosi and Carroll Borland as Count Mora and his predatory daughter Luna in *Mark of the Vampire* (1935)

ahead of it – the film gave Browning the opportunity to revisit an old property, just as James Whale was resurrecting an old friend in the Frankenstein picture. Theoretically, *Vampires of Prague* was a remake of Browning's 1927 silent *London After Midnight*. But when issued in May under the title *Mark of the Vampire*, it turned out to be a weird riposte to Browning's desultory work on *Dracula*.

Visoka, Czechoslovakia. On the death of Sir Karell Borotyn, vampires are reported to have taken up residence in his former home. Investigating Sir Karell's murder, Inspector Neumann and vampire specialist Professor Zelen discover that Baron Otto von Zinden is the culprit. The vampires, meanwhile, are revealed to be actors engaged to help in forcing a confession from him.

Since the reviled *Freaks*, Browning had been employed only on the bargain-basement John Gilbert vehicle *Fast Workers*. Back at the helm of what at least purported to be an A-picture, Browning was reunited with Lionel Barrymore, whose Professor Zelen emphasises fruity lines like "Miss Borotyn and her fiancé lie within the shadow of worse than death" with much tricksy business involving his pince-nez. As well as being a beetle-browed hoot, Barrymore's Zelen is also a pretty obvious clone of Edward Van Sloan's more grim-faced Van Helsing.

Though his motivation remains obscure, Browning's desire to offer a backward-looking commentary on *Dracula* is evident on a number of other levels. As several critics have pointed out, even the casting of demure British actress Elizabeth Allan seems to have been based on her physical resemblance to *Dracula*'s Helen Chandler. Above all, of course, third-billed Bela Lugosi is on hand to play the film's chief vampire; used for the most part as a mute, monolithic presence, he is actually better here than he was as the too-talkative Count Dracula.

Universal reportedly considered taking legal action over the similarities, which were hardly alleviated by screenwriter Guy Endore's rechristening of Dracula as Count Mora, or by Mora's somewhat frillier dress sense, a look apparently devised by Lugosi himself. Endore also posited an incestuous relationship between Mora and his spooky daughter Luna, involving her death at his hands and Mora's own death from a self-inflicted bullet wound. Any hint of this in the finished film was lost when M-G-M brutally excised 14 minutes' footage from the release print, leaving the hole in Mora's temple entirely unexplained, the film's rhythm fatally compromised and its narrative line exasperatingly unclear.

The film has to get by instead on its imagery, which fortunately is of a very high order indeed. As the horror cinema's first necrophile pin-up, Carroll Borland's Luna is shown off to ravishing effect by cinematographer James Wong Howe. Whether picked out in an unnatural glow as she lurks at the castle gates or drifting serenely towards the comatose Irena Borotyn across a fog-shrouded lawn, Borland's Luna makes an indelible impression. Late in the film, she has a startling moment of animal ferocity as she stoops to bite the heroine. By Borland's own account, Browning merely instructed her to growl like a wolf at this point; instead, she formed her face into a Kabuki mask, emitting a feral hiss that anticipates the Hammer vampire pictures of the 1950s and 60s.

The film remains unrivalled for its lushly realised Gothic atmospherics, though some of the shots (notably of Luna's strangely illuminated face peering in at Irena's window) are so effective Browning isn't above using them twice. The sequence in which Mora and Luna are first seen, gliding with unearthly purpose down a colossal staircase and passing miraculously through a vast spider's web, is a bona-fide classic – and modelled precisely on Lugosi's entrance in *Dracula*. The earlier film's marauding armadillos are replaced by a herd of beetles (Lugosi pauses to give them an appreciative second glance), while the diffident possum previously glimpsed in Dracula's crypt has now, we notice, made it above ground. We even get the same crummy spider scuttling along on the end of a string. Later, however, we're given a glimpse of something more freakish – a sort of crab-like arachnid beastie on numerous wires – when Zelen and Lionel Atwill's police inspector venture into the Borotyn vault.

Browning's creepy emphasis on vermin is relentless, even extending to the use of real South American fruit bats in addition to (extremely efficient) motorised ones. It's underlined by a dazzling sound design courtesy of M-G-M's recording guru Douglas Shearer, abounding in the sublimated squeaks of rodents and the low baying of wolves. Topped off with tremendous sets devised by Cedric Gibbons' art department, *Mark of the Vampire* works up a genuinely otherworldly atmosphere.

Then, of course, Browning goes and blows it all in the last reel by revealing the vampires as vaudevillians engaged to help catch a murderer, a resolution in line with his long-ago 'horrible possible' manifesto but totally illogical given what's gone before. It also makes Lugosi the butt of a feeble gag, essentially the industry in-joke about his being a 'ham'. "Did you watch me? I gave all of me. I was greater than any real vampire!" he boasts in the closing scene. "Sure, sure – but get off your make-up," laughs Borland in reply. In the opening reel, a toffee-nosed English tourist responded to the locals' muttered superstitions with "Ripping; they'd never believe that at the club." Depressingly, we realise at the end that Browning was in sympathy with the Englishman all along.

In a year of prestigious Metro hits like *Mutiny on the Bounty* and Garbo's *Anna Karenina*, there was little danger of M-G-M using Lugosi for anything other than exotic *Mark of the Vampire* set dressing. Moving from the sublime to the ridiculous, he went straight into a wretched Poverty Row potboiler for Imperial-Cameo called *Murder by Television*, in which a pioneering TV demonstration is complicated by the murder of its inventor. As Lionel Atwill had been in *The Sphinx* and Karloff soon would be in *The Black Room*, Lugosi was cast as twins.

The co-writer of *Mark of the Vampire*, Guy Endore, had been responsible for a gruesome 1933 novel called *The Werewolf of Paris*, an epic of the Paris Commune loosely founded on the Sergeant Bertrand necrophilia case. Though Universal were planning a picture with a very similar title, they didn't turn to Endore's novel – or, indeed, Endore himself – in fashioning it. Instead, they engaged playwright John Colton to concoct a peculiar original called *WereWolf of London*.

> *Collecting samples of the fabled mariphasa lupina lumino, a Tibetan flower that blooms only by moonlight, eminent botanist Dr Wilfred Glendon is attacked by a werewolf. Returning to London, he discovers that he's suffering from lycanthrophobia, that the mariphasa contains an antidote, and that his attacker was the Carpathian scientist Dr Yogami. As Glendon succumbs to feral fugues under the influence of the full moon, he enters into a deadly contest with Yogami for ownership of the flower.*

Colton was the conspicuously gay author of the sensational Broadway smashes *The Shanghai Gesture* and *Rain*; the latter had been filmed with both Gloria Swanson (1928) and Joan Crawford (1931). The tawdry, tropical exotica of Colton's stage plays is nowhere to be found in the staid *WereWolf of London*, though the film's Tibetan prologue, filmed at the familiar Vasquez Rocks, is enticingly done. "Our coolies tell us the valley we want to visit is filled with demons," says Glendon's fresh-faced assistant to a camel-riding, white-skinned holy man. "I've never been into that valley," nods the magus sagely, "and I've never known a man to return from it."

Viewers with Freudian leanings will appreciate the following scene, in which Glendon ignores the holy

Warner Oland and Henry Hull in a gruesome shot cut from *WereWolf of London* (1935); it did, however, make it into the trailer

WEREWOLF OF LONDON

Universal 1935
75 minutes
production began 28 January

Cinematographer: Charles Stumar; Art Director: Albert S D'Agostino; Editors: Russell Schoengarth, Milton Carruth*; Sound: Gilbert Kurland; Special Photographic Effects: John P Fulton; Make-up: Jack P Pierce*; Music: Karl Hajos; Screenplay: John Colton; Original Story and Associate Producer: Robert Harris; Executive Producer: Stanley Bergerman; Director: Stuart Walker

Henry Hull (Dr Glendon); Warner Oland (Dr Yogami); Valerie Hobson (Lisa Glendon); Lester Matthews (Paul Ames); Lawrence Grant (Sir Thomas Forsythe); Spring Byington (Miss Ettie Coombes); Clark Williams (Hugh Renwick); J M Kerrigan (Hawkins); Charlotte Granville (Lady Forsythe); Ethel Griffies (Mrs Whack); Zeffie Tilbury (Mrs Moncaster); Jeanne Bartlett (Daisy); uncredited: Reginald Barlow (Timothy); Egon Brecher (holy man); Vera Buckland (Yogami's housekeeper); Wong Chung (coolie); Alex Chivra (Yogami in werewolf form); Herbert Evans (Jenkins' assistant); Eole Galli (prima donna); Helena Grant (mother); Jeffrey Hassel (Alf); Boyd Irwin Sr (hotel manager); Noel Kennedy (boy); Connie Leon (Yogami's maid); Maude Leslie (Mrs Charteris); James May (barman); William Millman (John Bull); Roseollo Navello (maid); Amber Norman (beggar); Joseph North (Plimpton [Glendon's butler]); Tempe Pigott (drunken old lady); Harry Stubbs (Jenkins); David Thursby (photographer); Louis Vincenot (head coolie)

For those who like to feel their flesh creep this is first-class entertainment. It is highly unsuitable for children or even adults who are easily upset. It is well-directed. The photography reminds one of the Germans and is brilliant in parts. Hull and Oland bloodcurdle most successfully. Monthly Film Bulletin [UK]

***WereWolf of London* had a rather weakish but awfully nice director called Stuart Walker. And it had Henry Hull as the werewolf ... He was, of course, a very good and powerful actor, but ... he never really made it. So I think they were rather disappointed in that.**
Valerie Hobson [quoted in Mank, *Women in Horror Films 1930s*, 1999]

man's warning, pushes on into a cleft between the crags, starts to experience weird physical effects (as if penetrating uncharted dream territory) and finally locates the forbidden petals, only to pay a terrible price for handling them. Colton also brings a certain Freudian recoil to the explicitly female carnivorous plants on display at Glendon's garden party back in London; one, the so-called Madagascar carnalia, has lashing tentacles and a furry orifice that sucks down a hapless frog. There's also a submerged but unmistakable homoerotic frisson between the werewolf antagonists, who come across as martyrs to an 'abominable' craving (what Glendon calls "this mediaeval unpleasantness"), as well as confirming their fellow-feeling when Yogami fondles Glendon's arm to indicate how he came by the fateful bite.

Unfortunately, as antagonists the hard and flinty Henry Hull and the soft and mournful Warner Oland strike no sparks whatsoever. It's a critical commonplace, but there's no denying that the film would have been much improved with Karloff and Lugosi in parts seemingly tailor-made for them. (Lugosi's name had actually been mentioned for the Yogami role, and Universal had first prepared a treatment called *The Wolf Man* early in 1932, with Karloff earmarked for the lead.) Henry Hull, in particular, is a dead weight at the film's centre. Years before, he had been an engaging, fresh-faced presence in D W Griffith's *One Exciting Night*. Now, riding high on his Broadway success in Erskine Caldwell's *Tobacco Road*, Hull presents Glendon as such an unyieldingly cold fish that audience sympathy – normally the only thing that keeps werewolf films afloat – is never enlisted at any point.

Glendon's monomaniac absorption in his work is more akin to Dr Frankenstein than your average wolf man, and, in classic mad scientist style, he neglects his doting wife (played by Valerie Hobson, much better here than in *Bride of Frankenstein*) but is afraid he'll kill her when informed that werewolves go after the people they love most. Thanks to Hull's sour-faced performance, we never believe that Glendon loved Lisa in the first place, so the emotional impact of the film's closing stages is precisely zero.

At least two contemporary critiques considered *WereWolf of London* a familiar yarn, the *New York Times* opining that "the central idea has been used before" and Britain's *Monthly Film Bulletin* calling it "another story on the werewolf legend."[23] Given the paucity, and obscurity, of previous werewolf subjects (all of them discussed in Part One), it's reasonable to assume that these critics were alluding to the Jekyll and Hyde motif. The two themes are obviously connected and the film shows every sign of

wanting to pick up some of the lustre contained in Paramount's *Dr Jekyll and Mr Hyde*.

To underline the resemblance, *WereWolf of London* approaches lycanthropy – or 'lycanthrophobia' as it's called here – from an unusual science-fiction standpoint. Glendon has devised a complex apparatus to create artificial moonlight and also has a television-type device to warn him of laboratory visitors. (This last innovation would be replicated by Bela Lugosi, playing another scientist with an unwanted hair problem, in a 1942 quickie called *The Ape Man*.) Apart from a fleeting reference to Little Red Riding Hood, Colton's unfocused script eschews the legend's basis in folklore and tries to paper over its supernatural absurdities with a gloss of hi-tech modernity, resulting in a film crippled by a severe identity crisis.

Matters are made worse by the diffident direction of Stuart Walker and a host of half-hearted James Whale-isms – a London bobby complaining of fallen arches, a society matron repeatedly calling Yogami "Dr Yokohama", and a pair of gin-tippling comedy crones. (In a small mercy, neither of them is played by Una O'Connor.) There are virtues, however, notably typically deluxe Universal production design and a demonic monster make-up that looks plausibly like a wolf; Jack Pierce would opt for a more pig-like visage when called upon to create *The Wolf Man* six years later. A zoo sequence not only anticipates *Cat People* but also contains a first-rate shock when the werewolf's face is reflected in the mirrored powder-compact of his victim, and John Fulton's transformation sequences are top-notch for their time.

In addition to playing the persecuted Lisa Glendon, Valerie Hobson was cast as Edmund Lowe's fragmenting wife in Alan Crosland's *The Great Impersonation*, the last of ten films she made at Universal in 1934-5. This was another of the studio's straightforward melodramas (turning on espionage in this instance) mendaciously advertised as a horror picture. However, in adapting an E Phillips Oppenheim original, this one at least retained a spooky subplot that had been ditched in an earlier film version from 1921, and would be ditched again in Universal's own remake of 1942. Lowe's ancestral hall is fringed by the so-called Black Bog, the reputed 'ghost' of which is finally smoked out (literally) and revealed as none other than Dwight Frye.

SUPER-KARLOFF MELODRAMAS

Horror fanciers thinking wistfully of a *WereWolf of London* featuring Karloff and Lugosi rather than Henry Hull and Warner Oland would be placated by a new Universal shocker released a mere seven weeks later. After the phenomenal success of *The Black Cat*, it seemed natural to ally the stars' names to Edgar Allan Poe once more, but *The Raven* would go through seven writers (among them Guy Endore) before Universal felt they had a workable script. It was written by David Boehm, whose career at Warners had thrown up such imperishable titles as *Gold Diggers of 1933*.

The expertise of retired surgeon Dr Richard Vollin is called upon by Judge Thatcher when the latter's daughter Jean is injured in a car accident. Becoming obsessed with the recovered Jean, Vollin enslaves wanted criminal Edmond Bateman by disfiguring him in a way only Vollin can put right. A house party is then arranged at which the recalcitrant Judge Thatcher is to be punished with methods prescribed by Vollin's idol, Edgar Allan Poe...

Back in 1927, *Variety* had despaired of the horror content in Fox's *The Wizard* with the caveat that "the great American public brought it on themselves. They 'went' for the serials back in the early days of screendom, and it looks as if the cycle has come round again." Much the same could be said of *The Raven*, which Universal entrusted, not to an inspired maverick like *The Black Cat*'s Edgar Ulmer, but to a man who had previously directed only chapter-plays like *The Vanishing Shadow* and *The Red Rider*.

Louis Friedlander (later to style himself Lew Landers) was not the man, then, to prevent the film from disintegrating beyond repair in its second half, in which screenwriter Boehm offers so thorough a parody of serial cliffhangers that it's hard to resist the conclusion that he was laughing up his sleeve while writing it. As well as a basement bristling with torture devices lovingly modelled on Poe's original prescriptions, Dr Vollin's storm-tossed mansion turns out to be fitted with steel shutters that cover the windows at the flick of a switch, a telephone system that can be disconnected at the flick of another, even a credulity-busting bedroom that functions like an elevator. And Lugosi takes these baroque fixtures and fittings as his cue to go seriously over the top on his climactic cry of "What a delicious torture, Bateman! Greater than Poe! Poe only conceived it! I have done it, Bateman! Poe – you are avenged!"

This is a shame, because the first half of the film (and Lugosi's performance) is pregnant with possibilities. In a prologue very similar to that of the yet-to-be-released *The Crime of Doctor Crespi*, Friedlander cuts smartly to the chase. Some very effective model work sends Jean Thatcher's automobile tumbling over the brow of a hill, we see her stretched out in immaculate maquillage in the hospital, and finally

Ian Wolfe, Inez Courtney, Lester Matthews and Irene Ware are rudely awakened by Karloff and Lugosi in *The Raven* (1935)

THE RAVEN

Universal 1935
61 minutes
production began 20 March

Cinematographer: Charles Stumar; Art Director: Albert S D'Agostino; Editor: Alfred Akst; Sound: Gilbert Kurland; Make-up: Jack P Pierce*, Otto Lederer*; Music: Clifford Vaughan*; Choreography: Theodore Kosloff*; Dialogue Director: Florence Enright; Screenplay: David Boehm, Dore Schary* ('suggested by the immortal Edgar Allan Poe classic'); Associate Producer: David Diamond; Director: Louis Friedlander [later Lew Landers]

Karloff (Edmond Bateman); Lugosi (Dr Richard Vollin); Lester Matthews (Dr Jerry Halden); Irene Ware (Jean Thatcher); Samuel S Hinds (Judge Thatcher); Spencer Charters (Col Bertram Grant); Inez Courtney (Mary Burns); Ian Wolfe (Geoffrey ['Pinky']); Maidel Turner (Harriet Grant); uncredited: Raine Bennett ('Poe' in recitation); Jonathan Hale (Dr Cook); Arthur Hoyt (Mr Chapman); Walter Miller (Dr Hemingway); Madeline Talcott (nurse); Cyril Thornton (Vollin's butler)

nb: the on-screen cast list erroneously reverses the roles played by Spencer Charters and Ian Wolfe

Bela ('Dracula') Lugosi and Boris ('Frankenstein') Karloff, foremost US cinemonsters, first played together in *The Black Cat*, 'suggested' by Edgar Allan Poe's story. *The Raven*, 'suggested' by that frail, pathetic poet's best-known poem, suffers chiefly from the obligation its producers felt to give it more bloodcurdling situations and paraphernalia than *The Black Cat*. Consequently the picture is stuffed with horrors to the point of absurdity. *Time*

Screaming is an art, it was discovered during the filming of *The Raven* ... Inez Courtney ... was the screamer who passed with high honors. Her piercing scream almost scared the wits out of Karloff and Bela (Dracula) Lugosi, stars of the picture. It was conceded that to scare those two gentlemen you've got to be good. *from original pressbook*

overhear her father deciding to pay a personal visit on Dr Vollin. Then comes a marvellous introduction for Lugosi, beautifully realised by cinematographer Charles Stumar and ranking as one of the most memorable moments in the Universal canon. Lugosi's familiar Hungarian inflections are heard intoning Poe's titular poem as the ominous silhouette of a raven fills the screen. The camera pulls back to reveal Lugosi's corvine profile at left, exactly balancing that of the stuffed raven at right – and exactly fulfilling the script's description of the shot as "emphasizing [in Vollin] a certain sinister bird-like quality."[23]

For Lugosi fans, *The Raven* remains a delight. He may have received second billing and only $5000 to Karloff's $10,000, but he dominates the film with a uniquely flavoursome performance. Vollin's fascination for Jean (played by former 'Miss America' Irene Ware) begins in the operating theatre, when she's stretched out in a suitably Poe-like catatonic state and Stumar treats us to a very alarming close-up of Vollin's eyes, smouldering intensely above his surgical mask. Elsewhere, Vollin demonstrates that he knows how to show a girl a good time by serenading Jean with Bach's ever-popular Toccata and Fugue in D Minor, then sits in a theatre box to watch Jean's 'Dance Interpretation' of *The Raven*.

A very similar scene would appear in *Mad Love*, but where Peter Lorre suggests an explicitly sexual response to Frances Drake's stage performance, Lugosi looks on with a colder, more intellectual

absorption. In the meantime, a frankly poor recitation of the poem drones away on the soundtrack while Jean (actually Ware's dance double Nina Golden) leaps about in graceless circles.

Karloff's San Quentin escapee is, in actor parlance, decidedly 'low status' by comparison, though he has fun with a cod Cockney accent and a spectacular scene in which Bateman wakes from the operation Vollin has performed on him. Vollin has thoughtfully laid on a phalanx of full-length mirrors to maximise Bateman's shock on discovering the havoc wrought on his seventh cranial nerve, and Bateman repeatedly lisps "Fix my mouth" as if unaware of the highly unconvincing poached-egg eye applied by the normally immaculate Jack Pierce. Bateman's fate is a grisly sequel to his own self-fulfilling prophecy, expressed in lines that Boehm surely realised were ridiculous but which Karloff and Lugosi play with admirably straight faces. "Maybe if a man looks ugly he does ugly things," muses Bateman. "You are saying something profound," intones Vollin portentously.

As well as unusually pathetic comedy relief (chiefly supplied by Spencer Charters, just as unfunny here as he was in *The Bat Whispers*), *The Raven* is mainly distinguished by a pervasive aroma of sadism, as when Vollin relishes Bateman's account of his unorthodox use of an oxyacetylene torch in an Arizona bank. And this was to have far-reaching consequences. Though a box-office hit, the film was heavily cut by several local censorship boards, banned altogether in Ontario, and the subject of sustained newspaper sermonising in Great Britain.

In the meantime, horror fans could absorb the more literary pretensions of Fox's new version of *Dante's Inferno*, which told a moralistic tale akin to its 1924 predecessor and was decked out with a startling Inferno scene lusciously realised by painter-cum-director Harry Lachman, cinematographer Rudolph Maté and uncredited designer Ben Carré. On release at the end of August 1935, the film had begun production the previous December and reportedly employed 14,000 people, 3000 of whom were underclad extras in the purgatorical stews. The similarity of the film's Inferno to the erotic vision of Hell featured in Rex Ingram's *The Magician* is attributable, not only to the fact that Lachman had been Ingram's assistant, but to Hubert Stowitts, a lascivious faun in the Ingram film and unbilled choreographer here.

Also on view in August 1935 was a splendid Columbia melodrama called *The Black Room*. Though an original by Arthur Strawn and Henry Myers, this had sufficient literary heft and stateliness to move the young novelist Graham Greene to invoke the names of Mrs Radcliffe and 'Monk' Lewis in reviewing it. The film was the result of a one-picture deal Karloff had struck with Columbia soon after making *The Black Cat*; the delay in producing it was compensated for by an unwonted lavishness in its presentation. Like Lionel Atwill in *The Sphinx* and Bela Lugosi in *Murder by Television*, Karloff was cast here as twin brothers, always a fertile seedbed for uncanny effects. And the result counts as one of his most bravura showcases.

In 1834, Gregor de Berghman murders his mistress Mashka, deflecting the villagers' wrath by proposing to step down as the local squire in favour of his saintly twin brother Anton. This he does, but he also disposes of Anton in the notorious Black Room of the family castle. Resuming his dominion by carefully impersonating Anton (in particular a distinctive paralysis of the dead man's right hand), he then sets his sights on marrying the beautiful Thea...

That the film is to be a deluxe undertaking is immediately clear from its 18th century prologue, with an impressively looming tower and hordes of Tyrolean extras. When the arrival of twins is announced, the assembled grandees offer their congratulations to the fretful Baron de Berghman, but he demurs. "Don't toast this birth – please," he warns. (Simultaneously appearing in M-G-M's *Mad Love*, Henry Kolker is just as dignified a figure here.) Pointing to the de Berghman coat of arms – whose motto, 'Principio et Finem Similia', he helpfully translates as 'I End As I Began' – the Baron sets in train a tale of tragic inevitability revolving around a family curse.

The two boys are then seen as tots at their mother's grave – there is snow on the ground and a couple of ravens hover ominously – prior to a smart dissolve to the same boys some two decades later, heads downcast at their father's. After the lapse of another 20 years, nothing now remains but to introduce Karloff – playing, as the pressbook put it, "a Super Bluebeard ... with a Private Graveyard."

That graveyard takes the form of a hidden oubliette contained in the so-called Black Room. The pit itself is accessed by infernal machinery reminiscent of Poe's *The Pit and the Pendulum*, and when Katherine DeMille's village hoyden Mashka starts getting above her station it quickly becomes obvious that she will soon end up in it. In a terrific scene heavily freighted with sexual euphemism, Gregor chews nonchalantly on a pear and draws a near-the-knuckle parallel with Mashka's lubricious, yet disposable, charms. "A pear's the best fruit," he grins. "Lots of juice in a pear." Then: "Adam should have chosen a pear." And on this sardonic

Boris Karloff prepares to consign Katherine DeMille to the dreadful oubliette contained in *The Black Room* (1935)

THE BLACK ROOM

Columbia 1935
68 minutes
production began 6 May

Cinematographer: Allen G Siegler; Art Director: Stephen Goosson; Editor: Richard Cahoon; Sound: Edward Bernds*; Costumes: Murray Mayer; Musical Director: Louis Silvers; Screenplay: Arthur Strawn, Henry Myers; Story: Arthur Strawn; Producer: Robert North*; Director: R [Roy] William Neill

Boris Karloff (Gregor/Anton); Marian Marsh (Thea); Robert Allen (Lt Lussan); Thurston Hall (Col Hassel); Katherine DeMille (Mashka); John Buckler (Beran); Henry Kolker (Baron de Berghman); Colin Tapley (Lt Hassel); Torben Meyer (Peter); uncredited: John Beck (clerk of court); John M Bleifer (Franz); Bleifer Twins (Anton and Gregor when young); George Burr MacAnnan (majordomo); Sidney Bracy (hairdresser); Egon Brecher (Karl); Victor DeLinsky (Michael [Hassel's footman]); Helena Grant (Honor [Hassel's housekeeper]); Marion Lessing (Marie [Hassel's housemaid]); George MacQuarrie (Chief Justice); Robert Middlemass (prosecutor); Reginald Pasch (tailor); Joseph Singer (Raoul [Hassel's butler]); John Maurice Sullivan (Archbishop); Edward Van Sloan (doctor); Fredrik Vogeding (Josef); Phyllis Fraser, Lois Lindsey (bridesmaids); Abe Dinovitch, Ivan Linow (gatekeepers); Eric Mayne, Wilfrid North (gentlemen of the court); John George, Michael Mark, Bert Sprott, Paul Weigel (peasants)

Karloff ... carries the whole film, so far as acting is concerned, on his own shoulders. The direction is good: it has caught, as Mr James Whale never did with *Frankenstein*, the genuine Gothic note. Mrs Radcliffe would not have been ashamed of this absurd and exciting film. *The Spectator* [UK]

When filming began, it seemed to me that the pace was slow and that members of the cast, including Karloff, overacted. As we progressed, I began to see that I might be wrong ... Roy Neill and Boris Karloff knew what they were creating – and it worked.
Edward Bernds [Mr Bernds Goes to Hollywood, 1999]

invocation of original sin he brutally disposes of the girl, whom we next see when Gregor takes the unwitting Anton into the Black Room. Peering down into the pit – lorgnette dangling, paralysed right hand clutched characteristically to his lapel – Anton sees Mashka reposing at the bottom among a scattering of age-old skeletons. And, sure enough, he joins her there almost immediately.

Aided by seamless split-screen photography, Karloff differentiates between the two brothers with the simplest shifts in body language – Gregor slouching and sneering, Anton upright and open-faced. And, once Gregor's imposture as Anton gets under way, the two modes are marvellously intertwined when the trusting Colonel Hassel stumbles on Gregor's secret. Accused by Hassel over a game of chess, Gregor settles back in his chair and coolly uncurls his supposedly paralysed right hand. Moments later, in an extremely nifty parallel, Hassel's murder is discreetly shown merely through a close-up of his hand reaching for the bell-pull and then curling up in the paralysis of death.

Apart from the providential slip happened upon by Hassel, Gregor's impersonation is perfectly realised and begs disturbing questions regarding identity. At no time does anyone spot the black-hearted substance behind Gregor's smooth Anton façade, not even Marian Marsh's spirited and intelligent Thea. "My blood turns to ice when he touches me," she has said of Gregor-as-Gregor. Faced with Gregor-as-Anton, however, she has no relish in marrying him only because she loves another; the whiff of barely concealed brimstone

characteristic of Gregor passes her by entirely. "We can all be mistaken in people," Gregor piously assures her at one point – and still the penny doesn't drop.

To point up the theme of doubles and confused identities, Roy William Neill – whose direction is a model of imaginative precision throughout – has plenty of fun with mirrors. The walls of the Black Room itself are of mirrored onyx, Gregor transforming himself into Anton in its reflective surface just moments after killing him. Similarly, Gregor's indiscretion is spotted by Hassel in a huge mirror, the camera tracking smoothly into Gregor's reflection, then tracking precipitately away from him after a terrific reaction shot from Hassel. And the following morning, the discovery of the colonel's body is seen through yet another mirror, the housemaid happily preening herself in it prior to screaming in terror at her grisly find.

Apart from some slightly tacky back-projection in the climactic pursuit of the bogus Anton, *The Black Room* is beautifully done all the way, with especially luscious photography and production design from Al Siegler and Stephen Goosson respectively. It also has a pleasing circularity in its construction. When Gregor and Anton are united in death at the bottom of the fateful oubliette (and on the point of the same upturned dagger), the camera comes to rest once more on the legend 'Principio et Finem Similia' and the credits roll.

Prior to *The Black Room*, Roy William Neill had made the similarly titled *Black Moon* for Columbia. Completed on 3 May 1934, by 28 June the result was being memorably summarised by André Sennwald in the *New York Times*: "A hasty and deplorably incomplete inventory would show two blood sacrifices, two ordinary murders, incantations in three languages, a lunatic witch doctor, a white woman with a bad case of heebie-jeebies and a patriotic effort on the part of 2000 crazed natives to exterminate all white folk on the island, not counting the white goddess."

Unfortunately, the picture is by no means as exciting as Sennwald's summary makes it sound. The story is intriguing (and racist) enough. A well-heeled white woman (Dorothy Burgess) has been brought up among the natives of West Indian island San Christopher, finally returning there and becoming a voodoo priestess. When cheated of her husband (Jack Holt) and his adoring secretary (Fay Wray) as sacrificial victims, she is instructed by the High Priest to sacrifice her daughter (Cora Sue Collins) instead; "Nous demande le enfant pour le sacrifice!" he says in his pidgin French. There's a modicum of internal conflict here, with Burgess shedding a tear before uplifting the knife and being shot down by Holt in the nick of time. But the treatment is staid and superficial, with the jungle melodramatics played out more like Somerset Maugham's *The Letter* than Victor Halperin's *White Zombie*.

SHUDDERING WITH SADISTIC THRILLS

Cora Sue Collins, Jack Holt's imperilled daughter in *Black Moon*, turned up later as a tiny patient of Hollywood's newest mad scientist. Peter Lorre, the brilliant Hungarian star of Fritz Lang's *M*, had sailed for America, aged 30, on 18 July 1934, one day after completing work on Alfred Hitchcock's *The Man Who Knew Too Much* in London. He was to sit idle, however, until May 1935, when Columbia finally loaned him out to M-G-M for *Mad Love*. Loosely based on Maurice Renard's novel *Les Mains d'Orlac*, this was a remake of an 11-year-old Austrian picture called *Orlacs Hände* and was entrusted to director Karl Freund.

Yvonne, wife of the celebrated concert pianist Stephen Orlac, is a star of the Paris Théâtre des Horreurs and has a sensitive stalker in the form of Dr Gogol. When Stephen's hands are crushed in a train crash, Gogol grafts on the hands of guillotined knife-thrower Rollo instead, later convincing Stephen that he is responsible for the murder of his own stepfather. But when Gogol threatens Yvonne, Stephen puts his new-found facility with knives to good use.

Still unsure about horror subjects, M-G-M had gone elsewhere, not only for Lorre, but also for the film's other leads, borrowing Frances Drake from Paramount and Colin Clive from Warner Bros. Horror veteran John L Balderston, meanwhile, was called in for a last-minute script 'polish' and loaded the film with in-jokes, making it a kind of demented gazetteer of Hollywood's horror output thus far. Lines from *Frankenstein*, *The Mummy* and even the recently released *WereWolf of London* are shoehorned in wherever possible, a character from *Freaks* (played, what's more, by the same actor) makes a surprise appearance, and the mere presence of Colin Clive is a gag, given that here the former Dr Frankenstein gets to wear the Monster's stitched-on hands for a change.

The film begins in arresting style, with the glass-mounted credits abruptly smashed by an angry fist. A sardonic Balderston gag at the expense of his target audience is then played out by a courting couple in the foyer of Metro's thinly disguised version of the Théâtre du Grand Guignol; the girl resists going in, but the bloodthirsty boy is looking forward to "a fillip to jaded nerves, a new shudder." Inside, a female

"Whose hands *are* these?" Colin Clive appeals to Peter Lorre for post-operative therapy in *Mad Love* (1935)

cloakroom attendant is suited up to resemble a headless tuxedo, as droll a forecast of the film's decapitation angle as the candied guillotine sitting atop Yvonne's cake at the cast party. And before finding his way inside, Dr Gogol pauses to worship before a lifesize replica of Yvonne, only to seethe with jealousy when a nattily attired drunk does the same. "My card, monsieur," says the drunk. "I'm perfectly willing to give you satisfaction." The notion of grown men fighting a duel over a wax dummy is a suitably absurd cue for the necrophiliac madness soon to overcome Gogol.

Blessed with some terrific dialogue, Lorre's lovesick Gogol is a small masterpiece of steadily gathering lunacy, and a clear ancestor of the weirdly sympathetic psychopaths featured in films like *Psycho* and *Peeping Tom*. Sitting in his "lonely shadowed box" and watching *Torturée* for the 47th night in a row, his quietly orgasmic response to Yvonne's screams of mock-anguish make it immediately obvious that this is no ordinary stage-door Johnny. Later, his squint-eyed appraisal of Rollo's execution provides a coldly analytical parallel to the impassioned eloquence of his plot to unhinge Yvonne's already neurotic husband. His grisly masquerade as the supposedly resurrected Rollo – telling the impressionable Orlac that "They cut off my head, but that Gogol, he put it back!" – remains the film's macabre highlight. "The power of suggestion!" he crows later. "How easily it works!"

In Gogol's chambers, Freund's understated use of skewed angles and pools of shadow represents a refreshingly subtle tribute to the *Caligari* style, leading many years later to Pauline Kael's hotly contested claim that *Mad Love* was the inspiration for no less a picture than *Citizen Kane* (with which it shared cinematographer Gregg Toland). Freund also pulls off a couple of nifty montage sequences. In one of them, Orlac undergoes an intensive course of hand therapy, which anticipates the ghoulish regime of beautification undertaken by Norma Desmond in *Sunset Blvd*. The other – in which Yvonne dreams

MAD LOVE

M-G-M 1935
68 minutes
production began 6 May
UK title: The Hands of Orlac

Cinematographers: Chester Lyons, Gregg Toland; Art Director: Cedric Gibbons; Associate Art Directors: William A Horning, Edwin B Willis; Editor: Hugh Wynn; Sound: Douglas Shearer; Wardrobe: Dolly Tree; Music: Dmitri Tiomkin; Musical Director: Oscar Radin; Additional Dialogue: Leon Gordon*; Screenplay: P J Wolfson, John L Balderston; Screen Adaptation: Guy Endore (from the novel *Les Mains d'Orlac* by Maurice Renard, translated and adapted by Florence Crewe-Jones); Producer: John W Considine Jr; Director: Karl Freund

Peter Lorre (Doctor Gogol); Frances Drake (Yvonne Orlac); Colin Clive (Stephen Orlac); Ted Healy (Reagan); Sarah Haden (Marie); Edward Brophy (Rollo); Henry Kolker (Prefect Rosset); Keye Luke (Dr Wong); May Beatty (Françoise [concierge]); uncredited: Hooper Atchley (conductor); Agostino Borgato (stage door keeper); Maurice Brierre (cabbie); Julie Carter (nurse); Harvey Clark (station master); Cora Sue Collins (sick child); Nell Craig (Suzanne [nurse]); Frank Darien (Lavin); George Davis (chauffeur); Robert Emmett Keane (drunk in theatre foyer); Alphonz Ethier (second fingerprint man); Billy Gilbert (autograph hunter on train); Ramsey Hill (Duke in Torturée); Murray Kinnell (Charles [stage manager]); Edward Lippy (clerk); Rollo Lloyd (Varsac [fingerprint man]); Mark Lubell (Prince); Michael Mark (guillotine official); Sarah Padden (mother); Edward Norris (theatre patron); Matty Roubert (newsboy); Rolfe Sedan (traffic cop); Carl Stockdale (notary); Charles Trowbridge (Dr Marbeau); Clarence Wilson (creditor); Ian Wolfe (Henry Orlac)

nb: Isabel Jewell was billed fifth in the film's advertising but was deleted from the final print

At heart, *Mad Love* is not much more than a super-Karloff melodrama, an interesting but pretty trivial exercise in Grand Guignol. With any of our conventional maniacs in the role of the deranged surgeon, the photoplay would frequently be dancing on the edge of burlesque. But Mr Lorre, with his gift for supplementing a remarkable physical appearance with his acute perception of the mechanics of insanity, cuts deeply into the darkness of the morbid brain. *New York Times*

My recent role with Peter Lorre in *The Hands of Orlac* ... is still frankly in the horror class. I got no more enjoyment or artistic satisfaction out of playing it than I did out of the rest of my spine-chillers ... My only hope is that I may outlive this demand for horror pictures.
Colin Clive [reprinted in *Famous Monsters of Filmland*, May 1995]

of happier times – is used to bridge an awkward narrative lurch resulting from the excision of what, to preview audiences, must have been the film's most show-stopping scene. Rollo's bona-fide resuscitation in Gogol's lab was one of several items sacrificed to last-minute tampering, resulting in the loss of 15 minutes' footage.

The film has a few other problems, none of them fatal. Though excellent as Yvonne, Frances Drake is not so good at playing her own wax dummy, especially when a continuity gaffe shows the 'real' dummy in a quite different pose. Ted Healy's nosy reporter seems disturbingly like Lee Tracy's nosy reporter from *Doctor X* all over again. And the wrap-up is decidedly weak, with none of Orlac's problems satisfactorily resolved and Gogol expiring in ignominious silence.

"It is not conducive to sound sleep to watch him [Lorre] operating on little girls, shuddering with sadistic thrills at public executions, or slavering over the wax image of Mme Orlac,"[24] noted the reviewer for *Time* magazine. This was one of the milder responses to Freund's film. In the UK (where it retained its shooting title, *The Hands of Orlac*), the film's close proximity to Universal's *The Raven* caused the censor, Edward Shortt, to consider banning it. But, in the US as well as Britain, the picture succeeded in more or less suppressing itself. Of M-G-M's previous shockers, only *Kongo* had been cheaper to make. Yet, on release, *Mad Love* succeeded in losing M-G-M close to $40,000. With its febrile mixture of Grand Guignol histrionics, twisted eroticism and codified castration anxiety, the film was way ahead of its time and 1930s audiences were having none of it.

Indeed, in the summer of 1935 the debate regarding the desirability of horror pictures became a hot topic on both sides of the Atlantic. In the *New York Times* of 28 July, a reputable doctor was quoted to the effect that "a dozen of the worst obscene pictures cannot equal the damage that is done by such films as *Mark of the Vampire*," emphasising "the terrible effect that it has on the mental and nervous systems of not only unstable but even normal men, women and children ... In my opinion, it is a crime to produce and to present such films. We must guard not only our people's morals – we must be as careful of their physical and mental health."[12]

The passionate force of this and similar broadsides was founded on a curious paradox. Filmmakers had responded to the enforcement of the Production Code, not by shying away from horror subjects, but by meeting them head on, making 1935 a veritable orgy of bloodshed and sadism. The unfortunate repercussions of this would be felt in short order, with the response from Great Britain proving especially worrying.

Britain's antipathy to horror subjects was no secret; as noted above, the Rt Hon Edward Shortt, secretary of the British Board of Film Censors, had banned *Freaks* and *Island of Lost Souls* altogether, and to that august company he now added, incredibly, Universal's ridiculous quasi-documentary *Life Returns*. He had also removed over 1000 feet from Paramount's *Dr Jekyll and Mr Hyde* (reducing Miriam Hopkins' role to virtually nothing) and redubbed the Satanism in *The Black Cat* as 'sun worship'. Some local councils were even less accommodating than Mr Shortt. *Mad Love*, for example, was banned in Northampton, *The Raven* and *WereWolf of London* in Rotherham, and *Bride of Frankenstein* in both Birmingham and Exeter.

Describing the "tendency towards an increase in the number of films which come within the horror classification" as "unfortunate and undesirable," Shortt made himself very clear in the 4 July edition of *Kinematograph Weekly*. "I cannot believe such films are wholesome," he claimed, "pandering as they do to the love of the morbid and horrible ... I hope that producers and renters will accept this word of warning and discourage this type of subject as far as possible." The position became even clearer on 23 August, when the Associated Press ran the grim headline: HORROR FILMS TABOO IN BRITAIN – 'THE RAVEN' LAST. Another headline wittily represented the picture as THE FILM CENSOR'S 'NEVER MORE'.

Responses to this hardline stance came from some surprising sources. Faced with what was widely perceived to be Exhibit A – *The Raven* – the reaction of the London *Times* was unequivocal: "What artistic merit or legitimate entertainment value there may be in films of this kind I leave others to discover. Their capacity for harm would seem apparent to anyone. Certain mentalities are susceptible to morbid appeal. They will not resist these examples."[25] On the other hand, Graham Greene, reviewing *Mad Love* for the *Spectator*, noted that "If a horror film is bad, as *The Bride of Frankenstein* was bad, it isn't horrible at all and may be quite a good joke; if it is a good film, why should Mr Shortt narrow so puritanically the scope of an art? ... Must our pet vice be denied all satisfaction?"[26]

These competing claims – the one labelling horror as a harmless "pet vice" for the cognoscenti, the other branding it a dangerous example to "certain mentalities" (by implication, lower-class ones) – were to be repeated in similar controversies for decades, retaining their potency even into the 21st century. Back in the summer of 1935, however, the outcome would be felt within 12 months. Inspired in large part by the British ban, horror films would soon disappear altogether from Hollywood's production schedules.

LIGHTNING BUG AND DEATH ROW REVENANT

Presumably aware of the gathering opposition to horror subjects, Universal opted in their third Karloff-Lugosi vehicle to back-pedal on the expected Gothic mayhem, foregrounding instead the speculative science that had formed a persistent undercurrent in earlier pictures. Postponing a Karloff project called *Bluebeard* (written by Bayard Veiller of *The Thirteenth Chair* fame), Universal engaged John Colton to script a film that would be as much a vehicle for John Fulton's special effects as for Karloff and Lugosi.

Not one to waste a good formula, Colton came up with a thinly disguised retread of his *WereWolf of London* script and called it *The Invisible Ray*. Like Wilfred Glendon, Janos Rukh is a grim-faced over-reacher who contracts a dreadful 'disease' in an exotic location, becomes dependent on a hard-to-find antidote, and ends by threatening the young wife who has sought solace with another man.

> *In Africa, Dr Janos Rukh discovers Radium X, curing his mother's blindness with it but also acquiring the power to destroy by touch. An antidote prepared by Dr Felix Benet sends Rukh mad, and in Paris he determines to kill the men who stole his discovery and, in particular, the man who stole his wife. But the latter is saved when Rukh's mother disposes of the antidote, claiming that her son has "broken the first law of science."*

To underline the *WereWolf of London* resemblances, the film was initially earmarked for director Stuart Walker, later devolving upon Western specialist Lambert Hillyer. *The Invisible Ray* also marked the last time Karloff was billed merely as 'Karloff', with an especially grandiloquent expanded version – 'The Great Karloff' – being appended to much of the film's advertising. As usual, Lugosi's billing was more discreet, as was his remuneration, which fell short of Karloff's by nearly two thirds. And yet, as in *The Black Cat* and *The Raven*, Lugosi actually has the better part and walks away with the film.

Too much of the unappetising shade of Glendon clings to Karloff's Rukh; the indefinable Karloff charisma is obviously preferable to the granite inflexibility of Henry Hull, but Rukh never engages our sympathy as he should. He's dangerously mad from the outset, hardly requiring the dire effects of "the violent surcharge of poison and antidote" to send him over the edge. And, to beef up an unsympathetic character, Karloff tends to overplay, making Lugosi – a strange reversal, this – seem a model of restraint and sobriety. The indefinable Lugosi charisma helps to make something intriguing out of the normally thankless 'voice of reason' role; when Benet explains to Rukh the importance of his antidote, only Lugosi could put so ominous a spin on the line, "If you do not use the counteractive in time, you will literally crumble to an ash." Indeed, in Lugosi's hands, Benet comes across as a uniquely civilised and sophisticated individual, making Rukh look like a self-absorbed, atavistic oaf by comparison.

The rest of the acting is similarly accomplished, notably from the beautiful Paramount contractee Frances Drake, who, having replaced M-G-M's Virginia Bruce in *Mad Love*, was here deputising for Universal's Gloria Stuart. And when the action moves to Paris (a strangely popular locale in US chillers of the period, also featuring in *Svengali*, *Murders in the Rue Morgue*, *Mad Love* and the upcoming *The Devil-Doll*), we're treated to a host of interesting characters, from Georges Renevant's police chief to Lucio Villegas' hawk-faced butler. We also get clear evidence that Colton had realised his mistake in larding *WereWolf of London* with comedy crones; here there's just the one, and she's nicely sketched by May Beatty, formerly Peter Lorre's tipsy concierge in *Mad Love*.

With Rukh setting up his death ray in Mrs LeGrand's garret and training it on the stone saints of Notre Dame, the action provides a weird foretaste of *The Day of the Jackal*. There's also a hint of something very interesting when the immolation of these statues, in the words of a newspaper headline, causes "Onlookers [to] Faint and Pray." Unfortunately, altogether too many things in Colton's scattershot screenplay are merely hinted at. At the beginning, when Rukh prepares to give Benet and company a mind-bending "tour in time" from his Carpathian observatory, he points out that "Everything that ever happened has left its record on nature's film." Later, Benet achieves something similar when he photographs the dead eye of Rukh's first victim and finds an image of the killer imprinted on it. An improbable fusion of the mystic and the mechanical to equal anything in *The Hands of Orlac*, this is nevertheless tossed into Colton's stew of intriguing but undigested ideas and allowed to sink without trace.

Colton also makes little of the film's central contradiction, with Rukh descending into the Hellish flames of an African crater and coming out as a Messiah who cures his mother's blindness. The film's structure is all over the place too, with a first act set in the Carpathian mountains as a sop to the Laemmles'

Karloff looks broodingly on as Helen Brown thanks Lugosi for restoring the sight of her daughter (Anne Marie Conte) in *The Invisible Ray* (1935)

standard Gothicisms, a second set in darkest Africa to indicate that, if RKO and M-G-M could excel at jungle adventures, Universal could too, and a third that moves from a brief Carpathian curtain-raiser to the climactic business in Paris. The African section is especially episodic, with the longed-for newspaper headline "Benet Expedition Leaves Africa" coming a good 15 minutes later than the material, or the viewer, can stand.

Though for the most part unengaging, the film boasts an ace Karloff-Lugosi confrontation in its final reel, a stirring one between the disintegrating Rukh and his high-minded mother, and the aforementioned "tour in time," in which John Fulton's interplanetary visions paved the way for much that was to develop in science fiction pictures 20 years' hence.

Barely a month after completing his role as Janos Rukh, Karloff began work for Warner Bros on *The Walking Dead*, with which the studio resurrected a hard-hitting horror sideline that had lain dormant since *Mystery of the Wax Museum*.

In M-G-M's *Mad Love*, wisecracking Ted Healy had dreamt up the headline 'Man Without Head Kills Rich Jeweller' and quipped, "Why, that's the greatest story since Lindbergh flew to Paris!" Karloff's new picture not only involved a less sensationalist medical feat than the restoration of an executed man's head; it also included a much more topical reference to the heroic Charles A Lindbergh, whose historic transatlantic flight dated back to May 1927. He had since collaborated with Dr Alexis Carell in perfecting a mechanical circulatory system known as 'The Lindbergh Heart'. Warners duly featured a working model of the device in *The Walking Dead*, lending a touch of scientific topicality to a story otherwise preoccupied with more metaphysical matters.

THE INVISIBLE RAY

Universal 1935
80 minutes
production began 17 September

Cinematographer: George Robinson; Art Director: Albert S D'Agostino; Editor: Bernard Burton; Sound: Gilbert Kurland; Special Cinematographer: John P Fulton; Effects: Ray Lindsay*, David Horsley*; Make-up: Jack P Pierce*, Otto Lederer*; Gowns: Brymer; Music: Franz Waxman; Production Assistant: Alfred Stern; Technical Adviser: Ted Behr*; Screenplay: John Colton; Original Story: Howard Higgin, Douglas Hodges; Producer: Edmund Grainger; Director: Lambert Hillyer

Karloff (Dr Janos Rukh); Bela Lugosi (Dr Felix Benet); Frances Drake (Diana Rukh); Frank Lawton (Ronald Drake); Violet Kemble Cooper (Mother Rukh); Walter Kingsford (Sir Francis Stevens); Beulah Bondi (Lady Arabella Stevens); Frank Reicher (Professor Meiklejohn); Paul Weigel (Monsieur Noyer); Georges Renavent (Chief of Sûreté); uncredited: May Beatty (Mrs LeGrand); Helen Brown (French mother); Daisy Bufford (Zulu mother); Alex Chivra (cook); Anne Marie Conte (blind girl); Daniel Haines (headman); Winter Hall (minister); Paul McAllister (Papa LaCosta); Etta McDaniel (Zulu woman); Walter Miller (hobo); Hans Schumm (clinic attendant); Inez Seabury (Celeste); Lawrence Stewart (number one boy); Adele St Maur (Mme Noyer); Fred Toones (frightened native); Lucio Villegas (Benet's butler); Nydia Westman (Briggs [Lady Arabella's maid]); Charles Bastin, Ernest Bowern (newsboys); André Cheron, Alphonse Martell (Sûreté officers)

Nothing I have seen on the screen lately suggests more graphically the limitless range of screen art than this picture manages to do ... Its horror content is not as great as is usual in a Karloff picture, it handles its triangular romance with good taste, and presents us with some outstanding characterizations. *Hollywood Spectator*

Photographic effects never before attempted were accomplished successfully during the filming of *The Invisible Ray* ... After weeks of experimenting, studio camera experts headed by John Fulton evolveda method of ... [making] Karloff seem to pulsate with a weird incandescence like a big lightning bug. *from original pressbook*

Eerie revenant Boris Karloff, flanked by cemetery keeper Frank Darien and scientist Marguerite Churchill, in *The Walking Dead* (1935)

THE WALKING DEAD

Warner Bros-First National 1935
66 minutes
production began 23 November

Cinematographer: Hal Mohr; Art Director: Hugh Reticker; Editor: Thomas Pratt; Sound: Gerald Alexander*, Stanley L Jones*, Harold Shaw*; Mechanical heart devised by: Stanley Fox*; Make-up: Perc Westmore*; Gowns: Orry-Kelly; Musical Director: Leo F Forbstein*; Music: Bernhard Kaun*; Dialogue Director: Irving Rapper; Screenplay: Ewart Adamson, Peter Milne, with Robert Andrews and Lillie Hayward; Story: Ewart Adamson, Joseph Fields; Executive Producer: Hal B Wallis*; Director: Michael Curtiz

Boris Karloff (John Ellman); Ricardo Cortez (Nolan); Edmund Gwenn (Dr Beaumont); Marguerite Churchill (Nancy); Warren Hull (Jimmy); Barton MacLane (Loder); Henry O'Neill (Werner [DA]); Joseph King (Judge Shaw); Addison Richards (prison warden); Paul Harvey (Blackstone); Robert Strange (Merritt); Joseph Sawyer (Trigger); Eddie Acuff (Betcha); Kenneth Harlan (Stephen Martin); Miki Morita (Sako); Ruth Robinson (Mrs Shaw); uncredited: George André [de] Beranger (servant); Wade Boteler (guard); James P Burtis (second bodyguard); Edgar Cherrod (priest); Lucille Collins (girl in court); Frank Darien (cemetery caretaker); Gordon 'Wild Bill' Elliott (US announcer); Boyd Irwin (British doctor); John Kelly (Merritt's bodyguard [Joe]); Crauford Kent (British broadcaster); Isabelle LeMal (sob sister); Nick Moro (cellist); Alphonse Martell (florist); Spec O'Donnell (copy boy); Jean Perry (French broadcaster); James Pierce (gunman); William Wayne (trusty)

It is impossible for me to conceive of this production failing to intrigue a spectator ... There are many scenes of rare intensity, charged with emotional, spectacular thrills and possessing beauty of an uncommon sort. Conventional liberties at no time figure and suspense neatly is provoked almost at the start and sustained. *Hollywood Spectator*

Karloff heard that little Sybil [Jason] was about to pay him a call ... "Don't let that child on this stage!" he ordered. "She mustn't see me this way. She'll be scared out of ten years' growth!" ... But little Miss Jason slipped through a back door and ... burst out laughing. "Oh, Uncle Boris!" she giggled. "You look just too funny! What are you playing – a clown?" *from original pressbook*

Mild-mannered pianist John Ellman emerges from a ten-year prison sentence only to fall in with a group of racketeers who frame him and then stand by as he goes to the electric chair. Research scientist Dr Beaumont resurrects him, however, and Ellman succeeds in frightening his enemies to death merely by confronting them with their guilt. Shot down in a cemetery, he takes his life-in-death secrets with him to the grave.

Brilliantly directed by Michael Curtiz, *The Walking Dead* is a happier fusion of the hard-bitten Warners style with its otherworldly subject matter than the earlier Curtiz titles *Doctor X* and *Mystery of the Wax Museum*. It achieves this by the apparently crude device of just splitting the two down the middle and then bolting them together, whereas the other films had sassy newshounds threaded right the way through. To this end, the first half of the film has the agitated tempo, rat-a-tat dialogue and headline montages familiar from any number of Warner products, while the second settles for a more measured rhythm and the conjuring of a genuinely disquieting atmosphere.

The cross-over is effected as the persecuted Ellman goes to the electric chair. Here, cinematographer Hal Mohr comes up with a striking composition that

exactly anticipates film noir. Shot at a subtly skewed angle and striped with the spindly shadows of prison bars, Ellman's sombre Death Row procession is accompanied by his favourite composition, as played by a convict-cum-cellist. In making this last request, Ellman pointed out that "I always think of Heaven like that," an observation that, along with his firm conviction that "He'll believe me," introduces the film's surprisingly potent spiritual subtext.

Before dealing with that, however, Curtiz stages a dazzling resurrection sequence, observing the procedure from a multiplicity of angles as Beaumont and his assistants work diligently beneath a fusillade of arcing electrical currents. With Ellman's death and rebirth both brought about by electricity, it comes as no surprise when the doctor concludes with the now-obligatory nod to *Frankenstein*: "He's alive," he exults. "He will live!"

Karloff's Ellman remains one of his most sensitive creations – an all the more remarkable achievement given that, only days before production began, the script still painted the character as a sadistic, drug-addicted brute. In the finished film, he's a gentle and guileless soul drawn inexorably into the web of men infinitely more devious than he; he's meekly unresponsive even when his piano rendition of Rubinstein's 'Kammenoi-Ostrow' is rudely interrupted by the tuxedoed gangster, Loder.

Later on, Loder will be forced to hear the composition again when Beaumont stages a recital designed to smoke out the guilty racketeers. Aided by a riveting sequence of extreme close-ups, Karloff turns in his piano stool to direct his basilisk stare at each of the malefactors in turn, his eyes at the same time glistening with tears. This extraordinary combination of spiritual transcendence with unearthly malice must have stuck in the memory of Terence Fisher, whose very similar credits sequence for the 1960 Hammer film *The Curse of the Werewolf* dwells on a close-up of Oliver Reed's simultaneously hate- and tear-filled eyes.

Karloff really comes into his own when Ellman assumes his apparently God-given role as his victims' grimly unstoppable conscience. The well-heeled racketeers are a suitably despicable bunch, with the oleaginous Nolan (Ricardo Cortez) speaking for them all when he points out that "Murder ... is a very fine art. Covering up afterwards is even finer." Having ensured Ellman's fate by acting as his defence counsel, Nolan finally falls victim to a peculiarly satisfying stroke of poetic justice – along with the appalling Loder, he is electrocuted when their car smashes into an electrical pylon.

Crucially, Ellman does no actual violence to the guilty men; instead, faced with his brooding accusatory presence, the feckless hitman Trigger accidentally shoots himself, the venal Blackstone falls in front of an oncoming locomotive, and the rat-faced Merritt succumbs to a heart attack. The first two deaths are staged in the inky chiaroscuro of a rooming house and a railway siding respectively, but the third is played out in the dazzling whiteness of Merritt's Art Deco apartment as a thunderstorm rages outside. All three are brilliantly achieved, with Ellman stating an especially pertinent truth when dealing with Trigger: "You can't escape what you've done."

Karloff's great achievement lies in the otherworldly quality he brings to the resurrected Ellman. A forlorn, grey-faced revenant, he seems genuinely, as Beaumont puts it, to be "the instrument of some supernatural power." Delightfully played by Karloff's friend Edmund Gwenn, Beaumont shades imperceptibly from avuncular research scientist to stop-at-nothing over-reacher, telling the incredulous DA that, via Ellman, "secrets from the Beyond, things that no man has ever dreamt of, are within my reach." Beaumont is determined to answer no less a question than "What is death?" – and, in a moving exchange as his patient expires a second time, Ellman almost gets around to telling him. "It will never be known," Beaumont concludes sadly as the camera tracks into a rain-swept graveyard.

Released at the end of February 1936, *The Walking Dead* may have stirred memories in older picturegoers of two silents with remarkably similar plots, William Humphrey's *The Return of Maurice Donnelly* (1915) and Ernest C Warde's 1920 picture *The Devil to Pay*; the former, in fact, had been used as a propaganda picture by anti-capital punishment reformers. The Karloff film also recalled a Fox production released late in 1932. *Six Hours to Live* was one of the first American pictures directed by William Dieterle, who, as Wilhelm, had acted in Leni's *Das Wachsfigurenkabinett* and Murnau's *Faust* in his native Germany. With Warner Baxter as a League of Nations diplomat killed by rival politicians, Dieterle's film emphasises romance over metaphysics (never mind horror) and was aptly apostrophised in the review section of *Motion Picture*: "The novelty of the idea of a man brought back from death for six short hours has so many dramatic possibilities it is to be regretted that none of them were utilized."[27]

In March 1936, a horror picture went into production that, like *The Walking Dead*, stirred memories of a film made four years earlier. Unfortunately, Victor Halperin's *Revolt of the Zombies* falls pitifully short of its atmospheric progenitor, *White Zombie*. By now domiciled at the old Tec-Art studios, the Halperin brothers had recourse once again to the inspired cinematographer Arthur Martinelli, but to no avail. The result may once have held a few thrills for *Boy's Own* readers attracted by anything featuring Eastern idols and men in pith helmets, but to anyone else it's a cut-price and paralysingly slow production in which Armand Louque (Dean Jagger) searches for the lost city of Angkor and, back at his laboratory in Phnom Penh, recreates "the secret formula of the great king of the Khmers." With it he enslaves all his fellow researchers and Axis soldiers, the film entirely ignoring the usual definition of zombies as the risen dead.

The *New York Times*' Frank S Nugent drolly noted that zombies should "render a thanatoid service to an utter villain, not to a shilly-shallyer who cannot decide between a necrologic career and a blue-eyed blonde," concluding that the film's idea of zombies as "sleep-walkers or something" was likely "to imperil the very foundations of a grand spook legend." There are frequent reminders of the utter villain Nugent had in mind, however, given that Halperin superimposes close-ups of Lugosi's *White Zombie* eyes at every opportunity.

Dean Jagger is certainly no substitute. Though smoothly toupéed, he looks thoroughly sick about being in such a barrel-scraping embarrassment and reads his lines as if from an idiot-board. In a film overburdened with back-projection, at one point he is required to 'wade' through a rear-projected swamp, a tricky proposition calculated to tax any actor. Paraphrasing a Lugosi line from *White Zombie*, Louque frets that his hypnotic subjects "would all tear me limb from limb should I ever relinquish this control," and this they finally do in perhaps the least dynamic 'revolt' ever committed to film. Significantly, the writers of this farrago went uncredited. They were Victor Halperin, actor Rollo Lloyd (who was appearing in M-G-M's *The Devil-Doll* at the time) and sometime director Howard Higgin, who had recently co-written *The Invisible Ray*.

PRINCIPIO ET FINEM SIMILIA

Though *Revolt of the Zombies* showed some imagination in locating its action (however unconvincingly) in Cambodia, other 1936 releases followed the undying pattern of the 1920s spooky-house melodrama. Poverty Row outfit Chesterfield went through the usual whodunit paces in such films as Charles Lamont's *The Dark Hour* and Roland D Reed's *The House of Secrets*, the first of which was set off from the pack by the outré interpolation of a cross-dressing killer.

Two more interesting variants came from Canadian director Bob Hill – who, having co-written and served as assistant director on both *The Cat and the Canary* and *The Last Warning*, perhaps had more right than most to recycle the old elements. The first of these pictures, *A Face in the Fog*, has a glamorous drama critic (June Collyer) investigating the doings of a skulking hunchbacked killer who is equipped with poisoned bullets. The killer's victims are drawn from the cast of a threadbare musical comedy called 'Satan's Bride', which counts as a very forlorn reminder of the lush theatrical setting of *The Last Warning*.

Written by Al Martin, the film was released on 1 February. The day before, Hill began production at Reliable Studios on *The Rogues Tavern*, also written by Martin. Noticeably better looking and more imaginatively shot than *A Face in the Fog*, this one cast 'old house' veteran Wallace Ford alongside the skimpily attired Joan Woodbury and forgotten silent star Clara Kimball Young. In it, a gang of smugglers vies for attention with a murderous wolf-creature. The latter turns out, in a nod to the fanged snake's head of *Murders in the Zoo*, to be a human killer (Young) armed with a mocked-up dog's head, complete with canine false teeth.

Also in production in February 1936 was a Universal picture that was

Dean Jagger and expeditionary friends, plus a rear-projected Angkor Wat, in *Revolt of the Zombies* (1936)

something of a foregone conclusion after the enormous success of *Bride of Frankenstein*. Advertised with the inspired tag-line "She gives you that weird feeling," *Dracula's Daughter* was an inexpensive-looking programmer that nevertheless cost in excess of $278,000. Its tortuous gestation had involved the payment of substantial fees to people who did no work on the film (director Edward Sutherland) or whose work wasn't used (scenarists John L Balderston and R C Sherriff); even Bela Lugosi earned more for not appearing in the film than he had for starring in *Dracula*.

The project had originated in 1933, when David O Selznick purchased the rights to *Dracula's Guest*, the excised opening chapter of *Dracula*. Cannily selling it on to Universal, Selznick also sold them Balderston's extremely gruesome (and kinky) treatment. Universal chucked it out, however, and the film finally went into production with an incomplete script.

The spooky-house melodrama *The Rogues Tavern* (1936) managed to include an apostrophe in its advertising but not on screen

On the death of Dracula, Professor Van Helsing is arrested for murder and enlists the legal aid of his former pupil Jeffrey Garth. Countess Marya Zaleska, meanwhile, appropriates her father's corpse and ceremonially burns it, later victimising a young female model at her Chelsea studio. Garth and Van Helsing finally pursue Zaleska back to Castle Dracula, where she succumbs to a wooden-shafted arrow fired by her embittered amanuensis, Sandor.

Like *Bride of Frankenstein*, *Dracula's Daughter* starts exactly where its progenitor left off, with Van Helsing (here unaccountably renamed Von Helsing) having just put paid to Dracula and the dead Renfield sprawled at the foot of the Carfax staircase (actually the watchtower staircase from *Frankenstein*). That Van Helsing should be immediately arrested for murder is a logical enough development; less logical is the non-appearance of Harker and Dr Seward, whose testimony would have helped the poor chap no end. Instead, he falls into the hands of a couple of Cockney policemen who, as well as seeming strangely out of place in Whitby, indulge in laboured banter that plays like a hangover from the James Whale picture *Dracula's Daughter* was originally mooted as.

Whale having gratefully moved on to Universal's epic production of *Showboat*, the film fell to Lambert Hillyer, whose direction is as smoothly efficient but essentially anonymous as his work on *The Invisible Ray*. An atmospheric high point is reached early on, however, when the Countess stages a ritual cremation for her late father on, presumably, the Yorkshire moors. George Robinson's moody photography and a studio-filling pall of dry ice combine to create the sombre atmosphere that will follow Countess Zaleska throughout. The solemnity and desolation is memorably conveyed by Gloria Holden, a London-born actress whose Countess hates every moment of her undead existence, sublimating her unhappiness through macabre paintings.

Desperate to be "free to live as a woman," she returns from her nocturnal jaunts with forlorn instructions to her faithful manservant to clean her cloak because "There's blood on it again." Designed by Brymer, another of her outfits is swathed around her like the restricting bandages of a mummy, accentuating her ample bosom and emphasising her unhappy enslavement to "the curse of the Draculas."

Garrett Fort's script positions Zaleska as the screen's first reluctant vampire, offering a tentative psychological interpretation via the introduction of a smooth-talking psychiatrist. Ironically, Zaleska first latches on to Garth when he's discussing the presumed mental illness of Van Helsing. Showing a mordant wit, she observes that "There are more things in Heaven and Earth than are dreamed of in your psychiatry, Mr Garth," to which he replies with the sweeping statement that "Sympathetic treatment will release the human mind from any obsession."

So begins Zaleska's effort to rid herself of her compulsion, an unequal struggle that spells death for a waif-like model called Lili. "You won't object to removing your blouse, will you?" the Countess asks in preparation for a head-and-shoulders portrait. "Why are you staring at me that way?" asks Lili fearfully. "Won't I do?" "Yes," the Countess breathes in reply, "you'll do very well indeed." The Sapphic charge here is understated but inescapable, and it recurs at the end

Irving Pichel looms over Marguerite Churchill in a publicity pose for *Dracula's Daughter* (1936)

DRACULA'S DAUGHTER

Universal 1936
74 minutes
production began 4 February

Cinematographer: George Robinson; Art Director: Albert S D'Agostino; Editors: Maurice Pivar*, Milton Carruth; Sound: Gilbert Kurland; Special Cinematographer: John P Fulton; Make-up: Jack P Pierce*; Gowns: Brymer; Music: Heinz Roemheld*; Screenplay: Garrett Fort; Story: John L Balderston ('based on a work by Bram Stoker,' 'suggested by Oliver Jeffries'); Associate Producer: E M Asher; Director: Lambert Hillyer

Otto Kruger (Jeffrey Garth); Gloria Holden (Countess Marya Zaleska/Dracula's daughter); Marguerite Churchill (Janet); Edward Van Sloan (Professor Von [sic] Helsing); Gilbert Emery (Sir Basil Humphrey); Irving Pichel (Sandor); Halliwell Hobbes (Hawkins); Billy Bevan (Albert); Nan Grey (Lili); Hedda Hopper (Lady Esme Hammond); Claude Allister (Sir Aubrey); Edgar Norton (Hobbs); E E Clive (Sergeant Wilkes); uncredited: Agnes Anderson (Irena [bride]); Owen Gorin (best man); Gordon Hart (host); Guy Kingsford (radio announcer); George Kirby (bookseller); Eily Malyon (Miss Peabody); John Power (Grimes [police official]); Hedwigg Reicher (wife); Christian Rub (coachman); William Schramm (Zoltan [bridegroom]); Joseph E Tozer (Angus Graham); Fred Walton (Dr Bemish); Paul Weigel (innkeeper); Eric Wilton (Lady Esme's butler); Douglas Wood (Dr Townsend)

Gloria Holden is a remarkably convincing bat-woman, but we found ourselves wondering all through the picture how she managed to preserve so attractive an appearance – after sleeping in coffins and all – without the aid of a mirror ... Still, we suppose it's a minor objection to a cute little horror picture. Be sure and bring the kiddies. *New York Times*

Garrett Fort, author of the Universal screen play *Dracula's Daughter*, ... owns a $30,000 collection of works on black magic, voodooism and kindred occult matters. His library on these subjects is exceeded only by the late Houdini's collection ... Fort's books are in Hebrew, Greek, Latin, French and Hungarian. The secrets of the alchemists are guarded in cabalistic symbols. *from original pressbook*

when the Countess hovers over Marguerite Churchill's horizontal Janet, who, in a plot development lifted from *Bride of Frankenstein*, has been abducted to force Garth's co-operation.

Holden's striking presence was remarked upon by several contemporary critics. As well as noting that "the student of cinema will find a wealth of study material in the penetratingly intelligent synthesis of Miss Gloria Holden," Paul Jacobs insisted in *Hollywood Spectator* that "Her work bears the stamp of unguessable abilities. She is definitely a great find."[28] (In a later issue he nominated her Zaleska and Charles Laughton's Captain Bligh as the top performances of the year.) She's well supported by Edward Van Sloan (hypnotically effective in his old role of Van Helsing) and Irving Pichel, whose creepy manservant is a highly ambiguous figure; with his clammy pallor, painted eyebrows and heavily rouged lips, he looks like Carroll Borland's Luna after a none-too-thorough sex change. In addition, the lanky Gilbert Emery is very funny as an affable Scotland Yard man, resisting

Van Helsing's wilder theories with lines like "Just what new piece of asininity is this?"

With pleasing circularity, the film ends, as *Dracula* began, in Transylvania, with Albert S D'Agostino adapting sets from *The Invisible Ray* and resurrecting the castle's grand hall, complete with colossal spider's web, from the original *Dracula*. The film also boasts a fine, though uncredited, score by Heinz Roemheld, and a great deal of Benedick-and-Beatrice badinage from Otto Kruger and Marguerite Churchill. In a far cry from the vulgar repartee shared out between Lee Tracy and Fay Wray in *Doctor X*, these dialogues are written for a society psychiatrist and a Baronet's daughter, wittily anticipating the 'screwball' mode of the late 1930s but somewhat compromising the film's thoughtful and doom-laden tone.

While Dracula was acquiring a daughter at Universal, the director of the original *Dracula*, Tod Browning, was preparing a quite different picture at M-G-M. His last assignment, *Mark of the Vampire*, had netted Metro a respectable profit of $54,000. By March 1936, therefore, the studio was prepared to take another chance on him, a wise decision in that his next picture, *The Devil-Doll*, earned an even more respectable $68,000.

The source this time was a gruesome 1933 novel by Abraham Merritt called *Burn Witch Burn!* If Merritt was anticipating a more faithful adaptation than First National had previously accorded *Seven Footprints to Satan*, he was to be bitterly disappointed, for Browning was interested only in Merritt's basic theme of deadly homunculi created by a sexually ambiguous doll-maker. Beyond that, his concealed purpose seems to have been to remake another of his old pictures. Released in August, *The Devil-Doll* was *The Unholy Three* tarted up with a revenge plot and some science-fiction trimmings. But in making it, Browning gifted to posterity the remarkable spectacle of Lionel Barrymore in drag.

After 17 years in prison, framed financier Paul Lavond escapes and sets himself up in Montmartre as the kindly Mme Mandilip, proprietor of a quaintly old-fashioned toy shop. From a former cell-mate he has learnt the secrets of a miniaturisation process, with which he vengefully reduces the duplicitous Radin to 'devil-doll' dimensions. He then sets about the destruction of Coulvet and Matin, the other former associates responsible for his incarceration.

Though James Whale had tossed away the idea of miniaturised humans in one of *Bride of Frankenstein*'s more embarrassing asides, Browning was obviously determined to exploit it for all the macabre thrills it was capable of. The process work in *The Devil-Doll* isn't up to much; whether we're looking at a pony cavorting on a businessman's desk or the slinky Lachna smiling coquettishly at Lavond from the palm of his hand, the effect is never very convincing. But the film's use of freakishly enlarged sets is second to none. Again, the comic potential of the idea is never far away; after all, the last time such out-of-scale sets had been employed was in Laurel and Hardy's 1930 two-reeler *Brats*. But, as the reviewer for Britain's *Daily Sketch* observed at the time, "The suspense of watching these miniature creatures doing their fell work is truly horrifying."[29]

The miniaturised Lachna and Radin move through the massive sets with such feline grace, and Franz Waxman's score is so twinklingly suggestive, that there is real heart-in-mouth anticipation as they prepare to do their worst with the tiny envenomed stilettos provided them by Lavond. First, Lachna stalks across the counterpane of the slumbering Coulvet, then Radin tiptoes towards the spatted feet of Matin; the result in Coulvet's case is a permanent paralysis brought on by Lavond's poison, in the second a panicked confession from Matin. The lethal potential of these doll-like creatures is only enhanced by whimsical touches that even Whale might have envied – Lachna hauling a colossal string of pearls from Mme Coulvet's enormous jewel box, or Radin masquerading, absurdly, as a bizarre seasonal bauble, suspended precariously from Matin's Christmas tree.

The script is credited to horror veterans Garrett Fort and Guy Endore, with none other than Erich von Stroheim, by then a staff writer at M-G-M, adding various outré details of his own. Abounding with quotable lines, the screenplay is well served by an unusually strong cast, with the dapper Pedro de Cordoba a standout among Lavond's victims. And British imports Maureen O'Sullivan and Frank Lawton – together again after the success of M-G-M's *David Copperfield* – count as the least cloying romantic leads in a Hollywood horror picture to date.

Marcel, inventor of the miniaturisation process, is played on a note of haggard desperation by Henry B Walthall – a veteran, like Barrymore, of D W Griffith's earliest Biograph days, here making his last film. Having made a big impression in both *Grand Hotel* and *She Done Him Wrong*, Rafaela Ottiano is memorably mad as Malita, Marcel's widow and crazed guardian of his high-minded ideals. Hobbling about on a crutch, she provides a faint echo of Browning's old preoccupation with the disabled; sporting a white streak in her hair, she constitutes a much more obvious reference to Elsa Lanchester in *Bride of Frankenstein*. Indeed, the *Bride* link is made explicit, and

Lionel Barrymore, in drag for *The Devil-Doll* (1936), poses at Culver City alongside Clark Gable, Robert Montgomery and Paul Muni, in costume for *San Francisco*, *Trouble for Two* and *The Good Earth* respectively

THE DEVIL-DOLL

M-G-M 1936
70 minutes
production ended 29 April

Cinematographer: Leonard Smith; Art Director: Cedric Gibbons; Associate Art Directors: Stan Rogers, Edwin B Willis; Editor: Frederick Y Smith; Recording Director: Douglas Shearer; Photographic Effects: Warren Newcombe*; Wardrobe: Dolly Tree; Music: Franz Waxman; Choreography: Val Raset*; Screenplay: Garrett Fort, Guy Endore, Eric [sic] von Stroheim, Richard Schayer*, John Lee Mahin*; Story: Tod Browning (from the novel *Burn Witch Burn!* by Abraham Merritt); Executive Producer: E J Mannix; Director: Tod Browning

Lionel Barrymore (Lavond); Maureen O'Sullivan (Lorraine); Frank Lawton (Toto); Rafaela Ottiano (Malita); Robert Greig (Coulvet); Lucy Beaumont (Mme Lavond); Henry B Walthall (Marcel); Grace Ford (Lachna); Pedro de Cordoba (Matin); Arthur Hohl (Radin); Juanita Quigley (Marguerite [Coulvet's daughter]); Claire du Brey (Mme Coulvet); Rollo Lloyd (detective [Maurice]); E Allyn Warren (Commissioner); uncredited: Billy Gilbert (Matin's butler); Eily Malyon (laundry proprietress); Ines Palange (concierge); Frank Reicher (Matin's doctor); Evelyn Selbie (flower woman); Nick Thompson (police sergeant); Jean Alden, Paul Foltz (Apache dancers [ie, doubles for Lachna and Radin]); Christian J Frank, Sherry Hall, Francis McDonald (detectives); Robert du Couedic, Robert Graves, Edward Keene (gendarmes)

Metro-Goldwyn-Mayer's *The Devil Doll* [sic] exhibits great technical ingenuity and is most entertaining in its strange effects. I feel, however, that so much attention was devoted by the makers of this picture to reducing the characters that the plot was simultaneously and inadvertently reduced to practically nothing. *Hollywood Spectator*

I never realized how difficult it was to change sex. The make-up alone was an ordeal. I was never meant for wigs and dresses! When my false hair wasn't slipping out of place, my feet were getting entangled in the hem of my skirt. Changing my voice had its drawbacks, too, for I'm no soprano. Being a woman is hard work! *Lionel Barrymore* [quoted in original pressbook]

virtually actionable, when she goes berserk for the last time and Lavond paraphrases Dr Pretorius in his panicked cry of "Malita! Put that down! You'll blow yourself to atoms!"

Whether Browning was laughing up his sleeve at Whale's *Bride* will never be known. What's incontestable, however, is his desire to relive his biggest M-G-M hit, *The Unholy Three*. The older film is revisited in most of its essentials – a criminal dragged up as an old lady and casing the joints of his prospective victims by selling them, not parrots, but lifelike dolls, together with an extended suspense sequence in which a detective almost stumbles on concealed jewellery. In the Lon Chaney tradition, Lavond's artful disguise as Mme Mandilip is a delirious absurdity and played to the hilt by Barrymore. He also proves more than equal to the vengeful bitterness of a really powerful sequence in which he immobilises the full-sized Radin, and to a genuinely affecting coda in which he takes leave of his estranged daughter Lorraine atop the Eiffel Tower.

Many critiques of *The Devil-Doll* express regret over its sentimental tendencies and their imperfect

alignment with Browning's more fantastic elements. But the film scrupulously avoids taking the easy way out via a three-hanky reconciliation between Lavond and Lorraine. Instead, and with rare maturity, the logic of the story insists that Lavond not reveal himself to her, conferring his blessing by posing as a former cell-mate and then wandering off (it's strongly implied) to commit suicide. Beautifully played by Barrymore and Maureen O'Sullivan, the result is perhaps the most compassionate and moving scene in all the films considered in this book.

FIN DE SIÈCLE

Maureen O'Sullivan was an audience favourite as Jane in M-G-M's Tarzan pictures, and, having completed *The Devil-Doll* in April 1936, she was no doubt surprised to resume work on the third film in the series, *Tarzan Escapes*, in July. This had been completed the previous autumn, only to be withheld because of fundamental problems in its structure. Now it was more or less remade from scratch, and one of the casualties was a reportedly terrifying sequence in which Tarzan and Jane were assailed by giant vampire bats in a swamp. What *does* appear in the finished film, however, is a bizarre waddling bird played by Johnny Eck, the 'Half-Boy' of *Freaks*; making his second and last film appearance, he thus provided a weird echo of what Olga Baclanova was turned into in the earlier film.

Whether the vampire bats were excluded from *Tarzan Escapes* because of worries regarding local censor boards is unclear. But the gathering antipathy towards horror subjects certainly exercised a profound influence over *The Devil-Doll*, which Browning had planned as a voodoo subject called *The Witch of Timbuctoo* until objections came in from Great Britain regarding possible offence to its colonial subjects, prompting Browning to change the doll-making procedure to a mad science scenario.

In production at M-G-M at the same time as *The Devil-Doll* was another example of corporate cold feet. Robert Louis Stevenson's *The Suicide Club* – at one time mooted by Universal as a vehicle for Karloff and Lugosi – became in Metro's hands a vehicle for Robert Montgomery and Rosalind Russell called *Trouble for Two*. In it, the creepy stylings of director J Walter Ruben (and the forbidding presence of Reginald Owen as club president) were firmly subordinated to the glossy demands of a gung-ho Ruritanian romance.

In this pussyfooting context, the closing months of 1936 could offer horror fans no more than a graceless RKO parody of one of Karloff's finest films and a vaguely outré medical melodrama from Columbia. Made in May, Fred Guiol's *Mummy's Boys* is a handsomely appointed farce in which the inept labourers attached to an archaeological dig are the witless comedy duo Wheeler and Woolsey; the pair are eventually confronted with a bogus mummy. Shot in July, Harry Lachman's *The Man Who Lived Twice* involves a ruthless gangster (Ralph Bellamy) being transformed by brain surgery into a philanthropic doctor. Despite taking a thoughtful approach to its subject matter, the film was ballyhooed by Columbia publicists as "a hair-raiser" and the "strangest drama since *Dr Jekyll and Mr Hyde* startled the world!"

M-G-M, meanwhile, was shaken on 14 September by the premature death of the inspirational production executive Irving Thalberg. Given that, in his early days at Universal, Thalberg had been behind the production of *The Hunchback of Notre Dame* – later getting Lon Chaney and Tod Browning together at Metro and greenlighting the notorious *Freaks* – his death seems, in retrospect, like the end of an era for the horror genre as well as M-G-M.

More immediate indications of a genre in serious decline were provided by business affairs over at Universal City. Back on 1 November 1935, Carl Laemmle had sought to stave off financial ruin by arranging a loan from the Standard Capital Corporation of $750,000. There was an ominous proviso, however – that, if the necessary $5.5 million could be raised within 90 days, Standard Capital would take possession of the studio. When the money wasn't available by 1 February 1936, Laemmle made the suicidal gesture of granting Standard Capital an extension. The result was that, on 14 March, four days after the completion of *Dracula's Daughter*, the Laemmles lost control of their studio.

Carl Laemmle died, aged 72, on 24 September 1939. His son, meanwhile, had a brief flirtation with M-G-M in 1937 prior to retiring altogether at the age of 28. He died, aged 71, on 24 September 1979, 40 years to the day since his father's death. Junior Laemmle had never, perhaps, shown the flair of a Thalberg, but he had pushed through the first flood of all-talking horror pictures and was, as Edgar Ulmer put it, "a very, very strange producer ... [who] didn't have much education but had great respect for intelligence and creative spirit."[30] By April 1936, however, his duties were being shared out between men of a very different stripe. While launching the career of winsome teenage star Deanna Durbin, Charles R Rogers and William Koenig declared an unofficial moratorium on further horror subjects. To all intents and purposes, by the end of 1936 the horror genre was dead.

Part Four

Lycanthropy in the blood: Heather Angel, Bramwell Fletcher and (at rear) Eily Malyon minister to the wounded John Howard in *The Undying Monster* (1942)

Rising from the Past 1937-1942

By 1937, Franklin D Roosevelt was firmly established in his role as avuncular morale-booster to demoralised Americans, in particular via his famous 'fireside chats' on radio. But, faced with a government debt of $4 billion, he didn't flinch from a drastic reduction in public spending, precipitating a renewed slump. Hollywood, however, seemed untroubled by this downturn, achieving weekly US attendance figures of 75 million in both 1937 and 1938.

'Slump' is a perfectly apt word, however, for the state of the studios' horror output in those years, which was negligible. The unofficial British ban on such films – exemplified on 1 January 1937 by the BBFC's introduction of the 'H', for 'Horrific', certificate – had the desired effect in Hollywood but not, strangely enough, in Britain. There, a home-grown horror star, bred up in the lower-rent melodrama houses and carrying with him an agreeable whiff of old-fashioned brimstone, appeared in the shape of Tod Slaughter, whose rough-hewn films (none of them burdened with the baleful 'H') took canny advantage of the dearth of new Karloff and Lugosi vehicles in the nation's cinemas.

In the meantime, what Slaughter called "the desire for strong meat" was being pacified in America by pulp fiction and radio drama. H P Lovecraft died, aged 46, in March 1937, but *Weird Tales* lived on, hedged about now by competitors like *Dime Mystery*, *Terror Tales* and *Horror Stories*, all of which had sprouted between 1933 and 1935 in response to the popularity of Hollywood horror films. Along with *Spicy Mystery*, these new pretenders were, by the late 1930s, foregrounding a provocative mixture of sex and horror that would be unimaginable in the cinema for several decades.

Weird Tales would eventually gain a toehold in radio drama, with Lovecraft protégé Robert Bloch providing the scripts for *Stay Tuned for Terror*. The show was a one-series successor to *Lights Out*, which had a ten-year run from 1934 to 1943, managed first by Willis Cooper and then by Arch Oboler. There were several other popular radio anthologies, but much the greatest impact was made by 23-year-old enfant terrible Orson Welles, whose *Mercury Theatre of the Air* presented *Dracula* on 1 July 1938, with Welles in the unusual double-role of Dracula and Dr Seward. Then, on 30 October, the Mercury version of *The War of the Worlds*, relocating H G Wells' Martian invasion from

1898 Surrey to 1938 New Jersey, proved so uncannily persuasive it caused mass-delusional panic.

TREADING WATER

In Hollywood, the sudden dearth of horror product had a dire effect on the career of Bela Lugosi, who was so strongly identified with the genre that he quickly became a Hollywood version of Roosevelt's 'forgotten man'. Indeed, when *The Invisible Ray* wrapped on 25 October 1935, he disappeared from the screen almost entirely; prior to his return for *Son of Frankenstein* in November 1938, he appeared only in Universal's *Postal Inspector* and the serials *Shadow of Chinatown* and *SOS Coastguard*. Karloff's fate, however, was very different. Having already established his versatility via mainstream titles like *The House of Rothschild*, Karloff was able to follow his Warner Bros stint in *The Walking Dead* with several more assignments for the same studio. He also fulfilled engagements with Gaumont-British, 20th Century-Fox and Universal, and wasn't too proud to sign up with Monogram as well.

Of these films, H Bruce Humberstone's *Charlie Chan at the Opera* occupied Karloff during September 1936. Playing Gravelle, an amnesiac opera singer who escapes from a lunatic asylum, Karloff gets to wear an impressive Mephistopheles costume as chief red herring in Chan's latest investigation. (In a splendidly self-reflexive moment, the stage manager asserts that "This opera is going on tonight even if Frankenstein walks in.") The script was the work of W Scott Darling (later to write several Universal shockers) and *Mystery of the Wax Museum*'s Charles S Belden, who no doubt contributed the *Wax Museum*-like plot detail of Gravelle being presumed dead in a theatre fire.

Italian flyer for 20th Century-Fox's 'supergiallo', *Charlie Chan at the Opera* (1936)

Curiously, when Fox got around to *Charlie Chan at the Wax Museum* in May 1940 – with Warner Oland by this time supplanted as Chan by Sidney Toler – Belden was not involved. Instead, Lynn Shores' film features C Henry Gordon as a plastic surgeon who resculpts criminals' faces under cover of the titular waxworks. Other Chans with creepy accoutrements include *Charlie Chan in Egypt* (1935), with a mummified murder victim identified by X-ray, and *Charlie Chan's Secret* (1936), which features an old dark San Francisco seance complete with spectral apparitions.

Fox's 'Warner Oland vs Boris Karloff' extravaganza made it into the nation's cinemas in January 1937, a year in which horror fans had a decidedly lean time of it. They could sample the 'window dressing' horror elements in mystery-comedies like Benjamin Stoloff's RKO production *Super-Sleuth*, in which arch-criminal Eduardo Ciannelli maintains a Chamber of Horrors. Or they could turn to Mack V Wright's Republic horse-opera *Riders of the Whistling Skull*, which offered some meagre sustenance through its archaeological expedition, skull-faced desert topography and briefly perambulating mummy. In February, the more studiously inclined might have been attracted to Frank Lloyd's *Maid of Salem*, a Paramount production recalling *The Scarlet Letter* in its meticulous recreation of 17th century witch hysteria. Today, the film is notable for its foreshadowing of Arthur Miller's 1953 play *The Crucible* and for its deluxe cast, from top-liners Claudette Colbert and Fred MacMurray through to invaluable supports like Halliwell Hobbes, Pedro de Cordoba, Brandon Hurst and Gale Sondergaard.

Also featured in *Maid of Salem* was James Whale's old favourite, E E Clive. He appeared, too, in M-G-M's *Night Must Fall*, this time as a vulture-like tour guide, displaying the site of a gruesome murder to a gaggle of well-heeled Britons. "Remarkable, isn't it," he notes, "the interest shown in this lugubrious occurrence." Richard Thorpe – already a long way from his Poverty Row spooky-house picture, *Strange People* – was here entrusted with the film adaptation of Emlyn Williams' "Astonishing London and New York Stage Success," as the film's title card proudly dubs it.

Night Must Fall began shooting on 8 February 1937 and, like *The Old Dark House*, remains a prime example of a prestige British property being filmed in Hollywood with unwavering Britishness; happily, the instant Americanisation it would have suffered in future decades is nowhere in evidence. Indeed, four actors from the original West End production – Dame May Whitty, Merle Tottenham, Matthew Boulton

Unnerved old lady (Dame May Whitty) and soothing Welsh serial killer (Robert Montgomery) in *Night Must Fall* (1937)

and Kathleen Harrison – were specially imported, while the US dramatist John van Druten submitted Williams' play to the bare minimum of 'opening out'. The film's introductory image is the dark hulk of a tree; at its foot, a silhouetted figure works diligently while whistling 'Mighty Like a Rose'. Also discernible is a hatbox, which is to assume sinister significance in the ensuing action. (Speculating on its contents, the unwitting housekeeper observes that "It's too heavy for a hat.") The gnarled, darkened forest is returned to later, presenting a night-and-day contrast with the honeysuckle-covered cottage at its edge; the Gothic atmosphere is spoiled only by a sound design more suggestive of a Louisiana swamp than a Home Counties hideaway.

Previously partnered in Metro's *Trouble for Two*, Robert Montgomery and Rosalind Russell are excellent as a plausible Welsh psychopath and the spinsterish young woman who sees through him but remains strangely fascinated. The concluding passages, in which the vain old lady whom the Welsh boy has beguiled is left alone in the house, retain a queasy edge of suppressed hysteria, and both Montgomery and Whitty (making her screen debut, aged 72) were deservedly nominated for Oscars. By June 1941, Charles Vidor was recreating much of the film's atmosphere – with added fog – in Columbia's splendid *Ladies in Retirement*, which was also derived from a British stage original and also Oscar-nominated.

Back on 25 March 1937 – a week before *Night Must Fall* completed production – George B Seitz started work at M-G-M on a new film version of Bayard Veiller's old seance melodrama *The Thirteenth Chair*. Figuring Whitty as perfect casting in creepy stage adaptations, Metro accordingly cast her in the mediumistic role made famous by Veiller's wife Margaret Wycherly, while the dogged police inspector – comic relief in the play, Bela Lugosi in the 1929 version – was now poker-faced Metro stalwart Lewis Stone.

Unfortunately, films like Fox's *Trick for Trick* (1933) and RKO's *Their Big Moment* (1934) had filched enough of Veiller's plot mechanics to make Seitz's film appear decidedly old hat. Apart from the genuinely unsettling image of Henry Daniell propped up dead in his chair at the climactic seance, the film's misterioso qualities are derived almost exclusively from its recycling of musical cues from *The Devil-Doll*, starting with that film's beautiful theme over the opening titles. (The music credit, incidentally, goes to David Snell, which must have surprised Franz Waxman.) To make matters worse, Whitty plays Mme LaGrange for winsome sentiment rather than portentous weight, throwing away flavoursome lines like "There's hate in this house: I can feel it in me blood."

Despite this, in May the picture was slapped with the British censor's first-ever 'H' certificate, no doubt as a warning to others rather than as a true reflection of the picture's extremely mild content. With its very obvious severed head in a hatbox, *Night Must Fall* somehow avoided the same stigma; presumably the Board were just as intellectually bamboozled by its recent stage success as M-G-M had been.

In the absence of further horror product, no other American film would be so designated for almost two years; in the wake of *Son of Frankenstein*, however, there were several examples of the BBFC's hardline attitude. In 1939, the 'H' would be applied even to M-G-M's *On Borrowed Time*, a gossamer fantasy featuring a personification of Death no more threatening than a couple of earlier Paramount titles, *Death Takes a Holiday* and *Peter Ibbotson*. And, in a bizarre development, Frank Strayer's bewhiskered 1932 quickie *The Monster Walks* finally made it to British screens in 1941 – with the same deterrent certificate attached. "Dated in style to start with," observed Denis Gifford, "by then the poor little picture was so passé that the conscience-stricken distributor retitled it *The Monster Walked*."[1]

While M-G-M bravely took on heads in hatboxes, the so-called New Universal traded on its horror reputation only in pusillanimous and half-hearted fashion. In February 1937, Lloyd Corrigan's *Night Key* cast Boris Karloff in a sweet but forgettable crime yarn dressed up with some science-fiction trimmings. Universal also hooked up with the Crime Club to produce seven quickies based on books in that series, with vague horror elements worked into two of them. Released in January 1938, Otis Garrett's *The Black Doll* has C Henry Gordon as a venal businessman spooked

by the titular Mexican fetish, which briefly suggests that a former victim of Gordon's may have risen from the dead. The following year, Garrett's *Mystery of the White Room* featured a sightless man having a murder victim's corneas grafted on in order to identify the killer. Confusingly, another of the Crime Club series picked up the title of the old Universal's entirely unrelated silent *The Last Warning* – which, even more confusingly, was officially remade in March 1939 as *The House of Fear*, a slick and entertaining B-picture directed by Austrian émigré Joe May.

Back in 1937, horror fans subsisting on the meagre diet provided by *Night Must Fall* and *The Thirteenth Chair* had further cause for despondency when, on Friday 25 June, the 37-year-old Colin Clive succumbed to pulmonary pneumonia at Cedars of Lebanon Hospital. As Universal's original Dr Frankenstein, Clive's hysterical cries of "It's alive!" had become emblematic of Hollywood horror. By the same token, his sudden death seemed emblematic of a genre that had become thoroughly moribund.

Return of the Repressed

If 1937 had been a bad year for newly minted chillers, 1938 proved even worse; after the January release of *The Black Doll* there would be a very long wait until M-G-M provided the mild frissons of Edwin L Marin's *A Christmas Carol* in December. Yet, in the midst of the drought, Harry Coulter, assistant editor of the highbrow periodical *Cinema Progress*, somehow managed to write an investigation into Hollywood horror without once alluding to the fact that the supply had dried up.

Posing the question "Why do we Americans enjoy being scared to death?", Coulter quoted Bela Lugosi to the effect that "atavism has a great deal to do with it" and the opinion of 'a prominent psychologist' that "Horror as it is shown on the screen and as it is told in news accounts is a far cry from the nastiness of reality, since, in both cases, gruesome details cannot be presented in [their] entirety. The motion picture type of horror is made interesting, gripping, and dramatic. There is not the strict realism which in actual life makes crime loathsome and repelling."[2] Coulter didn't mention it, but liberal views of this kind were unlikely to cut much ice with the British censor. Coulter also recorded Lugosi's dictum that "The more unbelievable the part the more seriously the actor, himself, has to believe in it. The very moment he begins to play it from the 'outside', with his tongue in his cheek, he is lost." Again, there was no reference to the fact that the BBFC's attitude had denied Lugosi the opportunity to test his theory for close to three years.

Coulter was prophetic, however, in calling his article 'Cold Chills and Cold Cash', for the latter commodity was about to play a decisive part in reversing the anti-horror trend. After two years as Universal's vice-president in charge of production, Charles R Rogers had succeeded in losing the studio in excess of $3 million. In May 1938, therefore, he was replaced by Cliff Work, whose name was an apt one for an efficient and utilitarian regime dedicated to making good the disastrous losses incurred by Rogers.

With profits an urgent priority, the new Universal management inevitably sat up and took notice when a cash-strapped Beverly Hills exhibitor, E Mark Umann, scored an unexpected smash hit by triple-billing *Dracula*, *Frankenstein* and *The Son of Kong*. The combination opened for business at Umann's Regina Theatre on Thursday 5 August, and, hearing of the round-the-clock crowds clogging Wilshire Boulevard, exhibitors all over the country followed Umann's lead, dropping the whimsical *Kong* picture from the equation and sending Universal scrambling to strike 500 new prints of *Dracula* and *Frankenstein*.

By 16 October, the *New York Times* was commenting on the nationwide success of the double-feature in a piece bearing the suggestive title 'Revival of the Undead'. The following day, the grisly pairing achieved a showcase opening at New York's Rialto Theatre, again doing remarkable business. Also that day, Bela Lugosi told the *New York World-Telegram* about the time, two months earlier, when he first became aware of the minor revolution taking place at the Regina: "One day I drive past and see my name and big lines of people all around. I wonder what is giving way to people – maybe bacon or vegetables. But it is the comeback of horror, and I come back."[3]

Lugosi was correct in his assumption. Indeed, 17 October was also the day when pre-production began on an all-new Universal horror show. To write the script, Universal engaged Willis Cooper, who in 1934 had created the creepy radio anthology *Lights Out*. And to supplant James Whale they chose Rowland V Lee, who brought with him the suave South African-born actor Basil Rathbone, with whom he had recently worked on the British psychological thriller *Love from a Stranger*. Also on board were Boris Karloff and Bela Lugosi. As well as merely being grateful to be working, the latter rejoiced in an iconic role that was more or less made up from day to day thanks to Lee's determination to thwart Universal's front office, which had wanted to make use of Lugosi as quickly and cheaply as possible. The director's radical on-set rewrites made the production of *Son of Frankenstein* an

Boris Karloff's resurrected Monster re-enacts Lionel Atwill's childhood trauma in *Son of Frankenstein* (1938); the real child is Donnie Dunagan

SON OF FRANKENSTEIN

Universal 1938
96 minutes
production began 9 November

Cinematographer: George Robinson; Art Director: Jack Otterson; Associate Art Director: Richard H Riedel; Editor: Ted Kent; Sound: Bernard B Brown, William Hedgcock; Special Photographic Effects: John P Fulton*; Make-up: Jack P Pierce*; Gowns: Vera West; Musical Director: Charles Previn; Music: Frank Skinner; Assistant Director: Fred Frank; Screenplay: Willis Cooper ('suggested by the story written in 1816 by Mary Wollstonecraft Shelley'); Director-Producer: Rowland V Lee

Basil Rathbone (Baron Wolf von Frankenstein); Boris Karloff (The Monster); Bela Lugosi (Ygor); Lionel Atwill (Krogh); Josephine Hutchinson (Elsa von Frankenstein); Donnie Dunagan (Peter von Frankenstein); Emma Dunn (Amelia); Edgar Norton (Benson); Perry Ivins (Fritz); Lawrence Grant (Burgomaster); Lionel Belmore (Lang); Michael Mark (Ewald Neumüller); Caroline Cooke (Mrs Neumüller); Gustav von Seyffertitz, Lorimer Johnson, Tom Ricketts (burghers); uncredited: Betty Chay (maid); Clarence Wilson (Dr Berger); Ward Bond, Harry Cording (gendarmes); with Jack Harris

Success of the revival of horror pictures inspired this up-to-date chiller. The interesting thing about it is that the material is excellent, not cheaply done for commercial purposes. Boris Karloff, Bela Lugosi and Basil Rathbone work together with such an awesome effect of terror it is almost unbearable ... Prepare for nightmares. *Photoplay*

> **I could see the writing on the wall as to what was going to happen to the character of the Monster. There is just so much you can develop in a part of that nature, and it was a case of diminishing returns. The Monster was going to wind up as he did, a rather comic prop in the last act – and I thought, "Well, this isn't any good," and I wouldn't play him any more.**
> *Boris Karloff* [quoted in Lindsay, *Dear Boris*, 1975]

embattled slog that lasted from 9 November 1938 to 5 January 1939 – a mere five days prior to the film's pre-booked release date.

> *Wolf von Frankenstein travels from the new world to the mid-European village that bears his name. There he finds that his father's inheritance includes the sworn enmity of the locals and a still living, but comatose, Monster. Once Wolf has revived the creature, it embarks on a reign of terror at the behest of its vengeful friend, blacksmith-cum-bodysnatcher Ygor. To put a stop to this, Wolf finally topples the Monster into a boiling sulphur pit.*

Having opened to the monolithic strains of Frank Skinner's blood-curdling theme, the 'look' of *Son of Frankenstein* arrests the viewer's attention from the very first shot. Jack Otterson's stunningly idiosyncratic production design warps the vaguely mittel-European vistas of Universal's previous

Frankenstein pictures into an Americanised variation on the *Caligari* template, his extravagant creations limned in ominous shadow by George Robinson's equally impressive photography.

As the Frankenstein family take their breakfast in the tiny space between aggressively thrusting beams (a carved boar's head adorning each one), the effect is more akin to the angular abstractions devised by Anton Grot for First National than anything previously seen in a Universal film. (Given the *Caligari* connection, *Murders in the Rue Morgue* is perhaps its nearest relation.) The fixtures and fittings, too – even the props – are similarly outsized, if not grotesque: in the grip of a raging cloudburst, Wolf's elderly manservant struggles with a preposterously large umbrella, while Inspector Krogh has to manipulate a door-knocker almost as big as himself.

Acknowledging a rich heritage, Lee's direction throws in a few touches characteristic of Whale. In the train compartment occupied by Wolf and his wife Elsa, the camera passes magically through a connecting wall in the prescribed Whale fashion, and, on their arrival at the castle, firelight pulses on the walls in the hellish style featured in both *The Old Dark House* and *Bride of Frankenstein*. But the expert accumulation of foreboding in the film's opening reels is Lee's own. Memorable tableaux abound – the lashing rain and gnarled trees ranged on a diorama outside Wolf's compartment; the rain-slicked umbrellas of the townsfolk clustered at the railway station; the lightning piercing the night sky outside the Frankenstein library as the waterlogged Ygor lurches into view outside the windows.

The ominous atmosphere is bolstered even by the quaint Tyrolean jingle muttered by Elsa's nervous chambermaid: "If the house is filled with dread / Place the beds at head to head" – though this may also have been intended as a sarcastic means of appeasing the PCA, which wouldn't countenance even the most happily married couple sharing a double bed in a Code-approved picture.

We're quickly introduced, not just to Rathbone's quixotic, and heavily mascaraed, Wolf, but also to Lionel Atwill's embittered Inspector Krogh, a sublime performance that seems to lay bare the whole history of the man with the lightest of brushstrokes. Concealing Krogh's profound childhood trauma behind a brilliant bit of faux-nonchalant business with his monocle, Atwill is given one of the most memorable monologues in the horror genre, concluding with the grim admission that "One doesn't easily forget, Herr Baron, an arm torn out by the roots." Ironically, Krogh's robotic movements are close kin to those of the Monster that plucked away his arm, and his self-aware articulation of his prosthetic limb is a precise echo of Ygor's self-satisfied habit of rapping hollowly on his broken neck.

With these fetishistic displays of disability, Krogh and Ygor become parallel, and equally fascinating, figures. Certainly, Lugosi has the time of his life as Ygor. Cast well outside the Dracula rut for a change, Lugosi is nevertheless just as much a member of the living dead – hanged by the neck, Ygor somehow survived and now lives outside the legal reach of the pompous Burghers who condemned him. The weirdly rasping voice (caused, as Ygor puts it, because "bone get stuck in my throat"), the half-fawning, half-threatening interaction with Wolf, the touching concern and tenderness for his fellow undead, the Monster – all add up to a performance that vies with *The Black Cat* as Lugosi's greatest achievement. When Ygor describes the lightning strike that disabled the Monster and explains what his friend was doing out and about in the first place, only Lugosi could put such a masterful, and uniquely disagreeable, emphasis on the apparently innocuous line, "He was – *hunting*."

In this context, Karloff's Monster runs the risk of becoming a subordinate figure, functioning as a somnambulant Cesare to Ygor's conniving Caligari, being revived from a deep sleep only to do the murderous bidding of his master. Even so, Karloff contrives some marvellous moments, the best of them founded on the fact that Ygor, for all his manipulativeness, is more the Monster's friend than his master. When Wolf shoots Ygor to death, the Monster's discovery of the body – feeling blood under his cradling hands and throwing his head back in a primal scream of shock and despair – is derived from an understated Karloff moment in *The Old Dark House*, but is delivered here with a baroque intensity of extraordinary power. Karloff also has an affecting mime sequence with Rathbone in front of an articulated mirror, recoiling in disgust from his own reflection but inspecting Wolf's with a sad, questioning puzzlement.

Son of Frankenstein is a remarkably long film for the period, and, given the damaging censor- or studio-imposed cuts inflicted on so many earlier horror pictures, it seems churlish to wish that Ted Kent's editing team had had more time in which to reduce the film to a more manageable length. But, once the weasel-like Neumüller has been killed, the film's rhythm slips badly, with only a rousing finale on the brink of the sulphur pit to restore interest in the closing stages. (Here, in a truly inspired moment, the Monster replays Krogh's long-ago trauma by tearing off his prosthetic arm.) Overall, however, the film is a masterful fusion of the rough-hewn poetry of the films that preceded it and the crisply efficient narratives of the films that were to follow.

Thanks to Lee's perfectionism, *Son of Frankenstein* cost Universal some $420,000, almost twice what the studio originally had in mind. This hardly mattered, however, for the result was an all-conquering smash (even in the UK) and helped Universal turn a 1939 profit of $1,000,000. Indeed, the spread on the film published in *Look* magazine on 28 February bore a title that was to prove prophetic: 'The Son of Frankenstein Starts a New Horror Cycle.'

OLD PROPERTIES REFURBISHED

The British Board of Film Censors was naturally alarmed at Hollywood's resurrection of old monsters. On 4 November 1938, even before *Son of Frankenstein* began production, Board secretary J Brooke Wilkinson had urged the PCA's Joseph Breen "to use every possible endeavour to prevent production of any further pictures of this type intended for exhibition in this country."[4] Now, however, the obvious public appetite for horror – an appetite that had been stifled for the better part of three years – convinced Hollywood that the BBFC could safely be ignored. While social commentators speculated on the horror revival as a cathartic index to Adolf Hitler's increasingly aggressive manoeuvres in mainland Europe, film studios began hunting for creepy subjects with which to meet the demand.

First into the race was 20th Century-Fox, a relatively new operation forged from the old Fox Film Corporation and Darryl F Zanuck's 20th Century outfit. The chosen property, screamed the studio pressbook, was "one of literature's most shocking, spine-chilling mystery stories" featuring a "giant unearthly beast ... with blazing eyes and bared fangs, terrorizing the countryside, striking horror into the hearts of two young lovers and leaving a trail so terrifying that only Sherlock Holmes dare follow."

So it was that Basil Rathbone and Lionel Atwill moved straight from *Son of Frankenstein* into a revival of Arthur Conan Doyle's 1902 novel *The Hound of the Baskervilles*. Though the story had enjoyed an extensive career in German cinema as *Der Hund von Baskerville*, it had only been filmed twice in its native language, by British impresarios Oswald Stoll (1921) and Michael Balcon (1931). With nothing to fear from these earlier attempts, the Fox *Hound* not only had the benefit of a classic characterisation from Rathbone, it was also the most lavish Holmes picture yet made, with much of the money being spent on an astonishing Dartmoor set measuring 300 feet by 200 feet.

> *Sherlock Holmes sends his friend Dr Watson to Dartmoor to protect Sir Henry Baskerville from a family curse which has recently claimed the life of his uncle, Sir Charles. Keeping watch and looking into the case incognito, Holmes concludes that the eerie legend of the Hound of the Baskervilles conceals a more down-to-earth example of "refined, coldblooded murder..."*

"In all England there is no district more dismal" warns an introductory title, a prescription that art directors Richard Day and Hans Peters clearly took to heart. An arid expanse of grey crags and ground fog, their studio Dartmoor is an icy netherworld decorated only by a cluster of Neolithic menhirs and what Atwill's Dr Mortimer calls "the great Grimpen Mire, as treacherous a morass as exists anywhere." In this forbidding terrain, Nigel De Brulier – normally a specialist in more saintly roles, such as Dom Claude in Universal's *The Hunchback of Notre Dame* – cuts a very frightening figure as the escaped convict who hovers over Watson's investigations and turns out to have an intimate tie with the domestic staff at Baskerville Hall.

It is also, of course, the domain of the Hound itself, which was played by a Great Dane from the San Fernando Valley called Blitzen; thanks to growing anti-Nazi feeling, its name was quietly changed to Chief. "He tips the beam at 140 pounds, his keeper tells us, which is why he got the job," noted *Photoplay*'s studio correspondent Jack Wade. "The Hound, you'll recall, was a pretty ugly customer, with glowing eyes and dripping jaws – so you'll never recognise poor old Chief in the movie. They've rigged up a mask with phosphorous peepers to make him a sort of canine Karloff."[5] He sports no such embellishments in the finished film, making Sir Henry's post-savaging query – "What was it?" – seem faintly absurd, given that "it" was clearly a dog, rather than the more outlandish vision suggested in *Photoplay*.

Even so, it remains one of the more convincingly ferocious Hounds in the many adaptations of Doyle's story, and its hideaway – in a ruined, alfresco sepulchre – is suitably dank and forbidding. Unfortunately, the film's almost total absence of music takes the sting out of the creature's attacks, particularly its singularly unexciting toppling of the convict from a Dartmoor crag.

The London of the film's opening reel is more functionally presented. With splendid geographical implausibility, a stock shot of Big Ben cuts directly

to a gas lamp and a name-plate announcing "Baker Street W." Rathbone's Holmes is then discovered in epicene close-up, the familiar ratiocination routine with Dr Mortimer's cane immediately establishing a warm and engaging chemistry with Nigel Bruce's Watson. In later years Bruce would be encouraged into emphasising Watson's more buffoonish qualities; in this first film, however, he's an excellent foil and also genuinely funny, particularly when responding to one of Holmes' more provocative comments with a wonderfully huffy "Huff? I'm in no huff!" Atwill, too, is on excellent form, making Doyle's young and spare Dr Mortimer into a florid and bespectacled red herring of the first order.

Mortimer's account of the Baskerville curse cues a flashback to the 17th century Sir Hugo which is laughable in its (presumably Code-imposed) timidity; Sir Hugo and his cronies suggest mildly roistering club-men rather than the catalysts of an ancient evil. Mortimer is also the vehicle for one of the film's few notable deviations from the Doyle original, though the introduction of a seance sequence was perhaps a nod to Doyle's well-publicised interest in spiritualism. "I dabble a bit in the occult," Mortimer explains mildly. "Mrs Mortimer has very strong mediumistic qualities." The ensuing seance, nicely lit by flickering firelight, is spooky enough, with eerie wolf howls going up at Mrs Mortimer's every invocation to the late Sir Charles. Sir Charles himself, however, fails to contribute, casting Mrs Mortimer's mediumistic qualities in a dubious light and making the entire procedure seem pointless – as much of a token red herring as Dr Mortimer himself.

Having just been billed above Karloff and Lugosi in *Son of Frankenstein*, Rathbone was perhaps surprised to be billed here below the 20-year-old Richard Greene, whose fresh-faced Sir Henry is nicely played but no match for the corvine charisma of Rathbone's Holmes. The simple expedient of growing his hair longer and sweeping it back from his forehead (together with a much-reduced reliance on mascara) makes Rathbone appear older here than he did in *Son of Frankenstein*, helping to give his relatively limited appearances a scintillating blend of authority and self-possession. His closing cry of "Oh, Watson – the needle" comes out of nowhere, however, and must seem perplexing to non-aficionados unaware

THE HOUND OF THE BASKERVILLES

20th Century-Fox 1939
80 minutes
production began 29 December 1938

Cinematographer: Peverell Marley; Art Directors: Richard Day, Hans Peters; Editor: Robert Simpson; Sound: W D Flick, Roger Heman; Set Decorations: Thomas Little; Costumes: Gwen Wakeling; Musical Director: Cyril J Mockridge; Screenplay: Ernest Pascal (adapted from *The Hound of the Baskervilles* by Sir Arthur Conan Doyle); Associate Producer: Gene Markey; In Charge of Production: Darryl F Zanuck; Directors: Sidney Lanfield, Alfred Werker*

Richard Greene (Sir Henry Baskerville); Basil Rathbone (Sherlock Holmes); Wendy Barrie (Beryl Stapleton); Nigel Bruce (Dr Watson); Lionel Atwill (James Mortimer, MD); John Carradine (Barryman); Barlowe Borland (Frankland); Beryl Mercer (Mrs Jenifer Mortimer); Morton Lowry (John Stapleton); Ralph Forbes (Sir Hugo Baskerville); E E Clive (cabby); Eily Malyon (Mrs Barryman); Lionel Pape (coroner); Nigel De Brulier (convict); Mary Gordon (Mrs Hudson); Ian MacLaren (Sir Charles); uncredited: John Burton (Bruce); Douglas Gerrard (squire); Dennis Green (Jon); Kenneth Hunter (ship's officer); Vesey O'Donovan (steward); Rita Page (chambermaid); Ivan Simpson (shepherd); John Spacey (purser); Ruth Terry (Betsy-Ann); Evan Thomas (Edwin); David Thursby (driver); Peter Willes (Roderick); Mary Young (Betsy-Ann's mother)

The Hound of the Baskervilles is notable (a) for the romantic, misty impressionism of its settings – Dartmoor seen by Doré; (b) for a blood-curdling hound; (c) for a convincing, if rather young, Holmes from Basil Rathbone, and (d) for an amusingly stolid Watson from Nigel Bruce. The plot is well and, as far as I can remember, faithfully related; and the film very satisfactory if you feel in the mood. New Statesman [UK]

Ever since I was a boy and first got acquainted with the great detective I wanted to be like him. My desire to be an actor also began when I was a youngster, so it was only natural to combine the two ... To play such a character means as much to me as ten Hamlets!
Basil Rathbone [quoted in original pressbook]

Death on the moor: Nigel Bruce and Basil Rathbone stumble across Nigel De Brulier in *The Hound of the Baskervilles* (1939)

Potential murder victim Lionel Atwill, attended by butler Bela Lugosi and maid Patsy Kelly, in *The Gorilla* (1939)

of Holmes' fondness for cocaine; it was for many years cut, in any case.

20th Century-Fox also produced a new version (the third) of the old Ralph Spence play *The Gorilla*, which, though in preparation since October 1938, only went before Allan Dwan's cameras in March 1939. Lionel Atwill and Bela Lugosi were hired on as mere 'old house' set-dressing for what was basically a cut-price vehicle for the Ritz Brothers, a grotesquely unfunny vaudeville trio whose Fox career was drawing to a close. As the master of the house, Atwill has plenty of juicy close-ups as the minutes tick by to his predicted death, while Lugosi does what he can with a mock-sinister butler originally intended for Peter Lorre. The escaped ape – aptly named Poe – is played, not by the ubiquitous Charles Gemora, but stunt man Art Miles. The gorilla suit cost $2800 and, with an absurdly extravagant pompadour surmounting a surprisingly scary face and penetrating eyes, is a more effective melding of horror and humour than the film itself.

Strictly speaking, Fox's *The Gorilla* was the fourth rendition of Spence's original, given that in August 1937 First National had made a cephalopod variant called *Sh! The Octopus*. Playing fair, the film credited Spence alongside Ralph Murphy and Donald Gallaher, authors of the play *Sh, the Octopus*, a property First National had been sitting on ever since its brief Broadway run in 1928. (The Murphy-Gallaher play had obviously been designed as a 'tribute' to Spence's from the first, given that Gallaher had been producer of *The Gorilla* in its Broadway incarnation.) Transferring the action to a lighthouse and featuring the so-called Octopus of Crime rather than its anthropoid equivalent, William McGann's tedious film version is enlivened only by the climactic revelation that a fluffy old lady is the titular menace. She's played by Elspeth Dudgeon (formerly the peculiar Sir Roderick Femm of *The Old Dark House*) and the 'live' transformation effect is brilliantly achieved.

Fox's *The Gorilla* dutifully resurrected Spence's 'corpse dropping out of a closet' routine, itself a flagrant steal from Spence's model, *The Cat and the Canary*. To underline the fact, Paramount had acquired the screen rights to the latter, putting their modernised version into production shortly after *The Gorilla* finished shooting. The director was Elliott Nugent, who had written the Broadway hit *The Male Animal* with James Thurber and, as an actor, had appeared in the talkie version of *The Unholy Three*; he had also brought a surprisingly creepy emphasis to Paramount's 1935 teen murder-mystery *College Scandal*. Thanks to Nugent, the new *Cat* soared well beyond

the revised *Gorilla* by toplining, not a ramshackle trio of vaudeville clowns, but the slick and sophisticated Broadway comic Bob Hope.

Ten years after his death, the surviving relatives of Cyrus Norman gather at his isolated mansion in a Louisiana bayou. Soon after naming Joyce Norman as the heir, Lawyer Crosby is murdered, apparently by a lunatic who has escaped from a neighbouring asylum. With the aid of showbiz star Wally Campbell, Joyce discovers that her former sweetheart, Charlie Wilder, has been masquerading as the so-called Cat in order to drive her insane and claim her inheritance.

Nugent had already directed Hope in *Give Me a Sailor* and *Never Say Die*, but *The Cat and the Canary* was the picture that finally shot Hope to stardom. The Harold Lloyd-like figure played by Creighton Hale in the 1927 version had appeared slightly passé even then; Hope's Wally Campbell, by contrast, was as up-to-the-minute as possible. Many of his one-liners in *The Cat and the Canary* have become common currency, though frequently misquoted. For the best of them, Nydia Westman's diminutive Cicily acts as his twittering 'feed'. "Don't big empty houses scare you?" she asks over supper. "Not me," Wally replies. "I used to be in vaudeville." Later, the pair hang apprehensively over a banister as they peer into the darkness of the cellar. "Do you believe in reincarnation?" asks Cicily. "You know, that dead people come back?" "You mean like the Republicans?" replies Wally.

In addition to topicality and self-deprecation, Wally's gags serve another vital function, that of restyling a thoroughly clapped-out subgenre for a new generation. Hope's charming facility for commenting on the action would in later years assume virtually Brechtian proportions as he stepped beyond the 'fourth wall' to deliver knowing asides to the audience. Here, it's subtly employed to defuse audience impatience with conventions that had been done to death by pretty much every Poverty Row studio in Hollywood. "All this," Wally says at the outset. "Midnight, the alligators – I mean the heirs – and the family lawyer all gathering to hear the reading of the will: it reminds me of all the melodramas and murder-mysteries I've played in." You know and I know that this is a load of old cobblers, he seems to say, but let's trot through it again just for old times' sake.

Hope even manages to provide a self-reflexive introduction for leading lady Paulette Goddard, as well as letting the audience know exactly when the Act One 'curtain' occurs, later doing the same for Act Two. The genius of the film is that Hope's wisecracks

A staggering 'live' transformation effect for Elspeth Dudgeon in the otherwise negligible *Sh! The Octopus* (1937)

are so seamlessly integrated, never disrupting the atmosphere of what is, in other respects, an admirably straight retelling of a bewhiskered story.

Hope, in fact, is only the most conspicuous example of a modernisation process that is evident throughout. Rather than a German Expressionist castle overlooking the Hudson, Cyrus Norman's house has become a collapsed colonial mansion residing in the "strange solitude [of] the bayous of Louisiana." The creepy chatelaine of Martha Mattox has become a younger, and much sexier, Creole concierge played by Gale Sondergaard. Arthur Edmund Carewe's saturnine man-of-the-world has become a glib and graceless young oaf played by the discreetly toupéed John Beal. And so on. The Roaring Twenties have very visibly given way to an America poised on the brink of the smooth and facile 1940s.

In the kind of role in which she was soon to specialise, Sondergaard's Miss Lu is a delight, referring ominously to "my friends from the other world" and, when the lights flicker, noting that "Sometimes they get into the machinery." (Nugent even manages to kid the audience throughout the opening reels that Miss Lu and her feline familiar might be one and the same.) The film marked the genre debut of another favourite, Mancunian character star George Zucco, who contributes his unique brand of understated menace to the ill-fated Lawyer Crosby.

The Cat himself – ballyhooed in the film's pressbook as "a neat and nasty bogey-bundle" – now carries a very unpleasant flick-knife in his taloned hands. Spookily backlit, he advances on Goddard through low-beamed secret passages that are even more forbidding than the fetid bayou, overhung with

Paulette Goddard going through an old routine [see also pages 42 and 84] in the fourth film version of *The Cat and the Canary* (1939)

THE CAT AND THE CANARY

Paramount 1939
72 minutes
production began 29 March

Cinematographers: Charles Lang, Ted Tetzlaff*; Art Directors: Hans Dreier, Robert Usher; Editor: Archie Marshek; Sound: Philip Wisdom, Richard Olson; Interior Decorations: A E Freudeman; Costumes: Edith Head; Music: Dr Ernst Toch; Musical Adviser: Andrea Setaro; Screenplay: Walter DeLeon, Lynn Starling (based on the stage play by John Willard); Additional Dialogue: Wilkie Mahoney*; Executive Producer: William LeBaron*; Producer: Arthur Hornblow Jr; Director: Elliott Nugent

Bob Hope (Wally Campbell); Paulette Goddard (Joyce Norman); John Beal (Fred Blythe); Douglass Montgomery (Charlie Wilder); Gale Sondergaard (Miss Lu); Elizabeth Patterson (Aunt Susan); Nydia Westman (Cicily); George Zucco (Lawyer Crosby); John Wray (Hendricks [the guard]); George Regas (Indian guide); uncredited: William Abbey (The Cat); Milton Kibbee (photographer); Charles Lane, Frank Melton (reporters); Nick Thompson, Chief Thundercloud (Indian guides)

Paramount have done a very good job of work in this re-make. It has an 'H' certificate and deserves it; there really are thrills. Also there are laughs, all the more welcome as emotional relief ... This sort of thing is often done – and often badly. Here it is all done well; even the familiar 'gag' of the dead man falling out of the closet thrills. *To-Day's Cinema* [UK]

I had told her [Paulette Goddard] to scream, of course, thinking that I would get somebody else to match a scream with her lip movements later. But she surprised me. Right in the middle of the scene, she unleashed a blood-curdler that would have made Boris Karloff think twice.
Elliott Nugent [quoted in original pressbook]

Spanish moss, that lies without. When unmasked, he turns out to be the clean-limbed Charlie Wilder, whose first entrance brought forth an involuntary cry of "He's pretty, isn't he?" from Cicily. And therein, of course, lay the shock to 1939 audiences used to seeing Karloff and Lugosi in such roles. Looming into beetle-browed close-up, the classically chiselled Douglass Montgomery is almost as disturbing as Forrest Stanley in the silent version.

Thanks to Nugent's adroit handling – together with the nervous strings of composer Ernst Toch, Charles Lang's limpid cinematography and, above all, Hope's winning way with a wisecrack – *The Cat and the Canary* stands as arguably the classic example of horror-comedy. Only a further Hope-Goddard teaming – George Marshall's *The Ghost Breakers* – would surpass it. In the meantime, it triggered off a renewed rash of 'old house' comedies, notably Phil Rosen's Monogram potboiler *Murder by Invitation*. This June 1941 release is so self-aware it actually name-checks *The Cat and the Canary* at one point, as well as featuring that long-time resident of spooky houses, Wallace Ford, as the undying 'wisecracking reporter' stereotype.

Another throwback in mid-1939 was directed by the increasingly passé Tod Browning. Inactive since *The Devil-Doll*, he was back at M-G-M making *Miracles for Sale*, an engaging but minor-key adaptation of

the Clayton Rawson novel *Death from a Top Hat*. "Audiences are vastly different from those of the early days in pictures," Browning mused in the accompanying pressbook, adding that, "For fear, we relied somewhat on sound. Miss [Florence] Rice's scream in the night as she sees the supposed ghost of the dead demonologist is a perfect example of what such a scream can do. There are other fright-sounds ... [but] they must be handled carefully to avoid their verging over into comedy."

Sadly, the four weeks between 22 May and 22 June in which Browning made the picture effectively marked the end of his film career. He had no luck getting a film version of Horace McCoy's 1935 novel *They Shoot Horses, Don't They?* off the ground and finally retired in January 1942.

Miracles for Sale is in many ways an apt swan-song for Browning, with a debunking of professional psychics reminiscent of his 1925 picture *The Mystic* – and not a million miles removed from another 1939 release, Frank O'Conner's *The Mystic Circle Murder*, a Poverty Row exposé compéred by none other than Mme Houdini. Browning's film, of course, enjoys plenty of Metro gloss in telling a tale of two murders committed amid a Magic Circle-type community, with Robert Young as a dedicated debunker who exposes the killer as none other than Henry Hull. Appropriately, all the film's spooky set-pieces – a typewriter operating by itself, an ectoplasmic apparition smoked up from the mediumistic body of Gloria Holden, Hull sporting eerily opaque contact lenses, the aptly named Frederick Worlock lying dead within a pentacle – are made to conform to Browning's moth-eaten 'horrible possible' theory.

A similar set-up, also derived from a Clayton Rawson novel, would provide source material for Fox's 1942 murder-mystery *The Man Who Wouldn't Die*. With a memorably tongue-twisting tag-line ("The demon dick is out to manacle a maniacal phantom"), Herbert I Leeds' film indulges in some highly effective scenes of a resurrected Indian mystic who, it's finally revealed, wasn't dead after all, just exploiting his gift for self-induced catatonia. The same plot wrinkle would recur three years later in Monogram's *The Strange Mr Gregory*.

SYNTHETIC BLOOD, ARTIFICIAL HEARTS

The horror revival naturally came as a boon to Bela Lugosi. After *Son of Frankenstein* and *The Gorilla*, he went to England in April 1939 to appear in the Edgar Wallace shocker *The Dark Eyes of London*, returning to Hollywood in May for the Universal serial *The Phantom Creeps* and achieving the distinction in June of playing opposite Greta Garbo in Ernst Lubitsch's *Ninotchka*.

In the middle of all this, he missed out on Vincent Sherman's Warner Bros-First National production *The Return of Doctor X*. This was based on a William J Makin story called *The Doctor's Secret*, which had appeared in *Detective Fiction Weekly* on 31 July 1938 and been announced for filming the following October. The film was mentioned for Karloff as well as Lugosi but, when it finally went into production in the last week of May 1939, Bryan Foy – head of Warners' B unit – had scaled down his aspirations considerably, settling for John Litel as Dr Flegg and Humphrey Bogart as his undead associate Xavier. At the same time, Crane Wilbur's script – set, like Makin's story, in turn-of-the-century London – had been ditched in favour of a modern-day, Warners-flavoured treatment by Lee Katz.

> *Having discovered the corpse of stage star Angela Merrova in her hotel suite, young reporter Walter Garrett is surprised to find her up and about, if conspicuously pasty-faced, the very next day. His investigations lead to eminent haematologist Dr Francis Flegg, whose corpse-like assistant Marshall Quesne is actually the executed child murderer Dr Maurice Xavier. Flegg's consistent failure to devise an artificial bloodstream for the revived Xavier has resulted in a rash of vampire-type murders.*

The 39-year-old Bogart was at the time mired in second-string gangster parts, though his Warner contract occasionally yielded offbeat roles such as the sympathetic DA in *Marked Woman* and an enlightened prison governor in *Crime School*. The repulsive Marshall Quesne (pronounced Caine) was something else again, however, and was reportedly foisted on him as a punishment for his 'difficult' behaviour. The role was an unappetising one even by the standards of the horror genre, for we learn that, up until his execution in 1937, Quesne was the misguided medical genius Dr Maurice Xavier – "the skunk," as the reporter on his trail puts it, "who wanted to find out how long babies could go without eating."

Bogart's trademark habit of pulling his upper lip back over his teeth takes on new meaning in the role of the cinema's first fully fledged 'medical' vampire. Though unhappy with the part, he gives it all he's got, especially when eavesdropping, damp-eyed, on Dr Flegg as he confesses all to the young reporter. Nicely balancing an earlier scene in which the reporter spied through the same window on Flegg and Xavier, this is a genuinely moving moment. Here, too, John Litel is exceptional, concluding forlornly that "the magic element of life has eluded me" and

Dennis Morgan gets a bad feeling about shifty surgeons Humphrey Bogart and John Litel in *The Return of Doctor X* (1939)

THE RETURN OF DOCTOR X

Warner Bros-First National 1939
62 minutes
production began 24 May

Cinematographer: Sid Hickox; Art Director: Esdras Hartley; Editor: Thomas Pratt; Sound: Charles Lang; Make-up: Perc Westmore*; Gowns: Milo Anderson; Music: Bernhard Kaun*; Technical Adviser: Dr Leo Schulman; Dialogue Director: John Langan; Screenplay: Lee Katz (based on the story *The Doctor's Secret* by William J Makin); Executive Producers: Jack L Warner*, Hal B Wallis*; Associate Producer: Bryan Foy*; Director: Vincent Sherman

Humphrey Bogart (Marshall Quesne [Dr Xavier]); Rosemary Lane (Joan Vance); Wayne Morris (Walter Garrett ['Walter Barnett' in credits]); Dennis Morgan (Michael Rhodes); John Litel (Dr Francis Flegg); Lya Lys (Angela Merrova); Huntz Hall (Pinky); Charles Wilson (Detective Ray Kincaid); Vera Lewis (Miss Sweetman); Howard Hickman (chairman); Olin Howland (undertaker); Arthur Aylesworth (guide); Cliff Saum (Detective Sergeant Moran); Creighton Hale (hotel manager); John Ridgely (Rodgers); Joe Crehan (editor); Glenn Langan, DeWolfe Hopper Jr [later William Hopper] (internes); uncredited: Ian Wolfe (cemetery caretaker)

nb: the role of Moran is credited to Jack Mower in the film's publicity material

The Return of Dr X is a weirdly fascinating thing, a horror picture, to be sure, but one so intelligently presented that it will delight all classes of audiences ... It has a definite plot, an extremely novel and interesting one, and relies on high class production values for startling effect.
Hollywood Reporter

You can't believe what this one was like. I had a part that somebody like Bela Lugosi or Boris Karloff should have played. I was this doctor, brought back to life, and the only thing that nourished this poor bastard was blood. If it'd been Jack Warner's blood ... maybe I wouldn't have minded as much.
Humphrey Bogart [quoted in Gehman, Bogart, 1965]

that "my experiments have turned into madness." They're certainly a distinctive pair – Flegg prissily Mephistophelean in monocle and goatee, Xavier with his "cold graveyard look" and a skunk-like streak in his hair reminiscent of both Elsa Lanchester in *Bride of Frankenstein* and Karloff in *The Walking Dead*.

The film begins with an unusually lengthy disclaimer of the "Any resemblance to any person, living or dead, is entirely coincidental" variety. The reason isn't hard to guess; with an impressive sequence devoted to Flegg's resuscitation of a dead rabbit, Warners were obviously keen to deflect any suggestions that the dog-reviving Dr Robert E Cornish was the kind of man to have human vampires on his staff. Flegg comes out with many of the standard mad scientist pronouncements, notably "An effective surgeon can't afford the luxury of feelings" and a self-justifying reference to "the living, pulsing human heart ... held in a surgeon's hand" – the latter would be repeated, almost word for word, by the barking mad

Dr Rigas in Universal's *Man Made Monster*. But the final impression is of a sad and defeated over-reacher rather than a dangerously irrational one.

Indeed, Sid Hickox's brilliant cinematography conjures a disillusioned, shadow-saturated milieu not far removed from film noir. In this grim and despairing vision of New York, it isn't only the 'monsters' who are spookily lit from just below chin level; even the film's nominal lead, Wayne Morris, gets the treatment. As Walter Garrett, a fresh-faced newshound vaguely reminiscent of Lee Tracy in the original *Doctor X*, he also gets an unprecedented string of insults directed his way, from "Wichita brainchild" and "cornfed wizard" to "Kansas Sherlock" and "Wichita Frankenstein." Undaunted, his investigations lead him to Lya Lys, exotic star of Luis Buñuel's *L'Age d'or*, whose Angela Merrova has a capuchin monkey in her retinue and is clearly intended as a high-handed stage beauty in Sarah Bernhardt mould. Her appearance in the offices of the *Morning Dispatch* the day after her apparent murder carries a nasty necrophilic undertow; looking up from under the brim of her chic headgear, Merrova's unwavering stare – equal parts waxen and coquettish – instantly communicates the idea that something is deeply wrong.

Despite the PR department's flagrant misrepresentation of the film as a sequel to *Doctor X* (in which the quest for synthetic flesh constitutes the slimmest of parallels to Flegg's search for synthetic blood), *The Return of Doctor X* is a highly accomplished B-picture and also unusually gruesome for its time (in theme, if not execution). Even so, it doesn't quite escape the 'what kind of film are we making here?' confusion endemic to Warners' earlier attempts at horror – and in retrospect, of course, Bogart's casting only underlines the problem.

The finale, set in a tumble-down shack in fog-laden swamp country just outside Newark, is a case in point. In it, Xavier straps a pretty young nurse to a makeshift operating table in the very same "abandoned duck club" where his baby-starving experiments were conducted. With Xavier cooking up his blood-draining apparatus over an antiquated stove, the scene is pervaded by an unmistakable whiff of brimstone. "I wouldn't scream," he gloats, scalpel in hand. "No one can hear you." She screams anyway, her peals of terror initiating a climactic gun battle in which, disappointingly, Xavier is shot down like any common-or-garden gangster.

A month after Bogart began work as Dr Xavier, Boris Karloff embarked on a Columbia project called *The Man They Could Not Hang*, another film dealing with artificial bloodstreams. The screenplay was by Karl Brown, who had begun his career with D W Griffith before becoming a director in his own right. Though deftly structured and graced by excellent dialogue, Brown's script was hardly original; indeed, it took its second half almost lock, stock and barrel from a slick Columbia thriller of 1933 called *The Ninth Guest*. Directed by Roy William Neill, the earlier film was written by Garnett Weston (author of both *White Zombie* and *Supernatural*), who provided in it a blueprint for Agatha Christie's *And Then There Were None*. *The Man They Could Not Hang* did the same, only with the addition of a scientific necromancer as its leading character.

Dr Henryk Savaard has devised a means of reviving the dead but is arrested for the murder of a young volunteer before he can insert the artificial heart that will save him. Hanged, Savaard is himself revived by his assistant Lang, and before long six of the jurors who convicted Savaard have been murdered, apparently by hanging. Savaard's other enemies, meanwhile, are summoned to his abandoned house, where a sadistic game of cat-and-mouse ensues.

The script's borrowings did not end with *The Ninth Guest*. Its basic inspiration lay in the experiments of Robert E Cornish and the revolutionary Lindbergh Heart, both of which had already inspired Warners' *The Walking Dead*. Karloff duly undertakes the same Death Row procession he had previously experienced in the Warner picture, as well as devising a scheme of revenge closely allied to that of the juror-killing Ygor in *Son of Frankenstein*.

The very title would have served well had Ygor ever been given a film of his own – and, like Ygor, the resurrected Dr Savaard takes delight in drawing his enemies' attention to the paradox that they're dealing with a dead man whom the law cannot touch. "I am legally dead," he suavely informs the District Attorney who prosecuted him. "Your business is with the living." More specifically, the punishment meted out to the petrified jury foreman (impalement by spring-loaded needle concealed in telephone receiver) was previously the fate of both Brandon Hurst and Hale Hamilton in Frank Strayer's 1931 film *Murder at Midnight*.

The sense of déjà vu no doubt extended to the film's cinematographer Benjamin Kline, who had previously photographed *The Ninth Guest*. Kline is a key contributor, however, to the film's discreetly stylish look, whereby the workaday realism of director Nick Grindé is disrupted only at telling intervals. To introduce the Death Row scenes, for example, the pacing Savaard is seen as a giant shadow overlaid onto the bars of his cell. Moments later, his compact with Dr Lang having been made under the very nose of the prison warden, Savaard watches Lang depart through the foreground obstruction of a spiral staircase. And our first view of the post-mortem Savaard – wound round with bandages and a leather neck-brace, strapped firmly to an operating table and hovered over by the bird-like Lang – is strikingly shot from above, the camera peering vertiginously through a laboratory skylight.

On Savaard's awakening, his conference with the perspiring, post-operative Lang is rendered in massive, angled close-ups that point a powerful contrast between the two scientists. Lang is elated yet concerned with talking shop; of the heart apparatus, he points out that "The next one must be much stronger to force open the capillaries closed by rigor mortis." Savaard, however, clearly has more pressing matters on his mind than the propagation of a scientific miracle. "They won't come to learn, only to stare," he snarls. "I'll be a freak in a sideshow: Lazarus the Second."

Despite the hand-me-down nature of the material, Karloff's performance is a powerfully committed one throughout. When freed from his bandages and confronting his enemies, the 'new' Savaard looks little different from the old one; even at the beginning, Karloff was fitted with a white wig and a chalky make-up, giving him an intriguingly spectral quality. Now, however, Karloff subtly alters his body language to suggest a man lately recovered from a broken neck. (Though quite at home with mumbo-jumbo concerning capillaries and rigor mortis, screenwriter Brown was wise enough to skirt around the specifics of how this particular miracle was achieved, leaving Savaard to tell the police surgeon that it's "too long a story to tell you now.") Karloff is particularly impassioned when defending himself at his trial and when, later, he reflects on how all scientific advances have been somehow twisted by human "hate and greed" – providing an apt rationale for his climactic destruction of the apparatus.

Karloff, however, is pretty much the whole show. His assembled enemies comprise the three surviving jurors who didn't speak up for him, together with the cop on the case, the police surgeon, the DA, the judge, the nurse who informed on him, and a reporter who has stumbled into the affair – and none of them is especially interesting. To compensate for this, Grindé handles the cat-and-mouse business with suspenseful aplomb, as well as playing the scientific miracles on a brightly lit 'business as usual' note that confers unwonted realism on them.

THE MAN THEY COULD NOT HANG

Columbia 1939
65 minutes
production began 27 June

Cinematographer: Benjamin Kline; Editor: William Lyon; Sound: George Cooper*; Musical Director: M W Stoloff; Assistant Director: Thomas Flood*; Story: Leslie T White, George W Sayre; Screenplay: Karl Brown; Producer: Wallace MacDonald*; Director: Nick Grindé

Boris Karloff (Dr Henryk Savaard); Lorna Gray (Janet Savaard); Robert Wilcox ('Scoop' Foley); Roger Pryor (District Attorney Drake); Don Beddoe (Lieutenant Shane); Ann Doran (Betty Crawford); Joseph De Stefani (Dr Stoddard); Charles Trowbridge (Judge Bowman); Byron Foulger (Lang); Dick Curtis (Kearney [jury foreman]); James Craig (Watkins); John Tyrrell (Sutton); uncredited: George Anderson (warden); Sam Ash (pharmacist); Stanley Blystone (guard); Harlan Briggs (defense attorney); Stanley Brown (Bob); Flo Campbell (housewife); John Dilson (King); Frank Jacquet (fat man); Bill Lally (bailiff); Larry Lund (court clerk); Ian MacLaren (priest); Charles McAvoy (prison official); Charles Miller (Dr Avery); Cyril Thornton (butler); Franklin Parker, Walter Sande, Robert Sterling (newspapermen)

Boris Karloff is very much at home, of course, in the role of the scientist, and actually his performance dwarfs every other characterisation in the sheer 'meatiness' of his material ... As an unabashed thriller of the Grand Guignol school, it certainly has its merits of melodramatic punch.
To-Day's Cinema [UK]

I don't know whether we looked on it as a horror movie. It was just a movie. It happened to be a little strange. That was the kind of picture that Karloff made. You knew that, if you worked with Karloff, it would be strange.
Ann Doran [quoted in Scarlet Street, Winter 1995]

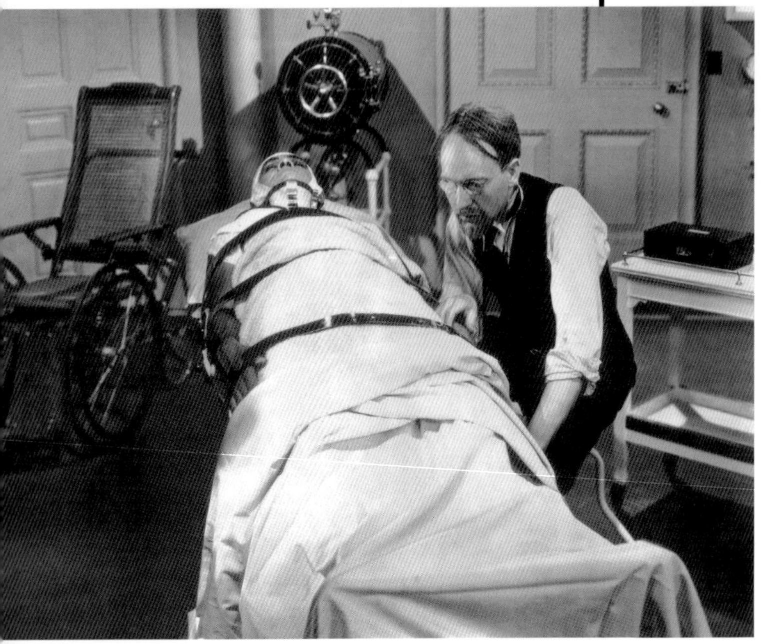
Byron Foulger prepares to prove that Boris Karloff is *The Man They Could Not Hang* (1939)

There are no wild displays of Strickfaden pyrotechnics here, just bulbous glass vessels, frothing liquids, a translucent coffin and icy plumes of cryogenic smoke. For all its borrowings, *The Man They Could Not Hang* is a lean and engaging thriller – and its déjà vu qualities were to be trumped, in any case, by two virtual remakes of it that Karloff would make for Columbia the following year.

Though credited with the original story for *The Man They Could Not Hang*, George W Sayre would go uncredited as fully fledged screenwriter of a Poverty Row quickie called *Torture Ship*, made in August by Producers Pictures Corporation (soon to corner the market in low-grade horrors under the modified name Producers Releasing Corporation). Picking up the shipboard setting of such films as *Black Waters* and *Terror Aboard*, this was directed with zero distinction by *White Zombie*'s Victor Halperin. In it, Irving Pichel is an unscrupulous endocrinologist who gets together a group of psychopaths for a sea voyage devoted to rehabilitating them by surgical means.

Despite the fascinating potential of Sayre's theme, the execution is strictly Am Dram. Even the mutinous criminals' decision to "maybe do a little operating ourselves" goes for virtually nothing, taking second place to a glutinous conclusion in which a female guinea pig responds to a successful operation with the line "I feel as if I had been born again." By this time more committed to directing than acting, Pichel walks through his part with every indication of indifference.

FROM MEDIAEVAL TO ULTRA-MODERN

By 1939, talk of remaking Universal's *The Hunchback of Notre Dame* had been going on at intervals for a decade. Among the actors mentioned for the title role at various times were the usual exotic suspects – Veidt, Lugosi, Karloff, Lorre – and some more surprising homegrown ones: Henry Hull, Edward G Robinson, Paul Muni. When the property passed to RKO, several other names cropped up: Claude Rains, Orson Welles, even Robert Morley. The final choice was closest to the Morley mould but, in fact, had first been nominated as long ago as 1934: Charles Laughton. Production began at the RKO ranch in the San Fernando Valley on 10 July 1939 and lasted 11 weeks.

The result was one of RKO's biggest hits and is routinely cited among the imperishable titles that made 1939 the banner year for the Hollywood studio system. (Others include *Gone with the Wind* and *The Wizard of Oz*.) William Dieterle's film can certainly boast astonishing grandeur, most memorably in its breathtaking climax, where the rebels storming the cathedral are met with a hail of molten metal from the agitated Quasimodo. It also has gorgeous cinematography (Joseph August) and art direction (Van Nest Polglase), a lovely Esmeralda in Maureen O'Hara and a delightful performance from Harry Davenport as Louis XI. "One shrinks from the ugly yet wants to look at it," he muses early on. "There's a devilish fascination in it. We extract pleasure from horror." The ugly is certainly on show – Laughton, an actor intensely conscious of his own ugliness, pulls off the difficult trick of making Quasimodo simultaneously cartoonish and deeply moving. But of horror there is virtually no sign, save for a *Freaks*-style moment in which Gringoire is introduced to the so-called Court of Miracles by a slithering vanguard of disabled beggars.

Worse, the film's plum part goes for almost nothing. The conniving Chief Justice, Frollo, is a psychotic racist and misogynist par excellence, closely resembling Angelo in Shakespeare's *Measure for Measure* – yet he's played on a single constipated note by Sir Cedric Hardwicke. One longs for the sulphuric evil of Brandon Hurst, who played the role in 1923; indeed, Hardwicke is out-acted by the saturnine George Zucco, who plays a lesser justice. A distinguished British stage star who never reconciled himself to being "situated 3000 miles from anything recognisable as the theatre," Hardwicke noted airily that "I had not known any community where it was easier to nod off to sleep."[6] The reciprocal effect on audiences was inevitable.

The Frollo role had originally been offered to the much more dynamic Basil Rathbone, but he was bound by Universal to appear as, coincidentally, a hunchback in Rowland V Lee's *Tower of London*, which began shooting on 11 August. This was a venture well outside Universal's usual rut but misleadingly pitched at Universal's usual customers; to entice the horror crowd, even Bela Lugosi was dragooned into appearing opposite Boris Karloff at the premiere, despite the fact that only Karloff actually appeared in the picture.

A lurid retelling of the Wars of the Roses focusing on the machinations of the future Richard III, it puts Rathbone's vulpine countenance to good use in the main role and has Karloff in one of his creepiest guises as Mord, executioner extraordinaire and Richard's right-hand man. First seen sharpening his axe with lip-smacking zeal, shooing his raven familiar from his shoulder and then nonchalantly loading another weight onto a supine torture victim, Karloff lords it over the stews with bald head, beetle brows and a very prominent club-foot. "Crookback and dragfoot," muses Richard. "Misfits, ey?" Their symbiotic relationship is not far removed from that of Ygor and the Monster in Lee's *Son of Frankenstein*, and it helps to enliven an over-careful historical epic that quickly becomes a deadening plod.

In compensation, the battles of Tewkesbury (soaked in rain) and Bosworth (swathed in mist) are ramshackle and brutal; the torture sequences are also surprisingly grisly. Karloff is on good form too, displaying an almost touching eagerness to go into battle and profound disquiet when ordered to kill the princes in the tower. For his part, Rathbone has a habit of inspecting a toy theatre in which are lined up a series of dolls representing the human obstacles to Richard's attainment of the throne. Unfortunately, the film takes on exactly the same toy-theatre aspect – and, to make matters worse, it inaugurated Universal's soon-to-be-exasperating habit of lifting great chunks from the *Son of Frankenstein* score.

Cast in the small but showy role of the Duke of Clarence was a 28-year-old Missouri native called Vincent Price, who 20 years later would assume a pre-eminent position in Hollywood horror films. In the meantime, less than six weeks elapsed between the completion of *Tower of London* and the start date of his next Universal assignment, *The Invisible Man Returns*. The chosen director was German émigré Joe May, who brought with him another – screenwriter Curt Siodmak, who was to become a crucial figure in 1940s horror. For the time being, however, Siodmak and May seemed unlikely choices for a film set in a colliery town in the north of England.

Due to be executed for murder, Sir Geoffrey Radcliffe literally disappears from his cell, having been rendered invisible by his doctor friend Frank Griffin with a formula devised by Frank's brother Jack – the same formula that drove Jack insane. Before the drug can have its inevitable effect, Geoffrey must establish his innocence by tracking down the real murderer. This turns out to be his cousin Richard Cobb, who meets his death when plunging from a coal skip.

The credits sequence of *The Invisible Man Returns* is an engaging one and was to prove highly influential – with the title formed from the exhalations of a test tube, it set the pattern for numerous smoked-up title cards to follow. The action is set nine years after the tragedy that befell Jack Griffin, with his brother Frank now in possession of Jack's invisibility serum and its name adjusted from Monocane to Duocane. Why this change was made is hard to guess, unless it was to indicate that there is hope for this particular Invisible Man. Price's Geoffrey Radcliffe never becomes the out-and-out monomaniac of the original, instead feeling the benefits of a last-minute antidote and being paired off with the appealing Nan Grey, making an attractive young 'duo' and furnishing what *The Invisible Man* conspicuously lacked: a happy ending.

Despite the clinch at the fade-out, the film's romantic subplot is by no means a conventional one. ("How does it feel to have a phantom fiancé?" Geoffrey asks at one point.) Elsewhere, Geoffrey's invisibility is played, not for the gallows humour of the original, but for vaguely saucy amusement related to nudity. Warned by his superior not to allow Geoffrey to remove his clothes, a panicked bobby mutters, "He won't do that, sir – there's a lady with him," later noting that the clothes have indeed been removed and saying "No wonder she fainted!" Perhaps inspired by the playful ghost hi-jinks of Norman Z McLeod's *Topper* and *Topper Takes a Trip*, the sadistic farce of *The Invisible Man* has also been toned down, the film's lighter touch being exemplified by a line that for Price would prove unusually prophetic. "If the worst comes to the worst," laughs Geoffrey, "I can always get a job haunting a house."

Exchanging sadistic farce for a more larkish tone obviously dulls the film's effectiveness as a horror picture, though a breath of cruelty is introduced into an overlong scene in which the transparent Geoffrey bedevils Cobb's right-hand man in a sunlit glade, later leaving him precariously balanced on a chair with a noose around his neck. The victim is played by Alan Napier (normally the last word in 'patrician' supporting actors) with an extremely variable North Country accent, emphasising the film's failure to create the provincial verisimilitude so effortlessly conjured by James Whale in *The Invisible Man*. One wonders why Universal bothered with so parochial a setting in the first place, given that it also entailed the considerable expense of building a life-sized colliery on the backlot. Cobb's 40-foot death plunge from the coal escalator is an impressive stunt, however, and draws a very conclusive line under a Cedric Hardwicke performance that's slightly less disengaged than usual.

John Fulton's special effects earned him an Oscar nomination and, though less thorough than the original in the invisibility scenes, are still highly impressive when first a guinea pig and then Geoffrey himself acquire substance through a slow accretion of sinew and bone. Fulton also takes advantage of one or two innovations, notably when Geoffrey's spectral outline is revealed, first by a downpour and then by the constabulary's massed smoke machines.

Geoffrey's sociopathic fugues are fruitily written and reveal something of why Curt Siodmak found himself in Hollywood in the first place. Here and there we're given direct echoes of R C Sherriff's lines in the original; where Griffin crowed about his new-found "power to walk into the gold vaults of the nations, into the secrets of kings, into the holy of holies," Geoffrey observes that "I could sit in on the councils of kings and dictators. It makes *me* King, it makes me Nemesis!"

Driven out of Germany by the Nazis, Siodmak was willing to call a spade a spade and introduce that telling word 'dictators'. "I'm beginning to get a new perspective on this crawling little animal known as man," Geoffrey continues, proposing a toast to "a new era, to a changed world with me as its guiding genius." In reply, Frank half-heartedly humours him with a cry of "Hail, invincible Leader!" Though Geoffrey's monomania has no practical application this time around – and Price plays Siodmak's lines with a kind of insanely boyish enthusiasm rather than the profoundly chilling purposefulness of Claude Rains – it's perfectly clear which Führer Siodmak had in mind while writing them.

When *The Invisible Man* was made in June 1933, Adolf Hitler had recently become German chancellor; by the time *The Invisible Man Returns* went into production, he had initiated a European war, made official by the British Prime Minister, Neville Chamberlain, on 3 September 1939. As a result, the film's scenes of caped policemen striding around in gas masks not only provide an amusing echo of Geoffrey's own bug-eyed disguise, they also seem uncannily prescient of the oncoming Blitz.

In the wake of *The Invisible Man Returns*, Universal put together a couple of inessential follow-ups. Both of these garnered Fulton further Oscar nominations, despite the fact that the invisibility effects in them were slipshod by comparison to his earlier efforts. *The Invisible Woman* was made in September 1940 by Edward Sutherland, who retained Charlie Ruggles from his earlier *Murders in the Zoo* in a cast toplined by Virginia Bruce and the tragically run-to-seed (and near death) John Barrymore. Though it carries H G Wells' name on its credits, the film has nothing to do with the Griffin saga; instead, it's little more than an unfunny screwball comedy predicated on the apparently risqué possibilities of Virginia Bruce in her (non-visible) birthday suit. "Phew!" she says at one point. "Kinda chilly. I wonder how the nudists stand it?"

THE INVISIBLE MAN RETURNS

Universal 1939
81 minutes
production began 13 October

Cinematographer: Milton Krasner; Art Directors: Jack Otterson, Martin Obzina; Editor: Frank Gross; Sound: Bernard B Brown, William Hedgcock; Special Photographic Effects: John P Fulton; Set Decorations: R A Gausman; Make-up: Jack P Pierce*; Gowns: Vera West; Music: H J Salter, Frank Skinner; Musical Director: Charles Previn; Assistant Director: Phil Karlstein; Screenplay: Lester Cole, Kurt Siodmak; Story: Joe May, Kurt Siodmak, Cedric Belfrage* ('a sequel to *The Invisible Man* by H G Wells'); Associate Producer: Ken Goldsmith; Director: Joe May

Sir Cedric Hardwicke (Richard Cobb); Vincent Price (Geoffrey Radcliffe); Nan Grey (Helen Manson); John Sutton (Doctor Frank Griffin); Cecil Kellaway (Sampson); Alan Napier (Willie Spears); Forrester Harvey (Ben Jenkins); uncredited: Billy Bevan (Jim [prison warden]); Matthew Boulton (constable at Radcliffe Manor); Louise Brien (Griffin's secretary); Harry Cording (miner); Rex Evans (Constable Briggs); Mary Field (Spears' neighbour); Edward Fielding (prison governor); Mary Gordon (cook); Leland Hodgson (chauffeur); Hugh Huntley (secretary); Bruce Lester (chaplain); Frances Robinson (nurse); Ivan Simpson (Cotton [butler]); Harry Stubbs (Constable Tukesberry); Dave Thursby (Bob); Eric Wilton (fingerprint man)

Universal make it abundantly clear here that a sequel can be every whit as entertaining as its predecessor ... It is impossible not to thrill to the gripping scenes of 'invisibility', and this macabre drama ... is agreeably leavened at times by scenes of compelling romance. *To-Day's Cinema* [UK]

He [Joe May] really couldn't speak any English at all ... He was a charming man – but very volatile, really uptight ... I don't think John Sutton understood a word he said, nor could Nan Grey. Cedric hated him, really hated him! Vincent Price [quoted in *Video Watchdog*, May-June 1992]

"How does it feel to have a phantom fiancé?" Fugitive nobleman Vincent Price with sweetheart Nan Grey in *The Invisible Man Returns* (1939)

Having been played for farce, the theme was then put at the service of wartime propaganda in Edwin L Marin's *Invisible Agent*, a Siodmak-scripted story of a Griffin descendant (Jon Hall) encountering Axis agents Cedric Hardwicke and Peter Lorre. Though lumpen and unexciting, the film's gung-ho wartime heroics struck an inevitable chord, ensuring an impressive gross in excess of $1 million on its release in August 1942; it seems worthwhile now only for its spirited Hungarian heroine Ilona Massey. Between these two Universal curios, Bryan Foy's Warner Bros B unit ground out an *Invisible Man* rip-off in August 1941 called *The Body Disappears*. Played, like *The Invisible Woman*, for farce, Ross Lederman's film has the delightful Edward Everett Horton as a professor whose serum for raising the dead in fact causes people to become invisible.

After appearing in both *Tower of London* and *The Invisible Man Returns*, Vincent Price and Nan Grey went on to a relatively sumptuous Universal adaptation of Nathaniel Hawthorne's 1851 novel *The House of the Seven Gables*, which began on 3 January 1940 and was put out, rather wastefully, as support feature to a film shot simultaneously, *Black Friday*. Telling Hawthorne's tale of a New England family curse in mannered but engaging style, Joe May's film strips away Hawthorne's vaguely supernatural undertones, settling for an interpretation in which the Pyncheons are "haunted by conscience, not by the calcified bones of Matthew Maule." George Sanders is the black-hearted Jaffrey Pyncheon, siphoning abolitionist money back into the slave trade and finally succumbing, like his father before him, to a strange throat haemorrhage, as predicted in Maule's dying curse: "God hath given him blood to drink." Margaret Lindsay is extremely affecting as Hepzibah, and Vincent Price's Clifford – railing against "this mausoleum ... [with] its rotting walls and decaying memories" – offers a youthful précis of the Poe roles he would make his own in the 1960s.

George Sanders, Margaret Lindsay and Vincent Price as accursed New Englanders in *The House of the Seven Gables* (1940)

MORE SCIENTIFIC BREAKTHROUGHS

Having written *The Invisible Man Returns*, Curt Siodmak went straight on to the Karloff-Lugosi vehicle *Black Friday*. In doing so, he inaugurated a theme that was to become a persistent one in his later work: brain transplantation. He also crafted a juicy part for Lugosi as the transplant pioneer and a double-role for Karloff as the man he experiments on. The film's three-week schedule began on 28 December 1939, but by that time Karloff's last-minute decision to play the surgeon rather than the guinea pig resulted in Lugosi's demotion to the ill-fitting role of a New York gangster. The plum part – or parts, given the split personality Siodmak envisaged as the inevitable consequence of brain juggling – was passed on to the little-known British actor Stanley Ridges.

> *En route to the electric chair, Dr Ernest Sovac explains that, to save the life of his academic friend George Kingsley, he gave him part of the brain matter of notorious gangster 'Red' Cannon. On learning that Cannon left $500,000 unaccounted for, he encouraged the submerged gangster in Kingsley to 're-emerge'. Five of Cannon's treacherous associates were killed as a result, and when Sovac's own daughter was threatened, he was forced to shoot his friend down.*

Given the opportunity to outshine both Karloff and Lugosi, Ridges grabbed it with both hands. The two facets of the rejuvenated Professor Kingsley – vague and lovable academic, cold and ruthless racketeer – are little more than stock figures, but they're endowed by Ridges with a rare humanity and, within the limits of a fantastic plot, believability. Kingsley is prone to quoting Tennyson and Cowper, even in the unfamiliar environs of a New York nightclub, and Ridges cleverly plants the seeds of Kingsley's mental disintegration with the innocent observation, apropos of the club's resident chanteuse, "I seem to know her. Could she be one of my former students?" When Cannon asserts himself, he laughs derisively at the notion that his other self is a lecturer in English literature, looks at his changed appearance in a mirror and grins, "Why doc, you're a genius – but you could've given me a better chassis."

Ridges is gripping to watch throughout, and is helped by a smoothly achieved 'transformation' scene

Boris Karloff faces execution (again) at the beginning of *Black Friday* (1940)

in which he holds his head in his hands, displacing his pince-nez in the process, and the phantom figures of Cannon's enemies swarm across the screen to signal the gangster's re-emergence. "Nobody'll know me like this," he beams, an admission that only makes one wonder, if the transformation isn't a physical one, why Jack Pierce went to the trouble of providing him with sleek black hair and a strangely waxen pallor. Ridges is memorably sinister in this modified guise, however, and the subtlety with which he distinguishes between the two characters makes one regret the final lap-dissolve that, in death, converts Cannon back into Kingsley. It's efficiently done, but the sudden interpolation of obvious camera trickery is at odds with what is otherwise a triumph of acting.

Playing opposite Ridges, Karloff is fitted with a fussy little moustache and a too-tight grey wig and glowers with all his usual panache. Sovac starts out as an avuncular figure but, on learning that $500,000 could be his if he plays his cards right, he becomes harsh, watchful and remorselessly exploitative. After *The Walking Dead* and *The Man They Could Not Hang*, Karloff is required yet again to walk 'the last mile' to the electric chair, and the self-satisfied voice-overs in which Sovac accounts for his behaviour do nothing to endear him to us. "Now I can actually bring to a realisation my plans for a great laboratory," he says of his scheme to get Cannon's money, "and give the world the benefit of my scientific knowledge." These sanctimonious rationalisations are accompanied by clichéd shots of his notebook whirring madly in space in the style of a Warner Bros newspaper montage, a clumsy device that, coupled with absurdly emphatic musical stings, quickly becomes boring.

Indeed, the film recalls a hard-bitten Warner gangster pic throughout its length, the horror elements artlessly integrated and the pacing sorely in need of the characteristic Warner vim. Director Arthur Lubin was keen to make an "un-horrid horror picture" but the film suffers from its glossy, workaday realisation. Some shadowplay for Cannon's first revenge killing, an eerie dappling of water during a tussle beside a reservoir, and frequent recourse to the *Son of Frankenstein* score can't, collectively, qualify the film as the horror proposition suggested by the presence of Karloff and Lugosi.

Lugosi, in particular, is grievously wasted as Cannon's treacherous associate, Eric Marnay. He's fine in the part – uttering such unlikely lines as "Mr Red Cannon now belongs to the history of crime: past tense" with perfect aplomb – but is firmly subordinate to the characters played by Ridges and Karloff. He's central, however, to the film's nastiest scene, in which Marnay is manoeuvred, somewhat ignominiously,

BLACK FRIDAY

Universal 1940
70 minutes
production ended 18 January

Cinematographer: Elwood Bredell; Art Directors: Jack Otterson, Harold MacArthur; Editor: Philip Cahn; Sound: Bernard B Brown, Charles Carroll; Special Effects: John P Fulton; Set Decorations: R A Gausman; Make-up: Jack P Pierce; Gowns: Vera West; Musical Director: H J Salter; Screenplay: Kurt Siodmak, Eric Taylor; Associate Producer: Burt Kelly; Director: Arthur Lubin

Boris Karloff (Doctor Ernest Sovac); Bela Lugosi (Eric Marnay); Stanley Ridges (Professor George Kingsley); Anne Nagel (Sunny); Anne Gwynne (Jean Sovac); Virginia Brissac (Mrs Margaret Kingsley); Edmund MacDonald (Frank Miller); Paul Fix (Kane); Murray Alper (bellhop); Jack Mulhall (barman); Joe King (Chief of Police); John Kelly (taxi driver); uncredited: Raymond Bailey (Devore); Franco Corsaro (head waiter); James Craig (reporter); Eddie Dunn (Detective Furnow); Harry Hayden (prison doctor); Frank Jaquet (fat man); Ellen Lowe (chambermaid); Jerry Marlowe (desk clerk); Edward McWade (archivist); Frank Sheridan (chaplain); Edwin Stanley (Dr Warner); Emmett Vogan (Detective Carpenter); Victor Zimmerman (G-man); Tommy Conlon, Wallace Reid Jr, Dave Willock (students); Dave Oliver, Harry Tenbrook (taxi drivers)

Patrons will vote this Universal picture as one of the most exciting thrillers they have seen ... It is a gripping recital of dual-personality villainy, and we can pay no higher tribute than to record the complete conviction with which the basically fantastic plot is put over. *To-Day's Cinema* [UK]

That rarest of all screen commodities, a new formula for making movies, is credited to Arthur Lubin, young Universal director. Lubin's formula is to make a horror picture without being horrid ... Lubin, one of Hollywood's 'young veterans' ... regards his un-horrid horror picture as his greatest achievement. *from original pressbook*

The iceman cometh: Boris Karloff with victims Byron Foulger, Stanley Brown, Hal Taliaferro and John Dilson in *The Man with Nine Lives* (1940)

into a kitchen cupboard and left to suffocate while Cannon throttles his duplicitous moll. This scene was the subject of a ludicrous publicity stunt in which it was suggested that Lugosi's agonies of suffocation were the real thing, implanted in the actor's mind via a controlled experiment by hypnotist Dr Manley Hall. Despite such old-style ballyhoo, *Black Friday* remains important mainly as a stepping stone to Siodmak's much-filmed 1943 novel, *Donovan's Brain*.

Universal's 1940-41 production programme included a further Karloff-Lugosi vehicle called *The Monster of Zombor*, trailed for exhibitors with an appetising tag-line that was presumably adapted from the Harry Coulter magazine article quoted on page 175: "Cold Sweat that Pays Off in Cold Cash." *Black Friday*, however, failed to rake in sufficient cold cash for Universal's increasingly cost-conscious management, and *The Monster of Zombor* was quietly dropped from the schedule. *Black Friday* endures, therefore, as the last Karloff-Lugosi picture produced by the studio that had made them famous. It's just a pity that the film's eleventh-hour cast changes left the pair without a single scene together.

Despite the eventual fate of *The Monster of Zombor*, Karloff's 'mad scientist' streak continued unchecked. On Friday 16 February 1940, exactly four weeks after the completion of *Black Friday*, he was back at Columbia for a loose follow-up to *The Man They Could Not Hang* called *The Man with Nine Lives*. And by 27 June he was churning out another, this one also fitted with a title confusingly similar to the original – *Before I Hang*. Like *The Man They Could Not Hang*, both of these were directed by Nick Grindé, photographed by Benjamin Kline, written by Karl Brown – and polished off in under three weeks each.

To avoid an 'H' certificate, *The Man with Nine Lives* was submitted to the British censor with six minutes missing, subsequently going out in the UK under one of its production titles, *Behind the Door*. It begins with a written foreword extolling science's "newest and most modern discovery – frozen therapy." Roger Pryor (previously the oily DA from *The Man They Could Not Hang*) is now research scientist Tim Mason, whose experiments in cryogenics lead him to an abandoned mansion on the Canadian border. "I've never seen a better specimen of a haunted house," he mutters on approaching it, and deep in its foundations he finds Karloff's Dr Leon Kravaal, preserved in ice for ten years. The flashback that follows ploughs the same furrow as *The Man They Could Not Hang*. Again, the doctor's medical miracle is frustrated by the blundering intervention of a fellow doctor and various police officials, with the twist that the entire group,

not merely Kravaal, is condemned to death prior to being scientifically revived.

With a limited cast and a confined setting, the film works up a suitably claustrophobic atmosphere seasoned with judicious doses of sadism. The flashback sees Kravaal's four antagonists trapped in an impregnable ice-chamber; on being thawed out by Mason a decade later, they find themselves trapped once again by Kravaal, who coldly refers to them as "laboratory animals." The arid whiteness of Kravaal's ice-chamber is nicely contrasted with the gloom of the outer rooms, which are spookily lit by the crackling flames necessary to the thawing-out process. Despite everything he's been through (tied up and gagged while his fiancée is experimented on in the ice-chamber), Mason nobly salutes "Dr Kravaal's intensity of purpose" in the final scene, and this seems reasonable in retrospect, given that the scientific miracles of both *The Man They Could Not Hang* (artificial hearts) and *The Man with Nine Lives* (cryogenic suspension) would later become reality. In the shorter term, the preservation-in-ice theme of *The Man with Nine Lives* – suggested, perhaps, by the old Harry Houdini melodrama *The Man from Beyond* – would soon be picked up in Universal's Frankenstein sequels.

Karloff's Columbia engagements began to succumb to the law of diminishing returns with *Before I Hang*, which was made under the more fanciful title *The Wizard of Death*. This one was concocted by Karl Brown in collaboration with Robert D Andrews, but scripted by Andrews alone; perhaps as a consequence, the film contains a great deal more scientific mumbo-jumbo than usual, with explicit reference made to Alexis Carell's real-life experiments. This time, Karloff is a bespectacled old duffer called Dr John Garth, who has developed a serum designed to arrest the ageing process but is sentenced to hang when an elderly patient fails to survive. Getting together with a prison doctor to perfect the formula, Garth experiments on himself with a serum prepared from the blood of an executed murderer. In an echo of the already well-worn *Hands of Orlac* routine, the reprieved (and rejuvenated) Garth starts strangling his old cronies, bitterly aware that "some awful force in the living cells I took into my body poisoned me with an urge to kill."

Rejuvenation gone wrong: Boris Karloff and frightened daughter Evelyn Keyes in *Before I Hang* (1940)

Kline's cinematography is as atmospheric as ever and Grindé's direction is sleekly efficient, but the end result lacks punch and conviction. Even so, the warning signals that presage Garth's homicidal fugues – a hand clamped to the back of his neck, a palm-rubbing motion, an obsessively twisted handkerchief – are creepily put over by Karloff, and among his victims are the always welcome figures of Pedro de Cordoba and Edward Van Sloan. It's particularly gratifying to see Karloff and Van Sloan, veterans of the first wave of Hollywood horror, labouring together in a shadow-laden prison laboratory. Indeed, the fourth-billed Van Sloan should really have been credited directly under Karloff, given that the actors who are – Evelyn Keyes and Bruce Bennett – play entirely negligible characters.

CASTILLO MALDITO AND THE HILL OF THE SEVEN JACKALS

Back on 12 June 1939, Paramount had inaugurated a so-called 'weird-chiller' series with Ernest B Schoedsack's *Dr Cyclops*, which, thanks to the complexity of its special effects, didn't go on release until April 1940. Schoedsack here swapped the gigantism of *King Kong* for the miniaturisation plot of *The Devil-Doll*, with the "gigantic radium deposit" of *The Invisible Ray* and bald-pated maniac of *Mad Love* thrown in for good measure. The egg-head this time is Dr Thorkel (Albert Dekker), "the greatest living authority on organic molecular structure," holed up in the Amazonian jungle and reducing a visiting scientific deputation to an average height of just over 13 inches.

The film begins in arresting style, with the letters of the title irradiated in a sickly green (an effect later appropriated by *The Thing from Another World*), the goggled silhouette of Thorkel bathed in stroboscopic blue light, and his quailing associate (Paul Fix) uttering the usual stuff: "What you are doing is mad, it is diabolic. You're tampering with powers reserved

Albert Dekker toys with his miniaturised enemies in *Dr Cyclops* (1939)

to God." And the Technicolor – no longer the two-tone compromise of Warners' early 1930s films, but the revolutionary three-strip variety introduced in 1935 by Rouben Mamoulian's *Becky Sharp* – is a delight to look at throughout. But the remainder is a strangely rhythm-less trawl through familiar *Kong* situations (with the towering Thorkel standing in for Kong and a marauding alligator for the dinosaurs), adopting a cartoonish approach to the miniaturisation theme at sharp variance to the profundities attempted in *The Incredible Shrinking Man* 17 years later.

Paramount then pencilled in Albert Dekker for a film version of H G Wells' *The Food of the Gods* (the enlarged animals of which would have formed a neat reversal of Dekker's *Dr Cyclops* procedure), but the project never got off the ground. Instead, Tim Whelan's *A Date with Destiny* began production in January 1940. When finally issued in February 1941, its release title – *The Mad Doctor* – ensured that critics overlooked its deluxe production values and dismissed it as just another horror picture. In fact, it's a gripping psychological thriller in which Basil Rathbone perfects the Bluebeard role he had essayed in the British *Love from a Stranger*. Whelan's film also includes an intriguing, PCA-dodging detail in that Rathbone's murderous Manhattan psychiatrist, though married to the unsuspecting Ellen Drew, is clearly in homosexual cahoots with the conniving Martin Kosleck.

The Bluebeard connotations of *The Mad Doctor* were in line with a persistent 1940s scenario that pitted quailing young brides against possibly psychotic husbands. The blueprint, as far as Hollywood was concerned, was the Oscar-winning Selznick International production *Rebecca*. Based on a Daphne du Maurier bestseller, this brought the British director Alfred Hitchcock to America for the first time and was completed in November 1939. Fresh from playing Emily Brontë's tousled Gothic archetype in William Wyler's *Wuthering Heights*, Laurence Olivier exchanged Heathcliff's histrionics for a thoroughly anaemic Maxim De Winter. This leaves *Rebecca* with little to recommend it beyond the luminescence of Joan Fontaine, the way George Sanders wipes the floor with Olivier in his too-few scenes, and the fetishistic absorption of Judith Anderson's Mrs Danvers. ("I keep her underwear on this side," she observes apropos the perfectly preserved boudoir of De Winter's first wife.) The remainder is crippled by a ridiculously inflated running time of 130 minutes and an intrusive Franz Waxman score.

The De Winter role might have carried more weight had it been played by the originally mooted William Powell, or for that matter by Basil Rathbone, whose career was yet to be blighted with the typecasting that followed his multiple appearances as Sherlock Holmes. Indeed, at the beginning of the 1940s Rathbone had no difficulty in exploiting

the two-faced potential suggested by *The Mad Doctor*, proving the point with a further 'borderline' horror, Charles Lederer's *Fingers at the Window*. Made at M-G-M just before Christmas 1941, this cast Rathbone as another psychiatrist, this time a bogus one who orchestrates an outbreak of axe murders in Chicago.

Paramount, meanwhile, had determined on making a loose follow-up to *The Cat and the Canary*, and in it Basil Rathbone would receive a memorable name-check. As well as reuniting Bob Hope and Paulette Goddard, the project retained several of the earlier film's key contributors behind the camera, notably cinematographer Charles Lang, art director Hans Dreier and dress designer Edith Head. On top of this, the chosen director, George Marshall, had recently scored notable hits with *Destry Rides Again* and the W C Fields vehicle *You Can't Cheat an Honest Man*. The source was the 31-year-old Broadway hit *The Ghost Breaker*, filmed twice in the silent era and here restyled *The Ghost Breakers*. Filming got under way in February 1940, and among Hope's supremely quotable one-liners was his unfazed response to a nocturnal New York skyline racked by an electrical storm: "Basil Rathbone must be giving a party."

Mistakenly thinking that he has killed a man, radio host Larry Lawrence hooks up with Mary Carter, who has just inherited a ruined pile situated on Black Island, off Cuba. Their visit to the baleful Castillo Maldito involves a perambulating ghost, a marauding zombie and the violent death of the shady Mr Parada. Their lives, too, are endangered when they discover that "a vein of silver as wide as the island" is at stake.

Arthur Hornblow Jr was one of Paramount's cannier in-house producers and *The Ghost Breakers*, like its predecessor, literally has his signature on it, following the *Cat and the Canary* template in most of its particulars. Again, Paulette Goddard is the heiress heroine and, again, she strips down to her slip for the benefit of the dads in the audience. (She also models a fetching bathing suit this time around.) Like George Zucco, Paul Lukas is smothered by a mystery hand in the shadow of a secret panel. Hope, meanwhile, conceals himself in Goddard's trunk; in the earlier film it was her wardrobe. An oddly worded jingle provides the clue to locating a hidden treasure, and once more the villain turns out to be a pretty-boy smoothie.

Above all, Hope's delightful persona – that of a cowardly braggart compelled by circumstance into showing an unwonted vein of heroism – is transferred intact. Indeed, one of his exchanges from *The Cat and the Canary* is repeated almost verbatim, though adjusted

THE GHOST BREAKERS

Paramount 1940
82 minutes
production began early February

Cinematographer: Charles Lang; Art Directors: Hans Dreier, Robert Usher; Editor: Ellsworth Hoagland; Sound: Harold Lewis, Richard Olson; Process Photography: Farciot Edouart; Interior Decorations: A E Freudeman; Costumes: Edith Head; Music: Ernst Toch, Victor Young*; Musical Adviser: Andrea Setaro; Screenplay: Walter DeLeon (based on a play by Paul Dickey and Charles W Goddard); Executive Producer: William LeBaron*; Producer: Arthur Hornblow Jr; Director: George Marshall

Bob Hope (Larry Lawrence); Paulette Goddard (Mary Carter); Richard Carlson (Geoff Montgomery); Paul Lukas (Parada); Willie Best (Alex); Pedro de Cordoba (Havez); Virginia Brissac (Mother Zombie); Noble Johnson (the Zombie); Anthony Quinn (Ramón Mederos/ Francisco Mederos); Tom Dugan (Raspy Kelly); Paul Fix (Frenchy Duval); Lloyd Corrigan (Martin); uncredited: James Blaine (police sergeant); David Durand (bellhop); Jack Edwards (ship's bellboy); Robert Elliott (Lt Murray); James Flavin (hotel porter); Jack Hatfield (elevator boy); Grace Hayle (screaming woman in corridor); Francisco Marán (head waiter); Paul Newlan (baggage man); Jack Norton (drunk on quayside); Kay Stewart (telephonist); Leonard Sues (newsboy); Blanca Vischer (Dolores); Emmett Vogan (announcer); Max Wagner (ship's porter); Douglas Kennedy, Robert Ryan (internes)

Of its type *The Ghost Breakers* is definitely good. If you liked *The Cat and the Canary* you will appreciate the thrills and humour in this one. Bob Hope is in great fettle. *Picturegoer and Film Weekly* [UK]

We establish the atmosphere ... Then the routine begins. It's the same as Poe, Conan Doyle and Lon Chaney employed. There are the shadows on the wall, lightning flashes, the baying dogs, the fluorescent eyes of the black cat ... As an antidote to this, the blundering butler falls down the stairs, the detective slips on a banana peel or the fat lady sits down where there is no chair ... In this way the tension never gets too hot. George Marshall [quoted in original pressbook]

Paulette Goddard encounters Castillo Maldito's resident zombie (Noble Johnson) in *The Ghost Breakers* (1940)

to avoid accusations of political bias. "A zombie has no will of his own," explains the youthful Richard Carlson. "You see them sometimes, walking around blindly, with dead eyes, following orders, not knowing what they do, nor caring." "You mean like Democrats?" retorts Hope. As the British critic and filmmaker Basil Wright put it at the time, the audience is "disarmed almost at once by the enchanting Bob Hope, before whose tilted nose and chatty wisecracks even an M R James visitant would turn tail."[7] One of these wisecracks, incidentally, is a concealed gag in which the film's screenwriter Walter DeLeon, who had written the 1922 version, tips his hat to the director of the original 1914 version. Surveying Havana harbour, Hope recites a publicity blurb about its exotic history and comments, "Sounds like a Cecil B DeMille script..."

The realisation of the film is deluxe right from the opening credits, which offer a forbidding view of Castillo Maldito as ectoplasmic shapes rise from the sea and coalesce into the letters of the title. The lightning bolts that rumble over New York in the introductory scenes recall a similar storm in the earlier Paramount chiller *Supernatural*; we're also quickly introduced to Pedro de Cordoba and Paul Lukas, whose differing brands of foreign suavity seem to be engaged in a 'spot the red herring' competition. Willie Best, too, is on hand as Hope's valet, going through his usual schtick but relatively free from the ultra-degrading tone imposed on him by such earlier films as *The Monster Walks* and *Mummy's Boys*. Another prominent black actor, Noble Johnson, is extremely impressive as the frog-faced zombie that corners Hope and Best in the decaying hallway of Castillo Maldito. In their generic, Hollywood-approved roles – quailing flunkey and monolithic zombie respectively – it's intriguing that Best and Johnson should be required to do battle in a location that was once the home of "Cuba's greatest slave trader."

Outdoing even *The Cat and the Canary*, Marshall lays the atmosphere on thick. The approach to Castillo Maldito is undertaken under broiling skies, with a swarm of bats to greet Hope and Best at the entrance. Inside, louvred doors spray spindly shadows across a monumental staircase and Don Santiago rises in a wisp of ectoplasm from a gilt-edged ottoman. (The brilliant effects work was by Farciot Edouart.) Matching the increased atmosphere stride for stride, Hope is provided with at least twice as many one-liners by his on-set gag writers, and the result is another seamless integration of comedy and horror. Is the scare potential of the ghost breakers' epic struggle with an armour-plated zombie compromised by Hope's absurd cry of "Quick, get the can opener"? Not in the least, and the point is underlined by the spell-stopped hush that falls upon the zombie when Goddard, done up as Mary's long-deceased ancestor María Ysobel Sebastian, floats ethereally down the staircase.

The film's atmospheric force is much enhanced by its soundtrack, which incorporates a Gilbert Wright invention called the Sonovox, an early form of voice-synthesiser that sounds similar to the Theremin (soon to predominate in US fantasy films). Even more intriguing, the script firmly repudiates the rationalist explanations that were so characteristic of the Broadway mysteries from which it sprang. "I can explain everything but that transparent ghost," Hope muses at the fade-out. In reply, the young Anthony Quinn states incontrovertibly, "That was a *real* ghost." And the same goes, presumably, for Noble Johnson's splendid zombie.

The voodoo ouanga directed at Paulette Goddard in *The Ghost Breakers* is a great deal creepier than anything featured in Arthur Leonard's *The Devil's Daughter*, which was shot in Jamaica and first seen in December 1939. Here, Nina Mae McKinney, the sometime 'black Garbo', indulges in "a little pocomania" in trying to scare her cosmopolitan sister off the family plantation. The word 'voodoo' is scrupulously avoided, 'obeah' taking its place. The film was a loose retread of another Kingston-based project, George Terwilliger's 1934 picture *Ouanga*, which at least features the raising of a couple of zombies – resolutely unfrightening ones, however, in that they meekly turn themselves in at the local police station in the final reel. Having been shot in a British colony, Terwilliger's otherwise thoroughly American film qualified under Britain's quota requirements and thus became arguably the weirdest of all the 'quota quickies'.

In the wake of *The Ghost Breakers*, Willie Best turned up regularly as terrified manservants in easy-going 'old house' retreads, though the racially insensitive antics imposed on him make for uneasy viewing today. Among these were Arthur Lubin's *Who Killed Aunt Maggie?* (1940) and Lewis Seiler's *The Smiling Ghost* (1941); produced by Republic and Warner Bros respectively, these were co-written by Stuart Palmer on the predictable but engaging lines of his earlier screenplay for *One Frightened Night*. In 1942, Best followed up with an amiable Fox vehicle for Milton Berle called *Whispering Ghosts* and Benjamin Stoloff's Warner mystery-thriller *The Hidden Hand*. Then, back at Republic, in March 1944 Best went through his usual paces in Howard Bretherton's 'cut off from the mainland' mystery *The Girl Who Dared*.

Alfred L Werker, director of *Whispering Ghosts*, assisted in the humiliation of Laurel and Hardy in

1942 by directing *A-Haunting We Will Go*, in which Stan and Ollie are deputed to accompany a coffin on a train trip, the occupant of which turns out to be a killer on the run. Quite apart from being stripped of creative control at 20th Century-Fox, Laurel and Hardy's childlike innocence was bound to seem out of time in a decade devoted to brash new talents like Bob Hope and Milton Berle.

Another such, Red Skelton, was caught up in a creepy Southern mansion in S Sylvan Simon's M-G-M comedy-thriller *Whistling in Dixie* (1942), which cast him in exactly the kind of 'radio personality' role played by Hope in *The Ghost Breakers* and Berle in *Whispering Ghosts*. The film was a sequel to Simon's *Whistling in the Dark*, in which the marvellous Conrad Veidt played the shady leader of a Long Island cult. Back in Hollywood after a long stint in the UK, Veidt had proved himself, as the *New York Times* put it, "as suavely satanic a figure as ever" in George Cukor's *A Woman's Face* (1941), a plastic surgery melodrama in which Joan Crawford's fire-damaged features recall *Mystery of the Wax Museum* and anticipate *The Face Behind the Mask*. In addition to *A Woman's Face* and *Whistling in the Dark*, Veidt would make six other Hollywood pictures prior to his untimely death, aged 50, in April 1943.

While *The Ghost Breakers* was enjoying its lucrative release in the summer of 1940, Universal were resurrecting a zombie of their own, albeit a cut-price bandaged one. In response to the extravagant budget over-runs necessitated by Rowland V Lee in the making of both *Son of Frankenstein* and *Tower of London*, the studio determined to subordinate future horror subjects to B-picture status. Setting the pattern, a measly $80,000 was apportioned to a fast-moving potboiler called *The Mummy's Hand*. The director was sometime Griffith protégé Christy Cabanne, but in many ways the most important contributor was screenwriter Griffin Jay, who conceived an elaborate Mummy backstory entirely unrelated to the events of Karl Freund's eight-year-old original.

In search of the tomb of Princess Ananka, a group of US archaeologists uncovers instead the mummy of Kharis, who in life attempted to revive Ananka with a brew of tana leaves. Now, Andoheb, latterday High Priest of the Temple of Karnak, applies the tana leaves to Kharis. Having killed two members of the expeditionary party, Kharis is about to get hold of a further draught of the tana brew when he is consumed by flames.

THE MUMMY'S HAND

Universal 1940
67 minutes
production began 29 May

Cinematographer: Elwood Bredell; Art Directors: Jack Otterson, Ralph M DeLacy; Editor: Philip Cahn; Sound: Bernard B Brown, Charles Carroll; Set Decorations: R A Gausman; Make-up: Jack P Pierce*; Gowns: Vera West; Musical Director: H J Salter; Screenplay: Griffin Jay, Maxwell Shane; Producer: Ben Pivar; Director: Christy Cabanne

Dick Foran (Steve Banning); Peggy Moran (Marta Solvani); Wallace Ford (Babe Jenson); Eduardo Cianelli (The High Priest); George Zucco (Andoheb); Cecil Kellaway (Mr Solvani); Charles Trowbridge (Dr Petrie); Tom Tyler (The Mummy); Siegfried [Sig] Arno (the beggar); Eddie Foster (Egyptian); Harry Stubbs (bartender); Michael Mark (bazaar owner); Mara Tartar (girl); Leon Belasco (Ali); uncredited: Frank Lackteen, Murdock MacQuarrie (priests); Jerry Frank, Kenneth Terrell (thugs)

With at least a nod at its Boris Karloff picture of seven years ago, *The Mummy*, Universal has whipped up another little pseudo-chiller for the same trade. It's calling this one *The Mummy's Hand* and it's transparently just a road company edition ... It's all strictly for the lesser duals [double-bills]. *Variety*

I never met Tom Tyler without his make-up ... and he couldn't talk with that make-up on, so I never heard his voice. So far as I was concerned, he really *was* the Mummy! ... When he picked me up and started carrying me around, I had the eeriest feeling.
Peggy Moran [quoted in Brunas/Brunas/Weaver, *Universal Horrors*, 1990]

Peggy Moran in the grip of Tom Tyler's ossified Kharis in *The Mummy's Hand* (1940)

The backstory may have dealt with Kharis and Ananka rather than Imhotep and Anck-es-en-Amon, but that didn't prevent Universal from clogging much of the film's opening reel with the flashback previously seen in *The Mummy*, with the handsome Western star Tom Tyler substituting for Karloff in the close-ups. The viewer has already gained a strong impression of recycled goods through a title sequence resounding, like much of the rest of the film, to music from *Son of Frankenstein*, and is no more encouraged by the cheapskate shots of Andoheb riding a camel through improbably verdant exteriors that are more Californian than Egyptian. But the conference between Eduardo Ciannelli's High Priest and George Zucco's Andoheb has a portentous solemnity that is much enhanced by an eerie string section – pilfered, again, from *Son of Frankenstein*.

Handing on his mantle to Zucco, Ciannelli seems to be in an advanced stage of Parkinson's Disease, pausing only for a garbled quotation from *Dracula* ("Do you hear? Children of the night. They howl about the Hill of the Seven Jackals") before slumping dead on his throne. (In a pleasingly abstract touch from cinematographer Elwood Bredell, the illumination on Ciannelli's face is snuffed out at the same time as his life.) Zucco, meanwhile, is even better value than Ciannelli. Like James Whale and Colin Clive, the 54-year-old actor had come to prominence via the original production of *Journey's End*, but his Andoheb would provide the cue for a lucrative sideline in horror pictures, his cultivated tones and strangely penetrating eyes bespeaking any number of unguessable perversions. As so often, this career turn was entirely accidental; the part had originally been mooted for Peter Lorre.

The rest of the cast, though personable enough, are not on the same level as Zucco. Dick Foran and Wallace Ford are a world away from the true-blue Britons featured in the archaeological digs of *The Mummy*. In the brash new light of the 1940s, slick and vacuous Americans were clearly deemed the only suitable identification figures for the juvenile audiences at which *The Mummy's Hand* was aimed. To this end, plenty of Brooklynese banter, and even a bar-room brawl, are shoehorned in for the delight of the groundlings.

Ford is a more florid and less engaging figure than he was in *Freaks* or *Night of Terror*, and his witticisms, such as they are, are exactly calculated to deflate any gathering audience apprehension. He refers crudely to "the Hill of the Seven Jackasses," dismisses an Egyptian beggar with a breezy "Hey, don't you ever take a shave?" and, in the film's tense closing moments, even undercuts Andoheb by calling him "Professor Andy." This is the cultured, pith-helmeted imperialism of the original film's Whemple expedition polished up to a philistine, wisecracking New World sheen, and it has dated badly.

Griffin Jay clearly had no time for the cerebral and dreamlike solemnity of *The Mummy*, even abandoning the Scroll of Thoth in favour of Andoheb's fanciful tana-leaf concoction, presumably for the benefit of adolescents who could grasp the drinking of a potion more readily than the ponderous reading of an incantation. Fortunately, the Mummy business, when it finally arrives, is efficiently done, with Tom Tyler proving a highly effective Kharis – gaunt, withered, horribly twisted, even overcoming the post-production handicap of having his eyes artlessly painted over as black blobs. His awakening before the horrified gaze of Charles Trowbridge's Dr Petrie is a spine-chilling highlight. Bredell's camera moves in for a close shot of Kharis' throat gulping down the life-giving tana brew, then observes the closing of his ancient hand over Petrie's as Kharis rises inexorably from his slab.

The ending, too, is memorable. As Kharis bears the unconscious heroine into the temple in which Andoheb awaits them, the camera pulls back to show the full extent of a truly monumental set, then smoothly closes back in to the sacrificial altar and the expectant Andoheb. The scope of the temple is a real eye-opener after the cramped confines in which the film has previously played out, but the set was actually a left-over from James Whale's *Green Hell*, a disastrous jungle melodrama that had cost some $600,000 more than *The Mummy's Hand*. Though roughly made in spots, the film benefits from some telling details, like the cloud of dust that goes up when the hero tussles with Kharis at the end. And, despite running some $4000 over budget, the result proved sufficiently successful to inspire no fewer than three similarly penny-pinching sequels.

GORILLA MEETS GANGSTERS

In July 1940, Paramount reunited the winning team behind *The Biscuit Eater*, a boy-meets-dog tale of rare distinction shot largely in Georgia. In light of the film's creepy incidental scenes of the dog being spirited away to a swamp, it seemed natural for director Stuart Heisler, producer Jack Moss and writer Stuart Anthony to have a crack at making a horror picture. Known in production as *The Avenging Brain*, the result cross-fertilised two Boris Karloff vehicles, *The Walking Dead* and *The Man They Could Not Hang*, with the brain transplant theme of another, *Black*

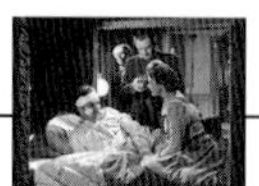

Prolific ape artist Charles Gemora becomes the experimental subject of Abner Biberman and George Zucco in *The Monster and the Girl* (1940)

Friday. On top of this, it recalled a much older source – Marshall Neilan's 1920 comedy-thriller *Go and Get It* – in selecting a gorilla as the unwitting recipient of an executed man's brain.

Having been tricked into marrying handsome gangster Larry Reed, Susan Webster is forced into a life of prostitution by his smooth boss W S Bruhl – and when Susan's brother Scot intervenes, Bruhl frames him on a murder charge. Prior to his execution, however, Scot agrees to donate his brain to research scientist Dr Parry, who transplants it into a large ape. Driven by Scot's vengeful instincts, the ape proceeds to pick off the guilty mobsters one by one.

Though rarely mentioned in histories of film noir, *The Monster and the Girl*, as it became known, contains many of the form's signifying features in embryo – a doomy voice-over, elaborate flashbacks, the 'wrong man' trapped in a sordid milieu, the demure girl exposed to the seaminess of same, masterful mood photography, a pervading aura of pessimism and despair. In fact, the doomy voice-over is replaced by a rather more tantalising device. After a credits sequence that scrolls down over the imposing pipes of a church organ, Ellen Drew's drained and defeated Susan Webster emerges from an oneiric mist to announce, "I'm Susan, the bad-luck penny." The story she introduces sets up her brother Scot as the generic 'wrong man' in a scene lifted from, of all things, the recent Paramount release *The Ghost Breakers*

THE MONSTER AND THE GIRL

Paramount 1940
64 minutes
production began 29 July

Cinematographer: Victor Milner; Art Directors: Hans Dreier, Haldane Douglas; Editor: Everett Douglas; Sound: Harry Mills, John Cope; Music: Gerard Carbonara*, John Leipold*; Musical Director: Sigmund Krumgold; Technical Adviser: Dr Francis Abdo*; Assistant Director: Stanley Goldsmith*; Screenplay: Stuart Anthony; Producer: Jack Moss*; Director: Stuart Heisler

Ellen Drew (Susan Webster); Robert Paige (Larry Reed); Paul Lukas (Bruhl); Joseph Calleia (Deacon); Onslow Stevens (McMasters [district attorney]); George Zucco (Dr Parry); Rod Cameron (Sam Daniels); Phillip Terry (Scot Webster); Marc Lawrence (Sleeper); Gerald Mohr (Munn); Tom Dugan (Captain Alton); Willard Robertson (Lieutenant Strickland); Minor Watson (Judge Pulver); George F Meader (Dr Knight); Cliff Edwards (Tips), and Skipper the dog; uncredited: Abner Biberman (Gregory [Parry's assistant]); Harry C Bradley (Reverend Russell); Florence Dudley (Madame); Emma Dunn (Aunt Della); Fern Emmett (woman organiser); Matty Fain (Wade Stanton); Charles Gemora (gorilla); Al M Hill (Bruhl's chauffeur); Maynard Holmes (Tim Harper); Corbet Morris (Claude Winters); Anne O'Neal (Julia); Emory Parnell (dumb cop); Frank M Thomas Sr (Janson); Oscar Smith (bootblack); Edward Van Sloan (warden); Emmett Vogan (apartment manager); Eleanor Wesselhoeft (housekeeper)

This is the season for horror thrillers and also screen duds. Which possibly explains the presence of this production in a first-run Broadway theatre. *Monster and the Girl* is a poor picture, strictly a routine gangster meller [melodrama] until the ape idea is dragged in. *Variety*

A scientific laboratory to end all scientific laboratories in the movies pulled more curious Paramount employees out to *The Monster and the Girl* stage during its filming than Claudette Colbert drew on the set next door ... Dr Francis Abdo was on hand at all times during the filming to act as technical adviser. *from original pressbook*

(even down to the casting of Paul Lukas as the heavy) – stooping over a murdered hoodlum in a hotel corridor, Scot is foolish enough to pick up the killer's discarded automatic.

In the courtroom scene that follows, Onslow Stevens' sneering DA presses Susan on "the nature of your occupation: how you live." Susan's eloquent silence, together with a preceding flashback in which we're shown her induction into Bruhl's 'white slavery' racket, stamp the film as a daring throwback to the pre-Code era; accordingly, censorship ructions followed it wherever it went, particularly in Britain. Though hardly calculated to raise an eyebrow nowadays, the film's 'morning after' flashback is still a potent cocktail of eroticism and brutality. Waking up in a honeymoon suite that looks as if a bomb has hit it, Susan stretches in sensual reverie and smiles at the dint in her absent husband's pillow. The man who disrupts her idyll is not her husband, however; he's an oily, trilby-hatted spiv who euphemistically describes her future place of work as "not the highest class cabaret."

Now, at the half-way point, the arrival of George Zucco (always welcome) signals the film's sudden switch from gangster frame-up to freakish revenge tragedy. A hearse drives smoothly up to a fog-shrouded Gothic pile and moments later Zucco is wheeling the deceased Scot down a shadowy corridor, past huge anatomical charts and into the hi-tech sterility of a colossal operating theatre. Another gurney is already in place, and there's a genuinely startling moment when Zucco lifts a concealing cloth to reveal its hirsute occupant. He also pulls back the creature's upper eyelids to introduce us to the weirdly phosphorescent eyes that are to dominate the remainder of the action. An assistant notes wryly that the ape "took his anaesthetic like a gentleman," to which Zucco replies, poker-faced, "This night's dreaming will step him up a million years in the pattern of evolution." A striking montage – revolving surgical implements, the faces of the guilty men, a skull in X-ray form – lets us know that Scot's vengeful consciousness is perfectly preserved within the recuperating ape, and now the stalking sequences can begin.

Played in an eerie silence, these scenes are small masterpieces of queasy chiaroscuro. Lurking on rooftops, trees and fire-escapes, the ape is turned into a moving shadow by cinematographer Victor Milner, with only those sparklingly mournful eyes to indicate Scot's methodical purpose. The ubiquitous Charles Gemora is the man in the ape suit, though it's quite unlike any of his usual gorilla get-ups; Paramount presumably decided, correctly, that Gemora's standard wardrobe had become debased by over-exposure. In any case, Gemora's damp-eyed performance and Heisler's sensitive handling succeed in making Scot's scheme of revenge a strangely moving one, culminating in the ape's dying attempts to communicate with the uncomprehending Susan. The achievement is all the more remarkable given the potentially mawkish inclusion at the crime scenes of Scot's beloved terrier Skipper, an affecting detail that was a foregone conclusion given Heisler's success with *The Biscuit Eater*.

The Monster and the Girl is a remarkable film across the board. As Bruhl, Paul Lukas is a smoother version of the gangster played by fellow Hungarian Bela Lugosi in *Black Friday*, and his death, like the other killings of the so-called 'Mangle Murderer', is gruesome and well-paced. Though borrowing much of its plot from other sources, the film's innovative theme of identity transplants and post-operative revenge would be picked up in the much later British picture *Frankenstein Created Woman*. Hans Dreier's production design is exemplary, and the comedy relief (from the two cops on the case and a sanctimonious police doctor) is nicely played and gratifyingly unobtrusive. Above all, the film conjures a dark and forbidding urban atmosphere that lingers long in the memory.

A more emphatic harbinger of film noir than Heisler's picture was a small-scale RKO production called *Stranger on the Third Floor*. Made in June 1940 by debutant director Boris Ingster, this features a wildly Expressionist nightmare sequence when the reporter who has ensured the 'guilty' verdict in a murder trial imagines a monstrously Kafkaesque trial of his own. It also has Peter Lorre as a malnourished psychopath who is determined not to go back to the place where "they put you in a shirt with long sleeves." Of the film's crew, cinematographer Nicholas Musuraca and composer Roy Webb would become vital components of the small horror unit RKO was to establish two years hence.

Charles Gemora's sad-eyed ape in *The Monster and the Girl* wasn't the only marauding gorilla being put through its paces in the summer of 1940. In August, a week after the Paramount picture began shooting, William Nigh started work at Monogram on a cut-price Karloff vehicle called *The Ape*. Here, screenwriter Curt Siodmak devised a story akin to Karloff's contemporaneous Columbia vehicles, casting him as a small-town doctor trying to cure the paralysis of his pretty next-door neighbour, Maris Wrixon. When a murderous ape escapes from a travelling circus,

Karloff has a chance to kill it and, dressed up in its skin, to take spinal fluid from an unwilling local donor (Philo McCullough).

"I ain't scared o' no crazy doctor," says a vainglorious little boy at the beginning, and it's hard to understand how Monogram imagined anyone would be, given Karloff's compassionate performance and Ray 'Crash' Corrigan's ridiculously cartoon-like get-up as both the real and fake gorillas. With its circus background and disabled young heroine, the film seems like a threadbare throwback to Tod Browning's familiar obsessions, while Siodmak anticipates a major strain of future horror films in Karloff's search for spinal fluid; any number of mad scientists would later be driven to gruesome lengths to restore a ruined girlfriend or daughter.

The Ape was filmed in one hectic week, during which director David Butler started production on a modish, and now severely dated, RKO horror-comedy called *You'll Find Out*. Here, Peter Lorre joined Karloff and Lugosi in support of the wildly popular NBC radio personality Kay Kyser. Cast as a professor, a swami and a judge respectively, 'The Three Horror Men', as the posters dubbed them, are involved in a dire plot to disinherit young Helen Parrish. Centre stage is given over to Kyser himself and his so-called Kollege of Musical Knowledge, and it's just a pity that a proposed number for Lorre, Lugosi and Karloff never reached fruition. Less of a pity, perhaps, is the fact that a mooted sequel – with Butler once again directing Kyser and the three menaces – failed to go into production.

Lorre, meanwhile, had decamped to Columbia, where in November 1940 he made a terrific little picture for Robert Florey called *The Face Behind the Mask*. As well as being distantly related to *Mystery of the Wax Museum*, this was another of Florey's 'fire-ravaged person in a mask' scenarios. As a painfully naïve Hungarian immigrant, Lorre is caught in a hotel fire on his first night off the boat, later going berserk in hospital with impassioned screams of "Where is my face? What did you do to my face?" By a strangely plausible sequence of unlikely circumstances, he becomes an eerily impassive crime lord in a vinyl mask, with some affecting sentiment introduced via his relationship with Evelyn Keyes' open-hearted blind girl. (In a brief rural idyll, he tells her sadly that "The face behind the mask [is] mutilated, hideous, a horrible nightmare out of which I can never awake.") The whole thing ends with a bizarre scene in which Lorre stage-manages the slow and painful death of his gangster enemies, and himself, in the Arizona desert.

Vinyl-featured Peter Lorre cradles the murdered Evelyn Keyes in *The Face Behind the Mask* (1940)

BELA LUGOSI AND BORIS KARLOFF WILL SEE YOU NOW

As already noted, Producers Releasing Corporation (PRC) had begun life as Producers Pictures Corporation, under which banner it had made the somnolent *Torture Ship* in August 1939. In that, Irving Pichel had erased memories of his sepulchral performances in *Murder by the Clock* and *Dracula's Daughter* by playing one of the most bland and boring mad scientists on record. Some 14 months later, as PRC's Sigmund Neufeld embarked on the first of many fully fledged horror quickies, he wasn't about to make the same mistake again. For *The Devil Bat*, Neufeld signed no less a performer than Bela Lugosi, ballyhooing his appearance in terms made all the more strident by the fact that the film had little else going for it.

In Heathville, Dr Paul Carruthers vows vengeance on the bosses of a local cosmetics firm, whose million-dollar success is founded on a cold cream devised by him. In his laboratory, he has perfected a means of enlarging bats to alarming proportions, and has trained them to kill in response to a scented after-shave. Four deaths and two near-misses later, Carruthers is himself doused in the after-shave by star reporter Johnny Layton, with inevitable results.

After the halcyon year of 1939, Lugosi had struggled again in 1940, completing *Black Friday* in January and then not making another film until *You'll Find Out* in August. Signing with PRC in mid-October, he

Bela Lugosi fusses over his winged familiars in *The Devil Bat* (1940)

THE DEVIL BAT

PRC 1940
68 minutes
production began 28 October

Cinematographer: Arthur Martinelli; Art Director: Paul Palmentola; Editor: Holbrook N Todd; Sound: Farrell Redd; Musical Director: David Chudnow; Production Manager: Melville DeLay; Screenplay: John Thomas Neville; Story: George Bricker; Associate Producer: Guy V Thayer Jr; Executive Producer: Sigmund Neufeld*; Producer: Jack Gallagher; Director: Jean Yarbrough

Bela Lugosi (Dr Paul Carruthers); Suzanne Kaaren (Mary Heath); Dave O'Brien (Johnny Layton); Guy Usher (Henry Morton); Yolande Mallott [later Yolande Donlan] (Maxine); Donald Kerr ('One-Shot' McGuire); Edward Mortimer (Martin Heath); Gene O'Donnell (Don Morton); Alan Baldwin (Tommy Heath); John Ellis (Roy Heath); Arthur Q Bryan (Joe McGinty); Hal Price (Chief Wilkins); John Davidson (Prof Raines); Wally Rairdon (Walter King)

nb: Billy Griffith (as 'coroner') is billed on screen but was deleted from the final print

As these pseudo-scientific chiller-dillers go, *The Devil Bat* is acceptable hocus-pocus ... With Bela Lugosi performing in style as the mad doctor, the picture moves along at [a] good pace under the direction of Jean Yarbrough ... The affair is not without humor, and doesn't take itself too seriously. *Hollywood Reporter*

I wasn't interested in being in a picture of that kind at that time; I was terribly snobbish! It was quick and it was fast; they were out to get the money as quickly as possible. It was one of those kind of pictures, a potboiler. *Yolande Donlan [quoted in Weaver, Poverty Row HORRORS!, 1993]*

was perhaps unaware that *The Devil Bat*'s Poverty Row status was to determine the course of his future career. Whatever Lugosi's personal apprehensions, *The Devil Bat* endures as the first of a lengthening line of cash-strapped quickies that remain watchable today for one reason and one reason only – Bela Lugosi.

The plot is similar to that of the minor Karloff vehicle *Night Key*. As an inventor who fancies himself duped out of a fortune, Lugosi's interviews with the venal Guy Usher are a close parallel to Karloff's with Samuel S Hinds in the earlier film, but the naïve old duffer portrayed by Karloff becomes predictably, and delightfully, Machiavellian in Lugosi's hands. Indeed, the whole film plays like a small-town 1940s fairy tale, complete with a written 'Foreword' that spells out the basic situation as clearly as possible. "All Heathville loved Paul Carruthers, their kindly local doctor," it reads. "No one suspected that in his home laboratory on a hillside overlooking the magnificent estate of Martin Heath, the doctor found time to conduct certain private experiments – weird, terrifying experiments."

In those experiments, Carruthers' dungeon-like laboratory crackles with sub-Strickfaden electrical gizmos. The film announces its cheerful lunacy early on, when Carruthers moves from one of these strenuous bat-enlarging exercises to answer a phone call with the words, "I'm very busy working on a formula for a new shaving lotion." Despite the *Night Key* parallel, Lugosi's Carruthers seems chiefly modelled on two of his previous roles, Ygor in *Son of Frankenstein* and Dr Mirakle in *Murders in the Rue Morgue*. From Ygor comes the remorseless campaign of revenge against people who have wronged him, utilising a 'monster' to do the dirty work. From Mirakle come the prolonged bouts of

animal experimentation, which mean that Carruthers is capable of creating his own avenger rather than relying, like Ygor, on someone else's.

In a weird parallel to one of *Rue Morgue*'s least convincing features, Carruthers' two enlarged bats are seen in mid-shot as inert downward-hanging monstrosities whipped up by the prop man, and in ill-matched close-up as real South American fruit bats. In this second-hand nature footage, the genuine bats even have a habit of giving toothy yawns that are disconcertingly similar to those of the genuine ape seen in *Rue Morgue*. That film is also recalled when the second 'Devil Bat' attempts to get into the bedroom of the film's vapid heroine, Suzanne Kaaren: the shadowed branches playing over her pillowed face recall the same set-up with Sidney Fox in the earlier film. Sadly, this is about the only striking visual that cinematographer Arthur Martinelli (who had done such remarkable work on another Lugosi vehicle, *White Zombie*) can squeeze from the grade-Z budget accorded him.

As a pioneering example of the 'body count' horror picture, the film's killings recur at frequent intervals but are rendered in unvarying style, with a massive bat swooping from Carruthers' attic and the victims struggling hopelessly to prise a low-flying lump of wings and fur from their jugulars. At least the filmmakers show some self-reflexive wit, having one of the characters sling together a wire-borne decoy Devil Bat that is no more or less convincing than the ones we're meant to take for 'real'. "Whoever constructed the strange-looking monster," pronounces a pompous radio pundit, "forgot to remove a label from the silk used on its left wing. That label reads: 'Made in Japan'."

Directing the first of several low-budget horror pictures, Jean Yarbrough has trouble investing any interest in the stiff, stock figures surrounding Lugosi or in moving the repetitive story at anything other than a snail's pace. Lugosi, however, remains the film's raison d'être and does not disappoint. Showing a sophisticated grasp of character comedy, he relishes the film's succession of ludicrous situations with an entirely straight face. His opening monologue is addressed, bizarrely, to the bat. "Ah, my friend," he beams exultantly, "our theory of glandular stimulation through electrical impulses was correct." Lugosi makes it clear that Carruthers isn't using the royal 'we' here; instead, he's sufficiently unhinged to see the bat as a conscious collaborator in a revolutionary scientific experiment. Later, his double-meaning farewells to his unwitting, cologne-daubed victims ("I don't think you'll ever use anything else," he informs one of them) are pure Lugosi and redeem an otherwise ridiculous film.

Lugosi polished off *The Devil Bat* (or rather, the other way round) in the first week of November; by the end of that month, Boris Karloff was back at Columbia for his fourth 'mad doctor' vehicle, *The Devil Commands*. This one departed from its interchangeably titled predecessors – *The Man They Could Not Hang*, *The Man with Nine Lives* and *Before I Hang* – not only in having a more distinctive title but also in being based on a recent work of fiction. This was an excellent 1939 novel called *The Edge of Running Water*, one of only two books written by Massachusetts novelist William Sloane. In another deviation from formula, the direction was entrusted, not to Nick Grindé, but to 32-year-old Edward Dmytryk, who was later to make such masterful thrillers as *Murder, My Sweet* and *Crossfire*.

Conducting research into brainwaves, Dr Julian Blair is traumatised by the death of his wife Helen in a car crash, subsequently holing up in the New England town of Barsham Harbor and dedicating his life to communicating with the dead by scientific means. He falls in, however, with phoney medium Mrs Walters, who assumes dominance over him when the handyman is reduced to a simpleton in one laboratory accident and, in another, the housekeeper is killed outright.

In a narrative trick that was soon to characterise film noir, *The Devil Commands* begins with a mordant female voice-over, in which Dr Blair's daughter sets the film's doom-laden tone by informing us that "For one brief moment, he [Blair] tore open the door to whatever lives beyond the grave." The film proper begins with another of those scientific demonstrations that, for Karloff, dated back to *The Invisible Ray* and the British production *The Man Who Changed His Mind*. Using his wife as a guinea pig, Dr Blair notes that "The wave impulse of woman, the so-called weaker sex, is much stronger and is much more regular than man's." Defying expectations, Mrs Blair doesn't die in the experiment, instead perishing in her car later that evening while Blair collects a birthday cake for their 20-year-old daughter. Though sketched only briefly, the scenes between Karloff and Shirley Warde are sufficiently warm and affectionate to make Blair's subsequent lapse from bereavement into derangement genuinely moving.

With Blair determining "to establish a controlled and scientific communication between the living and the so-called dead," the film's distinguishing feature becomes its adroit blend (lifted in large part from Sloane's original) of science and the supernatural,

Boris Karloff with experimental subjects Anne Revere and Ralph Penney in *The Devil Commands* (1940)

over-inquisitive housekeeper ventures into the laboratory at night. After the local sheriff's talk of several bodies having disappeared from the cemetery, it comes as no surprise to find the lab tenanted by five black-shrouded shapes. (Intriguingly, five was also the number of scientists who responded so enthusiastically to Blair's brainwave demonstration and so discouragingly to his metaphysical extension of it.) A glimpse of one of the parchment faces concealed beneath the shrouds sends the housekeeper blundering into the machinery, upon which an electrical vortex and preternatural wind cause the shrouds to be whipped off en masse and the corpses beneath to start gently nodding at one another.

This set-piece is much enhanced by plenty of inky chiaroscuro from cinematographer Allen Siegler. But the climactic seance is stranger still, with the corpses (kitted out, incidentally, like pulp-magazine astronauts) joggling uncontrollably in the teeth of the otherworldly wind and Blair himself ripped from his moorings, as a concluding voice-over suggests, by some mightily offended higher power. Unfortunately, despite Sloane's wildly imaginative premise and the film's equally bizarre realisation of Blair's experiments, the action trips itself up within sight of the finishing line. With just minutes to go, the script resorts to a straight-from-stock mob of angry villagers and a frankly muffed laboratory explosion by which Blair is finally reunited with his wife.

With the barely submerged soulfulness so characteristic of him, Karloff is the ideal interpreter for the bereaved Dr Blair, carefully pointing up the character's tragic self-delusion with lines like "This is science, Mrs Walters; there's nothing of the occult about it." Mrs Walters, in fact, is the only other character of substance, despite the fact that, by 1940, the phoney spiritualist was no less stereotypical than the angry mob. Anne Revere redeems the role, however, with an unflinchingly self-absorbed, coldly erotic performance that almost eclipses Karloff's.

In her role as strangely helmeted 'medium' in Blair's experiments, Mrs Walters provides an exact pre-echo of the poltergeist-ridden Barbara Judd in

THE DEVIL COMMANDS

Columbia 1940
65 minutes
production began 22 November

Cinematographer: Allen G Siegler; Art Director: Lionel Banks; Editor: Al Clark; Sound: P J Faulkner Jr*; Music: Frank Skinner*, Mischa Bakaleinikoff*; Musical Director: M W Stoloff; Assistant Director: George Rhein*; Screenplay: Robert D Andrews, Milton Gunzburg; Story [novel, *The Edge of Running Water*]: William Sloane; Producer: Wallace MacDonald*; Director: Edward Dmytryk

Boris Karloff (Dr Julian Blair); Richard Fiske (Dr Richard Sayles); Amanda Duff (Anne Blair); Anne Revere (Mrs Walters); Ralph Penney (Karl); Dorothy Adams (Mrs Marcy); Walter Baldwin (Seth Marcy); Kenneth MacDonald (Sheriff Willis); Shirley Warde (Helen Blair); uncredited: Ernie Adams (Elam); Lester Allen (Dr Van Den); Wheaton Chambers (Dr Sanders); Earl Crawford (Johnson); Harrison Greene (Mr Booth [baker]); Erwin Kalser (Professor Kent); Eddie Kane (Dr Hart); George McKay (station agent); Al Rhein (truck driver); John Tyrrell (postmaster); Jacques Vanaire (Dr Hartley)

Another grim study in the macabre by Boris Karloff ... The tale is wholly incredible, of course ... But, on the other hand, the incidental drama is sufficiently powerful ... to terrify all but the most blasé onlooker.
To-Day's Cinema [UK]

I remember meeting director Edward Dmytryk, a very nice man. He actually wanted someone more 'exotic' looking for *The Devil Commands* ... I actually did not enjoy making these kinds of movies and felt quite foolish doing some of them. Amanda Duff [quoted in *Classic Images*, April 1998]

a blend that was to reach fruition in later works like *Quatermass and the Pit* and *Ringu 2*. The blend, a borderline-blasphemous one by 1940s standards, includes an encephalographic version of automatic writing, through which Blair first becomes convinced his wife is not truly dead, and, at the climax, a memorably eerie techno-seance.

Our first glimpse of Blair's infernal machinery is contained in a queasy sequence in which his

Quatermass and the Pit. On top of this, she's a smooth and entirely remorseless operator, offering a modified bit of Edgar Allan Poe when she tells Blair that "Other men of science have turned to the occult for surcease from sorrow," then coolly citing such credulous dignitaries as Sir Oliver Lodge and Sir Arthur Conan Doyle to support her case. No sooner has Blair inadvertently reduced his handyman to a cretin than she gains total sway over him, modelling mandarin-collared gowns and chic little turbans, sashaying down shadowed stairways like Maine's answer to Lady Macbeth and only expiring when the electrical vortex becomes too much for her.

Straight after completing *The Devil Commands*, Karloff went across to New York to start work on Joseph Kesselring's black comedy *Arsenic and Old Lace*, which opened at the Fulton Theatre on Friday 10 January 1941 and proved a smash hit. Indeed, Karloff suspended all film activities in order to stay with the show, which he did until the last week of June 1942; after that he embarked on a 66-week national tour. Warner Bros, meanwhile, had engaged Frank Capra to concoct a film version, though stage producers Howard Lindsay and Russel Crouse insisted on keeping Karloff in the Broadway production. As a replacement, Capra hit upon Raymond Massey, who had co-starred with Karloff nine years previously in *The Old Dark House*.

Where the older film anatomised the British at home with a witheringly mordant wit, the new one would do the same for a similarly cracked US family with the skittish facility of screwball comedy. Dubbed "a Hallowe'en tale of Brooklyn," the film was built around Cary Grant (despite the fact that Capra himself would have preferred Bob Hope) and went into production on 20 October 1941. Having wrapped shortly before Christmas, it then came up against another Lindsay-Crouse stipulation designed to protect the Broadway show – it was withheld from release until September 1944, making the hurry to produce the picture, and the resultant loss of Karloff, seem completely pointless.

Massey, however, is a smouldering-eyed treat as the psychotic, and surgically altered, Jonathan Brewster, who memorialises one of his victims with the same in-joke line that brought the house down when uttered by the man himself on Broadway: "He said I looked like Boris Karloff!" His twittery maiden aunts turn out to be serial killers themselves, serving up a cocktail of arsenic, strychnine and cyanide in their home-made elderberry wine and depositing the bodies in the cellar. The film plays like a modified French farce, with concealed mistresses replaced by revolving corpses, and Grant is a hoot as Jonathan's drama critic brother, adopting an anthropoid stance almost throughout in order to express his comic horror over the old ladies' behaviour. Though overlong and ultimately over-involved, the film offers a last-minute bonus in the form of Edward Everett Horton, whose asylum superintendent fusses in trademark Horton style over the fact that "We're a bit short of Napoleons at present."

THE WORKER OF THE FUTURE

With Boris Karloff preparing to conquer Broadway, at the end of 1940 Bela Lugosi might reasonably have anticipated an uncontested run as Hollywood's top horror man. He was to be disappointed, however, for, with impeccable timing, Universal started production on a picture called *The Mysterious Doctor R* in the second week of December. On release, the film would be retitled *Man Made Monster*, shifting the focus away from Lionel Atwill's demented Dr Rigas and directing it instead onto a young actor whom Universal had hopes of grooming into a new Karloff.

This was the 34-year-old Creighton Chaney, who had long since bowed to the inevitable and adopted the name Lon Chaney Jr. After years of unrewarding slog in the lower reaches of the film industry, in August 1939 Chaney played the simple-minded itinerant Lennie in Lewis Milestone's film of the John

Scar-faced Raymond Massey and disgraced plastic surgeon Peter Lorre in *Arsenic and Old Lace* (1941)

MAN MADE MONSTER

Universal 1940
59 minutes
production began 9 December
UK title: The Electric Man

Cinematographer: Elwood Bredell; Art Directors: Jack Otterson, Harold H MacArthur; Editor: Arthur Hilton; Sound: Bernard B Brown, Charles Carroll; Set Decorations: R A Gausman; Make-up: Jack P Pierce*; Gowns: Vera West; Musical Director: H J Salter; Screenplay: Joseph West [George Waggner] (based on the story *The Electric Man* by Harry J Essex, Sid Schwartz, Len Golos); Associate Producer: Jack Bernhard; Director: George Waggner

Lionel Atwill (Dr Rigas); Lon Chaney Jr (Dan McCormick); Anne Nagel (June Lawrence); Frank Albertson (Mark Adams); Samuel S Hinds (Dr Lawrence); William Davidson (District Attorney); Ben Taggart (Detective Sergeant); Connie Bergen (nurse); Ivan Miller (doctor); Chester Gan (Chinese boy [Wong]); George Meader (Doctor Bruno); Frank O'Connor (detective); John Dilson (medical examiner); Byron Foulger (2nd alienist); Russell Hicks (warden); uncredited: Jessie Arnold (Mrs Davis); James Blaine (Charlie); Gary Breckner (radio announcer); Lowell Drew (jury foreman); John Ellis (Assistant DA); Douglas Evans (police radio announcer); Jack Gardner (reporter); William Hall (Mike); Wright Kramer (judge); Bob Reeves (guard); Mel Ruick (defense attorney); Francis Sayles (Frank Davis); Paul Scott (minister); Victor Zimmerman (dynamo operator)

Man Made Monster is a shocker that's in the groove for the horror fans. It makes no pretense of being anything but a freakish chiller, going directly to the point and proving mighty successful. *Variety*

After witnessing the torture my father endured in his various make-ups, I was more than ready to heed his advice about not doing that type of work. And yet, I suppose the fact that I'm here proves that some people just can't escape their destiny. *Lon Chaney Jr [quoted in original pressbook]*

Appropriately insulated, Lon Chaney Jr takes on a distinguished family mantle in *Man Made Monster* (1940)

Steinbeck novel *Of Mice and Men*. The film premiered in New York on Christmas Eve, increasing Chaney's prestige significantly. The previous month Chaney Jr had made another Hal Roach production, *One Million BC*, a fanciful tale of prehistoric times derived from a D W Griffith treatment called *When Man Began*. As Akhoba, cyclopean leader of the Rock People, Chaney managed not to be upstaged by the film's saurian parade of optically enlarged reptiles. Universal's decision to secure Chaney Jr's services may have been prompted by the fact that Lennie's uncomprehending murder of a flirty young woman smacked of *Frankenstein*, or because Akhoba was reminiscent of Chaney Sr's more brutish characterisations. Chiefly, however, it was motivated by his irresistible name.

Man Made Monster itself had a convoluted history, having originated as a 1935 treatment called *The Electric Man* (a title it would retain when eventually released in the UK). The treatment had been earmarked for production as a Karloff-Lugosi vehicle but came to nothing. Five years on, it was converted into a lean and efficient screenplay by George Waggner, a sometime silent screen actor and songwriter who had turned to directing in 1938. Putting the film together on a straitened budget of $86,000, Waggner ensured himself a crucial place in the conveyor-belt scheme of Universal's 1940s horror shows.

Five people are electrocuted when a bus ploughs into an electrical pylon. The only survivor, Dan McCormick, is taken in by the benevolent Dr Lawrence but experimented on by Lawrence's unhinged associate Dr Rigas. Driven to create a super-race, Rigas turns Dan into an electrified killing machine. Convicted for the murder of Dr Lawrence, Dan receives a massively invigorating jolt from the electric chair and heads off for a vengeful rendezvous with Rigas...

The film begins with an impressive piece of model work that recalls the car-crash opening of *The Raven*, a picture contemporaneous with *Man Made Monster*'s original treatment. (The films also have kindly character actor Samuel S Hinds in common.) Laid up in hospital, Dan happily recounts his sideshow days as 'Dynamo Dan the Electrical Man', Chaney Jr immediately establishing him as a big-hearted, likeable lunk. Transferred to Dr Lawrence's estate, he strikes up an instant rapport with Corky the dog, whose faithful monitoring of Dan's downward slide suggests that Waggner may have been given a sneak preview of Paramount's *The Monster and the Girl*.

In Lawrence's laboratory, the action conforms to the usual generic pattern, with Lawrence telling his

wild-eyed confederate Dr Rigas that "This theory of yours isn't science, it's black magic." Refreshingly, Rigas happily admits to being mad, as well as coming out with the well-worn justification that anaesthesia was considered a lunatic aspiration until relatively recently. Though recycling *The Invisible Man Returns* over the opening credits, Hans Salter's music is for the most part original and takes an effectively giddy turn for our introduction to Rigas. This and the other lab sequences carry none of the baroque flamboyance of Universal's Frankenstein pictures but they still crackle with an eye-catching fusillade of electrical pulses. And Dan's supercharged spells as a lethal human light-bulb benefit from the happy fusion of Jack Pierce's shrivelled make-up design and John P Fulton's effects, which inevitably recall his similar work on *The Invisible Ray*.

For all its borrowings, *Man Made Monster* would exercise an influence of its own. Rigas' position as scheming lieutenant to a high-minded scientist would be duplicated in *The Ghost of Frankenstein* (with Lionel Atwill again, the better to point up the similarity), while his plans for a whole race of electrified drones were to be echoed in George Zucco's plans for an army of werewolves in *The Mad Monster*. In the meantime, the material is lent a shadowy lustre by cinematographer Elwood Bredell and builds to a fine set-piece in which a bunch of farm workers fling themselves from a burning haywain after an encounter with the pulsating Dan. The only disappointment is the complete avoidance of the potentially show-stopping scene in which Dan breaks free of the electric chair; thanks to the censor, British audiences were denied even what little Universal deigned to include.

Lionel Atwill is ideally cast as Rigas, giving the role his gimlet-eyed all. Much of Rigas' dialogue, though fruity, is standard-issue mad scientist stuff, but Atwill is careful to introduce the kinky undertone that was uniquely his when cornering Anne Nagel in the final reel. All exposed teeth and eerie under-lighting, he explains crooningly that "I've always found that the female of the species was more sensitive to electrical impulses than was the male," moments later succumbing to Dan's lethal touch through the medium of a door-knob. Rigas is also made intriguing by the explicitly Nietzschean nature of his aspirations, which by the end of 1940 were readily recognisable as Nazi. Explaining his plans for "a race of superior men," he tells Lawrence that "half the people in the world are doomed to a life of mediocrity, born to be non-entities, millstones around the neck of progress." When his work reaches fruition, he gives a Wagnerian ring to the claim that "I have conquered Destiny!" and extols the rubber-suited Dan as "the worker of the future, controlled by a superior intelligence."

Interestingly, for all his fresh-faced straightforwardness, Dan comes out with similarly high-handed sentiments when reminiscing about his sideshow act. The stunts he performed were mostly phoney – "yokel-shockers," as he puts it, designed "to fool the peasants." Unfortunately, as the Universal production line ground on through the 1940s (with Chaney Jr as its frequently ill-suited star attraction), the suspicion that the studio's attitude to its horror pictures was identical to Dan's opinion of his "yokel-shockers" would become irresistible.

When *Man Made Monster* went into release on 28 March 1941, it was supported by another George Waggner picture; remarkably, *Horror Island* had started production a mere 25 days earlier. Reuniting Dick Foran and Peggy Moran from *The Mummy's Hand*, the result is a simple-minded but painless reiteration of spooky-house clichés, this time revolving around a tourist-trap 'haunted' castle off the Florida coast. The lost treasure turns out to be just as illusory as the ghosts, the gaunt Foy Van Dolsen cuts a striking figure as the so-called Phantom, and Elwood Bredell's photography is consistently diverting. In addition, the script contains nuggets of hoary doggerel ("When at length you find the chair / Place a dead man's body there") that anticipate Waggner's *The Wolf Man*.

Finishing production just as *Horror Island* began was a picture that brought Bela Lugosi back to Universal in the wake of PRC's *The Devil Bat*. This was Albert S Rogell's *The Black Cat*, a film that bears no relation to the studio's 1934 version and not much more to the original Poe story. Cast in the thankless role of a skulking gardener, Lugosi is required merely to be shot to death by the Edwardian beauty Gladys Cooper, who here plays the surprise killer in yet another 'who will get the inheritance?' scenario.

Just as *Horror Island* was obviously influenced by Paramount's *The Ghost Breakers*, so *The Black Cat* was a blatant attempt at stealing the horror-comedy thunder of the same studio's *The Cat and the Canary*; even the invaluable Gale Sondergaard, in a terrific showcase role and with "a puss like a lemon rinse," is on hand to play the housekeeper. Unfortunately, Universal's answer to Bob Hope was the excruciatingly awful Hugh Herbert. This leaves only a good-value cast headed by Basil Rathbone, and a 'stuff Anne Gwynne in the crematory' climax seemingly lifted from *A Shriek in the Night*, to keep the interest alive. Cooper, too, shows herself a world-class screamer, especially when engulfed in John Fulton's special effects flames at the end.

Straight after *The Black Cat*, Lugosi started work on his first picture for Sam Katzman's Banner Pictures Corporation, which would eventually supply the lowly Monogram with no fewer than nine Lugosi vehicles. *Invisible Ghost* began shooting on 20 March 1941, with Lugosi as kindly widower Charles Kessler, who is unaware that his errant wife (Betty Compson) is actually living in a brain-damaged state on his grounds. Her phantom appearances outside Kessler's window trigger homicidal fugues in which he murders a housemaid, a gardener and a hovering detective.

Director Joseph H Lewis, later to acquire cult status with films like *My Name is Julia Ross* and *Gun Crazy*, brings unwonted style to the proceedings, particularly when the butler (Clarence Muse) discovers the housemaid sprawled over her bed, an inane exercise class still droning on the radio. Betty Compson, too, is rivetingly strange as the wraith-like Mrs Kessler, and it's good to see Lugosi in so avuncular a role, uttering lines like "Apple pie? My, that *will* be a treat!" without a trace of his trademark portentousness. But the Helen and Al Martin script is a joke, the cobbled-together score an absurdity and the film as a whole a grim indication of the kind of thing that was to be Lugosi's lot while Universal concentrated on boosting Lon Chaney Jr. The judgment of *Variety*'s 'Hobe' was especially damning: "Except for Bela Lugosi's name for the marquee, this would-be chiller adds up to approximately zero. It's undoubtedly one of the feeblest pictures of the season."

Lugosi's second Monogram assignment followed in June and was even less auspicious. Though revealed as a mere magician, Lugosi is required to go through most of his Dracula paces in Phil Rosen's *Spooks Run Wild*, a dreary farce starring the East Side Kids, a repulsive bunch of 'comic' delinquents otherwise known as the Bowery Boys and the Dead End Kids. A rematch in February 1943 for William Beaudine's *Ghosts on the Loose* was even worse, though both films had a soon-to-be-illustrious name tucked away among the credits – screenwriter Carl Foreman on *Spooks Run Wild*, starlet Ava Gardner in *Ghosts on the Loose*. William Beaudine, by contrast, was a formerly illustrious name, his career having devolved from directing Mary Pickford in *Sparrows* to making Will Hay comedies in England and thence to a long sojourn on Hollywood's Poverty Row.

While the East Side Kids were running rings round Lugosi in *Spooks Run Wild*, Universal's latest money-spinning comedy stars, Bud Abbott and Lou Costello, were showing how spooky-house farces should be done in Arthur Lubin's *Hold That Ghost*. In this 'the ghosts are really gangsters' scenario, Bud and Lou inherit a tumble-down tavern that, according to the

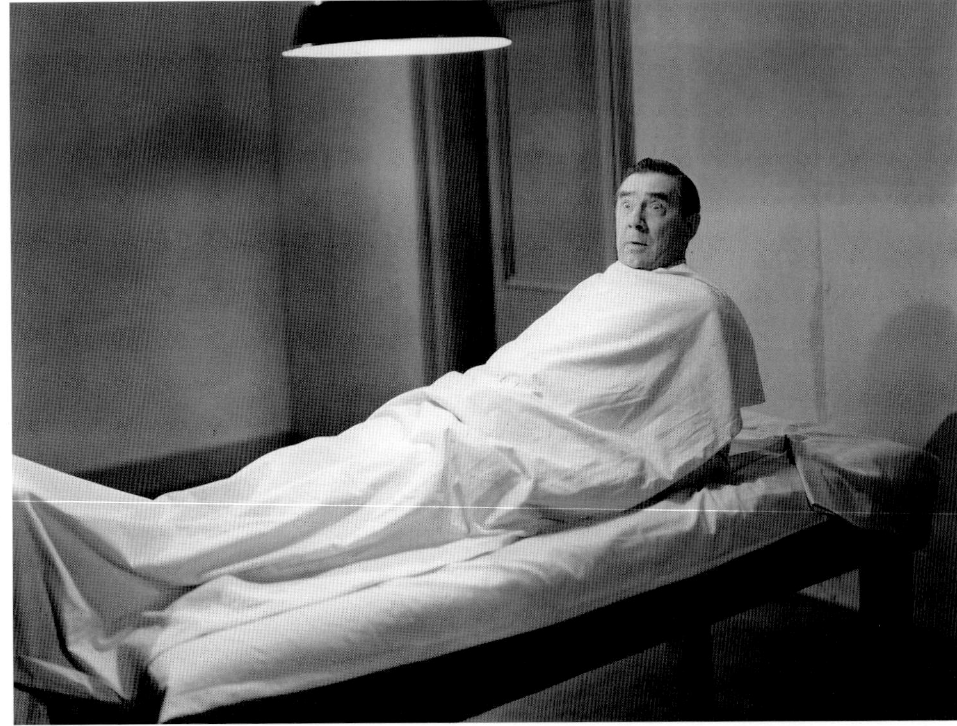

Consigned to the Monogram mortuary: Bela Lugosi plays to the camera on the set of *Invisible Ghost* (1941)

zany radio actress (Joan Davis) accompanying them, "looks like the setting for *The Death of a Howling Corpse*." Also along for the ride are Richard Carlson (imported direct from *The Ghost Breakers*) and the Chilean-born English actress Evelyn Ankers, who was to become omnipresent in Universal horror shows over the next few years. Even to those for whom a little Abbott and Costello goes a long way, the film is infectiously silly and contains such delightfully bad jokes as Lou's riposte to Bud's claim that a murdered gangster "had a gag in his mouth." "If he did," replies Lou, "he never had a chance to tell it."

HIGH GLOSS, LOW RENT

On 21 April 1941, while *The Monster and the Girl* was facing up to a censorship firestorm, its director, Stuart Heisler, began shooting *Among the Living* at Paramount. In this, Albert Dekker is John Raden, prodigal son of a deceased Southern capitalist, who gets a shock on returning to the town that bears his name – his twin brother Paul, presumed dead aged ten, is secretly in residence at the derelict family home.

Among the Living reveals itself as an unusually classy item from the word go, allowing a glamorously sunlit funeral to segue into a bone-shaking nocturnal thunderstorm, then revealing the straitjacketed Paul in a rocking chair as lightning flashes vividly through a skylight. Theodor Sparkuhl's moody lighting makes a small masterpiece of John's queasy tour of the old (and reputedly haunted) house, ending on a startling close-up of Paul's faithful servant, his mouth frozen open in death. Shrinking from the remembered screams of his brutalised mother, the child-like maniac is carefully underplayed by Dekker, who proves creepily effective even when passing a knife-grinder in the street and briefly handling a cleaver. And Heisler isn't above throwing in a smart in-joke, with Paul stopping in front of a cinema advertising Heisler's 'boy and his dog' film *The Biscuit Eater* as a legless man bowls by on a customised trolley, saying "Wanna buy a puppy, mister?"

Next door to the cinema is the River Bottom Café, where Paul encounters a peroxide glamour-girl (Jean Phillips) and, in a brilliantly edited tour de force, is driven to distraction by the wildly jitterbugging patrons. His subsequent pursuit of the girl through night-time alleyways is cut to an insanely energised tempo, and the film builds to a remarkable crescendo when the promise of a $5000 reward causes the blue-collar locals to go berserk. Predictably, John, not Paul, is mistakenly arraigned in front of a bloodthirsty kangaroo court, but not before the bedroom of the boys' late mother has been smashed to bits in the melee.

Town tease Susan Hayward shrinks from childlike maniac Albert Dekker in *Among the Living* (1941)

The film carries echoes of *M*, *Frankenstein* (Garrett Fort co-wrote the screenplay) and *Of Mice and Men*, benefiting, too, from a very sexy performance by Susan Hayward as an opportunistic local girl determined to "knock this neighbourhood cock-eyed." And, sensibly, the 'two Albert Dekkers in the same frame' scenes are kept to a minimum. Five years later, Robert Siodmak's somewhat similar *The Dark Mirror* benefited from state-of-the-art optical work in its 'two Olivia de Havillands for the price of one' highlights, but in other respects proved much less effective.

When Heisler began work on *Among the Living*, M-G-M had just completed a glamorous remake of *Dr Jekyll and Mr Hyde*, in which the opposing forces of John and Paul Raden were fused in the prestigious figure of Spencer Tracy. The project had originally been mooted for Robert Donat, the fey British star of M-G-M's *Goodbye, Mr Chips*. Transferred to the conspicuously American Tracy, the film was budgeted at over $1 million and entrusted to Victor Fleming, whose most recent credits were *The Wizard of Oz* and *Gone with the Wind*. The script was by John Lee Mahin, with no acknowledgment given to the writers of Paramount's 1931 version, which Mahin's parroted with scrupulous fidelity.

Disturbed by a vulgar outburst in church from a formerly law-abiding citizen, Dr Harry Jekyll determines to find a means of suppressing the man's evil instincts. But the man dies insane before the formula is perfected, so Jekyll tries it on himself. His own evil instincts become manifest as Mr Hyde, a sexual sadist who murders barmaid Ivy Peterson and Jekyll's prospective father-in-law Sir Charles Emery, eventually being shot down by Jekyll's friend Dr Lanyon.

Ingrid Bergman shows Spencer Tracy her whiplashes in *Dr Jekyll and Mr Hyde* (1941)

DR. JEKYLL AND MR. HYDE

M-G-M 1941
113 minutes
production began 4 February

Cinematographer: Joseph Ruttenberg; Art Directors: Cedric Gibbons, Daniel B Cathcart*; Editor: Harold F Kress; Sound: Douglas Shearer; Special Effects: Warren Newcombe; Montage Effects: Peter Ballbusch; Make-up: Jack Dawn; Gowns: Adrian; Men's Wardrobe: Gile Steele; Dance Direction: Ernst Matray; Music: Franz Waxman, Daniele Amfitheatrof*, Mario Castelnuovo-Tedesco*; Screenplay: John Lee Mahin (based on the novel by Robert Louis Stevenson); Producers: Victor Fleming*, Victor Saville*; Director: Victor Fleming

Spencer Tracy (Dr Harry Jekyll/Mr Hyde); Ingrid Bergman (Ivy Peterson); Lana Turner (Beatrix Emery); Donald Crisp (Sir Charles Emery); Ian Hunter (Dr John Lanyon); Barton MacLane (Sam Higgins); C Aubrey Smith (the Bishop); Peter Godfrey (Poole); Sara Allgood (Mrs Higgins); Frederick Worlock (Dr Heath); William Tannen (interne Fenwick); Frances Robinson (Marcia); Dennis Green (Freddie); Billy Bevan (Mr Weller); Forrester Harvey (Old Prouty); Lumsden Hare (Colonel Weymouth); Lawrence Grant (Dr Courtland); John Barclay (constable); uncredited: Jimmy Aubrey (hanger-on); Vangie Beilby (spinster); Lydia Bilbrook (Lady Copewell); Hillary Brooke (Mrs Arnold); Alec Craig (waiter); Al Ferguson (constable); Douglas Gordon (cockney); Winifred Harris (Mrs Weymouth); Brandon Hurst (Briggs); Olaf Hytten (Hobson); Claude King (Uncle Geoffrey); Doris Lloyd (Mrs Marley); Gwendolyn Logan (Mrs Courtland); Aubrey Mather (inspector); Alice Mock (soloist in 'See Me Dance the Polka'); Lionel Pape (Mr Marley); Milton Parsons (choirmaster); Yorke Sherwood (chairman); Pat Moriarty, Cyril McLaglen (drunks)

Dr Jekyll and Mr Hyde is a master screen work and a first-calibre dramatic hit. Magnificent are the performances of both Spencer Tracy and Ingrid Bergman, the thoughtful direction of Fleming, and the artful screenplay writing of John Lee Mahin. *Hollywood Reporter*

That scene where he [Victor Fleming] wanted a frightened distraught hysterical girl, faced by the terrifying Mr Hyde – I just couldn't do it. So eventually he took me by the shoulder with one hand, spun me around and struck me backwards and forwards across the face … But he'd got the performance he wanted. By the time the film was over I was deeply in love with Victor Fleming.
Ingrid Bergman [My Story, 1980]

That the full might of M-G-M was brought to bear on this new Jekyll and Hyde is immediately apparent from the gorgeous, pin-sharp cinematography of Joseph Ruttenberg. As well as favouring Tracy's female co-stars, Ingrid Bergman and Lana Turner, with breathtaking close-ups, Ruttenberg makes a small, gaslit masterpiece out of a nocturnal sequence in which Jekyll reverts to Hyde without recourse to his formula. The settings, too, are world-class, though several of them – notably Jekyll's laboratory and the flat in which Hyde accommodates Ivy – are patterned extremely closely on the equivalent designs in Rouben Mamoulian's version. To offset any invidious comparisons (and to ensure the new version an unimpeded crack at the nation's box-offices), M-G-M bought up all copies of the older film, even its negative, and buried them in their vaults, where they would remain until 1967.

The new film strikes out on its own, however, in an opening that dissolves from heavenly voices warbling "The Lord is My Shepherd" to the lofty spire of a cathedral. And it becomes clear at once that the big-studio gloss is to go hand in hand with a major dollop of big-studio pomposity. C Aubrey Smith's symbolically named Bishop Manners looms from the pulpit while speaking utter balderdash about the "way of life as exemplified by Victoria, our belovéd Queen" and "the ever-increasing flow of virtue and moral blessing" instigated by her. He also places the action in 1887, the year of Victoria's Golden Jubilee. This is a handy period in which to locate a critique of Victorianism, but the critique never develops. The man who disrupts the service – sniggering lewdly about "what a real man really thinks about" – is firmly identified as a nutcase, having been involved in a gas explosion that addled his brain. And the new Jekyll, sullenly played by Tracy, isn't nearly articulate enough to qualify as the social rebel featured in Mamoulian's version.

That the film should end up endorsing the Victorianism it nominally critiques is in part a result of the Victorian strictures of the Production Code. Now a barmaid rather than a prostitute, Ivy is demurely

dressed at her place of work (even her throat and wrists are firmly buttoned up) and is murdered in a morning room rather than in her boudoir, which we never see. Similarly, Jekyll's fiancée Beatrix reads a newspaper account of "deplorable housing conditions" in the East End, but not a hint of low-life grime is permitted to soil the preternatural gleam of Metro's production design; even the Palace of Frivolities, where Ivy works, is airbrushed to within an inch of its life. The problem is exacerbated by Donald Crisp's extremely low-voltage performance as Sir Charles. The intention was presumably to 'humanise' the Establishment blimp played by Halliwell Hobbes in 1931, but the result robs Tracy of an effective antagonist and is merely boring. As a forlorn footnote, Brandon Hurst (who in 1919 had brought real style to the equivalent role) is here reduced to a brief bit as Lanyon's butler.

In an attempt to subvert the film's tightly corseted good manners, Peter Ballbusch was engaged to create a couple of dream montages trading on Hollywood's modish interest in Sigmund Freud. In the first, Ivy and Beatrix are seen as fashion-plate steeds whipped onward by a frenzied Jekyll, with Ivy finally swallowed up in quicksand – presumably the primeval sludge of Jekyll's dirty mind. In the second (which corresponds to Mamoulian's 'bubbling pot' imagery), Bea is seen trapped in a bottle, with Ivy as the cork being methodically unscrewed by Jekyll's hand. When the cork is released, a volcanic eruption bursts out and the laughing Ivy is drenched in the flow. The splicey nature of these sequences makes it clear that they were originally even filthier, though the ejaculation imagery is so blatant as to appear childish.

Back in 1931, cinematographer Karl Struss had expressed reservations about the chimp-like make-up applied to Paramount's Mr Hyde; happily, Tracy's lighter make-up is more in line with what Struss had in mind. A widow's peak, a Roman nose, a toothy grin and reptilian scales under his eyes are all that differentiate Hyde from his upstanding alter ego, and Tracy's performance acquires a truly frightening edge of sociopathic mania. The gangsterish, shark-toothed swagger of James Cagney is occasionally detectable, particularly when Hyde flings a bunch of grapes in Ivy's face, echoing Cagney's similar utilisation of a grapefruit in *The Public Enemy*. Unfortunately, Tracy's rubber-masked stunt double, Gil Perkins, is laughably obvious in several scenes; he's evident, not merely when Hyde has to leap, but even when he has to run – an extreme case of Metro star-pampering.

Three years later, Ingrid Bergman's touching luminosity as Ivy was carried over into another M-G-M remake, this time of the British film *Gaslight*. Here, Charles Boyer plays the kind of role then associated with Basil Rathbone, a murderous husband bent on driving his fragile wife insane. (The part in Patrick Hamilton's original play had been taken on Broadway by the young Vincent Price.) For all the suspenseful grip of George Cukor's film (and the Oscar glory it conferred on Bergman), it cannot compete with the simpler, starker British original from 1940, though we're lucky even to have the opportunity to compare the two. As well as entombing Mamoulian's *Dr Jekyll and Mr Hyde* for nearly 30 years, Metro were only just prevented from destroying all existing prints of the original *Gaslight*. In the same way, Mervyn LeRoy's 1940 version of the Robert E Sherwood play *Waterloo Bridge* ensured the almost total extinction of James Whale's 1931 original.

A film as glossy, worthy and dull as M-G-M's *Dr Jekyll and Mr Hyde* was bound to garner an Oscar nod or two, and nominations duly went to Joseph Ruttenberg, editor Harold Kress and composer Franz Waxman. Another film graced with an Oscar nomination for its musical score came from the unlikeliest source imaginable – the decidedly low-rent Monogram Pictures Corporation. The film, too, was a wildly incongruous one to find in the Academy sweepstakes. After *The Devil Bat*, *King of the Zombies* was Jean Yarbrough's second attempt at horror, though, given that *The Ghost Breakers* was the film's obvious inspiration, it's as much a comedy as a horror film. It retains a certain historical significance, however, as the first wartime shocker to deal directly with the war. Though never explicitly stated, Dr Mikhail Sangre – "late of Vienna," spy master and zombie master combined – is the first of several Nazis to feature in Hollywood's horror output.

En route for the Bahamas, 'Mac' McCarthy's plane crash-lands on an isolated island, whereupon Mac, his friend Bill and Bill's valet Jefferson Jackson take refuge in the gloomy home of Dr Sangre. Not only is Sangre's retinue made up of zombies, he also turns out to be an enemy agent working with a voodoo priestess to wrest Canal Zone secrets from a kidnapped Admiral. Temporarily turned into a zombie, Mac kills Sangre during the 'Rite of Transmigration'.

Despite the Oscar nod, Edward Kay's unremarkable score – composed for the most part of thunderous voodoo drums – only acquires real distinction in one scene, which also happens to be the film's most visually striking. Some pleasantly scrapey strings and harps are overlaid onto the spectacle of the catatonic, white-draped Mme Sangre emerging from

Mantan Moreland and John Archer explore the catacombs by torchlight in *King of the Zombies* (1941)

KING OF THE ZOMBIES

Monogram 1941
69 minutes
production began 31 March

Cinematographer: Mack Stengler; Art Director: Charles Clague; Settings: Dave Milton; Editor: Richard Currier; Sound: William Fox, Glen Rominger; Musical Score and Direction: Edward Kay; Production Manager: Mack Wright; Screenplay: Edmond Kelso; Producer: Lindsley Parsons; Director: Jean Yarbrough

Dick Purcell (James McCarthy); Joan Woodbury (Barbara Winslow); Mantan Moreland (Jeff); Henry Victor (Dr Sangre); John Archer (Bill Summers); Patricia Stacey (Alyce Sangre); Guy Usher (Admiral Wainwright); Marguerite Whitten (Samantha); Leigh Whipper (Momba); Madame Sul-te-Wan (Tahama); Jimmy Davis (Lazarus); Lawrence Criner (Dr Couillie)

Except for those who enjoy an eerie and gruesome film, this is a most unpleasant one of its type, full of voodooism, black magic, graveyards, and walking dead. The best performances come from Manton [sic] Moreland as the scared Jefferson and Marguerite Whitten as a coloured maidservant, who play up to one another well. *Monthly Film Bulletin* [UK]

I enjoyed Monogram. They were fast B pictures, but the people were all good ... I liked having Mantan Moreland to work with – he was a funny guy who just cracked me up. John Archer [quoted in *Starlog*, May 1994]

an apparently solid bedroom wall. Mack Stengler's lighting casts striped beams of moonlight across the rear wall, making the scene play like a cash-strapped precursor of similar moments in RKO's *I Walked with a Zombie* and *Isle of the Dead*.

In other scenes, too, Stengler's cinematography shows far more care and attention than Poverty Row pictures could normally muster. The subterranean kitchen of Sangre's home is surmounted by a lattice-work of shadows, and when Bill and Jeff advance into the catacombs, desiccated mummies are teasingly glimpsed in Bill's flashlight beam before Mme Sangre comes into view; no longer merely death-like, she's now genuinely dead.

The film's plot takes *The Most Dangerous Game* as its springboard. Rather than ensnaring ships with rearranged buoys, Sangre diverts aeroplanes with phoney radio signals, and, in locating Sangre's island somewhere between Puerto Rico and Cuba, screenwriter Edmond Kelso seems to have anticipated the latterday Bermuda Triangle scare. In a role originally intended for Bela Lugosi or Peter Lorre, Henry Victor gives Sangre a robotic delivery that occasionally seems like an actor groping for his lines but is still strangely effective. The zombies in his charge are a monolithic and largely unscary bunch, though there's a curious foretaste of the cannibalistic undead of later decades when the sexy below-stairs kitchen maid (Marguerite Whitten) jocularly observes that "It's feedin' time, and they likes dark meat!" (As a result, when faced with two of them, the quailing Jeff blurts out, "Don't come close to me – I ain't no filet

mignon.") Sangre's climactic voodoo ritual is enjoyably absurd too, with the befeathered voodoo priestess (Madame Sul-Te-Wan) jigging insanely and Sangre himself being backed into a convenient fiery pit.

The nominal leads, Dick Purcell and John Archer, are little better than functional; the nominal heroine, Joan Woodbury, is pretty and sports a convincing German accent. The film belongs, however, to Mantan Moreland, whose name is listed below Purcell and Woodbury on the title card but is printed slightly larger – as if Monogram were unwilling to bill a black actor first but were prepared to acknowledge his importance in a different way.

As in the majority of his film roles, Moreland here plays the traditional frightened flunkey, but with the crucial difference that, rather than having mildly racist gags directed at him by his fast-talking employer, he makes the gags in charmingly self-deprecating fashion against himself. In *The Ghost Breakers*, Bob Hope tells Willie Best, in the midst of a power-cut, that "If this keeps up, I'm gonna have to paint you white." In *King of the Zombies*, Moreland comes to in a graveyard on crash-landing and responds to his employer's bland reassurances with "I thought I was a little off-colour to be a ghost." This nifty role-reversal gives the film such enduring charm as it possesses; the low-status figure of the black servant here occupies centre stage, with Moreland effectively assuming the Bob Hope role.

The effect would be lost, of course, if Moreland weren't a brilliantly engaging comedian, with a remarkable gift (not shared by Hope) for making his wisecracks sound ad-libbed. Some of them, in fact, could have been written for Hope. Towards the end, voodoo drums are heard and Bill asks "What does that sound like to you?" Jeff's reply – "I don't know, but it ain't Gene Krupa" – recalls Hope's panicked cry of "It ain't Baby Snooks!" when confronted with an out-of-control zombie. Moreland can make the simplest lines sound funny. Hypnotised by Sangre into thinking he's a zombie, he joins his undead fellows with an unfazed "Move over, boys, I'm one of the gang now." Later, tasting the thin gruel on offer in the kitchen, he mutters, "This bein' a zombie sure is a drawback." It's a delightful performance and well worth the price of admission on its own.

The stars of *King of the Zombies* were all kept busy at Monogram in the ensuing months. John Archer would play a fake hobo opposite Bela Lugosi in *Bowery at Midnight*, Joan Woodbury starred in *The Living Ghost* (a cheerful whodunit hyped for its virtually non-existent horror content), while Dick Purcell appeared in an underwhelming remake of *The Thirteenth Guest* called *Mystery of the 13th Guest*. Along with Woodbury and Mantan Moreland, Purcell also cropped up in *Phantom Killer*, another feeble retread of an early 1930s picture, this time *The Sphinx*.

All these titles were directed by the tireless William Beaudine, who also cast Moreland in the Dixie National production *Professor Creeps*. Playing a pair of penurious private detectives, Moreland and F E Miller encounter Professor Whackingham Creeps (Arthur Ray), who turns his niece's suitors into animals and keeps them in the cellar. Touting Moreland and Miller as the "sepia Abbott and Costello," the film was shot as *Goodbye, Mr Creeps* (as in the above-mentioned *Goodbye, Mr Chips*) and, on its release in February 1942, joined such titles as *Comes Midnight*, *Mr Smith Goes Ghost* and *Midnight Menace* as a so-called "all-Negro film." Later, Moreland would gain his greatest fame as chauffeur Birmingham Brown in Monogram's continuation of Fox's Charlie Chan mysteries, including such creepy entries as *Black Magic* (1944) and *The Feathered Serpent* (1948). The last of these was directed by – surprise – William Beaudine.

A Jury of the Damned

In addition to *Dr Jekyll and Mr Hyde* and *King of the Zombies*, another 1941 production with an Academy-nominated score was *All That Money Can Buy*, and the awards ceremony on 26 February 1942 duly saw the Oscar statuette conferred on Bernard Herrmann. The film was made at RKO in the aftermath of Orson Welles' *Citizen Kane* (for which Herrmann was also nominated) and was based on Stephen Vincent Benet's 1936 short story *The Devil and Daniel Webster*. The producer-director was William Dieterle, who in his native Germany had starred in F W Murnau's *Faust*. Emil Jannings' typically rotund Teutonic Devil in the Murnau film was countered in *All That Money Can Buy* by the brilliant Walter Huston, whose uniquely American Devil is wiry, plausible, clubbable, and has a shark-toothed grin a mile wide.

Cross Corners, New Hampshire – 1840. Cash-strapped farmer Jabez Stone strikes a bargain with the mysterious Mr Scratch, who offers him "all that money can buy" on the understanding that he will collect Stone's soul in seven years' time. Having become a boorish and high-handed landowner in the intervening period, Stone eventually realises his folly and enlists the celebrated Massachusetts senator Daniel Webster to plead his case before "a jury of the Damned."

With its background of New England farmers trying to form a union and thus outface the vampiric attentions of monied usurers, *All That Money Can Buy* had plenty of resonances for audiences emerging from the Great Depression. Yet those resonances went largely unremarked at the time, and the film lost RKO some $35,000. Uncertainty over the title can't have helped; there were several in contention (and even in release) as well as the one under which the picture was premiered. More damaging, perhaps, was the film's then-freakish mixture of tones. On the one hand, there's a wholesome dose of folksy naïveté to qualify it as a prime cut of costume Americana. On the other, the film boasts a selection of brilliantly realised supernatural set-pieces, stamping it as a bizarre efflorescence of the German Expressionism in which Dieterle had been trained.

Though a trifle longwinded, the Americana is superb in its detail, surprisingly caustic in its political subtext and beautifully played by James Craig, Anne Shirley, Jane Darwell and Edward Arnold. (The latter, fitted with a pair of furry caterpillars where his eyebrows should be, was a substitute for Thomas Mitchell, who had fractured his skull in an on-set accident.) The supernatural set-pieces are mainly congregated in the film's third act, but the threat of them is made manifest before this by Walter Huston's delightfully disreputable Mr Scratch. Twirling an ever-present cigar and cane, Scratch is a waggishly humorous confidence-trickster who somehow anticipates the anarchic creatures created later by Dr Seuss. Having made a nakedly materialistic appeal to Stone ("A soul is nothing; can you see it, smell it, touch it?"), he tempts him with a long-buried heap of Hessian gold which, obscenely, seems to move of its own accord, readily identifying itself as the root of all evil.

For his first entrance, Scratch comes out with a mellifluous greeting of "Good evening, neighbour Stone" and materialises from the hellish stripes of light at the rear of Stone's barn. The soundtrack reverberates to a panicked cacophony of crowing, whinnying, clucking, lowing – all of which Scratch silences by means of a peculiar whistling as he steps forward to offer Stone his card. (In a typically understated special effect, he discreetly incinerates it on the end of his cigar when Stone declines it.) The idea that Scratch occupies a separate plane of existence and has passed smoothly into Stone's is beautifully conveyed. The portal is the big, white square of the barn's inner door, and in its resemblance to a proscenium arch – with Scratch effectively penetrating the theatrical fourth wall – the scene is reminiscent of the moment in *Sparrows* in which Jesus passes from Mary Pickford's dreamworld into the barn in which she's sleeping.

Another Christ-like role-reversal is reserved for the film's climactic "jury of the Damned" sequence, in which Scratch summons a rogues' gallery of deceased jurors to decide Stone's fate. ("Dastards, liars, traitors, knaves," he calls them, adding satirically: "Americans all.") Presiding is the fearsome Judge Hawthorne, notorious for his involvement in the Salem witch trials and played, in an inspired bit of casting, by H B Warner, best remembered for playing Christ in Cecil B DeMille's *The King of Kings*. To add to the heady stew of Christ and anti-Christ references, Warner appears entirely bald, his parchment face, tear-stained eyes and bat-like ears making him look like an ethereal first cousin to Max Schreck's *Nosferatu*. The inclusion of Hawthorne is also apt given the lineage of Benet's story, which harks back to such 19th century writers as Washington Irving and Hawthorne's novelist descendant, Nathaniel.

Stunning though the trial scene is, it's matched in eeriness by two other remarkable sequences, both of which are beautifully choreographed literally as well as figuratively. The first is, as it were, a barndance macabre in which the partying locals are introduced to Scratch's kittenish confederate Belle (bewitchingly played by Simone Simon). Here, Joseph August's creepy underlighting is given to us in a brilliant series of quick cuts, with the hectic pace set in the editing room by future director Robert Wise and in the scene itself by Mr Scratch, who fiddles furiously while hissing "Faster! Faster!"

Later, Stone's newly built mansion is the scene of a supposedly swank housewarming attended only by what Belle calls "friends of mine from over the mountain." The otherworldly optical effects, the atonal undertow derived by Bernard Herrmann from the humming of telegraph wires, the demented carousel by which Belle dances Miser Stevens literally to death – all these contribute to a nightmarish scene which, as many commentators have observed, exactly foreshadows the 1961 cult classic *Carnival of Souls*.

Even more disturbing is Scratch's acquisition of Stevens' soul, which is represented by an oversized moth; very few of Scratch's clients, as he makes clear to the horrified Stone, end up as butterflies. (Another foreshadowing here; the piping plaint of the Stevens moth would be rendered cartoonish in the closing reel of Kurt Neumann's *The Fly*.) And as the vice closes around Stone, Huston expertly allows Scratch's face to harden into implacability – an implacability all the more frightening for his former skittishness – when he announces in massive close-up that "I'll give you until midnight ... but not one minute more." Balancing this is the film's dazzling final vignette, in which Huston casts about for a new victim and fixes impishly on the viewer. The effect is rather like those

"In the midst of life, one really hates to close these longstanding accounts..." James Craig and Walter Huston in *All That Money Can Buy* (1941)

"Your country needs you!" posters that featured Lord Kitchener in the UK and Uncle Sam himself in the US, and Huston's pantomime here is as brilliant a piece of comic acting as the cinema has to offer.

Prior to the casting of Walter Huston, the candidates for the role of Mr Scratch included Paul Muni and Claude Rains, who in 1946 would appear together in Archie Mayo's fanciful *Angel On My Shoulder*, Muni as a resurrected racketeer, Rains as an affable, man-of-the-world Mephistopheles. Even more svelte and epicene was Laird Cregar's Devil in Ernst Lubitsch's *Heaven Can Wait* (1943), which typified a strain of 1940s fantasy in which whimsical visions of Heaven or Hell were pressed into service for morale-boosting or heart-warming effect, a necessary catharsis in time of war. In 1942, for example, Stuart Heisler's *The Remarkable Andrew* furnished a spectral counterpart to the Daniel Webster of *All That Money Can Buy* in the form of Andrew Jackson (Brian Donlevy), who aids William Holden in his fight against small-town corruption. By the end of the decade, however, the Devil returned in the person of Ray Milland, ensnaring an upright District Attorney (Thomas Mitchell) in John Farrow's *Alias Nick Beal* (1948).

ALL THAT MONEY CAN BUY

RKO Radio / a William Dieterle production 1941
107 minutes
production began 25 March (suspended late April); resumed 28 May
preview title: Here is a Man
alternative release title: The Devil and Daniel Webster
reissue title [cut to 84 minutes]: Daniel and the Devil

Cinematographer: Joseph August; Art Directors: Van Nest Polglase, Al Herman; Editors: Robert Wise, Mark Robson*; Sound: Hugh McDowell Jr, James G Stewart; Special Effects: Vernon L Walker; Optical Effects: Linwood Dunn*; Set Decorations: Darrell Silvera; Costumes: Edward Stevenson; Music: Bernard Herrmann; Assistant Directors: Argyle Nelson, John Pommer; Dialogue Director: Peter Berneis; Screenplay: Dan Totheroh, Stephen Vincent Benet (from a story by Benet); Associate Producer: Charles L Glett; Director-Producer: William Dieterle

Edward Arnold (Daniel Webster); Walter Huston (Mr Scratch); Anne Shirley (Mary Stone); James Craig (Jabez Stone); Jane Darwell (Ma Stone); Simone Simon (Belle); Gene Lockhart (Squire Slossum); John Qualen (Miser Stevens); H B Warner (Justice Hawthorne); Frank Conlan (sheriff); Lindy Wade (Daniel Stone); George Cleveland (Cy Bibber); uncredited: Frank Austin (spectator); Walter Baldwin (Hank); Eddie Borden (gambler); Sonny Bupp (Martin); Bob Burns (townsman); Jeff Corey (Tom Sharp); Alec Craig (Eli Higgins); Eddie Dew (farmer); Patsy Doyle (Dorothy); Robert Dudley (Lem); Charles Herzinger (farmhand); Harry Hood (tailor); Harry Humphrey (pastor); Robert Pittard (clerk); Stewart Richards (Dr Simpson); Sherman Sanders (caller); Carl Stockdale (Van Brooks); Robert Strange (clerk of court); Jim Toney (farmer); Virginia Williams (baby Daniel)

Seldom does fanciful American folklore concern motion picture makers. William Dieterle dared to depart from formula ... Without doubt, this provocative feature deserves [a] place on any list of the year's ten extraordinary pictures ... Dieterle is to be congratulated for a masterly realization of a difficult and different theme. *Hollywood Reporter*

My part of the witch girl in *The Devil and Daniel Webster* was very short – and one of my big disappointments. I did that picture to meet the beautiful actor Walter Huston – and while I got to meet him during the shooting, I never had a scene with him! Simone Simon [quoted in Mank, *Women in Horror Films 1940s*, 1999]

MONSTERS NEW AND OLD

The affirmative response to *Man Made Monster* convinced Universal that, given the right setting, Lon Chaney Jr could be moulded into a brand-new horror star. A title first mooted in 1932 was accordingly dusted off, its original Robert Florey script junked entirely and the resourceful Curt Siodmak put to work on fashioning an alternative. Presiding over the project as director-producer was the studio's newest horror specialist, George Waggner, and a deluxe cast was assembled to bolster Chaney, among them old Universal hands Claude Rains and Bela Lugosi, plus the Moscow Art Theatre's Maria Ouspenskaya in the iconic role of gypsy matriarch Maleva. And, in a cheerfully cynical bid to recall past glories, Chaney's billing was discreetly adjusted to drop the 'Jr' from

THE WOLF MAN

Universal 1941
70 minutes
production began 27 October

Cinematographer: Joseph Valentine; Art Directors: Jack Otterson, Robert Boyle; Editor: Ted Kent; Sound: Bernard B Brown, Joe Lapis; Set Decorations: R A Gausman; Make-up: Jack P Pierce; Gowns: Vera West; Music: Hans J Salter*, Frank Skinner*; Musical Director: Charles Previn; Assistant Director: Vernon Keays; Screenplay: Curt Siodmak; Director-Producer: George Waggner

Claude Rains (Sir John Talbot); Warren William (Dr Lloyd); Ralph Bellamy (Colonel Montford); Patric Knowles (Frank Andrews); Bela Lugosi (Bela); Maria Ouspenskaya (Maleva); Evelyn Ankers (Gwen Conliffe); J M Kerrigan (Charles Conliffe); Fay Helm (Jenny); Forrester Harvey (Twiddle) and Lon Chaney [Jr] as The Wolf Man [Larry Talbot]; uncredited: Jessie Arnold (gypsy woman); Harry Cording (Wykes); Leland Hodgson (Kendall [butler]); Connie Leon (Mrs Wykes); Doris Lloyd (Mrs Williams); Ottola Nesmith (Mrs Bally); La Riana (gypsy dancer); Ernie Stanton (Phillips); Tom Stevenson (Richardson [gravedigger]); Harry Stubbs (Reverend Norman); Cyril Thornton (footman); Eric Wilton (chauffeur); Caroline [Frances] Cooke, Margaret Fealy (women on church steps); Gibson Gowland, Olaf Hytten (villagers)

This horror melodrama ... is a little too harrowing and somewhat depressing for the general run of picture-goer ... There are a few scenes that are properly frightening. And the production values are good, particularly the photography, which gives the picture an eerie atmosphere. Harrison's Reports

The kind of fog they used in those days ... was greasy stuff made with mineral oil. We worked in it for weeks and the entire cast and crew had sore eyes and intestinal trouble the whole time ... One other thing I remember was that Lon Chaney [Jr] was usually drunk. Philip Lathrop (camera operator) [quoted in Riley (ed), *Universal Filmscripts Series: Classic Horror Films Volume 12*, 1993]

"Some beast the gypsies left behind..." Lon Chaney Jr threatens unsuspecting Evelyn Ankers in *The Wolf Man* (1941)

his name. The strategy worked a treat. Going into production just before Hallowe'en 1941 with a modest budget of $180,000, *The Wolf Man* was issued in December and rapidly grossed a million.

After 18 years in the USA, Larry Talbot returns to his ancestral home on the death of his brother. Accompanying Gwen Conliffe and Jenny Williams to a local gypsy camp, he is bitten when Jenny falls prey to what appears to be a werewolf. He later becomes a werewolf in his turn, first killing a gravedigger and finally threatening Gwen, whereupon his father, Sir John, is compelled to kill him with a silver-topped cane.

Though all specific references to the location were deleted during production, Siodmak set his werewolf saga in Wales, formerly the site of *The Old Dark House*. The only giveaway in the finished film is the distinctively Welsh name Talbot, for Jack Otterson's brilliant production design is a crazy-quilt Gothic fantasia of no fixed abode, with Universal's longstanding Tyrolean village pressed into service alongside a solidly baronial mansion interior and a fog-shrouded forest of gnarled, soot-blackened trees. In a small nod towards English, if not Welsh, verisimilitude, Forrester Harvey, the sorely tried landlord of *The Invisible Man*, is on hand as a squeamish police official. At one point he makes a genuinely parochial reference to the famous Stanley Holloway monologue 'The Lion and Albert', mistaking Larry's wolf-headed cane for "a stick with an 'orse's 'ead 'andle."

With only a passing nod to folklore, Siodmak crafted most of his lycanthropic details from scratch, fashioning a whole new monster 'mythos' and creating a classic piece of doggerel in the lines, "Even a man who is pure in heart / And says his prayers by night / May become a wolf when the wolfbane blooms / And the autumn moon is bright." He also laced his script with a number of almost off-hand ironies. Early on, the unsuspecting Larry tries to chat up Gwen in notably ham-fisted fashion, letting us know that, in the then-popular meaning of the word (as a male equivalent to 'vamp'), he's clearly no good at being a 'wolf'. He later discovers that Gwen is already engaged to Frank Andrews, who turns out to be a gamekeeper, of all things, and makes his first entrance with a dog on a leash.

Siodmak also proposed that the reality or otherwise of Larry's condition should be left in doubt, with his wolf form only glimpsed by Larry himself in mirrors and the like. In the finished film, there is no such equivocation; the lycanthropic Larry stalks through the ground fog in a Jack Pierce make-up that is less impressive than the eerie stripes of moonlight applied to it in close-up by cinematographer Joseph Valentine. The script contains vestigial remnants of Siodmak's original, with Sir John offering a garbled account of schizophrenia and Dr Lloyd, more interestingly, drawing a parallel with "the stigmata appearing in the skin of zealots." More confusing still is the fact that Larry's attacker is a four-legged werewolf of the Alsatian variety – "I killed a wolf: a plain, ordinary wolf!" Larry insists, clubbing the floor with his wolf-headed cane for emphasis – while Larry himself turns into a two-legged werewolf of the humanoid variety.

These incongruities, however, seem to be of a piece with the never-never-land crafted by Otterson. We may question, for instance, what a bunch of Hungarian gypsies are doing in Wales, only to realise that their presence facilitated the happy casting of Bela Lugosi. Six years earlier, Lugosi had been earmarked for the Dr Yogami role in *WereWolf of London*; here, he finally got to play it, only this Yogami (called, appropriately, Bela) is bludgeoned to death in the act of infecting Larry, thus severely limiting his screen time. The gypsy subplot also facilitates some kneejerk xenophobia from the villagers, who respond to the gravediggers' murder with the theory that "It might be some beast the gypsies left behind." (Strictly speaking, of course, they're right.) And, just as *WereWolf of London* was indebted to the 1931 *Dr Jekyll and Mr Hyde*, so *The Wolf Man* gives a nod to its 1941 remake, with a 'surreal' dream sequence that plays like a poor man's reprise of the transformation montages seen in the M-G-M film.

Though overburdened with too many samey characters, Siodmak's script is immaculately constructed, with a satisfying undertow of tragic inevitability in that Larry's bludgeoning of Bela is framed in the same tree branches as Sir John's climactic bludgeoning of Larry. The uneasy relationship between Larry and his father is left teasingly vague; "tradition," Sir John points out, "insists that the Talbots be the stiff-necked, undemonstrative type, and frequently this has been carried to very unhappy extremes." As a result, the final, ferociously uninhibited father-son confrontation in the forest carries real emotional weight.

The effect is much enhanced by Chaney's anguished playing, together with that of Maria Ouspenskaya and Claude Rains as his diminutive mother- and father-figures. Larry is not a tragic hero in the classical sense; he is not a great man brought low by a single flaw in his nature, just a luckless lunk who has the misfortune to be bitten by a werewolf. But the schematic inevitability of his fate – and the frenzied violence of its staging – make *The Wolf Man*'s final reel one of the most powerful in Universal's repertoire.

The national release of *The Wolf Man* gave cinemagoers a belated opportunity to see *The Mad Doctor of Market Street*, which had been made back in July 1941 as *Terror of the Islands* and played as support to the Chaney picture. In this, Lionel Atwill goes the *Kongo* route of establishing himself as the 'God of Life' on a South Seas island, using his experiments in suspended animation to cow the assembled natives and uttering lines like "I'll be the greatest man who ever set foot on this earth; all will honour my name" with an unwonted nonchalance that borders on contempt. The result is indeed pretty contemptible, despite having the stylish Joseph H Lewis at the helm and the spirited Claire Dodd as the woman Atwill has his reptilian eye on. The 'bogus god in the South Seas' angle would be replayed, only this time for laughs, in Paramount's 1944 Dorothy Lamour vehicle *Rainbow Island*.

Early in October, Atwill was also engaged for William Nigh's *The Strange Case of Doctor Rx*, in which Universal's British import Patric Knowles starred just prior to making *The Wolf Man*. Just as the old Universal had done in the 1930s, the new Universal insisted on advertising non-horror subjects – in this case, a peculiarly lame whodunit – with a full battery of horror effects. Atwill himself is a red herring, aptly named Dr Fish, and the only nod to Universal's horror constituency is provided by a scene in which the cowled Dr Rx proposes to swap Knowles' brain with that of a caged gorilla. The latter was played by Ray 'Crash' Corrigan, with whom Nigh had recently collaborated on *The Ape*.

In December, Patric Knowles moved on to another murder-mystery sold as a horror picture, Phil Rosen's *The Mystery of Marie Roget*. This one at least had a period setting and a nominal source in Edgar Allan Poe. Cast as Poe's ratiocinative investigator Dupin, Knowles gets to the bottom of who disfigured the title character ("looks as if the face had been torn to a pulp by the claws of an animal," he muses) and dumped her body in the Seine. Though a good-looking picture, the result is valuable only for its glimpses of character actors like John Litel, Maria Ouspenskaya and Frank Reicher. Fans of high camp, however, will relish the casting of Maria Montez in the name part, caught here shortly before her brief celebrity in Technicolor extravaganzas like *Cobra Woman* and *Arabian Nights*.

THE GHOST OF FRANKENSTEIN

Universal 1941
67 minutes
production began 15 December

Cinematographers: Milton Krasner, Woody [Elwood] Bredell; Art Directors: Jack Otterson, Harold H MacArthur; Editor: Ted Kent; Sound: Bernard B Brown, Charles Carroll; Set Decorations: R A Gausman; Make-up: Jack P Pierce; Gowns: Vera West; Music: H J Salter; Assistant Director: Charles S Gould; Screenplay: W Scott Darling; Original Story: Eric Taylor; Producer: George Waggner; Director: Erle C Kenton

Sir Cedric Hardwicke (Frankenstein); Ralph Bellamy (Erik); Lionel Atwill (Doctor Bohmer); Bela Lugosi (Ygor); Evelyn Ankers (Elsa); Janet Ann Gallow (Cloestine); Barton Yarborough (Dr Kettering); Doris Lloyd (Martha); Leland Hodgson (Chief Constable); Olaf Hytten (Hussman); Holmes Herbert (magistrate) and Lon Chaney [Jr] as The Monster; uncredited: Harry Cording (Frone); Lawrence Grant (Mayor); Brandon Hurst (Hans); Teddy Infuhr (boy); Jimmy Phillips (Indian); Julius Tannen (Sektal); George Eldredge, Ernie Stanton (constables); Lionel Belmore, Michael Mark (councillors); Dwight Frye, Otto Hoffman (villagers)

All the tricks of chiller-dillers are employed and tossed on with emphasis, but the strain on the perpetrators is apparent throughout. Far from current film requirements, [the] picture ... only has a faint resemblance to the former issues of the Frankenstein series ... The clinical and surgical passages dip to the gruesome side, and are particularly untimely for audience consumption. *Variety*

I remember during *The Ghost of Frankenstein* they had me pose on the old Phantom stage and put a picture of Dad floating in the sky behind me ... It was tough enough with the 'ghost' of Dad floating around Universal, but when I had to take over the part of the Frankenstein Monster from Boris Karloff, the pressure was on. *Lon Chaney Jr [reprinted in Riley (ed), Universal Filmscripts Series: Classic Horror Films Volume 4, 1990]*

Bela Lugosi eavesdrops on a group of angry Vasarians, Brandon Hurst at their head, in a deleted shot from *The Ghost of Frankenstein* (1941)

Three weeks after completion of *The Wolf Man*, Lon Chaney Jr's Universal ascendancy was confirmed when work began on *The Ghost of Frankenstein*, in which he was required, symbolically, to occupy the asphalt-spreader boots of Boris Karloff. To perpetuate the studio's distinguished Frankenstein franchise into the 1940s, Universal selected screenwriter W Scott Darling and director Erle C Kenton, both of whom had been comedy specialists in silent days. Kenton, however, had directed the horrific *Island of Lost Souls* for Paramount, so was considered to have 'form' where scientific over-reachers were concerned.

When the Frankenstein castle is dynamited by angry villagers, the fleeing Ygor stumbles across the Monster and digs him out from the calcified remains of the sulphur pit. Decamping to Vasaria, Ygor contrives to have his brain transplanted into the Monster's skull by Frankenstein's unwitting second son, Ludwig. Struck blind in the process, the enraged Monster triggers off a blazing inferno...

The credits of *The Ghost of Frankenstein* are played out against the gnarled trees and fog-shrouded forest floor of *The Wolf Man*, after which the opening shot introduces us to the so-called Frankenstein Town Hall. This is the first of several Americanisms imposed by Darling. Inside, Lawrence Grant is still in place as the Burgomaster, only now he's called the Mayor. Among the rhubarbing throng of angry villagers are veterans Dwight Frye and Brandon Hurst; when the latter complains about "the curse of Frankenstein" (thereby predicting the first title in a future Frankenstein franchise), Grant rasps in reply, "This is nonsense, folks!" And, moments later, Hurst threatens him with the likely outcome of "the Fall election" should he not do something about the reputed curse.

This newly Americanised tone was no doubt introduced to make the film more palatable to its juvenile domestic audiences, and to the same end the action is precisely that – slick, fast-moving, audience-pleasing, with poetry in short supply. Though functional, the film's handling is nevertheless deluxe, with crystalline photography complementing a Jack Otterson production design that supplants his Expressionist extremes from *Son of Frankenstein* with realistic sets of an impressive solidity.

It's also a delight to re-encounter Bela Lugosi's Ygor, whom we first see through the

gossamer screen of a colossal spider's web. The spider itself is positioned screen left; Ygor sits in snake-charmer mode screen right, playing a weird tune on his even weirder horn while hovering expectantly over the hardened sulphur pit. Despite this telling introductory composition, Ygor turns out to be much less of a spider than he was first time around. Presumably to reduce the disturbing charge of unadulterated evil Lugosi had brought to *Son of Frankenstein*, Ygor has even had something of a personal makeover, with a slightly more presentable dress sense, much-improved dental work and a smoother haircut. In line with this new look, Lugosi's performance has less of the feral intensity he brought to the earlier film; even so, he's a joy to watch as he conspires with Lionel Atwill's Dr Bohmer to achieve world domination.

As Ludwig Frankenstein's sometime mentor and latterday assistant, Atwill is also on relishable form, snapping off his surgical gloves with wounded asperity when Ludwig tactlessly refers to the scandal that ruined his career, which he later passes off as nothing more than "a slight miscalculation." Cedric Hardwicke, however, seems visibly bored as Frankenstein's second son and Lon Chaney Jr makes the Monster little more than a bovine hulk. Clever, low-slung camera angles effectively emphasise the Monster's height and power, but Chaney brings no personality to the part whatever. In addition, Jack Pierce's famous make-up design is lamentably ill-suited to the cherubic contours of Chaney's face. (And Pierce was seemingly well aware of the fact; presumably willing to try anything in the attempt to salvage the situation, he applied cheekbone shadings that are visible in one scene and one scene only.) Unfortunately, one is left with the impression that, when deprived of the gallows features of Karloff for which it was specifically designed, Pierce's landmark design becomes pure comedy.

In a forlorn echo of the business with little Maria a decade earlier, this Monster strikes up a relationship with a Vasarian tot called Cloestine, and even expresses a desire to have her brain transplanted into his skull – a bizarre aspiration that goes for nothing in Chaney's inexpressive hands. When Ludwig enquires if the Monster is agreeable to having his brain transplanted, Ygor joyfully replies, "Can't you see? He is the first time happy in his life!" But, of course, we can't see anything of the sort.

The brain-swapping routine is a hangover from Curt Siodmak's *Black Friday* script, facilitating a startlingly gruesome moment when Bohmer wheels a bottled brain directly into the camera lens. (Just as grisly, by 1940s standards, are the shots of the Monster's face blistering in the heat of the final conflagration.) And there's a genuine chill when Ludwig realises that he has been duped: that the Monster has fetched up, not with the brain of "a man of character and learning," but that of the cunning Ygor. As Bohmer looks on with an obscenely self-satisfied Cheshire Cat grin, the Monster rises in triumph and announces that "I, Ygor, will live forever!" in the trademark rasp of Bela Lugosi. It's an instantly invalidated boast, of course, but makes for a truly memorable scene, nicely balancing a stunning moment at the beginning of the film when the Monster's neck electrodes take a direct, life-enhancing hit from a bolt of lightning. These, in fact, are the twin highlights of *The Ghost of Frankenstein*, which remains an efficient, unpretentious but not unlikeable potboiler.

Dr Bohmer's reference to "a slight miscalculation" was a resonant one, given that in May 1941 Lionel Atwill had testified in court regarding an apparently 'obscene' Christmas party at his Pacific Palisades home. Though exonerated – and despite the fact that his "slight miscalculation" entailed little more than the screening of a couple of 16mm stag films – Atwill would be indicted again in August 1942, this time for perjury. "This disastrous publicity and disgrace has wrecked me," he said, "and but for the courage and magnanimity of one particular studio, I guess I should be a dead egg now."[8]

MIND OVER MONSTER

While *The Ghost of Frankenstein* was in production at Universal, America was reeling from the impact of Sunday 7 December, "a day," as Roosevelt put it, "that will live in infamy." When 350 Japanese aircraft attacked the US naval base at Pearl Harbor, the result was a decimated Pacific Fleet together with the loss of 188 planes and over 2400 lives. And the sequel was swift to follow: by Tuesday the 9th, the USA was at war not only with Japan but also its allies, Germany and Italy. The great majority of the American public had remained staunchly opposed to intervention throughout the Nazis' all-conquering blitzkrieg in mainland Europe. Now, though, the inevitability of war was met with a kind of fatalistic resignation. If this mood seemed likely to preclude audience interest in the comparatively footling horrors purveyed by Hollywood, the impressive box-office returns of *The Ghost of Frankenstein* and, particularly, *The Wolf Man* seemed to indicate otherwise.

This, of course, was good news for Bela Lugosi, whose surprise casting in *Ninotchka* had failed to lead

Mad horticulturist (Bela Lugosi) and youth-hungry Countess (Elizabeth Russell) in *The Corpse Vanishes* (1942)

to a revived career in mainstream films. (As Tom Weaver memorably puts it, "By 1941, the only way Lugosi was getting into a straight picture was by buying a ticket."[9]) After his second stint as Ygor, and in the wake of Pearl Harbor, he went straight into William Nigh's *Black Dragons*, which was filmed in the final week of January 1942. For Lugosi fans, it was no doubt a new and faintly discomfiting thrill to hear him intone lines like "Anything I can do to hasten the establishment of our new order and to destroy the archaic democracies is an honour and a privilege." But the film, known in production as *The Yellow Menace*, is even more laboured, inane and confusing than the average Monogram. In the last reel, however, it adds to its veneer of spy-movie topicality a brief dash of horror: Lugosi is revealed as a German plastic surgeon who has altered the faces of six Japanese agents to make them appear Caucasian.

In mid-March, Lugosi was handed something much more attuned to his usual style. Wallace Fox's *The Corpse Vanishes* was Lugosi's fourth Monogram quickie and cast him as mad horticulturist Dr Lorenz. The film sets out its stall with admirable economy in its opening reel – a bride expires in the act of saying "I do," Lugosi grins insanely from the rear of a hearse as the body is wheeled inside, and a newspaper montage screams out such deathless headlines as "Police Baffled by Mysterious Theft of Altar Victims" and "Corpse Thief Believed Crank." The action bristles with implications of the foulest kind; what goes on in the back of the so-called "stiff wagon" we're left to speculate for ourselves. And even when the abducted brides are revealed to be alive (though catatonic), we're introduced to a grunting imbecile in Lorenz's employ who fetishistically strokes their hair.

With necrophilia on the menu, a number of vampire references are worked into the mix. Lorenz's wife, a Countess, is played by Elizabeth Russell, who bears more than a passing resemblance to Jeraldine Dvorak from Lugosi's *Dracula*. And, remarkably, the Lorenzes are discovered sleeping in twin coffins when a feisty reporter (Luana Walters) undertakes a nocturnal tour of their mansion. Informed of the Lorenzes' sleeping arrangements, the doctor 'hero' (played by the aptly named Tristram Coffin) blandly tells the reporter that "We often find it difficult to explain the peculiarities of some people" – a typical example of Harvey Gates' outstandingly clunky dialogue.

In an echo of the submerged secrets of Fort Marmaros in Ulmer's *The Black Cat*, Lorenz's bargain-basement laboratory is revealed as a private mausoleum with its own set of bride-filled morgue drawers. The film devolves into a truly risible climax, and is visibly under-budgeted throughout its length, but it would nevertheless prove massively influential. Lorenz, we learn, has devised a poisoned orchid with which to subdue his victims, thereafter drawing off their spinal fluid (or something) in order to restore the youth of his hysterical wife, a self-defeating process which inevitably requires repeated applications. Developing a hint provided by *The Ape*, *The Corpse Vanishes* thus presented a complete blueprint for such woman-fixated obsessives as Pierre Brasseur in *Les Yeux sans visage* and Peter Cushing in *Corruption*.

The week after *The Corpse Vanishes* started production at Monogram, work began at the even lowlier PRC on *The Mad Monster*, which plays like an extended retread of the same studio's *The Devil Bat*. The Lugosi role, however, is taken by George Zucco, whose smouldering Andoheb in *The Mummy's Hand* had made

a deep impression and effectively condemned him to a long stint on Poverty Row, starting with this picture. "My catalytic agent has brought about a complete transition from man to wolf," he exults, meanwhile proposing to offer the War Department "an army of wolf men, fearless, raging – every man a snarling animal. My serum will make it possible to unleash millions of such animal men."

As well as pirating *The Devil Bat*, *The Mad Monster* was an obvious riposte to Universal's *The Wolf Man*, with further Chaney Jr associations courtesy of Glenn Strange, whose simpering hayseed handyman is an embarrassing pastiche of Chaney's Lennie in *Of Mice and Men*. Having been injected with wolf blood by Zucco, Strange's werewolf persona has size and presence, but is hardly likely, as one character puts it, to have "scared Jed Harper so bad he went and got religion."

The swampy backwoods setting is effectively captured, but at an unusually lengthy 77 minutes the film becomes a paralysing bore; even Zucco, fitted with a silvery hairpiece, is betrayed into a samey and overpitched performance as the totally unhinged Dr Lorenzo Cameron. The part at least allowed him to get in some whip-cracking practice, which in July he would put to good use with another feral handyman in the super-glamorous B, *Dr Renault's Secret*. The British censor ensured that *The Mad Monster* remained unscreened in the UK until 1954, by which time the 'H' had been supplanted by the 'X', with exhibitors further enjoined to display a po-faced notice to the effect that "The public would be quite mistaken to think that any personal characteristics could be passed on by blood transfusion. Animal blood is never used for transfusions in the treatment of disease."[10]

Another 1942 production that would cause trouble at the BBFC was *Night Monster*, in which Bela Lugosi achieved top billing in a Universal production for the first time since *Dracula*; it would also be the last. For Ford Beebe, the film marked his feature debut after a long apprenticeship in Universal's serials. He polished it off in a mere 11 days in July, making the most of a highly peculiar scenario devised by Clarence Upson Young, whose only previous Universal credit was the anodyne *Strange Case of Dr Rx*.

Ingston Towers stands in close proximity to Pollard Slough, which is frequented by an apparition that causes the resident pond life to fall silent at its approach. The legless Kurt Ingston, meanwhile, is playing host to several guests, who are regaled by eminent yogi Agor Singh with a demonstration of matter materialisation. Ingston, it transpires, has been using the process to periodically grow legs and murder the doctors responsible for his disability.

Forty years prior to *Night Monster*, the Edison Company produced a skittish vignette called *The Mysterious Doctor*, in which a legless man has new limbs fitted by his physician and proceeds to skip around the surgery in transports of delight. Kurt Ingston in *Night Monster* is a much less congenial character, describing himself, as does the slithering Flint in *Kongo*, as "half a man." Made childish and cantankerous by his atrocious disability, he also nurses a bitter enmity towards the three doctors who "left him a misshapen thing that must hide even from the servants."

At a time when young soldiers were being routinely blown to bits in an international conflict, Universal's decision to back a picture in which the 'night monster' turns out to be a homicidal paraplegic was an unusual one to say the least. Even now, the film's high-gloss look (perfected by cinematographer Charles Van Enger, returning to horror for the first time since *The Phantom of the Opera*) is likely to take second place in viewers' estimations to Young's outrageously off-colour scenario.

Young isn't likely to have caught *The Mysterious Doctor*, but he may well have seen *Doctor X*, with its armless 'moon killer' committed to making "a crippled world whole again." In many ways, *Night Monster* is the missing link between *Doctor X* and the much later British film *The Abominable Dr Phibes*. All three feature an assemblage of shifty doctors (in *Doctor X* they're suspects, in *Night Monster* and *Phibes* they're methodically ticked-off victims), together with a physically ruined villain who can deconstruct himself at will.

Night Monster's most extraordinary scene comes towards the end, when Ingston is seen relaxing in bed, the black-gloved claw that is his right arm holding a book, the prosthetic device that is his left blithely removed before the astonished eyes of the hero and the investigating policeman, and the sheets thrown back to reveal pyjama-clad stumps where his knees once were. What's memorable here is Ingston's self-serving smugness; he performs this bizarre striptease not merely to establish his apparent alibi but also to gloat over the effect on the onlookers. The scene plays like a schlock riposte to the famous moment in Sam Wood's small-town melodrama *Kings Row* (released just five months prior to the shooting of *Night Monster*), in which Ronald Reagan realises that vindictive surgeon Charles Coburn has amputated his legs and asks Ann Sheridan, "Where's the rest of

Psychiatrist Irene Hervey and pulp novelist Don Porter meet various shady characters – Bela Lugosi, Leif Erickson, Nils Asther and (in wheelchair) Ralph Morgan – in *Night Monster* (1942)

NIGHT MONSTER

Universal 1942
73 minutes
production began 6 July
UK title: House of Mystery

Cinematographer: Charles van Enger; Art Directors: Jack Otterson, Richard Riedel; Editor: Milton Carruth; Sound: Bernard B Brown, Robert Pritchard; Set Decorations: R A Gausman, A J Gilmore; Make-up: Jack P Pierce*; Gowns: Vera West; Musical Director: H J Salter; Screenplay: Clarence Upson Young; Associate Producer: Donald H Brown; Director-Producer: Ford Beebe

Bela Lugosi *(Rolf)*; Lionel Atwill *(Dr King)*; Leif Erickson *(Laurie)*; Irene Hervey *(Dr Harper)*; Ralph Morgan *(Kurt Ingston)*; Don Porter *(Dick Baldwin)*; Nils Asther *(Agor Singh)*; Fay Helm *(Margaret Ingston)*; Frank Reicher *(Dr Timmons)*; Doris Lloyd *(Miss Judd)*; Francis Pierlot *(Dr Phipps)*; Robert Homans *(Cap Beggs)*; Janet Shaw *(Millie Carson)*; Eddy Waller *(Jeb Harmon)*; Cyril Delevanti *(Torque)*

The picture opens with promise in the eerie fog-bound mansion, but clarity, let alone plausibility, goes by the board with the introduction of Hindu mysticism or whatever ism it is that enables the killer to grow legs at will and carry out his campaign of revenge. Still, taken at its exuberant face value, it's [a] pretty good, if somewhat blood-thirsty, conventional 'who dunnit'. *Kinematograph Weekly* [UK]

Though it was a 'quickie', I always was kind of proud of it. Hitchcock, who was also making a picture on the lot [*Shadow of a Doubt*], screened a rough cut ... and ... couldn't believe the picture was shot in 11 days.
Ford Beebe [quoted in Bojarski, *The Films of Bela Lugosi*, 1980]

me?" It also provides a pre-echo of another *Phibes*-vintage British film, *Scream and Scream Again*, in which a hapless jogger has his limbs systematically removed in a mysterious clinic.

Night Monster is an unusual film from the start, with an opening exchange that is among the most intriguing in the genre. "How did you find the frogs at Pollard Slough, sir?" asks a grizzled gatekeeper of a lanky man in a white turban. "Quite well, thank you, Torque, quite well," returns the other, "but very uncommunicative." Indoors, we recognise the mansion interior from both *The Wolf Man* and *The Ghost of Frankenstein*, and encounter a grim-faced housekeeper scrubbing blood from the stairs while her frazzled mistress babbles about how "The whole house reeks of it." The weird ambience is maintained thereafter, particularly in Agor Singh's materialisation of a blood-dripping skeleton and Ingston's account of how "man can grow new tissues at will ... much as a lobster can grow a new claw to replace one he has lost in battle."

While Agor Singh's talk of reassembling matter provides a mystical forecast of *The Fly*, Ingston's little speech has a more immediate effect, blowing Young's denouement several reels too early. It doesn't detract, however, from the film's atmospheric set-pieces, which are of an extremely high standard indeed. Young's arbitrary idea that "the frogs quit croakin' when it [the monster] shows up" is exploited to maximum effect, with clouds of fog rolling in off the lake, the sudden cessation of the surrounding frog chorus, and the extremely spooky creaking of a garden door that separates Pollard Slough from the Ingston house. Finally, Ingston himself lurches into view, with murder in his eye and a pair of mind-over-matter feet at his extremities.

Curiously, the doctors themselves are all murdered indoors, with a marvellous point-of-view shot as the camera bears down on Francis Pierlot's fussy Dr Phipps, who bursts into a cold sweat and raises his hands to his throat while struggling for utterance. (Doris Lloyd, who plays Ingston's housekeeper, no doubt saw the finished film, because she would do something very similar the following year as one of the victims of *The Lodger*.) Of the other actors, top-billed Bela Lugosi and Lionel Atwill have nothing parts, the latter as a self-important doctor who doesn't even stick around for Singh's demonstration and the former as a sort of Hungarian-accented Malvolio. The part that might have gone to Lugosi in the previous decade is, of course, Agor Singh, nicely played by Swedish former heart-throb Nils Asther. And the film also has some unusually strong roles for women, chief among them the always-watchable Fay Helm as Ingston's quietly demented sister.

The *Motion Picture Herald* dismissed *Night Monster* as "a fair-to-middling production of its type, having appeal for mystery fans in particular," while trumpeting the virtues of its co-feature in no uncertain terms on the very same page: "Universal with this latest spine-chilling melodrama insures its reputation of leadership in the horror-drama field. In the best tradition of the company's Frankenstein pictures and the others of a long line, *The Mummy's Tomb* is meant to shock and does."[11]

Turhan Bey issues Lon Chaney Jr with his instructions in *The Mummy's Tomb* (1942)

Made a month in advance of *Night Monster*, Harold Young's *The Mummy's Tomb* is unadulterated computer product yet ended up as the chief attraction when the two films were paired as a double-bill. As a direct sequel to *The Mummy's Hand*, the film gobbles up a large portion of its running time with laboriously extended clips from its forerunner, while Dick Foran and Wallace Ford are unconvincingly smothered in talcum powder to indicate the passage of 30 years. Both are throttled, in authentically nightmarish scenes, by the revived Kharis, who has been transported to Massachusetts by a smarmy young High Priest of Karnak (Turhan Bey). The mummy also leaves his mouldy hand-print on dear old Mary Gordon, ensuring that his tally of victims is rather perplexingly confined to OAPs.

Lon Chaney Jr drags his way listlessly through the boring role of Kharis, who was apparently "only seared and twisted and maimed" in the previous film. The mob of angry villagers at the end is punched up with clips from *Frankenstein* and *Bride of Frankenstein*; the music, yet again, is cobbled together from *Son of Frankenstein*. The film represents a new and depressing development, in that Universal's contempt for its audience is detectable all through.

TWISTED ANIMAL JEALOUSY

As the *Motion Picture Herald* pointed out vis à vis *The Mummy's Tomb*, Universal remained unchallenged as a purveyor of screen shockers. On 26 June 1942, however, the *Hollywood Reporter* noted that Harry Lachman would start filming *Buried Alive* in ten days' time; though not Fox's first ever horror picture, as the *Reporter* claimed, it was certainly that studio's first contribution to the renewed horror cycle since *The Gorilla* in 1939. *Buried Alive* was presumably a 'smokescreen' title, given that it has no bearing on the content of the film Lachman actually began shooting on 6 July. This was *Dr Renault's Secret*, a straight-faced remake of Fox's old comedy-thriller *The Wizard*, itself derived from Gaston Leroux's *Balaoo*. It turned out to be Lachman's only attempt at fully fledged horror, a mode he'd merely flirted with in the earlier Fox productions *Dante's Inferno* and *The Man Who Lived Twice*.

Dr Larry Forbes arrives at the French château of Dr Robert Renault in order to take his fiancée, Renault's daughter Madelon, back to America with him. The household includes a strangely simian handyman called Noël, who is revealed as a Javanese gorilla whom Renault has subjected to a process of "experimental humanisation." Having gone berserk at the local Bastille Day celebrations, Noël finally turns on Renault, later killing the ex-con Rogell when he tries to kidnap Madelon.

Though failing to acknowledge him in its credits, *Dr Renault's Secret* switches the story back to Leroux's original France, as well as making the significant adjustment of humanising not only the ape-man but also his creator, who appear to have been about

Arthur Shields conducts a murder investigation, aided by J Carrol Naish and John Shepperd, in *Dr Renault's Secret* (1942)

DR. RENAULT'S SECRET

20th Century-Fox 1942
58 minutes
production began 6 July

Cinematographer: Virgil Miller; Art Directors: Richard Day, Nathan Juran; Editor: Fred Allen; Sound: Eugene Grossman, Harry M Leonard; Set Decorations: Thomas Little, Paul S Fox; Wardrobe: Herschel [McCoy]; Music: David Raksin, Emil Newman; Screenplay: William Bruckner, Robert F Metzler [from the story *Balaoo* by Gaston Leroux*]; Contributing Writer: Frances Hyland*; Executive Producer[s]: Sol M Wurtzel, William Goetz*; Director: Harry Lachman

J Carrol Naish (*Noël*); John Shepperd [later Shepperd Strudwick] (*Dr Larry Forbes*); Lynne Roberts (*Madelon Renault*); George Zucco (*Dr Robert Renault*); *uncredited:* Carmen Beretta (*Mrs LaRue*); Eugene Borden (*coroner*); Ann Codee (*passer-by*); Ray 'Crash' Corrigan (*ape*); George Davis (*contest proprietor*); Jean Del Val (*Henri [butler]*); Charles La Torre (*Marcel*); Mike Mazurki (*Rogell*); Louis Mercier (*bus driver*); Jack Norton (*Mr Austin*); Bert Roach (*proprietor of Le Chat Noir*); Arthur Shields (*Inspector Duval*); Charles Wagenheim (*Jacques [detective]*); Max Willenz (*Louis*)

Twentieth Century-Fox has gone the whole way in the matter of ape-men, achieving a harrowing film which sustains interest by reasonable progression once the original fantastic premise has been accepted. *Motion Picture Herald*

Even veteran waitresses ... gulped a few times when J Carrol Naish, made up as a savagely primitive human, dropped into the 20th Century-Fox commissary during the filming of *Dr Renault's Secret* ... Despite his horrible make-up, a young lady, a visitor from the East, exclaimed: "Oh, Mr Naish, you look just the same in real life as you do on the screen. I'd recognize you anywhere." Naish ... is still trying to figure that one out. *from original pressbook*

equally demonic in *The Wizard*. First up for inspection is J Carrol Naish's Noël, whom we encounter almost at once. No sooner has the visiting American doctor disembarked at a Gallic hostelry called Le Chat Noir than Noël shuffles subserviently into view and identifies himself as Dr Renault's handyman. Helped immeasurably by a subtle make-up job and a discreetly padded suit, Naish brings an affecting naïveté to this lost soul, especially when slumped sadly in his underground quarters and asking Renault the garbled but heavily loaded question, "Why you no let me like I was?"

Happily, the comic accoutrements of *The Wizard* have been stripped away almost completely. (And those that remain, such as Jack Norton's ill-fated American drunk, are sufficiently engaging not to break the spell.) Handled seriously, the theme can be more clearly seen as a variation on *Island of Lost Souls* and, before even that, the Lon Chaney silent *A Blind Bargain*. Indeed, the Fox publicists were presumably remembering the latter title – and entirely ignoring Universal's grand claims for Lon Chaney Jr – in asserting that "When it comes to portraying the grotesque, there probably never will be another Lon Chaney, but Hollywood casting directors today believe that the heir apparent to the Chaneyesque mantel [sic] is J Carrol Naish."

Renault is played by George Zucco, who had previously operated on a gorilla in Paramount's *The Monster and the Girl*. As frosty and gimlet-eyed as ever, Zucco makes Renault a self-absorbed prig whose attitude towards rehabilitation is demonstrably deluded. As well as retaining a former ape as handyman, he makes a point of having ex-cons in the posts of butler and gardener, conceitedly observing of the latter that "I've succeeded in eliminating every criminal instinct from his brain." Unfortunately, when he says this, we've already seen the oafish Rogell murdering the drunkard, and are later to see him conspiring with the butler to kidnap Renault's daughter Madelon. The basic problem with Renault's rehabilitation scheme is his harsh and unyielding application of it. Like Coriolos in *The Wizard*, he's extremely handy with a whip in Noël's presence and, though aware that Madelon's gentle influence "has accelerated the progress of my experiment to an amazing degree," seems unable to draw a moral from it.

Throughout all this, a somewhat dubious correlation is being drawn between the rehabilitation of criminals and the humanisation of Javanese gorillas, so Rogell's continued criminality makes it clear to the audience that poor Noël will finally 'revert' in his turn. His murderous lapse is triggered by love for Madelon (which Renault, typically, dismisses as "twisted animal jealousy"), and in the process the film's rather leisurely pace finally gets cranked up a few notches.

Vengefully targeting a waiter and a barber, Noël flings the first out of an upper window and, in a queasily ironic scene, demands that the other give him a shave before putting the straight-razor to a predictable use.

A noted post-Impressionist painter, the cosmopolitan Lachman (whose Paris apartment was requisitioned by the Nazis during shooting) was well placed to give these scenes a touch of Gallic verisimilitude. Much of his good work is undone, however, by the thick New York accent of Mike Mazurki, who, as Rogell, can't even pronounce the name of his unwilling conspirator Henri.

The film is crisply photographed by Virgil Miller, with Lachman's eye for painterly compositions lifting it well above the normal B-picture level. Midway through, however, it stumbles in spectacular style by showing Dr Forbes settling down with an anthropological tome, unaware that a knife-wielding hand has emerged from a sliding panel behind him. In fact, he never does become aware of it, which only emphasises what an unnecessary and ill-judged throwback to *The Wizard* this hoary piece of business is. To compensate, the film boasts an extraordinary sequence in which Forbes leafs through Renault's journal, disclosing a sequence of photographs in which a brutish gorilla shades slowly into the gentle Noël. The penultimate stage – showing a pair of fur-fringed eyes staring, almost human, from a lattice-work of bandages – is a haunting one.

Dr Renault's Secret was Lachman's final film and a product of Fox's B unit under its new head Bryan Foy, who had previously occupied the equivalent post at Warner Bros. Lachman's penultimate film, also a Fox quickie, had been *The Loves of Edgar Allan Poe*, which commenced production in mid-March 1942 under the much better title *The Romance of Annabel Lee*, with John Shepperd as Poe and Linda Darnell absurdly miscast as his ill-fated teenage bride Virginia. Screenwriter Samuel Hoffenstein, who had co-scripted Paramount's *Dr Jekyll and Mr Hyde*, rashly claimed (or, rather, the Fox pressbook claimed for him) that "because of the bold, tempestuous life Poe lived, there was no need ... to delve into the imagination for dramatic accent." And yet the rejection of *The Raven* (actually a huge success in Poe's lifetime) became the fulcrum of the plot. Something of the finished film's flavour is contained in the uniquely brainless tag-line, "The unknown story of Poe, known only to the women who loved him."

A much more interesting Poe film, albeit one lasting only 20 minutes, had come from M-G-M the previous year. Debutant director Jules Dassin crafted a small masterpiece out of *The Tell-Tale Heart* yet saw it consigned to the shelf until a Culver City exhibitor mislaid a newsreel and needed a substitute in a hurry. Doane Hoag's script judiciously fills in a few of Poe's blanks, making the young murderer (Joseph Schildkraut) a weaver in the autocratic employ of his wall-eyed old victim (Roman Bohnen). "You'll be dependent on me as long as I live," sneers the latter vindictively, setting up a remarkable scene in which Schildkraut steals into his bedroom and directs a strangely phosphorescent beam of lantern light at the old man's face. The dancing motes of luminescence, together with a stunning victim's-eye-view of the killer haloed in a starburst of kaleidoscopic light, confer a Messianic glamour on Schildkraut and make the murder seem like an act of deliverance.

In a virtuoso display of mounting hysteria, Schildkraut sweats profusely from start to finish. Cinematographer Paul Vogel provides him with massive close-ups as he tries to evade the judgmental scrutiny of the sheriff's men and identify the source of the metronomic beat in his head, the camera swerving to a clock pendulum, a dripping tap and a leaking water-butt by turns. Tellingly, the police officers (nicely played by Oscar O'Shea and Will Wright) are old men, just like the dismembered victim. And Sol Krandel's pulsing score reaches a marvellous crescendo on Schildkraut's climactic cry of "Tear up the planks" – then cuts out altogether, leaving the viewer just as relieved at the unburdening of his soul as Schildkraut himself.

THE NEW TYPE OF OTHER WOMAN

Apart from the monstrous make-up applied to Charles Laughton in *The Hunchback of Notre Dame*, the use of Karloff, Lugosi and Lorre in *You'll Find Out* and the folkloric Mr Scratch of *All That Money Can Buy*, RKO had so far avoided contributing to the 1940s horror boom. By 1942, however, the studio was struggling financially, with the commercial failure of Orson Welles' *Citizen Kane* widely taken to be at the root of the crisis. So, when Welles' champion George Schaefer was removed as vice president in charge of production, the incoming Charles Koerner was concerned to make modestly budgeted pictures that would turn a reasonable profit. Noticing how much money Universal were making with cheap-to-produce horror films, Koerner searched for someone to take charge of a new unit devoted to making similar subjects, and found him in the 37-year-old Vladimir Ivan Lewton.

Born in Yalta in 1904, Val Lewton had been brought up in artistic New York circles (his aunt on his mother's side was the celebrated tragedienne

Nazimova) and began his career as a journalist domiciled in Greenwich Village. Sometimes under a pseudonym, sometimes not, he had written novels, poetry, historical works, radio shows, even pornography. When approached by Koerner, he had been serving as David O Selznick's story editor for some eight years. Early in his Selznick association, he had supervised the Bastille sequences of Selznick's *A Tale of Two Cities*, an assignment that brought him into contact with Jacques Tourneur, son of the celebrated French director Maurice Tourneur. By the end of his Selznick stint, Lewton was overseeing preproduction on a mooted adaptation of *Jane Eyre*, in which capacity he encountered another man destined to make a key contribution to his horror pictures, playwright DeWitt Bodeen.

When Lewton took up his RKO duties on Monday 16 March 1942, Universal's *The Ghost of Frankenstein* had been in release a mere three days, while the zero-budgeted end of the market was represented by *The Corpse Vanishes*, which had just started production, and *The Mad Monster*, which was about to. *The Wolf Man*, however, was the all-conquering horror hit of the season, and it was with this in mind that Koerner hit upon the audience-tested title *Cat People* and handed Lewton a copy of the Algernon Blackwood story *Ancient Sorceries*. Another cat-themed tale considered for adaptation was Ambrose Bierce's *The Eyes of the Panther*, but in the end Lewton determined on an original story and screened several "run-of-the-mill weirdies," as he put it, in order to formulate what not to do.

Painstaking and highly literate, Lewton would outline his approach two years later as being "based on three fundamental theories. First is that audiences will people any patch of prepared darkness with more horror, suspense and frightfulness than the most imaginative writer could ever dream up. Second, and most important, is the fact that extraordinary things can happen to very ordinary people. And third is to use beauty of setting and camerawork to ward off audience laughter at situations which, when less beautifully photographed, might seem ludicrous."[12] He was also concerned, of course, to keep costs low, and among the strategies adopted in his maiden picture (which eventually cost $134,000) was the use of a brownstone interior left over from Welles' *The Magnificent Ambersons*, a New York street from *King Kong* and a zoo set previously seen in the Astaire-Rogers musical-comedies. The 31-year-old French star Simone Simon, who had made such an impact in *All That Money Can Buy*, was cast in the central role, and Lewton was ready to start *Cat People* by 28 July.

The marriage of Irena Dubrovna and Oliver Reed remains unconsummated thanks to Irena's fears regarding her Serbian heritage – namely, that uninhibited passion causes her to turn into a lethal panther. When Oliver falls in love with co-worker Alice Moore, Irena threatens them both in her panther form and later savages her psychiatrist when he tries to seduce her. Mortally wounded, she retreats in human form to the cat enclosure at the Central Park Zoo and dies there.

"You know, I never cease to marvel at what lies behind a brownstone front," observes Kent Smith's Oliver on first entering Irena's apartment house. The Manhattan setting of *Cat People*, so different from Universal's fanciful Vasaria, was instantly recognisable to the film's original audiences; operating much as Bram Stoker's *Dracula* had 45 years earlier, the film gained much of its impact from rooting an ancient evil in a workaday contemporary setting. "Val always insisted," recalled screenwriter DeWitt Bodeen, "that all his characters have occupations or professions *and be shown working in their jobs*."[13] Thus, a chic young fashion designer labours under a lycanthropic curse and a guileless ship's draughtsman enters into an unfortunate marriage with her.

Conforming to Lewton's dictum that "extraordinary things can happen to very ordinary people," Oliver and Alice are as clear-cut as Irena is (literally) impenetrable. By his own admission, Oliver is "a good plain Americano," while Alice is a smooth and efficient exemplar of the kind of young women swelling the workforce in wartime, describing herself as "the new type of other woman." The role reversal Alice invokes is an apt one; in conventional terms, Irena is just the kind of exotic vamp traditionally associated with erring husbands, yet here she becomes the wronged wife and the homewrecker role is taken by the apparently unthreatening Alice. Oliver and Alice are ordinary, too, in their blundering insensitivity when faced with the knotty problem of getting Irena out of the picture. Irena's well-justified resentment of their perfectly ordinary machinations means that her feline self is unleashed, not by sexual arousal as she had feared, but by its twisted near-relation, sexual jealousy.

In their masterful blend of suggestive sounds and images, the two sequences in which Alice is stalked by Irena were to prove enormously influential. In the first, Alice walks home at night through one of the Central Park transverses. The measured yet threatening tattoo of Irena's high heels becomes yet more threatening when it suddenly stops, Irena presumably having transformed in the interim. Alice, meanwhile, is isolated in the fitful

Kent Smith, Simone Simon and Jane Randolph – the tense triangle at the heart of *Cat People* (1942)

glare of the sodium lamps that punctuate Lewton's patches of prepared darkness. And, as her terror increases, an almost subliminal growl presages a loud hiss of air-brakes as a bus lurches unexpectedly into frame. Eliciting screams from wartime audiences, this simple yet revolutionary effect would be faithfully reproduced in all Lewton's films, the scenes being affectionately referred to by him as 'buses'.

Later, when the lights go out while Alice is taking a swim in the basement pool of the YWCA, a brilliant combination of relatively simple effects – the rippling light on the walls, the panther shadow lurking amid yet more prepared darkness, the frantic woman treading water, the rumbling growls on the soundtrack – creates an unforgettable vignette by the subtlest of means. Electrifyingly, Alice's climactic shrieks echo the piercing yowl of the cat and re-echo themselves in the claustrophobic confines of the indoor pool. The creative use of sound in Lewton's films was especially innovative, and the same applied to silence. "When D W Griffith saw the picture one night in a studio projection room," recalled Bodeen, "he commented upon the good use of silent passages, much to Val's pleasure."[13]

For all the shadowy suggestiveness applied to these sequences, the film makes no bones about the fact

CAT PEOPLE

RKO Radio 1942
73 minutes
production began 28 July

Cinematographer: Nicholas Musuraca; Art Directors: Albert S D'Agostino, Walter E Keller; Editors: Mark Robson, Robert Aldrich*; Sound: John L Cass; Photographic Effects: Vernon L Walker, Linwood G Dunn*; Set Decorations: Darrell Silvera, Al Fields; Gowns: Renié; Music: Roy Webb; Musical Director: C Bakaleinikoff; Animal Trainer: Mel Koontz*; Assistant Director: Doran Cox; Screenplay [and Dialogue Director*]: DeWitt Bodeen; Additional Dialogue: Edward Dein*; Executive Producer: Lou Ostrow*; Producer: Val Lewton; Director: Jacques Tourneur

Simone Simon (Irena); Kent Smith (Oliver); Tom Conway (Dr Louis Judd); Jane Randolph (Alice); Jack Holt ('Commodore' C R Cooper); uncredited: Henrietta Burnside (second woman); Alec Craig (zookeeper); Eddie Dew (street policeman); Elizabeth Dunne (Miss Plunkett [pet shop owner]); Dynamite (panther); Dot Farley (Miss Agnew [office concierge]); George Ford (whistling policeman); Bud Geary (mounted policeman); Mary Halsey (Blondie [pool receptionist]); Theresa Harris (Minnie [waitress]); Charles Jordan (bus driver); Donald Kerr (taxi driver); Connie Leon (woman); Dorothy Lloyd (cat voice); Murdock MacQuarrie (shepherd); Alan Napier ('Doc' Carver); Lida Nicova (patient); John Piffle (Belgrade proprietor); Betty Roadman (Mrs Hansen [pool concierge]); Elizabeth Russell (cat woman); Steve Soldi (organ grinder); Terry Walker (hotel attendant)

In line with the trend to tales of horror and anthropomorphism, RKO Radio has activated an old Balkan legend of women descended from cats, setting it in New York of today and wavering between phantasy and modern psychology for its explanations. The film, which has been admirably mounted and tightly directed and acted, ... can scarcely be termed pleasant entertainment. *Motion Picture Herald*

I'd like to have a girl with a little kitten face like Simone Simon, cute and soft and cuddly and seemingly not at all dangerous. I took a look at the Paramount picture *Island of Lost Souls* and after seeing their much publicised 'panther woman', I feel that any attempt to secure a cat-like quality in our girl's physical appearance would be absolutely disastrous.
Val Lewton [pre-production memo, reprinted in Cinefantastique, May-June 1982]

that Irena is a fully fledged werewolf. Revisionist comments attributed to Tourneur and others in later years, together with a general unwillingness on the part of highbrow critics to take shape-shifting seriously, has led to the widespread belief that the filmmakers somehow leave Irena's condition in doubt. The presence in the dramatis personae of a psychiatrist has helped to bolster the misapprehension that Irena's problem is merely psychological, despite the fact that Dr Judd is a slippery customer who talks a great deal of humbug and is chiefly motivated by a desire to get Irena into bed.

Given his intentions, Judd's sword-stick becomes an apt enough agent of Irena's death, penetrating her body just as Sir John's wolf-headed cane battered Larry Talbot's in *The Wolf Man*. Though Dr Judd is no more successful in assisting Irena than Dr Garth was in treating the similarly conflicted *Dracula's Daughter*, he nevertheless helps to establish the solemn tone of *Cat People* right at the outset, when the credits are succeeded by a written reflection on "ancient sin" purportedly extracted from his book *The Anatomy of Atavism*. The solemnity is garnished here and there (though never punctured) by discreet visual jokes. During Irena and Oliver's first romantic tryst in her darkened apartment, for example, she shies away from his observation that they have never kissed and becomes framed in the hulking shadow of a wing-chair, which forms the shape of cat's ears on the rear wall.

Another gently sardonic touch invokes an old and ossified horror property, *The Cat and the Canary*, when Irena returns Oliver's offered kitten to a pet shop, telling the twittering proprietress that "I'd like to exchange this kitten for a canary." The sequel, however, is far from gentle: its cage positioned directly in front of Irena's threatening panther tapestry, the bird dies of fright when Irena tries to handle it. Completing the food chain, she then throws the dead bird, which was Oliver's gift, to the male panther in Central Park Zoo.

Oliver and Alice have a fluffy white cat in their studio whom they quaintly call John Paul Jones, a Scots-American hero who contrasts starkly with the murky mid-European heritage bedevilling Irena. Guardedly unburdening herself to Oliver, Irena describes how her ancestors "bowed down to Satan and said their masses to him" when Serbia was overrun by the Mamalukes. Beautifully delivered by Simone Simon, Irena's monologue is given greater impact by a typically fastidious Lewton detail: above the mantel hangs a large-scale reproduction of a 1788 Goya portrait of a juvenile Spanish grandee, whose three pet cats squat at his feet while sizing up a caged bird. That they are perhaps the most malignant-looking cats in art history helps immeasurably.

The results of Irena's obsession are given to us in scenes of utter desolation – as when, on her wedding night, she is seen slumped at the bedroom door, unable to admit Oliver, reaching symbolically for the knob but withdrawing her hand when the panther howls warningly from outside. Later, after killing some sheep, she's shown weeping quietly in a claw-footed bathtub. Later still, she responds to Oliver's rejection first by speaking in tongues and then, in a telling parody of the sexual arousal she can never feel, scoring the sofa fabric with her fingernails.

In 1942, *Cat People* was a radically new type of horror film, abounding in subtle allusiveness and wearing its intellectual credentials on its sleeve. Of its many haunting vignettes, perhaps the most lingering is Irena's brief encounter with a fellow sufferer in the Serbian restaurant where her wedding reception is held. Elizabeth Russell (who had recently played Bela Lugosi's vampiric wife in *The Corpse Vanishes*) is a regal beauty who pauses en route to the exit to look at Irena and say simply, "Moia sestra." They're both 'Cat Women', of course. But, as DeWitt Bodeen observed in 1980, "If you write a scene between two strange women and one says to the other in a foreign language 'My sister,' you can bet your ass that there will be those who will say, 'Ah, lesbians.'"[14]

A CHOICE OF LYCANTHROPES

Though it was certainly the most sophisticated, *Cat People* was by no means the only response to Universal's money-spinning success with *The Wolf Man*. The lowly PRC had been first into the ring, making *The Mad Monster* in March, and some five months later 20th Century-Fox came up with a variation of their own. Made back-to-back with *Dr Renault's Secret*, *The Undying Monster* was in production at the same time as *Cat People*, enthusiastically embracing all the fogbound clichés that the RKO picture went out of its way to exclude. The director was German émigré John Brahm, a former theatrical producer who, as Hans Brahm, had made an atmospheric remake of *Broken Blossoms* in English exile at Twickenham. *The Undying Monster* is just as spooky, and also benefits from deluxe treatment more suited to an A-picture.

England, 1900. Helga Hammond enlists the aid of Scotland Yard detective Bob Curtis in investigating a savage attack on local girl Kate O'Malley. According to family legend, a Hammond ancestor who sold his soul to the Devil lives on in a secret room, periodically emerging

Nightwatchman Alec Craig, heroine Heather Angel and old retainers Eily Malyon and Halliwell Hobbes in *The Undying Monster* (1942)

to kill and hence prolong his existence. The truth is rather different but just as alarming: the family is subject to a lycanthropic curse that is currently vested in Helga's brother Oliver.

The Undying Monster starts in unusually arresting style. Credits over, we're shown a magnificent matte painting of the Hammond pile, perched giddily atop a cliff edge with the sea at its foot. The accompanying voice-over is not only uninformative but also drearily spoken; it gives place, though, to a striking sequence in which the 12 chimes of midnight are precisely shadowed by Lucien Ballard's mobile camera. These metronomic camera movements – taking in, among other things, a colossal mullioned window, a tattered heraldic hanging, a classical statue, the Hammond coat of arms and a baronial fireplace – build a peculiar kind of tension until exploded by the approaching tread of an elderly butler and the sudden lurch into wakefulness of a slumbering Great Dane.

The visual impact of the opening reel is underlined by a spooky shot of the phosphorescent sea and the gnarled tree positioned above it, also by the way Ballard's camera pulls right back to maximise the breathtaking scope of the mansion's interiors. In this way *The Undying Monster* immediately distances itself from the more claustrophobic *Dr Renault's Secret*, although the façade and front door of the Hammond mansion are recognisably a redressed version of Renault's château. The action abounds, meanwhile, in mysterious wolf howls, direful prophecies muttered by the domestic staff, and finally a startling sequence in which an ill-fated young woman is cornered in a cave under the cliff edge; she drops her lantern in terror and is savagely assaulted by the insane twitchings of a rapidly tracking camera. The effect is similar to a scene in *Night Monster* (shot the previous month), and Brahm would repeat it in both *The Lodger* and *Hangover Square*.

THE UNDYING MONSTER

20th Century-Fox 1942
60 minutes
production began 3 August
UK title: The Hammond Mystery

Cinematographer: Lucien Ballard; Art Directors: Richard Day, Lewis Creber; Editor: Harry Reynolds; Sound: George Leverett, Harry M Leonard; Special Photographic Effects: Fred Sersen*; Set Decorations: Thomas Little, Walter M Scott; Costumes: Billy Livingston; Music: Emil Newman, David Raksin; Dialogue Director: Robert Lewis*; Screenplay: Lillie Hayward, Michel Jacoby (from the novel by Jessie Douglas Kerruish); Executive Producer: William Goetz*; Producer: Bryan Foy; Director: John Brahm

James Ellison (Bob Curtis); Heather Angel (Helga Hammond); John Howard (Oliver Hammond); Bramwell Fletcher (Dr Geoffrey Covert); Heather Thatcher (Cornelia 'Christy' Christopher); Aubrey Mather (Inspector Craig); Halliwell Hobbes (Walton); uncredited: Matthew Boulton (coroner); Harry Carter (Warren); Alec Craig (Will); Douglas Gerrard (jury foreman); Holmes Herbert (constable); Eily Malyon (Mrs Walton); Charles McGraw (Frank Stradwick); Clive Morgan (Foster); John Rogers (Tom Clagpool); Donald Stuart (Charles Clagpool); David Thursby (Miles McGregor); Valerie Traxler (Kate O'Malley); Heather Wilde (Millie [maid])

At first view this seems another 'werewolf' picture ... However, the mood grows; and with it the conviction that the average audience will like it ... mainly because John Brahm has directed with great artistry, aided by Lucien Ballard, director of photography. There are scenes that deserve a pause for inspection as still pictures. *Motion Picture Herald*

We did things in those days that were very far out for the times. In mysteries and horror films, audiences will accept stuff they never would have accepted in a concert hall, because concert audiences are not that bright or sophisticated. But in a genre film they take dissonance and other modern techniques for granted.
David Raksin [quoted in Scarlet Street, Summer 1996]

Throughout, Brahm and Ballard leave no stone unturned in infusing a standard-issue story with visual interest. The atmosphere is laid on with a trowel, notably in a family crypt described by one character as "a sort of junior Westminster Abbey." Even the functional scenes in which Helga goes to Scotland Yard for help are given unwonted atmosphere by the torrents of rain splashing down outside the windows. Elsewhere, Brahm emphasises massively intrusive profile shots, whether of the peculiar butler and housekeeper, looming suspiciously behind stair rods, or the two Scotland Yard men conferring at a makeshift coroner's court.

At a time when British studios could muster only a modernised version of *Jane Eyre* called *The Night Has Eyes*, Brahm was here perfecting a Hollywood strain of mist-wreathed English Gothic that was soon to be consolidated by Roy William Neill in Universal's Sherlock Holmes pictures. The story was based on a 20-year-old novel by Jessie Douglas Kerruish, yet, with its family curse, husband-and-wife servants, savage animal attacks and pipe-smoking forensic detective, it's pretty clearly lifted from *The Hound of the Baskervilles* – with the crucial adjustment of making the youthful aristocrat, not a potential victim of the marauding hound, but the hound itself.

Peter Lorre finds his mark in Columbia's slapdash ghoul-farce, *The Boogie Man Will Get You* (1942)

Paying lip service to *The Wolf Man*, the venerable Halliwell Hobbes is given a hoary bit of homespun doggerel to the effect that "When stars are bright / On a frosty night / Beware thy bane / On the rocky lane." The werewolf itself, unfortunately, is only glimpsed at the climax, when a rather foolishly undercranked pursuit sequence features an insufficiently made-up stunt man, shinning up the cliff face in long shot. He finally emerges to reveal a hirsute face that has clearly been 'matted' onto his tweedy shoulders in order to facilitate a shaky transformation effect.

The film could also have benefited from stronger personalities at its centre than are provided by James Ellison and John Howard; the former, in fact, was deputising for the recalcitrant George Sanders. Ellison's Bob Curtis is no substitute for Sherlock Holmes (or, indeed, George Sanders), and the substance of his Holmes-Watson relationship with the horsey 'Christy' Christopher is sacrificed to Heather Thatcher's chief function of providing rather hi-falutin' comic relief. Much more impressive is Bramwell Fletcher, formerly the ill-fated junior archaeologist of *The Mummy* and now a splendidly shifty red herring called, appropriately, Dr Covert.

While *The Undying Monster* got by with only Halliwell Hobbes, Holmes Herbert and Bramwell Fletcher to remind viewers of past horrors, the more emblematic figures of Boris Karloff and Peter Lorre were over at Columbia making *The Boogie Man Will Get You*. Starting on 7 July, this was polished off in a mere fortnight by director Lew Landers, who had been known as Louis Friedlander when directing Karloff in *The Raven* seven years previously. Karloff had been briefly released from his stage commitment as Jonathan Brewster (the role was taken over by Erich von Stroheim), and the end product was aptly dismissed in the trades as "a poor man's *Arsenic and Old Lace*, crossed with a touch of *George Washington Slept Here*, and ... a waste of the talents of Boris Karloff and Peter Lorre."[15]

In completing his Columbia contract, Karloff was effectively sending up the four 'mad doctor' pictures he had made for the studio, joining with Lorre in a bungled attempt to create a super-race designed to "destroy Berlin [and] throttle Tokyo." The chosen vessel is cauliflower-eared powder-puff salesman Maxie Rosenbloom, while bungled prototypes reside in the cellar among the wines and cheeses. There's mild amusement to be had from Karloff's huffy objection to the word 'murder' ("Please, please!" he flaps, "the word is martyrised"), but Lorre is painfully unfunny and the same can be said for the film as a whole.

Bela Lugosi, meanwhile, was back at Monogram in August 1942, making a boring gangster melodrama called *Bowery at Midnight*, which has an ineptly executed 'horror' pay-off when Lugosi is set upon by his revived victims in what he calls his "dormitory of the dead." With Lugosi playing a college professor who moonlights as a social worker-cum-hoodlum ("I never saw a guy with so many angles," quips an associate), Wallace Fox's film plays like an East Side retread of Lugosi's British vehicle *The Dark Eyes of*

A meeting of monsters in Vasaria: Lon Chaney Jr and Bela Lugosi in *Frankenstein Meets the Wolf Man* (1942)

London. Remarkably, *Bowery at Midnight* triggered another warning shot from the British censor, who reported in November that the film would need major cuts, expressing concern, too, over Lugosi's previous film, *Night Monster.* Indeed, after the UK release of *The Ghost of Frankenstein* in May of that year, no further 'H' certificate films would be issued until the end of hostilities, when a large backlog of Hollywood horrors was released in a post-war rush.

Another film specified as troublesome by the BBFC in November 1942 had only just completed production. George Waggner's latest wheeze – a timely one given the increasingly clapped-out nature of Universal's Frankenstein franchise – was to get two monsters together in one picture, with the curious result that *Frankenstein Meets the Wolf Man* is a sequel to not one film but two – *The Wolf Man* and *The Ghost of Frankenstein.* (Decades later, the same philosophy would inform such millennial monster-mashes as *Freddy vs Jason* and *Alien vs Predator.*) To realise Curt Siodmak's script, Waggner had the good sense to engage Roy William Neill as director. Despite having made several vehicles for the Cockney comedian Max Miller during his recent stint in the UK, Neill reputedly had no grasp of comedy whatever, making him the ideal man to bring surprising gravity to a film saddled with such a ridiculous title.

FRANKENSTEIN MEETS THE WOLF MAN

Universal 1942
72 minutes
production began 12 October

Cinematographer: George Robinson; Art Directors; John B Goodman, Martin Obzina; Editor: Edward Curtiss; Sound: Bernard B Brown, William Fox; Special Photographic Effects: John P Fulton; Set Decorations: R A Gausman, E R Robinson; Make-up: Jack P Pierce; Gowns: Vera West; Musical Director: H J Salter; Assistant Director: Melville Shyer; Screenplay: Curt Siodmak; Producer: George Waggner; Director: Roy William Neill

Ilona Massey (Baroness Elsa Frankenstein); Patric Knowles (Dr Mannering); Lionel Atwill (Mayor); Bela Lugosi (Monster); Maria Ouspenskaya (Maleva); Denis Hoey (Inspector Owen); Don Barclay (Franzec); Rex Evans (Vazec); Dwight Frye (Rudi); Harry Stubbs (Guno) and Lon Chaney [Jr] as the Wolf Man [Larry Talbot]; uncredited: David Clyde (police sergeant); Jeff Corey (gravedigger); Charles Irwin (constable); Adia Kuznetzoff (singer); Doris Lloyd (nurse); Martha MacVicar [later Martha Vickers] (Margareta); Torben Meyer (Erno); Beatrice Roberts (Varja); Cyril Delevanti, Tom Stevenson (graverobbers)

To addicts of the Frankenstein saga, this is a Frankenstein job. To adherents of the Wolf Man, this is a Wolf Man number. To all and sundry, it's a meeting and a matching of the monstrosities ... that will put the producers of other horror pictures to test. Motion Picture Herald

Never make a joke in the studio. I was sitting down at the Universal commissary having lunch with George Waggner and I said, "George, why don't we make a picture [called] *Frankenstein Wolfs the Meat Man* – er, *Meets the Wolf Man.*" He didn't laugh...
Curt Siodmak [quoted in Brunas/Brunas/Weaver, *Universal Horrors,* 1990]

Providentially revived in his crypt, Lawrence Talbot escapes from hospital and journeys to Vasaria in search of Dr Frankenstein's diary, which he believes contains the secret of granting him eternal peace. Instead, he finds the Monster preserved in ice. Having trailed Talbot all the way from Cardiff, Dr Frank Mannering succeeds in restoring the Monster to full strength. Talbot, in werewolf form, and the revived creature are finally swept away by the dynamiting of a dam.

Waggner had crafted one of Universal's most powerful set-pieces for the closing reel of *The Wolf Man,* so Neill contrived to begin *Frankenstein Meets the Wolf Man* with another. The credits constitute a more elaborate version of the effect used in *The Invisible Man Returns* (the title is smoked up from the exhalations of an experimental beaker), and the opening shots rectify two of *The Wolf Man*'s more conspicuous omissions – first, we're given a view of the full moon, then a cemetery plaque ("Here Rest the Dead of Llanwelly") places the action very firmly in Wales. Ravens disport themselves on Jack Otterson's superb graveyard set (just as they did in Neill's earlier film, *The Black Room*) as two apprehensive bodysnatchers approach the Talbot family vault. Inside, the moon shines down on Larry's wolfbane-strewn corpse, whereupon a hand (its fingernails grown long in death) emerges to grasp one of the interlopers by the throat.

After this splendid opening, the action moves to the Cardiff hospital in which the delirious Larry has been confined, with Chaney Jr's performance, as in *The Wolf Man*, showing all the care and commitment he routinely denied his other monster roles. Patric Knowles, too, is smoothly professional in the thankless part of Dr Mannering, though Dennis Hoey is still playing Sherlock Holmes' associate Inspector Lestrade, whom he had recently created in Neill's first of nine Holmes pictures for Universal, *Sherlock Holmes and the Secret Weapon*. The film's first act also contains a man-to-wolf transformation that counts as much the most persuasive example of the normally unconvincing lap-dissolve technique, easily eclipsing the notably duff examples of the process in M-G-M's *Dr Jekyll and Mr Hyde*. This section winds up on an ominous note, with Mannering informed of Talbot's escape and that he "bit right through [his straitjacket]. Tore it to shreds with his teeth."

So far, as a direct sequel to *The Wolf Man*, the film is getting along just fine, with only the supporting actors' regional accents – which, when they remember to do them, sound vaguely Scottish rather than vaguely Welsh – striking a false note. Larry's journey to Vasaria brings with it the welcome reappearance of Maria Ouspenskaya's wise old Maleva, and his off-screen murder of an innkeeper's daughter is followed by a rousing werewolf pursuit in which Dwight Frye plays a prominent part. The castellated ruins of Ludwig's former home bear no relation to the building seen in *The Ghost of Frankenstein*, but no matter. Larry wipes the snowy residue from a subterranean ice-wall, the familiar Monster motif reverberates on the soundtrack and a startlingly evil, sneering face is disclosed to view when Larry chips the ice away.

On closer inspection, however, this turns out not to be Bela Lugosi (finally cast as the Monster after the near-miss of 1931) but a stunt double. The substitution recurs at frequent intervals, and is almost never convincing. Because Ygor had 'become' the Monster in the previous entry, Lugosi's casting made perfect sense. But in their cynical haste to make use of his name, Universal hadn't reckoned on the actor's advancing years. He turned 60 during production and, on 5 November, collapsed under the strain. To add insult to injury, Lugosi's dialogue was erased in post-production and, with it, all reference to the Monster's blindness, rendering his arm-waving performance inexplicable. Just one grace note survives this debacle; in the climactic experiment, the panicked Baroness Frankenstein has just told Mannering that "You're making him strong again!" when the Monster turns to look at the pair and is favoured with a colossal close-up. Not only is the Monster's triumphant leer an unmistakable Lugosi touch, it also makes it clear (to those in the know) that the Monster has now regained its sight.

Though the film's final act becomes bogged down in scientific mumbo-jumbo prior to its climactic battle of the Titans, there's plenty to enjoy elsewhere. Introduced in an astounding piece of Vera West headgear, the Hungarian beauty Ilona Massey is poised and personable as Ludwig's daughter Elsa, though it's ironic that, with a real mid-European cast as a Frankenstein for the first time, Universal suddenly chose to drop the 'von' from the family name. (It had been introduced, for no discernible reason, in *Son of Frankenstein*.) And Lionel Atwill, making his third Frankenstein picture, is on great scene-stealing form as the Mayor – particularly remarkable given the one-year suspended sentence that was handed down to him in the first week of production.

THE GLITTER OF PUTRESCENCE

A character actor labouring under a different sort of sentence was Dwight Frye, who had been condemned to an almost undeviating string of geeks, grotesques and ghouls since appearing in the original *Dracula* and *Frankenstein*. The month before making his small contribution to *Frankenstein Meets the Wolf Man*, he was featured in a cut-price PRC potboiler called *Dead Men Walk*, which began its six-day schedule on 11 September 1942. Like several of PRC's horrors, this was produced by Sigmund Neufeld and directed by his Anglicised younger brother Sam Newfield.

Top-billed for the first of only three occasions in his career (all of them for PRC), George Zucco plays doctor twins Elwyn and Lloyd Clayton, one of them undead and the other sporting a hairpiece. Elwyn, Lloyd explains, "always seemed an alien soul, even in childhood." Now he's a peculiarly salacious vampire, targeting his own niece (Mary Carlisle) and exulting in "the power [that] has been given me to draw everlasting life from the veins of the living." Fred Myton's script trots through all the usual *Dracula*-derived plot mechanics and dialogue, and the result is drearier even than the average PRC quickie, relieved only by Zucco's mad laughter and gloating pronouncements as Elwyn.

"You'll never leave here alive!" Dwight Frye takes a poker to George Zucco in *Dead Men Walk* (1942)

Frye is Zolarr, Elwyn's hunchbacked helper, a parodic combination of the roles that started it all (Renfield and Fritz) to which, commendably, Frye brings undiminished energy. In the quite impressive final conflagration (which puts paid to Lloyd, Elwyn and Zolarr at one stroke), there are some startling close-ups of Zolarr's mad face as he sets about Lloyd with a poker – forlorn reminders of similar shots of the torch-wielding Fritz in *Frankenstein*. Just over a year later, Frye was poised to appear in a long-awaited 'serious' film (a 20th Century-Fox biopic of Woodrow Wilson) when he succumbed to a heart attack, aged 44, on 7 November 1943.

Back at Hallowe'en 1942, the Val Lewton unit at RKO was embroiled in its second artful subversion of a lurid, audience-tested title. This one – *I Walked with a Zombie* – was cunningly attached to a disguised adaptation of *Jane Eyre*, a novel Lewton had become extremely familiar with while preparing a screen version for his old employer David O Selznick. Despite his association with Universal's *The Wolf Man*, Curt Siodmak was engaged to write the script (later revised by Ardel Wray and Lewton himself), and the result remains perhaps Lewton's most venerated title. Even so, Robin Wood's admiring claim that "To analyse the film is but to define its ambiguities"[16] was given an apt translation by Lewton biographer Ed Bansak: "Ultimately the film is more interesting to analyse than it is to watch."[17]

Betsy Connell is sent by an Ottawa recruitment agency to the Caribbean island of St Sebastian, where she is to nurse the cataleptic wife of sugar planter Paul Holland. Though rapidly falling in love with her employer, Betsy tries selflessly to restore Jessica to him first by electro-shock therapy, then by journeying to the Houmfort to consult the local voodoo priest. The latter, however, turns out to be in cahoots with Paul's bitter stepmother Mrs Rand.

Lewton's distaste for the title handed him is given smirking acknowledgment in the heroine's opening voice-over, in which she laughingly admits that it "does seem an odd thing to say." Moments earlier, the film's credits sequence has disclosed a rare, and appropriately half-concealed, instance of Lewton's pawky sense of humour in its 'no lawsuits please' disclaimer: "Any similarity to actual persons, living, dead *or possessed*, is purely coincidental." (Lewton's italics.) In line with this, the central ambiguity this time around concerns the exact status of the apparently braindead Jessica Holland. Has she been turned into a zombie, as Mrs Rand believes, or has

Christine Gordon combines Sleeping Beauty with the lost Lenore in *I Walked with a Zombie* (1942)

I WALKED WITH A ZOMBIE

RKO Radio 1942
69 minutes
production began 26 October

Cinematographer: J Roy Hunt; Art Directors: Albert S D'Agostino, Walter E Keller; Editor: Mark Robson; Sound: John C Grubb, Terry Kellum*, James G Stewart*; Set Decorations: Darrell Silvera, Al Fields; Music: Roy Webb; Musical Director: C Bakaleinikoff; Technical Adviser: LeRoy Antoine*; Assistant Director: William Dorfman; Screenplay: Curt Siodmak, Ardel Wray (based on an original story by Inez Wallace); Producer: Val Lewton; Director: Jacques Tourneur

James Ellison (Wesley Rand); Frances Dee (Betsy Connell); Tom Conway (Paul Holland); Edith Barrett (Mrs Rand); James Bell (Dr Maxwell); Christine Gordon (Jessica Holland); Theresa Harris (Alma); Sir Lancelot (calypso singer); Darby Jones (Carrefour); Jeni LeGon (dancer); uncredited: Richard Abrams (Clement); Vivian Dandridge (Melisse); Alan Edmiston (recruitment officer); Kathleen Hartfield (dancer); Norman Mayes (Bayard); Jieno Moxzer (Sabreur); Clinton Rosemond (coachman); Arthur Joseph (Ti-Joseph); Martin Wilkins (houngan); Melvin Williams (baby)

Lewton receives valued aid from the suspenseful direction by Jacques Tourneur. Their collaboration on *I Walked with a Zombie* stands an excellent chance of breaking the records that *Cat People* broke. In many respects it is a smoother entertainment. *Hollywood Reporter*

It was a small, close unit, comparable to today's independent. There wasn't too much Upstairs interference, except on the everlasting budget problem. And, if I'm not remembering falsely, [there were] some Upstairs fears that sock-it-to-them was being sacrificed for 'arty stuff'.
Ardel Wray [quoted in Siegel, *Val Lewton: The Reality of Terror*, 1972]

she merely succumbed, as the family doctor has it, to a fever well known to science?

The deceptive nature of appearances, and of the dividing line between life and death, has already been expounded by Paul Holland during Betsy's sea voyage to St Sebastian. "Those flying fish," he observes. "They're not leaping for joy, they're jumping in terror; bigger fish want to eat them. That luminous water. It takes its gleam from millions of tiny dead bodies – the glitter of putrescence. There's no beauty here, only death and decay." Unfortunately, this crucial speech is drawled out by Tom Conway (previously the oleaginous Dr Judd of *Cat People*) in the same cultivated monotone that characterises his entire performance, making Betsy's instant adoration for Paul seem inexplicable.

Indeed, of the leading characters, only Frances Dee's obscurely motivated Betsy makes a strong impression. As a result, St Sebastian's two maybe-zombies – Darby Jones' Carrefour and Christine Gordon's Jessica – become the black and white visual cornerstones of the picture. The pallid Jessica is a far cry from the raving Mrs Rochester of *Jane Eyre*; she's more suggestive of Sleeping Beauty or Poe's lost Lenore. Or even – though Lewton would no doubt have rebelled at the suggestion – Mme Sangre in *King of the Zombies*, another white-draped, catatonic consort to an ambiguous older man resident on a tropical island. Barely able to keep her eyes open, the conspicuously white Jessica presents a striking contrast to the bodeful black presence of Carrefour, whose thyroid-afflicted eyes seem frozen into eternal watchfulness by the state of living death.

Temporarily replacing Nicholas Musuraca, cinematographer J Roy Hunt slathers the action in slatted horizontal shadows that never succeed in suggesting the cloying heat of a Caribbean island; very quickly, the technique devolves into mere affectation. Set against this is Jacques Tourneur's masterful direction, which takes its cue from Paul's description of Betsy as "the nurse who's afraid of the dark," encouraging the viewer to gloss 'the dark' as a metaphor for the subconscious.

To this end, the film's catatonic pace is perfectly attuned to Jessica's trance-like state. A case in point is the short scene in which Betsy settles down on a

chaise-longue at the foot of Jessica's bed. Here, Hunt plasters the rear wall in the shadowed arabesques of an ironwork fence, with billowing white drapes agitating the strings of a foreground harp as a cue for Betsy to be enveloped by the lengthening shadow of Carrefour. The moment is given no garish emphasis, and as testament to its power the harp business was faithfully replicated by Italian director Mario Bava in his 1963 shocker *6 donne per l'assassino*.

The dream-like journey undertaken by Betsy and Jessica to the Houmfort applies the same principles. Only a rustling of sugar cane and the lowing of cattle register on the soundtrack as Hunt's gliding camera dispassionately observes their progress, alighting on various voodoo artefacts prior to coolly revealing Carrefour's foot in the pale beam of Betsy's torch. Tourneur even makes an intangible threat out of a cheery calypso singer, whose impudent song regarding the Hollands' tangled family relationships is allowed to encroach on the defenceless Betsy just as insidiously as the zombified Jessica did. This scene seems like Siodmak's subtle rewrite of an episode in his contemporaneous *Frankenstein Meets the Wolf Man* script; Paul's alcoholic half-brother Wesley flinches from the implications of the song in a mild-mannered parallel to Larry Talbot's fury at a rumbustious carnival singalong.

The calypso singer's stealthy approach, which completely belies his usual forelock-tugging demeanour, acts as an index to the uneasy truce between St Sebastian's native population and the colonial types lording it over them. A none-too-subtle symbol of the same theme is provided by the grim ornamentation fronting the Holland homestead – a slave-ship figurehead, popularly known as Ti-Misery, that takes the form of a black St Sebastian impaled on multiple arrows. One of these is eventually used by Wesley in his self-sacrificing murder of Jessica – who, rather disappointingly, has by this stage been identified as the stereotyped 'evil' influence whose feminine wiles have come between two upright young men.

The role of Betsy had originally been intended for Anna Lee, wife of the British director Robert Stevenson, with whom Lewton had been working on *Jane Eyre* when he was called to his post at RKO. Lee would finally act under Lewton's aegis in *Bedlam*, while the *Jane Eyre* project wound up at 20th Century-Fox after Selznick sold on the screen rights. Lewton was no longer involved but Stevenson remained in place as director, though the influence of Orson Welles (credited merely as playing Mr Rochester) hangs heavy over the finished product. This was remarked upon by critics at the time, with one New York reviewer noting that the film "broods darkly over the gloomier aspects of the story ... [and] by a change in emphasis the [Radio City] Music Hall patrons are given a horror drama – and an excellent one."[18] Of Welles' performance, another critic noted, with some justice, that "Almost any other actor in Hollywood, with the possible exception of Frank Sinatra, would have been a better choice for the role of the master of Thornfield."[19] The film opened in February 1944, a full year after it began production. Lewton, meanwhile, had polished off five more pictures.

Reverting to Type

When *I Walked with a Zombie* was completed on 19 November 1942, its forerunner, *Cat People*, had yet to be released. When it was, the results were astonishing, with estimates of its worldwide gross rising as high as $4 million. It had a particularly remarkable run at Hollywood's Hawaii Theatre, and by 12 April 1943 RKO had placed a self-congratulatory ad in the *Hollywood Reporter*. "Who Said a Cat Has Only 9 Lives?" it purred. "They're Still Feeding the Kitty at Hollywood's Hawaii ... Originally booked for 2 weeks, *Cat People* is now in its 13th week!"

The film had opened in New York City – at that established monster mecca, the Rialto – on 7 December 1942. Three days later, Ben Pivar's unit at Universal began production on *Captive Wild Woman*, which melded *Cat People* with another recent release, *Dr Renault's Secret*, and blithely stamped all over the kind of subtleties characteristic of Val Lewton. The film had been in development for some 18 months, so, if plagiarism was involved, it must have been of a distinctly eleventh-hour variety. Even so, if Universal had wanted to provide posterity with an object lesson in the stark difference between their approach and that of Lewton, they couldn't have done better than make *Captive Wild Woman*. On top of which, the film marked John Carradine's horror debut in a leading role – that of a driven scientist who, we're told, "has furthered not one but three attempts at racial improvement."

> *Endocrinologist Dr Sigmund Walters takes hormones from a female patient, and the brain from his assistant Miss Strand, and makes of Cheela the gorilla a glamorous young woman called Paula Dupree. Falling in love with circus lion-tamer Fred Mason, Paula finds herself reverting to animal form when watching him with his fiancée Beth. Targeting Beth for a further brain transplant, Walters is killed by Cheela, who is herself shot down while rescuing Fred from a horde of big cats.*

Captive Wild Woman is an efficient and fast-paced programmer aimed squarely at Universal's juvenile

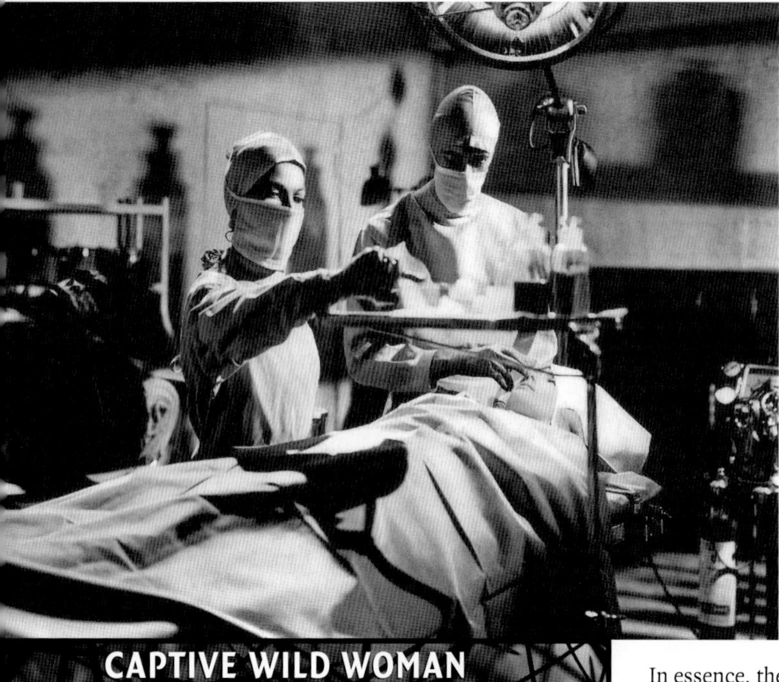

John Carradine and Fay Helm in pursuit of Martha Vickers' surplus sex hormones in *Captive Wild Woman* (1942)

CAPTIVE WILD WOMAN

Universal 1942
60 minutes
production began 10 December

Cinematographer: George Robinson; Art Directors: John B Goodman, Ralph M DeLacy; Editor: Milton Carruth; Sound: Bernard B Brown, William Hedgcock; Set Decorations: R A Gausman, Ira S Webb; Make-up: Jack P Pierce*; Gowns: Vera West; Music: H J Salter, Frank Skinner*; Screenplay: Griffin Jay, Henry Sucher; Story: Ted Fithian, Neil P Varnick, Maurice Pivar*; Associate Producer: Ben Pivar; Director: Edward Dmytryk

John Carradine (Dr Sigmund Walters); Evelyn Ankers (Beth Colman); Milburn Stone (Fred Mason); Lloyd Corrigan (John Whipple); Fay Helm (Miss Strand); Martha MacVicar [later Martha Vickers] (Dorothy Colman); Vince Barnett (Curley); Paul Fix (Gruen); and Acquanetta (Paula Dupree); uncredited: Turhan Bey (narrator); Ray 'Crash' Corrigan (Cheela [the ape]); Fern Emmett (spinster [murder victim]); Alexander Gill (waiter); Gus Glassmire (coroner); Joel Goodkind (boy); William Gould (sheriff); Harry Holman (clerk); Tom London (ship's captain); Charles McAvoy (cop); Frank Mitchell (handler); Ed Peil Sr (Jake); Joey Ray (attendant); Ray Walker (ringmaster); Anthony Warde (Tony); Grant Withers (veterinarian)

The production by Ben Pivar is an all-around good job, and its direction by Edward Dmytryk packs more conviction than is average in such subjects ... John Carradine gives an exceptionally smooth performance of the mad doctor, and Acquanetta is the shapely realization of his creation. Her role is completely without dialog, yet from the moment of her appearance she dominates proceedings. *Hollywood Reporter*

I know that they were testing various actresses at the studio. Yvonne de Carlo was one under consideration ... But, in any event, I tested and they said I was perfect for the role ... It was really interesting to work without speaking in *Captive Wild Woman*. It was more difficult, a challenge.
Acquanetta [quoted in Fangoria, July 1990]

constituency, directed with finesse by Edward Dmytryk and boasting an effectively restrained lead performance from Carradine. It seems to have owed its inception, not merely to a desire to fashion a sexy female version of *The Wolf Man*, but also to a more expedient wish to recycle footage from Universal's 1933 picture *The Big Cage*. To this end, Milburn Stone was briefly promoted to leading man status thanks to his resemblance to the earlier film's lion-tamer, Clyde Beatty.

Unfortunately, the recycled footage is allowed to run on and on – some of it even gets repeated – and this in a picture that only lasts an hour anyway. There is, however, an original sequence in which a tiger breaks loose and causes havoc at a quayside. This is an exciting and well-staged scene until the animal's recoil from Fred is achieved by the laughable trick of running the film backwards.

Where the film scores is in its scenes set at Dr Walters' Crestview Sanatorium, which is introduced to us via a name-plate over which shadowed tree branches wave ominously. In essence, the surgical sequences are little more than business as usual; Walters even gets to say the generic line, "Why should a single life be considered so important?" But they're moodily lit by George Robinson and feature some unusually off-colour details. Beth's ailing younger sister Dorothy, we're told, has "some sort of glandular trouble," but Dr Walters is more specific. She's suffering, he says, from "a rare case of follicular cyst which induces the secretion of unusual amounts of sex hormones." These are duly grafted into a female gorilla played by Ray 'Crash' Corrigan, retained from Universal's *The Strange Case of Doctor Rx*. The eroticised product of Walters' hormonal experiments is a big-breasted exotic whom the doctor christens Paula Dupree, and who is played by the 22-year-old Burnu Acquanetta.

Acquanetta is clearly J Carrol Naish of *Dr Renault's Secret* fused with Kathleen Burke from *Island of Lost Souls*, with some of Simone Simon's sexual hang-ups thrown in for good measure. As Dr Walters puts it, "Terrific emotion [is] the one thing I hadn't counted on." Paula's reaction when Fred and Beth exchange affectionate kisses is ascribed in the film to the same "twisted animal jealousy" referred to by Dr Renault in the Fox picture, but its origin in Paula's confused feelings of sexual arousal are clear enough. In response, she strides furiously into her dressing room and is horrified when she begins to revert to animal form. Jack Pierce's modified Wolf Man make-up is not among his best creations; it also leaves

large sections of Paula's exposed flesh – her legs, her midriff – untouched by encroaching fur, women's body hair presumably counting as a taboo subject.

Even more unfortunate, halfway through the transition Paula unmistakably turns black. This had happened previously in Mamoulian's *Dr Jekyll and Mr Hyde*, when it attracted no particular comment. In the midst of World War II, however, the situation was very different. In 1944, New York critic John T McManus was very clear on this point in his review of the film's first sequel: "In *Mein Kampf* Hitler calls the Negro a 'half-born ape.' *Jungle Woman* illustrates the point, changing a Hollywood glamor girl into an ape and vice versa with the Negro stage inserted right where Hitler says ... The 1943 version [ie, *Captive Wild Woman*] was challenged at the time of its production for its Nazi ideas, but Universal made it anyway. Apparently it is to be an annual outrage unless somebody passes a law against propounding Nazi race theories in America."[20] McManus' fellow critic Archer Winsten was less emphatic, merely drawing attention to "a couple of flashes of Burnu in an intermediate phase in which she resembles the Wolf Man in burnt cork."[21]

Given such accusations, it's ironic that the film should so blatantly present its chief villain as a neo-Nazi. Having just played Gestapo chief Reinhard Heydrich in Douglas Sirk's *Hitler's Madman*, Carradine was now, more or less, playing eugenics obsessive Josef Mengele. Indeed, Carradine's look – the gaunt features, the slicked-back hair, the discreet moustache – would be replicated when Gregory Peck played a superannuated Mengele in *The Boys from Brazil*. The connection is made very plain when Walters' ill-fated assistant Miss Strand – memorably played by Fay Helm – finally rebels against what she calls his "dreams of creating a race of supermen." Unfazed, Walters counters with the chilling observation that such dreams constitute "a laudable intent."

The film's sequels – *Jungle Woman* and *The Jungle Captive* – were churned out in February and September of 1944 respectively, and are as threadbare and cynical a pair of potboilers as Universal ever produced. In the first, Acquanetta is revived by J Carrol Naish (appropriately, given his own apish track record in *Dr Renault's Secret*), only to be killed by him in a climactic clinch. Directed by Reginald LeBorg, the film doesn't give us a good look at Paula's hirsute incarnation until the very end, presumably in a tragic attempt to 'ape' the elliptical Val Lewton approach. After this, the release of Harold Young's *The Jungle Captive* was withheld until June 1945. Just as trashy as its predecessor, it has mad biochemist Otto Kruger reviving a brain-damaged Paula in the new shape of Vicky Lane, who, unlike Acquanetta in *Jungle Woman*, is denied dialogue. "Lane," as critic Tim Lucas put it in 1998, "is not as visually striking as her predecessor, but she gives the role something Acquanetta could never quite muster – a performance."[22]

Back in December 1942, Bela Lugosi had gone the Acquanetta route in *The Ape Man*, a Monogram potboiler that began production only six days after *Captive Wild Woman*. Originally announced as *The Gorilla Strikes*, William Beaudine's film is widely held by Lugosi fans to be the crowning humiliation in a career that was beginning to proliferate with them. Just a few weeks after the debacle that was *Frankenstein Meets the Wolf Man*, Lugosi was plastered in excess hair and required to scuttle about in an ape-like posture as Dr James Brewster, the name presumably a nod to the stage role currently being played by his old rival Boris Karloff.

Minerva Urecal sympathises with her much-changed brother (Bela Lugosi) in *The Ape Man* (1942)

The story was based on a treatment by Karl Brown, author of Karloff's 'mad doctor' pictures for Columbia, and picks up a cue from Karloff's one-and-only Monogram horror, *The Ape*. Having dosed himself with simian spinal fluid, Lugosi's Brewster becomes convinced that "I must have human spinal fluid injected into me; it's my only chance." Hence the predictable murder spree, in which he is abetted by a bona-fide gorilla – as bona-fide, at any rate, as Emil Van Horn's ridiculous ape-suit will allow. For what it's worth, *The Ape Man* contains one or two legitimately funny lines (as when the murder detective suggests that "Whoever did it sure needed a hair-cut"), together with a self-reflexive pay-off that has to be seen to be believed. Ushering in the film's End title, an imbecilic little character who has been shadowing the action throughout is finally challenged to identify himself. "Me?" he beams, looking straight into camera. "Oh, I'm the author of the story. Screwy idea, wasn't it?"

Part Five

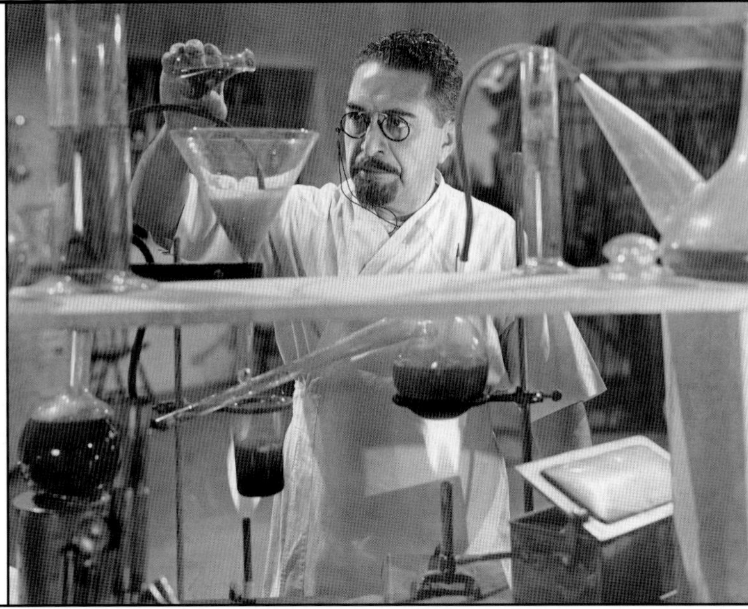

Mad scientist J Carroll Naish cooks up his bone-distorting formula in *The Monster Maker* (1944)

Diminishing Returns 1943-1945

Precipitated into war by the events of 7 December 1941, the American people saw radical changes during the ensuing four years – Roosevelt's New Deal programmes deprioritised, many of them discontinued altogether; unemployment almost eradicated in the interests of the war effort but poverty, paradoxically, on the rise; six million women joining the workforce to the tune of 'Rosie the Riveter'; a massive population shift that transplanted some 15 million Americans into urban centres. In the meantime, the first 12 months of the war brought some morale-boosting developments in the conflict itself, among them the Japanese fleet's expulsion from Midway in June 1942 and, starting in October, the Allied victories in north Africa co-ordinated by Field Marshal Montgomery and General Dwight D Eisenhower.

Gung-ho wartime propaganda inevitably became a staple in all Hollywood studios, horror pictures featuring Nazi villains as early as *King of the Zombies* in April 1941, with the Japanese following suit in *Black Dragons* the following January. Soon after this Universal's *Invisible Agent* cannily combined the two in the unlikely shapes of Sir Cedric Hardwicke and Peter Lorre.

In the same vein, Benjamin Stoloff directed *The Mysterious Doctor* for Warner Bros in March 1943, the result later being slapped with an 'H' in the UK for its opening scenes of a headless ghost roaming an English moor. At the time, the film was applauded by the *Hollywood Reporter* for containing "all the claptrap dear to the hearts of horror fans" and for "bludgeoning the nerves to a frazzle."[1] Seen now, however, it comes across as a mere cheat, with Stoloff's atmospheric efforts vitiated by a banal resolution in which the spook is exposed as a Nazi agent. The same galling plot twist (an up-to-date version of the old 'crooks disguised as bogies' gag) cropped up several times in contemporaneous British films. Starring local luminaries like Arthur Askey and Will Hay, these at least had the virtue of being comedies.

CENTRAL MIS-CASTING

1943 began at Universal with plans for a lavish Technicolor extravaganza budgeted at over $1.75 million. The notion of remaking *The Phantom of the Opera* had first arisen in the mid-1930s, director Anatole Litvak, ingenue Deanna Durbin and character

star Charles Laughton all being mooted for the project at various times in the interim. With George Waggner in charge, the final product started shooting on 21 January; Arthur Lubin was the director and centre stage was given over to M-G-M singing star Nelson Eddy. The title was crudely foreshortened to just *Phantom of the Opera*, with Claude Rains, fresh from *Casablanca*, making surprisingly little impression in the role.

To weaken him further, screenwriters Eric Taylor and Samuel Hoffenstein created a frankly banal backstory, rendered, not in flashbacks, but as a strictly linear feature of the main narrative. The result is that no atmosphere of mystery is built up around him; this Phantom is a pensioned-off violinist, Erique Claudin, who moves straight from a traumatic vitriol-splashing into the opera catacombs, apparently residing there for only a matter of days before being crushed in a climactic cave-in. (It's an ironic end given that he's just had the chance to utter the script's one-and-only resonant line: "Life here is like a resurrection.") And the vitriol episode proceeds from a ludicrous misunderstanding on Claudin's part; he merely *thinks* Miles Mander has misappropriated his concerto, whereupon he strangles him and receives the requisite face-full of acid. And the incident is staged with no excitement whatsoever.

Claude Rains coaches Susanna Foster in Universal's high-gloss remake of *Phantom of the Opera* (1943)

The same applies to the remainder of the action, with the Technicolor adding eye-popping lustre to the yards of red plush decorating Universal's refurbished Phantom stage but cruelly exposing the inch-thick pancake on the actors' faces and the plastic sterility of the sets. On top of this, the film's comic relief revolves around the superannuated Nelson Eddy and Edgar Barrier competing for the favours of 18-year-old diva Susanna Foster, plumbing mirthless depths undreamed of by all the 1930s' wisecracking reporters put together. The film was a smash, however, and its vulgarian attempt at 'high' culture inevitably garnered Academy recognition, resulting in Oscars for Color Art Direction, Color Photography and Set Decoration.

Preoccupied with *Phantom of the Opera*, George Waggner was unavailable to supervise the next stage in Universal's continuing saga of casting Lon Chaney Jr in inappropriate roles. Having spent the run-up to Christmas encased in the simian whiskers of *The Ape Man*, Bela Lugosi was reportedly furious about Universal's decision to star Chaney in *Son of Dracula*, a belated second sequel that, in fact, bears virtually no relation to the Lugosi original.

The script – eventually written by Eric Taylor – had originally been assigned to the reliable Curt Siodmak, but his participation was abruptly terminated when his competitive elder brother Robert came on board as director. The latter was an Ufa graduate who in 1944 would make an effective Universal adaptation of the Dr Crippen story called *The Suspect*, also proving himself a master of film noir in pictures like *Phantom Lady* and *The Killers*. Unsurprisingly then, *Son of Dracula* endures as perhaps the darkest and most beguiling of Universal's wartime horror pictures.

> *Kay Caldwell, heiress to a Southern plantation called Dark Oaks, secretly gets married to the undead Count Alucard. Learning of this, her fiancé Frank shoots his invulnerable rival but succeeds only in killing Kay. Kay, now undead, explains to Frank, now deranged, that her union with Alucard was just a ruse to gain eternal life, which she proposes to spend with Frank. Frank dutifully destroys Alucard in furtherance of her plan, but then sorrowfully destroys Kay too.*

Inspired, perhaps, by the latest version of *The Cat and the Canary*, the setting of *Son of Dracula* was presumably Taylor's gesture towards bringing vampirism into contemporary America (as Stoker had brought it to contemporary London), while still retaining a whiff of hothouse Louisiana exoticism. Unfortunately, there are no broiling Deep South histrionics such as Tennessee Williams would later make his own; the Caldwells are a mild-mannered bunch not so different from the Sewards featured in Universal's first Dracula film. Colonel Caldwell, for instance, is no blustering Big Daddy as per *Cat on a Hot Tin Roof*, he's a genteel invalid in a wheelchair

SON OF DRACULA

Universal 1943
78 minutes
production began 6 January

Cinematographer: George Robinson; Art Directors: John B Goodman, Martin Obzina; Editor: Saul Goodkind; Sound: Bernard B Brown, Charles Carroll, Edwin Wetzel*; Special Effects: John P Fulton; Set Decorations: R A Gausman, E R Robinson; Make-up: Jack P Pierce*; Gowns: Vera West; Music: H J Salter; Assistant Director: Melville Shyer; Screenplay: Eric Taylor; Original Story: Curtis [Curt] Siodmak; Associate Producer: Donald H Brown; Executive Producer: Jack J Gross*; Producer [and Second Unit Director*]: Ford Beebe; Director: Robert Siodmak

Robert Paige (Frank Stanley); Louise Allbritton (Katherine Caldwell); Evelyn Ankers (Claire Caldwell); Frank Craven (Doctor Brewster); J Edward Bromberg (Professor Lazlo); Samuel S Hinds (Judge Simmons); Adeline DeWalt Reynolds (Madame Zimba); Patrick Moriarity (Sheriff Dawes); Etta McDaniel (Sarah [maid]); George Irving (Colonel Caldwell); and Lon Chaney [Jr] as Count Dracula; uncredited: Charles Bates (Tommy Land); Joan Blair (Mrs Land); Jess Lee Brooks (Steven [valet]); Cyril Delevanti (Dr Peters); Robert Dudley (Jonathan Kirby); George Meeker (guest); Sam McDaniel (Andy [servant]); Charles Moore (Matthew [workman]); Jack Rockwell (Deputy Sheriff); Walter Sande (Deputy Matt); Emmett Smith (servant)

***Son of Dracula*, which arrived at the Rialto yesterday [5 November 1943], like its predecessors, is often as unintentionally funny as it is chilling ... But, as one of the principals remarks, "Gentlemen, the further we go, the crazier this gets." You can say that again, brother!** *New York Times*

In 1943 I had been in Hollywood for three years, doing what work I could get. Then Universal sent me the script of *Son of Dracula*: it was terrible – it had been knocked together in a few days ... [But] we did a lot of rewriting and the result wasn't bad: it wasn't *good*, but some scenes had a certain quality.
Robert Siodmak [quoted in Sight and Sound, Summer-Autumn 1959]

A Southern Gothic romance for Lon Chaney Jr and Louise Allbritton in *Son of Dracula* (1943)

who becomes Dracula's first US victim for reasons that are initially unclear.

The precise identity of the vampire, however, remains unclear throughout. The film's cherubic Van Helsing substitute, Professor Lazlo, suggests that he is "probably a descendant of Count Dracula," going by the name Alucard as a kind of anagrammatic joke. The ambiguity helps Chaney's performance, which is unlikely to satisfy anyone as a representation of Dracula but, taken on its own terms, presents a perfectly acceptable vampire and certainly a physically imposing one. For an actor who never looked at home in Larry Talbot's double-breasted suits, he carries off Alucard's more formal attire surprisingly well, also not disgracing himself when offered some scraps of modified Stoker dialogue. (As well as saying "I like old houses," Alucard observes that, in his homeland, "The soil is red with the blood of a hundred races.") Chaney lends desperate conviction, too, to Alucard's mortal panic when Frank locates his coffin in its fetid bayou hideaway and torches it.

Alucard's demise – a somewhat ignominious one, in that sunlight causes him to fall face-first into a pool of swamp water – is merely the most dynamic of several visual coups Siodmak pulls off in the course of the picture, coups that go hand in hand with some grandstanding innovations from John Fulton's special effects department. As well as seeing Alucard's outstretched hand reduced to its bare bones in the finale, we're also given the first of Universal's man-into-bat transformations (a slightly cartoonish animation effect, but none the worse for that) and some stunning shots of Alucard materialising from what Stoker called "a sort of pillar of cloud."

In one of these, his coffin rises to the surface of the swamp as vapour billows out of it, the reconstituted Count standing astride it as it glides inexorably towards Kay on the opposite shore. This is a startling vignette on several levels: as critic Dean Brierly puts it, "Siodmak's trademark forward-tracking camera imparts both a feeling of weightlessness and imminent sexual union."[2] On top of this, the Messianic 'walking on water' idea is as cogent a demonstration of the vampire's Anti-Christ status as anything Stoker dreamed up, while Hans Salter's score (excellent throughout) introduces a string-laden nautical theme to emphasise the scene's romantic sweep.

Alucard's reason for abandoning his Hungarian roots is much the same as the rationale Stoker gave Dracula for moving to London. The sagacious Dr Brewster describes the US as "a younger country, stronger and more virile," while Alucard himself describes his homeland as "dry and decadent" – and, tellingly, Chaney pronounces the latter word as "decay-dent." The link between the two worlds, Old and New, is provided by the film's most unusual character. Kay Caldwell's relationship with Alucard is a legacy of a recent trip to Budapest; she has also imported a toothless gypsy seer called Queen Zimba, an obvious clone of *The Wolf Man*'s Maleva

who quickly falls foul of Alucard's bat incarnation. (From the staging, it looks as if the bat puts the old woman's eyes out, though we later learn she died of a heart attack.) Kay's scheme is intriguing because it involves duping the supposedly all-powerful vampire – a genuinely surprising twist. But Kay herself is intriguing for what Lazlo calls her thanatophobia, which could just as easily be described as thanatophilia.

An infinitely more 'unhealthy' figure than *Dracula's Daughter*, Kay isn't struggling to free herself from a curse but, on the contrary, to bring it on. Unlike Luna in *Mark of the Vampire*, Kay prefigures the latterday 'Goth' youth cult in more than just her sepulchral appearance; she also has a whole philosophy worked out, ensuring that Queen Zimba's last-ever prediction – "I see you marrying a corpse" – seems to Kay not so much a threat as a promise.

After the unusually well-dressed role of Alucard, Chaney Jr would find himself back in the grimy wrappings of his least favourite role by the end of August. Reginald LeBorg's *The Mummy's Ghost* is another tired retread of the Kharis saga, with Chaney lurching through the sun-dappled Massachusetts night in a distressingly inexpressive face-mask. John Carradine is the swarthy High Priest on this occasion; his inappropriate passion for the heroine (who, in a forlorn echo of the Karl Freund original, is a reincarnation of Kharis' former love) leads to swift retribution at Kharis' mouldy hands. There's also a well-staged murder in the Scripps museum, with poor old Oscar O'Shea bashed against a plate-glass doorframe prior to being strangled.

Immediately prior to this, and for no readily apparent reason, there's an unusually self-reflexive, two-pronged reference to Lionel Atwill; as O'Shea relaxes in his office with a detective magazine, the narrator of a spooky radio drama mentions "the darkened study of Dr X, the mad doctor of Market Street." There are a couple of other scattered grace notes: a black cat crossing the heroine's path before her first encounter with Kharis, and the monster's shadow falling across hero and heroine as they neck in a parked car. Otherwise, the film is a by-the-numbers washout. It would take nearly 12 months to reach cinemas, going out in tandem with LeBorg's even less appetising *Jungle Woman*.

LATIN GLAMOUR AND FAMILY SKELETONS

In February 1943, while *Cat People* continued to make money and *I Walked with a Zombie* awaited release, RKO distributed Malcolm St Clair's vapid independent comedy *Two Weeks to Live*, which brought elderly radio comics Lum and Abner (Chester Lauck and Norris Goff) into contact with, among others, a statuesque Miss America, Rosemary LaPlanche, as herself and Luis Alberni as a comic Dr Jekyll. More importantly, the same month saw Val Lewton's RKO unit putting a third horror picture into production in a conscious attempt to capitalise on the meteoric success of *Cat People*.

Lewton had proposed Cornell Woolrich's novel *Black Alibi* back when the subject matter of *Cat People* was being debated some ten months earlier. It was pressed into service instead for *The Leopard Man*, which would turn out to be Lewton's last collaboration with Jacques Tourneur. Ardel Wray (daughter of the former director John Wray, who had acted in such shockers as *Doctor X* and *The Cat and the Canary*) was retained as screenwriter. This was slightly surprising in that – irrespective of the prominence given in his films to strong and resourceful female characters – Lewton reportedly had difficulty working with women.

> *During a nightclub engagement in New Mexico, promoter Jerry Manning arranges for his client Kiki Walker to make an eye-catching entrance with a black panther on a leash. Unfortunately, the animal gets loose and later kills young Teresa Delgado. When two further women die, Jerry theorises that a man is behind the latter killings, finally tracing them to Galbraith, a local academic who confesses to having been driven to kill by recurring visions of Teresa's mutilated body.*

Roy Webb's impressive score sets out the film's central motif in the opening credits, utilising a Hispanic flourish of castanets that resonates throughout the action. "When the dudes come out to New Mexico," explains a jaded nightclub cigarette girl in the opening scene, "they want to wallow in Latin glamour." The latter is provided by the sultry Clo-Clo, whose act is upstaged by Kiki's panther-toting entrance but who turns the tables in spectacular style by waggling her castanets in the beast's face and causing it to bolt. Moments before, the panther has been the subject of an especially good gag at the expense of one of the hoariest of genre clichés, the ominously opening door that admits only a harmless domestic cat. This time it admits a fearsome panther – safely corralled, however, by Kiki's hucksterish manager, Jerry Manning.

Once on the loose, the panther is central to a classic sequence that parallels *Cat People*'s nocturnal 'walk' and the elaborate variant featured in *I Walked with a Zombie*.

A child's shadowplay prefigures a night of terror for Margaret Landry in *The Leopard Man* (1943)

THE LEOPARD MAN

RKO Radio 1943
66 minutes
production began 4 February

Cinematographer: Robert de Grasse; Art Directors: Albert S D'Agostino, Walter E Keller; Editor: Mark Robson; Sound: John C Grubb, Terry Kellum*, James G Stewart*; Optical Effects: Linwood Dunn*; Set Decorations: Darrell Silvera, Al Fields; Music: Roy Webb; Musical Director: C Bakaleinikoff; Assistant Director: William Dorfman; Screenplay: Ardel Wray (from the novel *Black Alibi* by Cornell Woolrich); Additional Dialogue: Edward Dein; Producer: Val Lewton; Director: Jacques Tourneur

Dennis O'Keefe (Jerry Manning); Margo (Clo-Clo); Jean Brooks (Kiki Walker); Isabel Jewell (Maria); James Bell (Dr Galbraith); Margaret Landry (Teresa Delgado); Abner Biberman (Charlie How-Come); Tula Parma (Consuela Contreras); Ben Bard (Chief Robles); uncredited: Robert Anderson (Dwight); Jacqueline DeWit (Helene); John Dilson (coroner); Kate Drain Lawson (Señora Delgado); Dynamite (panther); Fely Franquelli (Rosita); Eliso Gamboa (Señor Delgado); William Halligan (Brunton); Ariel Heath (Eloise); Rose Higgins (Indian woman); Brandon Hurst (cemetery caretaker); Jacques Lory (Philippe); Charles Lung (Manuel [grocer]); Richard Martin (Raoul Belmonte); Mary McLaren (nun); Ottola Nesmith (Señora Contreras); Tom Orosco (window cleaner); René Pedrina (wounded waiter); John Piffle (flower seller); Betty Roadman (Clo-Clo's mother); Bobby Spindola (Pedro); Margaret Sylva (Marta); John Tettemer (minister); Rosita Varella (Clo-Clo's sister); Russell Wade (man in car); Joe Dominguez, George Sherwood (policemen)

Third of the psychological horror stories that Val Lewton has produced and Jacques Tourneur directed at RKO, ... *The Leopard Man* cannot hope to equal the grosses of its predecessors. Chiefly lacking in the plot adapted from Cornell Woolrich's novel, *Black Alibi*, is the element of legendary superstition that made the other two provocative. *Hollywood Reporter*

Personally, I don't like *The Leopard Man*. It's episodic, a series of vignettes. It got very confusing. After three pictures, RKO felt that, since Val and I worked so well together, we would work twice as well separately. They loaned me to Universal to do *Canyon Passage* and Val continued his series of films ... all fine pictures.
Jacques Tourneur [quoted in Cinefantastique, Summer 1973]

Clo-Clo having been dealt a death card by a blowzy fortune-teller, we fully expect the fateful 'walk' to be hers; instead, the focus shifts when she offers a cheery greeting to a teenage girl. Sent out by her mother to fetch cornmeal for her father's tortillas, every detail of Teresa's after-hours odyssey is expertly crafted: the distant train whistle and subliminal wind on the soundtrack; the dark expanse that disgorges a rolling tumbleweed; a sinister viaduct resonating to the methodical drip of water and pulsing with rippling light imported from *Cat People*'s pool sequence; the same film's hissing 'bus' reproduced to the power of ten by the sudden roar of an overhead train.

After so brilliant a succession of teases, it comes as a genuine shock when a massive close-up discloses the watchful panther hovering above her, and the shift to the interior of the girl's home, with the now unseen Teresa clamouring for admittance and her mother taking her own sweet time about going to the door, is agonising in the extreme. (A very nifty bit of dramatic irony from the mean-spirited mother here: "Just what she needs: someone to nip at her heels and hurry her up.") The sequel – a puddle of blood oozing under the still unopened door – is a real shocker, and was presumably derived from the same effect in *Le Système du Docteur Goudron et du Professeur Plume*, which was directed by Tourneur's father Maurice in 1912.

That life goes on is cruelly demonstrated when the busy shadow of a window-cleaner is cast on the girl's wake the following morning; her little brother, meanwhile, continues to make a cat-shaped silhouette with his hands, just as he did the night before. (This, perhaps, is a reference to Tourneur's claim – not an entirely credible one – that the panther shadow in *Cat People*'s pool sequence was created by his own fist.) The precariousness of human existence, a theme common to all Lewton's horror pictures, is aptly expressed back at the nightclub by the film's resident pipe-smoking boffin, Dr Galbraith. "I've learned one thing about life," he muses. "We're a bit like that ball dancing on a fountain. We know as little about the forces that

move us, and move the world around us, as that empty ball does."

Another philosophical character, roughly equivalent to the zookeeper in *Cat People*, is a cemetery caretaker played by the ancient Brandon Hurst. But it's James Bell's Galbraith who turns out to be the killer. His final monologue ("I saw her white face, the eyes full of fear ... the little frail body, the soft skin") is sufficiently nasty to redeem a dull third act in which Jerry and Kiki join forces to track down the culprit. Galbraith is apprehended at a strange procession commemorating the centuries-old massacre of a community of Native Americans by Spanish Conquistadors, a detail that links back to the colonial theme of *I Walked with a Zombie* but which is explained in expository dialogue so clumsy it's a wonder Lewton allowed it to pass.

The Leopard Man may be minor Lewton, with his suggestive strictures already seeming formulaic at only the third attempt. But its central stalking sequence is a tour de force, and it contains two others that are almost as good. In one of these, tree branches are shown bending over the high wall of a cemetery with an otherworldly purpose far outstripping the same effect in *Cat People*.

Over at Paramount, the influence of the Lewton unit was felt in a new project based on a successful novel by the Anglo-Irish writer Dorothy Macardle. To translate *Uneasy Freehold* to the screen, key positions were assigned to the English playwright and novelist Dodie Smith, who was yet to create her evergreen *101 Dalmatians*, and English actor Lewis Allen, who was studying filmmaking techniques under Paramount's aegis but had yet to direct a film. Another vital contributor to the project was Farciot Edouart, who built on the photographic slight-of-hand he had perfected in *The Ghost Breakers* to create a memorably baleful, ectoplasmic spirit. The result took as its title the name attached to the 'popular' edition of Macardle's book, *The Uninvited* – and was virtually unprecedented in that it employed its ghosts, not for comedy, but as crucial factors in a serious drama.

In 1937, composer Rick Fitzgerald and his sister Pamela buy an abandoned Cornish mansion at a knockdown price. The vendor, Commander Beech, seems strangely insistent that his grand-daughter Stella shouldn't enter the property, and the Fitzgeralds, assailed by supernatural manifestations, establish that Windward House is haunted by two ghosts – Stella's supposed mother, Mary Meredith, and her actual mother, Carmel. The first of these is a malevolent spirit that twice propels Stella to the edge of a precipitous cliff...

Critic Michael Brunas hit the nail on the head regarding Allen's debut film when he declared that "*The Uninvited* is probably the supreme example of a horror movie for people who don't like horror movies."[3] The film took its cue from RKO's success with *Rebecca* (for Mrs DeWinter, read Mary Meredith) but is wrapped in so suffocating a mantle of faux-English gloss that it turns its tale of a maleficent ghost into a peculiarly twee after-dinner anecdote. Something of its anodyne flavour is conveyed in the Fitzgeralds' first encounter with Windward House, when they gain entrance only because their boisterous terrier pursues a squirrel through one of its open windows.

THE UNINVITED

Paramount 1943
100 minutes
production began 14 April

Cinematographer: Charles Lang Jr; Art Directors: Hans Dreier, Ernst Fegté; Editor: Doane Harrison; Sound: Hugo Grenzbach, John Cope; Process Photography: Farciot Edouart; Set Decorations: Stephen Seymour; Make-up: Wally Westmore; Costumes: Edith Head; Music: Victor Young; Screenplay: Dodie Smith, Frank Partos (based on the novel [*Uneasy Freehold*] by Dorothy Macardle); Associate Producer: Charles Brackett; Director: Lewis Allen

Ray Milland (Roderick Fitzgerald); Ruth Hussey (Pamela Fitzgerald); Gail Russell (Stella Meredith); Donald Crisp (Commander Beech); Cornelia Otis Skinner (Miss Holloway); Dorothy Stickney (Miss Bird); Barbara Everest (Lizzie Flynn); Alan Napier (Dr Scott); uncredited: Norman Ainsley (chauffeur); David Clyde (boat hire man); Helena Grant (Edith [Dr Scott's maid]); Holmes Herbert (Charlie Jessup); Leland Hodgson (taxi driver); George Kirby (gas station attendant); Queenie Leonard (Mrs Taylor); Moyna MacGill (Mrs Coatsworthy); Ottola Nesmith (Mrs Carlton); Jessica Newcombe (Miss Ellis); Rita Page (Annie [Beech's maid]); Elizabeth Russell (ghost of Mary Meredith); Ivan Simpson (Hardy [tobacconist]); Evan Thomas (Colonel Carlton)

Whether or not you believe in ghosts, there are plenty of scary moments in the Globe Theatre's new picture ... The spooky angles of the story are handled seriously, and adroit direction, scripting and acting make it a thoroughly absorbing, if shuddery entertainment. *New York Journal-American*

Except for the English accent, all I had to do was be myself. To acquire the accent – five other girls with English accents were competing – Paramount drama coach Bill Russell locked me in a projection room. I saw *Pygmalion* four times, *Rebecca* twice, and *Young Mr Pitt* twice ... When I came out I had a British accent thicker than a London fog.
Gail Russell [reprinted in McClelland, *Forties Film Talk*, 1992]

Ruth Hussey and Ray Milland become aware of an uneasy presence in *The Uninvited* (1943)

Pamela's instant love affair with the house is tempered only by the discovery of an inaccessible upstairs room. "It's locked," observes Rick. "Family skeleton, probably." The film is engaging and efficient as it ticks off all the haunted house clichés that were fresh in 1943 but would later be beaten to death in such films as *Burnt Offerings* and *The Amityville Horror*. Among others, we have the crusty owner who states unequivocally that "No house is haunted" yet sells the property for a suspiciously reasonable £1200; the mystery room that turns out to be peculiarly damp, causing flowers to wilt and the male buyer to become inexplicably depressed; the mutterings in the nearby fishing village regarding the tragic fatality that took place in the grounds; the pungent scent that accompanies the supernatural manifestations; the eerie female sobbing that breaks out in the run-up to dawn.

This last effect (also featured in *I Walked with a Zombie*, which went on release just as *The Uninvited* went into production) is extremely well done, conjuring a tangible atmosphere of otherworldly dread as the Fitzgeralds lean over the banister in quest of its source. A memorable vignette is then punctured beyond repair when Rick dives back into bed and pulls the covers over his head, a reaction better suited to Johnny Arthur in *The Ghost Walks* than Ray Milland in a high-gloss Paramount production. Obviously, Allen's serious approach only went so far. The same undercutting is evident at the end, when it has been established (not too clearly) that Windward House is inhabited, not just by the shade of Mary Meredith, but also by her Romany love rival Carmel. Armed with this knowledge, Rick finally exorcises the malignant Mary by afflicting her with "the sound of laughter" and contemptuously flinging a candelabra at her, all of which would be fine were it not for the inanely self-satisfied grin Rick wears on accomplishing this feat.

Though barely discernible amid Edouart's tendrils of swirling ectoplasm, the ghost was played by the gaunt-faced Elizabeth Russell, who had made a big impact, in a very short space of time, as the chic 'Cat Woman' in *Cat People*. Her time here is just as short but her impact is diluted by a saccharine pay-off in which Rick goes into a clinch with Stella, which we've been prepared for, and Pamela does the same with the patrician Dr Scott, which we've not been prepared for at all. The whole thing wraps up on a tired gag from Rick: "I've had a narrow escape. She [the ghost] might have been my mother-in-law!" Suddenly, we're back in *The Ghost Breakers* after all.

Allen's light touch, of course, was ideally calculated to make *The Uninvited* a mainstream hit in the mid-1940s. He had to tread carefully, in any case, given that the mild frissons provided by the paranormal subject matter were under scrutiny from both the PCA and the Legion of Decency. The latter body, for instance, complained that "The spiritistic seance sequence is so constructed as to convey impressions of credence and possible invitation to spiritistic practices," as well as fretting over the more general observation that "in certain theaters large audiences of questionable types attended this film at unusual hours."[4]

The Legion was also concerned by one of the supporting characters. The hint of lesbianism conveyed by Elizabeth Russell's character in *Cat People* is perpetuated in *The Uninvited* by actress-playwright Cornelia Otis Skinner, who plays the discreetly butch head of an asylum called the Mary Meredith Retreat. Unfortunately, Skinner is dressed and made-up like Gloria Holden in *Dracula's Daughter* (another vaguely lesbian horror character), and is saddled with a tedious chunk of exposition and a wholly ludicrous lapse into madness.

Whatever its shortcomings, *The Uninvited* garnered an Oscar nomination for Charles Lang's cinematography and remains a popular ghost story to this day. More importantly, its relatively serious approach was a deviation from its contemporaries, where the spirit world was played either for laughs or wartime sentiment.

Traditional haunted house comedies were still available, such as *Henry Aldrich Haunts a House* (1943) and *Gildersleeve's Ghost* (1944), the latter featuring Charles Gemora in his usual gorilla get-up. But raffish sophistication was the order of the day elsewhere, the trend having been sparked off by Norman Z McLeod's *Topper* (1937), in which Cary Grant and Constance Bennett are screwball ghosts revolutionising the life of stuffed-shirt Roland Young; it sired two equally accomplished sequels in McLeod's *Topper Takes a Trip* (1938) and Roy Del Ruth's *Topper Returns* (1941). Derived, like *Topper*, from a story by Thorne Smith, René Clair's delightful *I Married a Witch* (1942) has Veronica Lake and Cecil Kellaway as father-and-daughter revenants who bedevil the descendant (Fredric March) of their Puritan persecutors.

The use of ghosts as an emotionally cathartic glimpse into the afterlife (together with the attendant danger of tipping over into schmaltz) had been foreshadowed pre-war by Irving Pichel's *Earthbound* and Edward Sutherland's *Beyond Tomorrow* (both 1940). In 1943, post-Pearl Harbor, Pichel followed up with Harry Carey as a spectral grandfather in *Happy Land*, Victor Fleming cast Spencer Tracy as a deceased bombardier in *A Guy Named Joe* and Edward A Blatt made *Between Two Worlds*; the latter was an updated

Jean Brooks under threat from Palladist assassin Feodor Chaliapin Jr in *The Seventh Victim* (1943)

version of Sutton Vane's play *Outward Bound*, previously filmed under that title in 1930. By 1945, even Universal were getting in on the act via Charles Lamont's winsome musical-comedy *That's the Spirit*. The same process, alternating between comedy and catharsis, was in train elsewhere; Britain, for example, yielded *Blithe Spirit* and *The Halfway House*. Post-war, Hollywood maintained the tradition in Joseph L Mankiewicz's *The Ghost and Mrs Muir* (1947) and William Dieterle's *Portrait of Jennie* (1948).

Missing Persons and Bleeding Hearts

After *The Leopard Man*, Jacques Tourneur was removed from the Lewton unit and promoted to supposedly more prestigious RKO pictures, including a glamorous but unconvincing *Gaslight* variant called *Experiment Perilous*. Lewton's choice to replace him was editor Mark Robson, who took on the challenge despite his conviction that Tourneur was "an extraordinary talent and [*I Walked with a*] *Zombie* is one of the most exquisite films ever made."[5] Robson's first assignment was *The Seventh Victim*, the research for which involved the film's co-writer DeWitt Bodeen sitting in on a meeting of genuine New York Satanists. He noted later that "they were exactly like the devil-worshippers in [Roman Polanski's 1967 film] *Rosemary's Baby* ... A bunch of tea-drinking old ladies and gentlemen, sitting there muttering imprecations against Hitler."[6]

Student Mary Gibson comes to Manhattan to locate her missing sister Jacqueline. She accompanies a private detective to the headquarters of La Sagesse, a cosmetics company formerly owned by Jacqueline, only for him to be murdered by an unknown assailant. Mary finally learns that her sister has fallen in with a cult of Palladists, who are now demanding that she kill herself in atonement for betraying the group to psychiatrist Dr Louis Judd.

The Seventh Victim opens on a stained-glass window and a quote from the 17th century metaphysical poet John Donne, setting the tone perfectly for a film more steeped in morbidity than anything since Ulmer's *The Black Cat* – "I runne to death, and death meets me as fast / And all my pleasures are like yesterday." As Mary sets out on her quest, the girlish atmosphere at Highcliffe Academy is punctured by several small portents. Off in the distance, a battery of teenage voices can be heard declining the French verb 'chercher', to search, while the cloistered Miss Gilchrist – who, along with headmistress Miss

THE SEVENTH VICTIM

RKO Radio 1943
71 minutes
production began 4 May

Cinematographer: Nicholas Musuraca; Art Directors: Albert S D'Agostino, Walter E Keller; Editor: John Lockert; Sound: John C Grubb; Optical Effects: Linwood Dunn*; Effects Cameraman: Harry Underwood*; Set Decorations: Darrell Silvera, Harley Miller; Gowns: Renié; Music: Roy Webb; Musical Director: C Bakaleinikoff; Dialogue Director: Jacqueline DeWit*; Assistant Director: William Dorfman; Screenplay: Charles O'Neal, DeWitt Bodeen; Producer: Val Lewton; Director: Mark Robson

Tom Conway (Dr Louis Judd); Jean Brooks (Jacqueline Gibson); Isabel Jewell (Frances Fallon); Kim Hunter (Mary Gibson); Evelyn Brent (Natalie Cortez); Erford Gage (Jason Hoag); Ben Bard (Bruins); Hugh Beaumont (Gregory Ward); Chef Milani (Mr Romari); Marguerita Sylva (Mrs Romari); uncredited: Joan Barclay (Gladys); Wally Brown (Durk); Feodor Chaliapin Jr (Leo); Kernan Cripps (policeman); Edythe Elliott (Mrs Swift); William Halligan (Radeau); Lloyd Ingraham (watchman); Milton Kibbee (Joseph); Lou Lubin (Irving August); Eve March (Miss Gilchrist); Marianne Mosner (Miss Rowan); Ottola Nesmith (Miss Lowood); Mary Newton (Mrs Redi); Betty Roadman (Mrs Wheeler); Dewey Robinson (conductor); Elizabeth Russell (Mimi); Sara Selby (Miss Gottschalk [librarian]); Ann Summers (Miss Summers)

Maybe it isn't essential that a plain horror picture make sense but at least the patron is entitled to know what the heck is going on. This writer claims, with modest candor, to have an average amount of brains, and we make it a point to pay attention whenever reviewing a film. But, brother, we have no more notion what *The Seventh Victim* is about than if we had watched the same picture run backward and upside down. New York Times

I think it would have been better if they had allowed it to be six or seven minutes longer. Certain things that should have been kept in the picture, and were shot, were edited out. And there are times, in my opinion, when the story that exists now doesn't make sense. It was the front office who did that – interfering again. DeWitt Bodeen [quoted in Brosnan, *The Horror People*, 1976]

Lowood, is the first of several possibly lesbian characters in the film – tells Mary that "One must have courage to really live in the world."

Mary's sister Jacqueline takes the opposite view, courageously reserving the right to die at a time of her own choosing by maintaining a tiny apartment furnished only with a noose and a chair. Jacqueline is a Greenwich Village counterpart to *Son of Dracula*'s Deep South thanatophiliac Kay Caldwell, sharing with her a luminously beautiful face framed by a severe, jet-black hairdo. Played by the bewitching Jean Brooks, her first appearance typifies the paranoid inscrutability common to all the strange, shadowy characters in the film – she appears fleetingly at a hotel door, silently appealing for discretion with a finger to her lips, then closes the door and disappears.

Later, framed under the guttering light of a wall-lamp, she has a brief interview with a consumptive woman from across the hall called Mimi (the name was presumably a nod to Puccini from the opera-loving Lewton), who understandably flinches from Jacqueline's observation that "I've always wanted to die, always." Then, as Mimi embarks on a final death-defying night on the town, she passes Jacqueline's door and we hear a chair overturning behind it. Though discreet, this was a flagrant contravention of the PCA's strictures regarding suicide. And it's the final shot of the film.

The latter-day Bohemians surrounding Jacqueline include Tom Conway's Dr Louis Judd, who has given up his practice in order to write but will presumably switch back again in time to treat Irena in the 'earlier' Lewton film *Cat People* (in which, it will be remembered, Irena kills him). Judd exhibits some of the sleaze factor familiar from *Cat People* (for no particular reason, he approaches a staircase with the words, "I prefer the left, the sinister side") and yet is required at the end to upbraid the gathered Satanists by invoking the Lord's Prayer.

Supremely civilised, the coven includes a silken society woman with only one arm, the formidable Mrs Redi (inheritor of Jacqueline's cosmetics business), a young cosmetician passionately devoted to the erring Jacqueline, and Bruins, a Humphrey Bogart lookalike who blandly observes that "If I prefer to believe in Satanic majesty and power, who can deny me?" Committed to non-violence, the Palladists gather like well-heeled vultures around Jacqueline in a riveting scene in which she is given a literally poisoned chalice – though, as we have seen, she prefers to kill herself on her own terms.

Smothered in Nicholas Musuraca's trademark chiaroscuro, the film's set-pieces are expertly crafted by Robson and remain among the queasiest in Lewton's portfolio. A private detective advances into a big, threatening block of darkness and is stabbed with a pair of scissors. Emphasising the unfathomable nature of everyone involved, Mary's shower curtain smudges her face into anonymity and, viewed from behind it, the threatening Mrs Redi becomes an impalpable, deep-voiced shadow. (That *Psycho* would provide a more visceral replay of this scene barely needs reiterating.) And Jacqueline's nocturnal flight from the Palladists, who have finally abandoned their "seemingly contradictory rules" by sending a hit-man after her, contains a couple of excellent 'buses' – a dustbin lid knocked over by a foraging dog and an unexpected burst of raucous merriment from the stage door of a local theatre.

The masks of comedy and tragedy embossed on the theatre entrance provide their own winsome commentary on the futility of existence, a futility which *The Seventh Victim* embraces, even revels in. Though written by others, the film seems uniquely personal to Lewton, being chiefly set on Perry Street, where he once lived as an aspiring writer, and featuring in its dramatis personae a feckless poet who hasn't published a book in ten years. And the nasty vignette in which Mary re-encounters the deceased private eye on a subway train was taken directly from Lewton's own experience.

Unfortunately, releasing so pessimistic a picture during wartime was almost as suicidal a gesture as Jacqueline's, and *The Seventh Victim* died a predictable death at the box-office. However, like the much later *The Wicker Man*, Lewton's film about a cult would soon inspire a cult of its own. According to Robson, the first adherents came along straight after the war in the clique-ish form of UK film directors Cavalcanti, Carol Reed and the Boulting brothers.

While *The Seventh Victim* was in production in May 1943, the Universal way of doing things was continuing unabated. In the unappetisingly titled *The Mad Ghoul*, Universal finally cast George Zucco in the mad scientist mould he'd made his own at PRC. Back in 1934, the film's director, James Hogan, had co-written the story of one of Universal's biggest embarrassments, *Life Returns*. He had moved on, however, to successful stints as a house director at Paramount and Columbia, casting Zucco to great effect in *Arrest Bulldog Drummond* and *Ellery Queen and the Murder Ring*. Hogan's third collaboration with Zucco was released on 12 November 1943 as support feature to *Son of Dracula*; sadly, Hogan had died of a heart attack eight days before, rendering the theme of his final picture unpleasantly apt.

Groping for fresh heart's blood: George Zucco turns to parchment in *The Mad Ghoul* (1943)

THE MAD GHOUL

Universal 1943
65 minutes
production began 13 May

Cinematographer: Milton Krasner; Art Directors: John B Goodman, Martin Obzina; Editor: Milton Carruth; Sound: Bernard B Brown, Jess Moulin; Set Decorations: R A Gausman, A J Gilmore; Make-up: Jack P Pierce*; Gowns: Vera West; Musical Director: H J Salter; Screenplay: Brenda Weisberg, Paul Gangelin; Original Story: Hans Kraly; Executive Producer: Joseph Gershenson*; Associate Producer: Benjamin Pivar; Director: James Hogan

David Bruce (Ted Allison); Evelyn Ankers (Isabel Lewis); George Zucco (Dr Alfred Morris); Robert Armstrong (Ken McClure), Turhan Bey (Eric Iverson); Milburn Stone (Macklin); Andrew Tombes (Eagan); Rose Hobart (Della); Addison Richards (Gavigan); Charles McGraw (Garrity); Gus Glassmire (caretaker); uncredited: Lillian Cornell (singing voice for Isabel); Gibson Gowland (detective); Hans Herbert (attendant); Mike Lally (reporter); Isabelle LaMal (maid); Gene O'Donnell (radio announcer); Bess Flowers, Cyril Ring (audience members); Lew Kelly, Bill Ruhl (stagehands)

Another mad scientist dies, screaming at his defeat. This time, it is George Zucco, many times a villain of polish, and still not tarnished ... It is another Universal 'horror' thriller, well done, but just that. Zucco's performance is the only one which will command audience attention. *Motion Picture Herald*

It was a pleasure ... to know George Zucco, David Bruce, and Milburn Stone, with whom I worked in *The Mad Ghoul*. All three were great troupers and, best of all, they were gentlemen, quite a unique characteristic in Hollywood in those days.
Evelyn Ankers ['The B and I', in McClelland, The Golden Age of 'B' Movies, 1978]

Dr Alfred Morris has identified a poison gas used in ancient times by the Mayans, discovering also that its 'zombifying' properties can be reversed, temporarily, by administering heart fluid taken from another subject. Morris has dishonorable designs on Isabel Lewis, fiancée of his star student Ted Allison. Once Ted has been deliberately exposed to the gas, there ensues a series of graveyard desecrations, in which Morris and the now parchment-faced Ted remove the hearts from fresh cadavers...

The Mad Ghoul is surprisingly unpleasant all round. The theme – harvesting bits of human bodies to keep an experimental subject looking presentable – is close kin to that of *The Corpse Vanishes* and not too far removed from the much older *Doctor X*. Also like those films, there are wisecracking reporters on hand to lend the grisly proceedings a wholly incongruous touch of *The Front Page* – or, given that newshound Robert Armstrong shares some of his scenes with arts correspondent Rose Hobart, a touch of that film's battle-of-the-sexes remake, *His Girl Friday*.

The film's nastiest scene is cleverly written, brilliantly performed, and directed by Hogan for the maximum brutality permissible. Armstrong's Ken McClure has worked out the modus operandi behind the 'mad ghoul' desecrations and arranges with an undertaker to lie in state overnight at a plushly appointed funeral home, the plan being to catch the ghoul red-handed. There's some delightful gallows humour as the mortician (played by the aptly named Andrew Tombes) takes his leave of the casketed McClure, then ominous shadows loom into view and McClure sits up, smartly levelling his revolver. Unfazed, Morris comes out with a bit of modified Mark Twain ("Reports of your death seem to have been greatly exaggerated") before pointing out that he has an accomplice stationed behind the coffin. "Why don't you stop?" sneers the disbelieving McClure. "Why, that gag's got whiskers." Upon which the impassive Ted shambles forward, his scalpel glinting wickedly, and stabs McClure in the back of the neck. Morris then wrestles the reporter out of frame and strangles him.

The power of this scene would be considerable under any circumstances, but all the more so in a modestly conceived Universal B-picture. (Robert Armstrong's ignominious demise is just the kind of thing that many comic-relief-phobic critics would like to have seen Lee Tracy suffer in *Doctor X*.) At the outset, however, the film gives no hint that it will develop along such remorseless lines. Indeed, the opening credits – complete with the usual *Son of Frankenstein* music and cartoon-like illustrations purporting to be part of an ancient Mayan mosaic – do not bode well. But as soon as Zucco's Dr Morris starts lecturing his students, we know at once that this college professor is a long way from the amiable character played by Stanley Ridges in *Black Friday*.

In some ways, Morris' vampiric relationship with his unfortunate protégé prefigures the teen-exploiting professor-types featured in the much later Herman Cohen productions *I Was a Teenage Werewolf* and *Horrors of the Black Museum*. (In the latter, Michael Gough refers to his basement torture chamber as "our private world," echoing Zucco's description of his laboratory as "my private universe.") But the gay subtext common to Cohen's pictures is conspicuously missing; indeed, Morris has his sights set firmly on Ted's porcelain fiancée Isabel.

When Morris realises that Isabel's enthusiasm for Ted has waned, Zucco is given some cherishable lines that he delivers in his own inimitable style. "It's perfectly natural now that you should turn to a more sophisticated man," he purrs to the always watchable Evelyn Ankers. "A man who could share your great joy in music. A man who knows the book of life, and could teach you how to read it." But the film presents us not only with the sad spectacle of a young man failing to register that his sweetheart has lost interest, it also shows us an old man whose romantic aspirations are entirely illusory and doomed to failure. And the same applies to Morris' crazy scientific breakthrough. At the end – having been vengefully exposed to the gas by Ted – there's a grim irony in the old man's vain gropings over a freshly dug grave, hopelessly calling "Ted! Ted!" as he breathes his last.

Apart from its sadistic set-pieces, the realisation of the film is merely functional, with corner-cutting in evidence here and there. That Universal's costumier Vera West was feeling the pinch of Universal's conveyor-belt schedule is clear from the fact that Evelyn Ankers briefly wears a spangled creation previously modelled by Louise Allbritton in *Son of Dracula*; presumably, the decision to recycle the dress was taken before the decision to double-bill the films. The picture appeared, complete with an 'H' certificate, some three years late in the UK, inspiring a memorable capsule comment from one English critic: "Scarcely a film to be recommended to those seeking pleasant relaxation after six years of total war."[7]

Though not among the listed actors, Veda Ann Borg dominated the advertising for *Revenge of the Zombies* (1943)

A third horror picture to go into production in May 1943 was Steve Sekeley's *Revenge of the Zombies*, a more than usually boring Monogram entry that seems to have arisen from producer Lindsley Parsons' conviction that the world needed a remake of *King of the Zombies*. In PRC's *The Mad Monster*, George Zucco proposed hurling an army of werewolves against the Axis powers; here, John Carradine's rather listless Dr Max Von Altermann is an Axis agent convinced that "even blown half to bits, undaunted by fire and gas, zombies would fight on."

Scripted once again by Edmund Kelso, the film reproduces all the essential ingredients of Parsons' previous zombie picture, only the sexy maid is less sexy, the sepulchral manservant (again called Lazarus) is less sepulchral, Madame Sul-Te-Wan is less demonic, and even the great Mantan Moreland is less funny, thanks chiefly to being given no amusing lines. Only Veda Ann Borg, as Von Altermann's zombified consort Lila, is an improvement. The other zombies,

mainly composed of pot-bellied middle-aged men in nappies, are a ridiculously unfrightening crew, with a particularly bizarre habit of yodelling at one another to induce wakefulness. Happily, producer Parsons' plans to make yet another zombie picture, *When Zombies Walked*, came to naught.

HOMICIDAL MANIA AND THICK FOG

Having completed *The Leopard Man* and *The Seventh Victim*, the Lewton unit at RKO was ready to press on with its 1943 production programme, as announced by the *Hollywood Reporter* at the end of June: "Val Lewton, the studio's mahatma of mayhem, is readying *The Curse of the Cat People*, *Ghost Ship* and *The Screaming Skull*."[8] Presumably an adaptation of F Marion Crawford's 1911 story of the same name, the latter title would go unmade. Instead, Lewton put Mark Robson's *The Ghost Ship* into production on 3 August, though the result dropped out of circulation for half a century thanks to an accusation of plagiarism from writers Norbert Faulkner and Samuel R Golding (costing RKO in excess of $25,000). The actual derivation, however, seems to have been Jack London's *The Sea Wolf*, which had been filmed in 1941 with Edward G Robinson as remorseless master of a ship called The Ghost.

Ann Carter as the six-year-old protagonist of *The Curse of the Cat People* (1943)

In Lewton's picture, young Tom Merriam goes to sea as third officer on the Altair and gradually realises that the philosophical Captain Stone's obsessive lectures about 'authority' are the rationalisations of a homicidal maniac. The title is justified in the most tenuous, and frankly inadequate, terms, with Stone's bird-like sweetheart Ellen (Edith Barrett) explaining to Merriam that he mustn't condemn himself, like Stone, "to a bloodless, ghostlike existence" as captain of "a ghost ship." The film accordingly becomes a study in the emotional paralysis of a certain type of workaday Fascist, offering a microcosmic view of the forces that, in 1943, were tearing the world apart. "Men are worthless cattle," explains Stone calmly, "and a few men are given authority to drive them." These sentiments are less baroque than the stuff Universal gave Lionel Atwill and John Carradine to speak, but the Nazi correlation is loud and clear nevertheless.

As a result, Russell Wade's Merriam becomes a kind of fresh-faced Resistance leader, the film's chief theme being the craven obeisance to authority that enables dictatorships to take hold in the first place. Richard Dix is appropriately stony-faced and stony-hearted, with occasional flashes of quirky gallows humour to indicate the mania that will reach full bloom at the end. The knife fight in which he eventually succumbs is unusually grisly; his opponent – a mute Finn whose gnomic thoughts, given to us in voice-over, punctuate the film in portentous but ineffective style – provides a rare showcase for Yorkshire-born bit player Skelton Knaggs.

Though for the most part rather glum, the film benefits from a couple of extremely memorable set-pieces. In one, a freshly painted, man-sized hook is left untethered at Stone's capricious command; its nocturnal swinging across the deck, smashing lifeboats and endangering sailors, is as much a metronomic memento mori as Poe's *The Pit and the Pendulum*. In the other, a chippy crew member (Lawrence Tierney) becomes conveniently trapped in the chain locker, his shouts drowned out by the racket of the chain itself as it coils inexorably on top of him. This one recalls the pit itself, as well as Poe's recurring themes of walling-up and premature burial.

The Ghost Ship finished shooting on 28 August; the most delicate and poetic of all Lewton's pictures, *The Curse of the Cat People*, had begun two days earlier. Though not as awkward as *The Ghost Ship*, this one ran into difficulties when the slow work rate of its original director, Gunther von Fritsch, caused Lewton to replace him with editor Robert Wise, who thereby made his directorial debut.

Saddled with a more than usually crass title, Lewton perversely chose to make a film in which the only 'curse' passed on by *Cat People*'s Irena is that of a vivid childhood imagination. DeWitt Bodeen's script relocates the now married Oliver and Alice Reed (Kent Smith and Jane Randolph) to the Tarrytown district of

New York, home of Headless Horseman legends and a half-mad old actress called Julia Farren. The Reeds' six-year-old daughter Amy (Ann Carter) stumbles upon the forbidding Farren house and is befriended by the old lady within, arousing the potentially psychotic jealousy of her grown-up daughter Barbara. Contriving her own curtain and footlights, the old lady relates the legend of Sleepy Hollow in a vignette electrifyingly put over by Julia Dean.

The heavily Victorian interior of the Farren house contains a stuffed lynx, complete with a bird crammed halfway down its throat. This, together with the reappearance in the Reeds' blandly modern home of the Goya canvas that used to belong to Irena, represents Lewton's only concession to the cat-themed shocker the front-office were expecting. Instead, the film is an intensely moving study in the fantasy life of a six-year-old described as "a nice girl, only a little different." Hedged about by her hidebound parents, a crashingly misguided teacher and the sad but sinister Barbara, Amy is inspired by a photo of Oliver and the dead Irena to create an 'imaginary friend' in Irena's likeness. Lewton's preferred title, in fact, was the obviously unsellable *Amy and Her Friend*.

The film is sufficiently ambiguous to allow for the possibility that Irena (played once again by Simone Simon) has genuinely returned as a ghost. Tellingly, she puts in her first appearance only when Oliver throws a cache of her photos on the fire, an attempted exorcism that has precisely the opposite effect. Escaping into the snow at Christmas, Amy returns to the Farren house in a dazzling sequence that involves the old lady sobbing her way through a fatal heart attack and Barbara (Elizabeth Russell) telling Amy that "Even my mother's last moments you've stolen from me." In this film, familiar Lewton devices (a threatening tattoo of the Headless Horseman's hoofbeats, for instance, are revealed as nothing more than a passing automobile) acquire unwonted power from the otherwise un-scary context in which they're embedded.

While Lewton coped with the director-swapping complexities of *The Curse of the Cat People*, 20th Century-Fox producer Robert Bassler was overseeing a lavish new screen version of Marie Belloc Lowndes' 1912 novel *The Lodger*, which had already been filmed twice in the UK. Remembering the wonders John Brahm had worked in the low-budget programmer *The Undying Monster*, Bassler engaged him as director while handing over the adaptation to Barré Lyndon, author of the hit plays *The Amazing Dr Clitterhouse* and *The Man in Half Moon Street*. Where the original story and the two British films had failed to identify the killer explicitly, Lyndon had no compunction in invoking the grim name of Jack the Ripper. On top of this, the film had an ace up its sleeve in the heavyweight form of character star Laird Cregar.

In 1888, a burly stranger takes up lodgings in the Montague Square home of Robert and Ellen Burton. With the Jack the Ripper killings in progress, the Burtons begin to fear that their lodger – a pathology student calling himself Slade – might be the killer. The Burtons' beautiful niece, Kitty Langley, is a music-hall star whose opening night at the Whitechapel Palace of Varieties is 'staked out' by Scotland Yard's Inspector Warwick, with fatal consequences for Slade.

As well as making an impact in films like *Blood and Sand*, *I Wake Up Screaming* and *Heaven Can Wait*, the 30-year-old Cregar had won fame on stage as Oscar Wilde. The fey quality Cregar brings to his Ripper was an intriguing development of the ambiguous figure featured in the two British versions, played on both occasions by the porcelain matinée idol Ivor Novello. In those films, Novello's Bosie-like protagonist turned out to be innocent. Cregar's bulky Slade, however, is much more akin to Wilde himself and the filmmakers make no bones about his culpability from the very beginning; Lucien Ballard's artfully ominous photography sees to that. A soft, spaniel-eyed recluse – often little more than a mellifluous voice issuing from a 20-stone silhouette – Cregar's killer is the very image of social exclusion as he peers forlornly around lace curtains or struggles to interact with the Burtons in their overstuffed morning room.

Instead of resorting to the kind of nudge-nudge intertitles featured in Alfred Hitchcock's 1926 version ("Even if he is a bit queer, he's a gentleman"), Lyndon's screenplay features a tantalisingly homoerotic scene that is made genuinely moving by the passionate intensity with which Cregar plays it. In an echo of Hamlet's "Look here upon this portrait, and on this," Slade promises his befuddled landlady that "I can show you something more beautiful than a beautiful woman," producing an exquisite miniature of a chiselled young man whom he claims was his brother but could just as easily have been Slade's very own Bosie. The boy was brought low, Slade claims, by his association with an actress – and, later, Inspector Warwick produces a corresponding miniature in which the boy, in a Dorian Gray-like touch, has turned into a degenerate, and possibly syphilitic, shadow of himself. As a psychological rationale for the killer, this is pretty elementary stuff, but Cregar's

quietly desolate repetition of "He need not have died" remains the emotional core of the film.

It was the PCA, of course, that necessitated the change of the Ripper's victims from East End prostitutes to down-on-their-luck actresses. The first of them is dispatched in an opening scene that set the fog-laden example by which all Ripper films would be judged. In a dazzling rabbit-warren of Whitechapel streets (cobbled together, in part, from sets designed for the 1937 picture *In Old Chicago*), mounted policemen move through the mist and the Weaver's Arms exudes a swarm of generic Cockneys (even a couple of Pearly Kings). Hugo Friedhofer's score then introduces a string motif modelled on the chimes of Big Ben, a strangely sinister touch that accompanies the victim as she weaves between gas lamps and finally disappears behind an imposing archway.

As a hue and cry is raised in response to her screams, Brahm throws in a couple of visual euphemisms for spilt blood – the woman's broken bottle lying on the cobbles, and later her outflung arm positioned above an overflowing drain. Both images connect to the Ripper's favoured mode of purification – "Deep water," he explains, "is dark and restful and full of peace" – and his eventual demise in the cleansing waters of the Thames.

In conjunction with Ballard's gorgeously moody photography, Brahm pulls off several other tours de force. The indoor murder of the blowzy Jenny (brilliantly played by the ubiquitous British character actress Doris Lloyd) is a truly disturbing vignette in which Brahm repeats a trick from *The Undying Monster*, tracking the camera bumpily towards her as she backs into a corner and finds herself – horrifyingly – unable to scream. The film's climax is set in the backstage area of a Whitechapel theatre, with Slade lurching directly into the camera's eye as he negotiates a precarious catwalk. Here, Ballard sends slatted shadows rippling across his advancing body like the water he so craves. And when he's finally cornered, Friedhofer's surging score cuts out completely, the better to emphasise Slade's stertorous breathing and the scary tracking shot that closes in on his wild, animalistic eyes.

The Lodger also boasts very nice supporting performances from Sara Allgood and a more-than-usually-animated Cedric Hardwicke, while Merle Oberon is lovingly photographed in the most literal sense; in 1946, she and Ballard would get married. The film belongs, however, to Brahm's masterful direction and Cregar's weirdly sympathetic psychopath. When he's seen in the audience during Kitty's frothy performance of the 'Parisian Trot', Cregar's perspiring

THE LODGER

20th Century-Fox 1943
84 minutes
production began 9 August

Cinematographer: Lucien Ballard; Art Directors: James Basevi, John Ewing; Editor: J Watson Webb Jr; Sound: E Clayton Ward, Roger Heman; Special Photographic Effects: Fred Sersen; Set Decorations: Thomas Little, Walter M Scott; Make-up: Guy Pearce, Allan Snyder*; Costumes: René Hubert; Music: Hugo W Friedhofer; Musical Direction: Emil Newman; Dance Director: Kenny Williams; Dialogue Director: Craig Noel*; Screenplay: Barré Lyndon (from the novel by Marie Belloc-Lowndes); Producer: Robert Bassler; Director: John Brahm

Merle Oberon (Kitty); George Sanders (John Warwick); Laird Cregar (Slade); Sir Cedric Hardwicke (Robert Burton); Sara Allgood (Ellen Burton); Aubrey Mather (Superintendent Sutherland); Queenie Leonard (Daisy); Doris Lloyd (Jennie); David Clyde (Sergeant Bates); Helena Pickard (Annie Rowley); uncredited: Jimmy Aubrey (cabbie); Billy Bevan (publican); Anita [Sharp-] Bolster (Wiggy); Edmond Breon (manager); Colin Campbell (Harold); Ruth Clifford (hairdresser); Harold de Becker (Charlie); Cyril Delevanti (stagehand); Douglas Gerrard (porter); Charlie Hall (comedian); Gerald Hamer (milkman); Lumsden Hare (Dr Sheridan); Forrester Harvey (cobbler); Stuart Holmes (Prince of Wales); Olaf Hytten (Harris); Crauford Kent (aide); Skelton Knaggs (carter); Connie Leon (woman); John Rogers (down-and-out); Montague Shaw (stage manager); Will Stanton (newsboy); Donald Stuart (concertina player); Walter Tetley (call boy); David Thursby (sergeant); Heather Wilde (girl); Frederick Worlock (Sir Edward Willoughby)

Mr Cregar or the director or the author or all three have decided to make the main character a rather diffident and sensitive maniac ... However, the book had a good deal of suspense, whereas the picture has rather little. More trick stuff than solid work has been used to establish atmosphere, and if it weren't for weird lighting and some trumped-up fog, there wouldn't be much to intimidate you. *The New Yorker*

I'd refer to the novel now and again, I suppose ... One thing I did was to go over to the Huntington Library and look into the newspaper reports in the London *Times* of that particular period. The reports are very restrained, but it was all in there. *Barré Lyndon* [quoted in *Focus on Film*, Summer 1975]

The very image of social exclusion: Laird Cregar as *The Lodger* (1943)

THE RETURN OF THE VAMPIRE

Columbia 1943
69 minutes
production began 21 August

Cinematographers: John Stumar, L W O'Connell; Art Directors: Lionel Banks, Victor Greene; Editor: Paul Borofsky; Sound: Howard Fogetti*; Special Effects: Aaron Nibley; Set Decorations: Louis Diage; Make-up: Clay Campbell*; Music: Mario C Tedesco; Musical Director: M W Stoloff; Additional Dialogue: Randall Faye; Screenplay: Griffin Jay, based upon an idea by Kurt Neumann; Producer: Sam White; Director: Lew Landers

Bela Lugosi (Armand Tesla); Frieda Inescort (Lady Jane Ainsley); Nina Foch (Nicki Saunders); Miles Mander (Sir Frederick Fleet); Roland Varno (John Ainsley); Matt Willis (Andreas Obry); uncredited: William Austin (Detective Gannett); Jeanne Bates (1918 victim); Billy Bevan (Horace); Sydney Chatton (Peters [desk clerk]); Sherlee Collier (Nicki as a girl); Harold De Becker (Horace's mate); Leslie Denison (Detective Lynch); Donald Dewar (John as a boy); Gilbert Emery (Professor Saunders); Olaf Hytten (butler); Nelson Leigh (Scotland Yard man); George McKay (cemetery guard); Ottola Nesmith (Elsa [housekeeper])

Rialto patrons can cringe in their seats through another romp with Old Man Dracula the next couple of weeks with *The Return of the Vampire*. He is not called Dracula this time – but what's the difference, Dracula or Tesla? It's still Bela Lugosi soaring around and biting people in the neck. After a few years of Dracula pictures, a movie critic gets so one bite in the neck seems about the same as another. *New York World-Telegram*

Bela was a real professional ... The rest of the cast was top notch – they were all imbued with their parts and Bela was the motivating factor ... The film cost approximately $75,000 and grossed for Columbia close to half a million dollars, and has not been off TV since the late 50s.
Sam White [quoted in Bojarski, The Films of Bela Lugosi, 1980]

Matt Willis hauls Bela Lugosi to his doom in *The Return of the Vampire* (1943)

combination of suppressed excitement and corrosive self-disgust signals the franker and more mature approach to psychopathology that would eventually throw up Hitchcock's *Psycho*.

The purifying waters of *The Lodger* became decidedly murky ones in André de Toth's *Dark Waters*, in which Merle Oberon graduated to the role of a young woman being driven insane by a bogus aunt and uncle in a swampy Louisiana locale. Made as an independent from 15 May 1944, the film is distinguished by a chalk-faced turn from Thomas Mitchell as the chief schemer ("I don't want any more blood on this floor," he says mildly in the closing stages) and a splendid demise for the shifty Elisha Cook Jr, subsumed screaming into a convenient quicksand. "I wanted to make it Gothic," de Toth explained, irrespective of the fact that "the seven producers I had on the show ... didn't understand what Gothic meant."[9] Aided by cinematographers Archie Stout and John (*Bride of Frankenstein*) Mescall, de Toth certainly succeeded in making it Gothic, but suspenseful or especially engaging? – no. The film is interesting, however, as a precursor of Hammer's 1960 thriller *Taste of Fear*.

VAMPIRISM AND VOODOO

Having made a small contribution to Monogram's *Ghosts on the Loose* in February 1943, Bela Lugosi returned to the stage, undertaking a brief tour of *Dracula* prior to assuming Boris Karloff's old role in *Arsenic and Old Lace* in San Francisco and Los Angeles. The latter engagement opened, to appreciative notices, at LA's Music Box Theater on Friday 20 August, the day before shooting began on Columbia's *The Return of the Vampire*. While playing Jonathan Brewster by night, therefore, Lugosi was finally reprising his screen Dracula during the day, albeit a Dracula cannily renamed Armand Tesla in deference to Universal's legal department. The film's credentials as a Universal pastiche were bolstered by the input of screenwriter Griffin Jay, the man who had revived the Mummy on Universal's behalf and also crafted *Captive Wild Woman* for them.

In 1918, occult scholar Armand Tesla – undead since the 18th century – is staked in London. Twenty-three years on, his body is unearthed by an explosion during the Blitz, and a couple of Civil Defence volunteers remove the stake in the belief that it's a piece of shrapnel. Returned to life, Tesla enslaves his werewolf associate Andreas once more and, assuming the identity of Dr Hugo Bruckner, embarks on a scheme of revenge...

Miles Mander, later to play an obstinately sceptical Scotland Yard official in the narrative proper,

introduces the film's extended prologue in voice-over, plunging us straight away into "a particularly gloomy, foggy night that was well suited for a visitation by the supernatural." The visitation, too, is sprung upon us straight away. In its anxiety to emulate Universal's *The Wolf Man*, the film dispenses with any elaborate build-up and has an extravagantly coiffured werewolf emerge through the mist (and into screen-hogging close-up) even before Mander has finished his spiel. The unfortunate Andreas is a lycanthropic Renfield, with a pooch-like face and an air of dog-like devotion, both of which are amusingly paralleled by a rather similar-looking, though much smaller, terrier belonging to the doe-eyed heroine.

The 1918 prologue is underpinned by a couple of pleasing ironies. First, that Tesla is destroyed by a man armed with vampire-killing information culled from a book written by Tesla himself some 200 years before. Second, that his destroyer never realises it's Tesla he's dealing with. The frontispiece of Professor Saunders' copy of *The Supernatural and Its Manifestations* is a glowering portrait of Tesla, yet Saunders doesn't make the connection on lifting Tesla's coffin lid.

Actually, this is hardly surprising, for the portrait is clearly an artist's impression of the publicity photo Lugosi circulated while campaigning to play Dracula 13 years earlier – and by 1943, the sexagenarian Lugosi didn't resemble the sexy Mephisto of 1930 one bit. He's unflatteringly photographed, looks faintly preposterous in a top hat, and doesn't have the benefit of the discreet hairpiece he wore in *Dracula*. And yet he remains a majestic presence, handling his paucity of lines with his trademark cadences intact and wisely eschewing any overt bids for sympathy. Addressing Andreas, he has one poetic line redolent of the weight of centuries: "Your fate is to be what you are, as mine is to be what I am..." He then returns smartly to undead megalomaniac mode by adding: "... your master."

In fact, this is an unusually remorseless vampire; in the footage set in 1918, he even stoops (literally) to victimising a five-year-old. Tesla's background, too, is intriguing. According to his chief antagonist, he was in life an 18th century diabolist hoist by his own petard; as Lady Jane puts it, "Tesla's morbid thirst for knowledge turned upon him."

The presence of a female Van Helsing figure is an unusual touch for 1943. The present-day action begins with Scotland Yard threatening Lady Jane with prosecution for her long-ago involvement in the staking of Tesla, just as Van Helsing was nearly arraigned in *Dracula's Daughter*. There are other echoes of that film, notably when Billy Bevan appears as a Civil Defence worker who stumbles on Tesla's exposed corpse and calls his fellow worker "chicken-hearted"; this is exactly what Halliwell Hobbes called Bevan when, as policemen, the pair stumbled across Dracula's corpse in the earlier film. Though this may have been a self-referential ad-lib thrown in by Bevan himself, it nevertheless seems as if Jay wanted to write the film Universal might have made had they retained Bela Lugosi in 1936.

Another veteran of *Dracula's Daughter*, actor-playwright Gilbert Emery, here plays Professor Saunders rather than the Scotland Yard inspector he played previously. Apparently unconvinced by his own vampire-hunting dialogue, he seems not to be acting but merely remembering his lines. The acting elsewhere is similarly stiff, though Miles Mander, in Emery's old role, does a priceless double-take when two subordinates dutifully tell him that a suspect "turned into a wolf, sir." The film is efficiently directed by Lew Landers, complete with the dreamlike rovings of a mobile camera and moody, mist-shrouded set-pieces that are second to none. It also benefits greatly from the unwonted topicality of its setting. There are stock shots of enemy bombers and anti-aircraft guns, together with specially staged scenes of ARP wardens ushering stoic Londoners into air-raid shelters.

For Lugosi, it was no doubt a relief to be working for Columbia rather than the cheeseparing Monogram – though, according to its producer Sam White, the film cost only $75,000. When Tesla raises his cloak in the familiar flying formation, horror fans who expected to see the kind of bat-like special effects they had just witnessed in *Son of Dracula* were inevitably disappointed. In compensation, the film has a grim and grey denouement in which Tesla is exposed to the dawn on the rubble of a bombed-out church. For British fans, however, the censor ensured that the scene's innovative 'melting head' effects were pared to a minimum.

On completion of *The Return of the Vampire*, Columbia announced in December 1943 that Griffin Jay had a sequel in the works called *Bride of the Vampire*. By the time the project began its 19-day schedule on 8 May the following year, it had transformed into something rather different, retaining Nina Foch from its progenitor rather than Bela Lugosi and substituting lycanthropy for vampirism.

Henry Levin's *Cry of the Werewolf* was written by Jay in collaboration with Charles O'Neal, co-writer of the Val Lewton production *The Seventh Victim*. As an attempt to cross-fertilise *The Wolf Man* and *Cat People*, the film is an embarrassing failure; as entertainment, it fares even worse. Set for the most part in a Washington occult museum, with occasional incursions to a New Orleans encampment of Transylvanian gypsies, the film casts Foch as Celeste, lycanthropic daughter of the notorious Marie La Tour, who, determined to stop an elderly researcher from publishing his account of her mother's life, changes into an Alsatian to do so.

As well as being a conspicuously suspense-free zone, the film boasts a shockingly bad performance as the researcher's quixotic son from Stephen Crane, who was best known at the time as Lana Turner's husband. It also has 'comic relief' policemen whose cross-talk is a trial to sit through. There's a tiny glimmer of interest in the misogynist fear inspired by the matriarchal gypsies, including the kinky undertone that creeps into Foch's scene with the equally glamorous Osa Massen, in which she promises that "To you shall be revealed all these [gypsy] secrets. You shall be my sister. It is in my power." Then again, the scene could well be meaningless, no more than an obligatory parroting of *Cat People*'s "moia sestra" routine.

On its release, the hopelessly derivative nature of *Cry of the Werewolf* was amusingly nailed by New York critic Archer Winsten, who wryly observed that "No happy chance permits anything unexpected to occur. When the wolf has finally been shot to death, it merely fades back to the body of Nina Foch. What a novelty it would have been, and really mysterious, to fade back to a gorilla or a black panther, though possibly an infringement of copyright on Universal or RKO Radio properties."[10]

Though the two films were premiered separately, *Cry of the Werewolf* later formed a double-feature with another Columbia clinker called *The Soul of a Monster*. Trumpeting the package as a "Supernatural Double-Horror Show," the ads laughably insisted that "Two Queens of Horror Explode a Double Dose of TNTerror in Your Heart!" Will Jason's film began shooting on 25 May and was written by Lewton alumnus Edward Dein. And, again, Winsten pounced in memorable style, calling *The Soul of a Monster* "the feeblest re-working of the Faustian legend up to Sept 8, 1944" and describing its nocturnal stalking sequence as "a honey, being composed of two pairs of legs on the street at night, one pair walking steadily after the other ... During it you occasionally wonder if a circular bit of film might not be going around and around like a phonograph record with a broken thread."[11]

What Winsten was describing, of course, was Jason's attempt at a Lewton 'walk'. This one involves a young pastor being stalked by a surgeon lately retrieved from death by diabolical means, and is indeed the "circular purgatory" specified by Winsten, lasting well over five minutes and concluding with a perfunctory flourish of the holy man's crucifix. It contains a few effective Lewton 'buses', however – a hydraulic lift clunking open on the sidewalk, a surprise appearance from an elderly cop, the roar of an overhead train – the latter effect previously used in *The Leopard Man*, which Dein co-wrote.

"If there's any zombie ghost in this place, we'll get him – or her." Comforting words for Stephen Crane and Osa Massen in *Cry of the Werewolf* (1944)

George MacReady is the bloodless, pulseless, soulless revenant and Rose Hobart the coldly alluring Satanic emissary who restored him, and at a late stage everything stops while a bunch of neighbourhood urchins trill 'Ave Maria'. The script contains metaphysical musings that verge on the pretentious, and springs a major surprise when Hobart is eventually run over by a truck – strange, given that her first appearance saw her miraculously unharmed by a speeding car. That Dein was warming over a well-worn theme is admitted even in his dialogue, with

the pastor (Eric Rolf) telling MacReady that "So many people have used the same plot: Boccaccio, Goethe ..."

Attempts at mimicking the Lewton style were not about to be made by Banner Pictures, the Sam Katzman-Jack Dietz outfit that was supplying Monogram with its Bela Lugosi vehicles. The sequence resumed in October 1943 with Phil Rosen's *Return of the Ape Man*, not a sequel to Lugosi's earlier embarrassment, *The Ape Man*, but in many ways just as ridiculous. Here, Lugosi is joined by John Carradine (giving a strictly phoned-in performance) as a pair of scientists who acquire a perfectly preserved Pithecanthropus from the Arctic and successfully thaw him out in Lugosi's basement. When Carradine unwillingly contributes his brain matter to the resurrected creature, Lugosi exults that "I have advanced his mind 20,000 years in a few hours!" The thing goes on the rampage in a couple of cardboard streets, kills three people (including Lugosi) and is finally torched in an empty theatre. The latter scene plays like a tragically threadbare repeat of *The Lodger*'s climax, just completed over at 20th Century-Fox.

Bela Lugosi and Frank Moran intimidate Judith Gibson (aka Teala Loring) in *Return of the Ape Man* (1943)

For what it's worth, Lugosi gets some very juicy lines, ranging from "Some people's brains would never be missed" as he sizes up the guests at a stuffed-shirt soirée, to a glib dismissal of Carradine's scruples with "Murder is an ugly word; as a scientist I don't recognise it." Notoriously, Frank Moran's Ape Man offers a rear view of his Y-fronts as he scrambles out of an upper window. And Poe's *The Black Cat* is strangely invoked when Lugosi takes some policemen into his basement only for the Ape Man to smash his way out from the wall he's imprisoned behind. Sam Katzman was clearly no respecter of actors; George Zucco, of all people, was originally cast as the Ape Man until (possibly feigned) illness supervened. A still of Zucco in the make-up seems to be all that survives of his brief time on the film, though this didn't stop Katzman from putting Zucco's name, in granite letters, just below Carradine's in the opening credits.

Though released first, William Beaudine's *Voodoo Man* went into production on 16 October 1943, a fortnight after *Return of the Ape Man* started. In it, Lugosi finally got to play a zombie master once more, having been unable to play Dr Sangre in *King of the Zombies* and Dr Von Altermann in *Revenge of the Zombies*. The result survives as arguably the best of the Lugosi Monograms, with the star on particularly good, emotive form as a courtly backwoods doctor, Richard Marlowe, who, with the aid of Zucco (saturnine gas-station proprietor) and Carradine (half-wit handyman), seeks to transfer the lifeforce of kidnapped young women into his deceased wife (Ellen Hall). "Somewhere," he insists, "there must be a girl with the perfect affinity."

Like the motorist-fooling lunatics of Roland West's *The Monster*, Carradine and fellow simpleton Pat McKee make use of a movable hedge and a 'Road Closed' sign to lure the women into Lugosi's clutches. One such (played by the glacially beautiful Louise Currie) catches sight of the catatonic Mrs Marlowe and enjoys a splendid exchange with her forbidding host. "Is your wife ill?" she asks. "She's dead," replies Lugosi. "She has been dead for 22 years." After this, Beaudine and cinematographer Marcel le Picard bring great style to a riveting exchange of massive close-ups as Lugosi works his hypnotic magic on Currie, and the ensuing voodoo ceremonies – with harps swooning on the soundtrack and Zucco invoking Ramboona in feathered head-dress and silken robe – are pleasingly ridiculous.

Currie makes a highly effective Sleeping Beauty, drifting through the California furze in a diaphanous Grecian gown, while four other zombie girls stand sentry in glass booths like the corpses in Ulmer's

The Black Cat. There's also fun to be had from Henry Hall's local sheriff, who describes Lugosi as "a peculiar old duck" and later says "Gosh all fish-hooks!" And the film is bookended by a virtually postmodern conceit, with our hero as a screenwriter for the Banner Motion Picture Company, presenting the aptly named 'SK' with a script called *Voodoo Man* and proposing it for Bela Lugosi: "It's right up his alley!"

The real SK gave a surprisingly unguarded interview a few days into the *Voodoo Man* schedule. "I call this a moron picture," he claimed. "I have made a number of these films and I claim there must be something wrong with anybody who goes to see 'em ... We dream up these hokey stories and we hire some actors and a fine director like Bill Beaudine. Then the money flows in as if we were great geniuses."[12] After *Voodoo Man*, however, Katzman failed to get a proposed version of Poe's *The Gold Bug* into production and accordingly brought his nine-film Lugosi sequence to an end. Indeed, Monogram would steer clear of horror subjects of any sort for some two years. The single exception was Beaudine's atrocious *Crazy Knights*, a 1944 'phoney haunted house' vehicle for superannuated comics Billy Gilbert, Shemp Howard and Maxie Rosenbloom.

YOU MEAN LIKE REPUBLICANS?

In October 1942, Curt Siodmak scripts were being filmed not only at Universal (*Frankenstein Meets the Wolf Man*) and RKO (*I Walked with a Zombie*) but also at Republic, where George Sherman directed *The London Blackout Murders*. This taut thriller, in which John Abbott is a homicidal doctor killing supposed German spies with a hypodermic, was succeeded 12 months later by a more momentous Siodmak-Sherman-Republic collaboration. Siodmak's novel *Donovan's Brain* had been issued in February 1943 to some acclaim, and by October a somewhat altered film version – starting with its title, which became, perplexingly, *The Lady and the Monster* – was in production at Republic.

The studio's only previous full-on horror picture was nearly ten years old, and even that – *The Crime of Doctor Crespi* – was a title they merely distributed. Republic had, however, produced the terrific 1940 serial *Drums of Fu Manchu*, in which Henry Brandon's bald-domed Oriental schemer was attended by zombie-like henchmen, all of them clearly bearing the scars of lobotomy. Mounting his first in-house horror feature, studio head Herbert J Yates stuck with the brain-tampering theme and turned to an actor who had 'form' where trephination was concerned: Dr Crespi himself, Erich von Stroheim.

When a tycoon's plane goes down near Professor Mueller's laboratory in the Arizona desert, the scientist removes the dead man's brain and uses electricity to keep it alive. Having established a telepathic link with Donovan's brain, Mueller's assistant, Cory, is taken over by it and travels to Los Angeles to handle the tycoon's unfinished business. Providentially freed from the brain's influence, Cory returns to Arizona, where both the brain and the insanely protective Mueller are destroyed.

Having just played Field Marshal Rommel in Billy Wilder's *Five Graves to Cairo*, Von Stroheim was perfect casting for Republic's paint-by-numbers attempt at a horror picture. In adapting Siodmak's novel, screenwriters Dane Lussier and Frederick Kohner clearly felt that its unremarkable protagonist, Dr Patrick Cory, wasn't exotic enough for mad scientist purposes. They therefore remodelled his reluctant associate, Dr Schratt, as a club-footed monomaniac called Professor Mueller, demoting Cory to the level of an assistant preoccupied with encephalographs.

Thus was raised the spectre of the Nazi scientist, with Von Stroheim presiding over an illicit brain operation, white cap and face mask leaving only his bespectacled eyes visible as he says "When you try to solve the mysteries of nature, it doesn't matter whether you experiment with guinea pigs or human beings." He then placidly calls for "instruments" and, after an infinitesimal hesitation from the attendant nurse, screams out "INSTRUMENTS!" in his best Crespi style. Von Stroheim, of course, is marvellous at moments like this, and he remains much the most striking thing about *The Lady and the Monster*. He benefits, too, from some discreetly humorous dialogue exchanges, as when Mueller hovers over Donovan's corpse and asks Cory to "sterilise the instruments." "Sterilise? What for?" replies Cory. "The man is dead." Earlier, Mueller's request for "all the necessary instruments for trephination" is supplemented by the deliciously portentous addendum, "And don't forget the gigli saw."

Best known for cheap Western programmers but now entertaining thoughts of studio gentrification, Herbert Yates presumably decided that, if a horror film was on the agenda, it wasn't to be done by halves, with a conspicuously healthy budget backing up the full fusillade of Gothic trimmings. The film begins, therefore, on an elaborate, though not particularly convincing, miniature of a castle (a decidedly odd thing to find in the Arizona desert), with smoke scudding across and a storm in full pelt. And, soon enough, Cory's struggles to extricate the dead Donovan from his crashed plane are impeded by as much troublesome tumbleweed as Republic's prop men could devise.

Arizona brain specialists Erich von Stroheim, Richard Arlen and Vera Hruba Ralston in *The Lady and the Monster* (1943)

Faced with Republic's tamperings, Siodmak disowned *The Lady and the Monster*, as he would all subsequent versions of his story. In truth, Republic's Gothic window-dressing not only makes *The Lady and the Monster* a more diverting experience than Felix Feist's flat and flavourless 1950s remake, it's also more in keeping with the spirit of Siodmak's original than he was prepared to admit. As a genuine SF proposition, the novel was aptly dismissed by John Brosnan on the grounds that "instead of investigating the reactions of the disassociated brain to its total sensory deprivation, Siodmak turns his story into yet another description of innocence being overcome by an evil supernatural force. What the original idea called for was a *science fiction* writer rather than one who was really, despite his customary trappings of pseudo-science, an exponent of Gothic horror, or rather Gothic soap opera."[13]

The 'supernatural force' part of Brosnan's critique is left to celebrated noir cinematographer John Alton, who contrives to underlight the possessed Cory's face in demonic shadows even when he's interacting with normal-looking characters; the effect is impressive at first but quickly becomes ridiculous. To make matters worse, Cory's dealings in LA with Donovan's conniving widow and attorney are repetitive and unengaging. And the film's mixture of science and

THE LADY AND THE MONSTER

Republic 1943
86 minutes
production began 18 October
UK title: The Lady and the Doctor

Cinematographer: John Alton; Art Director: Russell Kimball; Editor: Arthur Roberts; Sound: Earl Crain Sr; Special Effects: Theodore Lydecker; Set Decorations: Otto Siegel; Gowns: Adele [Palmer]; Music: Walter Scharf; Orchestral Arrangements: Marlin Skiles; Screenplay: Dane Lussier, Frederick Kohner (based on the novel *Donovan's Brain* by Curt Siodmak); Associate Producer and Director: George Sherman

Vera Hruba Ralston (Janice Farrell); Richard Arlen (Dr Patrick Cory); Erich von Stroheim (Professor Franz Mueller); Helen Vinson (Chloe Donovan); Mary Nash (Mrs Fame); Sidney Blackmer (Eugene Fulton); Janet Martin (café singer); Bill Henry (Roger Collins); Charles Cane (Mr Grimes); Juanita Quigley (Mary Lou); Josephine Dillon (grandmother); Antonio Triana, Lola Montes (themselves); uncredited: Billy Benedict (bellhop); Lane Chandler (ranger); Wallis Clark (warden); Herbert Clifton (butler); Harry Depp (cashier); Maxine Doyle (receptionist); Sam Flint (Phipps [bank manager]); Frank Graham (narrator); Harry Hayden (Dr Martin); Edward Keane (Manning); Jack Kirk (husky man); Lee Phelps (head waiter)

Republic has missed the boat in giving its latest thriller a corny title like *The Lady and the Monster*. Hidden under this conventional nomenclature is one of the most authentic hair-raisers screened this year at Broadway's horror house, the Rialto. *New York Herald Tribune*

Herbert Yates called me one day and said, "Siodmak, you are crazy! ... A scientist like Dr Cory, he doesn't live in a little hut in the desert. He lives in a *castle*!" He put a damn castle in the story, and von Stroheim running around it like a rat. "And," Yates went on, "I have a new title for you – *The Lady and the Monster*. And the lady will be *Vera!*' – Vera Hruba Ralston, the ice-skater, Yates' girlfriend. So I quit.
Curt Siodmak [quoted in Weaver, *Poverty Row HORRORS!*, 1993]

the supernatural is by no means as beguiling as the same combination in *The Devil Commands* – Cory is compelled by the brain to do a bit of automatic writing, and that's about it. The 'soap opera' part of Brosnan's prescription, meanwhile, is vested in the

Pith-helmeted padre Grant Withers, backed up by fellow vampire hunters Martin Wilkins, Emmett Vogan and Charles Gordon, in *The Vampire's Ghost* (1944)

blank-faced Vera Hruba Ralston, the Czechoslovakian ice-skating attraction of Republic's *Ice-Capades* and *Ice-Capades Revue*, cast here as Cory's sweetheart Janice. She was also Herbert Yates' mistress, and is given billing not only above Richard Arlen and Von Stroheim but even above the title.

Playing the 45-year-old Arlen's girlfriend was presumably no stretch for the 21-year-old Hruba Ralston, given that her real-life boyfriend was 63, but much else in the script is well beyond her scope. She gives her all to the spirited climax, however, in which Cory and Mueller engage in a lab-trashing brawl. The latter is shot down by the housekeeper even as he prepares to fling a chair in Cory's direction, and Janice finally smashes the brain's tank with a stool, the cerebrum hitting the deck in a cascade of spilled serum. This facilitates a suitably soapy voice-over in which all the loose ends are tied up: Mueller is described, inexplicably, as having "tried to distort an experiment of science into a diabolical plot to further his own personal gains" and Cory is said to have been given a brief prison sentence – but "Janice was waiting, so after all there was a happy ending to his experience."

Despite the success of *The Lady and the Monster*, Republic took a good 12 months before getting behind any further horror subjects, and slashed the budgets on them when they did. Designed as a double-feature, *The Vampire's Ghost* and *The Phantom Speaks* both went into production in October 1944, directed by Lesley Selander and John English respectively. The former features a vampire in darkest Africa, a former courtier of Elizabeth I who now operates a waterfront watering hole and in daylight takes the minor precaution of wearing shades: "I have to be careful," he says mildly, "I've got bad eyes."

The touches of originality in Leigh Brackett and John K Butler's script stand in stark contrast to its co-feature, written by Butler alone and cannibalised from a good half-dozen previous pictures, *The Lady and the Monster* among them. Here, a ruthless gangster goes to the electric chair prior to possessing a mild metaphysician and having him rub out various enemies. Siodmak's script for *Black Friday* had already sired a Monogram rip-off in the shape of Phil Rosen's *Man With Two Lives* (1942); now, Republic flaunted the suspicious similarity of *The Phantom Speaks* to *Black Friday* by casting Stanley Ridges in the same part (or parts) he'd played before. Richard Arlen, meanwhile, was retained from *The Lady and the Monster* to play the stolid journalist hero.

Taken together, *The Phantom Speaks* has production gloss, and Ridges' performance, to commend it but little else. *The Vampire's Ghost*, however, transcends its title (which would be uniquely stupid were it not for *The Mummy's Ghost*, made the previous year) by means of a highly unusual setting, a surprisingly saucy dance routine from Adele Mara, and such intriguing innovations as the vampire, having been wounded by a silver-tipped spear, drawing reviving sustenance from the moon. Unfortunately, there are plenty of atrocious lines like "We'll walk quickly through the dark shadows of Eternity" (quickly? through Eternity?), and the diminutive John Abbott is, outside of *Nosferatu* and his rat-like ilk, perhaps the least Byronic vampire on record. Which is ironic, given that Brackett had in mind Polidori's Byron-fixated novella *The Vampyre* when she concocted the story.

Much more interesting, potentially, than *The Vampire's Ghost* was a 1944 Howard Hawks project called *Dreadful Hollow*, based on an Irina Karlova novel of the same name and graced with a script by William Faulkner. A vampire story, the film had been earmarked by Hawks as a vehicle for his latest discovery, Finnish starlet Maila Nurmi, but it never made it into production. Appropriately, Nurmi would re-emerge in the 1950s as TV 'horror host' Vampira, while Hawks finally got around to a vampire picture in the up-to-the-minute form of *The Thing from Another World*.

MURDER IN LA MORTE ROUGE

After making *The Hound of the Baskervilles* and *The Adventures of Sherlock Holmes* for 20th Century-Fox,

the ideally matched Holmes-Watson team of Basil Rathbone and Nigel Bruce had repeated the trick in three successful radio series. Starting in October 1939, the sequence only wound down in March 1942 – and by 5 May of that year, Rathbone and Bruce were making the first of 12 modestly budgeted Holmes programmers for Universal. The studio's $300,000 deal with the Conan Doyle estate gave Universal title to the characters for a seven-year period in addition to rights in 21 of Doyle's original stories. The first batch of films, however – *Sherlock Holmes and the Voice of Terror*, *Sherlock Holmes and the Secret Weapon* and *Sherlock Holmes in Washington* – involved the pair in brashly up-to-the-minute espionage intrigues.

This changed with the studio's 1943 Holmes schedule, which kicked off in April with an item nominally based on Doyle's *The Musgrave Ritual*. *Sherlock Holmes Faces Death* was the third entry to be directed by Roy William Neill, who would go on to make all the remainder. In it, he had clearly decided to apply to the series some of the Gothic atmosphere he had perfected at Columbia in *The Black Room* and in the Gaumont-British production *Doctor Syn*. Here, a Northumberland pile called Hurlstone Towers, lately converted into a rest home for wounded soldiers, is the site of four murders (one of them bogus), as well as featuring a crypt familiar from *Dracula* and a neighbouring village that had recently done duty as Vasaria in *The Ghost of Frankenstein*. In addition, Neill's penchant for ravens (at least as persistent as Tod Browning's legendary interest in armadillos) is manifested in a particularly mischievous specimen resident in the local pub.

Evelyn Ankers and Alan Curtis shrink from an unseen threat in *The Invisible Man's Revenge* (1944)

The film was the second contribution to Universal's Holmes cycle by screenwriter Bertram Millhauser, who had got his start writing Pearl White serials and in 1928 had produced *The Leopard Lady* for the DeMille Corporation. In the next Holmes entry, he created an imperishable femme fatale in the form of *The Spider Woman*, which was shot in May 1943 and had the scintillating Gale Sondergaard in the title role. This amazing amalgam of a whole clutch of Doyle stories – among them *The Dying Detective*, *The Final Problem*, *The Empty House* and *The Devil's Foot* – concerns a rash of so-called 'pyjama suicides' initiated by the frosty Adrea Spedding, who uses lycosa carnivora, a spider whose venom impels its victims to take their own lives, in the furtherance of a fiendish insurance scam. The latter element relates the film to the British Lugosi vehicle *The Dark Eyes of London*, while the skin-crawling scene in which Holmes encounters a spider in his darkened bedroom is as much a precursor of *Dr No* as it is an echo of Doyle's *The Speckled Band*.

There's also a midget involved who seems derived not only from Doyle's *The Sign of Four* but also from *The Unholy Three* and *Freaks*; particularly the latter, given that 'Obongo from the Congo, the Prancing Pygmy' is played by *Freaks* veteran Angelo Rossitto. The creepiest participant, however, is seven-year-old Teddy Infuhr as Spedding's nephew Larry, a junior Renfield who communes with flies and secretes a potentially lethal poison gas in Holmes' fireplace. Even without these ghoulish accoutrements, the film would be cherishable for the crackling tension of its Sondergaard-Rathbone confrontations. Of her 'female Moriarty', Sondergaard noted that "the characterisation was up to me; she was not intricately conceived. Frankly, it was something to help pay the bills. I knew it wasn't art. I certainly didn't think it would outlast all my pictures other than [William Wyler's] *The Letter*."[14]

Before moving on to further Holmes subjects, Bertram Millhauser whipped up a belated addition to another Universal cycle in *The Invisible Man's Revenge*, which started under Ford Beebe's direction on 10 January 1944. This retained Jon Hall from *Invisible Agent*, casting him, however, as an entirely different Griffin, one who knows nothing about invisibility until stumbling across a fusty research scientist called Dr Drury (John Carradine). Drury claims to have "outstripped the immortals of science: Archimedes, Copernicus, Faraday, Darwin," but doesn't reckon on the fact that Griffin is a homicidal asylum escapee bent on getting even with a couple of landed gentry (Gale Sondergaard, Lester Matthews) in the mythical English county of Westshire.

About 50 minutes in, Millhauser introduces a particularly grisly twist, in that Griffin cannot regain his substance without draining the blood of someone else (all of it); he starts with Drury. ("Sounds a bit like Dracula, doesn't it?" he muses.) How Griffin does this without assistance or even a shred of medical know-how – or, indeed, how he accommodates two people's bloodstreams in one body – is never addressed. The film contains a reminiscence of James Whale's original in a protracted darts match set in the Running Nag public house, with one of Universal's most recognisable bit players, the uniquely raddled Ted Billings, cast as a barfly just as he had been in 1933. Elsewhere, we're asked to accept the grievously wasted Evelyn Ankers as Sondergaard's daughter, while John Fulton's effects (a bit hit-and-miss where plain invisibility is concerned) afford a couple of creepy moments in which Griffin smears his face in flour and trails his hand in water.

Fulton's effects work was back to full strength in *The Scarlet Claw*, which began shooting just two days after *The Invisible Man's Revenge*. In this, Universal's sixth Holmes picture, The Running Nag was refashioned as a mist-shrouded hostelry in darkest Canada. (And, inevitably, Ted Billings was recruited once more to prop up the bar.) Prior to production, the script – not a Bertram Millhauser concoction this time, instead being partly written by Roy William Neill himself – had gone by the nondescript title *Sherlock Holmes in Canada*. As well as carrying a faint echo of Doyle's *A Study in Scarlet*, the grisly release title was much better suited to a film that brought the Holmes series fully into line with Universal's continuing horror franchises.

In Quebec for a meeting of the Royal Canadian Occult Society, Sherlock Holmes and Dr Watson are called away to La Morte Rouge on the violent death of Lady Lillian Penrose. Though a phosphorescent monster haunts the outlying marshes, Holmes deduces that the killer is actually psychopathic actor Alastair Ramson – and that he has reason to hate two other residents of La Morte Rouge, the reclusive Judge Brisson and local hotelier Emile Journet.

The Scarlet Claw begins as it means to go on. As preternatural banks of fog scud across the benighted La Morte Rouge, a church bell tolls mournfully and the villagers huddled within the local pub mutter darkly of sheep having had their throats torn out. The resident pastor, meanwhile, pooh-poohs the villagers' fears on the principle that "There's no such thing as ghosts and monsters."

Over in plushly appointed Quebec, Sherlock Holmes expresses much the same view, angering the credulous Lord Penrose with his "ridiculous scepticism" even as Watson itemises two earlier cases, *The Hound of the Baskervilles* and *The Adventure of the Sussex Vampire*, that are to have a bearing on the case to follow. Holmes then receives a written appeal for help from Lady Penrose at the same time as he learns of her murder. (As a result, Gertrude Astor, formerly the gangling second female lead of Universal's *The Cat and the Canary*, is required to do no more than lie dead at the foot of a bell-rope.) Finally, and with a richly tantalising flourish, Holmes informs Watson that "For the first time, we've been retained by a corpse."

Despite its agreeably Poe-like name of La Morte Rouge, the film's location could just as easily be mittel-Europe or the Yorkshire moors for all the French-Canadian verisimilitude involved. The Holmes stock company – including Paul Cavanagh, Miles Mander, David Clyde and Gerald Hamer – is out in force, never disguising their British origins and contributing to an agreeable range of red herrings. As the only characters with French names, the American-born Arthur Hohl and Kay Harding make a token effort at French accents, though the uneasy relationship between Journet and his daughter is mainly memorable for the shocking unexpectedness of Marie's murder.

Having been miniaturised by Lionel Barrymore in *The Devil-Doll*, Hohl may have been conscious of a certain familiarity in the scenario here, which again required him to play one of three people targeted by a prison escapee. Unlike Barrymore's Paul Lavond, Hamer's Alastair Ramson is a psychopath who was justifiably imprisoned for the murder of a fellow actor. Like Lavond, however, he is a master of disguise who at one point drags up as a woman.

The murder of Mander's cringing Judge Brisson is perhaps the film's nastiest vignette, with Ramson, teasingly left in shadow but unmistakably dressed up as Brisson's prim housekeeper, advancing on his victim's wheelchair with an uplifted, five-pronged garden weeder. (A favourite murder implement at Universal, incidentally; a similar weapon had already featured in *The Mystery of Marie Roget* and would turn up again in *She-Wolf of London*.) To misdirect the audience, the scene cheats a little; the person seen closing Brisson's shutters moments before the killing is clearly the housekeeper herself, not a man impersonating her. But the transgressive charge of the murder is an obvious precursor of *Psycho*.

The film's atmospheric qualities are largely a result of Neill's potent collaboration with veteran

Holmes and Watson (Basil Rathbone and Nigel Bruce) collude with the local constabulary (David Clyde) in identifying *The Scarlet Claw* (1944)

cinematographer George Robinson. The latter had been adding lustre to Universal's horrors ever since the Spanish versions of *The Cat Creeps* and *Dracula* in 1930, but was here making his only contribution to the studio's Holmes sequence. Together with effects expert John Fulton, Neill and Robinson make a truly magical moment of Holmes' first foray onto the moors (actually California's Nagana Rocks), when an eerily phosphorescent humanoid figure appears at the top of a rocky incline and vaults downwards to illuminate the V-shaped fork of a gnarled tree.

Soon enough, of course, Holmes discovers a scrap of phosphor-painted clothing snagged on a branch (one of the story's several echoes of *The Hound of the Baskervilles*) and the threat is revealed as of human rather than supernatural agency. Unfortunately, when exposed at the end, Hamer's multi-faceted villain comes across as rather a paltry specimen, gabbling his lines in a robotic style that could be excused (if we're being charitable) as an attempt to show that actors as far gone as Ramson have no personality. It's also a shame that the granite-jawed and rather obnoxious Lord Penrose is entirely forgotten about in the film's closing reels, meaning that his clash with

THE SCARLET CLAW

Universal 1944
74 minutes
production began 12 January

Cinematographer: George Robinson; Art Directors: John B Goodman, Ralph M DeLacy; Editor: Paul Landres; Sound: Bernard B Brown, Robert Pritchard; Special Photography: John P Fulton; Set Decorations: Russell A Gausman, Ira S Webb; Make-up: Jack P Pierce*; Musical Director: Paul Sawtell; Dialogue Director: Stacey Keach; Screenplay: Edmund L Hartmann, Roy William Neill; Original Story: Paul Gangelin, Brenda Weisberg (based on the characters created by Sir Arthur Conan Doyle); Executive Producer: Howard Benedict*; Director-Producer: Roy William Neill

Basil Rathbone (Sherlock Holmes); Nigel Bruce (Doctor Watson); Gerald Hamer (Potts, Tanner, Ramson); Paul Cavanagh (Lord Penrose); Arthur Hohl (Emile Journet); Miles Mander (Judge Brisson); Kay Harding (Marie Journet); David Clyde (Sergeant Thompson); Ian Wolfe (Drake); Victoria Horne (Nora); uncredited: Harry Allen (Bill Taylor [storekeeper]); Gertrude Astor (Lady Penrose); Al Ferguson (attendant); Clyde Fillmore (inspector); Charles Francis (Sir John [chairman]); Olaf Hytten (hotel receptionist); George Kirby (Father Pierre); Charles Knight (assistant inspector); Norbert Muller (pageboy); Frank O'Connor (cab driver); Pietro Sosso (Trent); Tony Travers (musician); Eric Wilton (night clerk)

Although *The Scarlet Claw*, the Rialto Theatre's current bid for thrill-seekers, leans heavily on those old crutches, mist, murder, bogs and the supernatural, it departs sufficiently from routine to seem a little better than recent issues of the Sherlock Holmes series ... The chief source of new interest is a villain of great resourcefulness. *New York Post*

Nigel Bruce, the soft-spoken British actor, ... has always added greatly to the entertaining qualities of the Sherlock Holmes pictures, and in *The Scarlet Claw* he is said to be at his most amusing. And considering the volume of the genial gentleman's fan mail, there must be many horror film fans who welcome Nigel Bruce's skill in blending chuckles with chills. *from original pressbook*

Holmes over the existence of psychic phenomena is never resolved. Instead, the departing Holmes gets to utter a patriotic paean to Canada ("the lynchpin of the English-speaking world" etc) that Watson correctly identifies as a quote from Winston Churchill.

The Scarlet Claw finished production on 3 February 1944, and by 11 April Neill was at work on *The Pearl of Death*, in which Bertram Millhauser came up with the intriguing idea of temporarily disgracing Holmes when he inadvertently hands the coveted Borgia Pearl to rat-faced racketeer Giles Conover. Fresh from playing Judge Brisson, the former British film impresario Miles Mander shines in the low-life Conover role, while Evelyn Ankers is given a rare chance, brilliantly taken, to showcase her versatility as Conover's mistress-of-disguise right-hand woman. The film is also memorable for introducing the Hoxton Creeper in the awesome shape of real-life acromegalic Rondo Hatton.

By the end of May, Neill had polished off Universal's eighth Holmes adventure, *The Murder Club*, which was retitled *The House of Fear* on release. The script, by Roy Chanslor this time, confines the seven, steadily dwindling members of the titular club at Drearcliff, an eerie clifftop house on the Scottish coast. ("HORROR Stalking its Halls!" screamed the posters.) The action contrives to mete out several nasty deaths to series regulars like Holmes Herbert (exploded), Harry Cording (dismembered) and Paul Cavanagh (flattened) prior to revealing the 'murders' as part of the club members' efforts to collect on their communal insurance policy. Again, Neill lays on the Gothic atmosphere to plump up a thin and repetitive plot (much enhanced by Virgil Miller's outré camerawork), though far too much time is spent on Watson's nocturnal panic when assailed by spooky noises. This laboured 'comic' sequence makes his repeated stumblings into a bog in *The Scarlet Claw* seem almost dignified by comparison.

Subsequent to *The House of Fear*, only *The Woman in Green*, made by Neill in January 1945, maintained a foot in the horror camp, with five young women deprived of their forefingers as well as their lives in what are dubbed "the most atrocious murders since Jack the Ripper." There's also a riveting performance from femme fatale Hillary Brooke and a hypnotism subplot complete with John Fulton special effects. After that, the final Holmes pictures – *Pursuit to Algiers*, *Terror by Night* and *Dressed to Kill* – suffered from the law of diminishing returns, though only Rathbone's determination to renounce the role eventually put an end to them. He was, he explained later, "deeply concerned with the problem of being 'typed' ... My 52 roles in 23 plays of Shakespeare, my years in the London and New York theatre, my scores of motion pictures, including my two Academy Award nominations, were slowly but surely sinking into oblivion."[15] And, as a mournful postscript to the series, Roy William Neill went back to England at the end of 1946 and died there of a heart attack, aged 59.

EATING THE THING AWAY

One of the professional setbacks arising from Rathbone's identification with Sherlock Holmes befell him at Christmas 1943, just a few weeks before filming on *The Scarlet Claw* began. Like Laird Cregar, he found himself passed over for the role of Lord Henry Wotton in M-G-M's prestigious adaptation of Oscar Wilde's *The Picture of Dorian Gray*. The film was the brainchild of Albert Lewin, a former lecturer in English literature whose film career stretched back some 20 years. *Dorian Gray* was his dream project and in it he adhered to the spirit of Wilde's 1890 original with obsessive fidelity. The film finally went into production on 8 March 1944 and dragged on for some five months. Despite wearing its intellectual pretensions on its sleeve, the finished product would gross nearly $3 million worldwide.

> *London, 1886. Inspecting his recently completed portrait, Dorian Gray wishes his soul away in exchange for eternal youth. When music-hall singer Sibyl Vane commits suicide in response to his termination of their affair, Dorian embarks on a life of sin that somehow leaves no mark on his youthful features. The painting, however, takes on the aspect of "a sort of middle-aged, mad, gruesome uncle with a debauched face and blood all over him."*

The film's intellectual pretensions are proudly flaunted from the outset. An epigraph from the Rubáiyaát of Omar Khayyám is succeeded by a shot of Lord Henry reclining in a carriage, cigarette-holder firmly clenched and reading matter turned self-consciously to camera so that we can all identify it as Baudelaire's *Les Fleurs du mal*. (Moments later, he idly tosses the book to his uncomprehending chauffeur.) And the symbolism that follows is sufficiently bludgeoning to escape nobody. Warning Dorian that "The world is yours for a season," Lord Henry traps a butterfly under his top hat, drowns it in a dish of turps (we're even given a shot of the struggling insect superimposed over Dorian's impassive face) and then transfixes it decoratively to a card. Later, commenting on the death of Sibyl Vane, he tells his young protégé that "You must learn to see it in its proper perspective" while adjusting the controls of a hand-held stereopticon.

Hurd Hatfield encounters Leo Mostovoy's sandwich man outside The Two Turtles in *The Picture of Dorian Gray* (1944)

In his role as repugnant Mephistophelean tempter, George Sanders is fitted with a suitably Satanic moustache and goatee, though he throws away Wilde's bon mots with such rapid-fire insouciance that one regrets Basil Rathbone's missed opportunity. Naïve symbolism and Sanders' garbled epigrams aside, the film takes firm hold when Harry Stradling's Oscar-winning monochrome photography is briefly interrupted by a ravishing Technicolor glimpse of Dorian's portrait. It's a simple yet startling device, giving the impression that the placid pallor of Dorian's painted face, even the delicate lavender of his carnation, are more vividly alive than the man himself. The artist, Basil Hallward, has already referred to having been aware of "a power outside myself" when creating it – "as if the painting had a life of its own independent of me." And that power appears to be vested in the effigy of a cat, "one of the 73 gods of Egypt," that resides in Hallward's studio and is even featured in the portrait itself.

With the malefic influence of a cat firmly established, a canary can't be far behind, and she duly appears in the shape of 18-year-old Angela Lansbury, who gives a remarkably touching, Oscar-nominated performance as the doomed Sibyl Vane. At a Euston

THE PICTURE OF DORIAN GRAY

M-G-M 1944
110 minutes
includes 'colored inserts in Technicolor'
production began 8 March

Cinematographer: Harry Stradling; Art Directors: Cedric Gibbons, Hans Peters; Editor: Ferris Webster; Sound: Douglas Shearer, William R Edmondson*; Special Effects: Warren Newcombe*, A Arnold Gillespie*; Process Photography: Carroll L Shepphird*; Set Decorations: Edwin B Willis, Hugh Hunt, John Bonar; Make-up: Jack Dawn; Costume Supervision: Irene, Marion Herwood Keyes; Men's Costumes: Vallès; Music: Herbert Stothart; Paintings: Ivan Le Lorraine Albright [old Dorian], Henrique Medina [young Dorian]; Assistant Director: Gordon Wiles; Screenplay: Albert Lewin (based upon the novel by Oscar Wilde); Producer: Pandro S Berman; Director: Albert Lewin

George Sanders (Lord Henry Wotton); Hurd Hatfield (Dorian Gray); Donna Reed (Gladys Hallward); Angela Lansbury (Sibyl Vane); Peter Lawford (David Stone); Lowell Gilmore (Basil Hallward); Richard Fraser (James Vane); Douglas Walton (Allen Campbell); Morton Lowry (Adrian Singleton); Miles Mander (Sir Robert Bentley); Lydia Bilbrook (Mrs Vane); Mary Forbes (Lady Agatha); Robert Greig (Sir Thomas); Moyna MacGill (Duchess); Billy Bevan (Malvolio Jones, chairman); Renie Carson (young French woman); Lillian Bond (Kate); Devi Dja and Her Balinese Dancers; uncredited: Colin Campbell (shopkeeper); Lisa Carpenter (Lady Victoria Wotton); Edward Cooper (Ernest Harrowden); Pedro de Cordoba (pianist at Blue Gate Field); Natalie Draper (Mrs Vandeleur); Rex Evans (Lord Gerald Goodbody); Cedric Hardwicke (narrator); Carol Diane Keppler (Gladys as a child); Audrey Manners (Lady Alice Goodbody); Emily Massey (Parker); Leo Mostovoy ('Dr Look' sandwich man); Frank O'Connor (Gibson [Selby butler]); Anita Sharp-Bolster (Lady Harborough); Taylor & Sinclair (Mr and Mrs Ezekiel); Frederick Worlock (Francis [London butler]); John George, Skelton Knaggs (men at Blue Gate Field); with Jimmy Aubrey, Guy Belis, Gibson Gowland, Lumsden Hare, Stuart Holmes, Crauford Kent, Eric Mayne

There is a laudable attempt, within M-G-M's rather narrow limits, to treat the story realistically rather than as fantasy ... Much of the book's swishiness profitably disappears; most of the still more embarrassing purple patches have been unstitched from the fabric. And yet, overall, the movie does not come off. *Time*

The film didn't make me popular in Hollywood. It was too odd, too avant-garde, too ahead of its time. After all, Albert Lewin always said he had made it for six friends. The decadence, the hints of bisexuality and so on, made me a leper. *Hurd Hatfield [reprinted in McClelland, Forties Film Talk, 1992]*

Road music-hall called The Two Turtles (presumably turtle doves, given what develops), she sings 'The Little Yellow Bird' in a cascade of fake snow that looks like confetti, later receiving a canary in a cage from Dorian. The raffish atmosphere of The Two Turtles is alluringly conjured up; chairman Malvolio Jones is engagingly played by Billy Bevan (heading up a long list of horror veterans in the film's cast, among them Pedro de Cordoba, Skelton Knaggs and Lillian Bond) and an absurd novelty act on stage is announced as 'Mr and Mrs Ezekiel and Their Xylophone'. These two are energetically giving their all in the background when Sibyl, wearing a heart-shaped pendant, receives Dorian's cruel letter terminating their relationship.

After this emotional watershed, the film reaches a different kind of watershed – one it doesn't fully recover from – when, on the eve of Dorian's 38th birthday, Hallward insists on seeing the long-closeted painting. Again we have the Technicolor shock of the painted face, this time redoubled by what narrator Cedric Hardwicke calls "some moral leprosy ... eating the thing away." Dorian's savage stabbing of Hallward causes a hanging lamp to swing in graceful metronomic arcs, adding a strobe-like horror to an already nightmarish scene. It also suggests a pendulum counting down the final phases of Dorian's life, but those final phases, unfortunately, are crammed rather breathlessly into the film's remaining half hour. The narrative becomes clouded, in particular, by various male characters whose precise relationship to Dorian is left vague (in deference, of course, to the PCA) and by a last-minute removal to Dorian's country seat that disrupts the flow of an otherwise remarkably unified picture.

Edward G Robinson contemplates his doppelgänger in the triple-decker portmanteau, *Flesh and Fantasy* (1943)

Balancing Lansbury's birdlike Sibyl and Sanders' feline Lord Henry is the Dorian Gray of 26-year-old Hurd Hatfield, who portrays the social butterfly with a bare minimum of fluttering or, indeed, emotion. Many commentators have decried this apparent 'blank' at the film's centre, but the blankness of the performance is precisely what makes it work. Unmoved and virtually unmoving, Hatfield powerfully suggests the eerie, marbled inflexibility of someone who's had plastic surgery, aptly connecting Wilde's fin-de-siècle parable to a whole host of modern vanities Wilde could never have dreamed of. If, as Goya suggested, the sleep of reason produces monsters, the lust for eternal youth clearly produces robots – and it's all foreshadowed in Hatfield's glacial performance.

With its literary tone, fastidious attention to detail and wraparound M-G-M production gloss, Lewin's film could easily have seemed just as embalmed as Dorian himself. Instead, it overcomes its occasionally self-conscious artiness to hint at a profound and unfathomable horror of the soul. It's certainly light-years beyond Metro's starchy adaptation of *Dr Jekyll and Mr Hyde* – a book to which Wilde's, of course, had been an effetely philosophical riposte.

Oscar Wilde had already provided the source material for Metro's *The Canterville Ghost*, which gave Charles Laughton a fruity field-day and which Jules Dassin had completed in December 1943. With American GIs bringing the jitterbug to a straight-laced British community, the film is the exact opposite of Lewin's as far as fidelity to Wilde is concerned. Another Wilde story, *Lord Arthur Savile's Crime*, had been used as the second episode of a three-decker portmanteau picture called *Flesh and Fantasy*. The long-drawn-out production of this high-toned Universal special began at the end of July 1942, the result going out as a Hallowe'en attraction the following year.

Directed by Julien Duvivier of *Pepé le Moko* fame, the Wilde story is much the best in the picture, with

Edward G Robinson on top form as a self-absorbed lawyer, passing through London, who is told by an impish palm-reader (Thomas Mitchell) that he will commit a murder. Succumbing to an idée fixe, Robinson tries to rub out Dame May Whitty and C Aubrey Smith, finally fulfilling the prophecy by throttling Mitchell himself. Duvivier's realisation of the story is masterful, abounding in suggestive details. As Mitchell makes his prophecy, for example, the shrill of a train whistle is vaguely heard, swiftly followed by a hellish pall of locomotive smoke as Robinson takes his leave. Extremely creepy, too, is Duvivier's use of Robinson's mirror image, which, in the tradition of German doppelgänger dramas like *Der Student von Prag*, acts as a Satanic tempter.

Unfortunately, the other stories are distinguished by Duvivier's dazzling pictorial sense and little else. The first is described as "a tale about a gal with a detachable face" and begins arrestingly enough, with bat-winged demons clustering round a corpse, later revealing themselves as Mardi Gras mummers whose hectic revels form a backdrop to an elaborate *Cinderella* variant. Betty Field is a homely seamstress who acquires "the soft, sweet look that men seem to admire" via a Veronica Lake-style mask, eventually assuming a genuine beauty of her own when the mask is removed. There are a few creepy details, such as Lucrezia Borgia's death-mask nestled in a skein of cobwebs, but the eventual moral comes over as naïve and saccharine.

Worse, the third and final story is a total dud, with Barbara Stanwyck and Charles Boyer (who was Duvivier's co-producer on the project) indulging in a windy, and vaguely mystical, shipboard romance. (It's also hard to take this story seriously when one recognises the quayside sets from *Captive Wild Woman*.) Fortunately, the linking material is more engaging, with David Hoffman bearding the delightful Robert Benchley in a gentleman's club, the latter finally advising his companion to "Forget all these old bugaboos ... [because] superstition is for gypsies."

Flesh and Fantasy had been preceded by Duvivier's star-stuffed *Tales of Manhattan*. Released by 20th Century-Fox in August 1942, this involved Robinson, Boyer and Mitchell in a sequence of whimsical stories focused on a cursed tail-coat. As well as a precursor, *Flesh and Fantasy* would also have an appendage, a ditched fourth story that was salvaged by Universal in September 1944 and released (expanded to 65 minutes) as *Destiny*. With Alan Curtis as a feckless petty criminal who crosses a blind girl gifted with ESP (Gloria Jean), the film was credited solely to the director of the newly fashioned sequences, Reginald LeBorg. This seems a bit unfair given that the film's stand-out scene – a brilliantly realised preternatural storm, conjured by the girl to stop Curtis in his tracks – was all Duvivier's.

DESICCATION OF THE TISSUES

If Lon Chaney Jr seemed unsuited to some of the monsters he'd been saddled with, worse was to come. He had made his name as a lumbering simpleton in *Of Mice and Men*, yet, by 1943, Universal's increasingly laissez-faire executives saw nothing amiss in casting him as a suave, pencil-moustached academic – and not just one suave, pencil-moustached academic, but half a dozen of them. And, needless to say, this wasn't some high-minded exercise in showcasing the versatility of their so-called 'Master Character Creator'; it was merely an attempt to wring a few more dollars from his distinguished name.

This latest attempt came about through the resurrection of an old idea. Six years after linking up with the Crime Club for a seven-strong sequence of B-pictures, Universal made a similar deal with Simon and Schuster for a series of Inner Sanctum pictures. This time, though, they only acquired the use of the Inner Sanctum name, rather than any specific properties related to the book series or radio anthology of the same name.

The films were accorded budgets of $150,000 each, with schedules rarely exceeding 12 days. The first, *Calling Dr Death*, went into production at the end of October 1943, with Chaney as a neurologist whose adoring nurse (Patricia Morison) kills his wife (Ramsay Ames) with a poker prior to effacing her with acid; the details are coaxed out of her by hypnosis. An underwhelming beginning to a stubbornly underwhelming series, Reginald LeBorg's film would be followed in December by *Weird Woman* and, in 1944, by *Dead Man's Eyes* (March) and *The Frozen Ghost* (June), the latter directed by Harold Young rather than LeBorg.

Weird Woman is a good example of the limitations of the Inner Sanctum films. Chaney plays a super-rational academic who, appalled by his young wife's collection of voodoo artefacts, brings disaster on himself by burning them all. "Do you realise that you've been turning the hands of the clock back to the Dark Ages?" he asks Anne Gwynne at one point, a line typical of the supremely clunky dialogue in Brenda Weisberg's script. This was based on Fritz Leiber's excellent novel *Conjure Wife* (first published in *Unknown Worlds* as recently as April 1943), but with the witchcraft fetishes kept on as mere set dressing; Weisberg reveals the vengeful faculty wife orchestrating Chaney's downfall as a highly plausible

Lon Chaney Jr and Elizabeth Russell caught up in the campus conspiracy of *Weird Woman* (1943)

gossip-monger rather than a modern-day witch. She's played by Evelyn Ankers with a nice line in undercover spite, though without quite mustering the Jack the Ripper smile called for in the dialogue.

Two defining features of the Inner Sanctum series are heavily featured – a whispered Chaney voice-over played over shots of him earnestly cerebrating in furrowed-brow style, and a protracted flashback to his first meeting with his voodoo-fancying wife. The effect of both is unintentionally comic. Strangely shirking the expected Caribbean setting, the flashback presents its voodoo ceremonials as high-camp Polynesian; one half expects Fletcher Christian to blunder onto the scene rather than Chaney's jodhpured sociologist. Comparing these hula-girl hijinks with the convincingly frenzied rites in *I Walked with a Zombie* is as handy a way as any of illustrating the divide between the Universal technique and Val Lewton's.

By coincidence, Lewton alumnus Elizabeth Russell is on hand in an unusually meaty role as Ankers' unwitting accomplice, while doe-eyed student Lois Collier has to swoon over the bovine Chaney and apply to him such laughably inappropriate adjectives as "brilliant," "dynamic," etc. Stuff like this, together with the ridiculous South Seas flashback, helps to push *Weird Woman* into the 'kitsch classic' category, leaving the way clear for British company Independent Artists to produce the definitive *Conjure Wife* adaptation in 1961, under the title *Night of the Eagle*.

A bit of in-joke dialogue finds its way into *Weird Woman* when Collier is warned off Chaney by a fellow student, who jealously observes that "I know these educated wolves." Therein lies another defining feature of the Inner Sanctum pictures – though second to none at portraying werewolves, educated wolves were entirely beyond Chaney's grasp. Of the 1944 entries in the series, *Dead Man's Eyes* is another film that fails miserably to live up to its tantalising premise: Chaney's impecunious artist, having mistaken acid for eyewash, solves a couple of murders after a corneal transplant (an operation previously featured in Universal's Crime Club quickie, *Mystery of the White Room*). And *The Frozen Ghost*, set for the most part in a wax museum, is notable mainly as Evelyn Ankers' last Universal credit. It also boasts a creepy turn from German émigré Martin Kosleck as a disgraced plastic surgeon who has since become "a wizard with wax." Chaney, however, is as constipated as ever in the role of a stage hypnotist convinced he has willed Arthur Hohl and Tala Birell to death.

The Inner Sanctum series was echoed at Columbia in three further radio-derived B-movie franchises, with Richard Dix showcased in various roles in 'The Whistler' series, Warner Baxter as 'The Crime Doctor', and Jim Bannon and Barton Yarborough providing the connective tissue in a trio of 'I Love a Mystery' pictures. All three series featured plenty of weird atmospherics and outré details, notably the amnesiac wanderer of Lew Landers' *The Power of the Whistler*, the phantom apparition of Eugene Forde's *Shadows in the Night* (in which Baxter's Crime Doctor faced up to none other than George Zucco), plus the shrunken heads of *The Devil's Mask* and ominous Kentucky plantation of *The Unknown*, both directed by Henry Levin for the 'I Love a Mystery' sequence.

Though chiefly occupied with the Inner Sanctum pictures, Chaney Jr found time in February 1944 to suffer the humiliation of dressing up as a bear in Eddie Cline's *Ghost Catchers*, a grimly unfunny vehicle for Universal's grimly unfunny vaudeville duo Olsen and Johnson. Bela Lugosi, meanwhile, had just completed an 'old house' comedy that achieved the minor distinction of at least being painless. Distributed by Paramount, the independent production *One Body Too Many* began shooting in January, with Lugosi and Blanche Yurka as a butler and housekeeper forever urging poisoned coffee on their guests and getting no takers. "I assure you, this coffee will *not* keep you awake," Lugosi deadpans at one point.

A limp farce of the by-now bewhiskered 'will-reading with prowling murderer' variety, Frank McDonald's film is so hopelessly derivative it features a portrait of the deceased Cyrus J Rutherford that is the same one used for the deceased Cyrus Norman in Paramount's *The Cat and the Canary*; it also has actor Lucien Littlefield from an older version of the same

property. By June 1945, the same independent outfit, Pine-Thomas Productions, had an equally indifferent spook comedy on release, again via Paramount. *Scared Stiff* shares the same director, co-writer (Maxwell Shane), star (Jack Haley) – and Littlefield again, this time playing a creepy set of brothers.

While Lugosi was proffering coffee in *One Body Too Many*, Boris Karloff was at Universal for a pompous follow-up to the studio's recent *Phantom of the Opera* remake. George Waggner's *The Climax*, based by Curt Siodmak on a 35-year-old play by Edward Locke, has nothing to recommend it beyond Hal Mohr and W Howard Greene's stunning Technicolor photography. Slathered in indigestible cod-opera, the film casts Karloff as a theatre doctor, and reverse-Svengali, who is so determined on keeping *Phantom*'s Susanna Foster from fulfilling her destiny as a diva that he finally proposes to cut her vocal chords. In a kinky, Poe-like touch (two decades ahead of Roger Corman's *The Tomb of Ligeia*), we get a brief glimpse of a deceased flame of Karloff's, kept in a miraculous state of preservation in a sealed room. For horror fanciers, that – and Karloff's reading of lines like "I want to relax you before I examine your throat" – is pretty much all the film has to offer. In a doomed bid to attract a more high-class crowd, *The Climax* was put into New York's Criterion rather than the standard horror mecca, the Rialto.

The Rialto was occupied, anyway, by the film Karloff made as a means of concluding his one-off, two-picture Universal contract. *House of Frankenstein* had begun shooting (under the title *The Devil's Brood*) only a few days after completion of *The Climax*, and in it the two-monsters-for-the-price-of-one ethos of *Frankenstein Meets the Wolf Man* was taken to yet more cynical extremes. In addition to Count Dracula, the stew was spiced further with a hunchback and his mad scientist master, the latter role being the one earmarked for Karloff.

Receiving tuition on set from his distinguished predecessor, the latest occupant of the classic Monster make-up was Glenn Strange, a busy Western specialist who had made a physically impressive werewolf in PRC's *The Mad Monster*. That film was recalled, too, in a plot involving an embittered scientist's attempts to get even with the men who discredited him. This time, though, the murderous task falls to others, given that Strange's Monster remains supine and inoperative until moments before the end credits roll.

Prison escapee Dr Gustav Niemann commandeers an itinerant Chamber of Horrors and thereby acquires the skeleton of Count Dracula. When Dracula is revived, he gratefully kills Niemann's old enemy, Burgomaster Hussman, but is himself destroyed by the rising sun. Undaunted, Niemann moves on, reviving the frozen bodies of Larry Talbot and the Frankenstein Monster and promising Talbot a cure for lycanthropy. The party then journeys to Visaria to settle more of Niemann's old scores…

Rather than integrating the Universal monsters into a single story involving all of them, screenwriter Edward T Lowe went the easier route of featuring them in discrete segments, with only the Dr Niemann character providing some nominal narrative glue. Niemann, we learn, derives much of his inspiration from the fact that his brother was assistant to the great Dr Frankenstein. (One wonders if that brother was the unhinged Dr Otto von Niemann of *The Vampire Bat*, a film also scripted by Lowe.) Now, Niemann tells his hunchback assistant Daniel that "If I had Frankenstein's records to guide me, I could give you a perfect body." Unfortunately, Niemann proves so changeable and indecisive that poor Daniel never gets his wish. A similar plot point would turn up 14 years later in Hammer's *The Revenge of Frankenstein*, only there the doctor actually makes good on his promise.

That Niemann signally fails to achieve anything – vacillating endlessly over which of several brains to transfer into which of several bodies – is typical of Lowe's slack and baggy script, which is realised in functional and suspense-free fashion by director Erle C Kenton. The film begins very arrestingly, however, with a superbly staged prison breakout and a brief reminiscence of *Freaks* in the storm-tossed sideshow caravan stumbled upon by Niemann and Daniel. There's also a fruity cameo from George Zucco as the ill-fated showman, sagely warning his passengers that the nearby Reigelberg is "a town that doesn't care for horrors." Then Niemann inadvertently rouses Count Dracula from "the limbo of eternal waiting" and the action takes on the mechanical hue that will predominate thereafter.

From a strangely small skeleton, effects expert John Fulton conjures up a quite new Dracula and a sadly unpersuasive one, played by John Carradine with the neutered New World politesse of a poker player on a Mississippi steamboat. He doesn't last long, in any case. The Count has only just hypnotised the Burgomaster's daughter into rhapsodising, like *Son of Dracula*'s Kay Caldwell, over "a strange and beautiful land in which one may be dead and yet alive," when he's pursued by Lionel Atwill's mounted gendarmerie into the rays of the rising sun. This is an excitingly staged sequence and brings the film's first act to a thunderous close, with Dracula's runaway gig hurtling directly into the camera lens.

The action takes on a wider scope once Niemann quits the cloistered Reigelberg, with a particularly magnificent matte painting representing the distant ruins of Frankenstein's lab in Visaria. (Spelled Vasaria in earlier films, this is the least of the picture's inconsistencies.) In the ice caverns beneath it, Larry Talbot makes his entrance with a Lowe tongue-twister that Chaney Jr handles admirably, in the circumstances: "Why have you freed me from the ice that imprisoned the beast that lived within me?"

We also encounter gypsy girl Ilonka, who makes an undisguised show of revulsion when she realises Daniel is a hunchback. (Lowe, of course, had scripted Universal's *The Hunchback of Notre Dame* 22 years earlier.) A boring romantic triangle, of sorts, grows up between Ilonka, Daniel and Larry, enlivened only by the bizarre spectacle of Daniel taking out his frustration by energetically whipping the bound and uncomplaining Monster. Though sensitively played by J Carrol Naish, Daniel's incessant whingeing makes the Monster's first act on finally stirring into life – picking up the little pest and flinging him through the glass of a lofty skylight – an audience-pleasing high spot.

It isn't saying much, but Jack Pierce's Monster make-up looks better on Strange than it did on Chaney Jr or Bela Lugosi, with an unpleasantly seamed and withered look corresponding neatly with Niemann's observation that "the desiccation of the tissues has gone further than I thought." Having disposed of Daniel, however, all he does is drag Karloff's (extremely youthful-looking) stunt double towards a quicksand, whereupon Karloff takes over for an ending very similar to that of *Revenge of the Zombies*, in which John Carradine was forced into a bog by the rebellious Veda Ann Borg. Here, Kenton's abrupt final shot shows Karloff quite clearly thinking "OK then, here we go" before finally submerging himself under the viscous muck.

Shortly before meeting his end, Sig Ruman's pompous Burgomaster offers a pithy epitaph for the film, declining to look at Niemann's Chamber of Horrors on the principle that "to stare at a lot of idiotic humbugs" would be a waste of time. On the film's release just before Christmas 1944, any audience members disappointed that Chaney Jr's musty Kharis wasn't among the humbugs on display were perhaps mollified by the film's support feature, which was Leslie Goodwins' *The Mummy's Curse*. The last instalment in Universal's increasingly redundant Mummy sequence, this one was made over a 12-day stretch straddling July and August and at least has some smartly

HOUSE OF FRANKENSTEIN

Universal 1944
70 minutes
production began 4 April

Cinematographer: George Robinson; Art Directors: John B Goodman, Martin Obzina; Editor: Philip Cahn; Sound: Bernard B Brown, William Hedgcock; Special Photography: John P Fulton; Set Decorations: Russell A Gausman, A J Gilmore; Make-up: Jack P Pierce*; Gowns: Vera West; Musical Score and Direction: H J Salter; Assistant Director: William Tummel; Screenplay: Edward T Lowe (based on a story by Curt Siodmak); Executive Producer: Joseph Gershenson*; Producer: Paul Malvern; Director: Erle C Kenton

Boris Karloff (Doctor Niemann); Lon Chaney [Jr] (Larry Talbot); J Carrol Naish (Daniel); John Carradine (Dracula); Anne Gwynne (Rita); Peter Coe (Carl Hussman); Lionel Atwill (Arnz); George Zucco (Lampini); Elena Verdugo (Ilonka); Sig Ruman (Hussman); William Edmunds (Fejos); Charles Miller (Toberman); Philip Van Zandt (Muller); Julius Tannen (Hertz); Hans Herbert (Meier); Dick Dickinson (Born); George Lynn (Gerlach); Michael Mark (Strauss); Olaf Hytten (Hoffman); Frank Reicher (Ullman); Brandon Hurst (Dr Geissler); Glenn Strange (Monster); uncredited: Eddie Cobb (driver); Gino Corrado (sideshow patron); Joe Kirk (Schwartz); Belle Mitchell (Urla); Charles Wagenheim (prison guard)

It's Old Home Week among the monsters on the Rialto Theatre screen which provides a thoroughly amusing item called *The House of Frankenstein*. Chances are that Universal never meant this horror reunion to be funny, but the scenarists piled it on so thick that creepiness turns into comedy and ghoulishness into giggles. *New York Journal-American*

For the horror films at Universal, they used to have professional screamers on the sets ... Well, when the Wolf Man jumped out at me, I was so scared and screamed so wildly that they cancelled the professional screamer!
Elena Verdugo [quoted in Riley (ed), Universal Filmscripts Series: Classic Horror Films Volume 6, 1991]

"If you move, I'll send your soul back to the limbo of eternal waiting." Boris Karloff threatens John Carradine in *House of Frankenstein* (1944)

staged murders to commend it. Chaney, too, makes the persistent Kharis a more repulsive figure than before. Inexplicably, the swamp into which he sank in *The Mummy's Ghost* has somehow moved from Massachusetts to Louisiana, with the Cajun café around which the action revolves being very obviously lifted from the corresponding establishments in *The Invisible Man's Revenge* and *The Scarlet Claw*.

Virginia Christine pampers Lon Chaney Jr while filming *The Mummy's Curse* (1944)

Peter Coe is at once the smarmiest and most boring High Priest in the series, though he has a much more sinister cohort in the diminutive form of Martin Kosleck. And, to get rid of the Kosleck character in the final reel, Kharis finally does some major-league damage, pulverising an entire wing of a monastery set previously seen in *Tower of London*. The film also contains a sequence of such astonishing power that it validates the entire Kharis series all by itself. In it, Virginia Christine's deep-buried Princess Ananka emerges from her muddy grave in the wake of a bulldozer, groping blindly towards the rejuvenating waters of a nearby lake and drawing sustenance from the sun's rays as she goes. Christine's mime, coupled with Jack Pierce's clay-streaked make-up job, combine to create a memorably bizarre image of rebirth, and Goodwins has the courage to let it run on for close to four minutes.

The scene cut no ice, however, with contemporary critics. "It would seem to be impossible," wrote one, "to punctuate a film with stabbing, strangulation, swathed mummies stalking through the night and buried Egyptian maidens digging their way out of Louisiana swampland without creating a shudder or two. But there it is, and it will be at the Rialto until such time as the management can book an attraction."[16] Another aptly summed up the growing impatience with Universal's conveyor-belt productions, noting that "Because the big studios have first priority on available ray film, there is a shortage of film available for independents, educational films, etc. This is how one big studio expends its film ration."[17]

PENNY-PINCHING AT PRC

When J Carrol Naish and Glenn Strange made *House of Frankenstein*, they were fresh from a Poverty Row project that marked the return to horror of PRC's Newfield-Neufeld team after a hiatus of over a year. Made in February 1944, Newfield's *The Monster Maker* cast Naish as Dr Igor Markoff, who sees in Patricia – daughter of famed concert pianist Anthony Lawrence – a soul-stirring replica of his late wife. As a fiendish means of bending her father to his will, Markoff deliberately infects him with the genuine bone-distorting disease of acromegaly, the antidote to which is known only to Markoff. We also learn that he previously infected his beautiful wife out of jealousy and she committed suicide as a consequence.

In an otherwise pretty unimaginative picture (hobbled in particular by Naish's underwhelming Markoff), our first glimpse of Lawrence's deformity remains a memorably creepy vignette. When lilting piano music issues from Lawrence's study, the hope arises that his inexplicably swollen hands have got back to normal. We then, however, get a shadowy glimpse of one of them as it lifts the stylus from a record player. Light spilling from the hall then catches the distorted highlights of Lawrence's face, framed briefly underneath a noble bust of what looks like Beethoven.

The film's list of blatant borrowings is a long one. The pianist-losing-control-of-his-hands ploy is a direct steal from *Mad Love*, as is the 'it was only a record' gag. Edgar Allan Poe is in there too, for no particular reason. Markoff's lost wife is called Lenore; he quotes from *To One in Paradise* during his relentless pursuit of Patricia; there's a very long and boring sequence in which an ape threatens Markoff's doting assistant (Tala Birell) in images lifted straight from Universal's *Murders in the Rue Morgue*. And, of course, the whole 'deliberate disfigurement' plot was previously played out by Karloff and Lugosi in *The Raven*. But it's the acromegaly angle that gives *The Monster Maker* its particular patina of unpleasantness. Previously cast as a limbless maniac in *Night Monster*, Ralph Morgan gives, in the circumstances, an admirably dignified performance as Lawrence.

Some three weeks after finishing *House of Frankenstein* at Universal, John Carradine assumed the central role in a film that would buck the PRC trend and collect several admiring reviews. As noted in Part

Three, *Bluebeard* was a title first mooted at Universal while Edgar G Ulmer was shooting *The Black Cat* in 1934. Having devolved through East Coast ethnic pictures like *The Singing Blacksmith* and *Moon Over Harlem*, Ulmer resurrected the title on signing with PRC. For Carradine, the film offered an interesting parallel to his own professional circumstances. The homicidal Gaston Morrell finances his artistic puppet theatre by painting made-to-order portraits for an unscrupulous entrepreneur, just as Carradine sought to keep his Shakespeare repertory afloat by accepting demeaning roles in pictures like *Voodoo Man*.

Paris, 1855. Traumatised by the discovery that his muse, Jeanette, was a prostitute, artist and puppeteer Gaston Morrell strangled her. Despite knowing that Morrell now does the same to every woman he paints, unscrupulous art dealer La Marte urges him to keep painting, eventually getting strangled himself. Having killed her sister Francine, Morrell is on the point of strangling young modiste Lucile when the police hound him to a watery death in the Seine.

However long the *Bluebeard* title had been gestating, it seems pretty obvious that Ulmer's six-day wonder owed its existence to the recent success of Fox's *The Lodger*, sharing with it a serial-killing protagonist who's hung up on prostitutes (or, in Fox parlance, actresses) and who ends up drowning in a mighty river – the Thames in Brahm's picture, the Seine in Ulmer's. Both films offered an enviable showcase to their respective psychopaths, with Carradine as cunning and lanky as Cregar was guileless and bulky. And both gave gifted European directors the opportunity to apply their expertise to costumed prototypes of the 'body count' picture.

Ulmer's latterday reputation as the cash-strapped 'auteur' of Poverty Row is focused chiefly on his 1946 PRC production *Detour*, though there are plenty of distinctive Ulmer flourishes in *Bluebeard* too. Some are regrettable. Obsessed with marionettes, he sent to Philadelphia for the puppeteering team of [Wayne] Barlow and [Bob] Baker, who whipped up a Morrell production of *Faust* that Ulmer allows to run on interminably. Others – concocted in concert with another émigré, the innovative German cinematographer Eugen Schufftan – are genuinely striking, as when Morrell, fresh from throttling Francine, races downstairs and is caught, sad-eyed, in the cross-beams of a cruciform shadow.

The death of Francine is the centrepiece of a long and dynamic sequence in which the police stake out the business premises of Morrell's repulsive agent La Marte, only to bungle the operation in spectacular style. Trapped by Morrell in La Marte's upper room, the previously self-possessed Francine goes completely to pieces – an unlikely response for an undercover Surêté operative, but disturbingly well played by Teala Loring. Presaged by one of several riveting close-ups of Carradine's widening eyes, her death is marked by the stylish sweep of a tapestry enfolding her body (Ulmer may have picked up this effect from Jules Dassin's adaptation of *The Tell-Tale Heart*), after which Morrell indulges in a violent confrontation with La Marte. Showing off his *Faust* puppets, Morrell observed that his creations are "likenesses of people I've known," sardonically identifying the Mephisto figure as his business manager. Appropriately then, Ludwig Stossel's La Marte looks rather like Werner Krauss' demonic Scapinelli in *Der Student von Prag*.

Ulmer also contrives a dazzling last-minute flashback to the source of Morrell's neurosis, made weirdly memorable by the simple expedient of filming his disillusioning fling with Jeanette at a lop-sided angle. And he gets strong performances out of his players, even permitting an agreeable bit of Brooklynese comic relief when Iris Adrian swaggers into view and claims to have the same measurements as the Venus de Milo. The imposing Nils Asther makes a charming, if strangely lackadaisical, investigating detective; he's entirely absent throughout the stake-out sequence, but his cultured tones join with Carradine's to make *Bluebeard* an unusually mellifluous experience. Though often misused for cod-Shakespearean effect in other pictures, Carradine's voice here is expertly keyed to his restrained and sensitive interpretation, finally inspiring a twisted sort of sympathy for Morrell when he confesses that "Every girl I painted turned out to be Jeanette, and ... every time I painted her I had to kill her again."

For all its felicities, there's no ignoring the fact that *Bluebeard* is a PRC picture with all the drawbacks that implies. A charming continuity blunder occurs when the ill-fated Renée upbraids Morrell for his faithlessness; seated at first, she stands up in long shot prior to a close-up in which she's sitting down again and utters the unfortunate line, "I won't stand for it." In a judicial enquiry set up to identify the man who painted a portrait of one of the murdered girls, the first model to step up to the witness stand looks, confusingly, exactly like the woman in the picture, which is on show right next to her. And the film's papery Parisian verisimilitude is compromised by the fact that the actors don't appear to have reached a consensus regarding the pronunciation of words as simple as 'Albert'.

John Carradine takes off his cravat and strangles Sonia Sorel (Carradine's then-wife) in *Bluebeard* (1944)

Another blot on the film is attributable to Ulmer rather than PRC. Besotted by classical music, he conspired with composer Leo Erdody (or just 'Erdody', as he's pompously billed in the credits) to plaster the picture in grotesquely inappropriate music cues. Ulmer's *The Black Cat* had been similarly clogged, offering a pot-pourri of at least half a dozen classical composers. Erdody, by contrast, confined himself to souping up bits of Moussorgsky's *Pictures at an Exhibition*, and the result is so intrusive it occasionally makes the dialogue, and therefore the plot, hard to fathom.

The nascent 'serial killer' subgenre had already thrown up Hitchcock's *Shadow of a Doubt* (1942), in which Joseph Cotten's smooth small-town psychopath dwells disturbingly on his preferred victims as "horrible, faded, fat, greedy women." It would later produce Charles Chaplin's excoriating black comedy *Monsieur Verdoux* (1946), in which Chaplin elaborates, even more disturbingly, on the idea that "One murder makes a villain; millions, a hero." (This in the apocalyptic aftermath of World War II.) For his part, Edgar G Ulmer moved on from *Bluebeard* to *Strange Illusion*, a Californian *Hamlet* retread shot in October 1944. Here, Jimmy Lydon (the boyish lead in Paramount's 'Henry Aldrich' pictures) suspects, correctly, that his father was murdered by mom's new suitor, who turns out to be an asylum outpatient. In this role, the slumming Warren William is much the best thing in the picture.

A more typical PRC product, Terry Morse's engaging *Fog Island*, was also shot in October and was coupled with *Bluebeard* in some engagements; not a good match, given that its ex-con butler takes a watery death plunge obviously recycled from the Ulmer film. The picture remains valuable, however, as the only significant on-screen teaming of George Zucco and Lionel Atwill. The showdown between the two is grandstanding stuff; unexpectedly stabbed by Atwill, Zucco expires, gimlet-eyed, with the charmingly ironic line, "You've sealed your own doom. You've signed your own death wa – ."

By this time, the 'old dark house' routine had been given a fresh lick of paint by Agatha Christie's *And Then There Were None*; in fact, *Fog Island* plays very much like the Poverty Row answer to René Clair's glamorous 1945 film version of the Christie story. It's worth noting, however, that not only was *Fog Island* shot a few months before Clair's film, but the play on which it was based – *Angel Island* by Bernadine Angus – had itself anticipated Christie's novel, having premiered way back in 1937. Zucco had been down this route once before on PRC's behalf – in the May 1943 release *The Black Raven* – but *Fog Island* is much nastier, especially when Atwill and three other villains

BLUEBEARD

PRC 1944
73 minutes
production began 31 May

Cinematographer: Eugen Schufftan; Art Director: Paul Palmentola; Assistant [Art Director]: Angelo Scibetta; Editor: Carl Pierson; Sound: John Carter; Set Decorator: Glenn P Thompson; Properties: Charles Stevens; Marionettes: Barlow & Baker; Make-up: Milburn Moranti; Coiffeur: Loretta Francel; Wardrobe: James H Wade; Music: [Leo] Erdody; Production Manager: C A Beute; Assistant Director: Raoul E Pagel; Screenplay: Pierre Gendron; Original Story: Arnold Phillips, Werner H Furst; Associate Producer: Martin Mooney; Producer: Leon Fromkess; Director: Edgar G Ulmer

John Carradine (Gaston Morrell); Jean Parker (Lucille); Nils Asther (Inspector Lefèvre); Ludwig Stossel (La Marte); George Pembroke (Inspector Renard); Teala Loring (Francine); Sonia Sorel (Renée); Henry Kolker (Deschamps); Emmett Lynn (Le Soldat); Iris Adrian (Mimi); Patti McCarty (Babette); Carrie Devan (Constance); Anne Sterling (Jeanette); uncredited: Frank Darien (magistrate); George Irving (the Duc de Carineaux); the Barlow & Baker marionettes

nb: cinematographer Eugen Schufftan is erroneously credited on screen as production designer and his camera operator Jockey A Feindel as cinematographer

The psychological motivation in this gruesome but impressive film is not very convincing, but otherwise the production is of a high standard. The very first shot ... establishes an atmosphere of chilled suspense which skilful direction keeps up to the end. Monthly Film Bulletin [UK]

***Bluebeard* ... had a depth of characterisation which in that period in Hollywood was not often seen on the screen. In the early days of Hollywood, pictures were in black and white – black and white in more than one way ... Now we have human characters on the screen that have shades of evil and shades of good. There are greys. It took a while for Hollywood to learn this.** John Carradine [in *The Horror of It All*, PBS-TV documentary, 1983]

"I told you this island was no place for you..." George Zucco, Sharon Douglas and a plush PRC interior for *Fog Island* (1944)

are collectively drowned in a booby-trapped chamber. Here, however, the film is sufficiently PRC-cheap to recycle a close-up of Zucco's distinctively gnarled hand as if it were Atwill's.

Other PRC releases worked in horror elements as mere incidental trimmings, and sometimes only in their titles and advertising. The popular horse-opera team of Larry 'Buster' Crabbe and Al 'Fuzzy' St John encountered the *Wild Horse Phantom* in 1944, in which PRC's old *Devil Bat* prop was taken out of mothballs for added impact. Two of the team's later releases, *His Brother's Ghost* (1945) and *Ghost of Hidden Valley* (1946), went the usual route of invoking ghosts only to expose them as bogus trumpery. All three were directed by the tireless Sam Newfield, who was also responsible for the jungle adventures *Tiger Fangs* (1943) and *White Pongo* (1945). The former features presumed were-tigers that are revealed as real tigers modified by a mad Nazi scientist. The latter showcases "a beast with human instincts" that turns out to be the Missing Link and conceives an inappropriate affection for the lovely Maris Wrixon.

HOMO IMMORTALIS AND HOMICIDAL FUGUES

Paramount's *The Man in Half Moon Street* started production on 27 September 1943 and took just 24 days to shoot, yet it didn't open in New York until 19 January 1945. Resurrecting the theme of rejuvenation therapy handled long ago in such silent successes as *Black Oxen* and *The Young Diana*, the film cast an unchanged idol of the silent era, Nils Asther, as Julian Karell, whose glandular experiments have kept him looking around 35 despite a real age that's closer to 100. (The part had originally been mooted for both Alan Ladd and Albert Dekker.) Paramount's art department reportedly constructed a precise duplicate of Dr Serge Voronoff's Paris laboratory, while the leading character's name was suspiciously close to that of Nobel Prize winner Dr Alexis Carell; in Barré Lyndon's original play, the so-called 'homo immortalis' was plain John Thackeray.

Lyndon's version had played at the West End's New Theatre in 1939, and had never made it to Broadway despite Asther's personal interest in staging it. It was adapted for the screen by old hand Garrett Fort, who preserved a great deal of extremely literate dialogue but supplied director Ralph Murphy with precious few opportunities for visual excitement. Karell's experiments with the now ancient Dr Van Bruecken (Reinhold Schuenzel) are intended to "push back the barriers of Death forever," and he keeps a leather-bound diary grandiloquently embossed with the words 'Vita Immortalis'. Despite his growing alarm at Karell's ruthlessness (six medical students have been sacrificed in as many decades), Van Bruecken nevertheless offers a toast to his collaborator – but with a conspicuously shaky hand, a recent stroke having unfitted him for performing the latest life-preserving operation.

The intriguingly offbeat actress Helen Walker is wasted in the conventional role of Karell's love interest, and an oft-reproduced still of her sitting in a train compartment with the drastically wizened Asther turns out, on consulting the film itself, to be a scene that takes place in the dark. This is typical of the film's all-round reticence. It's a pleasant, if overlong, divertissement, but makes one long for the gaudy Technicolor of Hammer's 1958 remake *The Man Who Could Cheat Death*, which, though in many ways just as stodgy, at least worked some Grand Guignol grisliness into the mix.

While Paramount were preparing *The Man in Half Moon Street* for release, Barré Lyndon himself was at 20th Century-Fox, adapting a 1941 novel written by a literary acquaintance of his. Patrick Hamilton's *Hangover Square: a story of darkest Earl's Court* was redolent of the flyblown, fagged-out urban

LEFT: Noble Johnson poses an undead threat to Paulette Goddard and Bob Hope in *The Ghost Breakers* (1940)

BELOW LEFT: Bela Lugosi, starting a long stint on Poverty Row in *The Devil Bat* (1940) and *Invisible Ghost* (1941)

BELOW: RKO struck out in a new direction with the alluring *Cat People* (1942)

TOP LEFT: George Zucco presents J Carroll Naish to John Shepperd and Lynne Roberts in *Dr Renault's Secret* (1942)

TOP RIGHT: New horror star Lon Chaney Jr was the draw in Universal's *Son of Dracula* (1943)

ABOVE: Lobby card for the withdrawn RKO thriller *The Ghost Ship* (1943)

RIGHT: Lugosi on Poverty Row again, with Mici Goty and Ellen Hall in *Voodoo Man* (1943)

Above left: The first of several adaptations of *Donovan's Brain* was a loose one – *The Lady and the Monster* (1943)

Above right: Lugosi's character in *The Return of the Vampire* (1943) was called Armand Tesla, but this fooled no one

Below: Italian advertising for the Poe-like RKO chiller *Isle of the Dead* (1944)

Right: 'Midnite Mystery' novelisation of *The Climax* (1944)

"SHOULD ATTRACT HORROR FANS IN DROVES!" –BOXOFFICE

THE LAST WORD IN Shriek–and–Shudder SHOCK SENSATION!

Foul fiends stealing the dead by night so that medical students have bodies to dissect! . . . Even fouler fiends committing murder to get the young and beautiful for practice operations . . . in the dark days of early surgical research.

Boris KARLOFF in Robert Louis Stevenson's The BODY SNATCHER

GRAVES RAIDED! COFFINS ROBBED! CORPSES CARVED! MIDNIGHT MURDER! BODY BLACKMAIL! STALKING GHOULS!

WITH BELA LUGOSI HENRY DANIELL · EDITH ATWATER · RUSSELL WADE SHARYN MOFFETT

Directed by ROBERT WISE

GRAVES ROBBED! CORPSES CARVED! THE DEAD DESPOILED!

–in the most daring shriek-and-shudder shock sensation ever brought to the screen!

SEE COFFINS RIFLED! MIDNIGHT MURDER! BODY BLACKMAIL! STALKING GHOULS! MAD REVENGE! PANICKY THRILLS OF TERROR AND MACABRE MYSTERY!

and WITH ADS LIKE THIS YOU CAN'T MISS!

"DESERVES SPECIAL ATTENTION FOR BIG BOX-OFFICE!" — Film Daily

"SHOULD DO STRONG BIZ!" — Variety

"A REAL EXPLOITATION NATURAL!" — Showmen's Trade Review

RKO RADIO PICTURES

"FANS WILL GO FOR THIS!" — The Exhibitor

"TOPS IN HORROR FILMS!" — The Independent

"IT WILL CLEAN UP!" — Film Bulletin

"AN UNQUALIFIED LULU!" — Hollywood Reporter

"FAR SUPERIOR TO GENERAL RUN!" — Motion Picture Daily

ST. LOUIS TEST RUN HITS WITHIN INCHES OF ALL-TIME RECORD FOR FIRST-RUN MISSOURI THEATRE!

LET'S TOP THEM ALL IN THE MIGHTY 7th WAR LOAN

Ballyhoo from *Motion Picture Herald* for *The Body Snatcher* (1944)

ABOVE: Artwork in *Film Daily* publicising *The Beast with Five Fingers* (1945)

LEFT: British trade ad from *Kinematograph Weekly*, featuring Rosemary LaPlanche and John James in *Devil Bat's Daughter* (1946)

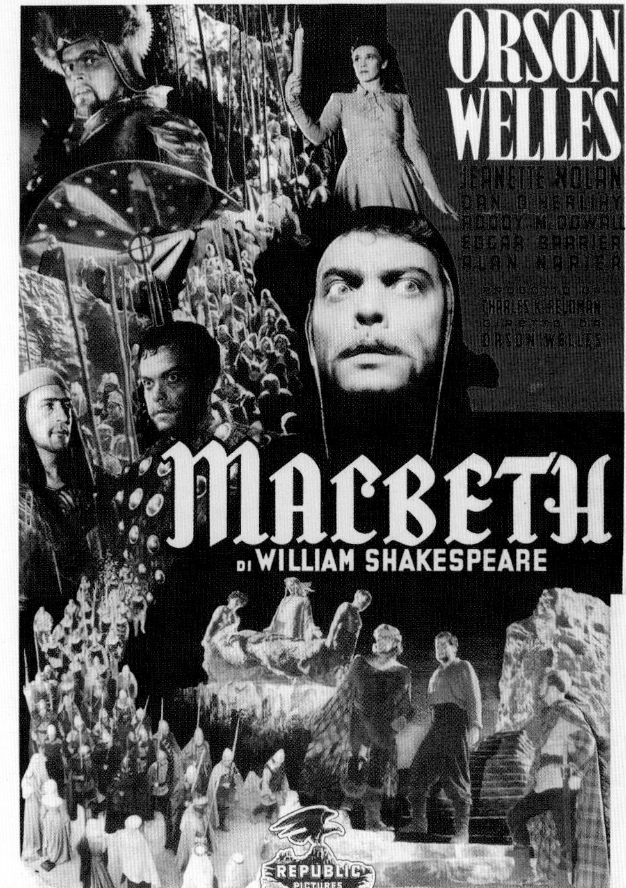

TOP LEFT: Italian poster for Orson Welles' highly atmospheric interpretation of *Macbeth* (1947)

TOP RIGHT: Belgian artwork for *Bride of the Gorilla* (1951)

ABOVE: Richard Stapley and Boris Karloff in UI's R L Stevenson adaptation *The Strange Door* (1951)

LEFT: Vincent Price and Paul Cavanagh talk art in *House of Wax* (1953); between them is Charles Buchinsky, later known as Charles Bronson

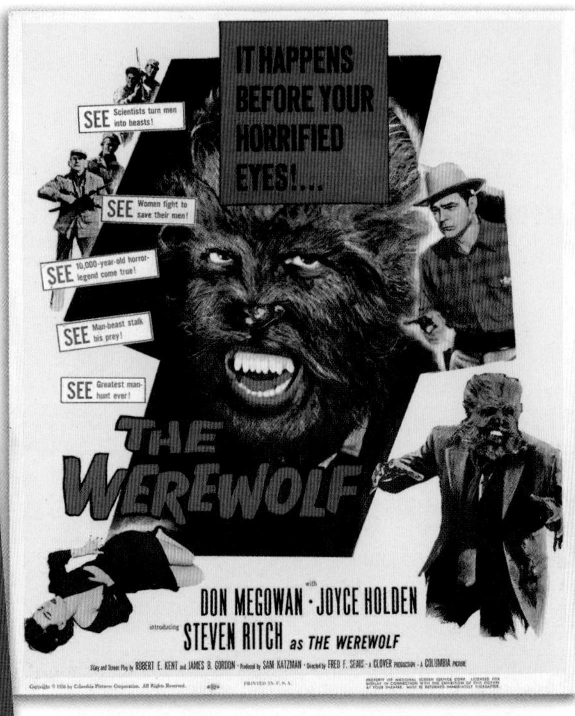

ABOVE LEFT: French pressbook for Warners' 'en relief' (ie, 3D) shocker *Phantom of the Rue Morgue* (1953)

ABOVE RIGHT: Lurid window card for *The Werewolf* (1955)

RIGHT: Lon Chaney Jr was just one of several horror veterans appearing in *The Black Sleep* (1956)

FAR RIGHT: Italian artwork showcasing femme fatale Allison Hayes alongside four of the *Zombies of Mora Tau* (1956)

ABOVE: Lush Belgian artwork for the un-lush *I Was a Teenage Frankenstein* (1957)

LEFT: Gloria Talbott as the much-sinned against *Daughter of Dr Jekyll* (1956)

BELOW LEFT: US lobby card claiming that *The Unearthly* (1957) is 'guaranteed to frighten'

BELOW RIGHT: French artwork for *House on Haunted Hill* (1958) depicting Carol Ohmart, Elisha Cook Jr and a frisky skeleton

ABOVE: Herbert Marshall, Vincent Price and little Charles Herbert witness the terrible end of *The Fly* (1958)

BELOW LEFT: The 1926 novelisation of *The Bat* was reprinted by Britain's World Distributors to accompany the 1959 remake

RIGHT: Dick Miller presents Antony Carbone with a disembodied head in *A Bucket of Blood* (1959)

BELOW RIGHT: Amy Fields gets a shock in her cinema seat in *The Tingler* (1959)

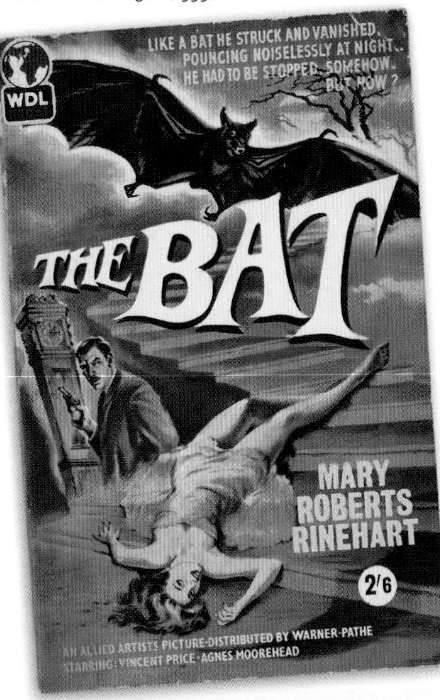

demi-monde that was Hamilton's stock-in-trade, but Fox had no interest in making a film in which the protagonist dreams of using a golf club to batter a Fascist adherent of Oswald Mosley. Nor did they intend to make a film set in the run-up to the Nazi invasion of Poland. Instead, they wanted to put the clock back to the turn of the century and produce a gaslit follow-up to *The Lodger*. They were no doubt mindful, too, of the recent success of M-G-M's adaptation of the Hamilton play *Gaslight*.

In addition to screenwriter Lyndon, the main players from *The Lodger* were all back in place: director John Brahm, producer Robert Bassler, and stars Laird Cregar and George Sanders. Cregar, in fact, had recommended Hamilton's novel in the first place, and was aghast when he saw the radical changes Lyndon had made. (No more so, however, than Hamilton was.) The female lead, meanwhile, went to the 20-year-old Linda Darnell, but only after Marlene Dietrich and Geraldine Fitzgerald had been mentioned for it. The latter casting would have made for a bizarre irony, given that Hamilton had been Fitzgerald's 'stalker' during the mid-1930s and the hateful Netta Longdon was a highly unflattering caricature of her.

London, 1903. George Harvey Bone is a brilliant young composer given to amnesiac fugues triggered by sudden, dissonant sounds. In one of these he murders a Fulham antiques dealer; in another he strangles the vain and capricious music-hall singer Netta, who has been conducting a self-interested romance with him. A watchful Home Office analyst finally faces him with his guilt and Bone goes up in flames during a private performance of his new concerto.

In 2005, the poet and novelist Iain Sinclair described *Hangover Square* as a "desecration of the novel" that "pulped [it] into the conventions of the shilling shocker," simultaneously acknowledging that "Brahm's film is a minor classic, a shotgun wedding of expressionism and surrealism."[18] Indeed: taken on its own terms, without regard to the violence it does to Hamilton's original, *Hangover Square* is a piece of virtuoso film-making.

Brahm begins in unapologetic *Lodger* mode, focusing on a hurdy-gurdy man, carousing Cockneys, a horse-drawn cab, and finally panning the camera upwards from a freshly lit gas lamp to an antique dealer's second-storey window. Gliding smoothly inside, we see Francis Ford (elder brother of the director John Ford) going through the 'retreating from twitchy oncoming camera' routine previously undergone in Brahm's films by Virginia Traxler and Doris Lloyd, after which this arresting preamble winds up with the first of three conflagrations. Thereafter, the film settles into a groove of its own, with fluid crane shots of a London square far more expansive than anything seen in *The Lodger*, plenty of indigestible psychobabble from George Sanders' Home Office pundit, and a music-hall sequence

HANGOVER SQUARE

20th Century-Fox 1944
77 minutes
production began 21 August

Cinematographer: Joseph LaShelle; Art Directors: Maurice Ransford, Lyle Wheeler; Editor: Harry Reynolds; Sound: Bernard Freericks, Harry M Leonard, Eugene Grossman*; Special Photographic Effects: Fred Sersen; Set Decorations: Thomas Little, Frank E Hughes; Make-up: Ben Nye; Costumes: René Hubert, Kay Nelson; Music: Bernard Herrmann; Piano Soloist: Ignace Hilsberg*; Choreographer: Hermes Pan*; Screenplay: Barré Lyndon (based on the novel by Patrick Hamilton); Producer: Robert Bassler; Director: John Brahm

Laird Cregar (George Harvey Bone); Linda Darnell (Netta Longdon); George Sanders (Dr Allan Middleton); Glenn Langan (Eddie Carstairs); Faye Marlowe (Barbara Chapman); Alan Napier (Sir Henry Chapman); uncredited: Jimmy Aubrey (drunk); J W Austin (Detective Inspector King); Frank Benson (news vendor); Clifford Brooke (watchman); Ann Codee (Yvette); Charles Coleman (man at bonfire); James Conaty (concert patron); Leslie Denison (bobby); Michael Dyne (Mickey); Francis Ford (Ogilby [antiques dealer]); John Goldsworthy (Williams [Sir Henry's butler]); Leland Hodgson (Lewis); Charles Irwin (publican); Connie Leon (maid); J Farrell MacDonald (street vendor); Roddy McDowall (voice of child); Leslie Sketchley (doorman); Frederick Worlock (Superintendent Clay); Ted Billings, Pat McKee (men in pub)

The Roxy's *Hangover Square* ... is blood-and-thunder melodrama, not unlike *The Lodger* in period or mood ... When Mr Brahm combines strange sounds and photography with the hero's mental turmoil *Hangover Square* is an effective shocker. The composer's sane moments, like his concerto and ballads, are less interesting. *New York Sun*

The picture which expedited his [Cregar's] demise was *Hangover Square* ... The change wrought in the story by the studio was too much for him and he refused to do the part. The studio, in accordance with its policy at the time, brought pressure to bear upon him and he finally succumbed. But a tragic resolve was born in Laird's mind to make himself over into a beautiful man who would never again be cast as a fiend.
George Sanders [*Memoirs of a Professional Cad*, 1960]

Laird Cregar's reluctant strangler with Gas Board employee Clifford Brooke in *Hangover Square* (1944)

in which Linda Darnell – all garter belts, fishnet stockings and flashing thighs – detonates a startling charge of hoydenish sexuality.

Top-billed this time, Laird Cregar remains front and centre throughout, giving a performance subtly different from his Slade in *The Lodger*, but no less powerful. His George Harvey Bone is a sombre yet good-natured presence, naïvely trusting and obstinately blind to Netta's true motives. His homicidal fugues are triumphs of acting, neatly fused with Joseph LaShelle's lighting and Brahm's inspired staging. A consignment of sewer pipes cascades into a ditch; the camera rushes in to examine Cregar's perspiring, pop-eyed response; he clasps his right hand to the sensitive area at the back of his neck (a gesture previously employed, incidentally, by Boris Karloff in *Before I Hang*) and we're shown a smeary-lensed point-of-view shot as his 'Hyde' persona emerges. In Hamilton's original, Bone had a feeling of being "in the tank of an aquarium or even at the bottom of the ocean – a noiseless, intense, gliding, fishy world," and these blurred visions, together with the bird-like cries of a piccolo on the soundtrack, are an effective translation of the idea.

Mad aristocrat Vincent Price ruminates over an empty crib in *Dragonwyck* (1945)

Netta is a black-hearted version of Miriam Hopkins' Ivy in *Dr Jekyll and Mr Hyde*, and the film's misogynist scheme insists that this classic destroyer of men be firmly dealt with; indeed, she isn't merely strangled but burnt at the stake. Like any self-respecting witch, she has a feline familiar that bolts at sound of her screams and is immediately run over, dying at the same instant as its mistress. ("Someone killed the cat," mutters an onlooker, inviting us to speculate on which cat he means.) Brahm has fun with the animal throughout, even indulging in a shot of Bone at the piano with Netta's pussy literally in his lap – a cheeky detail that sailed right over the heads of the PCA.

The burning of Netta is a masterful set-piece eclipsed only by the climactic burning of Bone himself. As Bone places Netta's inert body atop "the Dickens of a big bonfire over in Cheyne Yard," her 'penny for the guy' mask slips just enough to show us her dead pout beneath. And, this being 5 November, the 200 extras (resembling nothing so much as the torch-wielding villagers from Universal's Frankenstein films) are only too happy to help Bone in destroying the evidence. While this sequence is genuinely nightmarish, the ending achieves a genuinely moving grandeur, a marvellous synthesis of Cregar's end-of-the-line despair, Brahm's pyrotechnic direction and the mordantly powerful concerto composed for the film by Bernard Herrmann.

Determined to become straightforward leading man material, Cregar was on a crash diet during the shooting, his weight visibly fluctuating in the finished film in a weird parallel to Bone's schizoid tendencies. Tragically, only weeks after completing the film he submitted himself to a stomach-stapling operation and died of a heart attack five days later, on 9 December 1944.

Fox had had Cregar in mind for their upcoming production of *Dragonwyck*, which went ahead on 12 February 1945 with Vincent Price in the role; by coincidence, Price had delivered the eulogy at Cregar's funeral. Based on Anya Seton's recently published bestseller, the film was yet another instalment in the lengthening line of 'unsuspecting ingenue in clutches of loony husband' pictures. Set in the mid-1840s, it has Gene Tierney as Miranda Wells, a Connecticut farmer's daughter whose visit to a landed relative in upstate New York results in her marrying him – but only after his first wife dies in equivocal circumstances.

Screenwriter Joseph L Mankiewicz took over the direction from the originally mooted Ernst Lubitsch, crafting a gorgeously appointed potboiler in which Price's Nicholas Van Ryn prefigures his later Poe protagonists in every particular. "Do you hear it?" he babbles towards the end, referring to the strains of his grandmother's haunted harpsichord in the so-called Red Room; he has himself surrendered to opium addiction in the Tower Room, rightly convinced that he is the last of an enervated line.

Van Ryn's impatience with his wives' inability to produce an heir – together with his contention that "deformed bodies depress me" and his revulsion at Miranda's limping ladies' maid – provide an odd pre-echo of the serial killer soon to appear in *The Spiral Staircase*. Otherwise, *Dragonwyck* is Poe all the way, though seen through the prism of a Mills & Boon romance and with a political subplot grafted on that wouldn't have interested Poe in the slightest. Van Ryn's tenants are embroiled in an anti-rent rebellion reminiscent of the nascent trade union of *All That Money Can Buy*, while that film's Walter Huston is featured in an appetising cameo as Miranda's no-nonsense father. Faced with the aristocratic anomaly that is Van Ryn, he remarks pithily, "Since when do we have gentry in this country?"

After his exceptional performance in *Dragonwyck*, Price found himself in Alfred Werker's *Shock*, a so-so modern-dress suspense thriller in which a wife-murdering psychiatrist tries to eradicate a young witness (Anabel Shaw), eventually killing his conniving lover (Lynn Bari) instead. Price thereby added himself to the long line of dodgy psychiatrists proliferating in Hollywood films, chief among them Gregory Peck in Hitchcock's *Spellbound*. Another, played by the always engaging Edmund Gwenn, featured in an M-G-M curio called *Bewitched*, the first directorial effort of radio's Arch Oboler. A naïve case history in which split personality is more or less equated with demonic possession, this has Phyllis Thaxter as a well-bred young woman bedevilled by a grotesque second self and driven to kill a former flame with a pair of scissors. It remains memorable for Audrey Totter's extraordinary vocal performance as Thaxter's demonic inner voice.

Primitive Surgery and Septicaemic Plague

Over at RKO, in the wake of the magical fairy-tale atmosphere of *The Curse of the Cat People*, the Val Lewton unit had determined to make more films falling outside the horror bracket. Mark Robson's *Youth Runs Wild* was shot at the end of 1943 and put Lewton regulars Kent Smith, Jean Brooks and Elizabeth Russell into a high-minded 'social problem' picture about juvenile delinquency, while the following spring Robert Wise made *Mademoiselle Fifi*, a decorous Guy de Maupassant adaptation starring Simone Simon.

These diversions were soon brought to a halt, however, when Lewton was given a new overseer in the shape of "an abysmally ignorant and stupid gentleman called Jack Gross ... the man who has been making those Universal horror films and so had a particular grudge against me, as our pictures had shown up his films not only from an artistic standpoint, but also from a standpoint of profits."[19] Lewton's low opinion was confirmed when Gross instructed him to use Boris Karloff in his next picture, an actor who represented everything Lewton had set his face against. But, after the inanities of *House of Frankenstein*, Karloff was keen to be involved in more thoughtful subjects and quickly disarmed Lewton's prejudices.

Inspired by the period setting of *Mademoiselle Fifi*, Lewton would set his remaining thrillers in the past, albeit the fairly recent past (1912) in the case of his first Karloff venture, *Isle of the Dead*. This began shooting on 12 July but was shut down by a flare-up of the star's back trouble, necessitating an operation and a lengthy convalescence. To fill the gap before the film could be resumed in December, Lewton put *The Body Snatcher* into production just before Hallowe'en, for the first time taking a screenplay credit under his old nom de plume of Carlos Keith. Robert Louis Stevenson's short story – written in 1881 but only published at Christmas 1884 – dealt with the grisly subject of Edinburgh's 19th century resurrection men and, suitably adapted, provided a marvellous part for the recovered Karloff. The result turned out to be Lewton's biggest hit since *Cat People*.

> Edinburgh, 1831. *In the wake of the Burke and Hare scandal, Dr MacFarlane, a former pupil of Dr Knox, acquires bodies for medical research from a humble cab driver called John Gray. With graveyard security being tightened, Gray provides the doctor's newest subject by killing a street singer. Gray is himself killed when he threatens to blackmail MacFarlane about his past, after which the doctor takes the fateful decision to do his own grave-robbing in future.*

The Body Snatcher opens on a mezzotint of Edinburgh Castle, quickly fading to stock footage of the real thing. Moments later, however, we discover that the film's wet-behind-the-ears hero, as played by Russell Wade, is unable to pronounce Edinburgh correctly. He's in conversation at the time with Mary Gordon,

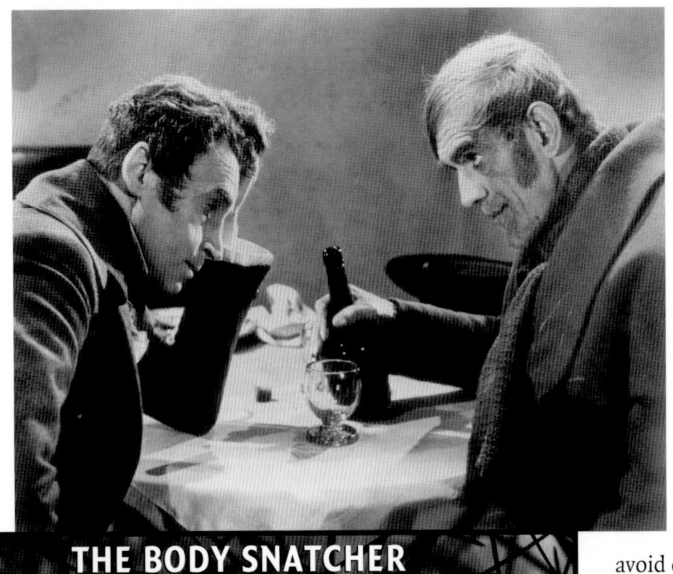

Henry Daniell and Boris Karloff prepare to exchange roles in *The Body Snatcher* (1944)

THE BODY SNATCHER

RKO Radio 1944
78 minutes
production began 24 October

Cinematographer: Robert De Grasse; Art Directors: Albert S D'Agostino, Walter E Keller; Editor: J R Whittredge; Sound: Bailey Fesler, Terry Kellum; Set Decorations: Darrell Silvera, John Sturtevant; Make-up: Frank LaRue*; Costumes: Renié; Music: Roy Webb; Musical Director: C Bakaleinikoff; Dialogue Director: Mrs Charlot*; Assistant Director: Harry Scott; Screenplay: Philip MacDonald, Carlos Keith [Val Lewton] (based on a short story by Robert Louis Stevenson); Executive Producer: Jack J Gross; Producer: Va Lewton; Director: Robert Wise

Boris Karloff (Gray); Bela Lugosi (Joseph); Henry Daniell (MacFarlane); Edith Atwater (Meg); Russell Wade (Fettes); Rita Corday (Mrs Marsh); Sharyn Moffett (Georgina); Donna Lee (street singer); uncredited: Robert Clarke (Richardson); Ainia Constant (maid); Mary Gordon (Mrs MacBride); Carl Kent (Gilchrist); Milton Kibbee (Dan); Ethan Laidlaw (drinker); Jim Moran (horse trader); Larry Wheat (street hawker); Bill Williams (student)

And if you're in the mood for a really superior hair-raiser, there's *The Body Snatcher* at the Rialto Theatre. It's well made, it's based on Robert Louis Stevenson's 19th century horror yarn, and the porter who robs graves to supply doctors with cadavers for medical research is played by Boris Karloff at his ghoulish best. *New York Journal-American*

This series that I have been doing has measured up to what I consider a worthwhile artistic standpoint. Three men, Mark Robson, Robert Wise and Val Lewton, have proved to be the very best working combination in my life ... I can't begin to tell you how happy this set-up makes me.
Boris Karloff [reprinted in Bojarski/Beals, *The Films of Boris Karloff*, 1974]

the diminutive Glaswegian actress best known as Mrs Hudson to Basil Rathbone's Sherlock Holmes, and later still we realise that hers is the only Scots accent in the whole film.

To bolster the film's otherwise tenuous flavour of Auld Reekie, Lewton and co-writer Philip MacDonald throw in a reference to Greyfriars Bobby (here called Robbie), the faithful terrier that watched over its master's grave for 14 years from 1858 onwards. But they also have some highly subversive fun with the legend. In Stevenson's original story, MacFarlane's antagonist was called merely Gray; the film adds the Christian name John, thus giving him the same name as Greyfriars Bobby's real-life master. Perversely, the fictional John Gray enters Greyfriars Kirkyard under cover of darkness and, to get at the body beneath, clubs Robbie to death with a shovel. This is a uniquely brutal scene, doing gleeful violence to a cherished piece of Edinburgh lore. It also leads to the film's most moving moment, when Gordon emerges from Greyfriars the next morning with the dog in her arms, sobbing, "They killed his wee doggie too – little Robbie."

Another piece of Edinburgh lore, though not such a cherished one, is the 1829 Burke and Hare scandal, which Stevenson's story handles directly. Lewton and MacDonald push the story forward a couple of years to avoid dealing with Burke and Hare, instead building up the character of Gray and his parasitic relationship with 'Toddy' MacFarlane. "You've become a cancer; a malignant, evil cancer," MacFarlane tells Gray. "I must cut you out." But Gray is no dull-witted Irish immigrant, as Burke and Hare reputedly were; he's a razor-sharp, shabby-genteel Englishman who is well aware of the film's subtext – that past events have caused him to more or less merge identities with his upright victim. "I am a small man, a humble man," he admits. "But so long as the great Dr MacFarlane jumps to my whistle, that long am I a man."

Gray and MacFarlane are beautifully played by Karloff and the halibut-faced British character star Henry Daniell, their mortal contest aptly staged in a pub that advertises itself as being "for Gentlemen and the Commonality." Karloff plays Gray as the most hateful form of embodied conscience; the smarmed-down hair, the silvery stubble, the calculating glitter in his eye, the frightful innuendos contained in his every lisping observation – all these add up to a source of terror that is recognisably human.

Daniell's MacFarlane is a buttoned-up exemplar of Regency rectitude, zealously over-compensating for the unspecified indiscretions of his youth to the point where he is unable to infuse his students with "the poetry of medicine," only with its nuts and bolts. When he's finally rid of Gray in the flesh (sending him, ironically, to the dissecting room), MacFarlane makes the fatal error of resurrecting him in spirit by determining to become his own body-snatcher, thus completing the fusion of their identities and precipitating a rousing climax that remains one of the most hair-raising in the genre.

The set-up is a classic one – the grisly business in Glencorse Kirkyard; the loading of a recently deceased woman onto a rain-lashed gig; the sheeted figure that lurches repeatedly onto both MacFarlane and his young assistant. Then, in a masterful use of sound typical of Lewton's films, the phantom voice that hisses "Never get rid of me!" in time to the hoof-beats; the lantern held up as the shroud is plucked aside; the percussive crash of lightning that illuminates a familiar, beetle-browed face. In Stevenson's original, Gray's corpse had indeed returned intactx from the dissecting room. Here, however, the concluding rationalisation – the horses bolt, MacFarlane is killed, and a female corpse is found beside him – forms the perfect coda to the film's portrait of a man destroyed by fear and guilt.

The film is highly literate but not stodgy, with an 1830s verisimilitude that may not stretch to anything specifically Scottish but is otherwise grimily convincing. And in Robert Wise, Lewton had found an apt pupil. Indeed, Wise fashions perhaps the best of Lewton's many 'buses' (given Gray's profession as a cab driver, this one could properly be called a horse-bus), together with a queasy scene in which an ill-fated street singer advances, like the private detective in *The Seventh Victim*, into a patch of prepared darkness, only for her song to be cut off with horrible abruptness.

Billed between Karloff and Daniell, though much less prominent, was none other than Bela Lugosi, who makes what he can of the lugubrious Joseph, a simple-minded janitor given to "sneaking about like a redskin." Lugosi had been signed to a three-picture deal by RKO, fulfilling the first of these commitments just before appearing in *The Body Snatcher*. Going into production on 11 September 1944, Gordon Douglas' *Zombies on Broadway* was a bizarre attempt to take the setting (St Sebastian) and two of the performers (Darby Jones and Sir Lancelot) from Lewton's *I Walked with a Zombie* and with them craft a horror-comedy in Abbott and Costello vein.

RKO's answers to Abbott and Costello were the less amusing (but also much less overbearing) Wally Brown and Alan Carney, here playing press agents sent to the South Seas to select attractions for a New York nightclub called The Zombie Hut. In particular, they're required to come back with a "hundred proof, 24-carat, A-1, unadulterated zombie" for display on opening night. As in the Lewton film, Jones lends his monolithic presence to the chief zombie, his thyroid problem from the earlier picture much exaggerated. So, too, Sir Lancelot sings a sweet-sounding calypso with a threatening undertow. As zombie master Professor Renault, the third-billed Lugosi is on great self-mocking form, doing battle with a Capuchin monkey trapped in a chest of drawers and wondering forlornly, "How can the natives do with their silly voodoo what I cannot accomplish by scientific means?"

Remarkably, the film actually makes an effort to be scary: there's a Lewton 'walk' through the jungle, complete with a strung-up panther and a 'bus' in the form of a couple of screeching parrots. And when Carney is temporarily zombified towards the end, the bug-eyed, baby-faced automaton that results is probably a lot more disturbing than the filmmakers intended. The film also boasts a charmingly funky theme by Roy Webb and a delightful heroine in Anne Jeffreys. The producer was Benjamin Stoloff, who 11 years before had directed Lugosi in *Night of Terror*; he directed the last three days of *Zombies on Broadway*, too, when Gordon Douglas was taken ill.

That voodoo and zombie-ism made good copy in the wake of *I Walked with a Zombie* was clear to studios other than RKO. Robert Webb's *The Caribbean Mystery*, for example, was made by 20th Century-Fox in January 1945 under the working titles *Zombies of the Swamp* and *The Voodoo Mystery* – despite a total lack of supernatural content. Lower down the scale, Monogram produced *The Strange Mr Gregory* in June

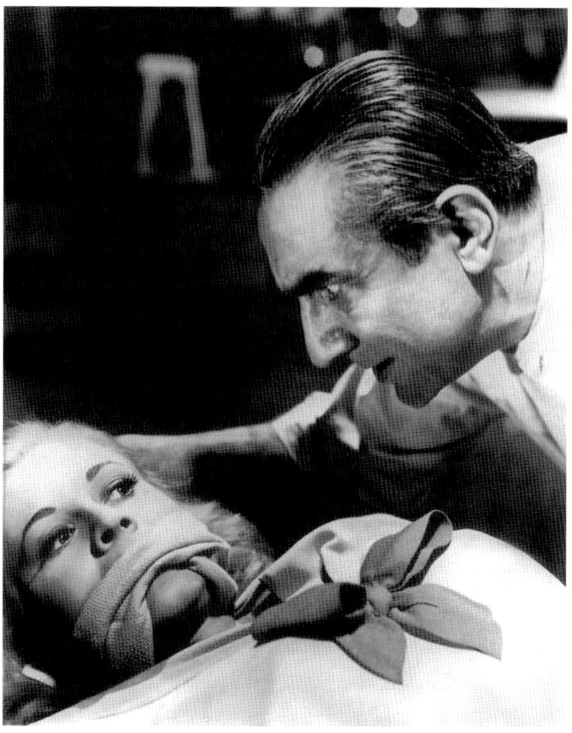

Bela Lugosi restrains Anne Jeffreys in a deleted scene from *Zombies on Broadway* (1944)

of the same year, with horror veterans Phil Rosen and Charles S Belden as director and screenwriter respectively. In this, Edmund Lowe recalled his long-ago role in *The Spider* (itself remade in 1945), playing a hypnotist who assumes a catatonic state in order to frame a man for murder, having already ensnared the man's wife with a voodoo doll impregnated with her blood.

In the meantime, Val Lewton's first film with Boris Karloff became the second, with the remaining 12 days of Mark Robson's *Isle of the Dead* schedule only completed in December 1944. This time Lewton took his inspiration from an 1880 painting by Arnold Böcklin which had already inspired Rachmaninov's 1909 symphonic poem of the same name; in addition, a reproduction of it had decorated the bedroom of Mrs Holland in *I Walked with a Zombie*. This self-referential touch was apt, given that the new film also reproduced the older one's island setting and horsey cataleptic woman wandering the night in white draperies.

During the 1912 Balkan War, the harsh General Pherides and Boston Star correspondent Oliver Davis become trapped on a Greek island when septicaemic plague breaks out among the handful of inhabitants. Under the baleful influence of a local woman called Madame Kyra, Pherides becomes convinced that the beautiful Thea is a vorvolaka, a psychic vampire and therefore responsible for the contagion. The ailing Mrs St Aubyn, meanwhile, slips into a cataleptic trance and is buried alive...

Isle of the Dead begins with a typically portentous Lewton title card, noting how "the people of Greece allowed their legends to degenerate into superstition" and citing "the Goddess Aphrodite giving way to the Vorvolaka" as an example. How this is likely to apply to Karloff's grim-faced General Pherides, shown in the opening scenes touring a corpse-strewn battlefield, keeps the film's first act consistently intriguing, with the expected echoes of earlier Lewton pictures adding further portent to the slate-grey atmosphere. When Pherides hands a pistol to a disgraced Colonel with the unspoken command to kill himself, the viewer is irresistibly reminded of the Palladists' efforts to will Jacqueline to death in *The Seventh Victim*, while Pherides' inflexible notions of his duty are an obvious reminiscence of Captain Stone in *The Ghost Ship*.

Neither of these comparisons is particularly flattering to Pherides, yet for much of the film Thea's observation that "The General is a cruel man; he has a bad name" seems exaggerated. Only when his rationalist friend Dr Drossos falls prey to the plague does Pherides' latent irrationality come roaring to the surface, though the transition is too complete, too sudden for even Karloff to make it entirely credible.

Faced with the thin-lipped Madame Kyra (memorably played by Max Reinhardt's widow, Helene Thimig), Pherides initially scoffs at her insinuations that the island contains "one who is pale and weak" alongside "one who is rosy and red and full of blood." He also maintains stoutly, in words reminiscent of Larry

ISLE OF THE DEAD

RKO Radio 1944
71 minutes
production began 14 July (suspended); resumed 1 December

Cinematographer: Jack Mackenzie; Art Directors: Albert S D'Agostino, Walter E Keller; Editor: Lyle Boyer; Sound: Jean L Speak, James G Stewart; Set Decorations: Darrell Silvera, Al Greenwood; Gowns: Edward Stevenson; Music: Leigh Harline; Musical Director: C Bakaleinikoff; Assistant Director: Harry Scott; Screenplay: Ardel Wray, Josef Mischel; Executive Producer: Jack J Gross; Producer: Val Lewton; Director: Mark Robson

Boris Karloff (General Pherides); Ellen Drew (Thea); Marc Cramer (Oliver Davis); Katherine Emery (Mrs St Aubyn); Helene Thimig (Madame Kyra); Alan Napier (St Aubyn); Jason Robards (Albrecht); Ernst Dorian [aka Ernst Deutsch] (Dr Drossos); uncredited: Sherry Hall (Colonel Kobestes); Erick Hanson (officer); Skelton Knaggs (Robbins)

The chill manner of Boris Karloff is air conditioning the blood vessels of Rialto audiences this week in a dark and mysterious affair called *Isle of the Dead* ... But you will have to grow mighty fond of weird lighting effects before you will get around [to] recommending this picture to a friend. *New York World-Telegram*

***Isle of the Dead*, which we just finished shooting, looks pretty hopeless, but we're going to apply to it the methods of despair and go absolutely, madly radical in our treatment of the film itself. It is the only thing that could possibly make it interesting.**
Val Lewton [reprinted in Siegel, Val Lewton: The Reality of Terror, 1972]

Boris Karloff succumbs to the superstitious promptings of Helene Thimig in *Isle of the Dead* (1944)

Talbot's sentiments in *The Wolf Man*, that "I put my faith in what I can feel and see and know about." By the end, however, he's babbling incoherently about "grave clothes – wings – face – eyes of death and evil." As with Stone in *The Ghost Ship*, the intention seems to have been to expose the posturings of authority figures as a flimsy cover for atavistic fears and neuroses. But given what's gone before, we don't really buy it.

The film is in some ways Lewton's subversion of the familiar *And Then There Were None* template, with a mixed bag of cut-off-from-the-mainland house guests being gradually picked off, not by a murderer or monster, but by septicaemic plague. The rhythm is seriously off, however, in that the film gets bogged down in talk just at the moment when it should start to get really exciting – when the plague begins to take its inexorable toll. Though it will be too late for some viewers, the third act recovers in fine style with a fusillade of top-notch Lewton set-pieces. As soon as the enfeebled Mrs St Aubyn lets slip her obsessive fear of premature burial, the viewer knows perfectly well that this is going to turn out to be a self-fulfilling prophecy, and the scenes showing her interment and subsequent rampage do not disappoint.

According to Karloff authority Paul M Jensen, a West Virginia exhibitor was well aware of the imbalance in the film, noting sagely that "The first part of the picture is boring, but the last part had my patrons screaming and shouting their heads off."[20] Indeed, these scenes were presumably the reason why *Isle of the Dead* was withheld from British distribution until 1956 – the camera closing in on the 'dead' Mrs St Aubyn's trembling lip when no one else is looking; the whimpers issuing from the packing crate in which she's been interred; the brilliantly timed scream and frenzied scratching at the lid; a world-class 'bus' when the lid finally lurches aside. As with several of Lewton's films, the inspiration here was clearly Edgar Allan Poe, especially when Kyra mutters "Hear her? Hear the wood splintering?" in a direct echo of the climactic passages of *The Fall of the House of Usher*.

The film also offers a self-reflexive repeat – muted, but still effective – of *Cat People*'s swimming pool sequence, when Thea advances into the claustrophobic darkness of the crypt, a childlike humming in her ears and any number of possible Mrs St Aubyns shifting in the shadows. The maddened Mrs St Aubyn's weapon of choice is a pocket-sized trident dug up by the mild-mannered archaeologist Albrecht; though strangely reminiscent of the five-pronged garden weeder so popular at Universal, it certainly makes short work of the film's twin repositories of blind superstition, Madame Kyra and General Pherides. The former goes completely unlamented but Pherides gets a sanctimonious send-off from Albrecht – "Back of his madness, there was something simple, good; he wanted to protect us" – that provides an apt coda to a film much stronger on visual atmosphere than coherent character development.

Rising to the Top

Robert Wise's first film outside the Lewton aegis was an inauspicious one, a wholly unnecessary remake of *The Most Dangerous Game* called *A Game of Death*. Released in November 1945, this changes the Russian aristocrat of the original into a Nazi renegade called General Krieger (Edgar Barrier), but is memorable only for an excess of chase footage lifted from the older picture; even the screams are Fay Wray's rather than issuing from new heroine Audrey Long. Barrier's quarry, the lanky John Loder, had also appeared for RKO in Max Nosseck's modestly effective *The Brighton Strangler*, in which he was an actor who becomes possessed by his role when his theatre is bombed in the Blitz. Loder was an Old Etonian whose career took some curious turns; having cropped up in German silents like *Alraune*, he returned to Britain (appearing opposite Boris Karloff in *The Man Who Changed His Mind*) prior to fetching up in Hollywood B-movies.

Though made in July 1944, *The Brighton Strangler* didn't open in Los Angeles until May of the following year, by which time Loder was starring in an unusually accomplished tribute to the Val Lewton style called *Woman Who Came Back*. An independent production distributed by Republic, the film was one of only half a dozen directed by the composer and former radio writer Walter Colmes.

> *Returning to the small Massachusetts town of Eben Rock, Lorna Webster is the only survivor of an accident that sends her bus crashing into Shadow Lake. Convinced that she shared her seat with Jezebel Trister – an elderly witch hanged 300 years earlier – Lorna begins to fear that she is the latest recipient of Jezebel's soul. Despite the best efforts of Lorna's doctor fiancé, the townspeople start to talk and strange events proliferate...*

Colmes had obviously studied Lewton's output carefully, putting us straight into *Cat People* country with a somewhat hollow opening voice-over. The sleepy town of Eben Rock, though a long way from the chic Manhattan inhabited by Lewton's Irena, was founded, we're told, by "settlers who brought to the New World the dark traditions they tried to escape in the Old." The Serbian devil worshippers haunting

Nancy Kelly mistakes rat poison for fish food, watched by Harry Tyler (second from left), in *Woman Who Came Back* (1945)

WOMAN WHO CAME BACK

Woman who Came Back Inc 1945
68 minutes
produced April/May

Cinematographer: Henry Sharp; Editor: John F Link; Sound: Percy Townsend; Set Decorations: Jacques Mapes; Music: Edward Plumb; Musical Director: Walter Sharf; Screenplay: Dennis Cooper, Lee Willis; Story: John Kafka (suggested by Phillip Yordan); Assistant Director: Barton Adams*; Production Manager: Bartlett A Carré; Associate Producer and Director: Walter Colmes

John Loder (*Dr Matt Adams*); Nancy Kelly (*Lorna Webster*); Otto Kruger (*Reverend Stevens*); Ruth Ford (*Ruth Gibson*); Harry Tyler (*Noah*); Jeanne Gail (*Peggy*); Almira Sessions (*Bessie*); J Farrell MacDonald (*sheriff*); Emmett Vogan (*Dr Peters*); *uncredited:* Jack Carr (*bus driver*); Elspeth Dudgeon (*old woman on bus*); Marjorie Manners (*blonde*); Twinkle Watts (*young girl*); Sam Ash, Frank Mills, Frank O'Connor (*townspeople*)

As the story of the supposedly bewitched young lady develops, it attains some speed but little logic, with clarity occasionally getting lost in its melodramatic wandering ... Produced and directed by Walter Colmes, the film, with its fine photographic treatment, is flavored to the tastes of thrill addicts who probably will find it satisfactory. *Motion Picture Herald*

John Loder ... had only one thought between 'takes' during the making of the picture. And that was the 'blessed event' he and his wife, Hedy Lamarr, were expecting. He was so excited about it ... that he declares they expect to have another child as soon as his wife's picture commitments will permit of more 'time out'. *from original pressbook*

Irena's imagination here become a coven of 17th century New England witches, all 15 of whom were zealously exterminated by Lorna's great-grandfather three times removed, Elijah Webster.

Unfortunately, the dire influence of Lorna's ancestry is spelt out for us in a crudely expository scene in which an arthritic housekeeper takes Dr Adams on a tour of the family portraits, flourishing her feather duster at all of them – slave trader, soldier of fortune, shady banker and the terrible 'hanging judge' himself. ("I get my fondness of the dark from him," Lorna explains later on.) Elsewhere, the script is prone to somewhat over-literal dialogue, as when the local parson joins Lorna at Shadow Lake and tells her that "Some people are like that: calm and peaceful on the surface and, underneath, full of dark little secrets." More discreetly, the same lakeside idyll is bookended by shots of ripples irradiating from pebbles thrown in the water, a simple but effective parallel to the agitation brewing in Lorna's unbalanced mind.

Though Colmes' poetic effects and the script's laboured literalness seem to be constantly at war, the impression of an outwardly rational community succumbing to the same mob hysteria that overcame it three centuries earlier is powerfully conveyed, and the subtext of "dark little secrets" is aptly vested in the villagers' tight-lipped ringleader, Ruth Gibson. Played by Ruth Ford with something of the asexual froideur exploited by Cornelia Otis Skinner in *The Uninvited* and Victoria Horne in *The Scarlet Claw*, Ruth's motivations are certainly pretty murky. A widowed single mother, her hysteria seems to be triggered by Lorna's imminent marriage to her brother.

The nocturnal opening of the film is especially memorable. The raddled old lady who climbs aboard a sleek Greyhound bus and hands the driver an ossified colonial bank note is played (uncredited) by Elspeth Dudgeon, who 13 years before had been the ancient Sir Roderick Femm in *The Old Dark House*. With the peculiarly precise diction familiar from Sir Roderick (and also ideally suited to a New England immigrant just off the Mayflower), Dudgeon's cackling crone is the story-book witch par excellence, and her brief interview with the severely spooked Lorna is uncomfortable in the extreme.

Lorna's ensuing delusions arise in large part from the fact that the old lady's body was never found among the crash victims, convincing her that her companion was Jezebel Trister returned from the grave. Sadly, the film abandons all ambiguity at the end, with the corpse finally discovered (totally unnecessarily) and identified as a geriatric asylum escapee who had an unhealthily encyclopaedic knowledge of local history.

As has been pointed out by several commentators, the film's plot device of a young woman being involved in a waterlogged auto accident, and passing thereafter into a different 'zone', would be echoed in Herk Harvey's 1961 film *Carnival of Souls*. Colmes' other set-pieces are firmly in Lewton vein, however, notably a brilliant sequence in which Lorna settles down in her darkened parlour to read a book recommended by the crusty Reverend Stevens, *The Origins of Superstition*. The room is lit by fitful bolts of lightning, the blustering wind agitates a pair of loose shutters, and the increasingly fearful Lorna sees the giant shadow of Jezebel Trister's canine familiar picked out by pulsing firelight on an opposite wall. By the time Ruth's little daughter turns up to shelter from the storm, the dog's shadow has mysteriously moved to the door, while Lorna is sufficiently distraught to look like the wild-eyed witch the villagers take her to be.

Technically, the film is compromised by some very poor model work at the miniature version of Shadow Lake and by a naïve superimposition of the old witch's face onto Lorna's when she looks in a mirror. In addition, John Loder's stolid performance helps to slow the film's already methodical pace; Nancy Kelly and Otto Kruger are much more engaging. But, in its thoughtful attempt at emulating the Lewton style, the film boasts two scenes that come close to bettering its instruction. In the first, Ruth is bedevilled by the subliminal jingling of a dog's lead and the endless procession of white picket fences against which she walks. Later, Lorna herself is briefly made uneasy by the most humdrum of Sunday morning sounds – passing bicycles, subdued gossip, even lawnmowers. In these scenes, Colmes has daringly gone Lewton one better, replaying the classic Lewton 'walk' in broad daylight.

The next bona-fide chiller from the Lewton unit turned out to be the last. The death in February 1945 of his RKO mentor Charles Koerner left Lewton more than ever at the mercy of Jack Gross, and it took until July for Lewton to get his next, typically high-minded project off the ground, albeit under the catchpenny title *Chamber of Horrors*. Taking its cue from the final image of Hogarth's eight-strong satirical sequence *The Rake's Progress*, the finished film – released as *Bedlam* – was budgeted at around $350,000, a substantial improvement on the $134,000 spent three years earlier on *Cat People*. Despite this, the squalid main hall of the St Mary of Bethlehem hospital had to be adapted from a quite different St Mary's, the Catholic church featured in RKO's sanctimonious Bing Crosby vehicle *The Bells of St Mary's*.

London, 1761. The St Mary's of Bethlehem Hospital is run with an iron hand by Apothecary-General Sims, whose clashes with the zealous reformer Nell Bowen lead to her trumped-up incarceration. When she is helped to escape by a dangerous inmate called Tom the Tiger, the other inmates put Sims on trial, though one of them – Dorothea the Dove – circumvents the judicial process by stabbing Sims with a stonemason's trowel.

The patina of respectability with which *Bedlam*'s stately historical horrors are imbued ensured it a major splash as a *Life* magazine 'Movie of the Week' and, in later years, a reputation as an overly fastidious costume bore. Certainly, the film has an uphill struggle to counteract the strange mixture of pedantry and pastiche in the screenplay, which is attributed to director Mark Robson and Lewton himself under his Carlos Keith pseudonym.

The opening reels play like a mildly diverting Restoration comedy, with the exaggerated courtliness of the so-called Age of Reason laid on with a stone-mason's trowel, the better to point up the shocking conditions in Bedlam itself. Unfortunately, the feckless Lord Mortimer is played by rotund comedian Billy House, who was clearly cast for his bulbous heft (ideal for Robson's painstaking reproductions of Hogarth imagery) rather than for his ability to convince as a pampered British nobleman. Similarly, Lewton regular Elizabeth Russell is ill-equipped to play a gin-tippling Cockney doxy, and when Richard Fraser turns up as a po-faced Quaker stonemason, the dialogue breaks out into a rash of "thees" and "thous" that pass from pedantry into preciousness.

BEDLAM

RKO Radio 1945
79 minutes
production began 18 July
banned in the UK

Cinematographer: Nicholas Musuraca; Art Directors: Albert S D'Agostino, Walter E Keller; Editor: Lyle Boyer; Sound: Jean L Speak, Terry Kellum; Special Effects: Vernon L Walker; Set Decorations: Darrell Silvera, John Sturtevant*; Gowns: Edward Stevenson; Music: Roy Webb; Musical Director: C Bakaleinikoff; Assistant Director: Doran Cox; Screenplay: Carlos Keith [Val Lewton], Mark Robson ('suggested by the William Hogarth painting 'Bedlam' Plate 8 *The Rake's Progress*'); Executive Producer: Jack J Gross; Producer: Val Lewton; Director: Mark Robson

Boris Karloff (Master Sims); Anna Lee (Nell Bowen); Billy House (Lord Mortimer); Richard Fraser (the stonemason [Hannay]); Glenn Vernon (the gilded boy); Ian Wolfe (Sidney Long); Jason Robards (Oliver Todd); Leland Hodgson ('That Devil' Wilkes); Joan Newton (Dorothea the Dove); Elizabeth Russell (Mistress Sims); uncredited: Polly Bailey (scrub woman); John Beck (Solomon); Hamilton Camp (voice of Pompey); Robert Clarke (Dan the Dog); Ellen Corby (Alfreda, Queen of the Artichokes); Frankie Dee (Pompey); Bruce Edwards (warder); John Goldsworthy (Chief Commissioner); Vic Holbrook (Tom the Tiger); John Ince (judge); Skelton Knaggs (Varney); James Logan (bailiff); John Meredith (maniac); Frank Pharr (commissioner); Foster H Phinney (Lord Sandwich); Victor Travers (Sims' friend); Larry Wheat (Podge); Betty Gillette, Donna Lee, Nan Leslie (girls); George Holmes, Jimmy Jordan, Tom Noonan (stonemasons)

Producer Val Lewton and Writer-Director Mark Robson wring some effective moments of pity and terror out of the assorted lunatics and, as in all Lewton films, the melodrama is used also for more serious purposes ... But sincere, artful and scary as the best of *Bedlam* is, its horror and high-mindedness don't always blend smoothly. *Time*

I think whoever was in charge at RKO wanted an American to play it – even though it was a very English part. I think it was Jane Greer whom they wanted. But anyway, Val fought for me and finally I did it. As far as I'm concerned, it was the best part I ever had – really a wonderful part.
Anna Lee [quoted in Mank, *Women in Horror Films 1940s*, 1999]

Anna Lee swaps epigrammatic insults with Boris Karloff in *Bedlam* (1945)

Happily, Sims is a role tailor-made for Karloff and he's well matched by Anna Lee, formerly his co-star in *The Man Who Changed His Mind* and now an unusually proactive heroine as actress-turned-reformer Nell Bowen. Lee perhaps overdoes Nell's assumed haughtiness in the early stages, particularly in her toffee-nosed dealings with the simple Quaker. But her authority gathers force as Nell's is gradually stripped away. Struggling against the Sims-like notion that "these people [her fellow inmates] are like beasts," she reaches a personal apotheosis on venturing into the cage of a dangerous lunatic and pacifying him merely by her presence. The impact here is dulled only by the lunatic himself; as played by Vic Holbrook, Tom the Tiger looks like little more than the fresh-faced young prizefighter Holbrook actually was.

Karloff's Sims is a scholarly figure who has suppressed his finer feelings in the drive to retain a precarious toehold in polite society. Convinced of his own intellectual discernment, he quotes from Thomas Dekker's 1604 play *The Honest Whore* while loftily dismissing him as "a second-rate dramatist of the last century." Moments later, however, he offers his own dramatic capabilities to Mortimer with the bottom-of-the-barrel promise that "I will prepare a masque of madness that will set you howling."

The ensuing performance takes place at a garden party in front of a tableful of powder-puffed grandees; it puts the modern viewer in mind of the Marquis de Sade's amateur theatricals at Charenton as dramatised by Peter Weiss in his 1963 drama *Marat/Sade*. Sims extols "our golden Age of Reason" and as its exemplar presents a mentally disturbed young man plastered in gold leaf. When a watching Whig politician points out the danger of suffocation, Karloff indulges in a masterfully smooth bit of black comedy, changing his description of the boy from "dying" to "dead" without batting an eyelid or even changing his tone.

The asylum environment is the source of a highly effective 'bus' or two, notably when the Quaker advances down a

darkened corridor that quickly bristles with out-thrust hands and a shrieking face. But it's mainly used as a sardonic microcosm of the wider world. Incarcerated there, Nell naturally gravitates towards a rarefied group whose mild-mannered spokesman rejects the idea of assisting the other inmates with the line, "Why should *we* help? We are the People of the Pillar." (In one of Lewton's most trenchant asides, the same unbalanced character is represented as an 18th century pioneer of motion pictures.) That the hierarchical structure of society is present even in Bedlam occasions Sims' bitterest reference to his thwarted ambitions, addressed to Nell in tones of the sincerest politesse: "It's a law of physics. The lighter elements, like scum, rise to the top."

This line may well have had a personal resonance for Lewton, a sensitive man whose serious approach to filmmaking was always at odds with the light-hearted froth better calculated to top the box-office charts. The film's philosophical aspirations may remain as half-realised as Sims' own, but it still builds to a haunting finale in which Lewton turns yet again to his old standby, Edgar Allan Poe. First, Sims is put on trial by his charges in a scenario reminiscent of Poe's *The System of Dr Tarr and Prof Fether*. Then he's stabbed in the back by a catatonic young woman, whose clandestinely filched trowel is clearly equivalent to the cataleptic woman's trident in *Isle of the Dead*. When the inmates proceed to wall Sims up, the reference appears to be to *The Black Cat* – until his eyes suddenly open just as the last stone is inserted, which takes us into *The Cask of Amontillado* and engenders a genuine chill of horror.

Any feelings of complacency among 1946 audiences regarding the nearly 200 years separating them from the action of *Bedlam* would be shattered by an exposé of modern mental institutions published the same year. Mary Jane Ward's bestseller *The Snake Pit* accordingly became an excoriating Fox production, shot in summer 1947, in which Olivia de Havilland was lumped in among the "strange animals" of an overcrowded asylum and was Oscar-nominated for her pains. Anatole Litvak's film would have its low-rent imitators, notably Budd Boetticher's *Behind Locked Doors*, in which Richard Carlson is a private dick going undercover in a sanitarium. And, despite the British censor's long-standing queasiness regarding depictions of mental illness, the Litvak film was deemed to have redeeming social value and therefore escaped being banned in the UK. No such leniency was extended to *Bedlam*, to which the irredeemable 'horror' taint presumably clung despite all Lewton's efforts to transcend it.

Karloff having completed three pictures for RKO, it remained only for Bela Lugosi to do the same. This he did in Leslie Goodwins' *Genius at Work*, a remake of RKO's eight-year-old mystery-comedy *Super-Sleuth*. Starting production in mid-August 1945 but withheld from release for over a year, this was the last vehicle for the comedy duo of Brown and Carney, with whom Lugosi had appeared in *Zombies on Broadway*. Also retained from that film was the beautiful Anne Jeffreys, with the added bonus of Lionel Atwill as criminal mastermind The Cobra. While Brown and Carney are as much of an acquired taste as before, Lugosi and Atwill are on fine form, particularly in an outrageous finale in which Atwill drags up as a wheelchair-bound old lady and Lugosi dons a false beard to portray 'her' husband.

While Lugosi and Atwill were guying themselves in *Genius at Work*, George Zucco was making his last film (of five) for PRC. Directed by Sam Newfield under the pseudonym Sherman Scott, *The Flying Serpent* was ballyhooed as a "Relic of an Ancient Terror Born a Billion Years Ago!" It had actually been born as recently as 1940, given that the winged Aztec god featured here – Quetzalcoatl, no less – is an extremely close relative to our old friend *The Devil Bat*, with a lethal homing instinct for his own plucked feathers rather than after-shave. In the old Lugosi role, Zucco is as watchable as ever, but the creature itself is a wire-borne hoot.

Despite this embarrassment, Zucco had several high-profile pictures ahead of him prior to his retirement in 1951. Bela Lugosi, however, would enjoy only one further major-studio assignment after *Genius at Work*, while Lionel Atwill was to appear in only one more film of any kind. After the completion of Universal's *House of Dracula*, in January 1946 he began work at the same studio on a serial called *Lost City of the Jungle*. He was unable to complete it. He died of throat cancer on Monday 22 April, aged 61.

SINS OF THE FATHERS

Like *The Flying Serpent*, Frank Wisbar's *Strangler of the Swamp* was produced at PRC in August 1945, but the result is a very different proposition. In it, Wisbar reached back to his 1935 film *Fährmann Maria*, a mystical tale of a young ferrywoman facing up to Death himself in order to save her fugitive lover. To play Maria, Wisbar cast Sybille Schmitz, the iconic, dark-eyed heroine of Carl Dreyer's *Vampyr*. At PRC, ironically, Wisbar got a much more Aryan-looking Maria in the shape of former Miss America Rosemary LaPlanche.

Like *Bluebeard*, *Strangler of the Swamp* is that rare thing, a PRC picture that has attracted a smattering of critical approbation, though most of the plaudits seem to spring from simple bamboozlement at the fact that PRC had briefly forsaken feathered serpents and backwoods werewolves for fetid atmospherics. Wisbar's story was somewhat retooled for PRC purposes, changing Maria's antagonist from a coolly acquisitive Death to a revenge-driven spectre, the ghost of a former ferryman who was hanged for a murder he didn't commit. When the phantom Douglass claims as his fifth victim the old man responsible for framing him, the latter's beautiful grand-daughter Maria returns to the village, assuming responsibility for the ferry and falling in love with another prodigal (played by future director Blake Edwards). When he too is targeted by the spectre, Maria – in a typically Teutonic, *Nosferatu*-style gesture – offers herself instead, thus breaking the curse.

The film's 'sins of the fathers' scenario, and its explicitly religious climax, is put over with disarming naïveté, while the studio-built swamp, swathed in a ton of dry ice, is a marvellously eerie setting. "The swamp makes me think of fairy tales, it's so lovely," Maria says dreamily at one point, emphasising the fact that she's almost as otherworldly a figure as Douglass. She's also a free spirit, and to that end is the most conspicuously braless horror heroine since Virginia Bruce in *Kongo* and Dorothy Burgess in *Black Moon*. The sometime Ming the Merciless, Charles Middleton, lends his sonorous voice to the strangler, and is photographed in a strikingly elliptical style by James S Brown Jr. Otherwise, it's hard not to concur with the contemporary opinion of Britain's *Monthly Film Bulletin*, which noted "a curiously amateurish quality about most of the acting, the photography, and the production as a whole, which may or may not be intended as a reflection of the unsophisticated story and its characters."[21]

In Hollywood's more reputable studios, the Welsh novelist Ethel Lina White, whose *The Wheel Spins* had served as the basis for Hitchcock's *The Lady Vanishes*, acquired a brief vogue in the mid-1940s, though she died in 1944 and was therefore not around to see the results. In May of that year, Paramount put *Fear* into production as a loose follow-up to *The Uninvited*, reuniting director Lewis Allen with heroine Gail Russell and releasing the finished product as *The Unseen* a year later. The source was White's novel *Midnight House* (called *Her Heart in Her Throat* in the US), though its story of Russell acting as governess to Joel McCrea's two obnoxious children is obviously indebted to *The Turn of the Screw*.

Ghosts are not the issue, however; instead, kindly doctor Herbert Marshall is revealed as the Massachusetts serial killer with whom McCrea's small son is in unwitting cahoots. The design of the film's Crescent Drive looks very similar to that of Montague Square in the just-released *The Lodger*; it even has a cobbled offshoot called Salem Alley to match the Fox picture's Slade Walk. There, however, all similarities end. *The Unseen* has a certain amount of atmosphere, and a single frisson when the little girl confesses that her odious brother "opens the front door so the man from the empty house can come in." But it's otherwise a boring misfire, hobbled by a spectacularly garbled script (co-written by Raymond Chandler) and a damp-squib resolution in which Russell's heroine, despite having been central to the intrigue all along, is patronisingly sent out of the room.

In August 1945, another Ethel Lina White serial killer was brought to the screen in an RKO picture that took advantage of numerous technicians, plus a couple of actors, from the Val Lewton unit. Directed by Robert Siodmak, the film benefited from an accomplished Mel Dinelli script that sought to apply psychological depth to the 'old house' routine popularised years before by Mary Roberts Rinehart. In the UK, at least one critic was keenly aware of this, and of the fact that the film's title closely echoed the Rinehart story that eventually mutated into *The Bat*. "Why *The Spiral Staircase?*" asked Campbell Dixon. "Why, I mean, the new title, which is likely to cause confusion with Mary Roberts Rinehart's *The Circular Staircase?* What was wrong with Ethel Lina White's original title, *Some Must Watch?*"[22]

1906. Traumatised by seeing her parents burned to death as a child, Helen is now mute and lives in the forbidding New England home of bedridden matriarch Mrs Warren, to whom she is a paid companion. A serial murderer is at large who preys exclusively on disabled young women, and Helen gradually comes to realise not only that she is marked to be the next victim but that the killer is inside the house.

Despite the new title, Siodmak goes all out to emphasise the voyeurism implicit in White's original, *Some Must Watch*. A gaggle of awestruck New Englanders are shown savouring an all-new form of voyeurism right at the beginning, with a room in the local hotel pressed into service as a makeshift nickelodeon. The silent characters on the screen provide a neat parallel to the voiceless girl sitting rapt in the audience, then Nicholas Musuraca's camera sweeps upwards to the room above and discovers a woman in her underwear limping to her closet to fetch a dressing gown. That the killer is in the closet

is a situation fraught with comic potential, but not as portrayed by Siodmak. In startling close-up, his remorseless eye looks daggers from the darkness, then a riveting point-of-view shot works a discreet gag on the silent picture being shown downstairs, the killer's eye (complete with lashes) forming a perfect, old-fashioned 'iris' shot.

The murder itself is shown only through the balletic contortions of the girl's upraised arms, another nice reversal in that the 'clutching hand' of silent melodrama has been transferred to the victim rather than the killer. This killer, in fact, is an altogether more modern creation; his hands are sheathed in the black leather gloves that would become an inescapable signifier of the Italian giallo pictures so popular in the 1960s and 70s. And, as well as scattering a healthy ration of red herrings, screenwriter Dinelli works hard to suggest that the killer is a kind of Everyman figure, thereby implicating even the voyeurs watching *The Spiral Staircase* itself. As James Bell's wiry police chief blandly puts it, the killer is "somebody in this town, somebody we all know, somebody we see every day. Might be me, might be you." Later, the officer's words are aptly turned around by Mrs Warren's insolent handyman, who notes of the people who fall prey to the killer: "It's never me, it's never you: it's always somebody else."

The Everyman serial killer is an especially disturbing concept given his repugnant rationale when he finally reveals himself. "There's no room in the whole world for imperfection," he explains, identifying himself as a Massachusetts prototype of the Nazi regime that had only just been overthrown when the film was made. He targets women with scarred faces, mental retardation, even pronounced limps, following his late father's dictum that "The strong survive, the weak die." Daddy was a big-game hunter (a portrait of him, pith helmet on knee, hangs above Mrs Warren's mantelpiece, which is itself adorned by a huge elephant's tusk), and the son's efforts to conform to "his concept of what a real man should be" have taken a cowardly and perverted turn. That sexual inadequacy is at the root of the problem is made very plain, and teasingly reinforced when both Mrs Warren and her starchy Irish nurse are described as being "as good as any man."

Simultaneously looking back to Mary Roberts Rinehart and forward to Mario Bava, *The Spiral Staircase* is a remarkable synthesis as well as a masterful thriller in its own right. Siodmak balances moments of surrealism (Helen, her mouth eerily erased, trapped in the iridescent swirls of the killer's pupils) with shadowplay to rival anything in the Lewton pictures (the ill-starred secretary trapped in the lumber room, obscured by a huge block of darkness, only her outflung arms visible as she too contorts in death). The sound design is exemplary,

THE SPIRAL STAIRCASE

RKO Radio / Vanguard Films 1945
83 *minutes*
production began mid-August

Cinematographer: Nicholas Musuraca; Art Directors: Albert S D'Agostino, Jack Okey; Editors: Harry Marker, Harry Gerstad; Sound: John L Cass, Terry Kellum; Special Effects: Vernon L Walker; Set Decorations: Darrell Silvera; Gowns: Edward Stevenson; Music: Roy Webb; Musical Director: C Bakaleinikoff; Production Assistant: Edgar Peterson; Assistant Director: Harry Scott; Screenplay: Mel Dinelli (based on the novel *Some Must Watch* by Ethel Lina White); Producer: Dore Schary; Director: Robert Siodmak

Dorothy McGuire (Helen); George Brent (Professor Warren); Ethel Barrymore (Mrs Warren); Kent Smith (Dr Parry); Rhonda Fleming (Blanche); Gordon Oliver (Steve Warren); Elsa Lanchester (Mrs Oates); Sara Allgood (Nurse Barker); Rhys Williams (Oates); James Bell (constable); uncredited: Erville Alderson (Dr Harvey); Ellen Corby (woman in hotel corridor); Myrna Dell (limping girl); Dickie Tyler (Freddy); Charles Wagenheim (hotelier); Larry Wheat (minister in dream sequence); with George Holmes, Irene Mack, Stanley Price, Leslie Raymaster

The intention of this film is that of the fat boy, to make the flesh creep, and it succeeds in its purpose. All that can minister to the sinister and eerie are here ... and if it is difficult to believe in the mental processes of the murderer, it is at least agreeable to meet in a film of this kind some attempt at a psychological explanation. The Times [UK]

Ethel Barrymore, First Lady of the Theatre, expects never to see herself on the screen ... She hasn't seen any of the pictures in which she has appeared, and they go back to early silent days. "It's not a superstition," she explains. "I just don't care to see myself in motion pictures. After all, I've never seen myself on the stage, either." *from original pressbook*

Some must watch: Dorothy McGuire as the 'imperfect' heroine of *The Spiral Staircase* (1945)

especially important given that a thunderstorm rumbles virtually from beginning to end, and Roy Webb's ominous score incorporates a spooky sound that was to predominate in 1950s fantasy films, that of the Theremin.

The house itself is a marvellous creation, its every turn-of-the-century knick-knack and writhing wallpaper arabesque adding to the oppressive aura of Helen's ordeal. The staircase of the title is sparingly used but, in its spiralling descent into darkness, precisely parallels the repeated close-ups of the killer's unfathomable eye. On top of all this, there are striking performances from Dorothy McGuire and Ethel Barrymore, the former memorably delineating post-traumatic stress, the latter required to gun down the killer in a predictably Oedipal but still satisfying conclusion.

Siodmak's film anticipated more than just the Italian giallo tradition. With its Victorian mansion, mummy's boy killer and bedridden old lady in an upstairs room, it also prefigures Hitchcock's *Psycho* in most of its important particulars save the cross-dressing – which, oddly enough, Ethel Lina White *did* include in a short story distilled from her original novel and titled *An Unlocked Window*. The story's killer-disguised-as-a-nurse motif had already been borrowed by Universal's Sherlock Holmes shocker *The Scarlet Claw*, and the story itself would finally be adapted as a striking 1965 episode of *The Alfred Hitchcock Hour* – filmed, with a pleasing circularity, in the *Psycho* house.

In the late summer of 1945, Hollywood studios, from PRC at the bottom end to RKO at the top, were working on in apparently untroubled, 'business as usual' fashion; the world, however, was emerging into an anxious new era. The war in Europe having ended on 8 May, the war in the Pacific was brought to a close on 6 August by the dropping of a uranium bomb on Hiroshima and, three days later, a plutonium bomb on Nagasaki; Japan's surrender was formalised on 2 September. After an unprecedented 12 years in office, Franklin D Roosevelt had died on 12 April, leaving the decision to utilise the newly developed weapons to the incoming president, Harry S Truman. The "draughts of blood" of the First World War, which Lotte Eisner cited as determining the collective nightmares of the inter-war period, had been replaced by a technological threat of unimaginable power, triggering a new set of collective nightmares that would coalesce into the rampant paranoia of the 1950s.

SATURATION EXPLOITATION

At Universal, the first part of 1945 was relatively quiet where new horror projects were concerned. The two final instalments of the Inner Sanctum series, however, were polished off in February and March. John Hoffman's *Strange Confession* is a tolerable remake of the 11-year-old *The Man Who Reclaimed His Head*, with Lon Chaney Jr substituting for Claude Rains and J Carrol Naish for Lionel Atwill, while Wallace Fox's *Pillow of Death* is a tiresome retread of the time-honoured 'phoney spiritualist' routine, with Chaney as a murderous lawyer haunted by his dead wife's voice.

This last entry was the only one, incidentally, to dispense with one of the series' major signifiers – a flute-faced guardian of the Inner Sanctum, oscillating weirdly in a crystal ball and offering a few prefatory remarks about "a strange, fantastic world controlled by a mass of living, pulsating flesh: the mind." Though retired from his Inner Sanctum duties, actor David Hoffman would turn up at the end of 1945 in Warners' *The Beast with Five Fingers*, recoiling from a mad killer while displaying a pair of nostrils to rival Ernest Thesiger's.

With Chaney Jr mired in these determinedly ho-hum programmers, the decision was finally taken to revive his iconic wolf man one more time in a film originally announced, some 18 months prior to production, as *The Wolf Man vs Dracula*. Unfortunately, the result, released as *House of Dracula*, provides further evidence of Universal's laissez-faire laziness. Though more or less recycling his *House of Frankenstein* script, writer Edward T Lowe proceeds as if that film never existed, offering no explanation for the revival of either Count Dracula or Larry Talbot. It also represents a final lapse into juvenilia for Universal's once-proud monster franchises; as critic Dorothy Masters put it at the time, the film is "positively guaranteed not to scare the pants off of anybody old enough to wear them."[23]

In rapid succession, Count Dracula and Larry Talbot appeal to Dr Franz Edelmann to lift from them the curses of vampirism and lycanthropy respectively. Having stumbled on the still-living body of the Frankenstein Monster, Edelmann is forced to kill Dracula when the treacherous vampire targets a beautiful young nurse. Dracula, however, has already transfused his own blood into Edelmann's veins. Talbot's treatment proves successful, but Edelmann himself becomes a fiend-like killer and determines on reviving the Monster...

House of Dracula begins with the Count looking up at a girl's window from a stone-flagged courtyard familiar from *House of Frankenstein*. The feeling of reheated goods persists throughout, as when Dr Edelmann extols "the undying monster: the triumphant climax of Frankenstein's genius," words

"A cold-blooded experiment to determine audience saturation point." John Carradine, Onslow Stevens and Martha O'Driscoll in *House of Dracula* (1945)

which, as well as namechecking a lycanthropic shocker made by rival studio 20th Century-Fox, were previously uttered by Dr Niemann in *House of Frankenstein*. Similarly, Martha O'Driscoll is given a monologue about Dracula's alluring shadow-world that was previously spoken by Anne Gwynne in the earlier film. The structure, too, is similar, never successfully integrating the monsters and getting John Carradine's Dracula out of the way first.

Again, Carradine doesn't quite cut it as Dracula, his baggy evening dress and rakishly angled top hat making him look like a consumptive Stage Door Johnny rather than an unstoppable King Vampire. He has one scene, though, that hints at what he could have done with the role in a more substantial vehicle, bringing an effective undertow of evil to his attempt to hypnotise O'Driscoll's Miliza at the piano. Even here, however, the choice of Beethoven's 'Moonlight Sonata' as the piece Miliza is playing stirs unwelcome memories of its use in one of Carradine's trashier Monogram pictures, *Return of the Ape Man*, in which Frank Moran's thawed-out throwback – bearing, as it happens, Carradine's newly transplanted brain – sits down at the pianoforte and, hilariously, launches into the same piece.

Carradine's Dracula is undercut, too, by the simplistic scientific explanation offered for his 'condition', with Edelmann pontificating about a "peculiar parasite" in his bloodstream. The same reductive nonsense is applied to Larry Talbot's lycanthropic tendencies, which Edelmann ascribes to a combination of self-hypnosis and pressure on the brain. Getting close to the popular analogy between werewolves and suddenly hirsute adolescent boys, Edelmann theorises that "the glands generate an abnormal supply of certain hormones, in your case those which bring about the physical transformation which you experience." Edelmann proposes to use the mould from a rare Bavarian flower to soften, not Larry's brain, but the cranium in which it's housed, thus enlarging the cavity and relieving the pressure. While boggling over this convoluted plan (which, incidentally, proves successful), the viewer with a long memory might also be reminded of the mysterious blooms that were central to the plot of *WereWolf of London*.

Though the script condemns him to sharing several listless romantic trysts with O'Driscoll, Chaney Jr nevertheless paints an affecting portrait of Larry Talbot as a sad and defeated older man, already a long

HOUSE OF DRACULA

Universal 1945
67 minutes
production began 21 September

Cinematographer: George Robinson; Art Directors: John B Goodman, Martin Obzina; Editor: Russell Schoengarth; Sound: Bernard B Brown, Jess Moulin; Special Photography: John P Fulton; Set Decorations: Russell A Gausman, Arthur D Leddy; Make-up: Jack P Pierce; Hair Stylist: Carmen Dirigo; Gowns: Vera West; Music: William Lava*; Musical Director: Edgar Fairchild; Assistant Director: Ralph Slosser; Screenplay: Edward T Lowe; Story: George Bricker*, Dwight V Babcock*; Executive Producer: Joseph Gershenson; Producer: Paul Malvern; Director: Erle C Kenton

Lon Chaney [Jr] (Lawrence Talbot); John Carradine (Count Dracula); Martha O'Driscoll (Miliza); Lionel Atwill (Inspector Holtz); Onslow Stevens (Dr Edelmann); Jane Adams (Nina); Ludwig Stossel (Siegfried); Glenn Strange (The Monster); Skelton Knaggs (Steinmuhl); uncredited: Joseph E Bernard (Brahms [coroner]); Fred Cordova, Casey Harrison (gendarmes); Dick Dickinson, Harry Lamont (villagers)

Universal has reassembled its old hobgoblin league for *House of Dracula* ... Even Frankenstein's monster is resurrected briefly, only to be destroyed again when the evil house goes up in flames. But don't worry, folks, you can count on Universal pulling the monster from the embers just as soon as they cool off. Frankenstein's little boy doesn't die easily. And, unfortunately, neither does this type of cinematic nightmare. *New York Times*

At the Pasadena Playhouse, I had become familiar with the Stanislavski 'method' of acting in serious drama. A horror film allowed you to become totally engrossed in what you were playing ... On *House of Dracula*, my memory is that they were all very serious actors, and they were sitting around, studying their scripts.
Jane Adams [quoted in Mank, Women in Horror Films 1940s, 1999]

way from the beaming boy who appeared in *The Wolf Man* a mere five years earlier. The film has a few other minor felicities, notably a clever bit of misdirection on our introduction to Edelmann's assistant Nina. Having treated us to a big, luminous close-up of Jane Adams, director Erle C Kenton then has her stand up and reveal that Lowe, in an intriguingly off-colour touch, has made this beautiful brunette into the hunchback of the piece.

What really makes the film watchable, however, is Onslow Stevens' performance as Edelmann. Overcoming the handicap of a conspicuously bad wig, Stevens makes the transformed doctor a very nasty, hollow-eyed psychopath, literally fading from view in his own mirror and then sadistically teasing his old retainer Siegfried as the latter rides into town; along with Carradine's hypnotism routine, this queasy sequence counts as the best in the picture. An inveterate magpie, Lowe reaches back to Paramount's *Dr Jekyll and Mr Hyde* for a scene in which Edelmann answers the laboratory door in his normal form only moments after having transformed into the abnormal one, while Kenton offers a visual reference to the same film in the giant running shadow that spreads over an exterior wall during Edelmann's pursuit by the local townspeople.

This exciting sequence helps to infuse some life into the film's leadenly paced third act. As usual, the comatose Monster is only infused with life in the final moments, quickly being incinerated in a selection of shots lifted wholesale from *The Ghost of Frankenstein*. An earlier Edelmann dream sequence similarly intercut shots of Glenn Strange cuffing various villagers with shots of Karloff doing the same in *Bride of Frankenstein*, and the clumsy appropriation is typical of the cheapjack expediency of the film as a whole.

"While there's always the possibility that *House of Dracula* may have been an attempt to write a few debits in Universal's income tax blank," continued Dorothy Masters in her *New York Daily News* column, "I'm afraid it was a cold-blooded experiment to determine audience saturation point." Audiences did indeed seem to have had enough of Universal's increasingly inane chillers, and John Carradine himself made a persuasive case as to why: "By the time they were finished [with] the script [of *House of Dracula*], millions of GIs were being shipped home. World War II had ended. Many of those GIs did not come home whole in mind and body. Thousands of families had their own horrors at home to contend with and the studios were running scared from any type of horror film."[24] In truth, the studios didn't catch on quite so quickly, for the rapid extinction of audience interest predictably triggered off an eleventh-hour splurge of over-production.

Even Monogram chose this inopportune moment to make their first full-on horror picture since 1943. Directed by the unstoppable William Beaudine, *The Face of Marble* started on 5 October and required Carradine to slip straight out of Count Dracula's evening clothes into the comfortable tweeds of bespectacled Professor Randolph, who, having stumbled upon a dead sailor on the beach, revives him electrically while proclaiming "the scientific fact [that] we have conquered death." The unbilled actor playing the experimental subject creates a mild frisson as he comes to marble-faced, eye-swivelling life, only to be snuffed out again by an unforeseen short circuit. Then, however, the film devolves into a boring and incoherent hodge-podge, with a voodoo-practising housekeeper precipitating the death of Randolph's young wife and a revived Great Dane succumbing to "haemomania: the blood craze," also turning see-through and passing through solid walls as a harp shudders on the soundtrack.

Cave canem: John Carradine and Robert Shayne at bay in *The Face of Marble* (1945)

Though more handsomely appointed than the average Monogram quickie, the film is only really interesting for a few blatant borrowings. Screenwriter Michel Jacoby had previously written *The Undying Monster*, and the opening shots here – a house perched above a craggy coastline, a dog slumbering by the fire, the heroine reposing on a sofa, the approaching tread of a family retainer – reprise the beginning of the earlier film in everything save Lucien Ballard's virtuoso camera moves. There's even a touch of the Val Lewtons visible: the shadowed bedroom and knife-wielding, white-draped woman seem to derive

from *Isle of the Dead*, while the forlorn 'footprints in the sand' ending is lifted straight from *I Walked with a Zombie*. This being Monogram, however, it's more a case of 'I Walked with an Ectoplasmic Great Dane'.

While *The Face of Marble* was in production, Arthur Lubin was directing *The Spider Woman Strikes Back* for Universal. Though alluding to the Sherlock Holmes entry *The Spider Woman*, this starred Gale Sondergaard, not as Holmes' adversary Adrea Spedding, but as the acquisitive Zenobia Dollard, a Nevada landowner rapidly running out of paid companions thanks to her habit of draining their blood to feed the carnivorous South American plants she keeps in the basement. "You're going to die, Jean, like all the others," she tells the latest incumbent (Brenda Joyce). "But it won't be really dying, because you'll live on in this beautiful plant."

The premise antedates by 12 years a British quickie called *Womaneater* (in which George Coulouris has dialogue almost identical to the Sondergaard lines quoted above), but the realisation of it degenerates rapidly into endless corridor-wandering and a hastily contrived climactic inferno. Sondergaard, however, is always good value, particularly in the film's one striking vignette. "You love Zenobia, don't you?" she croons to her favourite plant. "It's Zenobia gives you the food that makes you strong and virile." As the thing affectionately wraps its tendrils round her arm, Lubin has plumes of hellish smoke suffuse the rear of the frame while filming the bizarre exchange at a very slight angle.

Also in the background is Rondo Hatton as Zenobia's mute henchman Mario. Having lent his acromegalic features to *The Pearl of Death* and *Jungle Captive*, Hatton was now being given a big build-up by Universal. The idea, a frankly exploitative one, was to build Hatton into a new horror star – a horror star, moreover, who was in no need of elaborate assistance from the increasingly marginalised make-up maestro Jack Pierce. All this despite the fact, as the authors of *Universal Horrors* cruelly but not unjustly put it, that he "was probably the farthest thing from an actor that was ever manoeuvred in front of a movie camera."[25]

Either side of *The Spider Woman Strikes Back*, therefore, Hatton was pressed into service for two pictures directed by Jean Yarbrough and produced by Ben Pivar. In the first – *House of Horrors*, shot in September – Hatton's distorted features loom into massive close-up just in time for the mendacious credit, "Introducing Rondo Hatton as The Creeper." In fact, Hatton's Hoxton Creeper had already been seen in *The Pearl of Death*. Here, he's transplanted to New York and becomes the brutish accomplice to a prissy sculptor, memorably portrayed by Martin Kosleck. Soon enough, he's snapping the spines of the city's unfeasibly catty art critics, the kind that recommend "a cosy institution ... featuring hot and cold running straitjackets" for all artists of the abstract persuasion.

Of course, in depicting the German-accented Kosleck as a homicidal maniac by proxy, the film endorses this view, reserving clean-limbed-hero status for an insipid commercial artist played by Robert Lowery. There are engaging scenes of Lowery in his studio, painting a Varga-like portrait of the voluptuous Joan Shawlee in tennis gear that more closely resembles a bikini. And heroine Virginia Grey models a variety of "tricky" hats while rapping out some passably sassy wisecracks. The result is painless but uninspired, though later filmmakers seem to have been inspired by it. Milton Subotsky's similarly titled 1964 anthology picture *Dr Terror's House of Horrors* includes a story composited from the film's 'insufferable art critic' theme and the 'crawling hand' angle of another 1946 release, *The Beast with Five Fingers*. Tellingly, the Subotsky film was based on an unproduced script written by him in New York in 1948, when both films were relatively new.

The second of Hatton's tailor-made vehicles was shot in 13 days in November and called *The Brute Man*. By the time it was released the following October, Universal had merged with International and trashy B-pictures were deemed beneath contempt.

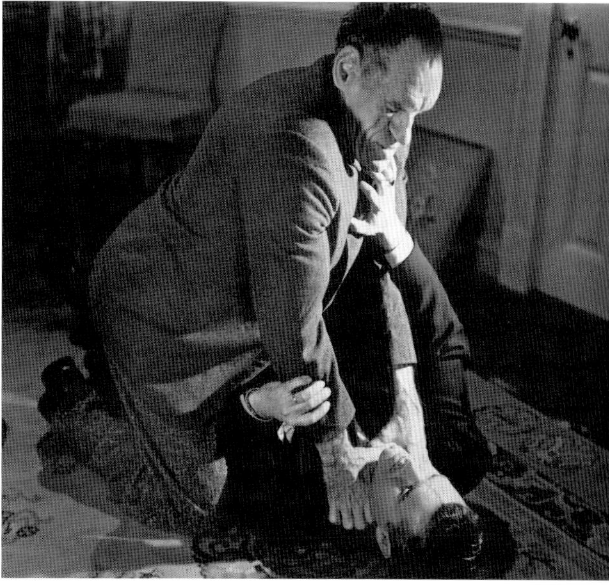

No make-up required: Rondo Hatton disposes of Tom Neal in *The Brute Man* (1945)

The Brute Man, therefore, was offloaded onto PRC, an appropriate destination given that studio's exploitation of acromegaly in *The Monster Maker*. The film posits a past for Hatton's Creeper as a short-fused college football hero disfigured by chemicals. "He may have killed Professor Cushman just because he kept him after class that day," muses one of his erstwhile classmates.

Hatton skulks around rain-slicked waterfront streets in his padded suit and absurd pork-pie hat, and that's all the horror the picture can muster. By this stage, however, Universal seemed to have decided that just photographing an unusually ugly man was all that it took. But since Hatton couldn't act, he fails completely to be scary. He scores zero in the pathos department too, despite a Frankenstein-style plot strand in which he's befriended by a blind musician (Jane Adams). *The Brute Man* is so dismal, formulaic and ultimately pointless that its few scraps of comic relief remain its most valuable feature, in particular Donald MacBride's droll performance as a lackadaisical police chief and a brief cameo from Oscar O'Shea as a bad-tempered grocer. Adding to the film's exploitative aura, Hatton's disease finally killed him on 2 February 1946, aged 51.

Before the full horror of *The Brute Man* became apparent, the Pivar unit, and director Jean Yarbrough, moved on to a glamorous programmer called *She-Wolf of London*, which was shot in a fortnight just prior to Christmas. The list of this film's superficial pleasures is surprisingly long – a gorgeous mansion interior, fluid camerawork and lustrous lighting (Maury Gertsman), an effective musical score (patched together by William Lava), a fetching ingenue (June Lockhart) and the requisite overdose of ground fog. The film also boasts a few diverting peculiarities – a nod to Hitchcock's *Suspicion* when the heroine's conniving aunt is seen ascending a staircase with a glass of milk, a denouement filmed (à la *Bluebeard*) at a lopsided angle, even an in-joke reference to the director of *The Hound of the Baskervilles* when the hero's father is name-checked as Sir Sidney Lanfield. On top of this, the caped London bobbies on show include not only the ubiquitous Frederick Worlock but also Laurel and Hardy's sometime nemesis, Jimmy Finlayson.

Unfortunately, all this production gloss is put at the service of a lamebrained story in which the heroine only imagines she's a she-wolf, being encouraged to think that way by the inheritance-hungry aunt, who is herself a different kind of she-wolf. ("The idea that a frail girl like you could literally tear a boy of ten to pieces is utterly ridiculous," she clucks at one point, meaning the exact opposite.) This flagrant cheat was perpetrated by Universal hacks George Bricker and Dwight V Babcock, and (by coincidence or otherwise) another Universal hack, Griffin Jay, came up with precisely the same story for a PRC potboiler that went into production less than five weeks later.

Savaged by the so-called *She-Wolf of London* (1945), Lloyd Corrigan is tended by bobbies Frederick Worlock and Jimmy Finlayson

This was *Devil Bat's Daughter*, which began on 9 January 1946 and was as much a follow-up to *Strangler of the Swamp* as *The Devil Bat*; the credits announce Frank Wisbar as the film's producer-director and the first actors we see are *Strangler* veterans Nolan Leary and Rosemary LaPlanche. The former is required to trot through a tedious resumé of Bela Lugosi's research work in *The Devil Bat* (with no reference to after-shave), while the latter is cast in the same thankless role essayed by June Lockhart in *She-Wolf of London*. This time, the person scheming to drive her insane (and to pin his wife's murder on her) is a conceited psychiatrist played with zero charisma by the hatchet-faced Michael Hale. The film is a dreary, dialogue-heavy bore, directed by Wisbar with no flair whatever. Absurdly, it even contrives to

exonerate the original film's extremely culpable Lugosi character in order to convince his traumatised daughter that she isn't insane.

Smell of formaldehyde: Ian Keith and Adrian Booth (aka Lorna Gray) in *Valley of the Zombies* (1945)

DEAD END

The closing months of 1945 saw an unexpected splurge of horror production not only from Universal, but also Republic. Shot in September, Philip Ford's *Valley of the Zombies* begins effectively on a mist-shrouded clocktower and a cloaked figure climbing over a parapet at its foot. The ubiquitous character actor Charles Trowbridge, so memorably throttled five years earlier by *The Mummy's Hand*, then falls prey to a presumed-dead mental case who "seemed to feel that periodic [blood] transfusions would guarantee him a kind of immortality." The splendidly named Ormand Murks, a former undertaker who thoughtfully embalms all his victims, has since visited "the land of voodoo rites and devil potions, the valley of the zombies" and has "discovered a world in between – a world of living death."

Murks, whose ancestral home smells of formaldehyde, is played by Ian Keith, a contender for Dracula back in 1930 but here coming over less like Lugosi than a wickedly accurate send-up of Lionel Barrymore. Unfortunately, Keith's deliciously sulphuric performance is the whole show, for the rest is given over to a hero and heroine who, like so many at this period, are an extremely poor man's version of Nick and Nora Charles from M-G-M's Thin Man films. The story owes an obvious debt to *The Return of Doctor X* and quickly becomes bogged down in farcical police procedurals, though it does find room for a pathetic attempt at a Lewton 'bus' involving a mooing cow.

Also shot in September and intended as *Valley*'s stable-mate on release, Lesley Selander's *The Catman of Paris* has writer Carl Esmond as chief suspect – but his benevolent business manager (Douglass Dumbrille) as the actual culprit – in an 1890s rash of werecat murders. This, too, has an arresting opening in which a black cat prowls hugely through a miniature of a Paris street, plus a halfway-decent scene in which priggish Adele Mara unwittingly invites the well-dressed werecat into her carriage. It also reveals its indebtedness to Val Lewton via the assurances of a credulous Prefet de Police that "There *have* been cat people." ("Such superstitions went out with the monarchy," his subordinate wittily replies.) An ancient text called 'Astrological Prognostications' offers a complicated backstory for the nine-times-reincarnated cat creature, but the thing itself looks like a pantomime Demon King and is laughably ineffective. Needless to say, any comparisons with the leonine beast of Jean Cocteau's *La Belle et la Bête* – which was being filmed in France at exactly the same time – would be invidious.

Also in 1945, Republic teamed up with independent producer W Lee Wilder to distribute a couple of items directed by future Western specialist Anthony Mann – *Strange Impersonation*, in which research scientist Brenda Marshall assumes Ruth Ford's identity via plastic surgery, and *The Great Flamarion*, a vaudeville thriller with lovelorn sharp-shooter Erich von Stroheim being double-crossed by Mary Beth Hughes. In November, it was PRC's turn to call on Von Stroheim, this time for a vaudeville subject co-written by the almost omnipresent Griffin Jay. And, like *The Great Flamarion*, the result recalled Von Stroheim's long-ago role in *The Great Gabbo*. Moody

Peter Lorre's grasp on reality crumbles when confronted by Robert Alda and Andrea King in *The Beast with Five Fingers* (1945)

absurdly pat ending, he finally trips over his own cat and onto a prop guillotine, which decapitates him.

Given this ignominious ending (and the fact that a PRC credit generally ranked as rock-bottom), it comes as no surprise to find the following note in the film's pressbook: "The master of sinister roles declares that with his performance in PRC's *Mask of Diijon* ... he has made his last picture in Hollywood. Having completed this role he expects to resume his French film career." Von Stroheim was as good as his word, only returning in 1949 for a ghoulish role in *Sunset Blvd* – directed, coincidentally, by W Lee Wilder's more famous brother, Billy.

THE BEAST WITH FIVE FINGERS

Warner Bros-First National 1945
88 minutes
production began 13 November

Cinematographer: Wesley Anderson; Art Director: Stanley Fleischer; Editor: Frank Magee; Sound: Oliver S Garretson; Special Effects: William McGann, H [Hans] Koenekamp; Special Optical Effects: Russell Collings*; Set Decorations: Walter Tilford; Make-up: Perc Westmore, Gene Hibbs*; Wardrobe: Travilla; Music: Max Steiner; Musical Director: Leo F Forbstein; Orchestral Arrangements: Hugo Friedhofer; Technical Adviser: Dario Sabatello; Dialogue Director: Jack Daniels; Screenplay: Curt Siodmak (from a story by William Fryer Harvey); Executive Producer: Jack L Warner; Producer: William Jacobs; Director: Robert Florey

Robert Alda *(Conrad Ryler)*; Andrea King *(Julie Holden)*; Peter Lorre *(Hilary Cummins)*; Victor Francen *(Francis Ingram)*; J Carrol Naish *(Ovidio Castanio)*; Charles Dingle *(Raymond Arlington)*; John Alvin *(Donald Arlington)*; David Hoffman *(Duprex)*; Barbara Brown *(Mrs Miller)*; Patricia White *(Clara)*; William Edmunds *(Antonio [butler])*; Belle Mitchell *(Giovanna)*; Ray Walker *(Mr Miller)*; Pedro de Cordoba *(Horatio)*; *uncredited:* Antonio Filauri *(bus driver)*; Count Stefanelli *(Giuseppe)*; Lottie Williams *(tourist)*; Gino Corrado, Franco Corsaro, Joseph Marievsky *(carabinieri)*; Symona Boniface, Edna Morris, Elinor Van Der Veer, Katherine Wallace *(professional mourners)*

Showmen who notify their customers that this mystery melodrama is a field day for Peter Lorre will be getting the news of first importance about the picture to the right people. It's an item in the suspense category, with the puzzlement carried well into the final minutes of play. Motion Picture Herald

I wrote *The Beast with Five Fingers*, not for Peter Lorre, but for Paul Henreid. Paul said, "You want me to play against a goddamned hand? I'm not crazy." I would love to have shot it with him, because I thought a man looking so debonair was a much more interesting murderer than that freakish Lorre. Curt Siodmak [reprinted in McClelland, *Forties Film Talk*, 1992]

but ponderous, Lew Landers' *The Mask of Diijon* stars Von Stroheim as a stage illusionist who develops a genuine hypnotic gift, impelling Mauritz Hugo to drown himself and then trying to will his wife (Jeanne Bates) into murdering her supposed lover. In an

In November 1945, while Von Stroheim was being decapitated at PRC and Universal busied itself in the doomed attempt to make a star of Rondo Hatton, Robert Florey was making an unusually distinguished horror picture over at Warner Bros-First National, enjoying, in the process, the benefits of a $750,000 budget. Fourteen years before, Florey had been bumped by the old Universal from the plum job of directing *Frankenstein*, so it was somehow appropriate that he should preside over *The Beast with Five Fingers*, a picture that applied a graceful full-stop to the horror cycle spawned by *Frankenstein*.

The project had originated in 1942, with Griffin Jay among the writers put to work on it. The more inventive Curt Siodmak provided the final screenplay, basing it on W F Harvey's 1919 story of the same name but picking up from it little more than the idea of a sentient severed hand getting loose in a private library. Harvey's unsettling notion of the hand being given to automatic writing – and his more larkish images of the hand sliding down banisters and strangling parrots – were deleted by Siodmak in favour of a story in which, as an opening disclaimer puts it, what happens only "seemed to happen."

Cantankerous concert pianist Francis Ingram, paralysed down his right side, dies suddenly and leaves a will favouring his nurse, Julie Holden. When Ingram's bookworm amanuensis Hilary Cummins learns of a lawyer's attempt to annul the will, he fears he will lose his beloved astrological volumes and kills the lawyer, convincing everyone that Ingram's revived left hand is responsible. He succumbs, however, to nightmare visions of the appendage and ultimately dies by his own hand.

That "seemed to happen" proviso bodes ill, suggesting the kind of rationalist cop-out that had afflicted too many US horror pictures of an earlier generation. In practice, however, it makes *The Beast with Five Fingers* akin to several of Val Lewton's films in being yet another disguised adaptation of Edgar Allan Poe.

As the film gears up for its famous third act fusillade of severed hand special effects, the accretion of warning signals that afflicts the increasingly deranged Hilary – a snapping guitar string, the chime of a clock, a book falling from its shelf – are clearly modelled on Jules Dassin's version of *The Tell-Tale Heart*, and it is as a Poe-like study in the hallucinatory horror of guilt that *The Beast with Five Fingers* really scores. When the hand's phantom piano-playing starts up towards the end, Hilary's shrieks of "Don't you hear it? It's bursting my eardrums! I can't stand it!" are as precise an echo of *The Tell-Tale Heart* as could be desired. Elsewhere, his cries of "It's alive! I tell you, it's alive!" provide a different echo, a poignant one for Florey given their inescapable connection to the landmark picture he'd missed out on in 1931.

Though a Poe devotee, W F Harvey had taken an entirely different tack in his waggishly gruesome story. There, the disembodied hand of a dead botanist – "moving quickly, in the manner of a geometer caterpillar, the fingers humped up one moment, flattened out the next" – bedevils two possibly homosexual young Englishmen and is established as a corporeal and incontrovertible fact. But the discrepancy hardly matters when the Siodmak version gives so invaluable a showcase to Peter Lorre, who, after *Mad Love*, was no stranger to paralysed pianists and severed hands. Siodmak claimed to have written the part with Paul Henreid in mind, though the role actually offered to Henreid was the spiv-like hero eventually played by Robert Alda. Either way, it's hard to see how the film's closing scenes could make such an impact without Lorre's saucer-eyed histrionics to balance the cold chill of the effects work.

Happily, the effects are state-of-the-art for their time. There are a couple of shots of a mechanical hand that looks like a motorised washing-up glove, together with another in which a wire is clearly visible. But the hand is for the most part a real one, with the anonymous actor's arm meticulously matted out. An image beloved of surrealists, the severed hand also rated a mention in Freud's 1919 analysis of *The Uncanny*, and his attribution of it to the castration complex is recalled here when the hand thrusts out a revoltingly phallic index finger, silently demanding that Hilary slide onto it the distinctive ring Ingram wore in life. First seen scrabbling its way out of a cigar humidor, the hand has an eerie, fleet-fingered spideriness that seems genuinely inhuman, especially when Hilary tears down a stack of books and Wesley Anderson's camera takes up a position behind the shelf, where we see the thing clinging tenaciously to the last remaining volumes.

So powerful is Lorre's battle with his embodied conscience that the film's first two-thirds seem like an entirely different picture. And, though leisurely paced, it's quite a diverting one, benefiting in particular from a marvellous performance by the Belgian character star Victor Francen. Curdled, like Kurt Ingston in *Night Monster*, into rancid bitterness by the slow shutdown of his physical faculties, Ingram is not only a monstrous exemplar of artistic temperament but is also presented as a vampire, one of his hangers-on telling Julie that "He draws his energy from your life. He'll never let you go." With an inappropriate passion for the hired help and a tendency to bark unreasonable demands from his wheelchair (plus a touch of sexual ambiguity provided by a vertiginous grey quiff), Ingram also recalls the supposedly crippled Mrs Bramson from *Night Must Fall*, and few actors could have equalled Francen's blazing intensity when Ingram attempts to strangle Hilary with his one good hand.

The film is further distinguished by a magnificent Max Steiner score, together with Florey's trademark use of chiaroscuro and eerily fluid camera moves. The second act dawdles somewhat, but the only real blot is provided by an inane coda that was inserted over Florey's strenuous objections. Here, J Carrol Naish's investigative Commissario (engaging enough elsewhere in the picture) is required to recoil from a hand swarming up his waistcoat and then laugh it off with a low-comedy cry of "How do you like that? [It was] my own hand!" As pay-off to a sequence as intense as Lorre's pitched battle with the severed hand, this gag is insulting in the extreme. As an image, however, of the classic American horror film ending as it began – with the potency of the genuinely scary stuff being thoughtlessly deflated by crass comedy – it couldn't be bettered.

Part Six

He's behind you... Lou Costello and Lon Chaney Jr in *Abbott and Costello Meet Frankenstein* (1948)

Post-war Permutations 1946-1956

Though begun in November 1945, the special effects complexities of *The Beast with Five Fingers* ensured that it was only completed in February 1946, after which it wasn't released until December. The delay was indicative of a sudden, and apparently complete, loss of interest in horror subjects among filmmakers and audiences alike. The war had ended not only with the apocalyptic shocks of Hiroshima and Nagasaki, but also with profoundly horrifying documentary evidence of Nazi war crimes that had previously only been guessed at. In light of the obscenities carried out in extermination camps like Auschwitz, and the insane racial theories of Josef Mengele and other SS doctors, the behaviour of movie mad scientists suddenly appeared at best trivial, at worst tasteless.

There were also more prosaic reasons for the drying-up of Hollywood horror product. "Horror," as Walter Kendrick has observed, "strangled itself, in typical Hollywood fashion, by riding a few once-successful types into the ground, exhausting their novelty and coaxing sighs instead of screams ... World War II may have had some impact, but the most likely culprit is boredom, born of repetition and reticence." The reticence Kendrick refers to was imposed on filmmakers by the PCA, but, according to Kendrick, "the blunting of horror for the sake of universal appeal led to the opposite outcome. Horror movies degenerated into feed for stunted appetites; viewers had to be crippled in some way if they could be satisfied by the dreck they were being served."[1] To what degree horror fans had become ghettoised by 1945 – and to what extent they qualified as 'stunted' and 'crippled' – is, to put it mildly, debatable. What's harder to argue, however, is the suitability of the word 'dreck' to the stuff coming out of Hollywood in the aftermath of the war.

January 1946, for example, not only saw the production of the atrocious *Devil Bat's Daughter* at PRC but also a braindead Universal programmer called *The Cat Creeps*. Slung together as the co-feature to *She-Wolf of London*, this one shows its poverty of imagination in every frame; even the title was filched from Rupert Julian's 1930 Universal talkie. It has all the usual ingredients: an old dark house, a stash of bootleggers' loot, an insufferable reporter 'hero'. Co-screenwriter, and Lewton graduate, Edward Dein adds a wholly inexplicable 'cat woman' to the mix

(she's actually an actress hired by the hero), and horror fans who had just suffered through Republic's *The Catman of Paris*, released a month earlier, will have experienced a wearisome shock of déjà-vu at the exposure of Douglass Dumbrille as the killer. "Who's directing this little production?" asks the reporter's equally irksome chum in a rare moment of self-reflexivity. In fact, it was Erle C Kenton, a very long way indeed from *Island of Lost Souls* and a fair distance even from *House of Dracula*.

TANGENTIAL THRILLS

The cessation of horror production inevitably posed problems for the actors most closely associated with the genre, and for Bela Lugosi the crisis must have seemed eerily reminiscent of his career hiatus of ten years before. In March 1946, he joined George Zucco at the Gordon Street facility for Christy Cabanne's *Accent on Horror*, a dismal Golden Gate quickie that finally went on release over 12 months later as *Scared to Death*. The picture was shot in the faintly putrid hues of Cinecolor, making it the only colour horror film for its sexagenarian stars. And that's pretty much all it has going for it, apart from the historical accident of prefiguring *Sunset Blvd* via the use of a corpse on a mortician's slab as a 'how did I get this way?' narrator.

Zucco is the bespectacled Dr Van Ee, Lugosi a cloaked hypnotist called Professor Leonide, and the virtually incomprehensible plot concerns a marauding green mask that finally causes Van Ee's daughter-in-law (Molly Lamont) to be, yes, scared to death. The script drags in meretricious references to concentration camps, the French occupation and Nazi firing squads, but the film's only value is to Lugosi completists, who can watch him in Cinecolor close-up as he intones such nonsense as "Laurette, Laurette, I'll make a bet / The man in green will get you yet."

Faring, as usual, a great deal better, Boris Karloff was simultaneously on display in the resplendent Technicolor of films like the smash Goldwyn comedy *The Secret Life of Walter Mitty* and Cecil B DeMille's Gary Cooper vehicle *Unconquered*. He also returned to Broadway, getting good notices in a couple of failed British imports before achieving a personal apotheosis as Captain Hook in *Peter Pan*, which opened in April 1950 and ran for over 300 performances.

Back in 1946, as well as picking over the various B-horrors made late the previous year, horror fans had *Bedlam* and *The Beast with Five Fingers* to sustain them, but very little else. In May they could sample the contrived seance hi-jinks of D Ross Lederman's *The Phantom Thief*, one of Chester Morris' 14 appearances in Columbia's 'Boston Blackie' detective series, and by August they were gifted with the marvellous Gale Sondergaard, on top form as a psychic housekeeper, in Universal's *The Time of Their Lives*. (The first of Charles T Barton's numerous Abbott and Costello vehicles, this was an unusual one, presenting Costello as an 18th century ghost and Abbott as the modern-day butt of his pranks.) October saw the release of M-G-M's *The Cockeyed Miracle*, in which director S Sylvan Simon dusted off the old 'friendly ghosts sorting things out for those left behind' plot, and the following month came James Tinling's *Dangerous Millions*, which resurrected the equally ancient 'millionaire spies on his prospective heirs' scenario, this time setting it in China.

More rewarding than any of these, the classic British anthology film *Dead of Night* was put out via Universal on 23 August in a 77-minute version, minus one of the original's five stories. Through British impresario (and major Universal shareholder) J Arthur Rank, Universal also acquired such titles as David Lean's *Great Expectations* and Laurence Olivier's ghost-haunted *Hamlet*, the latter picking up several Oscars, including Best Picture, in 1949. The previous year, a homegrown independent distributed by Universal, George Cukor's *A Double Life*, had picked up Oscars for composer Miklós Rósza and leading man Ronald Colman, the latter cast – in a more high-toned retread of RKO's *The Brighton Strangler* – as an actor driven mad by his role: Othello.

"When will you start acting normally for a change?" Roland Varno and Douglas Fowley upbraid Bela Lugosi's enigmatic Professor Leonide in *Scared to Death* (1946)

By this time, however, Universal had become a new entity called Universal-International (UI), the merger with the recently formed independent International Pictures having been announced on 30 July 1946. Something of an aesthete by movie mogul standards, new production head William Goetz was determined to handle prestige pictures in future, of which the well-heeled Rank acquisitions were an ostentatious sign. They were also about as Gothic as Goetz intended to get.

RKO, meanwhile, was facing upheavals of its own. As well as being hit hard by the post-war slump in theatre attendances, in May 1948 the studio came under the control of Howard Hughes, an implacable enemy of the studio system whose management practices were unpredictable to say the least. In the run-up to the Hughes handover, the studio closed down the Val Lewton unit on completion of *Bedlam*, putting out a feeble 'man poses as his own ghost' comedy called *Man Alive* in November 1945 and later resurrecting one of the hokiest of all mystery-thrillers, *Seven Keys to Baldpate*. Issued in June 1947, Lew Landers' film (the sixth adaptation of the Earl Derr Biggers-George M Cohan original) vitiates in witless light comedy an impressive opening that rounds up all the time-honoured old dark house clichés. Lewton himself mustered three non-horror credits, at Paramount, M-G-M and finally Universal-International, before succumbing, aged 46, to a heart attack on 14 March 1951.

Something of Lewton's style had found its way into an independent production, *No Trespassing*, made in the spring of 1946 by director Delmer Daves. Put out by United Artists as *The Red House* a year later, the film grabbed audiences by the throat in its opening reel with Edward G Robinson's guilt-ridden words, shouted despairingly over the racket of a rising storm, "Did you ever run away from a scream? You can't. It will follow you through the woods. It will follow you all your life!"

Though warned against it, surly teenage farm-hand Nath (Lon McCallister) plunges into Oxhead Woods regardless, and the nocturnal odyssey that follows squeezes maximum value from the agitated rustling of the trees and a series of subliminal wind-borne shrieks. Later, composer Miklós Rósza adds a discreet touch of Theremin to a daylight scene in which Nath's sweetheart Meg (Allene Roberts) ascends a wooded promontory and gets her first glimpse of the titular Red House, nestled in a lonely quarry and flanked by a tumble-down icehouse. Finally, her adoptive father Pete (Robinson) expiates his guilt by driving headlong into the icehouse, the waters rising up around him as a long-ago murder is laid to rest.

The Red House is unusual for its bucolic setting, captured almost entirely on location and radiantly photographed by Bert Glennon. It also has a great performance from Robinson as the pitifully conflicted Pete, who killed Meg's mother and her husband 15 years earlier and now nurses highly equivocal feelings for Meg herself. His terror of the Red House extends even to the idea of razing it to the ground – "They'd search the ashes and find her screaming," he babbles in his climactic breakdown. Unfortunately, at 100 minutes the film is seriously overlong, though this does allow for extended views of the young Julie London, whose remarkably sexy local hoyden points up the tragic repression of Pete himself.

The year after *The Red House*, Robinson gave another exceptional performance, this time opposite *The Uninvited*'s Gail Russell, in John Farrow's *Night Has a Thousand Eyes*, in which he plays a sideshow seer who is horrified when he seems to acquire the gift for real, accurately informing the fatalistic Russell that her death will be "within a few days, at night, under the stars." The source material was by Cornell Woolrich, who was also behind Maxwell Shane's similarly themed *Fear in the Night*, where the young DeForest Kelley

dreams a murder that then appears to have actually happened. In the same way, Lew Landers' 1948 quickie *Inner Sanctum* – not to be confused with the dreary series of Chaney Jr programmers lately concluded at Universal – features the elderly Fritz Leiber as blind mystic Dr Valonius, sagely informing a young woman that she will be murdered by her husband.

The connection of these films to the waning horror genre is pretty tangential, but tangential thrills were about all horror fans could expect in the latter part of the 1940s, and most of them came from the kind of pictures that would later be dubbed film noir. As well as *Fear in the Night*, in the summer of 1947 cinemagoers could sample Joan Crawford as a refined psychopath in Curtis Bernhardt's *Possessed*, Barbara Stanwyck as a standard-issue 'woman in peril' in Peter Godfrey's *Cry Wolf*, and Lucille Ball as bait to a Baudelaire-fixated serial killer in Douglas Sirk's *Lured*. (The latter offered juicy roles to horror veterans George Sanders, Boris Karloff, George Zucco and Cedric Hardwicke.) And the following year horror-starved filmgoers could try Hitchcock's limp Technicolor version of Patrick Hamilton's play *Rope*, loosely based on the Leopold and Loeb murder case of 24 years before and strung together from a sequence of uninterrupted, reel-length takes.

Louis Hayward silences Dorothy Patrick, permanently, in *House by the River* (1949)

Peter Godfrey, who had played Spencer Tracy's valet in M-G-M's *Dr Jekyll and Mr Hyde*, not only directed *Cry Wolf* in 1947 but also *The Woman in White*, an imprecise and overstuffed adaptation of Wilkie Collins' 1860 'sensation' novel, redeemed by lashings of Gothic atmosphere and a characteristically epicene Sydney Greenstreet as the monstrous Count Fosco. Though not released until May 1948, the film was produced between September 1946 and February 1947, much the same period in which *Uncle Silas*, a similar but considerably better 'sensation novel' adaptation, was being made in the UK. Also for Warner Bros, Godfrey was responsible for *The Two Mrs Carrolls*, which gave yet another airing to the popular 1940s plot in which newly wed wives begin to suspect they're married to psychopaths. Predictably, the blueprint for all of them – Rowland V Lee's British-made thriller *Love from a Stranger* – was subjected to a US remake in 1947, with the period shifted back to *Gaslight*-inspired Victoriana.

The Blanket of the Dark

The kinkiest of all the 'is my husband a psychopath?' pictures was Fritz Lang's *Secret Beyond the Door...* (1947), in which Joan Bennett marries British import Michael Redgrave. Obsessed with keys and concealment, Redgrave's cracked architect has constructed a sequence of fetishistic 'murder rooms' for the delectation of his house guests; one of them, however, remains locked and may just have been the site of his previous wife's untimely demise. Phoney Freudianising and all, this unconvincing Bluebeard variant was based on a novel called *Museum Piece No 13* by Rufus King, author of the long-ago *Murder by the Clock*.

After the failure of *Secret Beyond the Door...*, Fritz Lang worked with another old hand, Mel Dinelli, on *House by the River*, a cheap but much more intriguing programmer made for Republic in June 1949. Having based *The Spiral Staircase* on an Ethel Lina White original, Dinelli was working here from a novel by A P Herbert. The locked room that in *Secret Beyond the Door...* was representative of Redgrave's murky subconscious here becomes an ever-flowing river, symbolising the turbulent mind of a conceited turn-of-the-century novelist, Stephen Byrne (Louis Hayward), and eventually vomiting up the corpse of his murdered maid. Though Lang is well below his best in these straitened circumstances, the film still conjures a memorably bitter Gothic atmosphere; among the opening shots we see a stock-footage dead cow floating by, Byrne ruefully pointing out that "My manuscripts are like the tide out there: they always come back."

The first couple of reels are the best, in which Byrne gets turned on by the fact that the maid has used his wife's bath and perfume, then strangles her in an 'accidentally on purpose' sort of way, and finally inveigles his disabled brother into helping get rid of the body. The immersion of the maid, and her subsequent resurfacing, are the cue for a heavily symbolic fish to leap from the surrounding waters. (The film was made under the title *Floodtide*.) And Byrne's desperate efforts to recapture the body lead to an Ophelia-like tableau in which, as future director Bertrand Tavernier put it, "the condemned woman, surprised by death, floats with her hair unravelled in the current, like one of those forbidden scenes H P Lovecraft speaks of."[2] The remainder of *House by the River*, however, is only kept afloat by Hayward's shark's grin performance.

In addition to sponsoring fey fantasy-comedies like the March 1947 release *The Ghost Goes Wild*, Republic had anticipated putting Fritz Lang onto their books by accommodating the maverick genius of Orson Welles – apparently at the insistence of Vera Hruba Ralston, anodyne heroine of *The Lady and the Monster* and mistress of Republic's president, Herbert Yates.

Welles' signature RKO success, *Citizen Kane*, had carried its own overtones of American Gothic in its stunning opening shot of Charles Foster Kane's mist-wreathed domain, Xanadu, and in the ageing newspaper magnate's castellated isolation, dwarfed even by the cavernous breadth of his own fireplace. (The film had also helped crystallise the key personnel of the Val Lewton unit, gathering together, among others, effects expert Vernon L Walker, editors Robert Wise and Mark Robson, and set decorator Darrell Silvera.) Striking a deal with Republic, Welles proposed a film of Shakespeare's *Macbeth*, a 'voodoo' version of which, staged at Harlem's New Lafayette Theatre, had kick-started his career back in April 1935. To limber up for the film, in May 1947 Welles produced the play again in Salt Lake City, then went with his actors to Hollywood and had the picture in the can by 17 July. The result was an unashamedly Gothic *Macbeth* made for $700,000 and polished off in a mere 23 days; Laurence Olivier was simultaneously shooting *Hamlet* at J Arthur Rank's Denham studios and taking six months over it.

11th century Scotland. The treacherous Thane of Cawdor is executed and the loyal warrior Macbeth assumes his title, as foretold him by a trio of itinerant witches. Prompted by his ambitious wife, Macbeth then fulfils a further prediction – that he will succeed the elderly monarch, Duncan – by killing him. All-powerful yet increasingly paranoid, he next has his comrade Banquo assassinated and massacres the family of the absent Macduff. The latter returns from England and decapitates the usurper.

Making his last Hollywood studio picture – and in the reduced circumstances of Republic, to boot – Welles turned *Macbeth* into a small neo-Expressionist masterpiece, full of remarkable set-pieces that take their cue from Lady Macbeth's invocation to "the blanket of the dark." The film begins with the three witches crowing over their latest brew of viscous slop, fashioning from it a Macbeth homunculus which, at the end, will be briskly beheaded as an index to the fate of the man himself. Played mainly in voice-over by actors who elsewhere play Lady Macduff, the first murderer and Lady Macbeth's gentlewoman, the witches' faces are cannily withheld. Instead, the camera focuses on their slippery handiwork, as if they were malevolent midwives in at the birth of a new Macbeth, the Macbeth who abandons his loyalty to ambition and loses his soul in the process.

Welles' mastery of the medium is evident right here, from the use of a subliminal scraping sound as the witches wipe away the "hell-broth" from their Macbeth doll, to the brilliantly timed 'beat' inserted after the line "There to meet with...", the camera cutting in for a close-up of the doll as a whispered "... Macbeth" introduces the titles. Depicting Macbeth, quite literally, as a toy in the hands of "these juggling fiends," Welles sets the story up as a grim tragedy of predestination, then moves on to a powerful scene in which the treacherous (but harmless-looking) Cawdor is executed amid the crags of Dunsinane castle. During it, Macbeth and his wife are reunited – and share a kiss – in the shadow of a skeleton hanging in irons from a gibbet, a presentiment paralleled at the end when Macbeth goes into battle with his diminutive manservant, Seyton, dangling dead from a bell-rope.

Grisly ironies are emphasised at every opportunity. Reflecting on Cawdor's treachery, Duncan observes that "There's no art / To find the mind's construction in the face" even as he passes a spike surmounted by the very face he's referring to. Elsewhere, a subliminal buzz of bagpipes underpins Macbeth's musings on the fact that "If it were done when 'tis done, then 'twere well / It were done quickly," and Welles contrives a Lewton 'bus' when Lady Macbeth waits for news of King Duncan's death; starting at a sudden sound, she realises that "It was the owl that shriek'd." She later betrays a little orgasmic shudder as she seizes the blood-stained daggers from her traumatised husband, whereupon thunder peals out and a clangorous hammering at the castle gate is answered by the (sadly truncated) Porter.

The level of gruesomeness, presumably passed by the PCA because Shakespeare-sanctioned, is high. The Macbeths' Banquo-haunted banquet is claustrophobically staged in a low-roofed cave; the elongated shadow of Macbeth's pointing finger tracks

Orson Welles and hired assassins Brainerd Duffield and William Alland in *Macbeth* (1947); in the following decade Alland produced *Creature from the Black Lagoon* and several similar films

across to an eerie subjective shot in which the other guests are conspicuously absent, Macbeth seeing only Banquo in his appointed place, silently blinking away the blood from "twenty trenchéd gashes on his head." (That the cinema had acquired untold sophistication since the days when Spottiswoode Aitken groped his way out of Henry B Walthall's fireplace in *The Avenging Conscience* goes without saying.) Later, the massacre of Macduff's family – at which, contrary to Shakespeare, Macbeth himself is present – includes a gloating close-up of a helmeted soldier who obviously relishes killing children.

The film's final reels conjure an invading army from Republic's slim resources and are a tour de force. Birnam Wood comes to Dunsinane in a pall of slow-motion mist, the English soldiers and their lopped branches seeming like some strangely sentient, undulating monster as they oscillate onwards. The suicidal Lady Macbeth is granted a spectacular death plunge as she hurtles from the battlements, with the 'floppy-limbed dummy' problem normally endemic to such stunts entirely absent. And Dan O'Herlihy's Macduff, a silhouetted avenger backed by plumes of smoke, is electrifying as he bellows "Turn, hell-hound, turn," finally tossing "the usurper's cursed head" to the soldiers below in a supreme gesture of contempt.

The lowering photography, brilliant throughout, is by *Psycho*'s future cinematographer, John L Russell. Welles himself is a virile yet beautifully spoken presence (recasting Macbeth, as several critics have pointed out, in the grim-faced image of Attila the Hun), and Jeanette Nolan makes a splendidly vindictive consort. Though well acted, the film doesn't etch its characters too deeply, instead opting for a grimy visual sweep that is rarely less than riveting. And the over-literal idea of having the actors use Scottish accents works surprisingly well, though Republic would redub the film (and lop some 20 minutes from its running time) for a 1950 reissue, the film having bombed spectacularly on its original release in October 1948.

Inevitably, Welles made several fairly radical amendments to Shakespeare's text, including the creation of a composite character called 'a holy father'. He's played by Alan Napier as a craggily watchful presence, initially eliciting a vampiric hiss

MACBETH

Literary Classics Productions 1947
107 minutes [original release], 89 minutes [reissue]
production began 23 June

Cinematographer: John L Russell; Art Director: Fred Ritter; Editor: Lou Lindsay; Sound: John Stransky Jr, Gary Harris; Special Effects: Howard and Theodore Lydecker; Optical Effects: Consolidated Film Industries; Second Unit Photography: William Bradford; Set Decorations: John McCarthy Jr, James Redd; Make-up: Bob Mark; Hair Stylist: Peggy Gray; Women's Costumes: Adele Palmer; Music: Jacques Ibert; Conducted by: Efrem Kurtz; Assistant Director: Jack Lacey*; Dialogue Director: William Alland; Screenplay: Orson Welles*, based on the play by William Shakespeare; Associate Producer: Richard Wilson; Presented by: Charles K Feldman; Director-Producer: Orson Welles

Orson Welles (Macbeth); Jeanette Nolan (Lady Macbeth); Dan O'Herlihy (Macduff); Roddy McDowall (Malcolm); Edgar Barrier (Banquo); Alan Napier (a holy father); Erskine Sanford (Duncan); John Dierkes (Ross); Keene Curtis (Lennox); Peggy Webber (Lady Macduff); Lionel Braham (Siward); Archie Heugly (Young Siward); Jerry Farber (Fleance); Christopher Welles (Macduff child); Morgan Farley (doctor); Lurene Tuttle (gentlewoman); Brainerd Duffield (first murderer); William Alland (second murderer); George Chirello (Seyton); Gus Schilling (a porter); Brainerd Duffield, Lurene Tuttle, Peggy Webber (The Three)

Wonder-boy Welles has an imaginative way with a camera ... surrounding the plot with an atmosphere that makes all the crude violence believable; photographically, this mood is sustained. Dramatically, it is often violated, both by transpositions of text and by some of the performances. Time

On the first night [in Paris] there was a fight in the cinema ... Indifference would hurt me much more. After all, the film cannot be worthless if people like Jean Cocteau like it. On the other hand I don't take it as a compliment that the picture is having terrific success in Germany, where people are probably attracted by the mediaeval savagery of the subject.
Orson Welles [quoted in Sight and Sound, December 1950]

With John Baragrey out of action and June Vincent at his mercy, Onslow Stevens prepares to reveal himself as *The Creeper* (1948)

from the witches as he flourishes a cross at them but finally being impaled on the end of Macbeth's own spear. Welles also repeats a brilliant trick he first used in his Harlem *Macbeth* of 1935, shifting one of the witch's lines from Act I Scene III to the end title. "Peace," she mutters, "the charm's wound up."

YOUNG BLOOD – AND BRAINS

Also on release in the autumn of 1948 was a lame Jean Yarbrough picture called *The Creeper*, which had been shot in March by the independent Reliance company and was distributed by 20th Century-Fox. This was one of a tiny handful of films made by Universal producer Ben Pivar after his ignominious exit from that studio – and, despite its title, it bears no relation to the Rondo Hatton programmers Pivar and Yarbrough had made there. Instead, 'Creeper' is an unassuming laboratory cat that puts the wind up the highly strung June Vincent, who has returned from a research project in the West Indies with a severe case of ailurophobia.

The trip was in aid of some grade-A gibberish about serum extracted from cats and "cellular phosphorescence" designed to illuminate human organs during surgery. The sorry result is Onslow Stevens with a ridiculously fluffy cat's paw where his left hand should be, with which he savages Ralph Morgan, David Hoffman and Janis Wilson in quick succession. The scene in which he reveals his feline appendage is tensely done, with lots of queasy shadowplay as he tells the quailing Vincent that "The others who've seen this are dead. You and I will be the last." And veteran Universal cinematographer George Robinson lends style to several cat-ridden dream sequences. But the plot is virtually incomprehensible and the realisation of it bargain-basement. The most striking part of the film is a brief vignette directly after the credits, in which a black cat slinks purposefully along a gnarled tree branch. To get it, Pivar must have called in a favour from Universal, for it's taken direct from the opening of the 1941 version of *The Black Cat*.

Though genuine horror pictures were thin on the ground in the late 1940s, spoofs of them continued to be ground out on a regular basis. Columbia's Three Stooges added *If a Body Meets a Body*, *A Bird in the Head*, *Shivering Sherlocks* and *The Ghost Talks* to a roster of spooky farces that already included *Spook Louder*, *We Want Our Mummy* and *Three Missing Links*. Normally employed at PRC, Sam Newfield directed a horror-comedy for the African-American market, *Fight That Ghost*, at the behest of Atlanta entrepreneur Ted Toddy. And Monogram featured the Bowery Boys (aka the East Side Kids, aka the Dead End Kids) in *Spook Busters*, which the indefatigable William Beaudine directed in May 1946.

Having started in the haunted house vein as early as 1940 (in Joseph H Lewis' *Boys of the City*), and having subsequently encountered Bela Lugosi on two inauspicious occasions, the team would go over the same ground several times, growing ever more long in the tooth in *Master Minds* (1949), *Ghost Chasers* (1951) and *The Bowery Boys Meet the Monsters* (1954), only desisting with *Spook Chasers* as late as 1957.

For his part, Hal Roach tried to revisit the glory days of Our Gang and The Little Rascals by initiating a series devoted to the so-called Curley and His Gang. Only two entries were made, and the second of them, *Who Killed 'Doc' Robbin?*, put the urchins into a spooky house filled with laboratory paraphernalia. Shot in colour in September 1946 but not released until April 1948, Bernard Carr's film has brief turns from horror veterans George Zucco and Charles Gemora (in a gorilla suit, inevitably) and some grotesquely racist gags directed at the black boys in the gang, who are called Dis and Dat. Another offshoot of Our Gang was a brief series of PRC quickies devoted to the Gas House Kids, one of which – Edward L Cahn's *Gas House Kids in Hollywood* (1947) – stirred in the standard ingredients of a mad scientist, conniving gangsters, a hidden hoard and a supposedly haunted house.

For the new management at Universal, Bud Abbott and Lou Costello constituted just as depressing a reminder of the low-brow concerns of the previous regime as did the studio's recently retired horror franchises. The solution – *Abbott and Costello Meet Frankenstein* – was somehow inevitable, but the realisation of the film was so charming that a potentially humiliating project became a late-blooming celebration of the studio's monsters, and Abbott and Costello's most durable vehicle to boot. Originating as *The Brain of Frankenstein*, Charles Barton's film went into production on 5 February 1948 and was a major hit on its release in June; having cost UI some $792,000, it grossed over $3 million.

The monsters that had petrified audiences a mere 15 years ago – in the case of Lon Chaney Jr's Wolf Man, considerably less than that – here began the process by which they became little more than vaguely ominous old friends. Delightfully, Bela Lugosi (in his last role for a major studio) was retained to play Count Dracula for only the second time in his screen career, while Glenn Strange was back as the Monster, his make-up now handled, after the usurpation of Jack Pierce, by a new department headed by Bud Westmore. To accommodate all these menaces, Bud and Lou are cast as Chic and Wilbur, employees of a Florida baggage-handling company who are placed in charge of a hefty consignment bound for McDougal's House of Horrors. We therefore get an engaging replay of their 'moving candle' routine, mounted as it is on Dracula's unpredictable casket, and a sublime moment when the revived Monster catches sight of Wilbur and recoils in horror.

Wilbur is romantically involved with the glamorous Dr Sandra Mornay, but what she's really interested in, of course, is his brain, and in the climactic operating theatre scenes Lenore Aubert poses a formidable threat in surgical face-mask and black gloves, scalpel poised at the ready. Before she can do any damage, however, the Monster, presumably recalling his cavalier treatment of Daniel the hunchback in *House of Frankenstein*, flings her impatiently through a skylight. This is a surprisingly brutal detail in a final reel that also includes the surreal image of Lugosi slinging potted plants at the transformed Chaney, finally morphing into a bat only to plunge headlong into the sea in his pursuer's hairy grasp.

In addition to its marvellous sets, lustrous matte paintings, magisterial Frank Skinner score and welcome appearance from *Cat People*'s Jane Randolph as a pert insurance investigator, *Abbott and Costello Meet Frankenstein* is chiefly memorable for the mellow villainy of Lugosi, who, as the chalk-faced Dr Lejos (aka Dracula), relishes such faux-avuncular lines as "Oh, you young people, making the most of life – while it lasts." He also tells the uncomprehending Wilbur that "What we need today is young blood – and brains," and is briefly seen in a mirror as he vampirises the visibly rhapsodic Sandra. "There is no burlesque for me," Lugosi maintained during filming. "All I have to do is frighten the boys, a perfectly appropriate activity. My trademark will be unblemished."[3] And he was right.

Bela Lugosi puts his now 20-year-old moves on Lenore Aubert in *Abbott and Costello Meet Frankenstein* (1948)

After this imaginative and commercial high, Bud and Lou were matched with UI's full roster of pensioned-off monsters, but these further encounters showed a depressing slide in quality. *Abbott and Costello Meet the Killer, Boris Karloff* followed in September 1949, again directed by Charles Barton. Though the title would appear to blow the tiresome mystery at the film's heart even before it begins, Karloff's saturnine Swami Talpur turns out to be no more than a turbaned red herring, coping manfully with laboured lines like "You're going to commit suicide if it's the last thing you do."

The remaining titles suffer from a production-line sameness: *Abbott and Costello Meet the Invisible Man* was released in March 1951, *Abbott and Costello Meet Dr Jekyll and Mr Hyde* in August 1953, and *Abbott and Costello Meet the Mummy* as late as June 1955. All directed by Charles Lamont, these three have very little to recommend them, other than John Fulton's effects work in the first, a period setting and Karloff's smoothly villainous Jekyll in the second, and, in the third, an upgrade for stunt man Eddie Parker, who had played Mr Hyde uncredited but now received billing as the oddly named Klaris. Lamont moved on to a different UI comedy series, providing its seventh and last instalment with *Francis in the Haunted House* (1956), in which Mickey Rooney took over from Donald O'Connor as co-star to the titular talking mule.

THOSE WONDERFUL PEOPLE OUT THERE

In the aftermath of World War II, Hollywood's own history, particularly the lost world of silent pictures, had acquired a patina of antiquity that would find haunting expression in three high-profile films. The plots in each case revolved around psychotically self-absorbed performers, from carnival huckster Stanton Carlisle in *Nightmare Alley* to faded silent movie queen Norma Desmond in *Sunset Blvd* and phoney evangelist Harry Powell in *The Night of the Hunter*. All three chronicled a vanished, or vanishing, America with Gothic trimmings heavily informed by the classic horrors of an earlier generation.

Based on William Lindsay Gresham's 1946 novel, *Nightmare Alley* went into production at Fox on 19 May the following year, winding up ten weeks later and greatly upsetting Tyrone Power's legion of admirers on its release in November. The retired Tod Browning must have watched the finished product with great interest, recalling as it does his twin 1920s themes of sideshow workers and bogus spiritualists. Power's feckless but chiselled Stanton Carlisle is a direct descendant of John Gilbert's feckless but chiselled 'Cock' Robin in Browning's *The Show*, though his aspirations are considerably more baroque and his grimly inevitable downfall shocking in the extreme.

A different kind of unholy three: Tyrone Power, Coleen Gray and Mike Mazurki in *Nightmare Alley* (1947)

At the beginning of the picture, Carlisle observes the pitiful carnival 'geek' – a performer employed to bite the heads off live chickens – and says wonderingly, "I can't understand how anybody could get so low." The geek's hideous routine is discreetly handled but unmistakable ("Now folks, it's feedin' time," grins the barker as he tosses some poultry into the geek pit), and he goes berserk the same evening in a nightmarish scene resounding to his traumatised screams. As Carlisle begins his manipulative climb – appropriating a mind-reading act from an alcoholic associate prior to converting himself into society 'mentalist' The Great Stanton – the screams of the geek are subliminally repeated at regular intervals to telegraph the predestined end. "The spook racket," Carlisle grins. "I was made for it." At the

close, he stumbles, a blank-eyed hobo, into his former carnival and reassures the proprietor that "I know what a geek is," adding, "Mister, I was made for it." The moral is remorselessly punched home at the fade, when someone asks "How can a guy get so low?" and the proprietor says simply, "You reach too high."

Brilliantly directed by the veteran Edmund Goulding, *Nightmare Alley* sets up an intriguing parallel between the gullible rubes Carlisle cons in his first incarnation and the equally gullible toffs he scams later on. The film reaches its climax in a moving, magical scene in which Carlisle's chief victim, the septuagenarian Ezra Grindle (Taylor Holmes), is presented with the spirit of his deceased love Dorrie. In fact, it's Carlisle's reluctant wife (Coleen Gray) wandering in front of an ornamental fountain in Edwardian togs, complete with parasol. In Helen Walker's ice-cold psychiatrist, the film has a marvellous, sexually ambiguous femme fatale and in Ian Keith an equally impressive has-been carny. Power, too, is excellent in a role so far off the beaten track he had to fight to get the film made.

Carlisle's attempt to reunite Ezra Grindle with his lost love was echoed in 1948 by *The Spiritualist* (aka *The Amazing Mr X*), which Bernard Vorhaus started directing for independent producer Ben Stoloff on 7 January; the result went out in the last week of July. With a story by old hand Crane Wilbur, the film eschews the post-war bitterness of *Nightmare Alley* in favour of a hoary crime yarn harking back to Victor Halperin's *Supernatural*, only without the soul transference angle. "There's a millionaire right in this town [who] wouldn't buy a bag of popcorn without consulting his medium," sneers a medium-busting private dick, whose current case involves a beautiful young widow (Lynn Bari) and the oleaginous Alexis, a "psychic consultant" who bombards her with trumped-up reminders of her late husband.

With gorgeously diffused photography from his regular collaborator John Alton, Vorhaus makes the most of the spooky accoutrements surrounding the conniving Alexis, including his throaty raven familiar and a bogus disembodied hand that puts in an appearance at a rigged seance. The film also offers Turhan Bey, a slick but anodyne presence in several Universal horrors, a chance to show his mettle as the ultimately heroic Alexis. And it gives him a considerably more elaborate bag of tricks than Carlisle could muster – though the animated wedding gown that dances down on Bari like an ectoplasmic refugee from *The Uninvited* is never satisfactorily explained.

On 21 July 1948, D W Griffith succumbed to a cerebral haemorrhage, aged 73. Retired since 1931,

Cathy O'Donnell, Turhan Bey and Lynn Bari are joined by the legally dead Donald Curtis in *The Spiritualist*, which was rapidly reissued as *The Amazing Mr X* (1948)

he had been more or less forgotten by the town he had helped create, an unusually cruel instance of the 'chew 'em up and spit 'em out' ingratitude of the billion-dollar Hollywood machine. The eulogy at his sparsely attended funeral was spoken by writer-producer Charles Brackett, who immediately started work with his writer-director colleague Billy Wilder on a film called *Sunset Blvd*, which began shooting under Wilder's direction the following April.

"This is marked 'not to be missed' even for those young enough to associate silent movies with the Ark and puzzle over Gloria Swanson's name,"[4] observed a British critic on the film's belated release in August 1950. For in casting legendary silent star Swanson (still aged only 50) as legendary silent star Norma Desmond, Brackett and Wilder had fashioned a genuine Hollywood nightmare from the self-made grotesqueries of the movie capital.

Pursued by repo men, down-at-heel young screenwriter Joe Gillis stumbles upon a secluded palazzo of Hollywood's silent era, and finds it expedient to humour the faded movie star within. According to her forbidding butler Max, Norma Desmond was "the greatest of them all," and now she plans to make a comeback with her own script of Salome. *Joe, meanwhile, falls for a pretty young script reader called Betty Schaefer – and when Norma finds out, she takes violent action.*

The film's title is superimposed on a kerb stone, appropriately locating this melodrama of self-aggrandisement and self-disgust in the gutter. A special kind of tragic inevitability is set in train immediately,

"You don't yell at a sleepwalker..." Gloria Swanson faces the newsreel cameras at the conclusion of *Sunset Blvd* (1949)

SUNSET BLVD.

Paramount 1949
110 minutes
production began 18 April

Cinematographer: John F Seitz; Art Directors: Hans Dreier, John Meehan; Editorial Supervision: Doane Harrison; Editors: Arthur Schmidt, Frank Bracht*; Sound: Harry Lindgren, John Cope; Special Photographic Effects: Gordon Jennings; Process Photography: Farciot Edouart; Set Decorations: Sam Comer, Ray Moyer; Make-up: Wally Westmore, Frank Thayer*, Karl Silvera*; Costumes: Edith Head; Music: Franz Waxman; Assistant Director: C C Coleman Jr; Screenplay: Charles Brackett, Billy Wilder, D M Marshman Jr; Producer: Charles Brackett; Director: Billy Wilder

William Holden (Joe Gillis); Gloria Swanson (Norma Desmond); Erich von Stroheim (Max von Mayerling); Nancy Olson (Betty Schaefer); Fred Clark (Sheldrake); Lloyd Gough (Morino); Jack Webb (Artie Green); Cecil B DeMille, Hedda Hopper, Buster Keaton, Anna Q Nilsson, H B Warner, Ray Evans, Jay Livingston (themselves); Franklyn Farnum (undertaker); Larry Blake, Charles Dayton (finance men); uncredited: Gertrude Astor (courtier); Ken Christy (homicide captain); Ruth Clifford (Sheldrake's secretary); John Cortay (young gate man); Peter Drynan (tailor); Julia Faye (Hisham); Gerry Ganzer (Connie); Kenneth Gibson (sales assistant); E Mason Hopper (doctor); Gertrude Messinger (hairdresser); John Miller (electrician); Bert Moorhouse (Gordon Cole); Ottola Nesmith (woman); Robert Emmett O'Connor (Jonesy [older gate man]); Roy Thompson (Rudy [shoeshine boy]); Archie Twitchell (vicuña salesman); Yvette Vedder [later Yvette Vickers] (party girl on phone); Henry Wilcoxon (himself)

The picture is outstanding especially for a magnificent performance by a name which once was magic on any theatre marquee. Gloria Swanson, exhibitors can tell their customers, will once again give them their money's worth. For the older audiences who remember her with nostalgia she will be terrific and those who never saw her can now see for themselves what the movies had before they added sound. Motion Picture Herald

The tone of the piece was a mixture of Gothic eeriness and nostalgia for the old Hollywood ... The scene where Norma plays bridge with a few old friends came closest to giving us all the creeps ... "Waxworks is right," Buster muttered in his unmatchable deadpan.
Gloria Swanson [*Swanson on Swanson*, 1980]

the dead hero being fished out of a swimming pool and relating his story in flashback. (Even more outré: an excised prologue saw him discussing his predicament with several other corpses in the morgue.) Narrated in flip phrases that redefine the word 'jaded', Joe's struggle to keep hold of his 1946 Plymouth convertible winds up with a high-speed Hollywood car chase. So far, so noir. He then, however, suffers a blow-out, wheeling his car down a secluded turning and marvelling at the old house he stumbles upon, "the kind crazy movie people built in the crazy Twenties."

The 'car trouble' device is exactly what deposited the Wavertons at the Femm household in *The Old Dark House*, or the Alisons at Fort Marmaros in *The Black Cat*. And with Joe's arrival at "that grim Sunset castle," the film shifts into a horror pastiche more queasily effective than most genuine horror pictures, perfecting a funereal atmosphere that it never fully shakes off.

Norma Desmond herself is first seen as a spidery presence in black, bug-eyed shades, peeping out through Venetian blinds as Joe encounters her bullet-headed retainer Max, who – mistaking the interloper for, of all things, an undertaker – tells him, "If you need any help with the coffin, call me." The corpse in question is that of Norma's pet chimpanzee

(a miniature version of one of the most time-honoured horror menaces), and Norma's rhetoric over its body translates the bitterness of a forgotten star into the purple prose of a pulp thriller. "They took the idols and smashed them," she seethes. "But there's a microphone right there to catch the last gurgles, and Technicolor to photograph the red swollen tongue."

In creating Norma Desmond, Wilder, Brackett and Swanson anticipated an entire strain of 1960s horror cinema, in which female stars of a certain age were inserted into faintly prurient Grand Guignol plots; the strain was blueprinted by Robert Aldrich's *What Ever Happened to Baby Jane?* in 1962. But Wilder's imagery is rooted for the most part in ancient sources, with Joe himself invoking first *Great Expectations* and then Poe's House of Usher, describing 10086 Sunset Boulevard as "stricken with a kind of creeping paralysis ... crumbling away in slow motion." The wind whistles through the resident pipe organ (sounding very like a Theremin) and later Max will play Bach's Toccata and Fugue in D Minor on it, just as Karloff and Lugosi did in their 1930s Poe films. And the derelict swimming pool – in which "Mabel Normand and John Gilbert must have swum ... 10,000 midnights ago" – is now populated by rats.

Stoker's *Dracula* is powerfully evoked too, a parallel first proposed by Richard Corliss in his 1975 book *Talking Pictures*. William Holden's glib and feckless Joe comes across as a sort of hardboiled Jonathan Harker; ensnared in Norma's old-world web, his efforts to finesse her crazy screenplay (which he aptly calls "ghost writing") involve even more paperwork than Harker's property transfer. Both Norma Desmond and Count Dracula are faded grandees isolated in castles redolent of a bygone age, nurturing grand plans for a 'comeback' and displaying an ambiguous fascination for their young guests/prisoners, resorting to numerous subterfuges to keep them on the premises. Both indulge in lunatic monologues about their glorious past lives. And, in each case, three relics of their pasts materialise on occasion: three lubricious brides for Dracula, three bridge-playing "waxworks" for Norma.

There are smaller points of similarity, like Norma's home being devoid of locks just as Dracula's is of mirrors, and more fanciful ones: the evanescent beam of Norma's film projector, giving life to images of her decades-old self, recalls the motes of dust that gradually coalesce into Dracula's brides. And at the end, of course, Norma is fatally exposed to the 'light' of a newsreel crew. Above all, there's the predatory image of Swanson herself: all piercing eyes, cruel mouth and taloned fingers, she immortalises the confusion, so rife in her 1920s heyday, between 'vamps' and vampires. The film's advertising made no bones about this, depicting Swanson's toothy rictus in a blood-red wash, hovering hungrily over Holden and Nancy Olson, whose frightened embrace makes them look about as anodyne a pair of ingenues as David Manners and Jacqueline Wells in *The Black Cat*.

The film also includes a brief montage of Norma's fitness regime, in which she submits to "an army of beauty experts" in creepy images that simultaneously suggest the latex preoccupations of sado-masochism and the surgical procedures seen in *Mad Love*; the neck harness Norma subsequently wears seems like an explicit reference to that film. Among Norma's three faded, undead cronies is the miraculously preserved Anna Q Nilsson, a brilliant choice for a drama of living mummification given that she had starred in the silent rejuvenation fantasies *Vanity's Price* and *One Way Street*. And Erich von Stroheim – marvellously affecting as the faithful Max – is more or less playing himself, grimly enumerating Griffith, DeMille and 'Max von Mayerling' as the three directors who "showed promise" in the early days. Von Stroheim's casting was also apt, of course, given the number of horror films he appeared in after his fall from grace as a director.

Deftly winding up its tragic scheme, the film ends with a remarkable fusion of pity and terror. Having murdered Joe, Norma mistakes a newsreel team for the film crew of her longed-for comeback; descending the grand staircase in a spangled wrap as Franz Waxman's score swells on the soundtrack, she curls her arms in vampish arabesques before pausing to address the crew, assuring them that "There's nothing else. Just us, the cameras and those wonderful people out there in the dark..." The music surging again, she glides forward with grotesque come-hither hand movements as the cameras irradiate her face into a featureless, screen-filling blur. Profoundly disturbing, this is arguably the crowning achievement of Hollywood Gothic.

The grisly spectacle of Hollywood cannibalising itself in *Sunset Blvd* was paralleled in gentler terms by debutant director Charles Laughton, who on 15 August 1954 began shooting his own tribute to the silent era, and D W Griffith in particular, *The Night of the Hunter*. An independent production released via United Artists, the film was based on a Davis Grubb bestseller and, to prepare, Laughton screened several Griffith films; he also engaged Griffith's sometime muse Lillian Gish (then pushing 61) to play a sturdy exemplar of the kind of homespun values that by the mid-1950s were virtually extinct. In addition, he got from Robert Mitchum a chilling performance as sanctimonious West Virginia sociopath Harry Powell, justifying his murderous actions with the notion that even the Lord hates "perfume-smellin' things, lacy things, things with curly hair."

Powell is a kind of homicidal Tartuffe, moving up and down the Ohio River during the Depression and preying on unwary widows, remorselessly pursuing his latest victim's two children when they abscond with a hidden stash of $10,000. The children's lengthy upriver odyssey acquires mythic resonance from the limpid imagery created by Laughton and cinematographer Stanley Cortez; they seem to pass into a kind of bucolic fairyland, the nocturnal riverbank disclosing frogs, owls, turtles, rabbits and more. They also pass into the protection of gun-toting fairy godmother Rachel Cooper (Gish), who explains that "I'm a strong tree with branches for many birds" and is clearly a sexagenarian version of Mary Pickford's Mama Molly in *Sparrows*. She finally puts a bullet into the phoney preacher, who retires yelping like a fox driven out of a hen-coop.

Laughton's film seems to derive from Griffith mainly in the sincere sentimentality surrounding Gish and in its rigid demarcation between love and hate (the very words spelt out on Powell's tattooed fingers); visually, set-pieces like Powell's murder of the children's mother, surmounted by a triangular attic gable, seem more indebted to *Caligari* than *Broken Blossoms*. It failed miserably on release, demoralising Laughton profoundly, but endures as one of the most daringly off-centre American films of a too-conventional decade.

The film also takes vignettes from earlier horror pictures and infuses them with fresh power. Watching a stripper in a seedy burlesque house, Powell's combined sexual arousal and misogynist hatred parallels Slade's response to Kitty's music-hall act in *The Lodger*, only here they come together in the image of a suddenly erected flick-knife cutting through Powell's trouser pocket. And the anemone-like hair of the murdered maid in Lang's *House by the River* is redefined through an astonishing underwater tableau in which Shelley Winters sits in an abandoned Model T Ford, giant weeds waving in the current, shafts of sunlight piercing the water, "with her hair waving soft and lazy like meadowgrass under floodwater – and that slit in her throat like she had an extra mouth."

OLD HANDS, NEW WAVE

At the start of the 1950s, the traditional horror film may have been in abeyance but the filmmakers once associated with it still had an occasional chance to revisit past glories. The results, sadly, weren't always edifying.

Several such veterans (none of them yet 50) were involved in a Jack Broder production called *Bride of the Gorilla*, which started on 27 July 1951 and was polished off in seven days. Making his directorial debut, writer Curt Siodmak was here reunited with two actors indelibly associated with his signature successes of the 1940s – Tom Conway from *I Walked with a Zombie* and Lon Chaney Jr from *The Wolf Man*. From the first of these films comes a tropical setting, with voodoo trimmings; from the second – or, rather, from Siodmak's original concept for it – comes a burly protagonist whom we only see in animal form when reflected in ponds or mirrors. Boring and formless, the film never makes much of its 'power of suggestion' theme, mainly because Raymond Burr is a uniquely unappealing 'hero' and is effortlessly upstaged, in any case, by Barbara Payton's bullet bra. Conway, looking listless, is the local doctor. Chaney, looking rough, is a police chief who mutters vaguely about "a famous jungle demon that tears living animals to shreds" but is otherwise pretty peripheral.

Given that his Realart company was busy reissuing many of the old Universal classics, Jack Broder's next move after *Bride of the Gorilla* had a grim inevitability to it. Made in May 1952 and issued in September, the awful *Bela Lugosi Meets a Brooklyn Gorilla* reunited the ailing star with director William Beaudine. It also recalled *Zombies on Broadway* in casting him opposite, not a pair of Abbott and Costello wannabes, but a uniquely witless pair of Martin and Lewis clones called Duke Mitchell and Sammy

Lillian Gish and her teenage charge Gloria Castillo, shadowed by the psychopathic Robert Mitchum in *The Night of the Hunter* (1954)

Petrillo. Earning the personal apotheosis of having his name in a film's title (just as his old rival recently had with *Abbott and Costello Meet the Killer, Boris Karloff*), Lugosi is Dr Zabor, an evolutionary jungle researcher who turns Mitchell into a singing gorilla.

The real Dean Martin and Jerry Lewis, meanwhile, were appearing in a Paramount remake of *The Ghost Breakers*, with George Marshall directing once more and a title change to *Scared Stiff*. Starting production on 31 May 1952 and released the following spring, the result has glamour in the form of Lizabeth Scott and Carmen Miranda, plus a charming last-minute cameo from Bob Hope and Bing Crosby, but not a lot else.

Over at Universal-International, Boris Karloff was being saddled with the kind of parts Universal had dished out to Lugosi ten years previously. Joseph Pevney's *The Strange Door* started on 15 May 1951 and cast Karloff as Voltan, a faithful retainer in the 18th century household of Alain de Maletroit. In the latter role, Charles Laughton gives an entertaining but ill-thought-out performance, relishing lines like "I'll feed your liver to the swine" but otherwise adopting a scattershot approach that brings his Scarborough accent and campest mannerisms well to the fore. The latter, unfortunately, sit uneasily with the presumably heterosexual de Maletroit, who maintains the usual partitioned shrine to a lost female love. The dead Hélène's preference for de Maletroit's brother Edmond has sent him round the twist, with the result that Edmond has been imprisoned in the lower reaches; de Maletroit, meanwhile, plots to destroy Edmond and Hélène's daughter by marrying her to a libertine good-for-nothing.

Though no great shakes, the film is engaging enough as a lusty Gothic melodrama in the vein of the old Karloff vehicle *The Black Room*, though Laughton isn't required, as Karloff had been, to play both brothers. Instead, the incarcerated Edmond is played by Paul Cavanagh, whose regal features don't resemble Laughton's Yorkshire pudding-face one bit. The climax is pleasingly reminiscent of silent movie cliffhangers: an infernal machine in the basement causes the walls of Edmond's cell to close in, a touch of the Pearl Whites that's matched for absurdity by the sight of Karloff, mortally wounded, swimming to the rescue like Rin-Tin-Tin.

The Strange Door was based on a Robert Louis Stevenson story called *The Sire de Maletroit's Door*. A second UI attempt at reviving the Gothic strain, *The Black Castle*, was produced ten months later, starting on 12 March 1952. The screenplay was an original (of sorts) by the same screenwriter, Jerry Sackheim, and the producer was William Alland, a former associate of Orson Welles who had been involved both before and behind the camera in *Macbeth*. Like *The Strange Door*, the film contains undigested echoes of *The Most Dangerous Game*, with Stephen McNally's scar-faced Count Von Bruno an obvious antecedent of Count Zaroff. Richard Greene is an affable presence as 18th century English adventurer Sir Ronald Burton, who worms his way into Von Bruno's Black Forest stronghold with the intention of avenging the death of two of his friends.

"Drink this, and go with God..." Paula Corday, Boris Karloff and Richard Greene in *The Black Castle* (1952)

Set in a mock-courtly world of brocaded coats, lacy jabots and knee-breeches, the film is closer to the Gainsborough bodice-rippers produced in England in the 1940s than anything Universal had previously essayed in Gothic mode. Sackheim packs the proceedings with incident; in one sequence (extremely well staged), Greene gets to wrestle with a black panther in foggy terrain just as he had with *The Hound of the Baskervilles* 13 years earlier. The panther, of course, is also reminiscent of *Cat People*, as is a scene in which Burton and Von Bruno's unhappy wife inch their way around the eerily dappled walls overhanging an indoor alligator pool. Finally, as in *The Strange Door*, the action devolves into a "brief reunion" in a prison cell (the phrase appears in the dialogue of both films). The procedure this time, however, facilitates an echo of *Romeo and Juliet* when Karloff's kindly doctor puts the lovers into a catatonic state in order to evade the insane Von Bruno. This plot twist leads to a few very mild frissons when Burton's casket is being nailed down and low moans issue from within.

Karloff's underdeveloped role here, as Dr Meissner, hardly rates his being billed second, though poor Lon Chaney Jr fares even worse, playing a hulking mute manservant who climactically takes a tumble into the alligator pit. In addition to the casting of old hands like Karloff and Chaney, *The Strange Door* and *The Black Castle* hark back to an earlier era in their heavy reliance on music cues from Universal's now time-honoured chillers; in the latter film, Chaney Jr's every appearance is heralded by a lugubrious *Son of Frankenstein* fanfare.

The Black Castle, however, also pointed forward in that it was the directorial debut of former production designer Nathan Juran, who by the end of the decade would be responsible for such atom-age thrillers as *The Deadly Mantis*, *20 Million Miles to Earth* and *The Brain from Planet Arous*. These were late-ish entries in an industry-wide efflorescence of science fiction pictures, a form previously confined to 'once in a blue moon' titles like *The Invisible Ray* and *Dr Cyclops*.

In the wake of Hiroshima and Nagasaki, and sparked in particular by Soviet Russia's acquisition of an A-bomb in 1949, an increasingly fearful nation observed Communist expansion in China and mainland Europe with undisguised alarm. Almost a year to the day since Winston Churchill coined the term 'Iron Curtain', on 12 March 1947 President Truman laid the groundwork for anti-Communist paranoia in a speech that would be dubbed 'the Truman Doctrine'. Then, on 24 June of the same year, an Idaho pilot named Kenneth Arnold observed nine unidentifiable craft in the sky above Washington State. Before long, sightings of flying saucers, real or imagined, proliferated just as surely as the subversive Reds supposedly infiltrating the country.

Science fiction films began to proliferate, too, mainly via the canny expedient of splicing the two invasion threats together; the 1951 film *I Married a Communist*, for example, would lend its title seven years later to a classic of the form called *I Married a Monster from Outer Space*. It was a boom period memorably described by critic John Baxter as "springtime for Caliban," though he also called it a mere "galvanic twitch," noting that "The 'boom' ... was an illusory one. The public was not interested in pure SF but in the simpler fare of the movies."[5] Even so, for much of the 1950s science fiction films were big business, offering a skewed but still scary reflection of contemporary fears.

Unsurprisingly perhaps, several writers and directors formerly associated with Gothic horror made a smooth transition to the space craze. Irving Pichel directed the highly influential *Destination Moon*, while Edgar G Ulmer handled *The Man from Planet X*, Lesley Selander *Flight to Mars*, Robert Wise *The Day the Earth Stood Still* and William Cameron Menzies *Invaders from Mars*. Curt Siodmak, meanwhile, both wrote and directed *The Magnetic Monster*, later providing just the screenplay for *Riders to the Stars*. Other veteran scenarists contributing to the trend included John L Balderston and Anthony Veiller (co-authors of *Red Planet Mars*), Philip Wylie (author of the source novel for *When Worlds Collide*) and Barré Lyndon (*The War of the Worlds*). On top of all this, producer William Alland, who had recently completed *The Black Castle*, inducted Universal-International into the field via the eerie Arizona landscapes of Jack Arnold's *It Came from Outer Space*.

The portentous nature of the space craze wasn't lost on contemporary observers, among them British theatre critic Richard Findlater, who pondered the subject in an August 1952 issue of *Tribune*. The occasion was the belated UK release of a Hollywood chiller that garnered one of the British censor's first-ever 'X' certificates, a designation that had supplanted the old 'H' the year before. "If *The Thing* were only mildly entertaining nonsense, it wouldn't be worth discussing," Findlater began. "But it's only the latest arrival in a series of films which seems to me disturbingly dotty. Over us all hangs the threat of atomic murder ... and in these 'science shockers' from Hollywood, the universal nightmare is translated into Martian melodrama. We don't want to see what a napalm bomb does to a man, but it doesn't hurt to see an intellectual carrot being burned alive." Findlater's conclusion was that "The background to all these ga-ga films is the apocalyptic terror of the last day, the day of judgment."[6]

Findlater was reckoning without a number of films where the day of judgment was no mere background, but the essential theme; a persistent strain of post-apocalypse scenarios had been heralded by the sombre *Five*, which Arch Oboler shot in the autumn of 1950, and had since thrown up such disparate titles as Alfred E Green's *Invasion USA* and Stuart Gilmore's *Captive Women*. But for a combination of 'apocalyptic terror' and 'Martian melodrama', the film that prompted Findlater's remarks remains hard to beat. Produced under the aegis of Howard Hawks' company Winchester Pictures, the epic schedule of *The Thing* stretched from 25 October 1950 to 3 March the following year, with the title extended to *The Thing from Another World* when RKO distributed the film in April. The source material was *Who Goes There?*, a John W Campbell novella published in the August 1938 issue of *Astounding Science Fiction*.

To push the picture, Hawks indulged in a bit of phoney press-agent puffery to the effect that "It is important that we don't confuse the Frankenstein type of film with the science fiction picture."[7] The whole purpose of the film, however, was to do exactly that, sugaring the supposedly outmoded pill of Gothic horror with the fashionable sheen of science fiction.

November 1950. Investigating a flying saucer submerged under Arctic ice, the personnel of a US airbase use a thermite bomb to disinter it, but succeed only in destroying it. Thrown clear by the blast, the craft's pilot is taken back to camp in a block of ice, subsequently thawing out and embarking on a murderous rampage. Though humanoid in appearance, the thing is a super-intelligent vegetable that subsists on blood...

THE THING FROM ANOTHER WORLD

Winchester Pictures 1951
87 minutes
production ended 3 March

Cinematographer: Russell Harlan; Art Directors: Albert S D'Agostino, John J Hughes; Editor: Roland Gross; Sound: Phil Brigandi, Clem Portman; Special Effects: Donald Stewart; Special Photographic Effects: Linwood Dunn; Process Photography: Harold E Stine*; Set Decorations: Darrell Silvera, William Stevens; Make-up: Lee Greenway; Hair Stylist: Larry Germain; Ladies' Wardrobe: Michael Woulfe; Music: Dimitri Tiomkin; Screenplay: Charles Lederer, Ben Hecht* (based on the story *Who Goes There?* by John W Campbell Jr); Associate Producer: Edward Lasker; Producer: Howard Hawks; Director: Christian Nyby

Margaret Sheridan (Nikki); Kenneth Tobey (Captain Patrick Hendry); Robert Cornthwaite (Dr Carrington); Douglas Spencer (Scotty); James Young (Lt Eddie Dykes); Dewey Martin (crew chief [Bob]); Robert Nichols (Lt Ken MacPherson [Mac]); William Self (Corporal Barnes); Eduard Franz (Dr Stern); Sally Creighton (Mrs Chapman) and James Arness ('The Thing'); uncredited: Robert Bray (captain); Edmund Breon (Dr Ambrose); Nicholas Byron (Tex Richards); Billy Curtis (smallest Thing); John Dierkes (Dr Chapman); George Fenneman (Dr Redding); Paul Frees (Dr Vorhees); Everett Glass (Professor Wilson); Robert Gutknecht (Corporal Hauser); Ted Mangenes (smaller Thing); David McMahon (Brig Gen Fogarty); Norbert Schiller (Dr Laurence); Robert Stevenson (Captain Fred Smith); Lee Fung Too, Walter Ng (cooks); King Kong, Charles K Opunui, Riley Sunrise (eskimos); Ted Cooper, Allan Ray (lieutenants), with Gabriel Cubos, Ben Frommer, Tom Humphrey

nb: Robert Nichols' role is erroneously given on screen as Lt Ken Erickson

For science fiction addicts *The Thing* (London Pavilion) is indubitably the thing ... The film wants, like the Fat Boy in *Pickwick*, to make your flesh creep – and I dare say it will. *Daily Graphic* [UK]

We didn't finish until early March and the New York due date was in April! So Dimitri Tiomkin was composing the score from the rushes and from the rough cut of the film we had shot so far. When they showed us this rough cut ... I realised then what a witty picture it was, that this was not just an ordinary picture. It was very carefully made.
Robert Cornthwaite [quoted in *Filmfax*, August-September 1997]

The Thing from Another World has inspired over 60 years' worth of speculation regarding who actually directed it. It smacks of Howard Hawks from beginning to end, yet the director credit goes to Hawks' Oscar-winning editor Christian Nyby. Suffice to say that this combination of talents – together with a splendid ensemble cast and several RKO technicians familiar from the Val Lewton films – created a still-gripping horror thriller that was to exercise a profound influence on future films. And yet its antecedents are clear. The blizzard-tossed isolation of the North Pole is merely an imaginative variant on the standard, storm-wracked old dark house, while, to quote Findlater again, "the central character – the marauding carrot – is just like one of Boris Karloff's playmates in the dear old 'H' days."

Though facetious, Findlater's observation was spot-on. Despairing of a suitable make-up design for the Thing, Hawks reportedly instructed make-up man Lee Greenway to follow Jack Pierce's Frankenstein design of 1931, which Greenway modified by making the square-headed alien conspicuously bald. In the cyclical way of these things, the Frankenstein monster itself would go the hair-free route, looking very like the Thing, in a 1970 potboiler called *The Horror of Frankenstein*.

As an adaptation of Campbell's original, *The Thing* does more than shift the action from the Antarctic to the Arctic; it also drastically reduces the Thing's capabilities, which in the story included not only telepathy but a shape-shifting knack of assuming the appearance of its victims. The tentacles specified by Campbell – and any number of other freakish appendages – would turn up in squelchy

Robert Cornthwaite, Margaret Sheridan and Kenneth Tobey, opposing forces facing up to *The Thing from Another World* (1951)

abundance in a simultaneously sombre and hysterical new version directed in 1981 by John Carpenter. Here, however, they only appear figuratively and are attached, intriguingly, to the hero. Recollecting their former fling, 'Nikki' Nicholson tells Captain Hendry that "You had moments of kind of making like an octopus. I never saw so many hands in all my life."

The badinage here is slickly done, Margaret Sheridan and Kenneth Tobey giving such engaging performances that their scenes never come across as token romantic interludes. With a script concocted in part by Hawks' old associate Ben Hecht, the banter is obviously on a high level throughout, but, in some ways, the screenplay's plentiful wit works against the picture. The military men at the Pole maintain such an all-American sang-froid in the face of an abominable threat that the threat itself runs the risk of being diluted. As well as indulging in Howard Hawks in-jokes (one of the officers gears up for the siege with the observation that "I saw Gary Cooper in *Sergeant York*"), the Thing's potential victims are given several Thing-related quips that contribute to an almost larkish tone. "Where he came from they sure don't breed 'em for beauty" is just one such; in addition, Nikki refers to the invader as "that boogey man in the cake of ice," while the sardonic newspaperman, Scotty, calls it "one for Ripley" and "some form of super-carrot."

Margaret Field and 'alien' actor Pat Goldin in a gag shot for *The Man from Planet X* (1951)

Appropriately, the chief scientist at the base adopts a more reverential tone. "There are no enemies in science," observes Dr Carrington, "only phenomena to study." He also calls the Thing "our superior in every way," lauding the fact that it knows "no pain or pleasure as we know it, no emotions, no heart." Carrington – "who," as *Time* magazine put it, "is suggestively costumed to look like a Russian"[8] – is a postwar update of the old stop-at-nothing mad scientist, and as such is not to be trusted in the anti-intellectual ambience of a Howard Hawks picture. For the audience, however, he succeeds in subverting the tomfoolery of the soldiers, with the curious result that the viewer becomes more queasily apprehensive than the gung-ho characters on screen.

In particular, Carrington offers a round-table summation of the Thing's powers that is genuinely chilling, examining the creature's still-living severed arm in a crowded shot that accommodates no fewer than 17 significant characters. He also presides over a batch of newly grown vampire blooms, all of them hooked up to plasma bottles and emitting via stethoscope a sound "almost like the wail of a new-born child that's hungry." Cannily, the audience is prevented from hearing this for themselves, just as they're denied a view of Carrington's associates, throats slashed by the Thing and their bodies hung like steers from the greenhouse rafters. The imaginative power of these withheld horrors only lends greater weight to the film's big set-pieces, including a haunting view of the silhouetted creature making mincemeat of the huskies and proceeding to three shattering sequences in which the Thing makes shock appearances in doorways.

Even the film's opening title qualifies as a set-piece, with a scary oscillation of cymbals as *The Thing* literally burns itself into the screen and eerie shafts of light irradiate from each letter. At the opposite end of the film, the creature is 'cooked' in an electrical vortex reminiscent of the Strickfaden pyrotechnics of old. Employed in earlier films to infuse life, they succeed here in taking it away, reducing the Thing to a frazzle in a convincing effect that utilised three Things in total – all 6'7" of chief Thing James Arness, plus two stands-in of progressively smaller stature.

The Thing was preceded by a fleet-footed cash-in made in six days in December 1950. Though doing no damage to *The Thing*'s triumphal progress, Edgar G Ulmer's *The Man from Planet X* was first seen on 9 March 1951 and cleaned up spectacularly, having

been dashed off on a risible budget of little more than $40,000. Striking out as independent producers, the writing team of Aubrey Wisberg and Jack Pollexfen had imagined an enfeebled alien visitor who only turns nasty when a conniving scientist seeks to get answers out of him by, absurdly, beating him up. Presumably mindful of Ulmer's Gothic pedigree with *The Black Cat* and others, Wisberg and Pollexfen set their story in the forbidding environs of a Scottish broch, which gave Ulmer the ideal opportunity to smother the film's deficiencies in a very satisfying pall of ground fog.

A bolt of lightning from a lowering sky introduces the title, then the camera tracks smoothly towards the castellated tower as wraith-like plumes of mist curl around gnarled tree branches. It's a splendid opening – after *Macbeth*, cinematographer John L Russell was used to foggy Scottish landscapes – and Ulmer gets by on imagery of this sort for several reels. Where once stood the Deco hulk of Fort Marmaros now resides a dinky little spaceship, its occupant a diminutive mediaeval goblin, an eerily forlorn figure whose face is "a ghastly caricature, like something distorted by pressure." Unfortunately, conviction collapses completely on the arrival of some ridiculously unpersuasive locals, gibbering of "boogey doin's" and forming a small platoon of zombies at the alien's command. The film then devolves into a deadening plod until the inevitable military intervention.

RE-MAKE / RE-MODEL

The Thing from Another World was released on 6 April 1951, just three days before Lewton graduate Robert Wise began shooting *The Day the Earth Stood Still* for 20th Century-Fox, a film diametrically opposed to the blood-draining mayhem propagated by *The Thing*. In presenting a Christ-like, New England-accented alien (Michael Rennie), who comes to Washington DC with a message of disarmament but is immediately shot at for his pains, Wise's film took a bravely pacifist stand in a country increasingly possessed by Cold War paranoia.

"Our world at the moment," as a presidential aide puts it in *The Day the Earth Stood Still*, "is full of tensions and suspicions." The economic prosperity of the 1950s – with a new suburban culture eagerly snapping up such glamorous status symbols as television sets and baroquely styled automobiles – was set against the commencement of hostilities in Korea in July 1950 and, on his inauguration in January 1953, the anti-Soviet sabre-rattling of President Dwight D Eisenhower. The election campaign of 1952 had seen Truman accused of being "soft on Communism," a profoundly damaging claim given the recent ascendancy of Senator Joseph McCarthy. The creation of the House Un-American Activities Committee in 1947 had triggered a 'Reds under the bed' mania of which McCarthy had become the self-advertising figurehead. The HUAC's enquiries into supposed Communist sympathisers were focused, most famously, on the film industry, and, as Colin Shindler puts it, "the climate of fear and suspicion these investigations engendered in the film business led to a near-fatal sterility of ideas in Hollywood in the Fifties."[9]

In addition to the corrosive fear of the HUAC blacklist, the film industry was reeling from several other body-blows. The blatantly monopolistic practise by which the major studios (Paramount, 20th Century-Fox, M-G-M, Warner Bros, RKO) owned their own theatre chains was finally overturned by a court ruling in May 1948, leading to the rise of independent producers and the dissolution of the studio system. Audience figures, too – after an extraordinary post-war high of 100 million weekly admissions in 1946 – were plummeting alarmingly, with the migration to the suburbs separating Americans from the big downtown cinemas, many of which closed down as a result. And the impression of ungovernable upheaval, of the final extinction of old-style studio complacency, was exacerbated when United Artists defiantly issued Otto Preminger's 1953 film *The Moon is Blue* without a PCA seal. Thanks in part to the film's use of such prohibited words as 'virgin' and 'mistress', a $6 million gross was the result.

Beyond the film industry, the propensity for metaphorical book-burning of the HUAC variety became literal in the case of so-called horror comics. William Gaines' EC (Entertaining Comics) enterprise published three popular titles – *Tales from the Crypt*, *The Vault of Horror* and *The Haunt of Fear*, all three inaugurated in 1950 – that mixed sardonically humorous parables of sin and retribution with artwork that delved into the mechanics of putrefaction in unpredecented detail.

Gaines and his various competitors encountered their nemesis in the form of the German-born New York psychiatrist Dr Fredric Wertham, who whipped up a firestorm of moral panic on the dubious assumption that the EC product was being read by children. In 1954, Wertham published a massively influential book called *Seduction of the Innocent*, also taking the opportunity to testify before the Senate Subcommittee on Juvenile Delinquency. Despite an elegantly phrased put-down from Gaines himself – "It would be just as difficult to explain the harmless thrill of a horror story to a Dr Wertham as it would be to explain the sublimity of love to a frigid old maid"[10] – the hysteria resulted in the establishment of the Comics Code Authority in October of that year, a self-regulating body similar to the Production Code that had hamstrung the film industry for 20 years, right down to the necessity for a prominently displayed 'seal'. Among many others, all three of Gaines' titles ceased publication.

The hysteria surrounding *Tales from the Crypt* and its fellows can hardly have encouraged US film producers to venture back into the horror genre, and what horror pictures there were proved laughably anaemic by comparison to the EC titles. Even so, several old favourites were dusted off for early 1950s audiences, with variable results.

Made in under three weeks in March 1951, Seymour Friedman's *The Son of Dr Jekyll* was given as much period glamour as Columbia could muster. Cravenly, the studio also sought to perfume the project by removing screenwriter Edward Huebsch from the credits; despite being blacklisted by the HUAC, his case was upheld by the Screen Writers' Guild and Columbia were obliged to leave his name in place. Given that playwright Arthur Miller was soon to turn his own HUAC experiences into a drama about the Salem witch trials called *The Crucible*, it's intriguing that Huebsch's script should revolve around a smear campaign and give its title character the line, "Burning witches has always been a popular sport, hasn't it?"

Though the film's main action is set in 1890, it begins 30 years before – and, mindful of the fact that the story focuses on a son, an opening rubric advises us that Hyde's twilight existence in Soho involved a hitherto unsuspected wife, whose baby is rescued by satellite characters Utterson (Lester Matthews) and Lanyon (Alexander Knox) and brought up by the former. He grows into Louis Hayward, formerly the psychotic novelist of *House by the River* but here a quixotic do-gooder convinced that "Legends don't die; they have to be killed." To exonerate his father's memory, he therefore re-stages the older Jekyll's experiment, which entails little more than a brief close-up of his hand turning hairy.

The story proper revolves around a frame-up orchestrated by the embittered Lanyon, which, as already noted, is an intriguing, HUAC-style twist but succeeds in robbing the film of any horror. It's intriguing, too, that the new boy's very name – Edward Jekyll – makes him a fusion of his father's two personalities, but the film cheats on this promise, leaving only its opening and closing infernos to chew over, plus Doris Lloyd's cameo as a conniving old soubrette caught up in Lanyon's smear campaign. Released at Hallowe'en of 1951, the film can have given scant consolation to hard-up horror fanciers.

"Now you're looking at the man, not the legend." Louis Hayward expires in the fiery introduction to *The Son of Dr Jekyll* (1951)

Two Hallowe'ens later, audiences could see Louis Hayward's ex-wife, Ida Lupino, acting opposite her new husband, Howard Duff, in Joel Newton's *Jennifer*, an accomplished replay of the *Spiral Staircase* strain of 'old dark house' picture. With Lupino as concierge of an empty California pile, wondering anxiously what became of the previous incumbent, the film was shot in February 1953 and remains historically significant as marking the changeover from Monogram Pictures to the more high-sounding Allied Artists. A bit earlier, on 10 December 1952, something called *The Neanderthal Man* began

shooting; though ascribed to Global Productions, this one is a grotesquely bad farrago very much in the old Monogram tradition. Here, writer-producer Jack Pollexfen – co-writer of *The Man from Planet X* and *The Son of Dr Jekyll* – built on Rouben Mamoulian's old theories about Mr Hyde as a Neanderthal throwback, outlining the fate of a modern-day Jekyll and Hyde called Professor Clifford Groves.

Holed up in California's High Sierras, Groves is played very badly by Robert Shayne, formerly the assistant to John Carradine in a genuine Monogram, *The Face of Marble*. "They laughed," he raves, "that pack of thick-headed, egotistical stuffed-shirts at the Naturalists' Club." Groves has already converted a tabby cat into a sabre-toothed tiger (in some of its more feral moments, a chain is clearly visible round its neck); we are also shown, in a sequence of photographs, the conversion of his mute Mexican maid into a racist, *Captive Wild Woman*-style grotesque. The Professor's own primitive state is laughable in the extreme, though in it he kills two yokels and rapes waitress Beverly Garland. The cinematographer here was Stanley Cortez, less than two years away from shooting *The Night of the Hunter*. Even more remarkable, the director was E A Dupont, who had created such silent classics as the German *Varieté* and the British *Piccadilly*.

The shock of seeing Dupont's name attached to *The Neanderthal Man* was echoed in the darkest depths of Poverty Row by an incomprehensible clinker called *Mesa of Lost Women*, which was shot in two phases with distinguished old-time cinematographers attached to both – Karl Struss in 1951 and Gilbert Warrenton in 1952. In this, mad scientist Jackie Coogan's glandular experiments result in a barely mobile giant spider and a mob of sultry spider women – among them Tandra Quinn, who was soon to play the transmogrifying maid in *The Neanderthal Man*.

A couple of years after *The Neanderthal Man*, Jack Pollexfen began filming the similarly titled *Indestructible Man* on 11 November 1954, this time as producer-director. Retaining Robert Shayne, Pollexfen cast him this time as a researcher whose quest for a cancer cure resurrects Lon Chaney Jr, in the process making him "a vicious, brutal animal with an almost inconceivable amount of strength." Chaney is an executed gangster called 'Butcher' Benton, whose remorseless campaign of liquidating his former associates qualifies the film as a rip-off of the Karloff picture *The Walking Dead*; the 287,000 volts with which Shayne irradiates him qualify it, further, as a rip-off of Chaney's own *Man Made Monster*. As a director, Pollexfen defaults, when in doubt, to tediously repetitive close-ups of Chaney's

Resurrected gangster Lon Chaney Jr and spangled burlesque dancer Marian Carr in *Indestructible Man* (1954)

eyes, and the film is further clogged by a dreary voice-over from the resident cop and a tidal wave of verbal diarrhoea in the dialogue. Granted virtually none of the latter, the increasingly raddled-looking Chaney makes Benton a sufficiently baleful figure, providing a bear-like contrast to Marian Carr's sweetly spangled burlesque dancer.

Indestructible Man wasn't the only 1950s title to qualify as a disguised remake. Back in 1952, *King Kong* (suitably edited for delicate post-war sensibilities) had been reissued to the tune of a $3 million gross; the following year, a humble Mutual Films production called *The Beast from 20,000 Fathoms* was put out by Warner Bros and made very nearly $5 million. In modernising the *Kong* template (colossal prehistoric creature gets loose in New York City), Eugene Lourié's film made the significant adjustment of ascribing the dinosaur's resurrection to atomic tests. The film also borrowed from *The Thing from Another World*, casting Kenneth Tobey in a leading role and setting its introductory scenes at an Arctic military outpost. Most importantly, it introduced a worthy successor to *Kong*'s Willis O'Brien in stop-motion animator Ray Harryhausen.

Another 1953 makeover, beginning on 12 February and issued through United Artists in September, was Felix Feist's *Donovan's Brain*. The second screen version of Curt Siodmak's novel, this eschewed the castellated Gothic of *The Lady and the Monster* in favour of the bland and featureless monochrome of 1950s SF, though it benefits from the ironic casting of Lew Ayres, formerly MGM's clean-limbed Dr Kildare, as the possessed Dr Cory. Steve Brodie's sleazy tabloid newshound is good value (proffering Donovan's

Rampaging, remote-controlled, radioactive: a new kind of zombie (Karl Davis) in *Creature with the Atom Brain* (1954)

morgue photos, he points out suggestively that "I took the bandages off so you can see the stitches"), but Nancy Davis is remarkably stiff as Cory's wife and the deus ex machina climax, in which the brain gets fried by a tackily animated lightning bolt, is a suspense-free letdown. Though the Red Scare had lent new currency to the mind control theme, Siodmak himself didn't get a chance to develop it; initially pencilled in as the film's director, he was sacked before filming began.

Apart from a sombre Anglo-German remake in 1962 called *Vengeance*, the *Donovan's Brain* story now had nowhere to go other than the livid absurdities of exploitation pictures like *The Man Without a Body* and *The Brain that Wouldn't Die*. In 1954, however, Siodmak siphoned its themes, together with a dash or two of *Black Friday*, into a diverting little pulp programmer of his own. Produced by Sam Katzman and directed by Edward L Cahn, *Creature with the Atom Brain* was made in a week over the Hallowe'en period and advertised the following summer with the improbable tag-line, "Here is horror that can happen NOW ... TO YOU!"

The voodoo that had raised zombies in previous decades is replaced by Siodmak with a more 1950s form of black magic; as a pipe-smoking police scientist (Richard Denning) theorises, the walking dead here are "remote-controlled creatures, their brains powered by atomic energy." A vengeful gangster is rubbing out his enemies via bodies stolen from the morgue, their brain matter supplanted by a control device, their visual impressions relayed to HQ via television – all this achieved by a renegade German scientist whom the gangster hooked up with in continental exile. The film begins intriguingly with one of the creatures leaving radioactive fingerprints on its latest victim; it ends with a splendid pitched battle between zombies and the police. On top of this, the 'Ordinary Joe' look of the undead killers places *Creature with the Atom Brain* alongside a later Edward L Cahn picture, *Invisible Invaders*, as a precursor of the seminal 1967 film *Night of the Living Dead*.

Further retreads ranged from imaginative to slavish to tenuous in the extreme. In the first category, Fritz Lang's 19-year-old classic *M* was remade in June 1950, with David Wayne taking over from Peter Lorre as the compulsive child-killer and the locale shifted to noirish American gangland. By the time of the film's release in June 1951, its director, Joseph Losey, had fetched up on the HUAC blacklist, later decamping to the UK in order to keep working.

Under the 'slavish' heading, Hugo Fregonese's *Man in the Attic* was made by Fox subsidiary Panoramic Productions; it's a low-rent, virtually shot-for-shot and essentially pointless remake of the old Fox success *The Lodger*, with Barré Lyndon doing little to his original script other than abolishing its gay subtext. Indeed, the Ripper actually gets to share some romantic clinches with his intended final victim and, rather than being motivated by the loss of an adored brother, inveighs against a flighty actress mother who "had the face of Heaven and the wretched heart of Jezebel." In the end, he explains, "She had become a woman of the streets, and it was in the streets that she died." This is true enough – it's revealed in the final reel that she was his first victim. Here too, a standard-issue, hell-for-leather coach chase replaces the backstage theatre pursuit that had been so effective in the original film.

The film began shooting in the last week of August 1953, with Jack Palance fresh from his black-clad, Oscar-nominated turn in *Shane*; bringing newly fashionable 'Method' techniques to the killer Slade, he

thereby fumbles the role completely. By coincidence, the beautiful Irish ingenue Constance Smith had appeared four years earlier in a British variant on the story called *Room to Let*; here, her frothy 1950s production numbers (apparently, "the latest in saucy, delightfully wicked dances and songs") are laughably inappropriate to the 1880s setting. The scenes of cobbled streets and impenetrable fog are persuasively done, but Palance seems to be competing with his Scotland Yard nemesis, Byron Palmer, not merely for the romantic interest of Smith but also for top prize in a 'who has the biggest and oiliest 1950s quiff?' competition. Twenty years later, Palance would bring similar qualities to the title role in a CBS TV movie of *Dracula*, with similarly mixed results.

In complete contrast, Roy Boulting's engaging *Run for the Sun*, made in September-October 1955, qualifies as a remake of *The Most Dangerous Game* only by the slimmest of margins, with Count Zaroff transmuted into a couple of ex-Nazis (Trevor Howard and Peter Van Eyck, the former clearly identifiable as Lord Haw-Haw), but with the refined sadism that made the original a horror picture left out entirely.

Another old reliable, the 'curse-encrusted gems' plot, resurfaced in the autumn of 1953 when Abner Biberman directed the mild voodoo adventure *The Golden Mistress* in the full glory of Haitian travelogue Technicolor. Edgar Allan Poe, meanwhile, made only sporadic appearances in the early 1950s. Produced in May 1951, Fletcher Markle's M-G-M quickie *The Man with a Cloak* features Joseph Cotten as Poe's arch-ratiocinator Dupin, though the story (based on John Dickson Carr's 'locked room' mystery *The Gentleman from Paris*) includes a nifty twist revealing Dupin as Poe himself. *The Tell-Tale Heart*, meanwhile, enjoyed a striking new incarnation as an Oscar-nominated short from the UPA animation studio, released in December 1953 and graced by the feline tones of James Mason. A further echo of *The Tell-Tale Heart* followed in 1955, when W Lee Wilder's tacky nautical melodrama *Manfish* had the murderous Victor Jory becoming unhinged by air bubbles rising to the surface rather than by a phantom heartbeat. Also featuring Lon Chaney Jr, the rest of the film took its treasure hunt theme from Poe's *The Gold Bug*, with 'Manfish' turning out to be nothing more than the name of a boat. "*Manfish* has more holes in it than a soup strainer," opined one trade reviewer, "but the entire production is so inept it doesn't make much difference."[11]

For a more substantial Poe adaptation, a whole new technology would be pressed into service, the better to have a homicidal ape apparently bursting the bounds of the screen and threatening the viewers themselves. It would only be made possible, however, by the success of another dusted-off old chestnut, this time an all-new version of *Mystery of the Wax Museum*.

MULTI-DIMENSIONAL MENACES

As 1952 shaded over into 1953, the threat of television gave rise to the formulation of audience-grabbing gimmicks designed to lure audiences back into cinemas. The widescreen formats championed by Roland West over two decades before gained new currency with the advent of Cinerama and two more manageable processes, Fox's CinemaScope and Paramount's VistaVision. Stereoscopic photography was a less immediately durable but equally startling innovation, first catching the public imagination when the independent jungle adventure *Bwana Devil* appeared in the last week of November 1952. Produced on a shoestring by Arch Oboler, the film cleaned up in spectacular style, with the result that Warner Bros (initiators of the talkie revolution some 25 years earlier) determined to be the first major studio to use Polaroid's Natural Vision process in a major release.

Warners' 20-year-old shocker *Mystery of the Wax Museum* was accordingly brought out of mothballs for remake purposes, with a roster of eye-popping 3-D effects as its principal attraction. The new film went into production as *The Wax Works* (the title its originator, Charles Belden, had given the story back in 1932), was budgeted at some $680,000 and finished its 28-day shooting schedule on 20 February 1953. It was hustled out with remarkable speed, opening in New York on 10 April under the new title *House of Wax*. Six days later, the film's LA premiere featured an old horror star, Bela Lugosi, performing for the newsreel cameras in shades and evening dress while toting a 'gorilla' on a leash. More auspiciously, the film itself saw the advent of an entirely new horror star, Vincent Price.

> *New York, 1902. When the gifted, and apparently wheelchair-bound, sculptor Henry Jarrod sets up a House of Wax, the ghoulish exhibits include hanged stockbroker Matthew Burke, who, as Jarrod's business partner in a previous venture, caused Jarrod to be almost incinerated in a museum fire. When Sue Allen begins to suspect that the figures of Burke and others aren't mere facsimiles, she finds herself marked for waxen immortality as Jarrod's newest Marie Antoinette.*

A turn-of-the-century New York street, rain pouring down, a gas lamp on the left and, on the right, molten monolithic letters spelling out *House of Wax* while projecting intimidatingly into the stalls. It's certainly an arresting opening (particularly when seen in 3-D)

Watched from his wheelchair by Vincent Price, Phyllis Kirk takes Frank Lovejoy's investigation into her own hands in *House of Wax* (1953)

HOUSE OF WAX

Warner Bros-First National 1953
88 minutes
Warnercolor and Natural Vision 3-Dimension
production began 19 January

Cinematographers: Bert Glennon, Peverell Marley, Robert Burks*; Art Director: Stanley Fleischer; Editors: Rudi Fehr, James Kitchen*; Sound: Charles Lang; Visual Consultant: Julian Gunzburg MD; Natural Vision Supervision: M L Gunzburg; Natural Vision Consultant: Lothrop Worth; Set Decorations: Lyle B Reifsnider; Wax Exhibits: Katherine Stubergh*; Make-up: Gordon Bau, George Bau*; Wardrobe: Howard Shoup; Music: David Buttolph; Orchestrations: Maurice de Packh; Assistant Director: Jimmy McMahon; Screenplay: Crane Wilbur (from a story by Charles Belden); Producer: Bryan Foy; Director: André de Toth

Vincent Price (Professor Jarrod); Frank Lovejoy (Lt Brennan); Phyllis Kirk (Sue Allen); Carolyn Jones (Cathy Gray); Paul Picerni (Scott Andrews); Roy Roberts (Matthew Burke); Angela Clarke (Mrs Andrews); Paul Cavanagh (Sidney Wallace); Dabbs Greer (Sgt Shane); Charles Buchinsky [later Charles Bronson] (Igor); Reggie Rymal (barker); uncredited: Oliver Blake ('waxwork' man); Leo Curley (portly man); Frank Ferguson (medical examiner); Mary Lou Holloway (Millie); Lyle Latell (waiter); Grandon Rhodes (surgeon); Riza Royce (Mrs Flannigan); Philip Tonge (Bruce Allison); Merry Townsend (usherette); Ruth Warren (scrubwoman); Nedrick Young (Leon Averill); Richard Lightner, Jack Mower (detectives); Joanne Brown, Shirley Whitney (girlfriends); Darwin Greenfield, Jack Kenney (lodgers); Eddie Parks, Jack Woody (morgue attendants)

An intermittently gripping shocker, *House of Wax* ... calls for Polaroid spectacles. Although the Natural Vision is an improvement on that in *Bwana Devil*, it still becomes blurry at times, and there is often little illusion of depth, particularly in closeups ... The picture's writing and direction are also blurry, and the extra dimension is used primarily as a trick. *Time*

Just before I left Los Angeles to come to London [to make *Dr Phibes Rises Again*], they were reviving *House of Wax* at Grauman's Chinese Theatre. It was my first real horror movie, and it's still doing fantastic business. It was the best four weeks opening they'd had in ages, and the picture was made 18 years ago. Vincent Price [quoted in Films Illustrated, February 1972]

and dissolves, with a mellifluous harp glissando, to a view of Vincent Price massaging the waxen torso of a female work-in-progress. It all seems very *Mystery of the Wax Museum* so far but, on closer inspection, Jarrod's exhibits are not only much more Americanised than Ivan Igor's in the earlier film (John Wilkes Booth and Pocahontas substituting for Voltaire and Queen Victoria, for example), they're also considerably less convincing. The work of septuagenarian Burbank-based sculptor Katherine Stubergh and her namesake daughter, they make Paul Cavanagh's visiting art critic seem like a credulous idiot when he claims that "These groups are like dimensional paintings of the Old Masters."

They burn brilliantly, however, and director André de Toth builds on the equivalent sequence in *Mystery of the Wax Museum* to create an obscenely beautiful tableau of bodily corruption. The wax slithering down the dummies' cheeks makes them appear to be weeping – and, whether one finds the Stubergh figures convincing or not, the spectacle of one man's whole artistic output "going up like a paint factory" is indeed a powerfully moving one. De Toth includes a few refinements of

his own – crimped hair flying off in fiery strips, glass eyeballs plopping out onto waxen cheeks – and throws in a climactic gas explosion for good measure.

The script for *House of Wax* was written by Crane Wilbur, whose play *The Monster* had been filmed by Roland West nearly 30 years earlier. Unfortunately, in simplifying the congested subplots of *Mystery of the Wax Museum*, Wilbur made the fatal error of getting rid of Jarrod's arsonist business partner almost immediately, the better to have him put on display in Jarrod's establishment later on. When a character has apparently burned someone alive and moments later is strangled in his own office by a horribly burned interloper, no audience member can fail to realise that the killer is Jarrod himself. On top of this, the monster make-up is too precisely tailored to Price's own features to maintain any of the 'Mystery' specified in the original film's title.

Even so, the film winds up with a dutiful, though redundant, replay of the 'heroine beats on villain's face and smashes it' routine. Moments before, Jarrod has risen from his wheelchair and strode firmly across to the quailing heroine, an odd development given that his earlier pursuit of the girl in his slouch-hatted 'monster' guise involved a spastic, and frankly comical, waddle. It's a flagrant cheat reminiscent of the Bat's inexplicable foot-dragging in another Roland West film, *The Bat Whispers* – suggesting that Wilbur was too irretrievably immersed in the hokey horror motifs of an earlier age to successfully reinvigorate a property like *Mystery of the Wax Museum*. "*House of Wax*," opined critic John McCarten at the time, "has, I think, set the movies back about forty-nine years. It could have set them back farther if there had been anything earlier to set them back to."[12]

The film has other problems. Phyllis Kirk's Sue is a strangely somnolent heroine, apparently suffering from post-traumatic stress on the death of her ditzy girlfriend and only rousing herself from lethargy at the climax. Carolyn Jones is merely irritating as the ill-fated, wasp-waisted Cathy, and both actresses seem corseted into dreary roles that are considerably less free-spirited than the ones played by Glenda Farrell and Fay Wray in the original. Thanks no doubt to the Production Code, the figure of Jean-Paul Marat has been deprived of the knife thrust bloodily into its naked chest, and the sculptor's junkie associate has been demoted to a mere alcoholic. Conversely, the film makes it clear that the heroine is naked in her final ordeal, as Fay Wray clearly wasn't in *Mystery of the Wax Museum*.

The film remains significant for its promotion of the 41-year-old Vincent Price from a useful, if vaguely sinister, character player to the rank of fully fledged horror star. Indeed, some of Wilbur's dialogue has an ironic ring in retrospect, as when Price, himself a high-minded art collector, mutters "The morbidly curious? Ha! I won't cater to them." Elsewhere, he gives a nicely kinky touch of digit envy to his examination of an apprentice's hands ("What I wouldn't give to have those fingers of yours") and comes across as a soft and epicene figure, quite unlike the hard and unflinching character played by Lionel Atwill in 1932. His monster make-up, too, is pink and pliable – like bubble-gum – in sharp contrast to the wood-effect "African war mask" worn by Atwill.

The film itself, however, is a by-the-numbers simplification of the original, with only one moment suggesting a better and more ghoulish picture. As Sue investigates Jarrod's darkened workshop, a disturbingly lifelike wax face-mask, brutally cut off at the upper lip, juts out over the heads of the audience in eerie 3-D, anticipating the trophy-room obscenities of *The Texas Chain Saw Massacre* by two decades.

House of Wax was a huge success, easily outclassing Columbia's attempt at 3-D, *Man in the Dark*, a clumsy Lew Landers remake of *The Man Who Lived Twice* that was released only the day before. Inevitably, Warner Bros-First National ordered up a 3-D *House of Wax* follow-up, the film going into production at the end of September 1953. The director was Roy Del Ruth, who in 1928 had made another Warners' gimmick picture, the all-talking *The Terror* – and the choice of subject may possibly have been influenced by Bela Lugosi's embarrassing LA publicity stunt for *House of Wax*. To filmgoers with long memories, Bela Lugosi plus a guy in a gorilla suit recalled the Universal chiller *Murders in the Rue Morgue*, a film of roughly similar vintage to *House of Wax*'s progenitor, *Mystery of the Wax Museum*. The new film utilised the so-called 'All-Media' camera, a process developed in-house as a cheaper alternative to licensing Natural Vision, and the title, initially *The Phantom Ape*, became the much more alluring *Phantom of the Rue Morgue*.

In turn-of-the-century Paris, Inspector Bonnard is baffled by a series of gruesome killings. Though Bonnard arrests the youthful Professor Paul Dupin, it eventually transpires that Dupin's older colleague, combined zoologist and menagerist Dr Marais, has been avenging himself on showgirls who snubbed him by presenting each of them with a bracelet fitted with tinkling bells. Using his expertise in conditioned reflexes, Marais has trained his pet Madagascan gorilla, Sultan, to seek out and dismember anyone wearing such a trinket.

Though not nearly as well remembered as *House of Wax*, *Phantom of the Rue Morgue* is actually a much more lavish affair, with a dazzlingly colourful Can-Can sequence and art direction that recalls John Huston's recently released Toulouse-Lautrec picture, *Moulin Rouge*. Cinematographer Peverell Marley, who had collaborated with Bert Glennon on *House of Wax*, uses the same

PHANTOM OF THE RUE MORGUE

Warner Bros-First National 1953
84 minutes; WarnerColor and 3-Dimension
production began 29 September

Cinematographer: J Peverell Marley; Art Director: Bertram Tuttle; Editor: James Moore; Sound: Stanley Jones; Set Decoration: William Kuehl; Make-up: Gordon Bau; Wardrobe: Moss Mabry; Music: David Buttolph; Orchestrations: Maurice de Packh; Assistant Director: Frank Mattison; Screenplay: Harold Medford, James R Webb, from Edgar Allan Poe's The Murders in the Rue Morgue; Producer: Henry Blanke; Director: Roy Del Ruth

Karl Malden (Dr Marais); Claude Dauphin (Inspector Bonnard); Patricia Medina (Jeannette Rovere); Steve Forrest (Professor Paul Dupin); Allyn McLerie (Yvonne); Anthony Caruso (Jacques); Veola Vonn (Arlette); Dolores Dorn (Camille); Merv Griffin (Georges Brevert); Paul Richards (René); Rolphe Sedan (LeBon); Erin O'Brien-Moore (wardrobe woman); The Flying Zacchinis; uncredited: Baynes Barron (circus manager); Marie Blake (Marie); Nan Boardman (Camille's mother); Virginia Brissac (well-dressed woman); Edward Colmans (well-dressed man); Henry Corden (Mignaud); Charles Couch (trampolinist); Walter Coy (Gendarme Arnot); Charles Gemora (Sultan [gorilla]); Don and Dolores Graham (dancers); Creighton Hale (bystander); Tom Hernandez (Gendarme Lara); Henry Kulky (Maurice [sailor]); Frank Lackteen (Gendarme Chauvet); George J Lewis (Gendarme Duval); Carl Milletaire (artist); Belle Mitchell (concierge); John Parrish (bar tender); Leonard Penn (Gendarme Dumas); George Selk (lamp lighter); Tito Vuola (Pignatelli)

Americans setting out to chill your blood hold, like the Founding Fathers, certain truths to be self-evident and inalienable. A mad scientist is good. A killer ape is better ... I rate the film as worth, if not an A for Art, at least an E for Effort. The Censor's marking is X for horror, conscientiously earned. *Daily Telegraph* [UK]

Up-and-coming star Steve Forrest has a brother who has already arrived at the top – one, Dana Andrews. Incidentally it was Steve who sprained his back during the filming of *Phantom of the Rue Morgue* as a result of the most exotic accident in the annals of Warner Bros. He was injured on a set representing the Paris zoo by tripping over an elephant's foot while being chased by a lion! from original Warner Bros press notes, 1954

Patricia Medina encounters veteran ape artist Charles Gemora in *Phantom of the Rue Morgue* (1953)

WarnerColor process to confer an alluringly soft and unreal glamour on the film, while the startling 3-D effects range from cascading balloons, a knife-throwing act, trampolinists and trapeze artists to a blinking ostrich, a leaping lion and even a foregrounded dog skeleton. There's also a bloodcurdling score by David Buttolph. Most importantly, Del Ruth and his editor, James Moore, work hard to infuse unwonted ferocity into the murder sequences.

For the time, these scenes really are hair-raising – brilliantly staged, executed with bags of kinetic energy and containing a disturbingly eroticised undertow that in 1953 was quite new. In this way they anticipate the gorier shockers that would come out of Britain at the end of the decade and the still nastier giallo thrillers produced in Italy in the 1960s and '70s. The victims do an awful lot of high-decibel screaming and are subsequently discovered with ripped stockings and bloodily lacerated legs provocatively splayed; an attack in an artist's atelier becomes an action-painting shambles of which even Jackson Pollock might have approved. There are a few absurdities involved, such as an ape-shaped hole in the atelier's skylight that's worthy of a Warner Bros cartoon. But the murders still pack a punch.

Intriguingly, in the film's second half the action defaults to male victims, with bloody close-ups of Marais and his uncouth assistant Jacques, as if trying to atone for the sexualised extremes of the first half. Also in the final stages, Del Ruth comes up with a grim scene that gives us an idea of what the murder sequences might have been like had actual limb-ripping been permissible in 1953. Smashing his way into a dress shop, Sultan chops up a shop-window mannequin and the pursuing Marais pauses to pick up one of the severed limbs. As a visual parallel to what Sultan does to his living victims, the scene was Del Ruth's response to the euphemistic 'melting dummies' in *House of Wax*.

That *Phantom* was recalled in later years by British filmmakers as well as Italian ones is clear from a few of the film's incidental details. Sultan's final assault on Marais, for example, is replicated in the 1958 film *Horrors of the Black Museum*, while the Hammer Films writer-producer Anthony Hinds echoed the film's rooftop ape-chases in both *The Curse of the Werewolf* and *Dracula Has Risen from the Grave*, adding to the latter film a girl's bloodied body dropping shockingly from inside a huge church bell. This was presumably Hinds' recollection of one of the best moments in *Phantom*, a first-

class shock effect (derived from Poe) in which a girl's inverted, green-faced corpse slips into view from its hiding place in a chimney.

The all-important killer gorilla in *Phantom* was the veteran ape-suit specialist Charles Gemora, who had played the equivalent role in Universal's *Murders in the Rue Morgue* and here gave place to former acrobat Nick Cravat for the more physical scenes. Sultan not only benefits from Gemora's sad-eyed performance but also from one of his best ever ape suits. The Pavlovian business by which Sultan is motivated to kill proves that *Phantom*, though a big and brassy A picture, is indebted to the more threadbare Bs of the 1940s, with Marais' bell-fitted bangles recalling the aftershave of *The Devil Bat* and the plucked feathers of *The Flying Serpent*. As well as following Pavlov, Marais also (rather prematurely) invokes Freud, telling the investigating officer that "These days, Inspector, everything is Freud or it is nothing; Freud and the libido." He should know, given that he turns out to be the guardian of a shrine to his dead wife. As for Inspector Bonnard – though charmingly played by Claude Dauphin, he's a conspicuously intransigent dunderhead who puts his faith in Lombroso's theories of criminal physiognomy. "It's so much easier to find a criminal who *looks* like a criminal," he claims.

Vincent Price masquerades as The Great Rinaldi in *The Mad Magician* (1953)

Sadly, the film's main stumbling block remains the thoroughly miscast Karl Malden, who gives his all in the completely unaccustomed role of a cultured Gothic necrophile but just isn't the right man for the job. One can only imagine his relief on returning to the post-war naturalistic mode, of which he was a master, in *On the Waterfront*, which started shooting in New Jersey directly after *Phantom* finished.

In March 1954, horror fans thrilling to a 3-D Technicolor ape in *Phantom of the Rue Morgue* only had to wait until May to see another. Harmon Jones' *Gorilla at Large* was made, like *Man in the Attic*, for Panoramic Productions, mixing up an unusually good-value cast (Anne Bancroft, Lee J Cobb, Cameron Mitchell, Lee Marvin, Raymond Burr) in a tame circus murder-mystery. For his part, Vincent Price encountered no apes, 3-D or otherwise, in the wake of his *House of Wax* celebrity. He was courted instead by David Diamond, producer of the old Karloff-Lugosi vehicle *The Raven*, for a new film of that name to be written by the same screenwriter, David Boehm. The project never got off the ground; had it done so, Price would have made his Poe debut seven years ahead of time.

Price was free, therefore, to get together again with several of the key personnel involved in *House of Wax* – producer Bryan Foy, writer Crane Wilbur, cinematographer Bert Glennon, make-up man George Bau – for an independent quickie, distributed by Columbia, that eschewed the original's Technicolor and stereo sound but retained the 3-D. *The Mad Magician* started on 14 September 1953 and had John Brahm in the director's chair, an apt choice given the great chunks of *The Lodger* and *Hangover Square* that Wilbur had worked into his screenplay. The scenario also includes a lady crime novelist (charmingly played by Mrs Crane Wilbur, Lenita Lane) and an exhilaratingly crazed ending in which Price and Patrick O'Neal wrestle within inches of a blazing 'crematorium' device, an obvious nod to Wilbur's 1910s notoriety as Pearl White's leading man.

Price is Don Gallico, an inventor of elaborate stage illusions, struggling to establish himself as a magician in his own right ("I guess I'm just a ham at heart") but stymied by the intervention of his business partner, Ross Ormond (Donald Randolph). The latter is soon decapitated in a buzz-saw contraption, whereupon Gallico assumes his identity and later kills the so-called Great Rinaldi, assuming his in turn.

The trouble with all this, as in *House of Wax*, is that Price is so unmistakable he never looks like anyone other than Price, however elaborate the make-up. Presumably to counteract this problem, poor Donald Randolph is made to look like a taxidermist's dummy even when still alive. There's a lot to enjoy, however, notably John Emery's ridiculous French accent as Rinaldi, a hilarious sequence in which Gallico mislays a valise containing Ormond's severed head (he chases it in a hansom cab all over New York) and several really outstanding depth effects, extolled by 3-D historian R M Hayes as "some of the finest examples of stereoscopic cinematography ... [*The Mad Magician*] may be the clearest and sharpest 35mm 3-D feature ever made."[13]

CREEPY-CRAWLIES IN ALL SIZES

The Mad Magician wrapped on 3 October 1953; three days later, Universal-International began shooting *Creature from the Black Lagoon*, a contribution to the 3-D craze that spawned a classic monster in the time-honoured Universal tradition. Recalling an Amazon legend passed on to him by the cinematographer Gabriel Figueroa over ten years earlier, producer William Alland initiated what was known in production as just *The Black Lagoon*, utilising a brilliant Creature design created by former Disney artist Millicent Patrick.

The 'lost world' story devised in fulfilment of Alland's idea was unapologetically indebted to *King Kong*, starting with a taloned fossil hand being discovered by former silent heart-throb Antonio Moreno in "a limestone deposit dating back to the Devonian age." He takes it to Richards Carlson and Denning, smoothly professional actors who were fast becoming emblematic of 1950s science fiction, here playing a heroic scientist and his shiftless sponsor.

Julia Adams recoils from Universal's classic post-war monster, the *Creature from the Black Lagoon* (1953)

Their incursion into the Gill Man's domain faithfully follows *Kong* in portraying the Creature as a noble savage, rightly affronted by the arrogance of 'civilised' man and wreaking havoc in retaliation.

Director Jack Arnold had recently been responsible for Universal's 3-D summer smash of 1953, *It Came from Outer Space*, in which he displayed a remarkable gift for eerie desert landscapes. In *Creature*, this is transferred to the shimmering, marbled surface of the so-called Black Lagoon and, below it, the Creature's subterranean caverns, roiling with hellish plumes of white mist. Also below the calm surface of the lake is what Carlson aptly calls "another world," captured in underwater photography that's stunning by any standards but all the more so for being rendered in the astounding clarity of 3-D. The underwater sequences were taken by a second unit at Wakulla Springs in Florida; perfectly matched with the surface shots in Hollywood, the combination produces a genuine tour de force when the heroine goes swimming, unaware of the enraptured Creature matching her movements just a few feet below. The strange, ritualistic beauty of the sequence is capped by the crew's ominous discovery of a tattered net, clearly shredded by the Creature in a paroxysm of sexual frustration.

The film is full of similarly striking set-pieces, from the bludgeoning violence of the Creature's attack on Moreno's encampment to the uniquely eerie shots of the captured Gill Man looking up, gimlet-eyed and gasping, through the bars of his watery cage. The score includes a blaring, three-note trumpet motif that is repeated with mind-numbing iteration every time the Creature so much as shows a claw, and Julia Adams' role quickly devolves into a similarly mind-numbing screamathon. But neither of these drawbacks prevented the film – made for less than $464,000 – from rapidly raking in $3 million.

Earlier in 1953, the 3-D process had been pressed into service for a film that, like *Creature from the Black Lagoon*, pitted the ubiquitous Richard Carlson against an amphibian throwback. William Cameron Menzies' *The Maze* began shooting on 20 April and was on view in LA by the beginning of July; so early was it in the history of Allied Artists that its copyright notice is attributed to Monogram. The source was a 1945 novel by Maurice Sandoz that, like several of his books, was illustrated by Salvador Dalí. Dalí's participation in the film version was announced but didn't eventually happen; even so, Menzies created a bizarre picture that oscillates from surrealism to plain silliness and back again.

The plot proceeds from a long-lived premise; as in *Son of Frankenstein* and *The Wolf Man*, a young-ish American (Carlson) returns to his ancestral home in

Europe and uncovers a grim family legacy. But the film would prove prophetic in establishing another durable motif, that of 'the thing in the attic'. Where the upper reaches of Whale's *The Old Dark House* yielded a capering pyromaniac, *The Maze* goes further, showcasing a 203-year-old Scottish laird who suffers from "some sort of congenital illness." As a result, there's a touch of H P Lovecraft in Menzies' splendid nocturnal scenes of British ingenue Veronica Hurst quailing in her bed as *something* squelches about outside her door. The new note struck here is the suggestion that there's something out there that isn't merely dangerous, but somehow obscene.

True to his origins as a brilliant production designer, Menzies makes the most of Craven Castle's arid interiors and various fog-bound Highland settings reminiscent of Ulmer's *The Man from Planet X*. And, though the film moves rather too slowly for its own good, a palpable sense of dread is created as Menzies drops various ominous hints – a high view of the castle's ornamental maze as something takes a night-time tour of it; a clump of seaweed found in an upper room; webbed footprints on the stairs; the agitated Carlson consulting a book called 'Teratology', which later discloses a baleful subtitle: 'The Study of Monstrosities, Serious Malformations or Deviations from the Normal Structure in Man'.

Then there's the outrageous hilarity of the ending, in which Sir Roger Philip MacTeam is revealed as a man-sized frog, trumpeting his embarrassment like a bull elephant and plunging to his death from a high window in a crowd-pleasing orgy of 3-D. Sir Roger is a corridor-hopping absurdity, of course, yet there's something strangely moving, not only about Carlson's final tribute to him ("For over 200 years he suffered the torture of knowing he was a monster and feeling he was a man"), but also Menzies' sombre final shot, which shows the laird's freshly turned grave and a headstone reading 1750-1953.

In the wake of the unexpected high offered by *Creature from the Black Lagoon*, Universal-International came up with a boring *Cat People* makeover called *Cult of the Cobra*, directed by former editor Francis D Lyon. When, at the end of World War II, a bunch of airforce men cross an Indian snake cult called the Lamians, four out of the six don't get to enjoy their demob for very long (in a very 1950s-looking New York) thanks to the presence of a marauding cobra-woman.

To signal an oncoming transformation, there's an attempt at optically darkening the woman's face in the style of *Cat People*, while the various 'snake's eye view' shots are identical to the 'alien's eye view' shots in *It Came from Outer Space*. But the frustrated romance

Veronica Hurst and Katherine Emery wonder what seaweed can be doing in a Scottish castle in *The Maze* (1953)

between Faith Domergue and Marshall Thompson puts the Lewton film through a Mills and Boon filter of the "Oh Tom, if it could only be so simple" variety, and Domergue (deputising for Mari Blanchard) appears merely listless rather than doom-laden, falling well short of the figure of sexual terror she could have been. The monster, too, is a mere cobra, in no way fulfilling the trailer's definition of a Lamia as "the head and breast of a woman, the body of a serpent."

The film began shooting at Universal on 26 October 1954, just two days ahead of *Abbott and Costello Meet the Mummy*, with which it shares an impressive temple interior. The original snake ceremonial, in fact, is done with considerable verve, including a wildly erotic routine by dance group the Carlssons that was explicitly referenced 17 years later in the tiger-woman dance of *Vampire Circus*.

By this time, Universal had come under the control of Decca Records, paving the way for its ultimate absorption into MCA. Production-line efficiency still prevailed, however. Jack Arnold's *Creature from the Black Lagoon*, for example, spawned two rapid-fire sequels. Arnold's *Revenge of the Creature* began on 21 June 1954, followed by John Sherwood's *The Creature Walks Among Us* on 25 August the following year. The first is made interesting by its transferral of the chained creature to Florida's Marineland, thus pointing up the original story's *Kong* derivation and furnishing a remarkable image of affluent tourists fleeing in panic from the atavistic gill man. There are also engaging scenes of the creature stalking student ichthyologist Lori Nelson and busting up an evening of hot jazz at the Lobster House club. Unfortunately, an ill-advised adjustment to the creature's appearance was made by bugging out its eyes, and the film devolves into a ludicrous third act in which our smug hero, John Agar, joins the Coast Guard on a protracted creature hunt.

Forsaking the 3-D of its predecessors, *The Creature Walks Among Us* labours under a more straitened budget and an unusually high gibberish quotient, but it's otherwise a much more intriguing proposition than the first sequel. There's a laudable stab at profundity here, with a blandly unhinged scientist (Jeff Morrow) announcing that "The creature can be changed ... [to] bring a new species into existence." Suffering third-degree burns, the gill man is surgically altered to become more human; shots of its eyes peering dully from behind a screen of bandages are truly memorable. Dressed in a lumpen suit of sail cloth, the now gill-free creature foils a rapist and kills a mountain lion, finally going on a splendid rampage at Morrow's Sausalito home and escaping to a deserted headland. There, in a haunting final shot, it looks forlornly out to sea as if contemplating suicide by drowning.

As well as being modelled on *King Kong*, the 'undiscovered species in uncharted area' theme of *Creature from the Black Lagoon* and its sequels may well have derived greater topicality from contemporaneous reports about the fabled Yeti of the Himalayas, a creature duly featured in W Lee Wilder's *The Snow Creature*, Jerry Warren's *Man Beast* and Kenneth G Crane's *Half Human*. (The last of these was a hideous US bastardisation, with footage featuring John Carradine added, of a much more accomplished Japanese film, Ishirō Honda's *Jū Jin Yuki Otoko*.) These tacky potboilers would be effortlessly eclipsed in 1957 by a British thriller, made by Hammer, called *The Abominable Snowman*, which in many respects plays like screenwriter Nigel Kneale's more cerebral riposte to *Creature from the Black Lagoon*.

On the first day of June 1955, with *Revenge of the Creature* lately released to the nation's cinemas, Jack Arnold started work on another UI monster movie, the splendid *Tarantula*. In discreetly reworking H G Wells' *The Food of the Gods*, this one reached back ten years to Universal's inglorious attempt to make a star of real-life acromegalic Rondo Hatton. The bone-distorting horrors here are merely make-up, however, with scientist Leo G Carroll going the way of his deformed associates when his efforts to perfect an artificial nutrient result in acromegaly. They result, too, in a monstrously enlarged spider, climactically napalmed by jet pilot Clint Eastwood. Clifford Stine's special effects would reach greater heights in Arnold's exceptional *The Incredible Shrinking Man*, which was shot in June-July 1956 and pitted the miniaturised Grant Williams against a basement spider, among other things.

These inflated arachnids owed their inception to a remarkable Warner Bros picture called *Them!* Originally intended for 3-D, Gordon Douglas' film was shot at the same time UI were making *Creature from the Black Lagoon*, and on its release in June 1954 proved itself Warners' most lucrative film of the year. This despite the venerable Jack L Warner's withering judgment, after a preview at California's Huntington Park, that "Anyone who wants to make any more ant pictures will go to Republic!"[14]

The film followed Paramount's *The Naked Jungle* into release by only a few months, its success seemingly uncompromised by the fact that cinemagoers had already seen Charlton Heston doing battle with millions of South American army ants in the full glory of Technicolor. The difference, of course, was that the ants in *Them!* are the size of King Kong. At first confined to the New Mexico desert (mutated, inevitably, by post-war atomic tests), they finally hole up in the storm drains of Los Angeles, offering an eerily claustrophobic view of winged princesses gathered in the ultimate chamber moments before being flame-throwered to kingdom

Joan Weldon flees from an elephantine New Mexico ant in *Them!* (1953)

come. At the beginning of the film, Douglas conjures a different kind of eeriness, showing a traumatised little girl (played by the aptly named Sandy Descher) meandering through the Joshua trees and tumbleweed of an arid expanse (actually the Mojave Desert), still clutching her broken doll while the dunes resound to the weird keening of the unseen ants.

Ted Sherdeman's script is tightly constructed and full of quotable lines. "We may be witness to a Biblical prophecy come true," speculates the delightful Edmund Gwenn as elderly entomologist Dr Medford, excitedly unravelling a desert mystery that is laid out with immaculate precision in the opening reels. The wide-eyed wandering of the catatonic little girl, the weird preponderance of sugar at her missing parents' smashed-up trailer, the corpse of 'Gramps' discovered under a trapdoor in a similarly devastated general store – all these sinister portents lead up to an electrifying statement from the pathologist on the case. "And here's one for Sherlock Holmes," he deadpans. "There was enough formic acid in him to kill 20 men." The reference to Sherlock Holmes is apt, given that, as ominous curtain lines go, this one is right up there with Dr Mortimer's "Mr Holmes, they were the footsteps of a gigantic hound!"

WEST COUNTRY GOTHIC, COLD WAR ALIENATION

As well as 3-D, the other great innovation of the early 1950s was CinemaScope, memorably dismissed in Jean-Luc Godard's 1963 film *Contempt* as "only good for snakes and funerals." The speaker was Fritz Lang, whose first experiment in the new format, *Moonfleet*, had been shot at M-G-M from August to October 1954. Radically altered from J Meade Falkner's original novel, the film begins with a strikingly Gothic prologue, heavily influenced by David Lean's *Great Expectations*, in which a small boy wanders a lonely road in 18th century Dorset, stumbles upon the eerie, blank-eyed stare of an ornamental angel and passes out at the (entirely unexplained) intrusion of a clawing hand. He wakes to find himself ringed round by a grotesque bunch of smugglers, later encountering a hanged corpse in irons and, deep in his subterranean ancestral crypt, an exposed skeleton.

Elsewhere, widescreen Eastmancolor luxuriance is well to the fore and there's a typically smooth performance from Stewart Granger as the boy's equivocal guardian, "a man of bad character and evil reputation" who only does the decent thing when mortally skewered by George Sanders. Though smooth on screen, Granger was typically abrasive in his estimate of the finished film, saying, "I hated working with Fritz Lang – he was a Kraut and it was a bloody awful film. I wanted to produce and act it in Cornwall and made them buy the book ... [but] *Moonfleet* was not Lang's type of film – it is a romantic child's film."[15]

Despite signs of indifference on Lang's part, the result remains valuable as a swashbuckling English Gothic transferred intact to a Hollywood soundstage (together with various rugged locations around Laguna and Malibu), backed up by all the meticulous expertise of a big studio and with a whole roster of British character actors (including horror veterans Lester Matthews, Skelton Knaggs, Alan Napier and Elspeth Dudgeon) to authenticate the enterprise. Indeed, the film would exert a strong influence on bona-fide British pictures; its West Country contraband operation antedates such films as *Captain Clegg* and *Fury at Smugglers' Bay*, while its tempestuous gypsy dancer and hedonistic local gentry would be echoed in Hammer's 1958 version of *The Hound of the Baskervilles*. It also has gorgeously bogus painted panoramas of lowering skies and beetling rock formations, plus world-class glamour in the shape of Viveca Lindfors, Liliane Montevecchi and the smoky-voiced Ealing import Joan Greenwood.

The CinemaScope gaudiness of *Moonfleet* stood in marked contrast to the monochrome alienation of Robert Aldrich's *Kiss Me Deadly*, which wrapped two days before Christmas 1954 and gave a Cold War twist to the grisly Mickey Spillane thriller on which it was based. Forced (by, ironically, the still vigilant PCA) to ditch the drugs angle featured in Spillane's novel, screenwriter A I Bezzerides substituted a leather-bound box as the 'Great Whatsit' being tracked down by brutish detective Mike Hammer (Ralph Meeker). Albert Dekker's effete Dr Soberin describes what's inside it as "the head of the Medusa," warning the insatiably curious Gabrielle (Gaby Rodgers) that "Whoever looks on her will be changed, not into stone, but into brimstone and ashes." Explicitly likened by Soberin to the mythical Pandora, Gabrielle opens it anyway, unleashing a nuclear apocalypse from which Hammer either does or does not escape, depending on which cut of the film you see.

Amid the noirish, hard-boiled pulp of *Kiss Me Deadly*, the film's truly astounding ending touched one of the rawest nerves of 1950s America. Another was played upon with an expert hand by Don Siegel, who in March 1955 began shooting a film version of Jack Finney's novel *The Body Snatchers* for producer Walter Wanger. Finney's story had recently appeared in *Collier's Weekly*, the serialisation winding up just before Christmas, and it was set quite literally where he lived – in Mill Valley, not far from San Francisco. Though screenwriter

Daniel Mainwaring would invent a location of his own, the workaday 'where you live' immediacy of the original was faithfully – indeed, hair-raisingly – preserved in the finished film, which on release acquired the extended title *Invasion of the Body Snatchers*.

> *In the small California town of Santa Mira, little Jimmy Grimaldi claims tearfully that his mother is no longer his mother, while Wilma Lentz is adamant that her Uncle Ira isn't her Uncle Ira. These and similar claims are dismissed by a psychiatrist, Dr Danny Kauffman, as "an epidemic of mass hysteria." But the local GP, Dr Miles Bennell, comes to a different conclusion when he encounters weird, half-formed simulacra of his friend Jack Belicec and sweetheart Becky Driscoll.*

Though several Californian locations were employed, it was the picture-perfect Sierra Madre that stood in most conspicuously for the film's fictitious Santa Mira. With 'mira' sounding a little like 'mirror', Mainwaring's choice of name proved an apt one twice over, for the film not only exploited the time-honoured doppelgänger horror of people being replaced by mirror images; it also held up a mirror to American society in the context of a gripping thriller.

In fact, the film's over-riding theme – loss of identity via alien infiltration – is punched across so forcefully that the phrase 'pod people' has long since entered the language. These aliens get to Santa Mira's upstanding citizens while they sleep, replacing them with physically perfect but utterly soulless doubles hatched from large seed pods – "taking [them] over cell for cell, atom for atom." In a playfully subversive touch, their spokesman is the local psychiatrist, who sounds alarmingly plausible when pointing out that "There's no pain. Suddenly, while you're asleep, they'll absorb your minds, your memories. And you're reborn into an untroubled world." Distilled to its essence, his philosophy is "Love, desire, ambition, faith: without them, life's so simple."

As a paranoid parable *Invasion of the Body Snatchers* has few peers, though *Quatermass 2* – which Nigel Kneale was writing while *Body Snatchers* was in production – matches its power from a specifically British perspective. Where Kneale imagined an invasion by stealth that all too believably infected the Tory government, Finney, Mainwaring and Siegel were careful to exclude any overtly political angle. As a result *Body Snatchers* has remained open to entirely opposite interpretations, with the fear of being surrounded by 'them' glossed as both an anti-Communist statement and a coded attack on McCarthyism. Siegel himself considered the majority of Americans disturbingly pod-like even at the time, and it's as a more generalised warning against conformism that the film works best. "It's a malignant disease spreading through the whole country," says Miles. As he does so, Siegel gives us an aerial view of the town square; it's 7.45 on a Saturday morning and already multiple pods are being distributed in businesslike fashion from three trucks.

Lean and tautly paced, the film boasts more skin-crawling moments than any dozen of its contemporaries put together. Some are tiny, yet still powerful. Wilma Lentz's fears about Uncle Ira – "There was a special look in his eye; that look's gone" – are confided to Miles even as Ira himself calmly mows the lawn a short distance away. Siegel's mastery of his material is visible right here, conferring an indefinable breath of the sinister on the otherwise humdrum sight of a pipe-smoking middle-aged man methodically pushing a lawn-mower up and down.

Other creepy details proliferate rapidly. The first appearance of one of the half-formed pod people, prone on Jack Belicec's pool table, is looked down upon by a framed piece of artwork for (presumably) one of Jack's novels; the title, *Miroir noir*, emphasises the dark mirror represented by Jack's unborn doppelgänger – or, as Miles puts it, his 'blank'. The film's touches of humour are decidedly dark too, notably a bizarre Santa Mira soirée in which Becky's dad walks in with a seed pod and Miles' secretary recommends he put it in her baby's playpen, noting complacently that "There'll be no more tears." Later, our first look at one of the seed pods in action – suppurating obscenely as it squeezes out a human facsimile in Jack's greenhouse – comes in the midst of a supposedly cosy barbecue party, complete with Martinis.

The greenhouse horror acts as a cue for the film's frantic third act, in which Siegel ratchets up the tension to a nearly unbearable pitch as the townspeople pursue Miles and Becky into the hills. First, the lovers give themselves an impromptu burial, hiding beneath floor slats in an abandoned mine shaft. Later, Siegel supplements their last desperate embrace with huge, horrifying close-ups of Becky's dead-eyed stare and Miles' traumatised recoil. For Becky, we realise, has surrendered to sleep since we last saw her, filling the moment with a really potent mixture of pity and terror.

Miles' climactic meltdown on the freeway, desperately trying to flag down indifferent motorists while shrieking "You're next!" directly into camera, remains shatteringly effective despite the unwelcome presence of a tacked-on epilogue. Insisted upon by Allied Artists president Steve Broidy, this lame coda sought to draw the film's fangs by suggesting the

A greenhouse horror interrupts Martini time for Dana Wynter, Carolyn Jones, King Donovan and Kevin McCarthy in *Invasion of the Body Snatchers* (1955)

FBI would soon sort out the pod problem. Siegel's dynamic staging and Kevin McCarthy's terrific portrait of end-of-the-line despair are proof against this adulteration, however. Very different from the bovine male leads characteristic of 1950s SF, McCarthy is responsible, just as much as Siegel, for 'selling' Finney's nightmare premise. The film was a sizable hit and got good notices too. Britain's Margaret Hinxman, for example, called it "a triumph for a low-budget, black and white horror film," noting also that "If this were a grander film, Kevin McCarthy's performance would merit an Oscar nomination."[16]

Where Don Siegel used Sierra Madre as his Santa Mira duplicate, John Parker turned to the nocturnal streets of Venice California for what was undoubtedly the strangest film on display in 1955. *Dementia*, a 60-minute avant-garde nightmare made in mid-1953 but delayed by protracted censorship crises, explores the childhood trauma of a psychotic young woman identified only as 'The Gamin'. Intriguingly, the film contains no dialogue, instead resounding to a mesmerising score by George Antheil and the ethereal warblings of Marni Nixon, who sounds uncannily like a Theremin.

The girl (played by Parker's secretary, Adrienne Barrett) descends from her neon-lit bedsit to wander the streets, encountering, in addition to various Skid Row bums, *Freaks* veteran Angelo Rossitto in his real-life role of Hollywood news-vendor. In a mist-wreathed graveyard, she is accosted by a tall man in a black stocking-mask, who shows her primal scenes from her past – her father's killing of her mother, her own act of vengeful parricide – all restaged (domestic furniture and all) in the cemetery itself. She subsequently stabs a predatory fat man with a flick-knife, watches him plunge to the street below in a flotilla of dollar bills, and then hacks off his hand when she realises he's still clutching an incriminating pendant. The hand is stashed among the blooms in a flower-seller's basket but turns up later, still alive and clutching, in the girl's dresser-drawer – but not before she has been inducted into a nightclub playing host to jazz combo Shorty Rogers and His Giants.

The sustained surrealism of *Dementia* is occasionally naïve but rarely less than fascinating, and also downright eerie when the girl's attempt to hack off

INVASION OF THE BODY SNATCHERS

Walter Wanger Pictures 1955
80 minutes; SuperScope
production began 23 March

Cinematographer: Ellsworth Fredericks; Production Designer: Edward Haworth; Editor: Robert S Eisen; Sound: Ralph Butler; Sound Editor: Del Harris; Special Effects: Milt Rice; Set Decoration: Joseph Kish; Make-up: Emile LaVigne; Hair Stylist: Mary Westmoreland; Music: Carmen Dragon; Music Editor: Jerry Irvin; Assistant Directors: Richard Maybery, Bill Beaudine Jr; Screenplay: Daniel Mainwaring, based on the Collier's Magazine serial by Jack Finney; Producer: Walter Wanger*; Director: Don Siegel

Kevin McCarthy (Dr Miles Bennell); Dana Wynter (Becky Driscoll); Larry Gates (Dr Dan Kauffman); King Donovan (Jack Belicec); Carolyn Jones (Theodora 'Teddy' Belicec); Jean Willes (Sally [Miles' nurse]); Ralph Dumke (Nick [policeman]); Virginia Christine (Wilma Lentz); Tom Fadden (Uncle Ira); Kenneth Patterson (Stanley Driscoll); Guy Way (Officer Sam Janzek); Eileen Stevens (Anne Grimaldi); Beatrice Maude (Grandma Grimaldi); Jean Andren (Aunt Eleda); Bobby Clark (Jimmy Grimaldi); Everett Glass (Dr Pursey); Dabbs Greer (Mac Lomax [gas station man]); Pat O'Malley (baggage man); Guy Rennie (proprietor of Sky Terrace restaurant); Marie Selland (Martha Lomax); Sam Peckinpah (Charlie [meter reader]); Harry J Vejar (pod carrier); uncredited: Whit Bissell (Dr Hill); Richard Deacon (Dr Bassett); Robert Osterloh (ambulance

Utilizing a basic fiction that could have overtaxed the most cooperative fan's credulity under other handling, the producer [Walter Wanger] and his skilled director, Don Siegel, compound mystery, suspense and timing so expertly that the picture rides a high, swift road from starting point to pounding conclusion. The attraction is among the best the science-fiction field has yielded. *Motion Picture Herald*

Allied Artists had an old-fashioned credo that horror pictures couldn't have humor. I had a great deal of humor in the picture and, though they cut out a lot, they didn't totally succeed ... The main thing about the picture, however, was that it was about something, and that's rare ... People, without being vegetables, are becoming vegetables. I don't know what the answer is except an awareness of it. Don Siegel [quoted in *Cinefantastique*, Winter 1973]

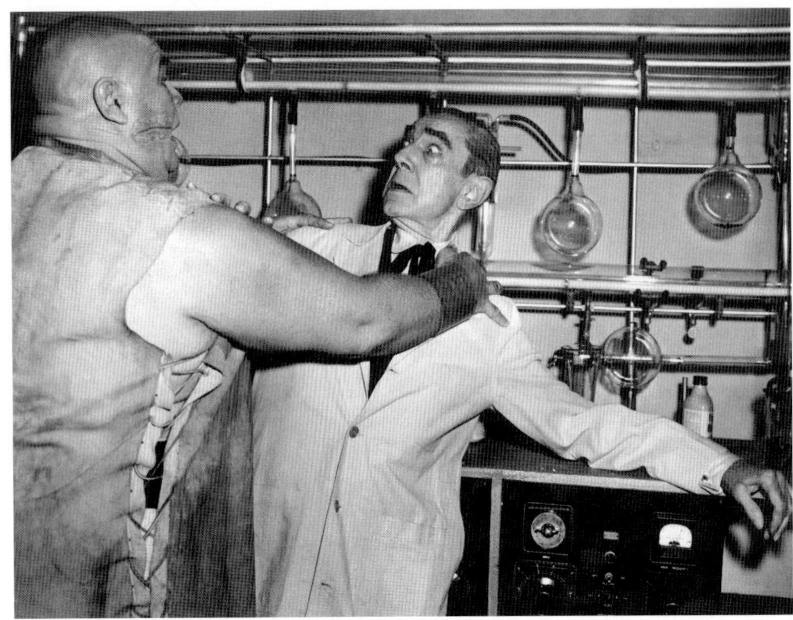

Tor Johnson rebels against the septuagenarian Bela Lugosi in *Bride of the Monster* (1954)

the fat man's hand is attended by a circle of well-heeled but stocking-faced onlookers. "Miss Electra's Avant Garde Phobia (Sexual, Of Course) is Legal though Gruesome," announced *Variety* on the film's eventual emergence in December 1955, though another two years would elapse before it was put out commercially. Entrepreneur Jack H Harris gave it a more sellable title – *Daughter of Horror* – and attached a cod-spooky voice-over spoken by TV personality Ed McMahon. "Come with me into the tormented, haunted, half-lit night of the insane," he begins, later identifying himself as 'The Demon' (ie, the blank-faced man in the cemetery), the similarly faceless onlookers as 'The Ghouls' and the jazzers in the nightclub as the girl's "kind of people" – that is to say, dangerous lunatics.

END OF AN ERA

Dementia was photographed (very handsomely) by William C Thompson, whose experience at the bottom of the barrel stretched back 20 years to Dwain Esper's *Maniac*. At the time of *Dementia*, he was also in league with a quixotic young filmmaker called Edward D Wood Jr, who in 1953 featured the ailing Bela Lugosi in the notorious *Glen or Glenda*. Mouthing inscrutable aphorisms as 'The Spirit', Lugosi apparently was unaware of the film's subject matter, which was transvestism and trans-sexuality. After a stint at the Silver Slipper Saloon in Las Vegas in *The Bela Lugosi Revue*, by October 1954 Lugosi was back in Wood's demi-monde orbit, playing the insane Dr Eric Vornoff in *Bride of the Atom*, who proposes, from the seclusion of his "forsaken jungle hell," to "perfect my own race of people, a race of atomic supermen which will conquer the world."

A cult has since grown up around the ineptitude of Wood's films, but *Bride of the Atom* (whose title was rapidly amended to *Bride of the Monster*) offers a genuinely moving envoi to Lugosi, whose last speaking role this was. Just turned 72, he drops his head in marvellously eloquent fashion when offered the chance to return to his homeland, muttering "I have no home" in tones of quiet desolation. He may look like a shadow of his former self, but the balletic precision of his hand movements (incorporating gestures dating back to *Dracula* and *White Zombie*) is as hypnotic as ever. The bald-pated Swedish wrestler Tor Johnson is on hand as Vornoff's mute henchman Lobo, a character analogous to the ape that attended Lugosi in *Murders in the Rue Morgue*. Inevitably, Lobo finally goes berserk and subjects Vornoff to his own process, whereupon Vornoff becomes an unnaturally tall, rampaging superman. It's actually Universal's old stunt man Eddie Parker in plainly visible platform boots, and it's Parker, too, who plays Vornoff's ignominious death scene, struggling with a prop octopus in Hollywood's Griffith Park.

When *Bride of the Atom* opened in Hollywood on 11 May 1955, the event was designed as a Lugosi benefit, for the previous month the actor had made headlines by voluntarily appealing for drug rehabilitation; persistent leg pains had long since made him a slave to morphine and other painkillers. By November, Lugosi's former co-star Boris Karloff was appearing on Broadway in Jean Anouilh's *The Lark*, garnering rave reviews, enjoying a run of over 200 performances and earning a Tony nomination. The recovered Lugosi, meanwhile, was pinning his hopes on an Ed Wood project called *The Ghoul Goes West*. It didn't happen.

Lugosi's old associate Sam Katzman – who had been behind the actor's long run of Monogram vehicles in the previous decade – was meanwhile going from strength to strength. Katzman's former Monogram

business partner, Jack Dietz, had made *The Beast from 20,000 Fathoms* and foolishly sold it on to Warner Bros. Katzman was cannier, manufacturing a slew of 'Jungle Jim' programmers prior to making *Creature with the Atom Brain* in late 1954. Twelve months later, Katzman's Clover Productions turned out another highly effective SF-horror hybrid. Called *The Werewolf*, its ten-day schedule began on 10 December 1955 and the location was California's Big Bear Lake, whose snow-covered expanses were to lend the proceedings a memorably forlorn atmosphere. Reaching cinemas the following July, the film was double-featured by Columbia with a more typical 1950s title, *Earth vs the Flying Saucers*. Both halves of the bill were directed by Fred F Sears and produced by Katzman.

Steven Ritch is Dr Duncan Marsh, who stumbles into the closed community of Mountaincrest and tells the kindly local GP that "Those other doctors did something to me." Chief among those other doctors is Morgan Chambers (George Lynn), who's introduced in the white coat and black goggles of Dr Rigas in *Man Made Monster* while wolves prowl in nearby cages like the lupine charges of Dr Cameron in *The Mad Monster*. Chambers' wolves, however, have been exposed to radiation, his ultimate aim being to create an elite group of humans to weather the inevitable apocalypse. The GP (Ken Christy) points up the moral in a homey speech that begins, "We don't feel it much up here in a place like Mountaincrest, but the world's a place of change." The film devolves into a prolonged wolfman hunt in which the plaid-jacketed gunmen seem like the missing link between Universal's torch-wielding villagers and the trigger-happy rednecks of *Night of the Living Dead*. But the glimmering monochrome of the forest vistas remains arresting, and in any case the film comes up elsewhere with some highly unusual scenes, notably a tearful reunion between the fugitive Marsh and his wife and son.

Though played for sympathy, Ritch's werewolf has a pleasingly fearsome, saliva-drooling visage similar to the more puppyish lycanthrope seen 12 years earlier in *The Return of the Vampire*. (It's possible that the unbilled make-up man in each case was the same: Clay Campbell.) Though seen for the most part in daylight, the monster makes its greatest impact when the malevolent Dr Chambers advances into Marsh's prison cell under cover of night. The resultant struggle makes for a terrific set-piece, played out against a backdrop of shadowed prison bars as Chambers is repeatedly smashed against the wall, and ending in a fusillade of off-screen shrieks as the local populace come running. According to Ritch, who is excellent as the tragic hero, a mooted sequel was quickly scotched.

In addition to Sam Katzman, two other independent producers putting out horror pictures in the mid-1950s were Howard W Koch and Aubrey Schenck of Bel-Air Productions. It was Koch and Schenck who, in February 1956, finally gave Bela Lugosi his first chance in three years to do a film for someone other than Ed Wood. *The Black Sleep* was shot in 13 days at American National Studios and the cast represented a feast for old-time horror fans, assembling, in addition to Lugosi, Basil Rathbone, Lon Chaney Jr and John Carradine, plus the Russian character star Akim Tamiroff as a more than acceptable substitute for Peter Lorre. Director Reginald LeBorg was a veteran of half-a-dozen Universal chillers from the mid-1940s, while the derivative but intriguing storyline was by Gerald Drayson Adams, who normally specialised in Westerns.

> *1872. Unjustly condemned to hang, Dr Gordon Ramsay eludes the gallows by means of an East Indian drug administered by his former tutor, Sir Joel Cadman. The drug induces a temporary state of living death, and, at Cadman's remote estate, Ramsay discovers that his benefactor is using it on living subjects in order to further his brain research. Cadman's aim is to revive his comatose young wife, but in the cellar reside several mutant martyrs to his work-in-progress...*

Adams had recently written a lurid melodrama for Bel-Air called *Three Bad Sisters*; in *The Black Sleep*, he had three ageing horror stars in Lugosi, Carradine and Chaney Jr and contrived to cast them, rather humiliatingly, as characters suffering from brain damage. Rathbone, more of a part-time horror star, was cast in the plum role of Sir Joel Cadman, a character patterned after the kind Lugosi played at Monogram in the 1940s, only with considerably more explicit dialogue. To restore his wife even for one day, he says, "I would put my knife into the brains of a hundred men, a thousand, and destroy them all." Relying for the most part on the seductive qualities of his voice, Rathbone presents a frozen Victorian façade, occasionally letting slip his obsessive love for his young wife, even some scattered touches of remorse, but mainly motivated by familiar quasi-Nazi notions like "In the interests of science, anything – anything is justified."

Set in 19th century England (alternating from an artist's studio in Limehouse to Cadman's converted abbey on the east coast), the film manages a surprisingly high level of verisimilitude, despite an

"If I fail, I'll destroy myself..." Basil Rathbone pledges himself to the catatonic Louanna Gardner in *The Black Sleep* (1956)

THE BLACK SLEEP

Bel-Air Productions 1956
85 minutes
production began 9 February

Cinematographer: Gordon Avil; Art Director: Bob Kinoshita; Editor: John F Schreyer; Sound: Joe Edmondson, Mike Pozen, Charles Cooper; Photographic Effects: Jack Rabin, Louis deWitt; Lighting Technician: Joe Edesa; Key Grip: George Fenaja; Operative Cameraman: Ben Colman; Set Decorator: Clarence Steenson; Property Master: Arden Cripe; Make-up created by: George Bau; Make-up: Ted Coodley; Characters designed by: [Nick] Volpe; Hair Styles: Cherie Banks; Wardrobe: Wesley V Jefferies, Angela Alexander; Music: Les Baxter; Music Editor: Sam Waxman; Assistant Director: Paul Wurtzel; Screenplay: John C Higgins (from a story by Gerald Drayson Adams); Executive Producer: Aubrey Schenck; Producer: Howard W Koch; Director: Reginald LeBorg

Basil Rathbone (Sir Joel Cadman); Akim Tamiroff (Odo); Lon Chaney [Jr] (Mungo); John Carradine (Bohemund); Bela Lugosi (Casimir); Herbert Rudley (Dr Gordon Ramsay); Patricia Blake [later Patricia Blair] (Laurie Munroe); Phyllis Stanley (Daphne); Tor Johnson (Curry); Sally Yarnell (Nancy); George Sawaya (K-6); Claire Carleton (Carmona Daly); uncredited: Louanna Gardner (Angelina Cadman); Peter Gordon (Sgt Steele); Clive Morgan (constable); Aubrey Schenck (coroner's aide); John Sheffield (Detective Redford)

An unoriginal horror piece weighed down by an overload of medical jargon. Direction and effects are unimaginative; though Cadman's cellar does yield up some moderately gruesome monsters, ruled over by a frenzied John Carradine. Basil Rathbone plays with drive and authority. The late Bela Lugosi, as the inevitable mute butler, mimes with touching and impressive conviction. *Monthly Film Bulletin* [UK]

There is Basil playing my part. I used to be the big cheese. Now I'm playing just a dumb part. I have no dialogue because I was a bit worried whether I could do justice to the expectations. I'm still recuperating.
Bela Lugosi [United Press interview, 15 February 1956]

opening title that announces the location as Newgate Prison while offering a view of the Tower of London. The plot is made up of odds and ends from a whole host of earlier films – the catalepsy-inducing drug from *The Crime of Doctor Crespi* and *The Black Castle*, the doctor going to extreme lengths to 'resurrect' a ruined spouse from *The Corpse Vanishes* and *Voodoo Man*, the zombie-like blonde and the nurse who silently adores her employer from *I Walked with a Zombie*. But the realisation of these hand-me-downs is surprisingly fresh, with LeBorg achieving a few off-the-wall effects like a subjective shot in which the rampaging Chaney Jr's hands appear to be attached to the camera.

The script wears its medical erudition rather self-consciously on its sleeve, and the Akim Tamiroff character – a polyglot gypsy tattoo artist who provides Cadman with his subjects – is amusing but never seems properly integrated into the action. (The film stops for an entire reel while he traps a past-her-best soubrette into sampling the so-called Black Sleep.) But Cadman's brain operations are surprisingly graphic, with trephining sound effects reminiscent of a woodwork class and a forebrain laid open in close-up, cerebral fluid running freely from its central fissure. Contemporary critics certainly took notice of the film's grue quotient; in *Variety*, 'Brog' observed that "Rathbone is quite credible as the surgeon, enough so that those brain operations he performs will horrify many viewers," while *Motion Picture Herald* suggested that patrons "are likely to find some of the brain-probing close-ups in this picture somewhat strong for their systems."[17]

The assembled horror veterans are given subordinate roles but are welcome nonetheless. Our first view of Lugosi, in which he peeks through a small partition built into Cadman's front door, is reminiscent of a memorable Lugosi moment in *Night of Terror*; elsewhere, he does little other than take people's coats and walk around with warming pans. Chaney, also mute, plays a lumbering retainer who was once a tutor at St Thomas' Hospital, as if Cadman's brain-tampering has caused the intellectual character Chaney habitually played in the Inner Sanctum pictures to revert to the bovine Lennie in *Of Mice and Men*. Carradine actually gets lines and is an absolute hoot, finally abandoning the reticence of most of his 1940s genre performances and acting up a storm. As a bedraggled troglodyte who thinks it's 1100 AD and fancies himself as Bohemund of Antioch, he raves about "defilers of the faith" and climactically mistakes Cadman for arch-infidel Saladin.

The make-up for the four mutants was applied by the Bau brothers from *House of Wax* and based on monster designs created by LA painter Nicholas Volpe (whose designs for *The Thing* had gone unused). The climactic uprising is a cut-price reprise of *Island of Lost Souls*, bringing the film to a crazy and untrammelled close – the devoted nurse goes up in flames, the female mutant shrieks with laughter throughout, Chaney Jr closes with the massive Tor Johnson in a fight to the death, and Rathbone and wife are finally hurled from a granite landing. Unfortunately, this last effect is slightly muffed, Rathbone's lack of dialogue when faced with the mutants proving a particular disappointment. Despite this, *The Black Sleep* is a diverting entertainment and distinguished by a doom-laden score (his first in what would turn out to be a long horror career) by Les Baxter.

The film was put out by United Artists in tandem with an extremely scary British import called *The Quatermass Xperiment*, which was retitled *The Creeping Unknown* for US audiences. One of the best-value double-features of the 1950s, the pairing opened at the Loew's Metropolitan in Brooklyn on 13 June 1956, and within two months had made the front cover of the *Hollywood Reporter*: "United Artists' combination bill of *The Creeping Unknown* and *The Black Sleep*, produced at a total cost of less than $400,000 for the pair, is headed for a domestic gross of better than $1,600,000."[18] Later still, the double-feature acquired a dubious distinction in Oak Park Illinois, as noted by *Variety* in November: "Family of a nine-year-old boy who died of a ruptured artery in a theater lobby here recently is suing the theater and a film distributor for admitting children to horror pix. Suit [for $25,000] blamed the death on fright."[19]

The Quatermass Xperiment was the break-out hit from the small British company Hammer Film Productions, which in November would start shooting an epoch-making shocker called *The Curse of Frankenstein*. That the Hammer personnel took a good look at *The Black Sleep* before embarking on their radical Frankenstein rethink seems incontestable. Rathbone's cold-hearted yet discreetly dandified researcher, the graphic brain operations, even some of the mutant make-ups (milky-white cataracts on one, half a head of hair on another) – all would find echoes in *The Curse of Frankenstein*.

Even the dialogue throws up an echo or two. At one point, Cadman offers his fellow doctor "hot toast, jam, marmalade," adding helpfully, "Teapot's under the cosy." This could well be the origin of the most famous line in Jimmy Sangster's Frankenstein script, when the super-suave Baron asks his fiancée to "Pass the marmalade." Sangster, however, had the dramatic sense to place the line directly after a scene of horrendous monster mayhem, whereas Cadman's version is just thrown in willy-nilly. A later Sangster script – for a non-Hammer item called *Blood of the Vampire* – would go further, picking up, consciously or otherwise, some of *The Black Sleep*'s plot.

Finally, however, these similarities amount to little more than details. *The Curse of Frankenstein* would benefit from a couple of dynamic actors new to the field, Peter Cushing and Christopher Lee, rather than the engaging but clapped-out crew featured in *The Black Sleep*. And the Hammer revolution would be further distinguished by an unprecedented emphasis on blood and sex, a certain sardonic sense of charnel-house humour and, of course, lurid Eastmancolor. *The Black Sleep*, by contrast, is bloodless, sexless, more or less humourless and literally colourless. Indeed, the script has Cadman attribute the conspicuous absence of blood in his operations to "the action of my anaesthetic." That Cushing's Baron Frankenstein lacked any such blood-suppressing agent would turn the horror genre on its head.

If *The Curse of Frankenstein* heralded the start of a whole new era in horror production, the end of the previous one had been signalled, only a few months before the Hammer picture started shooting, by the death of Bela Lugosi. Other than *The Black Sleep*, Lugosi's only film work in 1956 had involved some silent footage taken by his friend Ed Wood, possibly for a long-gestating project called *The Vampire's Tomb*; it would eventually turn up in Wood's legendary clinker, *Plan 9 from Outer Space*. Aged 73, Lugosi succumbed to a heart attack on Thursday 16 August, the funeral attracting no high-profile guests other than his film director countryman Zoltán Korda. John Carradine, however, offered a gracious tribute shortly afterwards. "Lugosi was a craftsman," Carradine maintained, "a considerate and kind gentleman. As for the parts we both played, he was the better vampire. He had a fine pair of eyes. Nobody will ever be able to fill his shoes. He will be missed by us all."[20]

AWAITING RESURRECTION

The filmmaking demi-monde that threw up Bela Lugosi's final collaborations with Ed Wood also harboured metaphysician Merle S Gould, who teamed up with the former M-G-M editor, and fellow metaphysician, Peter Ballbusch on a 1956 item called *You Live After Death*. Briefly seen under the release title *The Body is a Shell*, this threadbare tale – of a debunker of mediums who gradually comes to realise he's dead – was accurately perceived, by the few contemporary reviewers who caught it, as a vanity project. As a result, Gould's next Am Dram dud, *The Dead Talk Back*, in which a murder investigation seeks to communicate with the deceased via radio, went unreleased for 36 years, finally appearing on video in 1993.

Back in the sphere of professional filmmaking, Bel-Air Productions put Lee Sholem's *Pharaoh's Curse* into production in late March 1956, just a month after completing *The Black Sleep*. For this star-free but moderately intriguing riff on Universal's old Mummy pictures, painter Nick Volpe was on hand again, this time to create a gradually disintegrating young Egyptian, invaded by the spirit of a desecrated mummy at the moment his white-skinned masters cut the wrappings from its face. The boy's inscrutable sister (played by the beautiful Israeli actress Ziva Shapir) turns out to be a human manifestation of the feline deity Bubastis; the boy, meanwhile, picks off the invasive members of the expeditionary party one by one, becoming more and more horribly desiccated in the process. Among his victims is Kurt Katch, who 12 years before had fallen prey to Lon Chaney Jr in *The Mummy's Curse*. Here, he ends up with very nasty scratch marks on either side of his face.

The Death Valley locations look suitably barren, if not especially Egyptian, but what's interesting about the film is its script by Richard Landau, who had lately co-written *The Black Sleep*'s British stablemate, *The Quatermass Xperiment*. *Pharaoh's Curse* is in many ways a *Quatermass* retread transplanted to 19th century Egypt, with the boy's slow transformation echoing that of astronaut Victor Carroon in several particulars; even dialogue is lifted from the earlier film. "Something's happened," observes a medical officer. "There's been a change." He later identifies "a rapid acceleration of the ageing process: 50 years in a matter of hours," while the creature's victims are described as "completely deflated ... the whole body eviscerated."

Finally, the creature sheds an arm, just as Carroon sheds a spore-covered fragment of himself, and, during a gruesome autopsy on it, an aide says "That takes care of my appetite," paraphrasing Jack Warner in the Quatermass film. (The 'severed limb under analysis' scene was also derived from *The Thing* and would remain a popular device, amusingly replayed, for example, in the 1963 drive-in classic *The Horror of Party Beach*.) Landau obviously wasn't a man to waste a host of fascinating plot points, even if they were

"Unbelievable. The body disintegrating, turning into dust." Guy Prescott pronounces judgment, attended by Mark Dana, Ziva Shapir, Ben Wright, George N Neise and Robert Fortin, in *Pharaoh's Curse* (1956)

originated by someone else – in this case, the author of *The Quatermass Xperiment*'s TV source material, Nigel Kneale.

Landau's next Bel-Air script, *Voodoo Island*, borrowed from *The Quatermass Xperiment* yet again, albeit somewhat more sparingly. Here, the Carroon substitute is a catatonic man (one of four surveyors lately returned from a mysterious island) whose bizarre bio-rhythms are closely monitored by a team headed by none other than Boris Karloff, just about the only old-time horror star the Bel-Air people didn't squeeze into *The Black Sleep*. As a tediously sceptical TV pundit, Karloff heads straight for the island, with Elisha Cook and others in tow, finding voodoo fetishes and carnivorous vegetation but not much else. Reginald LeBorg's film, shot on the Hawaiian island of Kauai from 26 October 1956, is boringly devoid of wit or incident. It's enlivened only by Jean Engstrom as one of two women in the party, a lanky lesbian who tells Karloff's tight-lipped female assistant that "I could make you become alive, dear."

On 5 November, just over a week after Koch and Karloff started shooting in Kauai, Joseph Pevney's *Man of a Thousand Faces* began production at Universal. This thoroughly fictionalised Lon Chaney biopic features conspicuously poor, rubberised reproductions of Chaney's famous make-ups and an exceptional star performance from James Cagney – apt casting, given the Cagney-style direction Chaney might have taken had he lived past 1930. *Variety*'s judgment at the time – that it's "an unashamed soap opera tearjerker" and "not a film for the sophisticate or the discerning critic" – is hard to dispute.

While Universal were preparing this rose-tinted view of the 1920s, one of the most unusual items on offer in the nation's cinemas was a picture firmly rooted in the contemporary world. Released in September 1956, a good year after it had started shooting at Warner Bros, Mervyn LeRoy's film version of Maxwell Anderson's Broadway hit *The Bad Seed* retained six of the 12 actors involved in the original play. The inevitable result was scenery-chewing of a startlingly unrestrained order, particularly from the former *Woman Who Came Back*, Nancy Kelly, here playing the well-heeled mother of an eight-year-old psychopath. Flaxen-haired, beetle-browed Rhoda (Patty McCormack) is an outrageous caricature of "the perfect little old-fashioned girl," yet she dismisses the murder of a fellow pupil by saying, "I hit him with the shoes. What else could I do?" An old lady has been murdered by her before the film even begins, and she later incinerates the peculiar handyman (Henry Jones) who's wise to her wiles.

Patty McCormack as the small suburban serial killer of *The Bad Seed* (1955)

As a subversion of the squeaky-clean surfaces of 1950s suburbia, *The Bad Seed* had terrific impact; in it, the scientific horrors of the threatened apocalypse ("I'm not ready to be turned into a piece of chalk just yet," clucks a middle-aged landlady) suddenly paled beside the chill self-possession of McCormack. The script's unconvincing nature-vs-nurture debate is of the 'have your cake and eat it' variety, however, and the film also provided evidence of the continued influence of the PCA. The play's original downbeat ending (and that of the William March novel on which it was based) was exchanged for an audience-pleasing conclusion in which Rhoda is literally extinguished by a thunderbolt. And worse is to come. "At the film's end," noted a contemporary reviewer, "LeRoy makes his final obeisance to the stage: all the characters smilingly take their bows, and Nancy Kelly – as she did during curtain calls on Broadway – puts Patty across her knee and gives her a spanking."[21]

Though *The Bad Seed*'s fangs had been drawn, its demonic child scenario – as if the ill-fated Little Maria of *Frankenstein* had changed places with the Monster – would prove a prophetic one, pointing forward to pictures as varied as *Village of the Damned* and *The Omen*. For the time being, however, a pre-pubescent threat would remain an anomaly – for, in the latter part of the 1950s, your throat was much more likely to be torn out by a teenage werewolf. And a show of parental authority was unlikely to deter it, least of all a mere spanking.

Part Seven

Teenage monsters Gary Clarke and Gary Conway in classic Philip Scheer make-ups for *How to Make a Monster* (1958)

Teenage Kicks 1956-1959

In mid-October 1959, producer Rex Carlton was in the basement of the Henry Hudson Hotel on New York's West 57th Street. He was there to supervise the making of a small picture called *The Head that Wouldn't Die*, which by a strange anomaly would be released three years later as *The Brain that Wouldn't Die*. Emerging briefly from the basement – or, as *Variety* described it, "the blistering hot stage of the Lance Studios" – Carlton told the magazine's correspondent, Fred Hift, that "This kind of picture is aimed really at the teenage crowd. They aren't afraid of pictures like this. They laugh at them. It gives them a vicarious thrill, a release from reality." Filing his report, Hift concluded that "What it adds up to is that, with the majors cutting down so sharply on production, the small indies like Carlton are flourishing with exploitation product, which the majors in turn pick up to bolster their release skeds."[1]

With the 1950s drawing rapidly to a close, Carlton and Hift had put their fingers on the two crucial factors behind the explosion of exploitation product in the latter part of the decade. Independent producers were keenly aware – far more so than the ossified majors – that stay-at-home suburbanites who had lost the cinemagoing habit nevertheless had teenage children who now represented the lion's share of the audience. The evolving youth culture of the post-war period was to a large extent defined by its pulsing, parent-baiting music; so it was that, in the first week of January 1956, just a fortnight after they completed *The Werewolf*, producer Sam Katzman and director Fred F Sears began shooting *Rock Around the Clock*. Wasting no time, the pair had polished off a sequel, *Don't Knock the Rock*, before Twentieth Century-Fox got around to their own rock'n'roll showcase, *The Girl Can't Help It*, in September. The success of Katzman's pictures ensured that the benighted family man of *The Werewolf*, first seen by US audiences in July 1956, would be replaced within 12 months by the more up-to-date identification figure of *I Was a Teenage Werewolf*.

Alongside the rise of a thrill-hungry youth audience came a severe product shortage. Hit by declining audience figures and the fact that the Supreme Court's 1948 ruling deprived them of their own theatre chains, the major studios opted for a much-reduced production slate, focusing on great big swanky blockbusters for carefully staggered release at holiday times. This created huge gaps in what Hift called the 'release skeds',

threatening theatres, particularly smaller ones, with dissolution. Into this breach stepped independently produced exploitation double-features accompanied by strident, and conspicuously sensationalist, advertising. In fact, to paranoid social commentators fretting over supposed juvenile delinquency, the lurid come-ons were just as disturbing as the films' content.

In addition to the factors specified by Carlton and Hift, there were three others that ensured horror films a special place in the exploitation product aimed at teens. The release in May 1957 of the British import *The Curse of Frankenstein* – followed a year later by another smash from the same Hammer Films team, *Dracula* (or *Horror of Dracula* as it was known in the US) – reinvigorated the old Gothic icons with colour, carnality and, above all, class. In October 1957 Screen Gems released a package of 52 old Universal horror and mystery pictures to local TV stations under the umbrella title *Shock Theatre*, earning huge ratings and deifying the various ghoul-hosts who introduced the films. And in February 1958, consolidating the trend, came the first issue of Warren Publishing's *Famous Monsters of Filmland*, which required reprinting despite a hefty initial run of 150,000 copies. The magazine rapidly became a news-stand must for hordes of 'monster kids' craving what Rex Carlton called 'vicarious thrills'.

MONSTROUS FOR MONEY

"I'll say one thing for the horror pictures. The kids stay in their seats – [there's] none of this wandering up and down aisles the way they do during a fancy drawing room opus."[2] So said a grateful exhibitor when quizzed by *Newsweek* for a 1958 piece called *Monstrous for Money*.

Two men acutely attuned to keeping kids in their seats, and quite happy to be monstrous for money, were James H Nicholson and Samuel Z Arkoff, who in 1954 had gone into business together as American Releasing Corporation. By March 1956 the company name had been altered to American International Pictures (AIP); in the interim Nicholson and Arkoff had become involved with the young filmmaker Roger Corman. The latter had already enjoyed success as producer of Wyott Ordung's self-explanatory 1953 film *Monster from the Ocean Floor*, which had gone out via Lippert Pictures. For Nicholson and Arkoff, Corman produced David Kramarsky's *The Unseen*, a decidedly tatty alien-visitation saga, shot in April 1955 and released nine months later as *The Beast with a Million Eyes* – despite the fact that no million-eyed beast ever shows up, the threat remaining invisible and possessing various farmyard animals. That the film constitutes a kind of Poverty Row precursor to Hitchcock's *The Birds* remains its only interest.

It was clear, however, that even at this early stage Nicholson and Arkoff saw nothing incongruous about adding monsters to the more predictable teen diet of hot-rodders, rock'n'rollers and juvenile delinquents. And Corman's progress, in any case, was to be rapid, particularly when he opted to do the directing himself. This was the case with *Day the World Ended*, which added to its fashionable post-apocalypse scenario a hungry mutant designed (and acted) by the young effects artist Paul Blaisdell. Made in September 1955, the film was coupled on release with Dan Milner's embarrassingly threadbare marine-mutation melodrama *The Phantom from 10,000 Leagues*. With an eye to the teens patronising not only 'neighbourhood houses' but also the newly popular drive-in theatres, AIP were to become past masters at packaging such easily exploitable, value-for-money double-features.

In April 1956 Corman made *It Conquered the World*, casting Lee Van Cleef as an idealistic scientist unaware that the alien he has brought to Earth is by no means the peace-monger he imagines. As conceived by Blaisdell, the fanged, mind-controlling monster is a cheerfully absurd Venusian vegetable and is given way too much exposure in the comical finale. Shot a month after Corman's film and in due course forming a double-feature with it was Edward L Cahn's *The She-Creature*. "She comes from the beginning of time, huge and indestructible," exults a dodgy mesmerist while regressing his beautiful assistant (played by Elizabeth Taylor lookalike Marla English) into a prehistoric sea beast. More leathery-looking than in his heyday, Chester Morris is given some hypnotic close-ups reminding us that he was once considered for the title role in *Dracula*. And the monster, a kind of busty humanoid lobster, is another classic Paul Blaisdell creation.

Cahn's film exploited the 'regression to a past life' fad triggered by Morey Bernstein's bestselling book *The Search for Bridey Murphy*. In June 1956 the book was made into a major Paramount picture, simultaneously throwing up W Lee Wilder's small-scale Planet Filmplays production *Spell of the Hypnotist*. Despite an excellent film debut from Nancy Malone (playing a Manhattan neurotic who imagines herself as a key player in the 1889 Mayerling affair), this one only got bookings when retitled *Fright* and coupled with Wilder's terrible British film *The Man Without a Body*. Yet this outcome did nothing to impede the flow of Bridey Murphy-inspired pictures. Among them was a freakish, Ed Wood-scripted Allied Artists clinker called *The Bride and the Beast*, directed by Adrian Weiss

Morgan Jones and Beverly Garland commemorate a man who was *Not of This Earth* (1956)

in January 1957, in which Charlotte Austin's erotic interest in a gorilla derives from her past life as an ape.

After the perambulating turnip featured in AIP's *It Conquered the World*, Roger Corman moved on to an Allied Artists project in which the alien invader required only a pair of milky-white contact lenses. Written by Corman regulars Charles B Griffith and Mark Hanna, *Not of This Earth* conjures a genuine climate of eeriness from its workaday Los Angeles locations, through which passes a monolithic middle-aged man in suit and shades, determined to replenish his rapidly evaporating blood supply. He's actually "a fiend of the most diabolical kind," emissary of a vampiric alien race whose aim is "the conquest, subjugation and pasturing of the Earth sub-humans." Among his victims are a hapless trio of local hobos and a hepcat vacuum cleaner salesman hilariously played by Dick Miller, who does a marvellous triple-take in the gruesome basement prior to being killed by the alien's basilisk stare and consigned to the furnace.

Coolly photographed by John J Mescall, erstwhile cinematographer of *The Black Cat* and *Bride of Frankenstein*, the film lapses into unintentional comedy here and there, notably when a Blaisdell-designed bat-thing envelops a doctor's head. And it devolves at the end into a slightly listless chase sequence, enlivened only by Ronald Stein's atonal score. But the film gains much from its powerful imagery – a fridge stacked with plasma bottles, for example – and from the deadpan containment of Paul Birch as the alien. Exceptional, too, is Beverly Garland as the private nurse he employs; her gradual unravelling of the mystery stamps Garland as arguably the best, and most watchable, actress at work in low-budget fantasy during this period.

Having begun *Not of This Earth* on 7 June, Corman took a brief break prior to starting his next film, *The Trance of Diana Love*, on 26 July. Back with AIP for distribution purposes, Corman was here tapping into the *Search for Bridey Murphy* trend, shooting in a disused supermarket on Sunset Boulevard and completing the film on 9 August. When it was ready for distribution early the following year, however, the reincarnation craze had cooled and the picture acquired a misleading release title – *The Undead*.

Written once again by Griffith and Hanna, the film has a bespectacled academic dismiss the whole Bridey Murphy mania as "nothing but Sunday supplement nonsense" prior to sanctioning the hypnotic regression of prostitute Diana Love (Pamela Duncan). At this point the film becomes – as one of its cast members, Mel Welles, pithily put it – "a medieval spook picture requiring lots of fog blowing."[3] Diana, it seems, was an accused witch in a past life, with her eventual beheading forming the climax to a garbled intrigue in which Corman's Middle Ages re-enactment looks like a high-school production of *The Lady's Not for Burning*. The pastiche dialogue, written in blank verse, would be fine in a three-minute student skit but quickly becomes intolerable over 60-odd minutes. A curvaceous sorceress called Livia, for example, has this to say to Welles' bald-pated gravedigger: "Disturb me not, lummox. I must hasten to sweep these wandering ghosts back to their earthen homes before the Witches' Sabbat begins."

Livia is played by Allison Hayes, a former Miss America contestant for whom the word 'statuesque' might have been coined, here making her first of over half-a-dozen low-budget horror quickies. Like her uniquely irritating dwarf companion (Billy Barty), she has a tendency to turn into a tiny bat-like creature from time to time, though she raises the film's stakes a bit when decapitating innkeeper Bruno Ve Sota,

later offering the head as tribute to Richard Devon's pier-end Satan caricature.

The Undead may have been a clumsy entrée into Gothic horror for Corman, but his workaholic tendencies continued unabated. A few films later, he found himself on 26 November at California's Leo Carillo State Beach, there to start work on *Attack of the Crab Monsters*, an irradiated-crustaceans shocker that duly went out alongside *Not of This Earth*. *The Undead*, meanwhile, was coupled on release with Edward L Cahn's *Voodoo Woman*, which utilised a modified version of Paul Blaisdell's *She-Creature* monster suit. In this dreary recitation of jungle motifs and 'bad girl' clichés, the parchment-faced Tom Conway, sporting a very silly head-dress, effects a fusion of "white-man science and the black voodoo" by turning first Jean Davis and then Marla English into lumbering monsters.

A former editor, Edward L Cahn was known as, to put it mildly, a speed specialist. When he started shooting *Voodoo Woman* on 12 November 1956, a mere six days had passed since he finished work on his previous film, *Zombies of Mora Tau*, a film that had itself started shooting only nine days before that, on 29 October. Produced as *The Dead That Walk* (a title retained for UK release), *Zombies of Mora Tau* is largely uninspired but gets by on some effectively creepy scenes of waterlogged zombies, guardians of a hoard of African diamonds, rising seaweed-strewn from the waves to kill off the members of a modern-day salvage crew. The film also has a portentous rubric at the beginning that predicts the title of a 1960s television favourite ("In the darkness of an ancient world – on a shore that time has forgotten – there is a twilight zone between life and death"), together with *The Undead*'s Allison Hayes on top form as a heartless ball-breaker turned soulless zombie.

Zombies of Mora Tau was a Sam Katzman project produced back-to-back with another, Leslie Kardos' *The Petrified Man*. (The scripts in each case were by Bernard Gordon, who had to be billed as Raymond T Marcus thanks to his HUAC blacklisted status.) *The Petrified Man* preceded *Zombies* into production, on 12 October, and would form a double-feature with it on release, under the altered title *The Man Who Turned to Stone*.

It's considerably more interesting than its companion piece, featuring as it does the exploitational masterstroke of putting a bunch of centuries-old scientists in charge of a reform school for teenage girls. The scientists have discovered a means of transferring "bio-electric energy from one individual to another" and that "the best source of energy is in mature young women of child-bearing age." Hence the rash of strange fatalities at the detention centre, the girls going to their watery deaths in baptismal shifts.

The film runs out of steam sooner than the scientists do, with a climactic teen uprising going absolutely nowhere and Friedrich von Ledebur lumbering around indecisively as the most unbalanced of the crazies. (Von Ledebur, an Austrian Count in real life, was playing the lofty high priest in the Bel-Air production *Voodoo Island* almost simultaneously.) But the film at least has a great scene for the veteran English actor Paul Cavanagh, who rebels against the cruelty of his fellow scientists and rejects his latest 'fix', admitting sadly that "220 years is too long for any man to live" and finally turning into a living skull.

EVIL, BEAUTIFUL, DEADLY

Though most of them weren't likely to see 21 again, the sulky teen delinquents of *The Man Who Turned to Stone* were an indication of where the American horror film was heading. Teenage tearaways were

Ann Doran, Victor Jory and George Lynn assess Friedrich von Ledebur's bio-electric energy in *The Man Who Turned to Stone* (1956)

absent, however, from Edgar G Ulmer's *Daughter of Dr Jekyll*, which writer-producer Jack Pollexfen put into production on 7 November 1956. Previously involved with Columbia's *The Son of Dr Jekyll*, Pollexfen also drew inspiration from, of all things, *She-Wolf of London* and *Devil Bat's Daughter*, concocting a story in which plucky Gloria Talbott learns of her baleful heritage and is duped into thinking she's guilty of a local murder spree. Incredibly, the real killer has been introduced to us via direct-address right at the beginning. He's a gurning, snaggle-toothed Irishman with a face "like some perverted mask of evil out of a legend of horror" – and he looks suspiciously like the young woman's apparently benevolent guardian (Arthur Shields).

A few peculiarities surface along the way. Mr Hyde is explicitly identified as having been "a human werewolf," yet the outraged locals treated him like a vampire by staking him through the heart. (History duly repeats itself in a laughably unconvincing impalement scene.) And towards the end a 1950s cheesecake glamour girl intrudes into this turn-of-the-century story, pulling on her stockings to the tune of an Edison phonograph and succumbing to an interestingly staged murder. Beyond this the normally inspirational Ulmer can do nothing to curry interest in the film, other than smothering the ancestral mansion in mist and surrounding it with a frog chorus recalling the 1942 picture *Night Monster*. The result was put out by Allied Artists in July 1957 alongside Bert I Gordon's *The Cyclops*, in which an expedition to Mexico to find a woman's fiancé discovers that the missing man has become a radioactively mutated giant. This must have been a great double-feature for Gloria Talbott fans, given that she's the female lead in both.

Seriously deformed small-town doctor (John Beal) and doting nurse (Coleen Gray) in *The Vampire* (1956)

The Jekyll and Hyde motif was also present in Gramercy Pictures' *The Vampire*, which started at Hal Roach Studios on 10 December 1956 under a decidedly second-hand working title – *Mark of the Vampire*. Yet another attempt to graft Gothic horror onto the squeaky-clean surfaces of science fiction, Paul Landres' film has the slickly toupéed John Beal (formerly the surly third lead of Paramount's *The Cat and the Canary*) as a small-town GP who goes the way of Robert Shayne in *The Neanderthal Man*, taking so-called "regression pills [containing] a control serum extracted from bats" and becoming host to a saliva-borne virus that causes complete "capillary disintegration" in his victims. The *Neanderthal Man* comparison ends there, however, given that Beal's Dr Beecher is not only well acted but also a sympathetic character – he didn't devise the serum himself, only taking it by mistake on the death of a fellow researcher.

The regression angle places the film in the persistent Bridey Murphy subgenre, but the pseudo-scientific gibberish in Pat Fielder's script is just the usual faux-hip gloss applied to a time-honoured monster. Intriguingly, the serum is addictive, turning the conflicted doctor into a slobbering, frog-faced caricature of the generic dope fiend. A nocturnal exhumation reveals that one of his victims has turned into a half-fleshed skull in record time, while Dabbs Greer (playing Beecher's concerned associate) is unceremoniously jammed into a furnace – strong moments that would be echoed in Roger Corman's *Pit and the Pendulum* and Terence Fisher's *The Revenge of Frankenstein* respectively. Unfortunately, Beecher's transformations are achieved by some laughably clumsy lap-dissolves, and the picket-fenced site of his crimes stakes out suburban territory that would only be made genuinely creepy in John Carpenter's 1978 smash *Halloween*. The cinematographer was Jack Mackenzie, who had shot *Isle of the Dead* in 1944 but here overcomes the monochrome sterility characteristic of American SF films only in fits and starts.

Beginning production on the same day as *The Vampire* was a simultaneously bland and bizarre little film called *She Devil*, made by Robert Lippert's 20th Century-Fox subsidiary Regal Pictures. Here, a couple of scientists save a terminally ill woman from death by means of a rejuvenating serum derived from fruit flies;

she acquires the standard combination of vampish allure and homicidal mania, together with (a novel touch) the power to change her hair colour at will.

The premise smacks of the much-filmed German chestnut *Alraune* and, sure enough, roiling away under this straitlaced melodrama is a queasy terror of assertive women. "I did what I wanted to do," seethes Mari Blanchard, "and I'm going to keep right on doing it. And I'd like to see you stop me." The best Albert Dekker can offer in response is "Believe me, Kyra, we know what is best for you." As played by Dekker and Jack Kelly, the scientists are as patronising a pair of robotic stiffs as the era produced, and they end by effectively lobotomising their rebellious subject, with Dekker explicitly appealing to "a far greater and higher power." Inevitably, the moralistic God of 1950s conformity decrees that, the original experiment having been reversed, the consumptive Kyra should die instantly after all.

Co-written and (slightly drearily) directed by Kurt Neumann, *She Devil* is propelled by a familiar double-standard, covertly enjoying the liberated woman's depredations while siding with the blandly manipulative scientists. The veteran cinematographer Karl Struss gives the film what visual interest he can, resurrecting his old graduated-filter technique (previously used in *Ben-Hur* and Paramount's *Dr Jekyll and Mr Hyde*) when Kyra re-acquires the marks of ravaging illness, and also for the pretty astonishing scenes of her hair changing colour. Coincidentally, in the same month (December 1956) Mario Bava was borrowing the Struss technique for the instant ageing of Gianna Maria Canale in the pioneering Italian horror film *I vampiri*.

Another film made in December 1956 seemed to mock the misogynist message of *She Devil* with its hyperbolic title – *The Astounding She-Monster* – and the emphatic tag-line, "Evil... Beautiful... Deadly...!" Ronnie Ashcroft's film was actually called *Naked Invader* during production, and the result – in which the titular space female tangles with a scientist, an heiress and a bunch of kidnappers – is a hard-to-watch Am Dram effort recalling the work of Ed Wood, who's rumoured to have been involved in it. As *Box Office* magazine put it, "Shirley Kilpatrick makes an unusually eye-filling 'monster'"[4] – yet she doesn't hold a candle to the stunning poster image created by Albert Kallis when the film was picked up for distribution by AIP.

After completing *She Devil*, Kurt Neumann, Karl Struss and Regal Pictures moved on in January 1957 to a straight science fiction subject called *Kronos*, which would be bracketed with *She Devil* on release. Though specialising in B Westerns, Regal nevertheless turned out two further semi-horrors later that year, putting

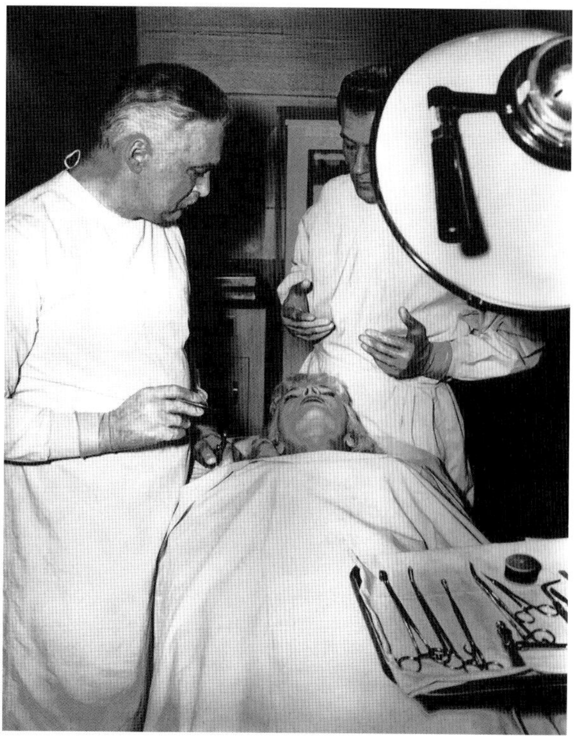

Patriarchal scientists Albert Dekker and Jack Kelly with female subject Mari Blanchard in *She Devil* (1956)

director Charles Marquis Warren to work on *The Unknown Terror* on 25 March and then whisking him straight on to *Back from the Dead* on 12 April. Sadly, Warren's rushed-off-his-feet handling makes for listless viewing in each case, a problem compounded when the two films were issued on the same bill.

The Unknown Terror involves an expedition to South America to find Mala Powers' missing brother, with the hoped-for chills revolving around "a remarkable fungus that reproduces by binary fission." Various zombie-like locals, infected by the fungus, disturb Powers' sleep, but the fungus itself, when encountered in the so-called Cave of the Dead, proliferates in drooling, drizzling gobs of what is clearly just washing powder. "We've got to seal it in this cave, otherwise it'll destroy the world!" we're excitedly told. Sadly, only a cameo appearance by 'King of the Calypsos' Sir Lancelot (15 years after *I Walked with a Zombie*) maintains interest – that and the plot's surface similarity to *The Cyclops*.

Back from the Dead has some unusually meaty female roles (it was based by screenwriter Catherine Turney on her recent novel *The Other One*), but the proceedings still take on a sexist *She Devil*-type flavour, with the dead protagonist identified as someone who "from the first set out to fascinate all men" and the poster tag-line clarifying this with "She Lived to DESTROY!" Having been drowned and eaten by a shark six years before, the baleful Felicia possesses Mandy, new wife of her widower. In life, it transpires, Felicia was involved with a Laguna Beach diabolist played (very woodenly) by Otto Reichow. Peggie Castle, as Mandy-Felicia, and Marsha Hunt, as Mandy's investigative sister, give it their all, but the limp ending – in which a barely glimpsed blood-draining ritual is broken up and the cowled diabolist is shot to death off screen – is typical of the film's all-round blandness.

"She Lived to DESTROY!" may as well have been the tag-line for the next male-chauvinist fantasy built around Allison Hayes. *The Disembodied*, which director Walter Grauman finished shooting on 8 March, cast Hayes as (to quote the actual tag-line) a "fiendish tigress of the jungle!" in a camped-up 1950s take on the old Columbia thriller *Black Moon*. Resplendent in silken Chinoiserie with a dinky little dagger affixed to her belt, Hayes plots to rub out her older husband (John Wengraf) in order to get at a handsome newcomer (Paul Burke), and to that end she changes into tasselled burlesque gear for an amusingly chintzy voodoo ceremonial. A vengeful native girl (Eugenia Paul) gets to deliver the coup de grâce, but the dapper Wengraf gets all the best lines – pointedly telling his wife, for example, that "There are only two backgrounds into which *you* fit properly: the jungle and the place where I found you first." Stodgy though it is, *The Disembodied* looks pretty good by comparison to its disastrous Allied Artists co-feature. Shot in May, Dan Milner's *From Hell It Came* – in which an executed Polynesian prince is revived by radiation as a murderous, ambulant tree monster – isn't even redeemed by a typically wild Paul Blaisdell creature design.

In April 1957, not long after completing *The Disembodied*, Allison Hayes was playing opposite John Carradine in something called *House of Monsters*, which on release would be retitled *The Unearthly* and coupled with Bert I Gordon's cut-price 'big bugs' extravaganza *Beginning of the End*. Produced, like its stablemate, by a short-lived film company put together by ABC Broadcasting and Paramount Theatres, *The Unearthly* was directed by Boris Petroff and taken from an 'original story' by his wife, Jane Mann. That word 'original' quickly becomes laughable as the film's thoroughly hackneyed action unfolds, with Carradine's shifty Dr Conway offering rest cures at his cosy clinic but actually experimenting on his patients to find the "secret of youth and eternal life."

The film's pulchritude level is high; in addition to the ubiquitous Hayes we have former Miss America Marilyn Buferd and recent *Playboy* Playmate Sally Todd. Offsetting this are Tor Johnson as Conway's hulking manservant (called Lobo, the same name Johnson's character was given in a couple of contemporaneous Ed Wood films) and a rather fetching mob of basement mutants who show up in the final reel. With his familiar lolloping gait and skeletal frame, Carradine is thoroughly swamped by his own suit and looks even more depressed than usual. "How could this have happened?" he gasps on inspecting the terrible mutant make-up applied to Todd. "I took every precaution!" Any halfway-attentive viewer will realise that it happened because Conway is arguably the stupidest mad scientist in this entire survey.

COHEN, CASTLE AND ZIV

Sally Todd wasn't the first *Playboy* Playmate drafted into a horror picture in the spring of 1957, for Dawn Richard – soon to appear in the magazine's May edition – had already played a sinuous high-school gymnast who comes to a bad end in *I Was a Teenage Werewolf*. This was a project originated by the 31-year-old producer Herman Cohen, who as assistant to Jack Broder had previously been involved with the unlovely duo *Bride of the Gorilla* and *Bela Lugosi Meets a Brooklyn Gorilla*. He had also put down roots in England with a 1952 Merton Park B picture called *Ghost Ship*.

Cohen pitched the werewolf idea to AIP co-head James H Nicholson on the grounds that "for a fledgling company which was trying to get the teenage market, it could be ideal."[5] And so it proved. Shot in March at Santa Monica's Ziv Studios, the film was issued in mid-June and became a smash hit. The title, meanwhile, passed into the vernacular even when the film was still current. "I came up with the title *Teenage Werewolf*," claimed Cohen, "and Jim Nicholson added *I Was a*."[6] The phrase actually originated in an issue of the comic teen magazine *Dig* that dated right back to May 1956. There, the waggish cover line 'I Was a Teenage Werewolf' jostled with 'You Can Be a Disc Jockey', 'Things Boys Don't Like About Girls' and – the one given banner prominence – 'Do You and Your Parents See Eye to Eye?'

Rockdale High School's most rebellious student, Tony Rivers, is urged by his girlfriend and a concerned police detective to seek help from consultant psychologist Dr Alfred Brandon – but he stubbornly refuses. Having attacked a friend at a Hallowe'en get-together, Tony is sufficiently shaken to consult Dr Brandon after all. Brandon, however, looks on Tony as "my perfect subject," using both hypnosis and a specially devised serum to "unleash the savage instincts that lie hidden within."

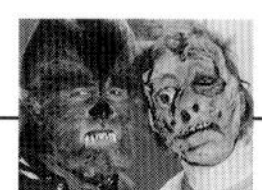

Teen gymnast Dawn Richard and aroused teen lycanthrope Michael Landon in *I Was a Teenage Werewolf* (1957)

The masterstroke in *I Was a Teenage Werewolf*, conscious or otherwise, was to exploit the contemporary teen audience by means of the werewolf myth, with its obvious parallels to the shape-changing angst of adolescence. Concocted pseudonymously by Cohen and the novelist and playwright Aben Kandel, the script takes a tip from the 1955 Warner release *Rebel Without a Cause*, deftly setting up Rockdale as stiflingly conformist and Tony as a convincingly disaffected teen who claims to "burn easy" because "people bug me." The philosophy expressed by his elders, given to us in broad but effective strokes, is predictably infuriating. According to Tony's widower father, "Sometimes you just have to do it the other's feller's way," while his sweetheart's dad insists that "You've got to bow to authority." The well-meaning ineffectiveness of Tony's father, the suffocating horror of life with Arlene's parents – both of these are nicely balanced by the sympathetic Detective Donovan, though even he proposes that Tony should "polish off the rough edges: adjust."

Another older man, Dr Brandon, indulges in a different, albeit familiar, kind of rhetoric: "I have penetrated the deepest secrets of creation, and I've achieved the first perfect case of regression." Yes, it's yet another film trading (rather belatedly in this instance) on *The Search for Bridey Murphy*, and teen audiences may have been forgiven for shifting impatiently in their seats as Brandon, creepily underlit, regresses the supine Tony via hypnosis. Even so, the smoothly professional Whit Bissell does his considerable best with Brandon's repetitive pronouncements, including all the usual guff about human guinea pigs being dispensable, together with some really outstanding garbage about reforming the human race by "hurl[ing] it back into its primitive dawn." He also claims that Tony is a suitable subject because "There were certain tell-tale marks on his body only I would recognise." This line hangs strangely until the homoeroticism that would become a Cohen-Kandel trademark comes into focus in later films.

I Was a Teenage Werewolf remains memorable for appearing genuinely simpatico with its target audience, rather than being the usual lumbering attempt at hipness by clueless middle-aged men. Much of the film's success can be attributed to Michael Landon's committed performance as Tony and also to debutant director Gene Fowler Jr, who struggles with the vacuous scenes set at the local teen drop-in but compensates with some really savage and sprightly attack scenes.

I WAS A TEENAGE WEREWOLF

Sunset Productions / American International 1957
76 minutes
production began 14 March

Cinematographer: Joseph La Shelle; Art Director: Leslie Thomas; Editor: George Gittens; Sound: James S Thomson, Henry Adams; Set Decoration: Morris Hoffman; Make-up: Philip Scheer; Hair Stylist: Fae Smith; Wardrobe: Oscar Rodriguez; Music: Paul Dunlap; Music Editor: Axel Hubert; Song: 'Eeny, Meeny, Miney, Mo' by Jerry Blaine; Assistant Director / Production Manager: Jack R Berne; Screenplay: Ralph Thornton [Aben Kandel, Herman Cohen]; Presented by: James H Nicholson, Samuel Z Arkoff; Producer: Herman Cohen; Director: Gene Fowler Jr

Michael Landon (Tony); Yvonne Lime (Arlene); Whit Bissell (Dr Alfred Brandon); Tony Marshall (Jimmy); Dawn Richard (Theresa); Barney Phillips (Detective Donovan); Ken Miller (Vic); Cindy Robbins (Pearl); Michael Rougas (Frank); Robert Griffin (Chief Baker); Joseph Mell (Dr Hugo Wagner); Malcolm Atterbury (Tony's father); Eddie Marr (Doyle); Vladimir Sokoloff (Pepe); Louise Lewis (Principal Ferguson); John Launer (Arlene's father); Guy Williams (Officer Chris Stanley); Dorothy Crehan (Arlene's mother); uncredited: Herman Cohen (plainclothes policeman with photos)

Injection of a youthful twist into one of the oldest of horror picture themes makes this spine tingler a praiseworthy parcel of middle bracket entertainment ... Because his [the doctor's] victim is an adolescent, the solidly constructed screenplay permits interpolation of the hepster antics and jive so dear to the hearts of the leather jacket set ... Assets include convincing performances by a young, new-faces cast, Herman Cohen's adequate production mountings and able direction by Gene Fowler Jr. *Box Office*

I put Michael [Landon] under personal contract to Herman Cohen Productions Inc ... Doing *Teenage Werewolf*, he did all the stunts. He almost killed himself! In a way, it was kind of weird. When he had the make-up on, he told me "I really feel like a werewolf." When he was chasing Dawn Richard in that gym to attack and kill her, we had to stop the camera and pull him off. He was really into it. *Herman Cohen [quoted in Scarlet Street, Winter 1995]*

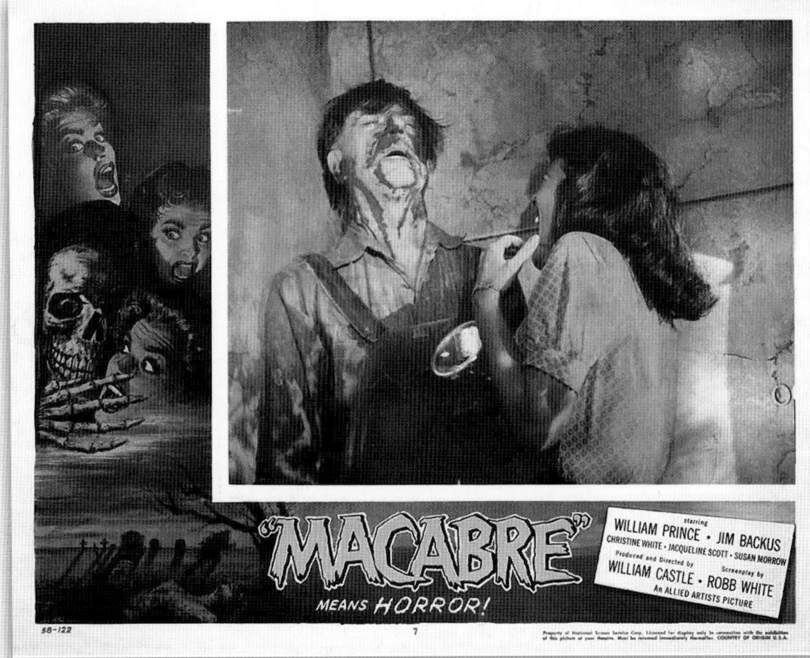

Jacqueline Scott stumbles across the deceased Howard Hoffman in *Macabre* (1957)

us exactly what to think of hypnotic head-shrinkers like Brandon.) At the final hurdle, however, Cohen's redefinition of the werewolf for a youth audience defaults to a disappointingly old-fashioned moral, with Detective Donovan, contemplating the bloody outcome of Brandon's self-proclaimed "world-shaking experiment," pointing out that "It's not for man to interfere in the ways of God."

Tony Rivers, of course, was to be only the first of several teenage monsters. Another film that initiated a franchise, of sorts, began shooting at Ziv on 29 July. This was an important date for the former Columbia contractee William Castle – after 14 years as a film director, he was finally going independent with a picture called *Macabre*. He'd recently experienced a Damascene conversion when watching H G Clouzot's dazzling French shocker *Les Diaboliques*. "The collective emotional release of all those screaming kids was exhilarating, incredible!" he claimed. "Leaving the theatre, I felt a strange sensation – a reawakening of some sort."[7] *Macabre*, personally financed by Castle and screenwriter Robb White to the tune of $86,000, was the result. Picked up by Allied Artists, it proved a major hit, with Castle promising each and every punter a $1000 Lloyds of London insurance policy "in case of death by fright" – a ploy cynically referred to by White as "the only thing the picture had going for it."[8]

An extremely mild adaptation of Theo Durrant's 1951 novel *The Marble Forest* (Durrant being the collective pseudonym for a dozen members of the Mystery Writers of America, writing a chapter each), the film focuses on the universally despised GP of an incestuous provincial community, whose three-year-old daughter has been kidnapped and reportedly stashed out of sight in a miniature coffin. From this rather unappealing plot premise there ensues a frantic search of the nearest cemetery, where the doctor's devoted nurse stumbles slap-bang into the elderly caretaker's bloodstained corpse – a splendidly orchestrated jolt but hardly likely to precipitate death

The drop-in is called The Haunted House and plays host to a memorably awful song'n'dance routine, boringly captured, like other scenes in the same set, in a single take without cuts. The werewolf action, however, is not only scarily realised but aptly expresses Tony's broiling unrest. The first victim, subjected to a highly effective 'Lewton walk' in nocturnal yet sun-dappled parkland, is unusually well played by Michael Rougas. The second is the inadvertently provocative Theresa (Dawn Richard), whose upended position on the gymnasium's parallel bars yields a startling POV shot of the aroused werewolf approaching her upside down. The beast man's sexual impulse had never been so frankly expressed in any previous werewolf film, and this scene retains all the bludgeoning impact it had in 1957. To add to its nerve-jangling qualities, Tony's change is initiated, not just by Theresa, but by an unexpected blaring of the school bell.

The film also boasts some queasy shadowplay from the distinguished cinematographer Joseph La Shelle and a classic werewolf make-up by Philip Scheer. There are even some good jokes, as when we're told that the pre-lycanthropic Tony was given to eating raw hamburgers, plus a strange but charming cameo from Vladimir Sokoloff as a displaced Carpathian janitor. (His old-country conviction that werewolfism only manifests "when the Evil Eye is on you" tells

by fright. More interesting than the supposedly creepy stuff is a surprisingly frank flashback to the fate of the GP's sister-in-law Nancy, who succumbed to some kind of bungled abortion. Radiantly beautiful and also blind, she's first seen in a speeding car, claiming jadedly that "I wanna live fast, love fast and die fast!" – death-wish sentiments given added piquancy by the fact that she's played (extremely well) by Christine White, sometime girlfriend of the tragically short-lived James Dean.

In Britain, where the film came out in August 1958 with a crucial graveside revelation cut to bits by the censor, it had the additional handicap of opening in the same week as Kurt Neumann's all-conquering *The Fly*. This was a minor blip, however, since Castle's second film in similar vein was about to start shooting.

For the staff at Ziv, Castle's graveyard emphasis must have induced a certain amount of déjà vu, for the studio had just played host to another low-budget independent set largely, like *Macabre*, in a cemetery. Albert Band's *Killer on the Wall* had begun shooting on 29 April 1957; the result was put out by United Artists over a year later under the more throat-grabbing title *I Bury the Living*. Here, Richard Boone plays Robert Kraft, incoming manager of the Immortal Hills cemetery, who is advised that black pins on the cemetery map indicate occupied plots while white pins denote paid-for but as yet untenanted ones. Inevitably, he accidentally applies black pins to the joint plot of a couple of newly-weds; their near-instantaneous death in a car crash triggers Kraft's rapid disintegration.

As more deaths ensue, Band builds up a climate of slow-burning eeriness with admirable economy, lending an almost sentient malevolence to the all-important map, the design of which seems to put forth watchful eyes as Kraft slips further and further under its influence. There's also a deliciously ominous score by Gerald Fried and a make-or-break central performance from Boone, who exudes clammy disquiet from beginning to end. Finally, Kraft decides that "If I have the power of death using the black pins, then I must have the power of life using the white ones..." Headstones topple, grave earth heaves – but it all turns out to be a huge tease, since the all-too-human culprit is implausibly revealed as the cemetery's murderous Scottish caretaker, ruining an otherwise exemplary little picture.

The film's writer, Louis Garfinkle, later called this cop-out ending "a criminal malefaction on the part of the UA executives, who sent down word from on high that 'audiences will never believe a map can have power of life and death over them' – the entire essence of my original story."[9] To make matters worse, the caretaker character, intended for the 80-year-old Finlay Currie, ended up with the 34-year-old Theodore Bikel, who never looks convincingly ancient despite all Jack Pierce's best efforts in the make-up chair.

FROM BLACKNESS INTO LIGHT

As their July 1957 double-bill of *The Vampire* and the 'giant molluscs threaten California' shocker *The Monster that Challenged the World* was unleashed nationwide, Gramercy Pictures were putting together a similar double-feature for release the following spring. One of the films, *The Flame Barrier*, was accurately characterised by SF historian Bill Warren as a dreary mix of jungle movie and (yet another) rip-off of Hammer's Quatermass pictures. Pride of place, however, went to a much more interesting item. *Curse of Dracula* went into production in the first week of September, with, as in *The Vampire*, Paul Landres directing and Pat Fielder scripting. Then in mid-April 1958, just before the film went on release, *Variety* noted a curious title change. By that time Gramercy, like everyone else in the industry, must have been aware of the major new British version of *Dracula* that was due to open a few weeks after theirs, which made the decision to retitle their film *The Return of Dracula* seem very odd indeed.

Hardly surprisingly, the lurid, gore-strewn impact of the Hammer version made Gramercy's pressbook claim that theirs was "the newest, and possibly most gruesome, of all the Dracula films" seem ridiculous. And yet *The Return of Dracula* has abundant charm and intelligence of its own.

> *In middle Europe, Meyerman of the European Police Authority is narrowly cheated of his quarry when a vampire's casket – maybe that of Count Dracula himself – turns out to be empty. Killing a humble artist called Bellac Gordal, the vampire assumes his identity and also his projected journey. Emigrating to a tranquil California town called Carleton, he's welcomed by Gordal's unsuspecting American relatives, particularly his impressionable young niece, Rachel Mayberry. But then Rachel's blind friend, Jennie Blake, becomes mysteriously ill and dies with shocking suddenness...*

Plot-wise, as Pat Fielder happily admitted, *The Return of Dracula* is modelled on Alfred Hitchcock's 1942 thriller *Shadow of a Doubt*, substituting Bellac Gordal for the homicidal Uncle Charlie and the guileless Rachel for Charlie's doting niece. This would be unusual enough, but Fielder loaded her script with numerous other

Francis Lederer isn't who Norma Eberhardt thinks he is in *The Return of Dracula* (1957)

intriguing features, including some extremely well-turned dialogue.

In addition to one direct Bram Stoker quote ("I have dined already"), the film's émigré bloodsucker fascinates his victims with such sacrilegious sentiments as "You shall arise reborn in me." When one such becomes a nascent vampire, Gordal reassures her with a sibilant croon of "That's right. It hurts to breathe again. But only for a moment." And when Rachel expresses disappointment at his indifference to being 'accepted' by the Mayberry family, he gets right to the heart of the conformist small-town milieu in which he's ended up by sneering, "There's a price for your acceptance – for me to conform." In another subversive touch, Fielder alludes to the recent McCarthy hearings when a supposed immigration official reflects on the political regime in Gordal's ancestral home, maintaining smugly that "Over here we don't like to investigate a man unless it's absolutely necessary."

Just as intriguing are some of Fielder's imaginative set-pieces, notably an extraordinary scene in which Gordal visits the blind Jennie and, prior to biting her, announces that "I can take you from the blackness into the light." Just as we're pondering the irony of this thing of darkness offering a blind person light, we realise that he's done exactly that – she momentarily regains her sight, meaning that the first and last person she sees is her Messianic killer. The sequel is another extraordinary scene in which Jennie (well played by Virginia Vincent) runs mad, repeatedly screaming "I've got to close the window!" before suddenly dropping dead. And that Meyerman, the vampire hunter on Gordal's trail, appears to be some kind of government official (or at least claims to be) brings to mind the dogged efforts of post-war Nazi hunters, with the contest between Gordal and Meyerman prefiguring the Nazi-hunting potboiler *The Boys from Brazil*. One person presumably unaware of this subtext was the film's property master, who, in a really bizarre blunder, supplied Gordal with a copy of the *Berliner Tageblatt* – a newspaper closed down by the Nazis in 1939.

THE RETURN OF DRACULA

Gramercy Pictures 1957
77 minutes
production began 3 September
UK title: The Fantastic Disappearing Man

Cinematographer: Jack Mackenzie; Art Director: James D Vance; Editor: Sherman A Rose; Sound: Jack Goodrich, Frank Moran; Set Decoration: Rudy Butler; Make-up: Stanley Smith; Music: Gerald Fried; Music Editor: George Brand; Dialogue Director: Dan Gachman; Assistant Director: Bernard F McEveety; Screenplay: Pat Fielder; Producers: Jules V Levy, Arthur Gardner; Director: Paul Landres

Francis Lederer ('Bellac Gordal'); Norma Eberhardt (Rachel Mayberry); Ray Stricklyn (Tim Hansen); John Wengraf (Meyerman); Virginia Vincent (Jennie Blake); Gage Clarke (Dr Reud Whitfield); Jimmy Baird (Mickey Mayberry); Greta Granstedt (Cora Mayberry); Enid Yousen (Frieda); uncredited: Mel F Allen (Mel [baggage man]); Dan Gachman (county clerk); Harry Harvey Sr (Eddie [station master]); Robert Lynn (Dr Paul Beecher); Belle Mitchell (Cornelia); John McNamara (Sheriff Bicknell); Norbert Schiller (Bellac Gordal); Charles Tannen (Mack Bryant [immigration official])

The Return of Dracula is a well-made little picture but it is somewhat short on its most marketable quantity – horror. Francis Lederer plays the title role with considerable restraint and it is not until the final reel that things get at all exciting. As a horror exploitation item, it could stand some juicing up. It could be, you might say, more full-blooded. *Variety*

I personally had a prejudice against these kind of pictures. My agent sent me to the studio, and they didn't have a script. I told them I never made that kind of picture. "Oh no, Mr Lederer. This will be a spoof!" That idea interested me tremendously, and so they engaged me. Then I got the script, and I was very discouraged. Francis Lederer [quoted in *Classic Images*, June 1997]

Yet the film is very definitely set in 1957, with the bland self-absorption of contemporary California providing a vivid contrast to the insidious old-world charm of Gordal. On top of this the noirish cinematography by Jack Mackenzie recalls his work on the Val Lewton production *Isle of the Dead*, despite Gordal's repeated visits to a somewhat over-bright graveyard. And, possibly in post-production deference to the Kensington Gore splashed all over Hammer's *Dracula*, for the staking of Jennie this otherwise monochrome picture breaks out into blood-pumping colour for a single shot. Yet the film remains too modest an enterprise to make full capital of its unusual ingredients. In particular, attempts at character development for the starry-eyed Rachel – as when she says, ostensibly about Jennie, "I just know how terrible it must be to be alone" – come to nothing. She remains a cipher, like everybody else in Carleton.

The film's power rests, instead, on a truly bloodcurdling score by Gerald Fried (patterned after a much-quoted mediaeval source, the *Dies Irae*), together with the two-sides-of-the-same-coin qualities of Francis Lederer and John Wengraf. Cast as Gordal and Meyerman respectively, these two middle-aged Austrian-born actors, with their noble faces and thrillingly mellifluous voices, lend the film a great deal of class merely by showing up. Ultimately, however, the fact that they never actually meet on screen proves a disappointment. Though the tireless Meyerman supervises the destruction of Jennie, it's left to Rachel's uninspiring boyfriend Tim to inadvertently propel Gordal into a stake pit.

Meyerman, incidentally, hedges his bets by referring to Gordal as "possibly Count Dracula himself," leaving Lederer's position in the pantheon of cinematic Draculas somewhat hazy. Either way, he remains a magnetic presence, and in 1971 he would have a less equivocal crack at Dracula in an episode of Rod Serling's *Night Gallery*.

A couple of years after he made *The Return of Dracula*, Lederer was on view in another horror picture, a US-Philippines co-production called *Terror is a Man*. Here he plays a former Park Avenue surgeon, Dr Girard, whose two-years' seclusion on a South Seas island has involved 53 major operations on a black panther. "I have chosen the animal," he says blandly, "to be the father of a new race of men." Of course, this is just another retread of H G Wells' *The Island of Dr Moreau*, with the book's community of tragic manimals reduced to one rebellious panther-man. Fortunately, as played by Flory Carlos and made-up by Remedios Amazan, he's a splendidly feral and pitiful creation, with particularly haunting post-operative close-ups of his tormented eyes that recall similar shots in *The Creature Walks Among Us*. At an early stage he escapes his confinement and spies on Girard's beautiful and unhappy wife (Greta Thyssen) as she tosses frustratedly in her bed. Inflamed, the beast-man proceeds to make short work of the local natives in a thrillingly staged killing spree.

Terror is a Man is overlong, dawdling somewhat in its middle section while Mrs G falls for the petroleum engineer (Richard Derr) who's been washed up on the island. But the film remains unusually compelling thanks to Paul Harber's clever script, Emmanuel Rojas' sumptuous monochrome photography and Lederer's exceptional performance. It also proved influential; a successful 1965 re-release as *Blood Creature* encouraged its producer, Eddie Romero, and director, Gerry De Leon, to fuse lush local colour with over-the-top mutant mayhem in such lurid Filipino titles as *Brides of Blood*, *Mad Doctor of Blood Island* and *Beast of Blood*.

A presentiment of those films is also visible in *She Demons*, a cut-rate Screencraft production that writer-director Richard E Cunha started on 25 September

Francis Lederer again, this time as a lightly disguised Dr Moreau in *Terror is a Man* (1959)

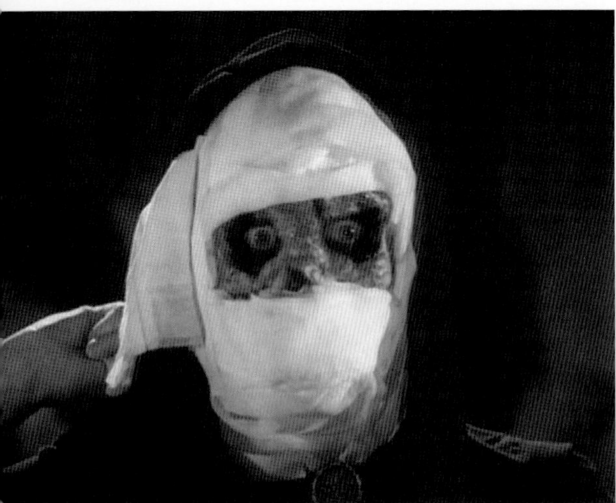

What remains of a renegade Nazi's disfigured wife in *She Demons* (1957)

1957. The ingredients here rapidly stack up into one of the most gob-smacking experiences the period has to offer – a stock-footage hurricane, a supposedly volcanic island, three shipwreck survivors, one of them a spoiled heiress played by Irish McCalla (TV's *Sheena Queen of the Jungle*), a sexy-chintzy bikini-clad dance troupe (the Diana Nellis Dancers), a torture compound staffed by displaced Gestapo officers wielding whips, a woman without a face, other women with heavenly bodies but the faces of animalistic demons, a smarmy Mengele type nicknamed The Butcher and amusingly played by Rudolph Anders ("Soon you will be beautiful again, my dear!"), a thrilling reveal of what lies behind the 'faceless' woman's bandages, a stock-footage volcanic eruption – and much much more. Recalling Poverty Row mad-scientist narratives of the 1940s while anticipating Georges Franju's *Les Yeux sans visage*, the end product isn't merely a hoot but also a bad-taste exploitation milestone.

Writing in *Variety*, 'Whit' was kind: "Mediocre film is actually more straight adventure than horror, although it fits adequately into the package top-bracketed by *Giant from the Unknown*." *She Demons*, in fact, had only come into being because Astor Pictures insisted on a supporting attraction when they agreed to distribute Cunha's first film, which he'd made on spec at the end of 1956 under the title *Giant of Devil's Crag*. The extraordinary sex-and-sadism cocktail of *She Demons* is nowhere to be seen in *Giant from the Unknown*. Instead we have a straightforward monster movie in which archaeologist Morris Ankrum hopes to add "a new chapter to the history of California" by uncovering the 500-years-dead Vargas, a "brutal, degenerate and depraved" Conquistador nicknamed the Diablo Giant.

There are an awful lot of boring expository scenes and sappy romantic ones in this too-long film, but Vargas himself is one of the most memorable monsters of the era. He gets a really terrific resurrection scene and stalks Joline Brand and Sally Fraser in scenes given real punch by Cunha's staging and Albert Glasser's stirring score. He's imposingly played, as the opening credits put it, by "Buddy Baer in makeup created by Jack Pierce" – a rare acknowledgment of Pierce's importance to the development of Hollywood's monster tradition. Sadly, Vargas is seen off with anticlimactic ease (the young hero sets about him with a stick), and he has tough competition, in any case, from the strangely ghoulish-looking old-time Western star Bob Steele, who plays the annoying local sheriff. Though released alongside *She Demons*, the film forms a more interesting companion piece to Fred F Sears' *The Werewolf*, having been filmed on much the same Big Bear locations 12 months after it.

The Filipino setting of *Terror is a Man*, much more exotic than Big Bear, wasn't the only foreign locale seen in American horror of the late 1950s. *Terror in the Midnight Sun*, for example, was a Hollywood-Stockholm hook-up that commenced production on 14 April 1958. With a US director (Virgil Vogel) and US leads, this is a real curiosity, filmed on snowbound Lapp locations and featuring a giant (and highly impressive) Yeti-type creature, recalling by turns *King Kong* and *Night of the Demon*. The hooded, white-faced aliens, who appear to be controlling the thing, reside in a spacecraft concealed in an icy cavern, thus invoking *It Came from Outer Space*, and the giant monster unleashes an orgasmic avalanche on first sighting the attractive heroine. Played by Barbara Wilson, she (or her body double) is granted a rather surprising nude shower scene and is told by the smug male lead to "Stay here and look pretty till we get back." Though much of the early action defaults to rather laboured scenes of figure skating, dinner dancing and torch singing (with Swedish pop icon Brita Borg the featured artist), the film's Arctic vistas and rampaging snow beast remain memorably eerie.

Known in Sweden as *Rymdinvasion i Lappland* (Space Invasion in Lapland), the film retained its English working title for release in the UK. In America, however, it had the misfortune to fall into the hands of Jerry Warren, who shoehorned John Carradine into it and came up with a disastrously re-edited atrocity called *Invasion of the Animal People*.

Another highly peculiar foreign co-production came from itinerant director-producer George Breakston, who, having got together with United Artists of Japan, started shooting *The Split* on

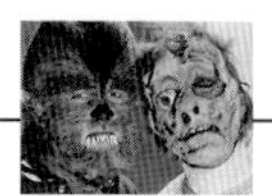

15 November 1958. Co-directed by Kenneth G Crane, this genuinely unhinged mad-scientist melodrama starts with a shaggy ape-thing laying waste to a pool of unsuspecting geishas in blood-spurting shadowplay, then introduces us to a thoroughly obnoxious American reporter called Larry Stanford and the shady Japanese scientist he wants to interview. The shaggy ape-thing, it turns out, was Dr Suzuki's transmogrified brother. The doctor's wife, kept caged in a subterranean laboratory, is a mutant too. Unaware he's been drugged, Larry acquires first a hairy right hand, then – in a strikingly surreal image – discovers a human eye winking out from his shoulder. Has Larry succumbed to some form of male pregnancy? Before this idea has time to sink in, the usual murder spree ensues. Having sprouted a subsidiary head next to his own, Larry finally splits into two beings and pluckily topples his anthropoid other self – "an alien thing, a species that's never walked this earth before" – into a volcano.

Just the first of *The Split*'s multiplying oddities is Breakston's importation of the soon-to-get-married English actors Peter Dyneley and Jane Hylton to play Larry and his downtrodden wife Linda. ("We met while making the same awful horror film in Tokyo,"[10] Hylton noted many years later.) On top of this, the film laces its mad-science scenario with a heavy dose of sleaze. To detain Larry in Japan, Suzuki (Tetsu Nakamura) distracts him with a string of willing geishas, and it's clear that, rather than altering Larry's personality, the drug has merely coaxed his sleazeball tendencies to the surface. The final freakish 'split', achieved with a bellowing intensity by Dyneley, is as sublime a fusion of horror and hilarity as 1950s exploitation achieved, which is saying a lot.

Tetsu Nakamura faces up to the two-headed Peter Dyneley in *The Split* (1958), aka *The Manster*

Retitled *The Manster*, the film appeared in the US in March 1962 as support to *Les Yeux sans visage*, itself ignominiously retitled *The Horror Chamber of Dr Faustus*. In the UK Breakston's film appeared under its working title, *The Split*, forming half of a United Artists double-bill in April 1961. The co-feature was a US-Brazilian Eastmancolor concoction called *Macumba Love*, which had been shot in São Paulo back in April 1959. Directed by Douglas Fowley, this is a dull-as-ditchwater musical-voodoo-travelogue, in which Walter Reed is the standard-issue "general debunker of mankind" who tangles with a remorseless voodoo priestess (Ruth de Souza). The film casts Eastbourne's most famous glamour model, June Wilkinson, as Reed's English-accented daughter, and there's a quite-good effect when the dead priestess morphs into an equally dead snake creature. The rest is a trial to sit through.

INSTRUCTION AND CONTROL

According to producer Herman Cohen, it was Robert O'Donnell of the Texas Interstate chain who suggested an *I Was a Teenage Werewolf* follow-up, asking that the film be ready for his theatres by Thanksgiving: 28 November 1957. He made this offer, according to legend, on Labor Day: 2 September. AIP's James H Nicholson then went one better by suggesting Cohen make, not just one follow-up, but two. As with the werewolf film, Cohen wrote the scripts in conjunction with Aben Kandel; he then assigned both films to director Herbert L Strock. With astonishing speed, Cohen had *Blood of Dracula* on the floor at Ziv Studios by 9 September, moving on to *I Was a Teenage Frankenstein* on 7 October. And he fulfilled O'Donnell's remit, with the double-feature getting a Thanksgiving launch at 75 Texan theatres prior to a staggered release elsewhere in December and January.

Pretty much every assessment of *Blood of Dracula*, starting right back in 1957, has asked why Cohen didn't do the sensible thing and call it *I Was a Teenage Vampire*. The story concocted by Cohen and Kandel laid down, more clearly than did *Teenage Werewolf*, what was to become their abiding motif – a hapless teen becoming the transmogrifying tool of an evil and sexually ambiguous authority figure. In this instance, 18-year-old Nancy Perkins (Sandra Harrison), forcibly enrolled at a boarding school on the remarriage of her father, comes under the influence of chemistry teacher Miss Branding (Louise Lewis) – whose name echoes the calculating Dr Brandon of *Teenage Werewolf*. And just as the earlier film's police station harboured an incongruous Carpathian caretaker, so Miss Branding hypnotises Nancy with a Carpathian amulet,

Another transmogrified teen: Sandra Harrison in *Blood of Dracula* (1957)

hoping somehow to promote nuclear disarmament (!) by demonstrating "that there's a power strong enough to destroy the world buried within each of us."

Commendably, Lewis plays the role absolutely deadpan, especially when explaining her quest for "a special kind of girl with special potentials." That Miss Branding is a lesbian is also alluded to in the film's first attack scene, when she wills on her protégée from an upper window, afterwards dabbing orgasmic sweat from her forehead. But, like everything else in the film, the notion is merely toyed with, then dropped. Worse, the action never works up any real energy, dwindling to a pathetically fudged ending in which Nancy's impalement isn't even shown.

A transformation in a cemetery, which leaves two victims piled up behind one gravestone, is reasonably well achieved, and Philip Scheer's make-up job for Nancy, like his previous werewolf design, is simultaneously ridiculous and a work of art. Another highlight of sorts comes when three local youths break into the girls' dormitory with (let's face it) rape on their minds, only to initiate a jaw-dropping rock'n'roll rendition of 'Puppy Love'. (Not the later Paul Anka hit; this one was written and lip-synced by Jerry Blaine.) And the script boasts at least one nifty double-entendre, when Nancy is told that the girls take turns dating the youthful groundsman as if he were "a jug of water on a lifeboat," with the pert clarification: "One swallow to each girl."

In AIP's new teen-horror package, *Blood of Dracula* was very definitely the secondary attraction, with punters lured in the main by the irresistible daftness of its companion's marquee-filling title, *I Was a Teenage Frankenstein*. Having been slung together so rapidly, both films are cruder, less polished and noticeably more claustrophobic than their werewolf forebear, and Strock's direction is slack and uninspired. Yet Cohen's teen Frankenstein remains arguably just as memorable as his teen werewolf, if only because on this occasion Cohen and Kandel really went for broke, piling absurdity on absurdity and coming up with a new kind of body-parts black comedy.

> *Visiting the US, England's Professor Frankenstein sets up a private laboratory and is able to take advantage of a couple of happy accidents. First, a nearby car crash yields a dead teenager; then a plane-load of high-school athletes goes down, yielding several more. Initially hideous, the resultant monster is given a handsome new face by Frankenstein, who proposes to show him off in England as "a wunderkind created by me, a teenage marvel."*

In the wake of Hammer's smash success with *The Curse of Frankenstein*, Cohen's choice of subject was a natural follow-up to *I Was a Teenage Werewolf*. Indeed, Philip Scheer's make-up for Cohen's latest boy wonder looks exactly like Philip Leakey's for Christopher Lee had it been reimagined by a six-year-old boy who'd read too many EC horror comics. The lumpen head taps into adolescent angst just as surely as *Teenage Werewolf* did; the secret shame this time is, not mysteriously proliferating hair, but rampaging acne. Intriguingly, this theme was relevant to the film even behind the scenes. Cohen's new creature, Gary Conway, was a 21-year-old novice who was at what he called "the great zit age" and fretted that theatrical make-up of any sort would make him "break out". He then noticed that the ubiquitous 47-year-old character actor Whit Bissell "had a wonderful smooth skin" and "decided that make-up couldn't be so bad."[11]

The other main ingredient of the film is its 'hapless teen controlled by tyrannical older man' scenario, a routine with obvious significance for the widening generation gap of the day. It had been briefly diverted onto women for *Blood of Dracula* but would now predominate in Cohen and Kandel's scripts – to the point where, in the 1973 potboiler *Craze*, Jack Palance comes right out with it, telling young Martin Potter that he was "a beggar when I picked you up – sleeping in Hyde Park, hustling old queens when you could turn a trick." In 1957 the homoeroticism was more of a subtext, with Professor Frankenstein responding to the

track team's plane crash with "Ah, tragic. All those fine young athletic bodies gone to waste..." To substantiate Frankenstein's words, the main criteria involved in casting his creation was obvious, as Cohen explained in the 1990s: "You know, *Teenage Frankenstein* had to have a good body; that was very important ... I could have gone down to Muscle Beach and picked 50 of them."[12]

As well as stating his Nazi determination to take "the principle of selective breeding one step further," this Frankenstein outlines a rationale just as barmy as those of the psychologist and chemistry teacher in Cohen's previous films. "If I can create out of different parts a youth whom I shall instruct and control," he points out, "I'll prove that only in youth is there any hope for the salvation of mankind." This kind of nonsense is put over with unflinching composure by the splendid Whit Bissell, whose Frankenstein refers to "you Americans" and even points out that "In England, you know, we have a little more respect for the older generation." And yet Bissell's mellifluous tones remain unmistakably American, despite Cohen's mistaken conviction that he sounded English.

Frankenstein has an impatient fiancée, Margaret, who is treated with a nasty misogynist distaste that would recur in all Cohen and Kandel's subsequent scripts. "Ah, perfidy – thy name is woman!" grumbles the Professor. To eradicate this too-inquisitive thorn in Frankenstein's side, the writers borrow a situation from *The Curse of Frankenstein*, unleashing the monster on her in arbitrary fashion, then – in an innovation of their own – consigning her to the alligator pool underneath the laboratory.

That Frankenstein, holed up in California's Huntington Park, has at least one alligator at his disposal is indication enough that Cohen and Kandel were laughing up their sleeves while concocting the script. The dialogue occasionally hints at deeper matters, as when the creature awakens behind his bandages and says forlornly, "It's dark in here. Dark." But by and large it's obviously parodic, as in the famous moment when Frankenstein urges the boy to "Speak! You've got a civil tongue in your head. I know you have because I sewed it back myself." There's room for discreet in-jokes too, as when Frankenstein proposes to deconstruct the boy and pack him off to England in a crate marked '113 Wardour Street' – the London HQ, not just of Cohen's associates at Anglo Amalgamated, but also Hammer Film Productions.

Cheap, slapdash, disposable – *I Was a Teenage Frankenstein* is all these things (it doesn't even include a creation scene), but it nevertheless finds room here and there for pulp surrealism of a high order. At one point Frankenstein and his protégé are seen in the shadowed recesses of a car, sizing up the necking couples in a Lover's Lane parking area. With Bissell

I WAS A TEENAGE FRANKENSTEIN

Santa Rosa Productions / American International 1957
73 *minutes*
production began 7 *October*
UK title: Teenage Frankenstein

Cinematographer: Lothrop Worth; Art Director: Leslie Thomas; Editor: Jerry Young; Sound: Al Overton, Kay Rose; Set Decoration: Tom Oliphant; Make-up: Philip Scheer; Wardrobe: Einar Bourman; Music: Paul Dunlap; Music Editor: George Brand; Assistant Director / Production Manager: Austen Jewell; Screenplay: Kenneth Langtry [Aben Kandel, Herman Cohen]; Presented by: James H Nicholson, Samuel Z Arkoff; Producer: Herman Cohen; Director: Herbert L Strock

Whit Bissell (Professor Frankenstein); Phyllis Coates (Margaret); Robert Burton (Dr Karlton); Gary Conway (teenage monster / Bob); George Lynn (Sgt Burns); John Cliff (Sgt McAfee); Marshall Bradford (Dr Randolph); Claudia Bryar (Arlene's mother); Angela Blake (beautiful girl); Russ Whiteman (Dr Elwood); Charles Seel (Mr Saxton [jeweller]); Paul Keast (car crash witness); uncredited: Larry Carr, William H O'Brien, Gretchen Thomas (witnesses in corridor); Pat Miller (police officer); Joy Stoner (Arlene)

Teamed with *Blood of Dracula* ... this is the stronger entry of the combo – in the purveying of spinal tingles, in production value, story and performances ... True, the screenplay – and it's about the crackpot croaker, what else? – defies all semblance of believability. But that can hardly be deemed a liability because the shoppers for horror certainly do not expect their purchases to be accompanied by logic. *Box Office*

Herman Cohen had a gimmick for *Teenage Frankenstein*. He was looking for a teenager – the ideal teenager. They were going to search across the country, one of those deals. I got it because I was around; I was just there ... I was not 'in the business' and following things. One day, I see this line all the way around the block. I look up and say, "I'll be damned! That's the movie!" I just couldn't get over it! *Gary Conway* [quoted in *Scarlet Street*, Winter 1995]

Gary Conway and Whit Bissell go cruising on Lover's Lane in *I Was a Teenage Frankenstein* (1957)

in a neat fedora and Conway in his outstandingly ugly monster make-up, it's a bizarre and memorable image. And what Frankenstein does next – taking the pretty face of one of the necking boys and successfully grafting it onto his creation – shows that Georges Franju may well have recalled the film when making his poetic masterwork *Les Yeux sans visage* early in 1959.

The self-parody encoded in *I Was a Teenage Frankenstein* turned to self-cannibalism in *How to Make a Monster*, which Herbert Strock started shooting – again, at Ziv Studios – on 2 April 1958. This time the studio gate actually appears in the film, with the Ziv sign replaced by a banner advertising the fictitious 'American International Studios'. AIP may not have had their own personalised studio, but they did have a production ethos that's self-regardingly mirrored in the Cohen-Kandel script. "The horror cycle is over," snarls an incoming producer. "There's no doubt about it. Monsters are finis." Balancing this, a kindly director points out, presumably with Hammer Films in mind, that "One picture can do it – maybe one of these foreign imports – and the whole monster cycle is on its way again." This wisdom comes too late for make-up master Pete Dumond, who has already started using a specially formulated foundation on his young *Werewolf Meets Frankenstein* stars (Gary Clarke and Gary Conway), causing them to enact his murderous revenge on the new-broom management.

Robert H Harris makes little impression as Dumond, though the role is so lazily written it's doubtful any actor could have done much with it. For the record, the homoeroticism is still vividly present, with Dumond reverently collecting photos of his charges and saying, "I enjoy working with these teenagers ... They put themselves in your hands." By the end of the film he's become (entirely improbably) a full-on drooling maniac; with a host of Paul Blaisdell's original creature creations on display in his inner sanctum, he predictably refers to the masks as "my family, my children" prior to the place going up in flames. Just as *I Was a Teenage Frankenstein* lurched into colour for the climactic frying of the creature, this whole last reel of *How to Make a Monster* is rendered in rather bilious hues, underlining the fact that it's really just *House of Wax* reduced to sub-bargain-basement level. The film could be taken as indicating Cohen and AIP's healthy gift for satirising themselves, or else their utter cynicism in fobbing off their teen audience with recycled goods. Probably both.

Early in *How to Make a Monster*, a studio tour guide tells his customers that "Our first stop will be on Stage 3, where they are now shooting *Horrors of the Black Museum*." Actually, *Horrors of the Black Museum* was just a title at the time; it didn't start shooting until October, when Cohen decamped to England and made it under the auspices of Anglo Amalgamated. With this film Cohen's standard teen-manipulating protagonist was inherited by the British actor Michael Gough, who in 1960 would do it all again in Cohen's 'enlarged ape' farrago *Konga*.

How to Make a Monster went out alongside a Roger Corman picture made under the title *Prehistoric World*, in which the titular world turns out to be post-apocalyptic rather than prehistoric. To Corman's horror, AIP retitled the film *Teenage Cave Man*. By the time Jerry Warren's jaw-dropping *Teenage Zombies* appeared in April 1960, the 'teenage monster' subgenre had run out of steam; teens, of course, were to remain an important feature of horror pictures, but the word 'teenage' was no longer a selling point. Warren's shoddy and almost unwatchable offering, in which femme fatale Katherine Victor schemes to convert decent Americans into unquestioning automata, had been on the shelf since 1957, and it certainly wasn't about to restore the word's box-office lustre.

ATOMIC REACTORS AND SPACE AGE VAMPIRES

Hollywood's horror output in 1957 wound down on a curious but uninspiring note, when Harold Daniels' *My World Dies Screaming* began shooting on 6 December. Here, a young newly-wed is disturbed to discover that her new Florida home is the same house that features in her recurring nightmares. The place, she tells us in introductory voice-over, is "silent, malignant: a place of unspeakable horror," a claim that would be easier to swallow if a big camera shadow didn't fall on the front door when we cross the threshold. Daniels' film claimed to be "the first picture in ... PSYCHO RAMA" – indicating that the proceedings are punctuated by various hokey instances of subliminal imagery. Otherwise it's a wall-to-wall talkfest, enlivened only by Cathy O'Donnell's engaging performance and a powerful score by Darrell Calker. For action it's entirely reliant on halfwit handyman John Qualen plunging over the banisters and a climactic axe fight in which the presence of two stunt men is painfully obvious. Swapping one hyperbolic title for another, a 1961 reissue went out as *Terror in the Haunted House*, a title that has clung to it ever since.

Over in England, Hammer Film Productions started work on *The Revenge of Frankenstein* on Monday 6 January 1958, with Jimmy Sangster smuggling into his script a delightful line in which Peter Cushing's Baron points out that his is "a large family ... remarkable since the Middle Ages for productivity. There are

Ill-fated flunkey Norbert Schiller and scar-faced mad scientist Boris Karloff in *Frankenstein 1970* (1958)

offshoots everywhere – even in America, I'm told." Sangster was clearly well aware that *I Was a Teenage Frankenstein* was not only an 'offshoot' of Hammer's success, but also that it proposed a US descendant of the original Frankenstein. (Albeit a US descendant inexplicably described in the dialogue as English.) No doubt Sangster had also spotted announcements in the trades during December 1957 regarding another American spin on the story, this one an Allied Artists project called *Frankenstein, 1960*. In the event, the film went into production just two days after *The Revenge of Frankenstein*, with its title rapidly changed during shooting to the even more perplexing *Frankenstein 1970*. And the utterly dismal level of the finished product ensured that Hammer could rest easy for a while yet.

Formerly the lynchpins of Bel-Air Productions, producer Aubrey Schenck and director Howard W Koch here took up residence at the Warner Bros studio, where they'd rented various baronial interiors built for Warners' just-completed Diana Barrymore biopic *Too Much, Too Soon*. Schenck also engaged the services of Boris Karloff, whose presence provided a forlorn reminder of past glories. There are a few ideas here that are interesting enough – a Frankenstein descendant (Karloff), having been disfigured by Nazis during the war and forced to ply his trade in Belsen, seeks to finance an atomic reactor by allowing a TV crew to film in his castle. Intriguing, too, is the positioning of Karloff's ultra-modern laboratory at a deeper level than the castle's cobwebbed crypt, suggesting that the horrors of modern science are infinitely worse than those of the Gothic past. But, apart from an atmospheric opening scene that turns out to be part of the show being made by the TV crew, the execution is bland and banal in all departments, vacillating between Frankenstein's super-talkative guests and extremely boring scenes of a visibly dispirited Karloff pottering about in his lab.

The co-writer was Richard Landau, who had several Hammer credits to his name, all of them pre-dating the company's Gothic breakthrough with *The Curse of Frankenstein*. And a few nods to Hammer are duly thrown in (a disembodied heart, a jar of eyeballs), but these are childishly gruesome asides in a film that can muster nothing better for a monster than a bandaged hulk – a hulk, what's more, who somehow gets to the heroine's bedroom door without the benefit of eyes. The heroine in question is Charlotte Austin, whose last film this was. In later years she summarised it quite nicely when pointing out that "I felt sorry for him [Karloff] having to be in a movie like *Frankenstein 1970*. It was degrading."[13]

While Karloff was limping and lisping his way around the *Frankenstein 1970* set, Edward L Cahn was directing a Vogue Pictures quickie called *It! The Vampire from Beyond Space*. Phenomenally speedy, in the last six years of his life Cahn made no fewer than 27 films for the producer Robert E Kent, together with a few more for other outfits. For his part, Kent had formerly been associated with Sam Katzman (for whom he wrote *The Werewolf*), and of the films he assigned to Cahn in 1958 four were horror pictures made for distribution by United Artists, starting with the space-vampire project in mid-January.

It! The Terror from Beyond Space, as the film was renamed on release, involves the first manned mission to Mars going AWOL and a second mission finding out the hard way what went wrong. A vampiric Martian, rogue relic of a lost civilisation, stows away in the rocket's oxygen ducts and the ensuing murders recall A E Van Vogt's 1939 story *Black Destroyer* while prefiguring the 1979 cinema smash *Alien*. To Cahn's credit, the thing's assaults, mainly seen in shadowplay, are executed with a flailing-armed savagery that helps establish it as a truly formidable threat. Cahn even manages a dash of suspense as 'It', holed up in the bowels of the ship, gradually smashes its way up through the various levels to get at the tasty human morsels above.

Shawn Smith in the three-clawed clutches of Ray 'Crash' Corrigan in *It! The Terror from Beyond Space* (1958)

When Cahn confines 'It' to brief glimpses, notably when the creature is skulking slime-faced through the duct system, 'It' does indeed resemble the more sophisticated monster of *Alien*. With three-clawed hands and a pig-nosed face loosely modelled on a vampire bat, Paul Blaisdell's monster suit (worn by gorilla specialist Ray 'Crash' Corrigan) is memorably repulsive, though it has a tendency to rumple in long shot and is introduced, ruinously, by a close-up of its absurdly taloned feet. Its victims' calcified husks, drained of "every ounce of edible fluid" in a process of "cellular collapse and dehydration," are pretty grim for the time, while the merely wounded are quickly infected with "an alien bacteria of some kind." In another detail picked up by *Alien*, the surviving crew members eventually contrive to asphyxiate the creature. "You and I would have thought of letting the air out of the ship in the first five minutes," asserted screenwriter Jerome Bixby. "A part of the commercial writer's art is to conceal the fact that his characters are part-time idiots. Otherwise half the yarns in existence would be one-liners."[14]

The next Cahn-Kent monster movie, which would be coupled with *It!* on release, kicked off on 24 March. Written by Bixby again, *Curse of the Faceless Man* involves Quintillus Aurelius, an ossified victim of Vesuvius who claimed in life to be "the son of Etruscan gods." Now he mimics the template laid down by *The Mummy*, pursuing a modern woman who is, inevitably, the reincarnation of his lost love. At the end he takes a powder, quite literally, when wading with her into the waters of the Bay of Naples, a pathetic anti-climax that is as artless and underwhelming as everything else in the film. When not afflicted by a droning voice-over narration, the viewer can at least take solace from a typically brooding Gerald Fried score, and the heroine (Elaine Edwards) gets one good line when wrinkling her nose in disgust and saying, "Thousands of years separate me from that thing." One British critic pointed out, rather indulgently, that "Quintillus is reminiscent of a Golem designed by [abstract sculptor] Mr Henry Moore."[15] Quintillus was actually designed by former ape specialist Charles Gemora, and he looks pretty effective when not (like the creature in *It!*) rumpling at inopportune moments.

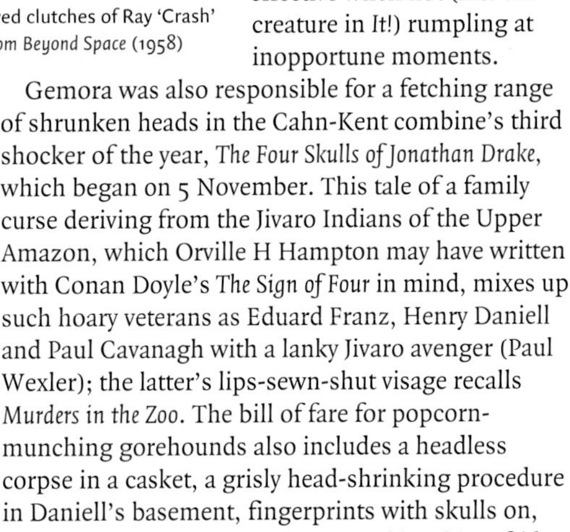

Gemora was also responsible for a fetching range of shrunken heads in the Cahn-Kent combine's third shocker of the year, *The Four Skulls of Jonathan Drake*, which began on 5 November. This tale of a family curse deriving from the Jivaro Indians of the Upper Amazon, which Orville H Hampton may have written with Conan Doyle's *The Sign of Four* in mind, mixes up such hoary veterans as Eduard Franz, Henry Daniell and Paul Cavanagh with a lanky Jivaro avenger (Paul Wexler); the latter's lips-sewn-shut visage recalls *Murders in the Zoo*. The bill of fare for popcorn-munching gorehounds also includes a headless corpse in a casket, a grisly head-shrinking procedure in Daniell's basement, fingerprints with skulls on, curare-tipped stilettos, and a severed head in a fridge.

Bob Bryant heads for the sea, with Elaine Edwards in his arms, in *Curse of the Faceless Man* (1958)

The 64-year-old Daniell, whose famous features needed no make-up in order to look convincingly embalmed, turns out to be the dead-for-180-years Dr Emil Zurich, a Swiss trader who is now just a head affixed to a Jivaro trunk. The curse, it transpires, can't be lifted "until the head of the white man is severed from the brown body," leading to a predictably gruesome but glumly downbeat conclusion. The touches of imagination in Hampton's script are enhanced here by Maury Gertsman's inky monochrome photography and by the baleful presence of Daniell himself, though even he looks ridiculous when decked out in an absurd, over-sized ritual mask.

Last in line for Cahn and Kent in 1958 was *Invisible Invaders*, which started shooting on 11 December and would fetch up as support feature to its predecessor, *The Four Skulls of Jonathan Drake*. Here, invisible aliens revive human corpses to form "a vast army [of] walking dead who kill but cannot be killed." John Carradine appears early on as a spokesman for the revenants, his normally sonorous voice as flat as a pancake – to indicate robotic undeath and also, quite possibly, his own bottom-of-the-barrel boredom. The rest of the film, complete with another droning voice-over narration and crudely appended stock footage of the world in chaos, is just as dreary. Even so, the 'regular guy' zombies and besieged protagonists, like those in Cahn's earlier film *Creature with the Atom Brain*, are a clear pointer towards George Romero's game-changing 1967 classic *Night of the Living Dead*.

Having said that, the idea of aliens resurrecting the dead wasn't quite new even when Cahn made *Invisible Invaders*. Ed Wood's notoriously inept *Plan 9 from Outer Space* had been given a Hollywood preview back in March 1957 under the title *Grave Robbers from Outer Space*, though whether Cahn's screenwriter, Samuel Newman, had seen Wood's film is unknown. The luckless Wood, incidentally, had meanwhile made a loose follow-up to *Bride of the Monster* and *Plan 9* called *Revenge of the Dead*, in which an apparently haunted house reveals a supposedly fake medium called Dr Acula. This had a few LA screenings in 1959 prior to disappearing entirely for some 25 years, re-emerging in the 1980s as an instant cult item called *Night of the Ghouls*.

Severed Heads and Floating Skulls

The 17th century head-on-another-man's-shoulders featured in *The Four Skulls of Jonathan Drake* had been anticipated earlier in 1958 by a film from Universal's B unit revolving almost exclusively around the severed head of a 16th century necromancer. Though starting production on 30 January as *The Water Witch*, Will Cowan's film would finally go out as *The Thing that Couldn't Die*, playing support to no less a genre monolith than Hammer's *Dracula*. The memorable image here is provided by British actor Robin Hughes, cast as the disembodied noggin of Gideon Drew – "the foulest and wickedest man who ever set feet upon earth." Having been dumped in California by Sir Francis Drake and

Robin Hughes projects the basilisk stare of *The Thing that Couldn't Die* (1958)

crew in 1579, he's finally reunited with his body when a psychic young farm girl (the water witch of the original title) successfully divines his resting place.

Much mind-control from beyond the grave ensues, together with a flashback to Drew's execution. Drew possesses three people in all – two women and a male simpleton, which says something about the sexist tendencies of David Duncan's script. Happily, Andra Martin, substituting for the originally cast Jill St John, is strikingly good as the first of the three. Though Drew is disposed of with anticlimactic ease just moments after popping his head back on, he at least gets some ripe dialogue. Surveying the assembled California stiffs, he hisses: "So this is what mankind has become? Hogs before the butcher, waiting to die!" This line recalls a speech of Dracula's from Bram Stoker's novel ("You think to baffle me, you – with your pale faces all in a row, like sheep in a butcher's"), though whether Duncan was aware of the echo is unclear. Either way, the film itself, underwhelming though it is, would be echoed in *El espanto surge de la tumba* (Horror Rises from the Tomb), a lurid Spanish shocker made 14 years later.

At the opposite end of 1958, Universal's B unit put *Affairs of a Vampire* into production on 10 December, changing the title to *Curse of the Undead* for its eventual release in support of another Hammer heavy-hitter, *The Mummy*. Here was an oddity – a horror-Western, albeit a horror-Western that would be compared unfavourably by the *Hollywood Reporter* to Vaughn Monroe's spooky No 1 hit of 1949, 'Ghost Riders in the Sky'. Michael Pate plays black-clad gunslinger Drake Robey, who's first seen nonchalantly climbing into a coffin already occupied by the newly deceased local doctor. The sexual ambiguity only intensifies when he hovers over a female victim, sucking rather oddly on her cheek prior to fastening on her neck. After this, a flashback to 1860 reveals that he's actually called Drago Robles and owes his undead state to the fact he committed suicide in atonement for having killed his own brother.

The film was directed by Edward Dein, who co-wrote it with his wife Mildred. Having worked in the 1940s on the Lewton picture *The Leopard Man* and the Lewton pastiche *The Soul of a Monster*, Dein duly inserts a Lewton 'walk', with a heroic young padre (Eric Fleming) being bedevilled by running footfalls at dead of night. Coincidentally, there's also a scene in which Drake tries to throttle the padre over a desk, a situation with a direct parallel in the film's stablemate, *The Mummy*. And that the Deins were trying to reconfigure, not just the vampire's environment, but also his personality, is clear when Drake says disarmingly, "You should pity me." But, excepting some atmospheric touches from cinematographer Ellis W Carter, the film is blandly realised and fails to make the most of its cross-fertilisation of horror and Old West motifs.

This was a combination that had yielded several titles in previous decades, but in the 1950s *Curse of the Undead*'s predecessors numbered only three. The most recent, *The Fiend who Walked the West*, had been made by Gordon Douglas in April 1958 as *The Hell-Bent Kid*. The title change, according to the film's star Robert Evans, had been decreed by "Charlie Einfeld, the Neanderthal marketing and distribution genius at Fox" on the principle that "We'll get both audiences – the rednecks who go for oaters and the horror freaks."[16] Sadly, it's an uninspired remake of Henry Hathaway's peerless 1947 noir *Kiss of Death*, dialled back to 1876 and with Evans making a reasonable stab at following in Richard Widmark's serial-killer footsteps. It's interesting to speculate, however, on how it might have turned out had one of Evans' fellow auditioners won the role – namely Anthony Perkins, future star of *Psycho*.

The two other horror-Westerns from the 1950s, *The Beast of Hollow Mountain* and *Teenage Monster*, were very different propositions. The first, directed by Edward Nassour and Ismael Rodríguez at Mexico

City's Churubusco facility early in 1955, is a colourful Mexican co-production in which rival ranchers encounter a cattle-munching stop-motion dinosaur. (The story idea was credited to the venerable *King Kong* animator Willis O'Brien.) The second, produced and directed by Jacques Marquette, began shooting as *Monster on the Hill* on 12 August 1957 before settling on a release title obviously pitched at the *I Was a Teenage Frankenstein* demographic. Under any title, the result is among the very feeblest products of the period, with a young miner's son, afflicted by a meteor strike, growing up to be a gurning, hirsute absurdity with homicidal tendencies. Sadly, the film was a humbling experience for three Universal veterans – Anne Gwynne (leading lady), Jack Pierce (make-up) and Gil Perkins (pushing 50 and playing the title character). In Britain, the BBFC rejected the film in March 1959, presumably because of its mental retardation angle.

Just a month before making *Teenage Monster*, Jacques Marquette had served as producer-cinematographer on the ridiculous alien-possession quickie *The Brain from Planet Arous*, in which John Agar is inhabited by a homicidal extraterrestrial brain called Gor; the two films would in due course go out as a double-feature. The director of *Arous* was Nathan Juran, hiding his shame under the pseudonym Nathan Hertz, as he also did when reuniting with Marquette in January 1958 to make *Attack of the 50 Foot Woman*. This one, which started shooting on the same day as *Frankenstein 1970*, boasts the delirious spectacle of Allison Hayes – as a wronged suburban wife who encounters a mysterious alien sphere – growing big enough to take a Godzilla-style revenge for her marginalisation.

For writer Mark Hanna, this was just a sex-switched reverse on his 1957 script for Bert I Gordon's *The Amazing Colossal Man*, in which Glenn Langan's giantism was triggered by a plutonium bomb. And just as Albert Kallis had immortalised the amateurish *Astounding She-Monster* with an iconic poster, so Reynold Brown provided *Attack of the 50 Foot Woman* with an alluring advertising image vastly superior to the actual product. Produced by Bernard Woolner of the Louisiana drive-in chain Woolner Bros, the film was just one of numerous instances of exhibitors seeking to plug the product shortage by producing films themselves.

Just as exhibitors could make their own pictures, so actors could make their own work. In March 1958 the former Universal contractee Alex Nicol directed an unusual film that would eventually be picked up by AIP. *The Screaming Skull* is a chamber-piece for five characters, rather too talky for its own good, in which the excellent Peggy Webber plays Jeni, a delicate newly-wed, fresh from a nervous breakdown, who arrives at a palatial but eerily empty LA estate supposedly haunted by her husband's first wife.

The premise is as clichéd as can be; it was last done just a few months earlier, in *My World Dies Screaming*. But Nicol adds a few grace notes, notably a skull's canted POV shot of the house and the dreadful screaming that goes up when the dead woman's hideous self-portrait is ritually burned. Jeni is unusually well characterised; she reads Henry James and confesses that "When I was a little girl I used to wanna be a caterpillar." (Her confidant is the halfwit gardener, played by Nicol himself.) And the veteran cinematographer Floyd Crosby contrives a highly effective double-exposed greenhouse ghost when the late wife comes back. For the novelty here is that the fortune-hunting, ghost-faking husband (John Hudson) comes up against a real spectre and has his throat bitten out in the lily pond by a disembodied skull.

The film was made just when William Castle's *Macabre* was cleaning up at US box-offices, with its hokey promotional offer of a $1000 insurance policy. Accordingly, *The Screaming Skull* not only offered punters a free burial should they die of fright, it even had a brief prologue appended, set in a funeral parlour and suggesting that watching the film "may kill you." Similarly, composer Ernest Gold appears to have quoted the *Dies Irae* in response to Gerald Fried's recent

Peggy Webber succumbs to the standard 'scheming new husband' scenario in *The Screaming Skull* (1958)

use of it in *The Return of Dracula*. AIP paired the finished product with Robert J Gurney's tatty *Terror from the Year 5000*, in which a time-travel device provides a portal for, as the ads leeringly put it, "a hideous she-thing" from the future. In an alternative pairing, Gurney's film went out with *The Brain Eaters*, a clumsy misappropriation of Robert Heinlein's 1951 alien-takeover novel *The Puppet Masters*; the director was Bruno Ve Sota, a tubby regular in Roger Corman's acting ensemble.

Two other 1958 productions with a Corman connection were Bernard L Kowalski's *Night of the Blood Beast* and Charles R Rondeau's *Devil's Partner*. The first of these, produced by Corman and his brother Gene in May, is a tacky *Quatermass Xperiment* retread, with an astronaut returning to Earth as "a dead man with a brain and a body kept alive artificially to feed a generation of monsters." The chief interest here is the gruesome detail; the astronaut is incubating alien embryos and the doctor attending him is found dead, his body inverted and drizzling blood onto the floor. Shot in October, *Devil's Partner* has Ed Nelson as a grizzled hermit who converts himself via black magic into his own nephew, a slickly Mephistophelean figure who quips that "I'm really the Devil. It got kinda hot down there." Well acted and modestly effective in creating the sweat-stained rural community of Furnace Flats, the film rises briefly to brilliance when Nelson gives local wino Byron Foulger a Jekyll and Hyde-style demonstration of his transformative powers; shrieking his way out of the shack, Foulger is immediately trampled to death by a possessed horse. Belatedly picked up by the Corman brothers' Filmgroup outfit, the film was only released in 1961.

Semi-saurian: Robert Clarke stalks Nan Peterson in *The Hideous Sun Demon* (1958)

SQUALID AND MALEVOLENT

In the early months of 1958, Alex Nicol's *The Screaming Skull* wasn't the only example of an actor directing a low-budget horror. Convinced he could make something better than *The Astounding She-Monster*, in which he'd appeared at the end of 1956, Robert Clarke devoted 12 weekends and some $10,000 to making *The Hideous Sun Demon*, a Jekyll-Hyde story in which a whisky-guzzling scientist is exposed to radiation and becomes susceptible to a process of reverse evolution. "His whole appearance has changed into something scaly, almost lizard-like," we're told. "The catalyst is sunlight."

As co-writer, director and star, Clarke infuses a degree of demented energy into the doctor's rampage around various LA locations in a pleasingly grotesque monster suit, with library music later used in *Night of the Living Dead* also maintaining interest in these scenes. Amusingly, Clarke's Dr McKenna is a man who transforms, not at night, but in the blaze of day, so he feels safe when trysting with Nan Peterson's voluptuous nightclub singer in the shadows of a local bar – only to dally with her too long on the beach and flee in transmogrifying horror when the sun comes up. He finally takes a tumble from the top of a Long Beach gas storage tower, but the non-lizard sections of the film are bitty and sluggish. For some reason, the film's British distributor retitled it *Blood on His Lips*, facilitating a memorable tag-line: "He had ... *Blood on His Lips* ... But you'll have SCREAMS on yours!"

The Sun Demon was designed by Dick Cassarino, but Clarke's first port of call had been former Universal employee Jack Kevan, whose price proved considerably too high. Another memorable monster of the period resulted from Kevan and Irvin Berwick – who had been make-up artist and dialogue director, respectively, on *Creature from the Black Lagoon* – going into business together as Vanwick Productions. Their feral first cousin to the *Creature*, called *The Monster of Piedras Blancas*, was budgeted at just under $30,000 and involved writer-director Berwick and his crew descending on the California coastal resort of Cayucos on 26 March 1958.

Clumsily written and awkwardly acted, the result is mainly notable for the unusually high grue levels applied to the seaside murder spree of a so-called Diplovertebron, which climactically, or rather anticlimactically, takes a death plunge from the top of the Point Conception lighthouse. There are a few diverting quotes in the film – young lovers clinching in the surf as in *From Here to Eternity*, a grieving father advancing down the main street with his headless daughter in his arms, echoing *Frankenstein*. But the film remains memorable mainly for the hideous thing itself (cannibalised from various monster designs Kevan had executed at Universal over the years) and such envelope-pushing imagery as the daughter's

Patricia Owens commiserates with Al Hedison on the lab set of *The Fly* (1958)

severed head lying discarded in a cave mouth with a crab scuttling over it.

While *The Hideous Sun Demon* worked through its on-again off-again schedule at the beginning of 1958, plans were afoot to make a similar mutation shocker at the Fox subsidiary Regal Pictures, though when *The Fly* went on the floor in March 1958 it had become instead a fully fledged Fox production costing over $300,000. The source, initially published in the June 1957 issue of *Playboy*, was a George Langelaan story in which a scientist ends up with the combined facial features of a bluebottle and a domestic cat. Even with the removal of Langelaan's cat particles in favour of a simple fly-headed horror, the story's gruesome details made it perfect for a film industry newly receptive to extremes of gruesome spectacle. And to add a memorable touch of incongruity Fox lavished on it such ultra-glamorous accoutrements as stereo sound, CinemaScope and De Luxe Color.

THE FLY

20th Century-Fox 1958
94 minutes; De Luxe Color and CinemaScope
production began 17 March

Director: Jack Gertsman; Screenplay: James Clavell, based on a story by George Langelaan; Producer-Director: Kurt Neumann

Cinematographer: Karl Struss; Art Directors: Lyle R Wheeler, Theobold Holsopple; Editor: Merrill G White; Sound: Eugene Grossman, Harry M Leonard; Special Photographic Effects: L B Abbott; Special Effects: James B Gordon*; Set Decorations: Walter M Scott, Eli Benneche; Make-up: Ben Nye; Hair Stylist: Helen Turpin; Costume Designer: Adele Balkan; Executive Wardrobe Designer: Charles LeMaire; Music: Paul Sawtell; Assistant

Al Hedison [later David Hedison] (André Delambre); Patricia Owens (Hélène Delambre); Vincent Price (François Delambre); Herbert Marshall (Inspector Charas); Kathleen Freeman (Emma); Betty Lou Gerson (Nurse Andersone); Charles Herbert (Philippe Delambre); uncredited: Eugene Borden (Dr Ejoute); Harry Carter (doctor); Arthur Dulac (footman at Athenaeum Club); Torben Meyer (Gaston); Franz Roehn (police doctor); Charles Tannen (male nurse)

***The Fly* (Rialto, 'X') is not so blatantly sadistic as some recent films – the British *Dracula*, for instance. It is more in the vein of the SF series about giant apes and ants, and Things from other Worlds ... It's a tribute to the ingenuity of writer and director that the climax, as hokum goes, is extraordinarily effective.** *Daily Telegraph* [UK]

***The Fly* ... was just plain ridiculous. There was one scene there which I told the director, Kurt Neumann, was crazy. They had the figure of a man reduced to the size of a fly, and the fly talked. And they made the man say "Help me! Help me!" in a tiny voice. Oh gee! It was as bad as the monkey Hyde.** *Karl Struss [quoted in Reid, CinemaScope Two: Twentieth Century-Fox, 2005]*

When Hélène Delambre pulverises her scientist husband André with two 50-ton strokes of the steam press at Montreal's Delambre Frères, the dead man's elder brother, François, collaborates with Inspector Charas in working out Hélène's motivation. Breaking her silence, Hélène reveals that André had perfected a means of matter-transmission – disintegrating an object's atoms in one place and seamlessly reintegrating them in another. All went well until André experimented on himself, oblivious to the fact that a house fly had joined him inside the disintegration booth...

The men charged with realising this ghastly story were producer-director Kurt Neumann and the now 71-year-old cinematographer Karl Struss, who not long before had collaborated on Regal's *She Devil* – another film featuring fly experimentation, oddly enough. In their hands the film's buttoned-up bourgeois setting (transplanted from Langelaan's France to a sleekly contemporary Canada) smacks of a lush Douglas Sirk melodrama in which the emotional high point is a fit of screaming hysterics at sight of a monstrous man-fly.

The Modigliani that hangs discreetly in Francois' study isn't just a cheerful nod to the art expertise of the actor playing him (Vincent Price); it's a mark of the monied and rather prissily cultivated milieu occupied by the Delambres. Indeed, everyone looks immaculate and squeaky-clean – in stark contrast to the film's man-sized incarnation of what Mark Twain once called a "squalid and malevolent creature" whose chief purpose is to "walk over food and gaum it with filth and death." Thanks to this contrast, the film's climactic reveal of André's transmogrified appearance – the hirsute fly face, the pulsing proboscis, the white lab coat from which a shaggy fly's claw protrudes – achieves a rare blend of the ludicrous and the genuinely horrific. As well as recalling Kafka's *Metamorphosis*, the image is redolent of Surrealist painting, particularly the hideous, humanoid owls and horses of Max Ernst's wartime canvases 'The Robing of the Bride' and 'The Anti-Pope'.

The film's bland surface sheen hides not only a revolting fusion of man and insect but also a bristling host of illogicalities. The steam press set-piece, for example, is genuinely gruesome – yet an autopsy would immediately reveal the shameful fly parts that the suicidal André wished to erase for eternity. And the unfeasibility of a man with a fly's head and a fly with a man's head has been anatomised so frequently there's really no need to reiterate it here. To his credit, the film's debutant screenwriter, James Clavell, blithely ignores such objections and instead laces the film with some unexpectedly interesting asides. The use of tall cabinets in André's experiments, for example, recalls the origins of science in sorcery. ("Have you turned magician?" asks Hélène. "In a way," André replies.) Similarly, the image of André concealing his mutated head beneath a black drape echoes the procedures of early photographers, while the whole principle of his atom-reassembly experiments, with their appalling consequences, is patterned on that of cinema's hated rival, television.

A further discussion between husband and wife – about the fact that, with matter-transmitters, "humanity need never want or fear again" – suggests that, had André not been squished by a steam hammer, he would instead have been crushed by the same self-interested capitalists ranged against the idealist inventor in the 1951 film *The Man in the White Suit*. And, after a visit to the ballet, a frisky moment between Hélène and André ("You're in an unscientific mood...") is quickly forgotten when André teleports first a champagne bottle and then a guinea pig. This neutered moment of coitus interruptus is echoed later by the freakish image of the man-fly trying to give the unconscious Hélène a kiss, after which the futility of the exercise provokes him into an orgasmic orgy of lab-trashing destruction.

Most importantly, Clavell shrewdly preserves the plot motor of Langelaan's story, with an opening half-hour that, for the uninitiated, forms a really gripping mystery. (Why on earth did Hélène use the steam hammer? And why is she obsessed with flies?) There follows a 50-minute flashback carried by Patricia Owens' Hélène and Al Hedison's boyish André, culminating in a justly celebrated shot from the man-fly's multi-faceted POV, in which multiple Hélènes scream in unison right across the CinemaScope frame.

Finally, a 15-minute coda shows us François and Charas encountering the André-headed fly in a spider's web. The sight of André squealing "Help me!" as the spider closes in is another astonishing blend of horror and hilarity, with neither response compromising the other. In a nasty final detail, Charas' despairing use of a large stone to end André's torment comes rather late; the spider's mandibles connect with André a second or two before the stone does.

The Fly has other memorable features – notably the eerie, disembodied yowling of the Delambres' pet cat when it's accidentally converted into "a stream of cat atoms," and an authentically Kafkaesque moment when the conflicted, voiceless man-fly scrawls out the chilling observation, "Brain says strange things now." For 20th Century-Fox, however, the film's greatest achievement was its blockbuster success. (An outcome Kurt Neumann didn't live to see; he died, aged 50, in August.) Yet this didn't convince Fox to lend their production imprimatur to any further metamorphosis shockers. In the spring of 1959 *Return of the Fly* and *The Alligator People* went straight to the studio's Regal subsidiary, as had originally been intended for *The Fly* itself, though Robert Lippert had by this time changed Regal's name to Associated Producers. Both films were pegged for monochrome rather than luscious colour and, to underline their similarities, they would be put out together, hitting 1600 cinemas on 13 July as "2 Super-Monstrous Double-Chill Sensations!"

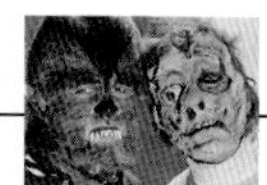

Another semi-saurian: Richard Crane and concerned wife Beverly Garland in *The Alligator People* (1959)

Writer-director Edward Bernds began shooting *Return of the Fly* on 3 March, with his script flashing forward some 15 years to, presumably, 1973. Price's François is now a greying elder statesman, his little nephew Philippe is now the handsome Brett Halsey, and the action begins as they attend the damp and dreary funeral of Philippe's mother Hélène. Despite Francois' time-honoured warnings – the boy's father, he insists, "ventured into areas of knowledge where man is not meant to go" – Philippe quickly gets the cobwebbed machinery up and running again, with hokey but watchable complications provided by his scheming assistant, nicely played by the British actor David Frankham.

Because Philippe is trying out something André never thought of – namely, "delayed reintegration" – the nasty assistant is able to elude a pursuing detective by splicing him with a previously disintegrated guinea pig. The resultant rodent with tiny human hands is much creepier than the stricken detective sporting furry great paws, but both images accurately replicate the horror-hilarity quotient of *The Fly*. Unfortunately, when Philippe finally goes the way of his father, the fact that the theme has turned almost instantly to schlock is signalled by his ridiculous fly's head, which is about six times bigger than André's was. And then the film exhausts the viewer's patience with an utterly silly man-fly rampage through the surrounding woods and nearby town.

The Alligator People went into production six weeks after *Return of the Fly*, on 13 April 1959, with Roy Del Ruth in the director's chair and Karl Struss (late of *The Fly*) lending his trademark luminosity to the film's fetid Louisiana setting. Here, Beverly Garland is the plucky new wife of a gradually mutating husband; in a faint echo of *Doctor X*, researcher George Macready has been harvesting hydrocortisone from the local alligators and reconstituting various maimed or mutilated human subjects, but with predictably grisly long-term results. As a cross-fertilisation of *The Fly* with *The Wolf Man*, the film has the wit to cast Lon Chaney Jr as a gator-hating drunken lech with a highly unconvincing hook for a hand. (He even ends up spectacularly electrocuted in a nod to the long-ago thrills of *Man Made Monster*.) Elsewhere the film tries for a hothouse vibe that simultaneously recalls *Creature from the Black Lagoon* while foreshadowing the 1971 film *Frogs*, together with a forlorn whiff or two of Tennessee Williams.

Among the film's plus points is a very interesting performance from the aptly reptilian Macready, who characterises the surrounding bayou as "the cradle of life where we all started: the slime and the ooze, the bottom of a swamp." No prizes for guessing that that's exactly where the hapless husband ends up, sucked down by the primordial glop in an absurd gator suit devised by *The Fly*'s make-up artist, Ben Nye. By this time, however, the film has hobbled itself in exactly the same way *Return of the Fly* does – with an utterly laughable monster run-around that completely shatters the promise of an atmospheric build-up. Beverly Garland, however, is as compelling as ever, particularly during a rain-lashed ordeal in which she stumbles over real gators and fake ones with equal aplomb. "I just played her the way you would if you were married to an alligator,"[17] she deadpanned in later years.

NOT THE MAN SHE FELL IN LOVE WITH

In the latter half of the 1950s, the displacement of horror motifs into science fiction reached its height. As noted on page 308, film historian John Baxter dubbed this period "springtime for Caliban," though precious few SF films featured monsters with the redeeming humanity of Shakespeare's "mis-shapen knave". Instead, the threats tended to be as impersonal and inhuman as the frightening technological advances they stood in for. Even the humanoid aliens characteristic of *The Thing from Another World*, *The Man from Planet X* and *Invaders from Mars* were quickly superseded, with utterly non-human monsters surging forth in alarming numbers to offer a symbolic warning against overweening science. "To American audiences the havoc wreaked on their homes by various dinosaurs is as welcome as the lash to a flagellant,"[18] noted Baxter.

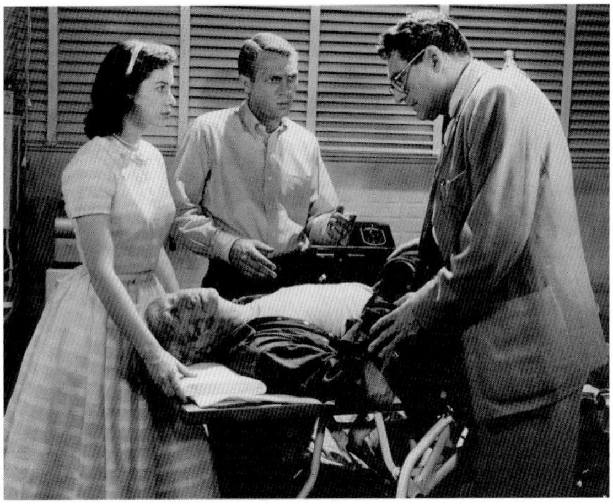

Inflated creepy-crawlies of one kind or another performed a similar cathartic service. Cued by *Them!* and *Tarantula*, they aggravated an 'end times' nerve in Nathan Juran's *The Deadly Mantis*, Edward Ludwig's *The Black Scorpion* (which benefited from the involvement of *Kong* veteran Willis O'Brien), Kenneth G Crane's *Monster from Green Hell*, Roger Corman's *Attack of the Crab Monsters*, Arnold Laven's *The Monster that Challenged the World* and Bernard L Kowalski's *Attack of the Giant Leeches*. As late as 1959 debutant directors Monte Hellman and Ray Kellogg contributed to the trend, Hellman with *Beast from Haunted Cave* for Roger and Gene Corman's Filmgroup company and Ray Kellogg with a back-to-back duo made for the Dallas exhibitor Gordon McLendon – *The Killer Shrews* and *The Giant Gila Monster*. There was also the work of a specialist in the field, the quixotic Bert I Gordon, who, in addition to making *King Dinosaur*, *Beginning of the End*, *Earth vs the Spider* and *Attack of the Puppet People*, had a persistent habit of enlarging humans too, as in *The Cyclops*, *The Amazing Colossal Man* and *War of the Colossal Beast*.

Variations on the routine included the Ray Harryhausen-animated octopus of Robert Gordon's *It Came from Beneath the Sea*, the humanoid mole men of Virgil Vogel's glamorous Universal B, *The Mole People*, and the ludicrous enlarged turkey of Fred F Sears' Sam Katzman quickie *The Giant Claw*. And there were other films that removed their threats from any vestige of humanity more comprehensively than even the 'big bug' cycle. Kurt Neumann's remarkable *Kronos* features an energy-slurping alien juggernaut thundering its way across the USA. John Sherwood's charming *The Monolith Monsters*, derived from a story by Jack Arnold, concerns a meteor-borne invasion of crystalline obelisks, and Irvin S Yeaworth's *The Blob* goes from hard to soft courtesy of a gelatinous monstrosity from outer space.

Aneta Corsaut, Steve McQueen and Stephen Chase examine the stricken Olin Howland in *The Blob* (1957)

The Blob, in fact, created a genuine pop-culture artefact, a people-eating ooze that emerges from a meteorite and threatens to envelop small-town America, only to be stymied by a plucky teenager played by the 27-year-old movie debutant Steve McQueen. The genesis of the project was almost as bizarre as the Blob itself, given that it involved Philadelphia distributor Jack H Harris getting together with the Methodist filmmakers of Valley Forge Film Studios and convincing their minister, Yeaworth, to direct a monster movie. Having been sold to Paramount, the film was released in September 1958, over a year after production, and made a mint. When shooting the film Harris had recently acquired the avant-garde oddity

Dementia, retooling it as *Daughter of Horror* – and this is the film that's playing as part of a 'Midnight Spook Show' when the Blob invades a movie theatre.

Paramount bought *The Blob* purely to support a recent production of their own, though in practice *The Blob* took precedence in most situations. Yet the other film, *I Married a Monster from Outer Space*, is a moody small-scale gem that picks up from *Invasion of the Body Snatchers* in restoring a human angle to SF. Director-producer Gene Fowler Jr had been inspired to put the story together by the unexpected smash success of his previous shocker, *I Was a Teenage Werewolf*. Like that film, the title was as simultaneously absurd and iconic as anything the 1950s produced, though in this instance it was self-imposed by Fowler and his screenwriter, Lou Vittes.

Having left his stag party early, Bill Farrell is waylaid by an alien presence and the next morning he's conspicuously late for his own wedding. The bride, Marge, is spooked by Bill's out-of-character behaviour on their honeymoon, and a year later she writes to her mother claiming that "Bill isn't the man I fell in love with" – though the letter remains unsent. Soon afterwards, suffering a sleepless night, Marge spots Bill venturing into the woods and decides to follow him...

I MARRIED A MONSTER FROM OUTER SPACE

Paramount 1958
78 minutes
production began 21 April

Cinematographer: Haskell Boggs; Art Directors: Hal Pereira, Henry Bumstead; Editor: George Tomasini; Sound: Phil Wisdom, Charles Grenzbach; Special Photographic Effects: John P Fulton; Set Decoration: Sam Comer, Robert Benton; Make-up: Wally Westmore, Charles Gemora*; Hair Stylist: Nellie Manley; Wardrobe: John Noble*, Hazel Hegarty*; Assistant Director: William Mull; Screenplay: Louis Vittes; Producer-Director: Gene Fowler Jr

Tom Tryon (Bill Farrell); Gloria Talbott (Marge Bradley Farrell); Peter Baldwin (Officer Frank Swanson); Robert Ivers (Harry Phillips); Chuck Wassil (Ted Hanks); Valerie Allen (Francine [B-girl]); Ty Hungerford (Mac Brody); Ken Lynch (Dr Wayne); John Eldredge (Chief Collins); Alan Dexter (Sam Benson); James Anderson (Weldon); Jean Carson (Helen Rhodes); Jack Orrison (Officer Schultz); Steve London (Charles Mason); Maxie Rosenbloom (Grady [bar tender]); uncredited: Tony Di Milo (Mr Potter [Western Union clerk]); Darlene Fields (Caroline Hanks); Bess Flowers, Harold Miller (wedding guests); Charles Gemora (alien); Helen Jay, Sherry Staiger (girls at country club bar); Arthur Lovejoy (minister); Ralph Manza (waiter); Mary Treen (Mrs Bradley)

This latest addition to the current cycle of science-fiction-horror melodramas is just as fantastic as the others in its category, but it is more imaginative than most and should prove to be a good supporting feature ... It is, as I said, fantastic stuff, but thanks to the expert direction and good performances the action unfolds in suspenseful fashion and holds one's interest well all the way through. Harrison's Reports

I liked it when I was making it, as opposed to [*I Was a Teenage*] *Werewolf*, which I really had no faith in ... I came up with the title *I Married a Monster from Outer Space* because it was so exploitable. And we tried to make the best movie we could with this ridiculous title. There again, I tried to put characterization into the monster. The so-called monsters, the aliens, were very sad people. Gene Fowler Jr [quoted in *Fangoria*, July 1983]

The opening reel of *I Married a Monster from Outer Space* presents a gently scathing parody of conventional 1950s attitudes to romance. Outside a country club, a couple are necking in a parked open-top car and don't even pause when someone playfully bangs on the door. Inside, a couple of single girls sit at the bar, looking across at a group of males and complaining that "Those guys ain't even giving us a hard look." The men in question are in the midst of a rather glum stag do; the recommended tipple is called 'Freedom on the Rocks' and Bill's friend Harry, looking at his retreating back, sighs, "Aw, he's such a nice guy. It's a shame it has to happen to him." The next day, Marge and the late-arriving Bill indulge in a prolonged kiss, causing Marge's mildly scandalised mother to twitter, "Marge, dear! Marge: you're not married yet!"

Marge doesn't know it, but the borderline impropriety of that kiss was caused by the fact that 'Bill' is no longer Bill; he's an alien concealed inside a projected facsimile of Bill's body, and naturally he's a very long way from getting the hang of this love-and-marriage business, as conceived by humans. The tone

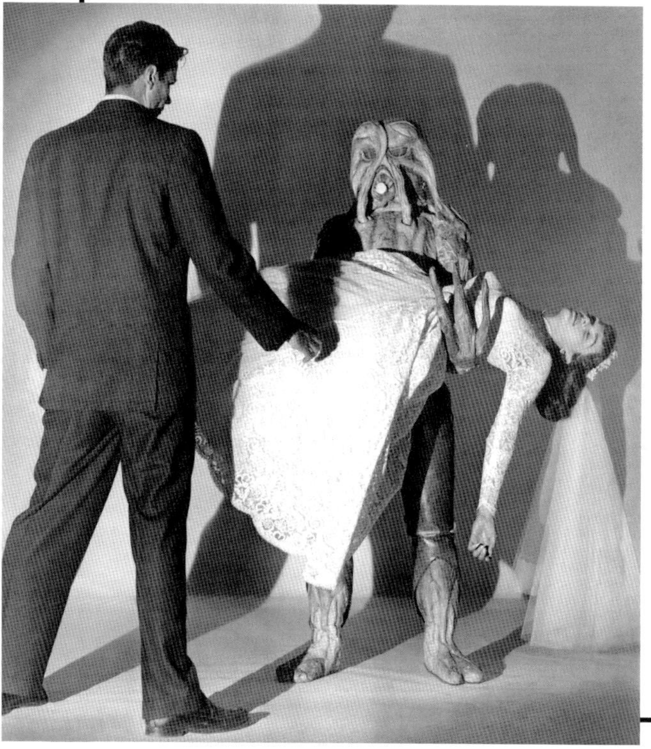

Husband Tom Tryon and wife Gloria Talbott, plus an alien designed (and reputedly played) by Charles Gemora, advertising *I Married a Monster from Outer Space* in 1958

inevitably darkens on the honeymoon, when the clink of champagne glasses is accompanied by an ominous roll of thunder across the bay. In this film, consummation is accompanied, not by crashing waves, but by flashes of lightning. One such interrupts the signal from Bill's spaceship, causing his face, ever so briefly, to take on the repulsive features of his alien host. It's a chilling and brilliantly timed moment, coming, as it does, just before he resolves to go back to Marge and 'do his duty'. As Peter Nicholls pithily puts it, the film addresses "the one question previous films on the theme had politely evaded. What would it be like to have sex with, ugh, a 'thing', without knowing it when you began?"[19]

Clearly, then, this supposed exploitation film touches on deep-rooted anxieties about sex and male-female relations. Twelve months into her marriage, Marge frets that Bill is "almost a stranger," even wondering – in a telling phrase – if he might be "Bill's twin brother from some other place." The film becomes close kin to the 'young wife being driven insane' thrillers initiated by Patrick Hamilton's *Gaslight*, with Marge being pooh-poohed and disbelieved by those around her just as if she were the heroine of a classic film noir. To this end, Fowler and his cinematographer, Haskell Boggs, come up with a wealth of brooding black-and-white compositions, reminding us that Fowler, a sometime editor, had been a close associate of Fritz Lang.

Further anxieties crowd in as Marge worries about her fertility; as it turns out, the aliens have yet to master how "to mutate female human chromosomes so we can have children with them." The final ironic twist comes when Bill, much to his surprise, starts to

Joanna Moore recoils from her severely regressed fiancé in *Monster on the Campus* (1958)

feel "human desires [and] emotions," causing him to reproach the increasingly distant Marge. "The past few weeks you've changed," he mopes, "as though you've gone away." In this way the film throws the viewer for a loop, switching from the feminist nightmare undergone by Marge to a resolution in which our sympathies are engaged, to some degree, by the aliens, whose women have become extinct and who are seeking only to keep their race alive.

The film boasts exceptional special effects and a truly hideous alien design, credited to veterans John P Fulton and Charles Gemora respectively. As Marge and Bill, Gloria Talbott and Tom Tryon are perfectly cast as the supposedly ideal Eisenhower-era couple. (Tryon, incidentally, would later enjoy success with a doppelgänger tale of his own, the 1971 bestseller *The Other*.) And in the midst of Marge's travails we get a truly disturbing scene in which another young woman – a so-called B-girl – propositions a faceless, anorak-wearing figure standing immobile in front of a toy shop. On top of all this, the ending is unusually gruesome, with plenty of blood-pumping alien windpipes and rivers of viscous goo as the creatures disintegrate. It's possible that someone involved had seen a sneak preview of the British film *Fiend Without a Face*, which has a similarly extreme final reel.

Finally, it's worth pointing out that, amid all the grue and marital angst, the film finds room for some waggish humour, as when Bill consorts with other bogus townsmen who are just as boorishly clubbable as their human counterparts. One of them, Sam, complains about "wearing this thing" (a human body) because "the design's pretty lousy." Elsewhere, normal sexual relations are invoked in a really world-class double-entendre, when Marge's friend Caroline recalls "wrestling with Ted in the back seat of that darned old convertible." "I never could manage to get the top down," Ted replies.

Universal's latest B, *Monster in the Night*, went into production just three days after *I Married a Monster from Outer Space*. On release the title was adjusted to *Monster on the Campus*, presumably to convince teen audiences that there would be some teens in it. Incredibly, someone at Universal thought that it would be worth their while to make a more glamorous retread of the trashy 1952 film *The Neanderthal Man*. Even more incredibly, the studio felt that juvenile junk like this was a suitable project to foist onto Jack Arnold after his high-toned triumph with *The Incredible Shrinking Man*. And inevitably he found it impossible to give David Duncan's by-the-numbers script any weight whatsoever. With a college professor (Arthur Franz) becoming infected by the blood of a gamma ray-treated

coelacanth and regressing into "a beast far more intelligent than an ape and yet not quite human," it's just yet another of the period's numerous Jekyll and Hyde knock-offs.

Like *I Married a Monster from Outer Space*, the film contains a subtext regarding male-female relations, only this time it's barely developed. Professor Blake's first line, surveying his incapacitated fiancée, is "A female in the perfect state: defenceless and silent." It therefore makes sense that this smug '50s chauvinist should subsequently string up a woman, caveman-style, by her hair. (At the climax he has a good yank at his fiancée's hair too.) In fairness, the understated reveal of the first victim, her tresses lashed to a tree branch, is effectively done, and there's a startling moment when an unfortunate Forest Ranger gets an axe in the head. But the project is entirely sunk by such ludicrous conceits as the boggle-eyed coelacanth and an inflated prehistoric dragonfly, not forgetting the rubber-masked absurdity that Blake periodically turns into. The film went out as support to a Universal acquisition from the UK, the gruesome Hammer imitation *Blood of the Vampire*.

Donald Murphy submits Sandra Knight to yet another Jekyll-Hyde serum in *Frankenstein's Daughter* (1958)

In considerably lower climes, Richard E Cunha, the former industrial filmmaker who had made the effective *Giant from the Unknown* and jaw-dropping *She Demons*, started directing *Frankenstein's Daughter* on 30 April. This Astor release has Donald Murphy, as the original Frankenstein's grandson Oliver, telling his elderly mentor (Felix Locher) that "The Frankensteins were masters who brought life from death." "I think you're a strange boy," comes the straight-faced reply.

In the early stages, Oliver doses up the old man's niece Trudy (Sandra Knight) with still another of those ubiquitous Jekyll-Hyde serums, resulting in a she-monster running around in a white dressing gown and black swimsuit. Forty years later, US critic Tim Lucas likened this plot point to modern concerns about date-rape drugs; whatever it may be, it's quickly reduced to a side-issue when Oliver inserts the brain of seductive Suzy (Sally Todd) into a custom-made body. The result, apparently, is another she-monster, though the fact that it's played by the so-called 'ugliest man in pictures', Harry Wilson, is embarrassingly obvious. Oliver eventually receives a face-full of acid and the monster bumps into a Bunsen burner (!) and is consumed by flames. Despite some distinctly gruesome touches, the film quickly devolves to the point where a pool-party performance by the Page Cavanaugh Trio ranks as a distracting highlight.

Following *Frankenstein's Daughter*, Cunha moved on in June to directing its double-feature stablemate, the laughably inept *Missile to the Moon*, then in January 1959 he photographed Ralph Brooke's *Bloodlust!* – in which, a few grisly details notwithstanding, the old *Most Dangerous Game* plot plummeted straight to the bottom of the barrel. After that, Cunha departed the horror scene as quickly as he'd arrived.

TRUMPED-UP GHOSTS AND ANTI-AGEING REMEDIES

By August 1958, William Castle and his combined screenwriter and co-producer, Robb White, were ready to capitalise on the recent smash success of their first collaboration, *Macabre*.

Castle's hucksterish wheeze for promoting his new project was far more elaborate than the mere insurance policy he'd offered for *Macabre*. For *House on Haunted Hill* he came up with something called Emergo, which entailed a phosphorescent plastic skeleton being winched out from the proscenium at

Vincent Price shows off the creepy statuary and cosmetic cobwebs of the *House on Haunted Hill* (1958)

HOUSE ON HAUNTED HILL

Susina Productions 1958
['a William Castle-Robb White production']
75 minutes
production began 3 September

Cinematographer: Carl E Guthrie; Art Director: David Milton; Editor: Roy Livingston; Sound: Ralph Butler, Charles Schelling; Special Effects: Herman Townsley; Set Decoration: Morris Hoffman; Make-up: Jack Dusick; Hair Stylist: Gale McGarry; Wardrobe: Roger J Weinberg, Norah Sharpe; Music: Von Dexter; Music Editor: Jerry Irvin; Assistant Director: Jack R Berne; Associate Producer / Screenplay: Robb White; Producer-Director: William Castle

Vincent Price (Frederick Loren); Carol Ohmart (Annabelle Loren); Richard Long (Lance Schroeder); Alan Marshal (Dr David Trent); Carolyn Craig (Nora Manning); Elisha Cook (Watson Pritchard); Julie Mitchum (Ruth Bridgers); Leona Anderson (Mrs Slydes); Howard Hoffman (Jonas Slydes); skeleton – by himself

Severed heads and vats of acid in a farrago, enjoyable in an infantile way, about a night in a ghost-ridden mansion. At the end an illuminated skeleton of plywood or some kindred material is swung towards the circle, and the audience can go home with the tenuous satisfaction of having seen what the advertisements call Emergo. *Sunday Times* [UK]

The night of the sneak preview ... there were no young people in the theatre. I looked at the man next to me. An elderly, baldish, bespectacled man, constantly fidgeting in his seat ... "Stop fidgeting," I whispered. Turning to me, he whispered back, "The biggest piece of shit I've ever seen." ... For the next preview, I made sure there was a young audience present, and the results were just the opposite – the response was wildly enthusiastic. William Castle [*Step Right Up! I'm Gonna Scare the Pants Off America*, 1976]

a climactic moment and juddering above the audience's heads. No matter that the stunt was confined to the swankier first-run houses, or that the more inventive teens quickly worked out that the skeletons were vulnerable to air-gun pellets and other projectiles. In an era of unrestrained ballyhoo echoing cinema's roots in travelling fairs and medicine shows, it was this outrageous selling point that set Castle apart as *the* master showman. As Kevin Heffernan puts it, "The carnival barker, for a time banished to the sidewalk outside the theatre, [had taken] over the director's chair."[20]

Having hired a reputedly haunted mansion for the night, the acerbic millionaire Frederick Loren invites its nervy owner, Watson Pritchard, and four other guests to a "spend-the-night ghost party" for Loren's fourth wife, Annabelle. To add to the atmosphere, Loren has offered each of his guests ten grand if they can stay put

till morning. The whole scenario is met with general bemusement – except by Pritchard, who maintains that "Only the ghosts in this house are glad we're here."

House on Haunted Hill was Castle and White's self-amused but legitimately scary update on ancient properties like *The Bat* and *The Cat and the Canary*, with the ghoulish accoutrements revealed as mere set dressing for a murder intrigue borrowing from Castle's much more recent inspiration, *Les Diaboliques*. As such it's a superlatively well-oiled commercial machine that still exudes plenty of raffish charm.

To put his young audience in the right Hallowe'en spirit, Castle begins with a black screen riven by random shrieks and chain-clankings and generalised moaning-of-the-damned, after which the disembodied heads of Elisha Cook, as the twitchy Pritchard, and Vincent Price, as the unruffled Loren, pop up to warn us about what's in store. The credits play out over some icy exterior views of Frank Lloyd Wright's extraordinary Ennis House; perched on a Los Feliz hilltop, it was only 34 years old when Castle's crew filmed there, providing a modernist contrast to what we see when the camera tracks in through the front door – a business-as-usual Edwardian interior on a soundstage. In a token effort to match the interior to the exterior, art director David Milton adds some Mayan Revival columns to the cellar, of all places. Elsewhere, the house's immaculately preserved fixtures and fittings are garnished with occasional cobwebs, cobwebs so cosmetic one imagines Loren himself might have sprayed them on for effect. Of the uncobwebbed ornaments, Castle particularly likes gliding the camera past a sculpted hunting horn, which looms pleasantly in the foreground and thus provides the main room with unexpected depth.

A good example of the design team's attention to detail can be seen in Annabelle Loren's boudoir. As her husband serves champagne and they wonder who might be poisoning who, we notice that the ice bucket is decorated with a pair of hissing snakes going head to head. The civilised loathing between the Lorens gets a grand showcase in Robb White's splendid dialogue, which plays like acid-tinged Noël Coward. "Of all my wives you are the least agreeable," sighs Loren. "But still alive," twinkles Annabelle in reply. After the star-free zone that was *Macabre*, Castle realised he needed a name to really push his latest film, and, with *The Fly* cleaning up all around the country, Price was the obvious candidate. The Loren role allows Price's epicene brilliance full scope (as his passive character in *The Fly* definitely didn't), and Carol Ohmart is just as good as the "so beautiful, so greedy, so cold" Annabelle.

Annabelle, of course, is a textbook femme fatale, conforming exactly to the unwritten rule that autonomous and sexually arousing young women should receive a grisly comeuppance in the final reel. (In this case it's provided by the kind of acid vat recently popularised by *The Curse of Frankenstein*.) Her opposite number is the dreary, doe-eyed ingenue Nora, who's about as uninspiring as the other guests – stodgy test pilot Lance, middle-aged journalist Ruth and a smoothly toupéed "saturnine psychiatrist" called Dr Trent. Pritchard, however, is another matter. Constantly babbling about the seven people murdered in the house (and the fact their heads were never found), he's given the full force of Elisha Cook's trademark mannerisms and is a hoot.

The characters, however, are secondary to Castle's parade of hokey horrors, with Nora being assailed by a weirdly gliding crone and finding a severed head in her suitcase even before midnight has struck. Though the head looks like a crudely carved chunk of glacé fruit, the shock appearance of the grinning crone had a gratifyingly pants-wetting effect on the film's original audiences. Castle also contrives a highly effective apparition of the (apparently) hanged Annabelle, hovering glassy-eyed outside Nora's window, together with a barnstorming finale in which Annabelle is confronted by a mobile skeleton on the brink of the acid vat. Cutting smartly between Annabelle's screaming mouth and the jeering, slack-jawed rictus of the skeleton, this of course is the fabled Emergo moment, though it's rapidly undercut by the revelation that Loren was controlling the skeleton with an absurd contraption of wires and pulleys. Ridiculous though it is, the reveal of Loren-as-puppetmaster is an apt one, given that Price himself was to be the puppetmaster in more than a decade's worth of further horrors.

With *House on Haunted Hill*, incidentally, Castle's dominion almost extended into television, with Allied Artists' TV subsidiary, Interstate, gearing up to shoot an episodic spin-off, *Tales of the Haunted House*, as soon as the film wrapped. The projected pilot never happened, however, and the idea was abandoned.

Shortly before Castle's film went into production, Jack H Harris got back together with Irvin S Yeaworth and the other Pennsylvania Methodists at Valley Forge Film Studios to make *4D Man*, a film that in due course would be picked up by Universal. When the film started, on 18 August, the previous Harris-Yeaworth collaboration, *The Blob*, had yet to come out, but the two men were sufficiently confident to shift focus from the juvenilia of *The Blob* to an unusually mature and well-thought-through screenplay by Theodore

Edgar Stehli, cornered by the vengeful Robert Lansing in *4D Man* (1958)

Simonson and Cy Chermak. Here, Robert Lansing, in his film debut, gives a really terrific performance – nuanced, believable and properly scary when called for – as Scott Nelson, a priggish young scientist who has his girlfriend Linda stolen from him by his younger brother Tony, prompting him in turn to steal Tony's research. The result? He becomes *The Fourth Dimensional Man* (the film's working title), able to pass through walls and drain people's lifeforce purely by touch, ageing them to death and thus replenishing himself.

This modified vampire story gives Lansing hair-raising confrontation scenes with Edgar Stehli (as Scott's fastidious but venal employer) and a recent Miss America, Lee Meriwether (as the conflicted Linda). He also has a queasy meeting with the 11-year-old Patty Duke that quotes from both *Frankenstein* and *The Quatermass Xperiment*, plus a disastrous liaison with a nightclub glamourpuss (Chic James) recalling the similarly ill-fated B-girl of *I Married a Monster from Outer Space*. The special effects are variable, and the action becomes predictable after Tony's horrified realisation that "A man in the fourth dimension is indestructible." But the De Luxe Color is just that and Ralph Carmichael's snappy jazz score is refreshingly unconventional.

As 1958 gave way to 1959, the focus turned from a science-mutated man to a couple of women in a similar predicament – though their attempts to regain their youth are motivated by normal ageing rather than the youth-draining effects of inhabiting the fourth dimension. The films in question revived, in a schlock format, whimsical rejuvenation fantasies of the silent era like *The Young Diana* and *Vanity's Price*. The first, *The Wasp Woman*, even contrived to squeeze in a reference to the fact that "30 years ago a bunch of quacks were treating people with monkey glands." Written by actor Leo Gordon and directed by Roger Corman at Kling Studios in December 1958, this casts Susan Cabot as the 40-year-old head of a major cosmetics firm who sees sales slipping even as her own personal glamour fades. (Or so the film would have us think; quite apart from the difficulty of seeing someone of 40 as over the hill, Cabot was in any case only 31 at the time.) She turns to a maverick old chemist (played by Michael Mark, the grieving father, many moons before, in *Frankenstein*) and overdoses on his revolutionary new serum – which, ominously, is derived from wasp enzymes.

Making her last film, Cabot is an imposing presence but her increasing desperation is the only thing that adds weight to the proceedings. The script's major plot complication – when the elderly expert who could help our protagonist becomes incapacitated – seems to have been lifted from an older film on the same theme, *The Man in Half Moon Street*. And, as usual with Corman, there are various droll asides that retain interest. But technically the film is a big let-down, particularly where Cabot's ludicrous wasp-head transformation is concerned. (Neck and legs, by the way, are visibly unaffected.) And only in the demented climax does Corman work up any of the energy that was normally his trademark.

Barely had Corman and Cabot finished work on *The Wasp Woman* than director Edward Dein and star Coleen Gray went into *The Leech*, a Universal B shot in February 1959 and released as *The Leech Woman*. Dein was fresh from directing *Curse of the Undead*, and Gray was delighted to be working with him: "Eddie Dein was the genius on that one, and that picture was ten days of sheer joy ... I got to camp all over the place."[21] Camp or not, the passionate conviction that Gray brings to her role is the mortar that holds the whole ramshackle structure together. Without her, *The Leech Woman* would have little to recommend it.

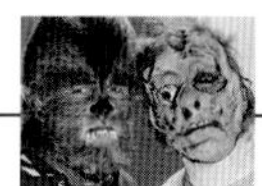

Gray and Phillip Terry are a self-confessed "cruddy pair" – alcoholic 50-year-old wife and smug endocrinologist husband respectively – whose encounter with a wizened old African woman (Estelle Hemsley) leads the film into a grievously padded 'jungle trek' middle section. But when the old woman's tribe is located, the rejuvenation ritual turns out to be, yes, camp but also surprisingly brutal. Gray inflicts the ceremonial lancing of the pineal gland first on Terry, then John van Dreelen and finally Arthur Batanides. Poor Gloria Talbott is also added to the roster of victims, with Gray herself ending up as a defenestrated crone sprawled among patio furniture.

The make-up applied to Gray is almost never convincing, and the action anticipates another rejuvenation fantasy, *Countess Dracula*, in a couple of interesting ways – not only does the rejuvenated Gray impersonate her own niece, she also has a bedroom-farce tendency to degenerate whenever sexual consummation is in view. "For a man, old age has rewards," observes the venerable African matron. "But for the aged woman there is nothing." Despite this brief flash of insight, a heady cocktail of ageism and sexism is encoded in the film itself. At 37 Gray was presumably thought to be a useful halfway-house between the two 'faces' of her character, yet Phillip Terry, who was in reality 13 years her senior, is cast as someone ten years her junior. Universal were perhaps unimpressed by the result, withholding it from release until June 1960, when they put it out as support to the lavish Hammer hit *The Brides of Dracula*.

Dismayed by her deteriorating mirror image, Coleen Gray is *The Leech Woman* (1959)

DEAD BAT, DEAD CAT

If rejuvenation fantasies like *The Wasp Woman* and *The Leech Woman* echoed, however distantly, the silent era, another film came along in the spring of 1959 to make those echoes explicit. Having already recalled his old cliffhanging days by writing *House of Wax* and *The Mad Magician*, the 72-year-old Crane Wilbur now got to direct as well as write a new version of *The Bat* for Allied Artists, putting it into production on 27 April.

Sadly, so ossified – virtually moribund – a property required a much more vibrant hand at the helm in order to appeal to youthful cinemagoers, though *Box Office* magazine suggested that, by "asserting a nostalgic appeal, it will attract hordes of oldsters."[22] The familiar story of a masked interloper searching out hidden loot in an old dark house is here given a few extra details; the lady currently occupying the estate is now a crime novelist (author of, among others, *The Private Morgue of Doctor X*) and the Bat's victims look "like their throats had been ripped out with steel claws." Fans of Italian exploitation might be interested in the way the killer's blank face and taloned glove anticipate future giallo pictures, and the film boasts engaging performances from Agnes Moorehead and the increasingly typecast Vincent Price. But otherwise it comes up dismally short on wit, atmosphere, excitement and, above all, novelty.

All four of those qualities would burst forth in abundance from a film that began shooting just two weeks after *The Bat*. Forty years Crane Wilbur's junior, Roger Corman had got together with his regular screenwriter, Charles B Griffith, and visited the Co-Existence Bagel Shop in North Beach, epicentre of San Francisco's burgeoning Beat movement, after which they toured similar hang-outs on LA's Sunset Strip. In one of these, Chez Paulette, actress Sally Kellerman was working as a waitress and made some helpful suggestions about the story Griffith was crafting. It was a pointed little satire about the aspirant artists, self-absorbed poets and pretentious hangers-on endemic to such establishments, and by extension a satire of the hollowness and gullibility of the art scene generally. And in plot terms it took a substantial tip or two from *House of Wax*.

Walter Paisley is a humble busboy at the Yellow Door café, aching with unrequited love for the pretty Carla and longing to be as cool as the resident improvisatory poet, Maxwell H Brock. At his humble lodgings one night, Walter is making a crude attempt at sculpture when he realises his landlady's cat is trapped behind the wall. Trying to free Frankie, he accidentally impales him instead. The next day he drops into the Yellow Door with a sculpture he guilelessly calls 'Dead Cat'.

Dick Miller admires his disturbingly lifelike 'Dead Cat' sculpture in *A Bucket of Blood* (1959)

A BUCKET OF BLOOD

Alta Vista Productions / American International 1959
66 minutes
production began 11 May

Cinematographer: Jack [Jacques] Marquette; Art Director: Dan Haller; Editor: Anthony Carras; Sound: Wally Nogle; Sound Editor: Leonard Corso; Properties: Dick Rubin; Make-up: Bob Mark; Wardrobe: Marge Corso; Music: Fred Katz; Music Editor: Jerry Irvin; Saxophone Solo: Paul Horn; Songs: 'Gari, Gari' by Gene Raskin*, 'The Ballad of Tim Evans' by Ewan McColl*; Assistant Director: Paul Rapp; Screenplay: Charles B Griffith; Executive Producers: James H Nicholson*, Samuel Z Arkoff*; Producer-Director: Roger Corman

Dick Miller (Walter Paisley); Barboura Morris (Carla); Antony Carbone (Leonard De Santis); Julian Burton (Maxwell H Brock); Ed Nelson (Art Lacroix); John Brinkley (Will); John Shaner (Oscar); Judy Bamber (Alice); Myrtle Damerel (Mrs Swickert); Burt Convy (Lou Raby); Jhean Burton (Naolia); Bruno Ve Sota (art collector); Lynne Storey (Sylvia); uncredited: Alex Hassilev (folk singer); Paul Horn (saxophonist); Henry Travis (art critic)

A Bucket of Blood is a 66-minute joke compounded of beatniks and gore. It's too comic to be a typical horror film and the horror is too explicit for it to be a comedy ... It's perhaps idle to speculate on what Corman might have come up with had he had more time and money ... The film will sell as is. But it might have been a very satisfying satire. *Variety*

This was truly a fast-paced romp from the start, almost like a party. It didn't feel like work ... The audience at the sneak [preview] laughed throughout the film and applauded at the end. I had made a successful comedy that also commented on the ambitions and pretentions of the art world. When a critic wrote that the art world was a metaphor for the movie world, I didn't deny it. *Roger Corman [How I Made a Hundred Movies in Hollywood and Never Lost a Dime, 1990]*

Corman's new film was shot in May under the nondescript title *The Living Dead*, presumably referring to the living death Maxwell confers on his various clay-covered victims. Quite late in the day, at the end of August, this was changed to *A Bucket of Blood*, a more apposite title given that one of the funniest scenes in the film involves a stream of blood drizzling into a bucket from a corpse Walter has stashed out of sight above his kitchen cupboards. It was also more apposite in that it flagged up the fashionably sick humour that gave, and still gives, the film its distinctive flavour. Indeed, a 1958 book by the *Village Voice* cartoonist Jules Feiffer, *Sick Sick Sick: A Guide to Non-Confident Living*, would in due course give AIP a handy tag-line for the film: "You'll be *sick, sick, sick* – from LAUGHING!"

That Walter Paisley is non-confident is patently obvious from the first servile, cringing tic in Dick Miller's expert comic performance. "Everyone listened to my new poem," muses the impossibly pompous Brock. "But do you think they really *heard* it?" One person who lapped up every line, repeating them later on word for word, is the impressionable Walter, whose delusions spring, not from the overweening self-regard of the beatniks around him, but from a slow-witted desperation to belong, to be accepted. His clumsy attempts at kneading clay in his apartment ("Come on, be a nose!") are pitiful to behold, and at first we root for him when he turns the accidental death of Frankie to his advantage. Especially painful is a dismissive line delivered by Leonard, Walter's venal young employer, when 'Dead Cat' is presented to him the following morning. "You're a real artist now," he concedes. "Now go in back and scrub down those garbage cans."

Brock's response, however, is rather different; he announces loftily that "You may call me Maxwell." Even the engaging and seemingly sensible Carla is pretentious enough to say, apropos of the Frankie sculpture, "Look at the expression on its face" – when it clearly has no expression at all. Griffith's witty deconstruction of artistic snobbery takes no prisoners, extending from Leonard's willingness to market Walter's sculptures despite having stumbled on their gruesome method of manufacture, to a snooty art critic who talks about "a one-man return to realism" and values one of Walter's creations at $5000. Fred Katz's eccentric jazz score complements the action perfectly, and Griffith has the beat patois down to a tee, as when a heavy-breathing groupie tells Walter he's touched "something deep down inside of my prana." But the film's real charm springs from

the fact that its broader target – artistic onanism in all its forms – is eternal, rendering the action simultaneously of its time and yet timeless.

Once Walter becomes fêted for his bogus art works the action slips into an amusing 'Emperor with no clothes' groove, altering Walter's dress sense to underline the point. As well as sashaying into the café in a beret and cravat and toting a zen stick, Walter is later seen lording it over the beats in a paper crown and with a toilet plunger for a sceptre. But Corman doesn't skimp on the horror either, crafting a bludgeoning highlight when Walter brains an undercover cop (the subsequent split-cranium statue, dubbed 'Murdered Man', is a genuine grotesque), together with a suspenseful scene in which Walter prepares to strangle an acid-tongued life model called Alice.

It's here, unfortunately, that the film appears to run out of script, leaving no room to explore our complicated response to Walter's lapse into homicidal mania. Alice is killed out of wounded pride, a factory worker from the expedient need to keep 'creating' ("I gotta do something before they forget"), and even the venerated Carla is targeted when Walter realises she doesn't love him. This is a nasty customer all of a sudden and by no means the delightful Walter we used to know. Corman rallies, however, with a thrillingly dynamic nocturnal chase, in which the beatniks discover Walter's secret and the killer is haunted, like Richard III, by the spectral voices of his victims. The final joke is predictable but satisfying – Walter becomes "his [own] greatest work." Yet here, as Dick Miller regretfully confirmed, time and money ran out, with the dead Walter bearing just a few streaks of clay on his face rather than becoming a fully fledged statue.

Though he wrapped it up in just six days, Corman demonstrated so complete a command of his material in *A Bucket of Blood* that it rated as a breakthrough film; indeed, according to the trade papers he was due to follow it on 22 May with an ambitious project called *The Haunted House of Usher*. The film was postponed, however, allowing Corman to go to Puerto Rico in June to make *Last Woman on Earth* (a threadbare, albeit Eastmancolor'd, post-apocalyptic three-hander) and *Creature from the Haunted Sea*, an aquatic horror-comedy splicing the Cuban uprising with a burping, boggle-eyed sea monster. There followed a brilliant black comedy in *Bucket of Blood* vein, *The Little Shop of Horrors*, filmed over a weekend in late December, and only in January 1960 did Corman mount his momentous assault on Edgar Allan Poe with *House of Usher*.

On the same day *A Bucket of Blood* got under way at Amco Studios, AIP put *Drag Race* into production on an adjoining stage. Directed by William Hole and released as *Ghost of Dragstrip Hollow*, this is a simple-minded teen-appeal quickie that locates squeaky-clean hot-rodders in a supposedly haunted house, with a closing rock'n'roll party numbering none other than Paul Blaisdell among the guests. It's actually Blaisdell in a modified version of his iconic costume from *The She-Creature*, and when the head is pulled off he gets to utter a lachrymose lament for his brief glory days as AIP's monster-maker in chief. "Of course you've seen me before," he blubs. "I scared you to death – to *death* – in *Day the World Ended*. You shivered when you saw me in *The She-Creature*. The shame of it. The indignity. They didn't use me in *Horrors of the Black Museum*, after my years of faithful service. They just discarded me." Rarely has art imitated life so painfully, for this peculiar moment of self-parody was the 31-year-old Blaisdell's last notable work for AIP, and for the film industry in general.

Back on 19 January, *Dragstrip Hollow*'s William Hole had been at Carthay Studios to start directing a strange little film for Rex Carlton Productions called *The Naked Goddess*. Its scripted title was *Witchcraft*, a better one given that the only naked goddess in the film is a mildly erotic sculpture of Linda Christian. Indeed, Christian herself smoulders quite splendidly throughout the finished product and is the only real reason to watch it. She plays the standard-issue "beautiful, evil witch," part of "an ancient cult of worshippers who believe sacrifice brings immortality." The former silent movie heart-throb Neil Hamilton is its leader and Robert Alda is the smarmy dullard who gets lured into the coven's clutches by Christian. Reducing the credibility of an already tedious film, Hamilton's machinations are channelled through some of the feeblest voodoo dolls on record.

Linda Christian lures Robert Alda into a diabolist cult in *The Devil's Hand* (1959)

Much more interesting than the film itself is the court case that arose when Rex Carlton and others (among them Christian and Alda, who appear to have had money in the film) were accused of misusing a $20,000 donation. The deliberations of the Los Angeles Superior Court resulted in control of the film passing to the plaintiff, a Tennessee music publisher called Alvin Bubis, who by late March 1959 had retitled it *Devil's Doll*. When it finally came out in September 1961, the title had changed yet again to *The Devil's Hand*, with Rex Carlton and his production company entirely erased from the credits.

THE WALLS ARE CLOSING IN

Three days after *A Bucket of Blood* and *Ghost of Dragstrip Hollow* began, William Castle started directing *The Tingler*, first fruit of the newly inaugurated William Castle Productions. Robb White's screenplay, initially called *The Chiller*, was built around one of the most harebrained horror plots ever devised, and to help sell it the urbane presence of Vincent Price was once again deemed essential. An audience-grabbing gimmick was also de rigueur, of course, and this time Castle came up with what he called Percepto. "I'm going to buzz the asses of everyone in America by installing little motors under the seats of every theatre in the country," he enthused, noting later that "In the final count, I think we must have buzzed 20,000,000 behinds."[23] Given that only first-run houses were Percepto-fitted, and even then only in selected seats, this was a typically Castle-esque exaggeration. But it certainly made good copy.

Researching death by fright, pathologist Dr Warren Chapin theorises that a lobster-like parasite in the human body is fed by fear, growing in size and eventually – if the emotion is unrelieved by screaming – causing death by crushing the host's spine. When called upon to conduct an autopsy on Martha Higgins, a mute middle-aged woman who ran a silent-movie revival house, Chapin has the chance to encounter a 'tingler' in the flesh…

The multiplying absurdities of *The Tingler* are not only essential to its entertainment value but also make one wonder what White and Castle were 'on' when they concocted it. As it happens, the story involves LSD, with Price's Dr Chapin making experimental use of it and, in what was very likely a cinema first, experiencing a paranoid 'trip' on camera. White claimed to have given it a go himself, under medical supervision at UCLA, and explained the effects to Price in some detail. "In the movie," White lamented, "he jumped around and did the same goddam thing he always did!"[24] Price's display of gathering hysteria – recoiling from a skeleton, repeatedly wheezing "The walls!" and finally pitching forward over a hospital gurney – is really just a way-out drama-school exercise captured on film, and a source of delight to Price cultists everywhere.

Providing the stiffest possible test for the viewer's suspension of disbelief, the lunacy starts early. A cadaverous little wisp of a man, Ollie Higgins, introduces himself with the telling phrase "I'm nobody, Doc" and proceeds to sit in on his own brother-in-law's autopsy. Chapin, what's more, lets him. The just-executed brother-in-law was a two-time murderer and the autopsy involves a cosy discussion of the corpse's mysteriously shattered spine. Later, the ever-placid Ollie will sit in on another of Chapin's autopsies; this time the subject is Ollie's wife Martha. In the meantime we've been misdirected into thinking that Chapin dosed up the perpetually fearful Martha with LSD in order to bring about her death and thus get his hands on a fully developed tingler. The truth turns out to be rather different – the outrageously elaborate 'visions' Martha experienced were somehow engineered by Ollie himself. In White's defence, his original script did indeed point the finger at Chapin, with the blame switched to Ollie via subsequent rewrites. As a result, Ollie's charade demands a leap of the imagination almost as gymnastic as the idea that tinglers have somehow never been noticed by any previous pathologist.

As for the tingler's spine-snapping strength, it's encapsulated by a line in which White tips his hat to Price's role in *The Fly*; explains Chapin, "I felt as though my arm were in one of those hydraulic presses." With magpie abandon, White also throws in witty quotes from *Doctor X* (a sheeted corpse sitting upright on its slab) and the much more recent French hit *Les Diaboliques* (a Castle favourite), when Martha expires of fright in a dingy bathroom. In this instance, the film's prevailing monochrome incorporates startling, sludge-like red as the sink and bathtub fill with blood.

Martha is memorably played by Judith Evelyn, a former Broadway co-star of Price's who was cast at his suggestion. Martha suffers quite clearly from obsessive-compulsive disorder and, with her dumb-show means of communication, is every bit as 'silent' as the cinematic phantoms that people her movie house. "You'd be surprised at how many people come to see these old pictures," says Ollie. "Not just to make fun either." That this apparently ultra-modern shocker pays tribute to silent films is one of its most charming features, though it's just as well it does given the fusillade of irredeemably

Straight out of the 1920s: one of the nightmare visions experienced by Judith Evelyn in *The Tingler* (1959)

hokey 'old house' apparitions devised by Ollie. (A hairy anthropoid arm, brandishing a hatchet, is straight out of the 1920s.) Though presumably coincidental, even the casting of Patricia Cutts as Chapin's scheming wife connects the film to the silent era; her father was the British film pioneer Graham Cutts.

The soapy, hate-filled sparring between the Chapins gives White the opportunity to recycle a key dynamic from *House on Haunted Hill*, and Price and Cutts play it to the hilt. The female characters – the viperous married 'tramp' in silver lamé, the submissive younger sister who will make Chapin's lab assistant a good wife, and the traumatised middle-aged woman who literally has no voice – are a stereotypical trio, but really the entire dramatis personae are just a bunch of stick figures that pale beside the charming, and visibly wire-manipulated, tingler.

At the end, the film quotes *The Blob* by letting the thing loose in a movie theatre (the one in the film and, by implication, the one patronised by Castle's teen audience), causing pandemonium during a screening of the 1921 Richard Barthelmess vehicle *Tol'able David*. It even gets into the projection booth, crawling in slug-like silhouette across the whited-out screen and finally being deposited for safe keeping in, of all things, a film can – wonderfully pulpy devices suggesting that the tingler is a slimy metaphor for exploitation cinema generally.

After Castle completed *The Tingler*, another master showman, Bert I Gordon – cinema's cut-rate master of enlarged insects – changed tack completely, starting production on an atmospheric ghost story at Hal Roach Studios on 12 August. In *Tormented*, the excellent Richard Carlson is a conceited "piano genius of jazz" who fails to assist his voluptuous mistress (Juli Reding) when she's dangling from the uppermost platform of a lighthouse. The resultant haunting is apparently born of Carlson's guilt, though the film seems rather confused on this point, since several other characters appear to be aware of it too. Gordon's imagery ranges from the startlingly surreal (Reding's body, washed up on the beach, morphing into a colossal clump of seaweed) to the hilariously hokey (various dodgy special effects scenes involving her severed hand and head). Somewhere between these two extremes is Carlson's disastrous wedding,

THE TINGLER

William Castle Productions 1959
82 minutes
production began 14 May

Cinematographer: Wilfrid M Cline; Art Director: Phil Bennett; Editor: Chester W Schaeffer; Sound: John Livadary, Harry Mills; Set Decoration: Milton Stumph; Make-up: Monty Westmore*; Hair Stylist: Hazel Keats*; Wardrobe: Robert Spencer*, Roselle Novello*; Music: Von Dexter; Assistant Director: Herb Wallerstein; Associate to the Producer: Dona Holloway; Screenplay: Robb White; Producer-Director: William Castle

Vincent Price (Dr Warren Chapin); Judith Evelyn (Martha Higgins); Darryl Hickman (David Morris); Patricia Cutts (Isabel Chapin); Pamela Lincoln (Lucy Stevens); Philip Coolidge (Oliver 'Ollie' Higgins); uncredited: Gail Bonney, Clarence Straight (audience members); William Castle (himself); Pat Colby, Amy Fields (young couple in audience); Bob Gunderson (condemned man); Dal McKennon (projectionist)

The Tingler ... could use a little gore, even with those palpitating ads. For some time producer William Castle has been serving some of the worst, dullest little horror entries ever to snake into movie houses. This one, which he also directed, is about a rubbery-looking lobster ... It failed to arouse the customer seated in front of this viewer yesterday – a fearless lad who was sound asleep, snoring. Just keep us awake, Mr Castle. *New York Times*

I kicked a lot of kelp on Malibu Beach trying to figure out how to make an ugly rubber worm into a feature movie ... As shooting went on we agreed that the picture was sadly in need of *something*, but we couldn't think of anything to help it until Bill [Castle] came in one morning with a small vibrator, which eventually saved the picture and gave it *The Tingler* for a title. Robb White [*Oh the Horror of it All*, in *Monsters from the Vault*, Summer 1999]

with the winsome bride (Lugene Sanders) shrieking in horror as her corsage spontaneously wilts. Despite all these bells and whistles, the chilly beachfront atmosphere is quite memorable, and the circularity of the ending – with Carlson and Reding entwined, dead, in the surf – is even poignant.

As the 1950s hastened to a close, Allied Artists commissioned a film called *The Hypnotic Eye*, assigning George Blair to direct it and putting it into production on 10 September. This one effected a bizarre fusion of several exploitation strands, splicing the time-honoured 'evil hypnotist' motif, which had picked up renewed steam with the recent Bridey Murphy fad, with the trend for audience-grabbing, William Castle-style promotional gimmicks. In short, the evil hypnotist is himself the gimmick, propagating so-called 'HypnoMagic' via a couple of direct-address spiels to the audience, spiels that have the unfortunate effect of completely torpedo-ing the narrative, in one instance for a whopping nine minutes. Added to the mix is a third exploitation strand, a new one never given quite such gloating emphasis before – a mean-spirited parade of mutilated women, beginning with an attention-grabbing pre-credits vignette in which an entranced blonde beauty sets her own head on fire.

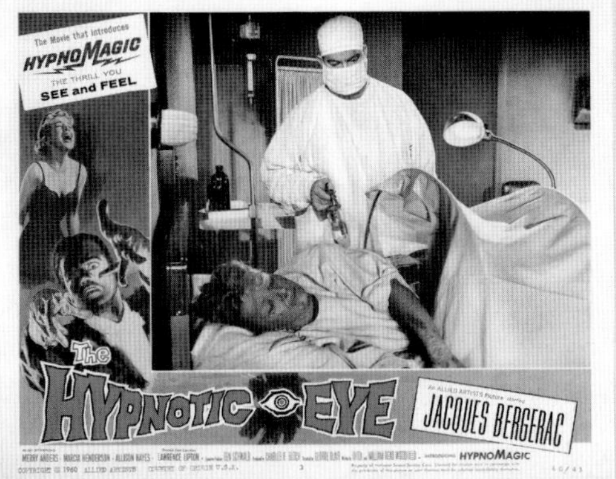

Merry Anders, hospitalised with self-inflicted acid burns in *The Hypnotic Eye* (1959)

Among the other casualties of post-hypnotic suggestion we have Merry Anders giving herself an H_2SO_4 facial and Carol Thurston revealing crude but nastily effective 'eyeless' make-up when interviewed by the stodgy investigative heroes. The culprit is The Great Desmond (Jacques Bergerac), whose beautiful assistant – none other than Allison Hayes – ends up teetering on a theatre gantry, screaming "If you like my beautiful face so much, you may have it!" prior to ripping off her 'face' to reveal the hideous disfigurement beneath. It's a rare moment of pulp panache in an otherwise threadbare product, though the misogynist impulse behind 'unmasking' Hayes' monolithic glamour in this way is disturbing, to say the least. There was clearly something unpleasant in the air, given that an almost exactly contemporary British shocker, *Circus of Horrors*, traded in similar disfigurements. (A later British film, *Devil Doll*, dropped the mutilations in favour of explicitly echoing Desmond's smarmy stage act.) Aside from its horror highlights, the film echoes *A Bucket of Blood* with a bit of hipster padding in which 'King of the Beatniks' Lawrence Lipton, just turning 60, says "I was a teenage movie monster" in the midst of a coffee-shop poetry recital; the scene was, for some reason, cut in the UK.

On release in February 1960, *The Hypnotic Eye* got by on its hucksterish ad campaign, proclaiming "HypnoMagic is the first movie audience participation gimmick!" The film also distinguished itself when censors in Memphis, Tennessee coupled it with the British import *Jack the Ripper* in calling for a statewide ban. Beyond its mean-spirited grue factor, however, *The Hypnotic Eye*'s arrival at the outset of a new decade seemed emblematic of an uncomfortable truth – that, with a glut of cheap horror pictures cluttering up US cinemas, and an increasingly hysterical range of gimmicks being used to sell them, the impetus provided by AIP and other companies had exhausted itself in record time.

Indeed, the emphasis on teen audiences, once so invigorating and revolutionary, had by this time dwindled to the level of juvenilia. *Ghost of Dragstrip Hollow*, for example, has frequently been cited as a precursor to AIP's 1963 film *Beach Party* and its half-dozen charmingly inane successors. One solution to this impasse was to take a tip from the mature and sumptuously upholstered horror pictures coming in from England's Hammer Films – or, for that matter, from that rare instance of a handsomely appointed Hollywood shocker, *The Fly*. Before that could happen, however, American horror would sink to a level even lower than Poverty Row, courtesy of maverick producer Rex Carlton.

THE ULTIMATE HORROR

As noted at the beginning of this chapter, in mid-October 1959 Rex Carlton – presumably unfazed by accusations of financial irregularity on his last film, *The Devil's Hand* – was in a New York hotel basement, making something called *The Brain that Wouldn't Die*.

The mad scientist here is called Dr Cortland; the surname, consciously or otherwise, is a virtual anagram of Carlton. Written and directed by Joseph Green, the end product contains curious echoes of two foreign pictures made earlier in the year – curious

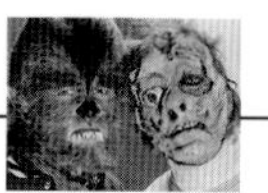

because it's highly unlikely he could have seen them yet. Like Professor Génessier in *Les Yeux sans visage*, Cortland is struggling to reconstruct a female loved one after a tragedy brought about by the doctor's dangerous driving. Like Professor Abel in *Die Nackte und der Satan*, Cortland's fiancée Jan is reduced to a living head propped up in a dish of preservative and surrounded by a forest of tubes.

As a cult movie, Green's film has pretty much everything, from crudely mismatched inserts to laborious dialogue scenes captured in unvarying mid-shot, even a closing title that contradicts the film's opening by calling the film *The Head that Wouldn't Die* – which, as pointed out earlier, was the working title. For what it's worth, Virginia Leith's disembodied, and splendidly vindictive, Jan remains the film's pièce de résistance. Her glacial, angular beauty – severely framed in a tight-fitting bandage – bestows a truly indelible image on an otherwise Z-grade picture. "Like all quantities, horror has its ultimate," she sneers. "And I am that."

For all its ineptitude, the film was years ahead of its time in the titillation and gore departments and had to wait until August 1962 for an emasculated release via AIP. Cortland is a total sleazeball whose search for a suitable body with which to supplement Jan's head involves cruising clipjoints and beauty parades. ("We've got a stripper and a model in this show," Carlton boasted to *Variety*. "Abroad we can give 'em a little more."[25]) And at the climax Cortland's crippled assistant has his one good arm torn off and Cortland himself has a sizable chunk bitten out of his neck. The final conflagration, however, is open-ended, underlining Carlton's claim during production that he was "already planning a sequel – *The Return of the Head that Wouldn't Die*."[26] It didn't happen, but the film nevertheless pointed forward to the 1963 release *Blood Feast* and other full-colour gore movies from Herschell Gordon Lewis.

By the time *The Brain that Wouldn't Die* came out, Jan's contention that she is the 'ultimate' horror had long been disproved, in any case, and by no less an industry titan than Alfred Hitchcock. As well as being stung by the success of the Hitchcock-like *Les Diaboliques*, Hitchcock was keenly aware of (a) the horror wave unleashed by Hammer and (b) the money-spinning manoeuvres of William Castle. He therefore initiated a film adaptation of Robert Bloch's uncompromisingly adult novel *Psycho* and arrived at California's Golden State Freeway on 30 November 1959 to start shooting it. Sinister though the meeting between a nervous motorist (Janet Leigh) and a saturnine highway patrolman (Mort Mills) may have been, there was far worse to

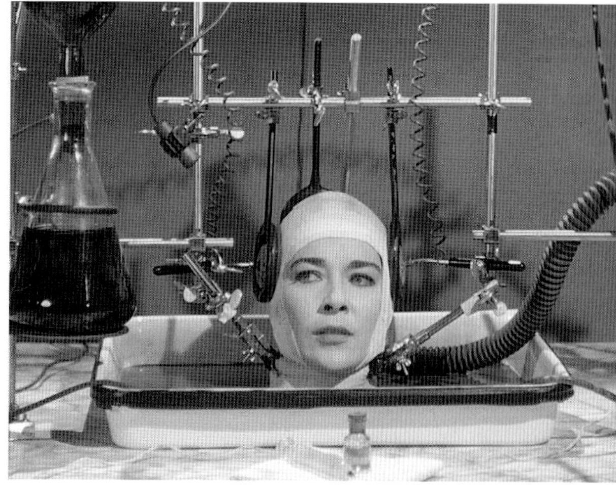

Virginia Leith as the vindictive living head of a car crash victim in *The Brain that Wouldn't Die* (1959)

come on the Universal backlot, where Hitchcock's design team had erected a new and improved version of America's traditional old dark house.

And, just as Hitchcock was apparently lowering his game with a low-budget black-and-white horror picture, so AIP were significantly raising theirs with a luridly coloured return to Edgar Allan Poe's original old dark house. With their 'two cheap pictures on the same bill' strategy having long since been tarnished by other companies, Jim Nicholson and Sam Arkoff looked at the glamorous Hammer releases and reasoned that more expensive films were likely to be the way forward. They therefore gave the go-ahead for Roger Corman's lush-looking *House of Usher*, cannily casting Vincent Price in the lead and putting the film into production on 18 January 1960.

At the turn of the 1960s, then, the American horror film was ready to rise from the doldrums of market saturation and strike out in radically new directions. But the foundations of the *Usher* and *Psycho* houses had been firmly laid in the six decades' worth of more naïve, but equally intriguing, screen shockers that preceded them. With its dual emphasis on silent movie houses and LSD experimentation, Castle's simultaneously nostalgic and forward-looking *The Tingler* remains an appropriate film with which to draw a line under a strain of American horror that was about to undergo profound change. The mutations involved would have been unimaginable even to the pantheon of mad scientists who'd featured in *The Tingler*'s distinguished forebears – Richard Vollin, Henryk Savaard, Lorenzo Cameron, Sir Joel Cadman – even unto Dr Warren Chapin himself.

But that's another story.

Source Notes

Part One
American Horror in Embryo

1 Gilbert Seldes, *Movies for the Millions: An Account of Motion Pictures, Principally in America*, London 1937
2 review of *Life Without Soul*, *Moving Picture World* 4 December 1915
3 quoted in *Famous Monsters of Filmland* October 1963
4 Richard Willis, 'The Edwin Booth of the Screen', *Motion Picture Classic* June 1916
5 quoted in Kevin Brownlow, *Hollywood: The Pioneers*, London 1979
6 reprinted in Denis Gifford, 'Pictures of Poe', in *The Edgar Allan Poe Scrapbook*, London 1977
7 Lotte H Eisner, *L'Ecran démoniaque*, Paris 1952 (UK reprint: *The Haunted Screen*, London 1969)
8 reprinted in John Kobler, *Damned in Paradise: The Life of John Barrymore*, New York 1977
9 quoted in David Robinson, 'Conversation with Lillian Gish', *Sight and Sound* Winter 1957-58
10 Terry Ramsaye, *A Million and One Nights: A History of the Motion Picture*, New York 1926
11 quoted in Myrtle Gebhart, *The New Theda Bara*, *Picture-Play* September 1925
12 Mary Roberts Rinehart, *My Story*, New York 1931
13 J C Trewin, *The Gay Twenties: A Decade of the Theatre*, London 1958
14 Kevin Brownlow, *Hollywood: The Pioneers*, London 1979
15 reprinted in Philip J Riley, *A Blind Bargain reconstructed*, Atlantic City 1988
16 Laurence Reid, 'The Celluloid Critic', *Motion Picture Classic* November 1922
17 Lionel Collier, 'Shop for Your Films', *Picturegoer and Film Weekly* 5 October 1940
18 *New York Sun* 25 March 1924; reprinted in Scott MacQueen, 'Roland West', in *Between Action and Cut: Five American Directors*, Metuchen NJ 1985
19 Mary Astor, *My Story: an Autobiography*, New York 1959
20 Denis Gifford, *A Pictorial History of Horror Movies*, London 1973
21 'The New Pictures', *Time* 10 September 1923

Jeanne Bates offers a prayer to Satan and gets sultry Rose Hobart in *The Soul of a Monster* (1944)

Part Two
Silent as the Tomb

1 'The Shadow Stage', *Photoplay* December 1924
2 *Life* 3 September 1925; reprinted in Anthony Slide, *Selected Film Criticism Volume Two: 1921-1930*, Metuchen NJ 1982
3 quoted in *Stoll Herald* 17 August 1925
4 'Box-Office Film Reviews', *The Bioscope* 5 March 1925
5 Lionel Barrymore, *We Barrymores*, London 1951
6 Welford Beaton, untitled review, *The Film Spectator* 9 June 1928
7 Norbert Lusk, 'The Screen in Review', *Picture-Play* November 1926
8 quoted in Margaret Chute, 'The Wind', *The Picturegoer* January 1928
9 quoted in Booton Herndon, *Mary Pickford and Douglas Fairbanks – The Most Popular Couple the World Has Known*, New York 1977
10 Joan Dickey, 'A Maker of Mystery', *Motion Picture Classic* March 1928
11 quoted in Welford Beaton, 'From the Editor's Easy Chair', *Hollywood Spectator* 20 June 1936
12 Sally Benson, 'The Screen in Review', *Picture-Play* August 1925
13 John S Cohen Jr, 'The New Photo Plays', *New York Sun* 13 June 1927; reprinted in David J Skal and Elias Savada, *Dark Carnival: The Secret World of Tod Browning*, New York 1995
14 reprinted in Philip J Riley, *London After Midnight reconstructed*, New York 1985
15 William K Everson, *Classics of the Horror Film*, Secaucus NJ 1974
16 Herbert Howe, 'An Evolution Trial in the Zoo', *Photoplay* October 1925
17 Welford Beaton, 'Julian Makes Good with *Leopard Woman*' [sic], *The Film Spectator* 7 January 1928
18 Donald Beaton, 'As They Appeal to a Youth', *The Film Spectator* 5 January 1929

19 Edwin Schallert, 'The Talk of Hollywood', *Picture-Play* July 1928
20 quoted in Jeanne Stein, 'Fusspot and Fortune's Fool: Edward Everett Horton', *Focus on Film* January-February 1970
21 'Box-Office Film Reviews', *The Bioscope* 31 October 1928
22 John Cabourn, 'Terrorised Critics', *The Bioscope* 31 October 1928
23 'Box-Office Film Reviews', *The Bioscope* 24 July 1929
24 Walter Ramsey, 'It's Sound Appeal Now', *Picture-Play* January 1930
25 quoted in Ruth Waterbury, 'The True Life Story of Lon Chaney', *Photoplay* February 1928
26 Welford Beaton, 'In Talkie Form All the Absurdities Become Apparent', *The Film Spectator* 30 August 1930

Martin Kosleck and Rondo Hatton as chalk-and-cheese conspirators in *House of Horrors* (1945)

Part Three
Children of the Night

1 Donald Beaton, 'Another Point of View', *The Film Spectator* 28 March 1931
2 'The Picture Parade: Reviews of the Newest Pictures', *Motion Picture* June 1931
3 Dalton Trumbo, 'Trumbo Reviews: Murder and Magic', *Hollywood Spectator* November 1931
4 reprinted in James Curtis, *James Whale: A New World of Gods and Monsters*, Boston 1998
5 Burness Martin, 'Listen, Boris – Your Face May Be Your Fortune But – ', *Picturegoer Weekly* 13 February 1932
6 Welford Beaton, 'An Achievement', *Hollywood Spectator* February 1932
7 quoted in William Stull, 'Concerning Cinematography: Common Sense and Camera Angles', *American Cinematographer* February 1932
8 reprinted in Mark A Vieira, *Sin in Soft Focus: Pre-Code Hollywood*, New York 1999
9 Charles Grayson, 'In Gaga Disguise', *Motion Picture* February 1931
10 'More Screen SHOCKS and SHIVERS', *Picturegoer Weekly* 13 February 1932
11 Leonard Wolf, *Horror: A Connoisseur's Guide to Literature and Film*, New York 1989
12 reprinted in *The AFI Catalog of Motion Pictures Produced in the United States: Feature Films 1931-40*, Berkeley and Los Angeles 1993
13 'Letters from Our Readers', *Motion Picture* May 1932
14 reprinted in Phillip Lopate (ed), *American Movie Critics: An Anthology from the Silents until Now*, New York 2006
15 'The Picture Parade: Reviews of the Newest Pictures', *Motion Picture* December 1932
16 Kathryn Dougherty, 'Close-Ups and Long-Shots', *Photoplay* January 1933
17 'The Vampire Bat plays to big business in America', *Kinematograph Weekly* 15 June 1933
18 quoted in Faith Service, 'He's the Mental Lon Chaney!', *Motion Picture* July 1933
19 quoted in Danny Peary (ed), *Close-Ups: The Movie Star Book*, New York 1978
20 reprinted in Anthony Slide, 'Censored Screams! Horror Films and the Production Code in the 1930s', *Filmfax* April-May 1999
21 George E Turner and Michael H Price, *Forgotten Horrors: The Definitive Edition*, Baltimore 1999
22 review by 'JWUT', *Monthly Film Bulletin* May 1935
23 reprinted in Gregory William Mank, *Karloff and Lugosi: The Story of a Haunting Collaboration*, Jefferson NC 1990
24 'The New Pictures', *Time* 22 July 1935
25 review in the *Times* 4 August 1935; reprinted in Tom Johnson, *Censored Screams: The British Ban on Hollywood Horror in the Thirties*, Jefferson NC 1997
26 review in the *Spectator* 9 August 1935; reprinted in Graham Greene, *The Pleasure Dome: The Collected Film Criticism 1935-40*, London 1972
27 'The Picture Parade: Reviews of the Newest Pictures', *Motion Picture* January 1933
28 Paul Jacobs, 'Its Acting Saves It', *Hollywood Spectator* 9 May 1936
29 reprinted in *The Devil-Doll* UK pressbook
30 Edgar G Ulmer interviewed by Peter Bogdanovich, in Todd McCarthy and Charles Flynn (eds), *Kings of the Bs: Working Within the Hollywood System*, New York 1975

Part Four
Rising from the Past

1 Denis Gifford, *A Pictorial History of Horror Movies*, London 1973
2 Harry Coulter, 'Cold Chills and Cold Cash', *Cinema Progress: The Film and Life*, May-June 1938
3 reprinted in Gary Don Rhodes, 'A Hunger for Horror: The 1939 Revival of a Genre', *Scarlet Street* Fall 1997
4 reprinted in Anthony Slide, 'Censored Screams! Horror Films

Researchers Nancy Davis, Lew Ayres and Gene Evans scrutinise what's left of a multi-millionaire in *Donovan's Brain* (1953)

and the Production Code in the 1930s', *Filmfax* March-April 1999

5 Jack Wade, 'We Cover the Studios', *Photoplay* April 1939

6 Cedric Hardwicke [as told to James Brough], *A Victorian in Orbit: The Irreverent Memoirs of Sir Cedric Hardwicke*, London 1961

7 Basil Wright, 'The Cinema', *The Spectator* 9 August 1940

8 reprinted in Gregory William Mank, *Hollywood's Maddest Scientists: Lionel Atwill, Colin Clive, George Zucco*, Baltimore 1998

9 Tom Weaver, *Poverty Row HORRORS! – Monogram, PRC and Republic Horror Films of the Forties*, Jefferson NC 1993

10 reprinted in Denis Gifford, *A Pictorial History of Horror Movies*, London 1973

11 Paul C Mooney Jr, 'Showmen's Reviews', *Motion Picture Herald* 24 October 1942

12 press release for *The Seventh Victim*; reprinted in George E Turner, 'Val Lewton's Cat People', *Cinefantastique* May-June 1982

13 DeWitt Bodeen, 'Val Lewton', *Films in Review* April 1963

14 quoted in Gregory William Mank, *Hollywood Cauldron: Thirteen Horror Films from the Genre's Golden Age*, Jefferson NC 1994

15 'Idea Doesn't Pay Off In Production', *Hollywood Reporter* 1 April 1943

16 Robin Wood, 'The Shadow Worlds of Jacques Tourneur', *Film Comment* Summer 1972

17 Ed Bansak, 'Fearing the Dark: The Val Lewton Legacy', *Midnight Marquee* Spring 1990

18 Alton Cook, 'Jane Eyre Adds Horror, Retaining Novel's Pattern', *New York World-Telegram* 4 February 1944

19 Kate Cameron, 'Music Hall Offers Treat in Jane Eyre', *New York Daily News* 4 February 1944

20 John T McManus, 'Jungle Woman', *New York PM*, 16 July 1944

21 Archer Winsten, 'Jungle Woman Gets Rough on Rialto Theatre's Screen', *New York Post* 15 July 1944

22 Tim Lucas, 'Video Tapevine: Frankenstein Created Paula the Ape Woman', *Video Watchdog* # 48, 1998

Part Five
Diminishing Returns

1 'Mysterious Doctor OK for Horror Fans', *Hollywood Reporter* 24 February 1943

2 Dean Brierly, 'Robert Siodmak: The Uncrowned King of Forties Film Noir', *Filmfax* August-September 1997

3 Michael Brunas, 'The Uninvited', *Scarlet Street* Fall 1993

4 quoted in Anthony Slide, 'Censored Screams! Part Two: Horror Films and the Production Code in the 1940s', *Filmfax* May-June 1999

5 quoted in Joel C Siegel, *Val Lewton: The Reality of Terror*, London 1972

6 quoted in John Brosnan, *The Horror People*, London 1976

7 unsigned review, *Monthly Film Bulletin* February 1946

8 '12 RKO Producers Ready 22 Features', *Hollywood Reporter* 29 June 1943

9 quoted in Anthony Slide (ed), *De Toth on De Toth*, London 1996

10 Archer Winsten, 'Cry of the Werewolf Sounded at the Rialto', *New York Post* 12 August 1944

11 Archer Winsten, 'The Soul of a Monster Bared at Rialto Theatre, Where Else?', *New York Post* 9 September 1944

12 reprinted in Gregory William Mank, 'Louise Currie: l'amour of The Ape Man', *Monsters from the Vault* Fall 1997

13 John Brosnan, *Future Tense: The Cinema of Science Fiction*, London 1978

14 quoted in Boze Hadleigh, 'Last Kiss of the Spider Woman', *Scarlet Street* Summer 1993

15 Basil Rathbone, *In and Out of Character*, New York 1962

16 Bert McCord, 'The Mummy's Curse', *New York Herald Tribune* 31 March 1945

17 John T McManus, 'The Mummy's Curse', *New York PM* 1 April 1945

18 Iain Sinclair, 'Pulped Fictions', *The Guardian* 12 March 2005

19 reprinted in Joel C Siegel, *Val Lewton: The Reality of Terror*, London 1972

20 reprinted in Paul M Jensen, *Boris Karloff and His Films*, New York 1974

21 review by 'GMD', *Monthly Film Bulletin* 31 October 1946

22 Campbell Dixon, review of *The Spiral Staircase*, *Daily Telegraph* 11 February 1946

23 Dorothy Masters, 'A Bloodthirsty Trio Presented at Rialto', *New York Daily News* 22 December 1945

24 introduction to Philip J Riley (ed), *Universal Filmscripts Series: Classic Horror Films Volume 16*, Absecon NJ 1993

25 Michael Brunas, John Brunas, Tom Weaver, *Universal Horrors: The Studio's Classic Films, 1931-1946*, Jefferson NC 1990

Part Six
Post-war Permutations

1 Walter Kendrick, *The Thrill of Fear: 250 Years of Scary Entertainment*, New York 1991
2 Bertrand Tavernier, 'Lettre de Bruxelles', *Cahiers du Cinéma* June 1962
3 quoted in Thomas F Brady, 'Old Ghoulish Friends Roam the Sets at Universal', *New York Times* 14 March 1948; reprinted in Gary Don Rhodes, *Lugosi*, Jefferson NC 1997
4 Elspeth Grant, review of *Sunset Blvd*, *Daily Graphic* 18 August 1950
5 John Baxter, *Science Fiction in the Cinema 1895-1970*, London 1970
6 Richard Findlater, 'Seen and Heard', *Tribune* 22 August 1952
7 reprinted in George E Turner, 'Howard Hawks' The Thing', *Cinefantastique* July-August 1982
8 'The New Pictures', *Time* 14 May 1951
9 Colin Shindler, 'Cold War Cinema', in Ann Lloyd (ed), *Movies of the Fifties*, London 1982
10 reprinted in Jack Sullivan (ed), *The Penguin Encyclopedia of Horror and the Supernatural*, New York 1986
11 Milton Luban, 'Manfish a Slipshod, Inept Motion Picture Production', *Hollywood Reporter* 8 February 1956
12 John McCarten, 'The Current Cinema: Cheaters Aren't the Answer', *The New Yorker* 18 April 1953
13 R M Hayes, *3-D Movies: A History and Filmography of Stereoscopic Cinema*, Jefferson NC 1989
14 reprinted in Steve Rubin, 'Retrospect: Them!', *Cinefantastique* Winter 1974
15 quoted in Brian McFarlane, *An Autobiography of British Cinema*, London 1997
16 Margaret Hinxman, 'Stepping Out Tonight?' / 'Picturegoer Parade', *Picturegoer* 6 October 1956
17 William R Weaver, 'The Product Digest', *Motion Picture Herald* 23 June 1956
18 'Another Little Bonanza', *Hollywood Reporter* 10 August 1956
19 'Parents Sue on Horror Pix After Boy, 9, Dies', *Variety* 6 November 1956
20 reprinted in Tom Weaver, *John Carradine: The Films*, Jefferson NC 1999
21 'The New Pictures', *Time* 17 September 1956

Part Seven
Teenage Kicks

1 Fred Hift, 'Rex Carlton, a 1959 Shoestringer, Rides Today's Product Shortage in Quaint and Wondrous Ways', *Variety* 28 October 1959
2 unsigned, 'Monstrous for Money', *Newsweek* 14 July 1958
3 quoted in Roger Corman, *How I Made a Hundred Movies in Hollywood and Never Lost a Dime*, London 1990
4 unsigned, 'Feature Reviews: The Astounding She-Monster', *Box Office* vol 73 # 8, 16 June 1958
5 quoted in Mark McGee, *Fast and Furious: The Story of American International Pictures*, Jefferson NC 1996
6 ibid
7 William Castle, *Step Right Up! I'm Gonna Scare the Pants Off America*, New York 1976
8 Robb White, 'Oh the Horror of it All', *Monsters from the Vault* # 9, Summer 1999
9 quoted in John Brunas, 'Shock Drive-In presents I Bury the Living', *Scarlet Street* # 12, Fall 1993
10 quoted in Dermod Hill, 'A New Kind of Happiness for Jane Hylton', *TV Times* 15 July 1972
11 quoted in Jessie Lilley, 'How to Make a Movie Star: Gary Conway', *Scarlet Street* # 17, Winter 1995
12 quoted in Jessie Lilley, 'How to Make a Monster Movie: Herman Cohen', *Scarlet Street* # 17, Winter 1995
13 quoted in Tom Weaver, *It Came from Weaver Five*, Jefferson NC 1996
14 quoted in Don Cullen Smith, 'Jerome Bixby' [interview], *Fangoria* # 25, February 1983
15 unsigned, 'Shorter Notices: Curse of the Faceless Man', *Monthly Film Bulletin* vol 25 # 298, November 1958
16 Robert Evans, *The Kid Stays in the Picture*, New York 1994
17 quoted in John Brunas, 'Shock Drive-In presents The Alligator People', *Scarlet Street* # 10, Spring 1993
18 John Baxter, *Science Fiction in the Cinema 1895-1970*, London 1970
19 Peter Nicholls, *Fantastic Cinema: An Illustrated Survey*, London 1984
20 Kevin Heffernan, *Ghouls, Gimmicks and Gold: Horror Films and the American Movie Business, 1953-1968*, Durham NC 2004
21 quoted in Michael Brunas, 'Riding High on Nightmare Alley: Coleen Gray', *Scarlet Street* # 31, Summer 1998
22 unsigned, 'Feature Reviews: The Bat', *Box Office* vol 75 # 17, 17 August 1959
23 Castle, op cit
24 quoted in Tom Weaver, 'Weaver's World', *Scarlet Street* # 7, Summer 1992
25 quoted in Hift, op cit
26 ibid

Veteran make-up artist Jack P Pierce converts Buddy Baer into the *Giant from the Unknown* (1956)

Alternative Titles

Listed below are films with alternative titles, excluding those already alluded to in the text. The country-of-origin title is listed first, with variations for US and/or UK distribution, together with reissue titles where applicable.

- 6 donne per l'assassino : Blood and Black Lace (US / UK)
- Abbott and Costello Meet Frankenstein : Meet the Ghosts (UK)
- The Abominable Snowman : The Abominable Snowman of the Himalayas (US)
- The Adventures of Sherlock Holmes : Sherlock Holmes (UK)
- Alias Nick Beal : The Contact Man (UK)
- The Ape Man : Lock Your Doors (UK)
- Behind Locked Doors : The Human Gorilla (reissue)
- The Black Cat (1934) : The Vanishing Body (reissue)
- The Black Sleep : Dr Cadman's Secret (reissue)
- The Bridge : aka The Spy
- Condemned to Live : Demon of Doom (reissue)
- The Corpse Vanishes : The Case of the Missing Brides (UK reissue)
- The Dark Eyes of London : The Human Monster (US)
- The Devil's Daughter : aka Pocomania
- Drums o' Voodoo : aka Louisiana / She Devil / Voodoo Drums
- El espanto surge de la tumba : Horror Rises from the Tomb (US)
- The Flying Serpent : Killer with Wings (reissue)
- Gaslight (UK version, 1940) : Angel Street (US)
- Gaslight (US version, 1944) : The Murder in Thornton Square (UK)
- Ghosts on the Loose : Ghosts in the Night (UK)
- House of Horrors : Joan Medford is Missing (UK)
- House of Usher : The Fall of the House of Usher (UK)

The Monster Walks, with Vera Reynolds and Martha Mattox, was made in January 1932 and reached the UK nine years later as *The Monster Walked*

- The Jungle Captive : Wild Jungle Captive (reissue)
- The Lady and the Monster : Tiger Man (reissue)
- The Last Performance : aka The Last Call
- The Little Red Schoolhouse : The Greater Law (UK)
- The Living Ghost : aka A Walking Nightmare
- The Lodger (1926) : aka The Case of Jonathan Drew
- The Lodger (1932) : The Phantom Fiend (US)
- Lola : Without a Soul (reissue)
- Manfish : Calypso (UK)
- Man Made Monster : Atomic Monster (reissue)
- The Man Who Changed His Mind : The Man Who Lived Again (US) / Dr Maniac (US reissue)
- The Master Mystery : aka The Houdini Serial
- Midnight Warning : aka Eyes of Mystery
- The Murder in the Museum : The Five Deadly Vices (reissue)
- The Mystery of the Mary Celeste : Phantom Ship (US)
- Mystery of the White Room : aka Murder in the Surgery
- The Mystic Circle Murder : aka Religious Racketeers
- Die Nackte und der Satan : The Head (US)
- Night of the Demon : Curse of the Demon (US)
- Night of the Eagle : Burn Witch Burn (US)
- Oliver the Eighth: The Private Life of Oliver the Eighth (UK)
- One Million BC : Man and His Mate (UK) / Cave Man (US reissue)
- Ouanga : aka Crime of Voodoo / Drums of the Jungle / The Love Wanga
- Pharaoh's Curse : aka Curse of the Pharaoh
- Quatermass 2 : Enemy from Space (US)
- Quatermass and the Pit : Five Million Years to Earth (US)
- Rasputin and the Empress : Rasputin the Mad Monk (UK)
- Revenge of the Zombies : The Corpse Vanished (UK)
- Revolt of the Zombies : aka Revolt of the Demons
- Riders of the Whistling Skull : The Golden Trail (UK)
- Sherlock Holmes and the Great Murder Mystery : aka Sherlock Holmes in the Great Murder Mystery
- She-Wolf of London : The Curse of the Allenbys (UK)
- Strange Confession : The Missing Head (reissue)
- The Strange Mr Gregory : aka The Great Mystic
- Le Système du Docteur Goudron et du Professeur Plume : The Lunatics (US)
- Taste of Fear : Scream of Fear (US)
- Their Big Moment : Afterwards (UK)
- The Time of Their Lives : aka The Ghost Steps Out
- Uncle Silas : The Inheritance (US)
- Vampyr : Castle of Doom (US)
- Vanity's Price : This House of Vanity (UK)
- Vengeance : The Brain (US)
- Voodoo Island : Silent Death (reissue)
- Das Wachsfigurenkabinnett : Waxworks (UK), The Three Wax Works (US)
- White Pongo : Adventure Unlimited (UK)
- Zombies on Broadway : Loonies on Broadway (UK)

Title Index

Film titles are given in bold type; stage, television and radio plays in italics; novels, stories, poems etc in regular type.

Numerals in bold type indicate illustrations. Numerals followed by an asterisk refer to the 16 pages of colour illustrations, while ep1 and ep2 indicate stills contained in the front and back endpapers.

Don Haggerty and Arthur Franz restrain the suicidal Peggie Castle in *Back from the Dead* (1957)

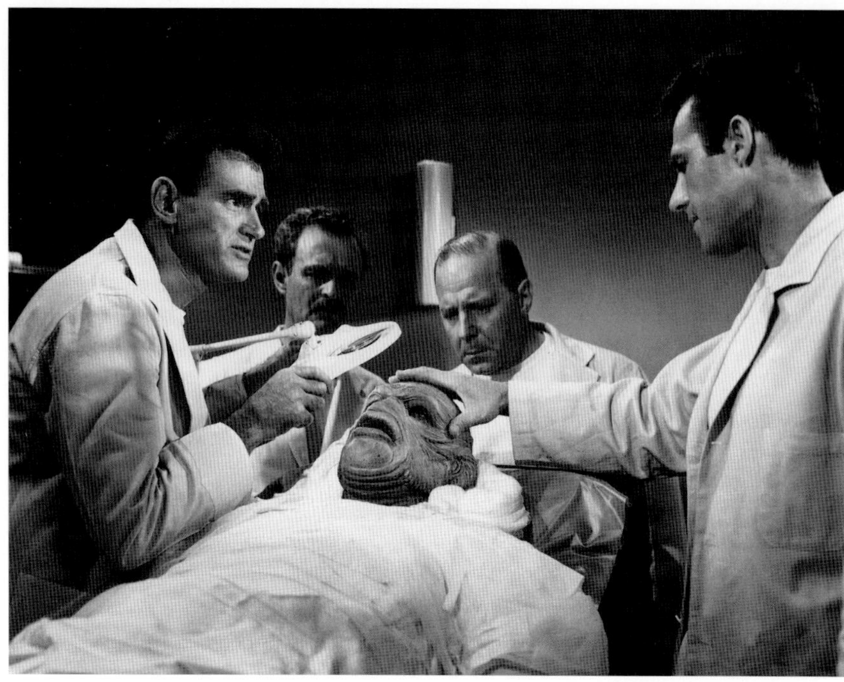

Scientists Jeff Morrow, James Rawley, Maurice Manson and Rex Reason, with experimental subject Don Megowan in *The Creature Walks Among Us* (1955)

First National ballyhoo for the second screen rendering of the Broadway success *The Gorilla* (1930)

William R Dunn spies on May McAvoy and Edna Young in *The House of the Tolling Bell* (1920)

What remains of a diplovertebron's pre-teen victim in *The Monster of Piedras Blancas* (1958)

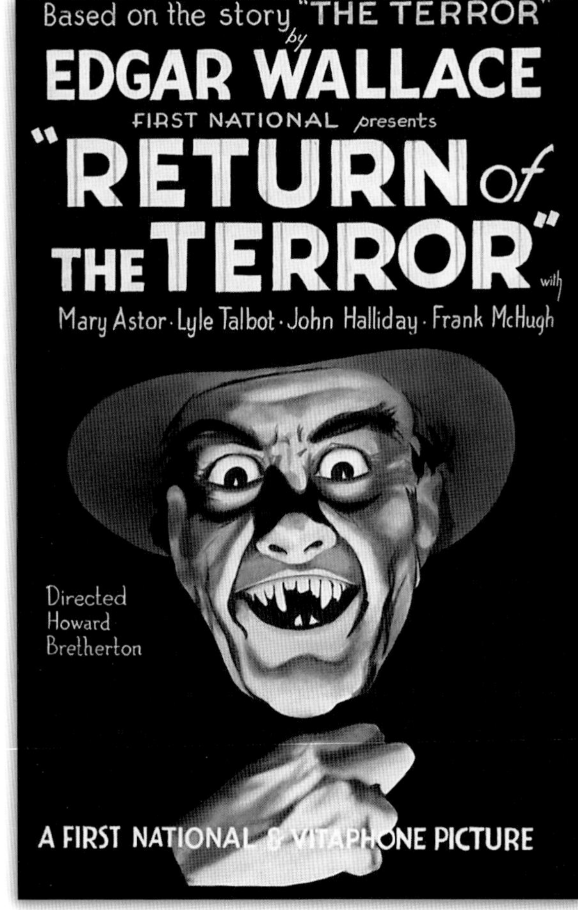

British trade ad for the uninspired spooky-house melodrama *Return of the Terror* (1934)

Jack Lambert patrols an ancient Cuban castle and Lizabeth Scott is *Scared Stiff* (1952)